中国企业改革

Chinese Industrial Firms under Reform

Edited by
William A. Byrd

PUBLISHED FOR THE WORLD BANK
Oxford University Press

Oxford University Press

OXFORD NEW YORK TORONTO DELHI
BOMBAY CALCUTTA MADRAS KARACHI
KUALA LUMPUR SINGAPORE HONG KONG
TOKYO NAIROBI DAR ES SALAAM
CAPE TOWN MELBOURNE AUCKLAND
and associated companies in
BERLIN IBADAN

© 1992 The International Bank for
Reconstruction and Development / THE WORLD BANK
1818 H Street, N.W., Washington, D.C. 20433, U.S.A.

Manufactured in the United States of America
First printing February 1992

The findings, interpretations, and conclusions expressed in this
publication are those of the authors and should not be attributed
in any manner to the World Bank, to its affiliated organizations,
or to members of its Board of Executive Directors or the
countries they represent. The denominations, classifications,
boundaries, and colors used in the map do not imply on the part
of the World Bank any judgment on the legal or other status of
any territory or any endorsement or acceptance of any boundary.

The cover design, by Beatrice Sito, incorporates the Chinese characters
meaning "China's enterprise reform." The calligraphy is by Booker Lee.

Library of Congress Cataloging-in-Publication Data
Chinese industrial firms under reform / edited by William A. Byrd.
    p.   cm.
"Published for the World Bank."
Includes bibliographical references and index.
ISBN 0–19–520875–7
    1. China—Industries—Case studies.   2. China—Economic
policy—1976–   I. Byrd, William A.   II. International Bank for
Reconstruction and Development.
HC427.92.C467218 1992
338.0951—dc20
                                                    91-32401
                                                        CIP

中
国
企
业
改
革

Contents

Acknowledgments   ix

Exchange Rates   xi

Preface   xiii

1 Chinese Industrial Reform, 1978–89   1

William A. Byrd

Chinese Industrial Reform: A Topical Review   1
Achievements and Problems   13
Industrial Performance, 1978–88   18
Prospects for Reform   27
Notes   30
References   31

2 Summary of Research and General Observations   33

William A. Byrd

Methodology   33
The Case Studies   37
Common Themes   47
Notes   56
References   57

3 The Chongqing Clock and Watch Company   58

William A. Byrd and Gene Tidrick

Introduction and General Background   58
Analysis of Main Reforms   68
Enterprise Response, 1980–82   87
Implications of Chongqing's Experience   103
A Postscript on Subsequent Developments   111
Notes   114

References 117

4 The Qingdao Forging Machinery Plant 120
Chen Jiyuan, Xu Lu, Tang Zongkun, and Chen Lantong

Historical Background 121
Supervisory Structure 123
Reforms in Planning and Marketing 126
Improving Economic Performance 130
The Labor and Wage System 135
Technical Transformation and Development of New Products 141
Editor's Supplementary Observations and Postscript 144
Notes 148

5 The Shenyang Smelter 149
William A. Byrd

Industrial and Historical Perspective 149
Main Problems 161
Response to Problems 176
Organizational Reforms 192
General Observations 200
Later Developments 209
Notes 221
References 225

6 The Qinghe Woolen Textile Mill 228
Lora Sabin

An Introduction to the Industry and Enterprise 229
Qinghe's Response to the Changing Economic Environment 238
Conclusions and Implications 266
Notes 271
References 273

7 The Nanning Silk and Ramie Textile Mill 276
Josephine Woo

General Background 276
Reforms and Changes in the Nanning Mill's Environment 282
Effects of Reform on Nanning's Behavior 290
Limitations of Enterprise Reforms 295
Notes 300
References 302

8 The Anshan Iron and Steel Company 303
William A. Byrd

Issues and History 304

The Supervisory System   309
The Financial System and Incentives   316
Mandatory Planning and Marketing Controls   320
Vertical Integration versus Administrative Fragmentation   329
Internal Organization and Management   340
Labor and Wages   347
Renovation and Modernization   356
Conclusions   361
Notes   365
References   368

9 The Second Motor Vehicle Manufacturing Plant   371
   William A. Byrd

China's Motor Vehicle Industry and Number Two's Development   372
Administrative Supervision   382
Planning, Supply, and Marketing Controls   388
Business Environment, Strategy, and Practices   395
The Dongfeng Corporation   407
Conclusions   418
Notes   423
References   425

Index   427

Acknowledgments

NUMEROUS PEOPLE AND ORGANIZATIONS contributed to the research on which this volume is based. The wholehearted cooperation of the enterprises surveyed was invaluable to the success of the project, as was that of their supervisory authorities and the State Economic Commission. The project was managed by Gene Tidrick of the World Bank and Chen Jiyuan of the Institute of Economics of the Chinese Academy of Social Sciences. Other members of the research team were William Byrd, Chen Lantong, David Granick, Tang Zongkun, Josephine Woo, Xu Lu, and Zheng Guangliang. Chinese researchers from the graduate school of the Institute of Economics gathered most of the primary data, and Shahnaz Rana assisted with preparation of the manuscript. Finally, a number of readers made helpful comments on the full volume and on individual studies.

Exchange Rates

THE CHINESE currency unit is the yuan or renminbi, for which the abbreviation Y is used in this volume. Average exchange rates (yuan per U.S. dollar) for recent years, taken from the International Monetary Fund's *International Financial Statistics Yearbook* (Washington, D.C., 1990), are given below. All references to dollars in this book are to U.S. dollars.

1978	1.68
1979	1.56
1980	1.50
1981	1.71
1982	1.89
1983	1.98
1984	2.32
1985	2.94
1986	3.45
1987	3.72
1988	3.72
1989	3.77

Preface

THIS BOOK ANALYZES reforms in Chinese industry from the perspective of twenty state-owned industrial firms that underwent changes starting in the late 1970s. The analysis is based on detailed case studies, the fruits of in-depth empirical research conducted jointly by the Institute of Economics of the Chinese Academy of Social Sciences and the World Bank from 1983 to 1985 as part of an ongoing collaborative research program. Although internal organization and management of firms were examined, researchers mainly studied the administrative and economic environment, firms' motivation and incentives, their response to reforms and other developments in the economy, and the effect of environment, motivation, and responses on enterprise behavior and performance.

In-depth interviews conducted at a carefully selected sample of twenty Chinese state-owned industrial firms (see Tidrick and Chen 1987, pp. 11–38) were the main source of data for the research. Detailed quantitative information on these firms also was gathered, as were regional, subsectoral, and national industrial statistics and background information from press reports and journal articles. Information from interviews and firm-level quantitative data, collected in 1983 and 1984, covered the period from 1975 to 1984, with an emphasis on 1979–82.

The case study method allowed researchers to gain a good understanding of the industrial milieu in China and the changes that affected enterprises from the late 1970s onward. Such research provided insights into the implementation of Chinese industrial reforms, which often differed greatly from their official descriptions or comments about them in secondary sources. The case studies were useful in developing hypotheses and buttressing generalizations about Chinese industry as a whole; they also are inherently interesting and have considerable historical value. (See chapter 2 for a more detailed discussion of the case study method and its advantages and drawbacks.)

An important publication based on this research project was Tidrick and Chen (1987), which contains papers prepared by Chinese and World Bank researchers for an international conference held in Beijing in August 1985. Other publications include Granick (1990) and three case studies of particular firms, Byrd and Tidrick (1984), Chen Jiyuan and others (1984), and Byrd (1985). Revised, updated versions of these studies appear as chapters 3, 4, and 5 of this volume. The remaining case studies in this book were written in 1987–89, after the fieldwork and initial analysis for the project were completed; these rely to some extent on information gathered after 1984. The studies are presented in the order in which they were written.

This volume substantially augments the earlier products of the research project and provides a fresh perspective on China's industrial reforms. The case studies contain a wealth of detail and full coverage of illuminating episodes left out of Tidrick and Chen (1987) because of length constraints. As a result, the book supports and strengthens many of the general arguments made in the earlier volume. Some general analysis and topical discussions that were omitted or condensed in Tidrick and Chen are also included.

Every effort has been made to extend the information base and analysis into the late 1980s, with some degree of success in nearly all chapters. In any case, the experiences described in this volume are still relevant to current policy issues in China and shed light on current problems. Many of the difficulties encountered by firms in the late 1970s and early 1980s still plagued China's state-owned industrial sector in the late 1980s. Although numerous policy changes and administrative reorganizations have occurred, a certain continuity in systemic features is evident. Manifestations of this continuity include the orientation of firms toward workers, the soft budget constraint, and the fragmentation of industrial administration. The fundamental problems faced by sample firms as well as by the state-owned industrial sector as a whole did not change so quickly as to nullify the analytical value of these earlier experiences.

The experiences of sample enterprises in the late 1970s and early 1980s are particularly relevant today because most of the selected firms were engaged in advanced reforms. Although this characteristic may have made them somewhat unrepresentative of Chinese state-owned industry as a whole in those years, their experiences and problems may be similar to those of most firms in the late 1980s. Numerous examples of advanced pilot reforms that were widely adopted later are included in the case studies.

Finally, the case studies have considerable historical value. During the late 1970s and early to mid-1980s, Chinese industrial reform went through an important early phase, achieved some success despite numerous problems, and set the stage for the much publicized second phase of reform ushered in after 1984. This crucial early period cannot be adequately understood through aggregate statistics, quotations from official documents, Chinese articles, or visitors' reports. The fuller, more accurate picture developed by the case studies in this volume therefore forms an indispensable contribution to an understanding of industrial reform in China.

References

Byrd, William A. 1985. *The Shenyang Smelter: A Case Study of Problems and Reforms in China's Nonferrous Metals Industry.* World Bank Staff Working Paper 766. Washington, D.C.

Byrd, William A., and Gene Tidrick. 1984. "Adjustment and Reform in the Chongqing Clock and Watch Company." In William Byrd, Gene Tidrick, Chen Jiyuan, Xu Lu, Tang Zongkun, and Chen Lantong, *Recent Chinese Economic Reforms: Studies of Two Industrial Enterprises.* World Bank Staff Working Paper 652. Washington, D.C.

Chen Jiyuan, Xu Lu, Tang Zongkun, and Chen Lantong. 1984. "Management Reforms in the Qingdao Forging Machinery Plant." In William Byrd, Gene Tidrick, Chen Jiyuan, Xu Lu, Tang Zongkun, and Chen Lantong, *Recent Chinese Economic Reforms: Studies of Two Industrial Enterprises.* World Bank Staff Working Paper 652. Washington, D.C.

Granick, David. 1990. *Chinese State Enterprises: A Regional Property Rights Analysis.* Chicago: University of Chicago Press.

Tidrick, Gene, and Chen Jiyuan, eds. 1987. *China's Industrial Reform.* New York: Oxford University Press.

1

Chinese Industrial Reform, 1978–89

William A. Byrd

BACKGROUND INFORMATION on Chinese industrial reform and performance since the late 1970s will provide a useful context for the detailed analysis of industrial enterprises that forms the core of this volume. The following discussion reviews reforms and structural changes and highlights some important achievements and problems. The quantitative performance of Chinese industry during 1978–88 is broadly summarized, and the prospects for industrial reform are assessed in the light of the economic and political changes that have occurred in China since June 1989.

Chinese Industrial Reform: A Topical Review

Pervasive inefficiency and the need to shift from Soviet-style extensive growth to intensive growth based on improved resource allocation contributed to the emergence of Chinese economic reforms in the late 1970s. In the early years reforms progressed more rapidly in agriculture than they did in urban state-owned industries. Dynamic rural nonstate (collective and private) industries became increasingly important, however, and beginning in 1984 reforming urban state-owned industrial firms received more attention and was given high priority.

Chinese industrial firms fall into the following main categories: (1) large state enterprises, relatively tightly controlled by the government planning and administrative apparatus, small in number but accounting for large shares of industrial output, profits, assets, and so forth; (2) smaller state enterprises, under the jurisdiction of county or municipal governments, whose share in industrial output has been declining; (3) urban collective firms, nominally owned by urban community entities but actually controlled by various government agencies; (4) generally small rural firms owned by township and village governments, which have proliferated during the past decade; and (5) private enterprises, mostly in rural areas, which greatly increased in number after 1984 and now account for a significant share of total industrial output. Joint ventures involving different types of enterprises as well as firms with direct foreign investment have emerged.

Each type of firm has somewhat different institutional characteristics, calling for different reform strategies and measures. All except the private enterprises, however, are under the jurisdiction of government supervisory agencies, such as industrial ministries; provincial, municipal, or county industrial bureaus; or organs of urban neighborhood committees or rural township and village governments. Many sizable private enterprises also have close ties to local governments and officials. Some rural private firms even registered as collectives in the early 1980s to minimize their political visibility and any possible ideological problems (Byrd and Lin 1990).

The history of Chinese industrial reform since the late 1970s is a confusing plethora of measures, implemented amid evolving economic behavior and institutions. Under these circumstances, the effect of specific reforms has been understandably difficult to trace.

No overall blueprint or plan for reform has guided the process. Instead, reforms have been headlong and unpremeditated, sometimes haphazard, often seemingly chaotic, and highly ad hoc in implementation, with considerable regional variation. Typically, reforms began with "experiments"; where these were deemed successful, usually after only a short period of implementation and a superficial evaluation, they were often rapidly instituted nationwide.

It is important to understand the underlying impetus and direction of the reform movement to help explain this mass of detail. Despite the lack of overall guidelines, a basic package of industrial reforms can be identified that reflects coherent logic and is manifested to some extent in implementation patterns. This underlying coherence is only implicit and appears to have emerged more from experience over time than from conscious advance planning.

The entire decade of industrial reform can be understood as an effort to "marketize" the industrial sector—to shift from a system in which planning and administrative directives guided the allocation of resources to one in which resource allocation was determined largely by interactions in the market among autonomous, competitive, profit-oriented economic agents. (See Perkins 1988, pp. 613–21, for an analysis of Chinese urban industrial reforms from this perspective.)

Marketization was intended to be partial in many respects; government supervision was to be circumscribed and oriented more toward economic rationality, but not abolished. Whereas it was increasingly recognized that the market mechanism should become the dominant mode of allocating industrial goods, market-based allocation of factors of production (labor, capital, and land) was far more limited, and government bodies retained considerable influence in such areas as finance and technology.

The first reforms of state enterprises promulgated in the late 1970s contained three main elements: (1) greater decisionmaking autonomy for enterprises in production and, to a lesser extent, in investment; (2) reinstitution of financial incentives for enterprises and individuals;[1] and (3) expansion of the role of markets in the allocation of industrial goods and corresponding reductions in the role of planning and administrative allocation (see Byrd 1983). The components of this initial package were closely related and mutually reinforcing. Considerable progress was made in implementing the second of these elements and, with the onset of buyers' markets in many industries, also the third. There was initially much less progress with the first, especially in the sphere of investment.

This package also generated a need for certain related reforms. Price reform was needed so that market prices could reflect scarcity values in the economy. Reforms in the systems for determining wages, bonuses, and labor allocation were required to provide credible incentives to workers. Reform of investment financing mainly involved shifting funding of investment projects from the government budget to bank loans and enterprise-retained funds. Another important component of Chinese industrial reforms was the opening up of the industrial economy to international economic relations (trade, technology transfer, direct foreign investment, and so forth), in order to increase foreign exchange earnings, strengthen competition, and encourage technological modernization.

Financial Reforms in State Enterprises

Initial reforms in state-owned industrial enterprises were intended to transform financial arrangements and incentives. These reforms got off to a modest start in a few factories in Sichuan Province as early as October 1978. Subsequently a number of local pilot reforms sprang up, culminating in the national "experiment in expanding enterprise autonomy," promulgated in July 1979. The core of these early reforms was restoration of profit retention by enterprises (10 to 30 percent of above-quota profits in the case of the national system). There were also experimental profit tax systems, "dividend" systems, and other variants. Most enterprises were allowed to retain a higher proportion of their depreciation funds as well.

Profit retention spread rapidly, and by the end of 1980, 6,600 state-owned industrial firms, accounting for 16 percent of their total number but 60 percent of the total value of output of such firms and 70 percent of their profits, had instituted some form of profit retention, although incentives were still weak because of low and unstable retention rates. Moreover, many firms complained about ratchet effects, whereby good performance in one year was, in effect, punished by higher targets in subsequent years.

In 1981–82 various forms of the "economic responsibility system" were instituted. This system specified targets for profits to be turned over to the government by enterprises, with high retention rates from above-quota profits (often 60 to 80 percent, sometimes 100 percent). Since targets were based on negotiations between firms and their supervisory agencies and could be adjusted from year to year or even within each year, the new system provided considerable flexibility in the face of market or other shocks. Its ad hoc nature, however, weakened incentive effects. Moreover, the system apparently led to a hemorrhage of government revenue, since firms and supervisory agencies could effectively conspire to reduce flows of profits to the public finance system.

The culmination of the first phase of state enterprise reform was the gradual move to a profit tax system in 1983–85, a development that was in part a reaction against the excesses of the economic responsibility system. Various experimental profit tax systems had been instituted in some firms from as early as 1980.[2] Starting in 1983 a nationwide profit tax system was implemented; profit tax carried a uniform rate of 55 percent, but because of price distortions and other "objective factors" that caused variation in profits across firms and industries, an enterprise-specific "adjustment tax" also was imposed on most large or medium-size enterprises. Firms in industries with very low profitability paid tax at rates effectively well below 55 percent, or in some cases none at all. Despite these problems, the profit tax system represented an important step toward creation of a genuine tax system, and adjustment tax rates for most firms were gradually reduced. By 1985 the bulk of state enterprises were at least nominally operating under the new profit tax system.

Financial reforms in state enterprises clearly were successful in shifting substantial amounts of profits from government to enterprise control. The total amount of profits retained by state enterprises (nonindustrial as well as industrial) jumped from Y2 billion in 1978 to Y10 billion in 1980, Y17 billion in 1982, Y28 billion in 1983, and an estimated Y31 billion in 1984 (World Bank 1988, p. 85).[3] According to a different source, state-owned industrial firms that kept separate financial accounts retained a total of Y32.3 billion in profits in 1988 (up from Y22.8 billion in 1986), which amounted to 36 percent of total before-tax profits of these firms.[4]

These large increases in retained profits seem not to have had a commensurate effect on performance. Retained profits did provide the funding for massive spending by enterprises on housing, public facilities, and welfare for employees, whose real standard of living increased markedly. One striking feature of Chinese state industry has been the heavy social responsibilities of firms for their employees' welfare. These responsibilities include medical care, pensions, housing, education, food service, and, in many cases, local public services and infrastructure.

Another important aspect of financial reforms in state enterprises was a significant shift in the pattern of investment financing, from reliance primarily on government budgetary grants to extensive use of bank loans and funds retained by enterprises (profits and depreciation allowances). Because of unusual (by international standards) provisions for repayment of loans, as well as frequent postponements of loan repayments, incentives for enterprises to borrow were very strong. Hence one of the main objectives of loan financing—to encourage firms to exercise greater care in making decisions about investments and to become more cautious and restrained in their demand for investment funds—was not achieved.

Financial incentives do not work well unless enterprises are subject to a certain degree of financial discipline. The early profit retention schemes were "soft" and negotiable, and they weakened rather than strengthened financial discipline. In addition to "harder" financial incentives, the solution to weak financial discipline would involve effective sanctions against poor performance, culminating in bankruptcy for unviable firms. A bankruptcy law was promulgated in 1986, but it went into effect only later. Although a tiny number of smaller urban collective firms began or completed bankruptcy procedures, bankruptcy has not become a real threat to sizable state enterprises. Among rural nonstate industrial enterprises, by contrast, exit has been relatively easy for many types of firms, either through switching product lines or through going out of business. In any case, the ability of rural township or village governments, with their limited resources, to subsidize their enterprises was extremely small.

Reform of Markets and Prices

The effort to increase the share of the market mechanism and reduce the role of directive planning in the allocation of industrial goods made some progress in the early years of reform. This occurred, however, mainly as a result of changing market conditions rather than through explicit reform measures. Cutbacks in investment, along with government adjustment policies emphasizing consumption and increased living standards, caused market conditions for many industrial producer goods (that is, goods used by industry in production), especially machinery and equipment, to shift from excess demand to excess supply. In the case of textiles and many consumer durables, high prices stimulated expansion by existing producers and the entry of many new firms, which also led to excess supply. Under these circumstances government agencies in charge of procuring and distributing industrial goods tended to abdicate their responsibility, forcing enterprises to market their output directly. This in turn led many producers to respond positively by improving quality, developing new products, promoting sales, providing warranties and better after-sale service, and so forth (see Byrd 1987b).

Market conditions tightened after the early 1980s, but the share of markets expanded further for many industrial goods. The rapidly growing rural nonstate industrial sector contributed significantly to this trend, as did various efforts to release state enterprises from mandatory planning. By the late 1980s the share of output directly marketed by firms had become quite sub-

Table 1.1. Share of Enterprises' Direct Marketing in Total Sales of Selected Industrial Products, 1987–88
(percent)

Product	1987	1988
Industrial producer goods		
Pig iron	12.8	45.1
For steelmaking	5.4	34.7
For casting	41.0	52.2
Rolled steel	22.5	29.1
Metal-cutting machine tools	70.7	75.6
Motor vehicles	53.3	51.8
Trucks	57.9	58.2
Large and medium-size tractors	37.1	47.0
Small tractors	55.2	56.9
AC generators[a]	79.9	80.8
Machine-made paper and paperboard	—	64.8
Sulfuric acid	23.3	49.7
Sodium bicarbonate	27.5	33.6
Soda ash	49.3	32.3
Tire inner tubes	47.2	43.7
Tire outer parts	42.1	35.2
Cement	52.4	62.3
Plate glass	62.3	64.5
Raw timber	37.8	36.1
Coal	20.0	20.5
Crude oil	1.3	1.6
Heavy oil[b]	9.5	7.5
Gasoline	12.6	17.1
Diesel oil	12.2	13.7
Consumer goods and inputs		
Bicycles	—	64.0
Sewing machines	—	55.0
Televisions	—	73.0
Color televisions	—	73.2
Radios	—	73.9
Tape recorders	—	85.3
Cameras	—	76.2
Electric fans	—	74.5
Washing machines	—	75.8
Refrigerators	—	68.3

(Table continues on the following page.)

Table 1.1 (*continued*)

Product	1987	1988
Cloth	—	51.9
Pure synthetic	—	57.0
Nylon thread	—	70.7
Woolen thread	—	65.8
Leather	—	82.3
Cigarettes	—	24.5

— Not available.
a. Shares calculated in terms of generating capacity.
b. 1988 figure is for fuel oil, which may cover a slightly different universe than heavy oil.
Source: State Statistical Bureau 1988, pp. 460–72; 1989b, pp. 379–80.

stantial for most industrial producer goods and even higher in the case of consumer durables (table 1.1). The rise in the share of markets was naturally accompanied by a decline in the proportion of production subject to allocation under the state plan. Table 1.2 shows decreasing state plan shares for some important industrial producer goods in the 1980s. In some cases there were precipitous drops, in others more gradual reductions.

The opening of the industrial economy to international economic relations had multiple objectives, among them growth in exports to provide foreign exchange with which to import advanced technology and equipment, the involvement of firms in exports as a means of stimulating competitiveness and improving quality, and specialization through foreign trade. Although much of Chinese industry remained poorly integrated with the international economy, the performance of exports has been impressive, and industry has benefited from an influx of foreign equipment, technology, and, to a lesser extent, investment.

Changes in pricing were related to market-oriented reforms. An early de facto loosening of price controls for many industrial producer goods was cut short by restored controls at the end of 1980, a development that also stymied efforts to adjust state-set prices of such goods. The environment in the early 1980s was not conducive to free-market pricing, and many enterprises resorted to various barterlike arrangements involving exchanges of products and inputs. From 1984, however, price controls became progressively weaker; first increases of up to 20 percent in prices for output produced by firms above the plan amount were permitted, and then, in early 1985, such prices were freed to find their own levels in the marketplace. By the mid- to late 1980s market prices for industrial producer goods in numerous cities were being widely reported, and available evidence indicates that these prices were not subject to systematic controls (see Byrd 1991, chapter 8). Overall, although adjustment of government-controlled prices was usually limited and was hindered by the opposition of vested interests, considerable

Table 1.2. Share of State Plan in Output of Principal Industrial Producer Goods, for Selected Years, 1980–88
(percentage of total domestic production)

Product	1980	1985	1986	1987	1988[a]
Coal	57.9	50.6	42.3	—	—
Timber	80.9	30.7	30.0	27.6	25[b]
Rolled steel	74.3	56.9	53.1	47.1	42[c]
Cement	35.0	19.4	16.2	15.6	14[b]
Nonferrous metals[d]	86.4	—	61.4	—	—

— Not available.

a. Estimated.

b. Based on share of state plan contracts in total output. Contracts were substantially underfulfilled in 1988, so shares of actual deliveries of goods for distribution under the state plan were even lower.

c. Based on reported percentage decline in state plan contracts and increase in production.

d. Copper, lead, zinc, and aluminum (presumably combined weight).

Source: Byrd 1991, table 3.1.

progress was made in releasing prices from controls and in the emergence of a two-tiered price system. As a result, most industrial producer goods were transacted at least partly through the market mechanism, at largely market-determined prices (see Byrd 1987a).

The functioning of the market has been problematic, and informal ceilings on "market" prices of some products have been imposed at times. Many firms have continued to engage in barter (even though direct sales at market prices were legitimized) for various tax and accounting reasons. There is evidence that markets for industrial goods have been at least somewhat segmented as a result of administrative as well as infrastructural barriers. Nevertheless, the mere existence and (however imperfect) functioning of markets for industrial producer and consumer goods marks a significant change.

Reform of Labor and Wages

Allocation of labor remained the least reformed part of the system, but certain changes deserve mention. Beginning in 1986, most newly hired regular workers in state-owned industrial enterprises were given fixed-term (usually three-year) contracts. This measure was intended to increase labor discipline, strengthen performance-based incentives for workers, and weaken the traditional "iron rice bowl" system, under which workers were effectively guaranteed the right to keep their jobs for their entire career. The contracts were renewable, but in principle workers whose performance was unsatisfactory could be terminated when their contract expired. In practice, this happened extremely rarely, and contract renewals became largely a pro forma exercise.[5]

A more important development was the authority given to managers in the mid-1980s to rationalize their work force within the enterprise, by taking surplus workers out of production and segregating them in separate teams engaged in miscellaneous tasks or training. Poorly performing workers tended to be assigned to these teams, and even though wages continued to be paid, the loss of bonuses and possibly other benefits must have served as a potent incentive for all workers to perform well. By this time some differentiation in bonuses was increasingly accepted, although it remained impossible to terminate regular employees.

State enterprises gained additional flexibility through hiring various kinds of nonregular employees, often on a temporary basis. Parceling out activities to rural concerns was another way of achieving the same objective—that is, lowering average labor costs and enhancing flexibility in an environment that did not permit outright layoffs of regular workers but in which market competition was becoming more severe.

Rural industrial enterprises present a stark contrast to state enterprises in the area of labor. Although rural labor markets are fragmented and geographic mobility is limited, temporary flows of labor from poorer to better-off areas have been increasing, as has migration to cities. Perhaps most important, rural nonstate industrial firms have greater latitude in dismissing or penalizing poorly performing workers, and in reducing the size of the labor force in the face of business difficulties.

State enterprises increasingly relied on pay-related incentives for workers. The bonus system, whose restoration had begun in 1978, had become virtually universal by 1979. Widespread experimentation with different types of bonus and work-related pay schemes occurred in the early stages of reform. Ceilings on wages and bonuses limited the total compensation that could be paid to workers, however, and it was difficult to differentiate bonuses sharply among workers. Bonuses rapidly came to be viewed by workers as a fixed income supplement, which could not be reduced except in response to clear-cut violations or absence from work. Under these circumstances, attempts to experiment with piece-rate wages ran into opposition from the workers. In contrast, in rural township and village enterprises piece rates and other forms of performance-related pay were widely adopted as incentives.

In the mid-1980s incentives offered to state enterprises and their employees were combined with the system for allocating labor. Under the so-called linkage between financial results and total wage bill, ceilings on wages and bonuses were removed and the total wage bill of an enterprise was linked to its remittance of profits and payment of taxes to the government. If profit remittances and tax payments increased, total wages also could rise, usually in a specified ratio to the increase in taxes and in profit remittances. Moreover, since total wages no longer depended on the number of workers employed, average compensation per worker could be increased by reducing the size of the work force through attrition. Although labor productivity undoubtedly increased as a result, growth in employment must have suffered.

Increasing the Authority of Factory Directors

The authority of the enterprise director was also increased during the reform period, especially after 1984. Although early reforms gave firms greater latitude in making decisions, the question of who would exercise this power remained unresolved. Supreme decisionmaking power was vested in the enterprise party committee, headed by its secretary, in the prereform period. Some enterprises experimented with internal control through the Workers' Representative Assembly and the election of factory directors by the workers.

The general trend, however, was for the factory director, whether elected or appointed, to assume the role of ultimate decisionmaker and representative of the enterprise in dealings with outside agencies. The Regulations on the Work of Factory Directors in State-Owned Industrial Enterprises, issued in September 1986, gave final operational authority to factory directors, although directors were enjoined to consult with other actors on major decisions. Perhaps most important, directors were granted authority over personnel decisions within enterprises.

The "factory director responsibility system" and the "factory director fixed-term goal responsibility system" were manifestations of this new emphasis. The former began as an experiment in 1984—in the Nanning Silk and Ramie Mill, among other places—and by 1986 had been implemented in 27,000 state-owned industrial firms. This program, which foreshadowed the regulations for factory directors that were promulgated later, stipulated that managerial rewards could exceed the pay of the average worker by 100 to 300 percent; the mechanism for determining managerial pay, however, remained unclear. The fixed-term goal responsibility system involved setting specific tasks and targets for factory directors, against which performance was evaluated at the end of their terms in office. The system was designed to combat the tendency of directors in fixed-term jobs (introduced in September 1984) to pursue short-term goals at the expense of the long-term development of their firms.

Contractual Responsibility Systems

A group of reforms known as the contractual responsibility systems was important in the reform effort during the late 1980s.[6] These schemes, which began in 1986 and were widely implemented in 1987–88, included leasing of smaller firms, the contract management responsibility system (later made into the dominant "umbrella" scheme), the enterprise management responsibility system, and the asset management responsibility system.

Despite considerable variation, these programs shared some common elements. First, all of them involved a contract-based relationship between the enterprise, usually represented by its director, and its supervisory agency. In theory, the contracts were between equals and were entered into voluntarily, a sharp departure from earlier schemes. In order to succeed, these schemes required the factory directors to be in positions of authority, and hence they often led to a substantial increase in their de facto powers.

The directors also assumed substantial risk in these programs, and their rewards were linked to performance. Under the asset management responsibility system, for example, directors' rewards could exceed the average worker's pay by as much as 1,000 percent. The most radical schemes involved open selection of enterprise directors, based on applications, interviews, and decisions by personnel committees. Finally, most of the systems had multiyear targets and incentives, in order to weaken ratchet effects.

The contractual responsibility systems achieved some success, especially in the small number of firms where they were implemented as experimental schemes. Specifically, the programs increased the autonomy of factory directors and improved their ability to effectively manage the work force. Many directors gained credibility among workers, in part because they took personal responsibility by signing contracts and pledging some of their own personal assets as a "guarantee" to be forfeited in the event of poor financial performance. The systems also permitted directors to reorganize their management teams and sometimes even to demote middle-level managers to ordinary workers. More generally, the reforms promoted a businesslike attitude on the part of both management and workers.

Nevertheless, the systems had numerous problems. The contractual arrangements divided the interests of directors and workers. Resistance by workers was sometimes open, more often hidden. Managerial incentives were not well defined or fully credible, particularly since directors bore only a negligible portion of the enterprise's risk and their personal assets were seldom confiscated in the event of failure. Open selection of factory directors, a significant advance, was not widely implemented. More generally, international experience shows that legal contracts are not the most appropriate mode of structuring the positions and incentives of corporate management. Finally, in many cases the contractual responsibility systems undermined the profit tax system. By the late 1980s reformers came to recognize that these programs could be only transitional mechanisms.

Radical Reform Efforts after the Mid-1980s

By the mid-1980s industrial reform clearly had begun to move beyond the initial phase. The need to contemplate deeper and more wide-ranging reforms and to take into account the relations among various parts of the system became apparent to many in government and industry.

Restructuring the ownership of state enterprises became a reform issue. This did not (except in smaller firms) involve wholesale privatization but rather stronger and more responsible exercise of the functions of ownership by government agencies. The more advanced contractual responsibility systems reflected this orientation, as did experiments with share ownership.

Share ownership differed from stock ownership in other countries in that shares generally carried limited or no rights to participate in decisionmaking, and transfer was typically restricted or prohibited. The stock system, however, with its partial ownership rights for workers and public agencies, was viewed as a means of diversifying the ownership structure and regularizing ownership functions with respect to state enterprises.

Smaller state and urban collective enterprises instituted more radical measures. Some firms were sold outright to individuals, others to their workers or a group of employees. Such privatization was more common in retail commerce than in industry, but it reached substantial proportions in the latter as well.

Another popular practice was "leasing" small state and, especially, collective enterprises to individuals or management teams. In this arrangement the lessee typically paid a fee to the government "owner" of the enterprise and was allowed to keep most or all of the financial proceeds from improved performance during the lease period. Leasing was also used to rehabilitate failing enterprises run by rural township and village governments. In many cases leasing served as a prelude to privatization.

Efforts were made in the late 1980s to ease the social burden of state enterprises. Pensions of state enterprise employees, which had been paid directly by their employers, were pooled at the municipal level. Enterprises contributed a portion of their wage bill to a specialized municipal organization, which then paid workers' pensions. Efforts to reduce the responsibility of enterprises for the heavily subsidized housing system also got under way slowly.

By the late 1980s Chinese industrial reform was in a ferment, in some ways similar to the initial phase of local experimentation in the late 1970s, but it had become more advanced and sophisticated. Recognition of the nature and complexity of barriers to dynamism and efficiency in Chinese state industry led to a search for deeper, more fundamental solutions.

Inflationary Pressures in the Late 1980s

In 1988 a massive surge of inflation threatened to derail the second phase of industrial reform in China. The two-tier pricing and distribution system for industrial goods described earlier requires a fairly stable, not excessively inflationary macroeconomic framework in order to function effectively and promote marketization and concomitant improvements in industrial efficiency. (Otherwise inflationary pressures will result in sharply rising market prices, increasing the gap between them and plan prices and exacerbating tendencies toward arbitrage and corruption that are already present in the system.) Such a framework had been present in the early 1980s, but it largely unraveled in 1987 and 1988.

The main inflationary mechanism was rapid growth of bank credit, primarily to enterprises; although the overt fiscal deficit was not high, bank credit was used to finance government-sponsored investments that had previously relied mainly on budgetary funds (see Naughton 1990). Credit expansion accelerated in 1984, but for a time the inflationary effect was held back by increases in the share of output of many industrial goods sold on the market (see Byrd 1991, chapter 8)[7] and by a half-hearted effort to restrain credit growth in 1986. By 1988, however, inflationary pressures became reflected in sharply rising market prices of both producer and consumer goods.

In September 1988, the government responded to the macroeconomic crisis by sharply cutting back credit and taking other harsh anti-inflationary measures, which were inimical to industrial reform. Price controls were tightened, mandatory planning was extended to more products (its scope had been sharply reduced earlier), and enterprise-level reforms were put on hold. Priority in the allocation of materials and finance was given to large state enterprises in critical basic industries; as a result the more market-oriented parts of Chinese industry, such as the rural nonstate industrial sector, suffered disproportionately in terms of access to resources (but not necessarily in terms of performance). The reform-oriented wing of the government leadership was increasingly on the defensive and was forced to retreat from radical proposals that had been circulating during the previous year.

The austerity policy quickly began to affect inflation, production, and financial performance in the industrial sector. There was undoubtedly conflict within the government over how severe and long-lasting restrictions should be. Nevertheless, there was no sign of any relaxation in late 1988 and early 1989. Then the political crisis of May–June 1989 intervened and removed the strongly proreform wing (the Zhao Ziyang faction) from the government, which permitted the restrictive macroeconomic stance to continue and tighten even further. Only in late 1989 and early 1990 was renewed expansion of credit allowed. In sum, further progress of industrial reform in China was stalled and existing reforms were threatened in 1988–89 by macroeconomic instability and its inflationary consequences. Political change then reinforced the antireform trend.

Achievements and Problems

It is important to review qualitative progress and changes in the relative importance of different economic arrangements and transactions in Chinese industry during the period from the late 1970s through the late 1980s, as a prelude to the case studies that follow. A discussion of some of the most salient problems that have emerged during the reform process is also necessary to provide a context for later chapters.

Achievements

In retrospect, it is clear that reforms have transformed the industrial land-scape in China since the late 1970s. Change has often moved in unintended directions, and new distortions and problems have emerged, but the industrial system in 1988 differed significantly from that of 1978. The most striking successes are related to the main components of the initial reform package discussed earlier.

First, directive planning and administrative allocation of industrial goods has declined sharply, while the role of markets and marketlike mechanisms has greatly expanded (see tables 1.1 and 1.2). Such marketization was initially impelled by weakening market conditions; however, direct marketing remained strong following the reversion to sellers' markets that occurred after 1982. The increased importance of markets, even in the face of excess demand, reflected the renewed emphasis on urban reforms beginning in 1984. The two-tier pricing system, legitimized at the beginning of 1985, accentuated the trend of marketization, which brought with it more meaningful competition among firms in many industries.

Another striking achievement was the inculcation in enterprises and their managers of a strong orientation toward profits. Changes in attitudes and the evolution of business and administrative practices in the state-owned industrial sector, as well as profit retention schemes, contributed to this shift. The new profit orientation, however, was also based on deeper objectives and considerations, which in many respects differed radically from those at work in the industrial market economies. For example, in many firms profits were valued primarily because they could be used to improve workers' living standards, through bonuses, welfare, and enterprise-provided housing.

The least progress was made in achieving genuine autonomy for enterprise directors in making business decisions. Even in this area, however, there were some advances, through the director responsibility system, the various contractual responsibility systems, and a general weakening of the supervisory apparatus. The position of the factory director as supreme decisionmaker within the enterprise was strengthened, and the role of the enterprise Party Committee in the business and administrative sphere diminished. Management became stronger in its dealings with workers, even though layoffs were not allowed and jobs and incomes were guaranteed.

An important achievement of reform was the rapid growth of rural township, village, and private industries into a businesslike and profit-oriented sector that functioned largely within a market environment and was independent of the government bureaucracy. Rural nonstate industry increasingly influenced state industries through the medium of market competition, as well as through commercial and other transactions. This was especially true of smaller state enterprises that competed directly in similar product lines,

Table 1.3. Ownership Structure of Chinese Industry, for Selected Years, 1971–88
(percentage of total value of industrial output)

Category	1971	1975	1978	1980	1981	1982	1983	1984[a]	1985	1986	1987	1988
State	85.9	81.2	77.6	75.1	74.3	73.8	72.6	67.6	75.9	62.3	59.7	56.8
Urban collective	10.9	13.7	13.7	14.4	14.1	14.3	14.4	15.9	15.9	15.1	14.6	14.3
Urban private[b]	..	..	..	0.0	0.0	0.1	0.1	0.2	0.3	0.4	0.6	0.6
Urban other[c]	..	..	..	0.5	0.6	0.7	0.8	1.1	1.2	1.5	2.0	2.7
Rural nonstate	3.2	5.1	8.7	10.0	11.0	11.2	12.1	15.2	17.7	20.8	23.1	25.6
Township	1.6	2.6	4.8	5.4	5.9	6.0	6.3	7.7	7.8	8.8	9.3	10.1
Village	1.6	2.5	3.9	4.6	5.1	5.2	5.8	6.0	6.8	7.5	8.4	9.3
Below village[d]	—	—	—	—	—	—	—	1.5	3.1	4.5	5.4	6.2
Individual firms	—	—	—	—	—	—	—	—	1.5	2.5	3.3	4.0

.. Negligible.

— Not available.

Note: Percentages for 1971–80 are based on data on value of industrial output, in 1970 constant accounting prices, for 1981–83 in 1980 constant prices, and for 1984–88 in current prices. Since these figures are based on data compiled by the State Statistical Bureau, they show slightly lower shares for rural nonstate enterprises than Ministry of Agriculture statistics would imply.

a. In the absence of current-price data for forms of ownership other than rural nonstate industry, the shares of various forms of urban ownership were calculated on the basis of their constant-price shares. There may be some inconsistencies between 1984 data and earlier and later data, which are from different sources.

b. Includes partnerships and individual firms.

c. May include some rural firms. Most of this category is accounted for by joint ventures among different forms of ownership, including foreign capital.

d. Includes production team firms and private enterprises (both partnerships and individual firms). By the mid-1980s most production team firms had gone out of business or had been privatized in one way or another, so the bulk of this category came to consist of private enterprises.

Source: State Statistical Bureau 1983, 1985a, 1985b, 1986a, 1986b, 1987a, 1987b, 1987c, 1987d, 1988, 1989b.

but the rural nonstate sector was also beginning more generally to serve as an example for the reform of state enterprises.

Important changes in the ownership structure of Chinese industry also occurred during this period, as shown in table 1.3. The share of the state sector in total national gross value of industrial output (GVIO) markedly declined, from 77.6 percent in 1978 to 56.8 percent in 1988. The share of urban collective firms remained roughly constant at about 14 percent, while rural township and village industry boomed especially from 1984, nearly tripling its share from 8.7 percent in 1978 to 25.6 percent in 1988. Within the rural industrial sector, private enterprises increased their share of national GVIO from negligible levels in the late 1970s to 6 percent by 1988. Although price and other distortions may cause these figures to somewhat overstate the extent of structural change, there is no doubt that it has been substantial, with important implications for Chinese industrial planning, market development, and regulation.

The size distribution of Chinese industrial firms has changed less than would be suggested by the dramatic shift in ownership. Between 1978 and 1988, the share of enterprises classified as large in total national GVIO declined from 24.1 percent to 23.5 percent, while that of medium-size firms fell from 17.6 percent to 15.1 percent, and that of small firms rose from 58.3 percent to 61.4 percent.[8]

The relative shares in total output, employment, and fixed assets of industrial enterprises by number of persons employed are shown in table 1.4, which indicates that China's industrial structure remains somewhat top-heavy despite the burgeoning growth of the rural nonstate industrial sector. Firms with more than 500 employees, for example, accounted for about 52 percent of national GVIO, about 41 percent of employment, and an estimated 70 percent of fixed assets. Although most rural nonstate firms are small, some have successfully expanded to substantial size.

Problems

Despite these accomplishments, little progress was made in a number of areas; moreover, new distortions and difficulties were engendered by partial reform. Although in many respects reforms in various parts of the system seemed to be moving forward in the mid- to late 1980s, the gap between reality and reformers' aspirations was large, and the situation in a few spheres may have regressed.

Goods markets remained fragmented and distorted, and price anomalies persisted despite progress in deregulating the price system. Competition among enterprises was weakened by the continuing lack of financial discipline in the state sector and the inability to force out poor performers. The two-tier price system created strong incentives for arbitrage between plan and market segments and for rent-seeking behavior by enterprises as well as government

Table 1.4. Structure of Industry by Size of Firm, 1987
(percentage of total)

Size or category of firm (number of employees)	Number of firms	Share of total number of firms	Share of GVIO (1980 constant prices)	Share of employment	Share of fixed assets[a]
More than 10,000	302	0.0	9.6	8.6	24
1,000–10,000	9,203	0.1	29.9	21.4	35
500–1,000	15,157	0.2	12.6	11.4	11
100–500	107,078	1.5	21.8	25.3	17
50–100	73,310	1.0	4.2	5.8	3
Fewer than 50	212,854	2.9	3.6	5.0	2
Nonindependent accounting units[b]	75,700	1.0	4.6	22.5	3
Rural village and lower-level firms[c]	6,821,500	93.3	13.7		5
Total	7,315,104	100.0	100.0	100.0	100

GVIO, gross value of industrial output.

a. Very rough estimates, in the absence of reliable data for fixed assets of nonindependent accounting units and rural firms below the village level. Fixed assets are valued at original purchase and installation cost.

b. These are industrial firms that do not keep separate financial accounts of their own. The bulk of these firms are not in the state sector, but the few state enterprises among them probably account for most of the GVIO and fixed assets of this category.

c. These firms were not previously included in the industrial sector, although they produce industrial goods. Most are extremely small, but a few village enterprises are sizable, with hundreds of employees.

Source: State Statistical Bureau 1988, pp. 44, 154, 377; 1989a, pp. 25, 293. Information from fieldwork.

agencies. As already mentioned, barterlike exchange arrangements and informal local controls on distribution hindered the functioning of the market. Mandatory planning remained dominant in such basic industries as steel and nonferrous metals, affecting the industrial sector as a whole through interindustry linkages.

Reform in the labor system of state enterprises has not been very effective in improving workers' incentives and discipline, or in encouraging more efficient allocation of labor. These difficulties are fundamentally the product of the lifetime employment system in state enterprises, along with the concomitant burden of providing social services to workers. Changing demographics, however, will make the responsibility of finding employment for workers' children less onerous for state enterprises.

The incentives and mechanisms for allocation of financial capital continued to suffer from many shortcomings. Banks remained overresponsive to government agencies in their lending decisions, and capital markets were only beginning to function. Flows of capital among firms, localities, regions, and administrative hierarchies were impeded. Changes in the sources and mechanisms of investment finance have tended to stimulate rather than restrain enterprise demand for investment, exacerbating macroeconomic difficulties.

Financial incentives at the enterprise level remained soft and easily manipulated, despite efforts to instill a sense of financial discipline in state enterprises. Pressures to control costs, especially those related to labor, remained weak. The culture and habit of regularly paying direct taxes was not established in most firms. Loan repayment schedules had even less credibility, and payments were frequently delayed on the slightest pretext.

Weak financial discipline resulted from the lack of a credible threat of bankruptcy for state enterprises, except for very small firms. Even shrinkage of poorly performing state-owned firms was difficult, particularly if this involved reducing the size of the labor force through methods other than attrition. Other sanctions, such as changing management or reducing pay, worked only imperfectly.

Finally, the hierarchical apparatus for industrial supervision remained in place despite some changes, and the bureaucratic subordination of state enterprises to government agencies was left largely untouched. Reforms in industrial administration, whether they took the form of decentralization, centralization, transformation of industrial bureaus into "corporations," or others, have not yielded positive results and instead have often had adverse side effects. Moreover, numerous government agencies continued to intervene in the business affairs of enterprises, although for the most part with less authority than in the prereform period. Until the links between state enterprises and the massive government bureaucracy are severed, or at least substantially weakened, further progress in reforming state industry will be difficult.

Industrial Performance, 1978–88

Chinese industry performed well during the decade of economic reform, despite the problems cited in this chapter.

Growth of Output

Growth of GVIO has been impressive, averaging nearly 13 percent a year in 1978–88 (table 1.5). Net value of industrial output, basically equivalent to value added, has grown more slowly (10 percent a year). Industry grew somewhat more rapidly overall in the 1980s than earlier, although the degree of acceleration was modest. The composition of GVIO has shifted slightly in favor of light industry (primarily consumer goods) during the reform period. Marked year-to-year fluctuations in the industrial growth rate are evident in table 1.5.

Growth rates for individual products vary widely, with most producer goods showing respectable increases (table 1.6). In a few cases, such as metal-cutting machine tools, low growth reflects overproduction in 1978 and masks improvements in quality, technology, and other product characteristics during the decade. The production of large tractors declined as a consequence of the decollectivization of agriculture into small plots; demand for small, two-wheeled tractors has increased very rapidly. Perhaps most remarkable, all forms of energy production have increased slowly in relation to the aggregate industrial growth rate, reflecting substantial progress in energy conservation.

The production of basic industrial consumer goods has grown steadily, and that of consumer durables has increased rapidly, as shown in table 1.7. Although the base of existing production for many of these goods was extremely small in 1978, by the late 1980s ownership of consumer durables in the population at large had reached respectable levels by the standards applied to developing countries, especially in urban areas (table 1.8). This massive provision of consumer durables to the population should be considered an important achievement of reform. Housing for the urban population also has greatly increased in quantity and improved in quality.

Some analysts have suggested that distortions in Chinese statistics may have resulted in a substantial overstatement of industrial growth since the

Table 1.5. Annual Industrial Growth, 1952–88
(percent)

Year	Total	Real GVIO Heavy industry	Light industry	Share of light industry in total	Real net value of industrial output
1952–78[a]	11.4	13.8	9.3	—	11.5
1957–78[a]	9.9	11.2	8.4	—	9.6
1979	8.8	8.0	10.0	43.7	8.1
1980	9.3	1.9	18.9	47.2	10.9
1981	4.3	−4.5	14.3	51.5	1.7
1982	7.8	9.9	5.8	50.2	6.0
1983	11.2	13.1	9.3	48.5	9.8
1984	16.3	16.5	16.1	47.4	14.9
1985	21.4	20.2	22.7	47.4	19.6
1986	11.7	10.2	13.1	47.6	9.6
1987	17.7	16.7	18.6	48.2	13.0
1988	20.8	19.4	22.1	49.3	17.4
1978–88[a]	12.8	10.9	15.0	—	11.0

— Not available.

GVIO, gross value of industrial output.

a. Data are compound average annual growth rates between end points of the period concerned. Although generated by data converted into constant-price series, the conversion from fixed accounting prices of one year to those of another is crude and mechanical and probably results in overstatement of long-term growth trends.

Source: State Statistical Bureau 1989b, pp. 30–31, 52–54.

Table 1.6. Output of Industrial Producer Goods, 1978–88

Item	Unit	Level of output 1978	Level of output 1988	Annual growth of output, 1978–88 (percent)[a]	Output per capita[b] 1978	Output per capita[b] 1988	Output per capita[b] Unit
Coal	Million tons	618	980	4.7	0.64	0.89	Tons
Crude oil	Million tons	104	137	2.8	0.11	0.13	Tons
Natural gas	Billion cubic meters	13.7	14.3	0.4	14	13	Cubic meters
Electric power	Billion kilowatt-hours	257	545	7.8	267	497	Kilowatt-hours
Crude steel	Million tons	31.8	59.4	6.5	33	54	Kilograms
Finished steel	Million tons	22.1	46.9	7.8	23	43	Kilograms
Cement	Million tons	65.2	210.1	12.4	68	192	Kilograms
Sulfuric acid	Million tons	6.61	11.11	5.3	6.9	10.1	Kilograms
Soda ash	Million tons	1.33	2.61	7.0	1.4	2.4	Kilograms
Caustic soda	Million tons	1.64	3.01	6.2	1.7	2.7	Kilograms
Nitrogenous fertilizer[c]	Million tons	7.64	13.65	6.0	7.9	12.5	Kilograms
Phosphatic fertilizer[c]	Million tons	1.03	3.69	13.6	1.1	3.4	Kilograms

	Unit						
Tires	Millions	9.39	29.91	12.3	9.8	27.3	Units per 1,000 persons
Metal-cutting machine tools	Thousands	183	192	0.5	0.19	0.17	Units per 1,000 persons
Mining equipment	Thousands	243	384	4.7	0.25	0.35	Units per 1,000 persons
Power generating equipment	Megawatts	4,838	11,093	8.7	5.0	10.1	Watts
Motor vehicles	Thousands	149	645	15.8	0.15	0.59	Units per 1,000 persons
Tractors	Thousands	99.3	47.2	−8.4	0.10	0.04	Units per 1,000 persons
Hand tractors	Thousands	324	1,336	15.2	0.34	1.22	Units per 1,000 persons
Locomotives	Units	521	844	4.9	..	..	n.a.
Freight wagons	Thousands	717	23	3.2	..	..	n.a.
Passenger wagons	Units	784	1,980	9.7	..	..	n.a.

n.a. Not applicable.

.. Negligible.

a. Compound annual growth rate between 1978 and 1988 (between end points of the period).

b. Based on year-end population figures.

c. Calculated in terms of 100 percent effectiveness (nutrient content).

Source: State Statistical Bureau 1989b, pp. 87, 298–301.

21

Table 1.7. Output of Industrial Consumer Goods, 1978–88

Item	Unit	Level of output		Annual growth of output, 1978–88 (percent)	Output per capita[a]		Unit
		1978	1988		1978	1988	
Yarn (cotton and synthetic)	Million tons	2.38	4.66	6.9	2.47	4.38	Kilograms
Cloth (cotton and synthetic)	Billion meters	11.0	18.8	5.5	11.5	17.1	Meters
Silk	Thousand tons	29.7	51.0	5.6	30.9	46.5	Kilograms per 1000 persons
Bicycles	Millions	8.54	41.4	17.1	8.9	37.8	Units per 1000 persons
Sugar	Million tons	2.27	4.61	7.3	2.36	4.21	Kilograms
Watches	Millions	13.5	66.6	17.3	14.0	62.7	Units per 1000 persons
Refrigerators	Thousands	28	7,576	75.1	0.03	6.91	Units per 1000 persons
Washing machines	Millions	400[b]	10.47	176.6	—	9.55	Units per 1000 persons
Electric fans	Millions	1.38	44.96	41.7	1.4	41.1	Units per 1000 persons
Radios	Millions	11.7	15.5	2.9	12.1	14.1	Units per 1000 persons
Tape recorders	Thousands	47	25,404	87.6	0.05	23.2	Units per 1000 persons
Televisions	Millions	0.52	25.05	47.4	0.54	22.9	Units per 1000 persons
Cameras	Millions	0.18	3.12	33.1	0.19	2.85	Units per 1000 persons

— Not available.

a. Based on year-end population figures.
b. 400 units only (not millions).

Source: State Statistical Bureau 1989b, pp. 87, 296–98.

late 1970s. Although in-depth research would be required to resolve all aspects of this question, a few observations can be made. There is no evidence of outright falsification of data at higher levels of government, although lower levels may be under some pressure to report high GVIO (to meet targets, gain promotions, and so forth). The ability to falsify data on physical output, however, is limited.

The extremely rapid growth of rural nonstate industrial output may in part reflect activities that were not previously reported. Structural changes, most notably the rising market share of small firms, may also have caused distortions. Price indexes appear to underestimate the true rate of inflation, and the use of different prices in calculating real GVIO (fixed accounting prices of 1980, plan prices, local "temporary" prices, and market prices) may have resulted in overstatement of real growth. At the same time, incentives to underreport production, especially as a means of avoiding taxes for rural and small firms, may have led to downward bias. All in all, it is unlikely that any upward bias in the reported industrial growth rate is so large as to change our general evaluation of Chinese industrial performance.

The physical output figures in tables 1.6–1.8 provide a partial check on the GVIO data. Production figures could lag behind GVIO data because of development of new products, innovations in existing products, and improvements in quality. In any case, although perhaps not fully consistent with the reported real GVIO growth rate, indicators of physical output suggest overall industrial growth of at least 9 to 10 percent a year.

Table 1.8. Ownership of Durable Consumer Goods, 1978 and 1988
(average per 100 persons)

Product	1978 (total)	1988 Total	1988 Urban[a]	1988 Rural[a]
Sewing machines	3.5	11.8	19.5	10.6
Bicycles	7.7	30.4	48.9	21.8
Watches	8.5	47.0	81.1	34.2
Electric fans	1.0	13.4	32.4	—
Washing machines	—	6.8	20.2	—
Refrigerators	—	1.8	7.7	—
Televisions	0.3	13.2	28.4	6.4
Tape recorders	0.2	8.3	17.7	—
Radios	7.8	23.9	—	10.6
Cameras	0.5	1.7	4.4	—

— Not available.

a. Data are based on urban and rural household surveys conducted by the State Statistical Bureau, with the original data divided by average household size to derive per capita figures. The urban and rural figures hence may not be strictly comparable with each other or with the nationwide averages.

Source: State Statistical Bureau 1989b, pp. 724, 726, 737, 742, 745.

Employment and Wages

China's total labor force in industry grew from 60.9 million in 1978 to 96.6 million in 1988 (State Statistical Bureau 1989b, p. 102). Industry's share in the total national labor force rose from 15.2 percent to 17.8 percent during this period, and average annual growth of industrial employment was 4.7 percent a year. Although respectable, employment growth evidently lagged far behind output growth.

These figures seem significantly to underestimate the number of persons employed in rapidly growing small rural industrial enterprises, often on a part-time or seasonal basis. Ministry of Agriculture statistics indicate that the number of employees of rural nonstate firms outside of agriculture (including construction, transportation, and commerce as well as industry) rose from 22 million in 1978 to more than 87 million in 1987, an increase of 65 million (Ministry of Agriculture 1989a, p. 292, 1989b, p. 192), compared with an increase of only 41 million according to statistics on the national labor force.

Although the Ministry of Agriculture figures may overstate the growth of full-time equivalent rural nonagricultural employment, they do suggest that the official statistics on the labor force are too low. The implications of underreporting could be significant; for example, if industrial employment was really 10 million more than the official figure in 1988, its share in the total national labor force would rise to nearly 20 percent.

Nominal and real wages of industrial workers increased rapidly in the decade of reform (see table 1.9). Average wages for employees increased 11.0 percent a year in state-owned and urban collective industrial enterprises and 13.7 percent in rural township and village enterprises (nonindustrial as well as industrial). During the same period the official cost of living index for urban employees rose 6.6 percent annually, which indicates that real wages increased about 4 percent a year for state and urban collective employees

Table 1.9. *Average Annual Wages of Employees, 1978 and 1988*
(yuan)

Item	State industry	Urban collective industry	Rural township and village enterprises[a]
Average wage, 1978	681	499	306
Average wage, 1988	1,931	1,419	1,106
Average annual increase (percent)	11.0	11.0	13.7

Note: Figures apply to all workers and staff (including managers).

a. Data exclude private enterprises.

Source: State Statistical Bureau 1989b, pp. 142, 146, 240; Ministry of Agriculture 1989b, p. 286.

and at a higher rate in rural industry. The index may understate inflation, but industrial workers' standard of living has clearly improved.

Capital

Healthy levels of industrial investment and substantial growth of capital stock occurred during 1978–88. Estimates by Chen and others (1988a) indicate that between 1978 and 1985 the nominal value of the capital stock of state-owned industrial firms increased 8.7 percent a year, whereas real growth was about 5 percent. Nominal growth of the capital stock in 1985–88 was much faster, 14.9 percent a year, which reflects increased investment activity during 1984–85 and higher inflation in construction costs (the average cost per square meter of factory buildings rose 12.3 percent a year in 1985–88, compared with 10.0 percent in 1978–85).

The capital stock of rural firms owned by township and village governments (nonindustrial as well as industrial) grew 21 percent a year in nominal terms from 1978 to 1988. Although inflation in investment costs may have been somewhat higher in rural areas, this increase still represents an impressive real rate of growth. Rural industry began with a tiny base of capital assets in the late 1970s, and subsequent growth in production was much higher than in the state sector.

Exports

China's manufactured exports increased rapidly from the mid-1970s through 1988, despite some fluctuations. Total merchandise exports were valued at less than $10 billion in 1978 but nearly quintupled to $47.5 billion by 1988, an average annual increase of more than 17 percent. Manufactured exports increased 16.3 percent a year in nominal dollar value between 1981 and 1988, starting from a much larger base than in 1978.[9] Growth in volume was somewhat lower, given inflation. In 1987 total exports rose 27 percent in dollar value, and manufactured exports rose 33 percent. In 1988 export growth continued at a rapid pace, with total exports increasing 21 percent and manufactured exports 26 percent. Export performance in the late 1980s has been particularly impressive given the substantial adverse effect of declining oil prices. (Petroleum and petroleum products accounted for about 7 percent of total exports in 1988, down sharply from 25 percent in 1985.)[10]

Financial Performance

Financial rates of return declined somewhat in Chinese state-owned industry between 1978 and 1988 (table 1.10), whereas financial losses as a percentage of gross profits first dropped and then climbed sharply in the late 1980s.

Deteriorating financial performance reflected disproportionate price increases for raw materials and energy and increased wage costs, as well as some degree of inefficiency. Increased competition among state enterprises and especially between urban state and rural nonstate enterprises also contributed to lower profit margins. Labor productivity in state enterprises increased sharply, at an average annual rate of nearly 5 percent a year in real terms in 1978–88. This solid performance is not surprising given the rapid growth of production. Finally, although costs of production of state enterprises fell in the early years of the reform period, they rose sharply from the mid-1980s, reflecting general price inflation in the industrial sector.

Technological Progress

The technological capability of Chinese industry has risen considerably since the late 1970s, although many industries remain outdated and inefficient. Improvements in domestically produced capital goods (some of them embodying advanced technology obtained through joint ventures or licensing with foreign companies), as well as a large influx of imported equipment, played important roles in contributing to technological progress.

Table 1.10. Selected Financial and Cost Indicators for State-Owned Industrial Firms, 1978–88
(percent)

Year	Profit-capital ratio	Ratio of profit and tax			Ratio of losses to profits	Increase in real labor productivity	Change in production cost of comparable products
		To capital	To fixed assets	To GVIO			
1978	15.5	24.2	24.8	24.1	8.3	12.3	−4.6
1979	16.1	24.8	24.9	24.2	6.5	6.4	−0.3
1980	16.0	24.8	24.3	24.0	5.9	2.1	+1.1
1981	15.0	23.8	22.9	23.9	7.9	−1.8	+1.2
1982	14.4	23.4	22.2	23.4	8.0	2.3	+0.4
1983	14.4	23.2	21.7	22.8	5.0	7.5	−0.2
1984	14.9	24.2	22.3	23.2	3.8	7.8	+2.0
1985	13.2	23.8	22.4	23.6	4.4	7.2	+7.7
1986	10.6	20.7	19.9	22.3	7.9	2.5	+7.3
1987	10.6	20.3	19.7	22.6	7.8	7.9	+7.0
1988	10.4	20.6	20.2	17.8	9.2	8.3	+15.6

GVIO, gross value of industrial output.

Note: Data are from independent accounting units only. Independent accounting units are firms that keep separate financial accounts of their own. They account for the bulk of the output, employment, assets, and profits of state industry.

Source: State Statistical Bureau 1989a, pp. 48–50; 1989b, pp. 326, 327, 333, 335.

China's large government research and development program has become more responsive to market demands because of increased reliance on payments from industrial clients in the face of budget cuts. Rapidly increasing industrial exports and greater domestic competition may have provided stronger incentives for enterprises to modernize technology. Nevertheless, major problems remain in this area.

Growth of Factor Productivity

A basic measure of efficiency in production is the relation between value of output and value of a suitable index of factor inputs, which generates an index of total factor productivity or multifactor productivity. Using revised capital stock estimates and eliminating nonproductive capital (workers' housing and public facilities) and labor (employees who provide various services rather than contribute to industrial production), Chen and others (1988b, p. 585) calculated the growth of total factor productivity in Chinese state-owned industry. According to these estimates, productivity of state-owned industry increased 5 to 6 percent annually on average in 1978–85, compared with only about 1 percent a year in 1957–78.[11] Although similar estimates have not been made for urban collective industry or rural industry, available data indicate even higher productivity growth for rural industry during the period of reform.

Prospects for Reform

As noted earlier in this chapter, worsening macroeconomic imbalances in 1988 led to government actions that adversely affected industrial reform. Hence prospects for continuing reform were in doubt even before the occupation of Tian An Men Square in Beijing by Chinese prodemocracy activists in May 1989 and their subsequent violent suppression by the military. These events were followed by significant changes in China's leadership and policies. Although these political changes were not caused directly by economic forces, they had substantial economic consequences, at least in the short run. There was a sharp reaction against political and radical economic reform; moreover, the country's top leadership for a time tried to use traditional planning solutions to deal with macroeconomic imbalances. The new political configuration did not immediately stabilize, engendering considerable uncertainty.

In the wake of these developments, economic policy became unclear. For instance, observers found Premier Li Peng's statements that no changes would be made to policies in such areas as the rural responsibility system (in agriculture), the contract responsibility system and director responsibility systems in enterprises, center-province fiscal relationships, private business, and preferential treatment for foreign investors unconvincing. Some leaders made strong antireform comments, which, however, were not translated into concrete directives at lower levels of government.

The general atmosphere became one of sharply reduced political support for urban and industrial economic reform, which inevitably also affected implementation of existing reforms at the enterprise level. Private enterprises were placed under political and ideological pressure, and some even went out of business as a result. The central government gave renewed emphasis to direct controls, such as price controls, to counter macroeconomic instability and inflation. The widely publicized campaign against corruption may have been selective and probably inhibited legitimate business activities and entrepreneurship, especially in the private sector.

Given the extent to which the Chinese economy has been changed by reform, there were limits to how much regression could occur without damage to industrial performance. This is most obvious in the case of rural nonstate (township and village) enterprises. Earlier critical comments by Chinese leaders were softened, and local governments strongly defended this sector, which contributes greatly to rural employment and incomes. Although credit granted to rural nonstate industry by state banks was cut sharply and the sector's output growth slowed, it remained considerably faster than the growth of Chinese industry as a whole. State enterprises were told that existing reforms would continue, although it was not clear in exactly what form.

The prospects for industrial reform at the end of the 1980s depended on interpretation and decisionmaking at lower levels of government, as well as firms' perceptions of the political and ideological climate. This could result in variable outcomes throughout industry. For example, local governments tried to protect rural industry, the engine of growth in many areas, from restrictions imposed by the central government. In the case of state industry, however, lower levels of government may have been less inclined to support existing reforms and experimental programs; instead they would probably subsidize local state enterprises in trouble and try to protect them from competition.

The possibility that China will return to the more reform-oriented political regime and economic policies that prevailed until 1988 should not be ruled out. For this reason it is important to assess whether industrial reform, as it was proceeding in the mid- to late 1980s, would ultimately have been successful. If so, the experience of the 1980s will provide useful guidance to future reform efforts in China and may also be helpful to other centrally planned economies in the process of transition.

Although it is impossible to provide a conclusive assessment of economic reform in China during the 1980s, the experience does suggest some fruitful directions for future action. Some of these were already being explored, if only hesitantly, before 1989,[12] and in a small number of enterprises reform objectives appear to have been largely achieved. Severance or drastic weakening of the hierarchical ties between firms and their supervisory agencies appears to be a critical prerequisite for success. Market conditions need to be sufficiently weak and unstable that enterprises must pay attention to sales and demand. Substantial direct marketing of products by enterprises also seems to be required. Many enterprises have fulfilled the requirements related to market conditions and direct marketing, at least temporarily.

China's experience with industrial reform clearly shows that progress will be limited and the danger of reversals great in the absence of a reasonable degree of macroeconomic stability. This is broadly true of any market-oriented reform strategy, not just the particular approach taken in China in 1984–88, based on the two-tier plan-and-market system of pricing and allocating industrial goods.

In the years before 1989 there had been increasing recognition of the serious, fundamental nature of the problems of state enterprises. Policymakers had begun to consider initial measures to reform administrative supervision, institutional arrangements, and even ownership. A tiny number of firms had begun to implement such measures, but the effort was cut short in 1988–89.

Of more immediate interest is the question of whether further progress with industrial reform could occur under the post-1988 policy regime. Obviously, the environment for reform became less favorable than in the late 1980s. Little or no progress occurred in state enterprise reform, and rural nonstate industry for a time was under political and ideological attack. Given the antireform attitude of Chinese leaders and many bureaucrats, even the prospects for maintaining existing reforms were in doubt. Perhaps most important was the exit of the most creative, radical reformers from positions of influence in the government, which led to a dearth of new ideas as well as vulnerability of existing reforms because of the lack of strong protectors within the government.

Certain mitigating factors limited the damage, however. Since a harsh reversal of reform policy would seriously curtail industrial performance, which already was lagging, Chinese leaders were under some pressure to refrain from sudden changes, or at least to relax restrictions once their adverse effects became apparent. Another factor inhibiting centralization of authority was the entrenched interests and power of local and provincial governments. These forces could be weakened by the central government through appointment of provincial leaders, as well as direct recentralization measures, but it appears that such efforts were not very effective in the context of a fragmented and complex power structure. Finally, and somewhat paradoxically, the restrictive government macroeconomic policies instituted in 1988 may have weakened market conditions for many industrial products. The shift from sellers' markets to buyers' markets, as mentioned earlier, probably aided the success of reform in the early 1980s and conceivably might also encourage decontrol in the post-1989 situation. Overall, the environment faced by many Chinese state-owned industrial firms may not have changed too much from that in the early to mid-1980s.

Notes

1. Chinese industrial firms, unlike their Soviet counterparts, were not allowed to retain any profits in the prereform period, and bonuses for workers were taboo. Profit retention schemes had been abolished in the 1960s, and bonuses were commuted to fixed wage supplements during the Cultural Revolution period.

2. The Chongqing Clock and Watch Company and the Qinghe Woolen Textile Mill, two of the firms analyzed in this volume, were among the earliest to implement experimental profit tax schemes in 1980 (see chapters 3 and 6).

3. One billion equals 1,000 million.

4. Data are from State Statistical Bureau (1987a, p. 272, and 1989b, p. 327). These figures probably refer to retained profits after subtraction of various levies and repayments of bank loans, whereas those cited earlier may refer to profits net of taxes but including these other expenditures.

5. In fact, the contract system could sometimes be used by workers to their own advantage: they could learn a skill during the initial contract period and then go into business for themselves or take a higher-paying job elsewhere (see Byrd and Tidrick 1987, p. 70). This was reported to have occurred at the Nanning Silk and Ramie Mill (see chapter 7), which implemented a trial contract labor system in 1980.

6. See Byrd (forthcoming) for a detailed review of contractual responsibility systems in Chinese state-owned industrial enterprises.

7. Given market prices higher than plan prices, an increase in the share of supply sold at market prices will lead to higher average prices and additional absorption of liquidity from the system (though net absorption depends on how the extra earnings of suppliers are spent).

8. State Statistical Bureau (1987a, pp. 130, 220; 1987b, p. 185; 1989b, pp. 265, 266, 273, 277). Figures are shares in GVIO at constant prices. Classification of firms as large, medium-size, and small is based on production capacity and varies across industries. Moreover, the criteria occasionally have been revised, which means that the figures cited may overstate the degree of structural change. The small category includes many firms that would be considered relatively large by international standards.

9. Breakdowns by sector from 1978 onward, based on statistics from the Ministry of Foreign Trade, are not strictly comparable with customs data that are available for the years from 1981 onward.

10. In response to the sharp decline in international prices and high domestic demand, exports of petroleum and petroleum products dropped from more than 36 million tons in 1985 to less than 31 million tons in 1988. The unit value of crude oil exports fell from $174 a ton in 1985 to $99 in 1988 (State Statistical Bureau 1987a, p. 526, 1989b, p. 640).

11. Although corrections were made in the labor and capital data series to eliminate distortions, such corrections were not made in the output series. If the latter overstates industrial growth, productivity estimates would be biased upward.

12. Scholarly discussions often went further than the schemes implemented, in some cases proposing such radical measures as privatization, worker ownership, replacement of bureaucratic privilege with ownership stakes in the state-owned econ-

omy, and the use of multiple currencies in different regions. But some of the schemes actually implemented also involved striking departures from the existing system.

References

Byrd, William A. 1983. "Enterprise-Level Reforms in Chinese State-Owned Industry." *American Economic Review* 73(2): 329–32.

———. 1987a. "The Impact of the Two-Tier Plan/Market System in Chinese Industry." *Journal of Comparative Economics* 11(3): 295–308.

———. 1987b. "The Role and Impact of Markets." In Tidrick and Chen.

———. 1991. *The Market Mechanism and Economic Reforms in China.* New York: M. E. Sharpe.

———. Forthcoming. "Contractual Responsibility Systems in Chinese State-Owned Industry: A Preliminary Assessment." In David Brown and Sylvain Plasschaert, eds., *Advances in Chinese Industrial Studies.* Vol. 2. Greenwich, Conn.: JAI Press.

Byrd, William A., and Lin Qingsong, eds. 1990. *China's Rural Industry: Structure, Development, and Reform.* New York: Oxford University Press.

Byrd, William A., and Gene Tidrick. 1987. "Factor Allocation and Enterprise Incentives." In Tidrick and Chen.

Chen Kuan, Gary H. Jefferson, Thomas G. Rawski, Wang Hongchang, and Zheng Yuxin. 1988a. "New Estimates of Fixed Investment and Capital Stock for Chinese State Industry." *China Quarterly* 114 (June): 243–66.

———. 1988b. "Productivity Change in Chinese Industry: 1953–1985." *Journal of Comparative Economics* 12(4): 570–91.

Ministry of Agriculture. 1989a. *Zhongguo Nongcun Jingji Tongji Da Quan (1949–1986)* (Statistical Compendium on China's Rural Economy, 1949–1986). Beijing: Nongye Chubanshe.

———. 1989b. *Zhongguo Nongye Tongji Ziliao (1987)* (Statistical Materials on Chinese Agriculture, 1987). Beijing: Nongye Chubanshe.

Naughton, Barry. 1990. "Economic Reform and the Chinese Political Crisis of 1989." *Journal of Asian Economics* 1(2): 349–61.

Perkins, Dwight H. 1988. "Reforming China's Economic System." *Journal of Economic Literature* 26(2): 601–45.

State Statistical Bureau. 1983. *Statistical Yearbook of China 1983.* Hong Kong: Economic Information and Agency.

———. 1985a. *Statistical Yearbook of China 1985.* Hong Kong: Economic Information and Agency.

———. 1985b. *Zhongguo Gongye Jingji Tongji Ziliao 1949–1984* (Statistical Materials on China's Industrial Economy, 1949–1984). Beijing: Zhongguo Tongji Chubanshe.

———. 1986a. *Statistical Yearbook of China 1986.* Hong Kong: Economic Information and Agency.

———. 1986b. *Zhongguo Nongcun Tongji Nianjian 1985* (China Rural Statistical Yearbook 1985). Beijing: Zhongguo Tongji Chubanshe.

———. 1987a. *Statistical Yearbook of China 1987*. Hong Kong: Orient Longman.

———. 1987b. *Zhongguo Gongye Jingji Tongji Ziliao 1986* (Statistical Materials on China's Industrial Economy 1986). Beijing: Zhongguo Tongji Chubanshe.

———. 1987c. *Zhongguo Nongcun Tongji Nianjian 1986* (China Rural Statistical Yearbook 1986). Beijing: Zhongguo Tongji Chubanshe.

———. 1987d. *Zhongguo Nongcun Tongji Nianjian 1987* (China Rural Statistical Yearbook 1987). Beijing: Zhongguo Tongji Chubanshe.

———. 1988. *Zhongguo Tongji Nianjian 1988* (Statistical Yearbook of China 1988). Beijing: Zhongguo Tongji Chubanshe.

———. 1989a. *Zhongguo Gongye Jingji Tongji Nianjian 1988* (China Industrial Economy Statistical Yearbook 1988). Beijing: Zhongguo Tongji Chubanshe.

———. 1989b. *Zhongguo Tongji Nianjian 1989* (Statistical Yearbook of China 1989). Beijing: Zhongguo Tongji Chubanshe.

Tidrick, Gene, and Chen Jiyuan, eds. 1987. *China's Industrial Reform*. New York: Oxford University Press.

World Bank. 1988. *China: Finance and Investment*. Washington, D.C.

2

Summary of Research and General Observations

William A. Byrd

THIS VOLUME IS BASED primarily on detailed empirical research on enterprises; it consists of extensive case studies of seven Chinese firms. An overview of the methodology and data base on which this study depends, as well as a summary of important findings, will provide a useful context for the analysis that follows.

Methodology

Methods of collecting and analyzing data for this project were shaped by its objectives and by constraints on obtaining Chinese economic data in the early 1980s. A review of the basic methodology and sources of data used in the project will illuminate the strengths and weaknesses of case studies.

The Case Study Method

The case study approach strives to build a foundation of specific knowledge that can serve as a basis for different levels of generalization. The method requires obtaining a detailed understanding of a small number of firms and their experiences, primarily through extensive interviewing; broader observations can then be made concerning the particular enterprises, the sample, the industries to which firms belong, or the state-owned industrial sector as a whole.

Data for the project were obtained through in-depth interviews with enterprise management and supervisory agencies, as well as with such other concerned organizations as commercial units, finance bureaus, planning departments, and banks. Interviews were supplemented by detailed quantitative data collected through distribution of questionnaires to each firm.[1]

Interviews gave priority to key facets of enterprise structure and operations: production, marketing, supply, investment, financial incentives and profit tribution, labor and wages, relations with supervisory agencies, and so on. Although interviews followed general guidelines, researchers were free to pursue topics of special interest or importance for the firm. Thus the interview information inevitably is uneven, with different emphases and degrees of detail depending on the enterprise, the managers who were interviewed, and the interviewers.

When possible, important episodes in the enterprise's history were examined through interviews with individuals both within and outside the enterprise, thus allowing researchers to prepare subcases on topics from different perspectives. Visits at each enterprise were long enough to allow follow-up on specific topics, and reinterviews were conducted subsequently at nearly all firms. The detail on particular events elicited in this way often provided insights into motivation, incentives, and constraints that could not have been achieved otherwise.

Analysis of the interview data began with careful perusal of interview notes, quantitative data, and other sources of information to develop a broad picture of the enterprise, its main activities, and its economic and administrative environment. Within this framework, researchers could pursue questions of enterprise motivation, changing incentives and constraints, the link with enterprise decisions and behavior, and the performance of the enterprise. Only after researchers understood the particular circumstances of individual firms could they make generalizations based on the firms' experience.

Information gathering was based to some extent on implicit working hypotheses that were reflected in the written guidelines for interviewers. For the most part, however, working hypotheses were developed during the research process, after initial interviews and data gathering. The sequence from case studies to generalizations was sometimes reversed in the promulgation of research results; four of the seven studies in this volume were written after the synthesis in Tidrick and Chen (1987). Nevertheless, the process of analysis usually proceeded from episodes and enterprise histories to generalizations.

Sources of Information

The interview notes and the quantitative questionnaires for each enterprise constituted the main data base for the project. The notes usually ran to more than 100 pages, subdivided according to interviewee. For most firms two sets of interview notes based on different visits were produced. Although notes were not transcribed verbatim, the record generally followed the flow of conversation at each interview and there was no subsequent editing, so as to preserve the character of the notes as primary data.

The quantitative questionnaire was six pages long and contained thirteen categories of information, with a total of about 200 different items. Most of the data requested could be obtained by the enterprise from its own accounts. Information for each year from 1975 to 1982 was requested for most items, as well as for several earlier years such as 1965. About 1,600 pieces of quantitative data were generated for each firm, although some records were incomplete since a few enterprises came into existence after 1975 or did not fill out the questionnaire properly.

Other sources of information supplemented and updated the main data base, to varying degrees for different firms. These included articles from Chinese journals and books, statistical information from various sources (such as the *Statistical Yearbook of China*, yearbooks of industrial statistics, and the industrial census), and, for a few firms, subsequent visits. Although this additional information was uneven, it provided a useful supplement to the detailed data from interviews.

Advantages and Disadvantages

The case study method as applied in this project had the advantage of allowing researchers to gain a good understanding of the institutional organization, administrative environment, and unquantifiable social or cultural aspects of enterprise management and industrial administration. These insights would have been extremely difficult to obtain using any other research method. The case studies also permitted researchers to track the implementation of state enterprise reforms, which often differed greatly from their formal provisions and from accounts in the press and in journals.

Rapid changes in organization, incentives, administration, and markets in the 1980s meant that the information base had to be frequently updated. This could be accomplished by following particular firms over time. Although the research project did not undertake a longitudinal study, for some enterprises other sources of data and reinterviews did permit follow-up over periods of up to a decade. This augmentation enriched some of the case studies considerably.

The case study approach also provided the opportunity to observe enterprise behavior directly, rather than relying on statistical indicators or aggregated data. Direct observation of behavior and response in enterprises allowed more confident judgments about causation than could be inferred from statistics. Conversely, case studies could sometimes signal that inferences from quantitative or aggregated data or from perusal of formal reform provisions were questionable.

Case studies are also often useful in buttressing general conclusions. A well-chosen example can sometimes illuminate a point more effectively than presentation or manipulation of statistics. In addition, case studies can be a fertile source of ideas for further research and can generate a multitude of testable hypotheses. Finally, case studies can be a useful teaching aid, depicting concrete examples and real-life situations.

The case study approach also has some drawbacks. The most important limitation of the method is the difficulty of reaching general conclusions based on the experience of one or a few firms. The degree to which a small sample can be representative of broader trends and patterns in Chinese state-owned industry must be considered in the design of research and analysis of data. The experiences and anecdotes that emerge from studies of particular firms are based on characteristics specific to enterprises, locations, and industries, which might well be different in other circumstances. Although the representativeness of the twenty-firm sample in a statistical sense can be ascertained (see Tidrick and Chen 1987, pp. 11–38), this does not allow disentangling many enterprise-specific aspects that are difficult to quantify or not amenable to statistical analysis with such a small sample.

To adjust to this limitation, caution must be used in generalizing from interview data. Knowledge of the industries concerned and of overall trends reduces the likelihood of inaccurate generalizations. In any case, the general observations made in the case studies should be viewed not as definitive conclusions, but rather as tentative hypotheses requiring further testing.

Whether interview data can always yield an accurate description of an enterprise is doubtful. Depending on the interviewees and the reforms and policies in vogue, unintentional inaccuracies or, rarely, deliberate prevarication may result in a distorted picture of the enterprise under study.

The interview method used in the research project was designed to minimize these problems. Researchers spent a week or longer at each firm and interviewed large numbers of managers working in different parts of the enterprise. As mentioned earlier, central government organizations as well as local supervisory agencies and other relevant entities also were interviewed. This process provided a check against distortions based on any single interview.

Biases due to the timing of interviews were counteracted by scheduling several contacts with the enterprise over a period of time and by supplementing interview data with other sources of information. Researchers visited some firms as many as three times over a period of four years and in most cases made use of articles or books dealing with the enterprise concerned. Quantitative data supplied by firms, carefully checked for accuracy and consistency, also served as a check against distortions.

Additional measures were taken to improve the reliability of the information base:

1. Detailed notes were taken on all interviews, and where two or more research team members were present at a particular interview, notes were cross-checked before being put into final form.

2. Reinterviews were conducted at eighteen of the twenty sample firms,[2] dur-

ing which researchers could check inconsistencies or fill in gaps from initial interviews, pursue new questions, and trace the evolution of the enterprises over time.

3. Interviews dealt with specific situations, decisions, and actions, not just the general opinions of interviewees.

4. Researchers asked follow-up questions to amplify points that were unclear or vague.

The Case Studies

The selection of the seven case-study firms from the sample of twenty was based on several criteria. First, extensive and reliable information about the firm was a prerequisite for selection. The quantitative questionnaire that was distributed before interviewing had to be completed fully and accurately, and interviews had to be detailed and informative as well as carefully recorded. Some consideration also was given to the availability of data from other sources.

The need for adequate information resulted in a tendency for authors to write about firms that they themselves had visited. Since six of the seven case studies were written by researchers from the World Bank, selection was weighted toward enterprises that had been visited by the World Bank team. In fact, of the seven firms where World Bank researchers conducted interviews, six are the subject of case studies.[3]

Second, there was a preference for enterprises whose experiences provided illuminating insights related to Chinese industry and reform. The Chongqing Clock and Watch Company and the Shenyang Smelter were outstanding in this respect, although all seven had experiences with broad applicability. Unfortunately, some enterprises with exceptionally rich histories could not be included because data were lacking.[4]

Third, the selected enterprises were supposed to demonstrate variety in such attributes as industrial subsector, size, technology, ownership and level of government jurisdiction, reform experience, growth, and financial performance. The diversity of the enterprises and their experiences is evident in the brief introductions in this section and is even more apparent in the case studies themselves.

The interplay among these considerations can be seen in the seven enterprises selected. While priority was given to the first criterion, the second and third considerations were well satisfied in most respects. Only two of the firms are in the same industrial subsector, and these produce quite different products (one woolen textiles, the other ramie textiles). The seven enterprises are located in six different provinces (see map 2.1), and there is great variety in their administrative jurisdictions and experiences during reform.

Chongqing Clock and Watch Company

The Chongqing Clock and Watch Company is a medium-size producer of clocks and watches, situated in the large, heavily industrialized city of Chongqing in Southwest China's Sichuan Province. The company was originally established under municipal jurisdiction as a musical instrument factory in 1952. It began producing clocks in 1958 and, on an experimental basis, watches in 1970. Full-scale production of watches commenced only in 1977. Output grew rapidly in the late 1970s and early 1980s in response to strong demand; the enterprise improved efficiency and benefited from government readjustment policies providing increased financial and other resources to producers of durable consumer goods. The company eased resource and market demand constraints by becoming a corporation and by engaging in a number of joint ventures and associations with other firms.

By 1982 market conditions had turned sharply against the enterprise. The clock market was saturated, and expansion by existing producers and widespread entry of new firms into the industry were beginning to create an oversupply of watches. The response of planning authorities slowed but could not stop the shift from a sellers' market to a buyers' market; commercial agencies discontinued guaranteed procurement of output, forcing such enterprises as Chongqing to fend for themselves in a deteriorating market.

The company responded successfully to market problems, becoming more customer-oriented and developing new and improved products. By the mid-1980s it had virtually discontinued clock production and was in a relatively good position to take advantage of rebounding demand for watches.

Chongqing is of great interest for a number of reasons. First, it is a producer of consumer durables, which benefited from the readjustment policies of the late 1970s but were subject to the wide market fluctuations typical of such industries. The company's response to changing market conditions was similar to that of Chinese consumer goods industries in general when the prevailing sellers' market became a buyers' market in the early 1980s. Chongqing also provides an example of unsuccessful government intervention in an attempt to mitigate the impact of changing market conditions.

The firm's experience illustrates the importance of provisions for repayment of bank loans in influencing investment incentives for enterprises and their choices about investment financing. Because both principal and interest repayments were deducted from before-tax profits, and tax and depreciation funds were diverted to loan repayment when necessary, the enterprise had a strong incentive to engage in loan-financed, rather than self-financed, investment.

Chongqing oriented its behavior toward workers and strongly manifested the so-called family motive.[5] The firm's most striking actions in this area were its widespread employment of workers' children and massive construction

Map 2.1. Location of the Sample Firms

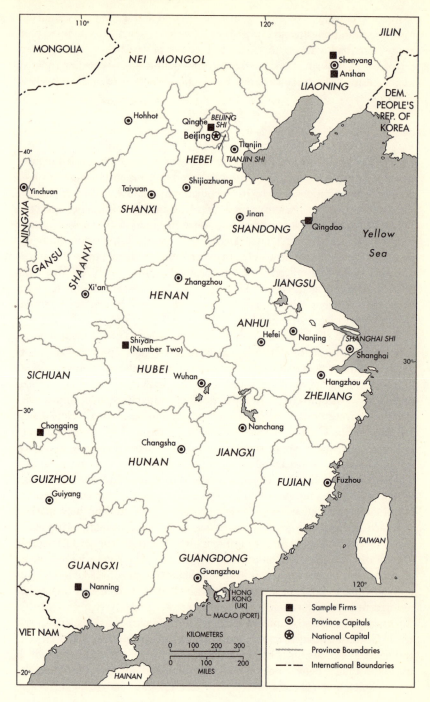

of workers' housing. Since the total wage bill and average wages were subject to ceilings, and housing and other benefits were financed from retained profits, workers had a strong incentive to increase profits; hence, the company expanded rapidly when the market permitted. Indeed, Chongqing's motive for increasing profits probably arose mainly from its desire to promote workers' interests.

Qingdao Forging Machinery Plant

This producer of twin-disc friction presses traces its history through a number of predecessors to before 1949. In 1960 the plant began manufacturing its current set of products, which embodied an inefficient, highly energy-intensive technology no longer used elsewhere in the world. The enterprise suffered from chronic inefficiency and waste in production and was plagued by problems with quality; large amounts of materials, products, and self-produced factory equipment were useless and eventually had to be discarded. Qingdao faced a severe problem with demand in the late 1970s, when the central government discontinued guaranteed procurement and state-sector users, increasingly selective and financially constrained by readjustment policies, were no longer attracted by the enterprise's products.

To cope with this situation, Qingdao first appealed to government supervisory agencies for assistance; when help in the form of procurement of its products did not materialize, the firm made vigorous efforts to promote sales. Ultimately Qingdao was forced to change its product mix and make small presses for rapidly growing light industries and proliferating small rural collective and private firms; it also sought contract business and developed new products. Thus Qingdao passed through the characteristic three stages of response to a weak market noted by Byrd (1987, pp. 243–44)—passivity, sales promotion, and demand-oriented changes in products and practices.

The change in the mix of products sharply depressed profits because the margin on small presses was much lower than the margin on large ones, but the shift did allow the enterprise to survive by tapping new markets in which demand was growing. Moreover, as occurred in many other firms, much of the burden of declining profits was borne by the government as a result of reduced profit remittances by Qingdao. The enterprise also made a number of changes in management and improved incentives for work units and individuals. These measures, along with efforts to reduce slack and waste, resulted in higher efficiency.

Qingdao is of special interest because of its "multiheaded leadership system." Government agencies at county, municipal, provincial, and even central levels at various times had partial jurisdiction over the enterprise, which was often caught between conflicting objectives and directives. For example, county and municipal authorities disagreed on Qingdao's target for gross value of output; county officials set unrealistically high goals and then criticized Qingdao for failing to achieve them. An administrative reorganization in the mid-1980s apparently ameliorated but did not fully resolve the problems with multiheaded leadership.

Over the longer term, Qingdao faces the dilemma that its outdated products and technology cannot survive much longer in the Chinese market. Its attempt to overcome this problem by producing beer cans and the machinery for making them encountered obstacles related to loan financing and administrative approval. Enterprise management, striving to maintain its position in the conflict between county and municipal authorities, found it difficult to concentrate on long-term strategy.

Shenyang Smelter

The Shenyang Smelter is China's oldest nonferrous metals smelter, established in the 1930s under Japanese occupation. Its main products are electrolytic copper, lead, and zinc; it also produces sulfuric acid, gold, and silver as by-products of smelting operations. Considerable expansion occurred until the mid-1970s, after which growth slowed.

The Shenyang Smelter faced problems of increasing severity during the period under study. The smelter was located in the middle of the largest city of China's electricity-short Northeast, far from its scattered sources of raw materials. The firm was by far the largest polluter in Shenyang City, and its pollutants included highly toxic agents such as lead and arsenic. The enterprise's location and cramped site between other factories hindered expansion, as well as production, and raised costs.

Augmenting these physical and technical constraints were some severe administrative problems. Although it was a very large enterprise, the smelter had been decentralized to provincial and then municipal control during the Cultural Revolution period. Since raw materials came primarily from distant sources and were allocated by the central government, and outputs continued to be distributed through the state plan, decentralization led to numerous conflicts and problems. There were often serious inconsistencies between targets for output and profits, and chronic problems of supply were exacerbated by the involvement of numerous agencies at different levels. The perceived shortage of needed investment funds was also related to control by multiple agencies.

A reorganization and centralization of China's nonferrous metals industry took place at the end of 1983, exemplifying attempts to find administrative solutions to the problems of a fragmented, decentralized system. The Shenyang Smelter was subsequently placed under the "subsectoral responsibility system" for nonferrous metals, one of a number of such programs instituted for various heavy industries. Contrary to reform goals, however, both centralization and, to a lesser extent, the new incentive system bound the smelter more tightly to administrative control. As a consequence, reforms did not progress rapidly in most spheres and did not yield significant benefits.

More fundamental than the problems of multiheaded leadership, serious as these were, was the continued predominance of mandatory planning, which largely removed marketing from the control of the enterprise. Mandatory planning prevented the smelter from producing alloys instead of pure metals, even though production of alloys often would have been economically more efficient. One harmful effect of mandatory planning and the smelter's lack of market orientation was an overemphasis on quality: the enterprise produced goods whose quality exceeded the legitimate needs of customers in order to maintain a good reputation and win awards.

The Shenyang Smelter provides an illuminating case study of a firm facing serious physical, technical, and administrative problems, struggling to survive and operate from day to day. In this situation, dynamism, expansion, and a strong market orientation were impossible. By its efforts to improve efficiency and reduce pollution at the firm level, the smelter may have hindered the development of a more fundamental solution involving some form of exit or relocation.

Qinghe Woolen Textile Mill

This is the oldest firm in the sample, dating from the first decade of the twentieth century and boasting a variegated history as a public enterprise under Qing Dynasty, warlord, Japanese, and Kuomintang control. After 1949 the mill expanded greatly, partly through infusions of foreign equipment and technology. Although Qinghe was a mature enterprise by the late 1970s, the firm was in a good position to take advantage of the new opportunities for the woolen textile industry presented by the readjustment policies. Moreover, the enterprise was selected to participate in pilot programs in enterprise and tax reform. Qinghe also made great advances in the reform of its internal management.

Like the other textile mills in the sample, Qinghe was buffeted by sharp fluctuations in both domestic and international markets, exacerbated by a 15 percent reduction in local-currency prices for woolen textiles procured for export in 1983. Hence this case study provides insights into enterprise response to a weakening and rapidly changing market situation. Management complained that its freedom of action and scope for quick, flexible response were severely hindered by persistent bureaucratic controls and restrictions.

In the early 1980s, somewhat earlier than most other enterprises, Qinghe gradually strengthened the position and authority of its director at the expense of the enterprise party committee and party secretary. This development was accompanied by an effort to strengthen line management in the workshops and work units, which had been weakened by the strong party structure within the enterprise. Qinghe was largely successful in these endeavors, and by 1984 the power and authority of the director had reached a level substantially greater than at most other state enterprises.

Qinghe also exhibited worker-oriented behavior. It refused to embark on a major expansion project until the authorities insisted that the project was a prerequisite to receiving permission to construct new housing and public facilities for its employees. The firm also maneuvered to increase bonuses beyond state-imposed ceilings, primarily through awards for productivity and for the development of new products.

In one respect the incentive system faced by Qinghe differed markedly from that of most other state enterprises: bank loans had to be paid from after-tax profits rather than from before-tax profits. This diminished Qinghe's incentive to engage in loan-financed investment projects and may also have contributed to its reluctance to expand in the case just cited.

Qinghe also experienced problems with the supply of various inputs, both domestic and imported, stemming largely from continuing administrative control over their allocation. Qinghe was forced to market directly a large share of its output, especially goods produced for export. (Although export transactions were concluded with Chinese foreign trade corporations rather than directly with foreign customers, Qinghe had to seek out export opportunities rather than wait for orders from foreign trade authorities.)

Qinghe provides a good example of a reforming enterprise that made great progress in some spheres, particularly internal management, but whose dynamism and flexibility were harmed by continuing government interference. Although its status as a model enterprise undoubtedly helped Qinghe in certain respects, it also led to an increase in the number of government agencies involved in its business affairs and to jealousy on the part of the local government supervisory organ.

Nanning Silk and Ramie Mill

The Nanning Silk and Ramie Mill is a medium-size plant in the Guangxi Autonomous Region, a relatively lightly industrialized area in Southeast China. Established in the mid-1960s, later than most other firms in the sample, it was originally designed to be a silk textile mill for processing cassava cocoons. The enterprise changed product lines early in its history because of shortages of raw materials and lack of demand. The firm also experienced problems with quality, which were resolved only in the late 1970s.

Eventually the mill became a producer of pure and blended ramie textiles. It was included in a pilot program in enterprise reform in 1979 and subsequently underwent rapid growth that lasted for about two years. Exports, which began in the early 1970s, made up a significant proportion of total output.

National overproduction as well as price changes early in 1983 led to sharply declining profits. Although in 1982 the enterprise's worsening financial performance was mitigated by a steep fall in profits remitted to the government, in 1983 the profit remittance target was hardened, forcing the mill to make extraordinary efforts to improve performance. The enterprise developed new products such as blended fabrics of ramie and polyester yarn, improved quality, and increased the share of exports.

The weak market of 1982–83 led to a sharp rise in the proportion of directly marketed output, which made up half of the total in 1982 and nearly four-fifths in 1983. The increased responsiveness to market signals, particularly in 1983, illustrates the growing importance of market forces.

The factory director responsibility system, instituted at the mill in 1984, strengthened the authority of the director in relation to the enterprise party committee; this in turn facilitated decisionmaking, allowing the director to institute a number of measures to improve efficiency and contributing to the enterprise's sharp turnaround and improved performance in 1984.

The enterprise, in collusion with local authorities, was able to circumvent central government directives imposing financial levies of one kind or another. Although such behavior was evident in other enterprises as well, the Nanning Mill represents an extreme in this respect. One example was the enterprise's outright refusal to pay the bonus tax in 1984, with confidence that it would not be penalized as a result.

Finally, the mill's experience provides insights into local government practices with respect to enterprise loan repayments. Since use of before-tax profits to repay loans adversely affected local government revenue, the Nanning Municipal Finance Bureau insisted on several occasions that the mill delay loan repayments to ensure that the municipality could meet its target for collection of revenues. Local banks had little choice but to comply, and loan maturities were stretched without penalty to the mill.

Anshan Iron and Steel Company

The Anshan Iron and Steel Company, the largest firm in the sample and the largest employer in Chinese industry, was founded in 1909 in the northeastern province of Liaoning. Before the mid-1940s it was under Japanese control. Large-scale expansion occurred in the 1950s, when Anshan was built up with a large infusion of Soviet advisers, investment, and technology. Subsequent growth was much slower, and Anshan was decentralized to provincial and, for a time, municipal control during the early 1970s. By the late 1970s the enterprise faced serious difficulties because of its backward technology, aging facilities, and crowded site.

A number of factors make Anshan especially interesting as a case study.

First, the strategy and design of modernization at Anshan have broad implications. The strategic choices it faced, such as whether the enterprise should be modernized in the first place and whether production should continue at full capacity during the renovation process, are typical of those involved in many major investment decisions in Chinese industry. Modernization was hindered by financial constraints as well as by the bureaucratic obstacles that permeate China's administrative system for approval, financing, and implementation of investment projects.

Second, Anshan's large size affected internal organization, transfer pricing, incentives at the subordinate factory or work-unit level, and other elements of management. Beginning in the mid-1980s decisionmaking was substantially decentralized to subordinate factories. These units were also given strong profit incentives and some authority over smaller investment projects. Flows of depreciation funds were decentralized as well, with potentially serious consequences.

For a large enterprise such as Anshan, the issue of vertical and horizontal integration is important. Upstream, ancillary, and downstream activities were frequently transferred between the enterprise and various government agencies, and protracted bureaucratic conflicts sometimes ensued. The firm suffered because of this instability in the scope of its activities. Because the range of choice included only integration and planning but not market-based allocation, all solutions tended to be inefficient as well as unstable.

Anshan is also noteworthy because of its many subsidiary collectives, firms and individuals that were part of the Anshan community but had a distinctly secondary status within it. With more than 160,000 employees, Anshan's collective sector was massive. The main goal of setting up subordinate collectives was to provide jobs for the large numbers of children of Anshan workers coming into the labor force, most of whom could not be placed as regular state workers.

Anshan's interactions with the central planning system and the Ministry of Metallurgy, its supervisory agency, are of great interest. The bulk of Anshan's steel output continued to be allocated through mandatory planning. Moreover, the chronic sellers' market for steel and widespread resort to "exchange" (something akin to barter) of steel for inputs and consumer goods needed by Anshan meant that direct marketing did little or nothing to make Anshan more customer-oriented and responsive to the market.

Anshan was placed under the steel industry's subsectoral responsibility system in 1984, which involved fixing targets for production of goods for the state plan over several years. The system had the adverse effect of binding Anshan more tightly to mandatory planning and ministerial supervision. Management complained about substantial increases in the amount of steel products levied from it at low prices and shortfalls in the supply of certain ancillary inputs, which necessitated purchases on the market at high prices.

Anshan is an important example of the most weakly reformed part of Chinese state industry: large, centrally controlled enterprises in heavy industries, the bulk of whose production remained subject to allocation under the central plan. Although few in number, these firms account for a substantial share of total national production of like products and through interindustry linkages have a disproportionate effect on aggregate industrial performance. The discrepancy between Anshan's huge size and obvious economic importance and the degree of administrative control over it throughout the 1980s forms an interesting contrast.

Second Motor Vehicle Manufacturing Plant

This enterprise, one of the most entrepreneurial in the sample, rose to become China's largest truck manufacturer during the period under study. The Second Motor Vehicle Factory came into being as the result of a bold transfer of staff, expertise, and technology from the First Motor Vehicle Factory in northeast China to a remote, mountainous region in northwestern Hubei Province, as part of the "Third Front" strategy.[6] The enterprise experienced difficult conditions and lacked adequate transport facilities until after 1975, resulting in a long delay in beginning truck production.

In response to mounting financial pressures in the late 1970s, the central government announced that it would stop investing in the Second Motor Vehicle Factory and may even have considered closing it. Faced with this crisis, enterprise management made several counteroffers involving lenient financial treatment but no new state investment, the last of which was accepted by the government.

With this leeway, the enterprise made extraordinary efforts to increase production and improve quality. The factory was successful, and the relatively lax profit remittance quota allowed it to reinvest in expansion and modernization. It weathered a period of weak demand in the early 1980s, as well as a subsequent wave of truck imports from Japan. By the late 1980s the Second Motor Vehicle Factory had become China's largest truck producer, with ambitious plans for further expansion, new product development, and technological modernization.

Among the most interesting aspects of the enterprise was its Dongfeng (East Wind) corporation linking 200 associated producers of parts and components as well as small producers of trucks. The corporation became a means of expansion and partial rationalization of China's motor vehicle industry through consolidation and specialization. Its success spawned imitators and undoubtedly influenced subsequent campaigns to promote horizontal associations between firms and the formation of enterprise groups.

The Second Motor Vehicle Factory's aggressive efforts to expand, modernize, export, and relocate some of its operations all are suggestive of a kind of entrepreneurial dynamism seen in few of the other sample firms.[7] A central question addressed in this case study is the source of this dynamism, which was intimately related to the enterprise's ability to escape from hierarchical ties to government supervisory agencies. Another important question is how the enterprise was able to maintain its customer orientation even when market conditions reverted to excess demand after 1982. This type of behavior may well be crucial to the success of state enterprise reforms. Finally, the case study explores the drastic reduction in mandatory planning and in allocation of trucks by the central plan, which for the most part occurred in a sellers' market.

Common Themes

From the diversity of experience illustrated by the case studies emerge a number of common themes, patterns, and problems, which suggest wider issues for consideration in analyzing Chinese industrial reform. Many of these issues are also reflected in evidence from other sources, and some of the observations made below echo the discussion in Tidrick and Chen (1987). They also complement the introductory survey of Chinese industrial reforms presented in chapter 1. All of these generalizations, however, are made more concrete through their linkage to the detailed case studies.

The Importance of Market Conditions

The effect of market conditions on enterprise incentives, behavior, and performance is evident in each of the case studies (also see Byrd 1987, pp. 244–45). The effectiveness of reform in promoting improved efficiency has been severely hampered by chronic sellers' markets for industrial products. In the late 1970s and early 1980s, shifts in market conditions from chronic excess demand to excess supply or rough equilibrium (buyers' markets) had a more beneficial impact on enterprise behavior than did the specific provisions of the reform program. In many cases reforms allowing direct marketing by enterprises became meaningful only with the emergence of a buyers' market. Where market conditions quickly reverted back to excess demand, the impact on enterprise behavior tended to be ephemeral.

The experience of sample firms after the early 1980s, however, indicates that the importance of market conditions must be qualified in certain respects. Market conditions are not the sole determinant of enterprise behavior and the success of reform; in any case substantial excess supply cannot be maintained indefinitely. Thus it is simplistic to view a sustained buyers' market as the essential, sufficient condition for successful enterprise reform, even though it undoubtedly is of great importance, and periods of weak demand have stimulated appropriate responses on the part of producers.

The critical ingredient to successful and sustained reform seems to be a sufficient degree of uncertainty about the adequacy of demand for firms' products over a long enough period of time, so that customer-oriented behavior becomes part of the organizational structure as well as the culture of the enterprise. Once this is achieved, temporary resumption of excess demand does not have adverse effects. The clearest example of this dynamic is the Second Motor Vehicle Factory, whose case also suggests that even in a strong market, enterprises eager to expand market share may orient their behavior toward customers and develop new products.

Mandatory Planning

The effect of mandatory planning on reform is related to but distinct from that of market conditions. On the one hand, firms compelled to deliver most of their output for distribution under the state plan have had great problems implementing reforms. On the other hand, it is extremely difficult if not impossible for authorities to maintain mandatory planning in the face of a sustained buyers' market, because purchasers will bypass the planning system and buy directly on the market at greater convenience and usually at lower prices as well.

In a chronic sellers' market a high share of mandatory planning is possible but not inevitable. Authorities have sometimes released firms from mandatory planning even when there have been shortages, and the government has often failed to reinstate mandatory planning when a buyers' market has reverted to a sellers' market. Hence a fortuitous combination of release from mandatory planning and the existence of enterprise dynamism (perhaps learned when the market was weak) could promote attainment of the objectives of reform even in the face of a sellers' market.

The Second Motor Vehicle Factory provides a good example of this pattern. It should be kept in mind, however, that the enterprise faced a difficult domestic market for a time and considerable import competition in the mid-1980s. The factory's strong drive to expand its market share and the lessons learned from the time of weak market demand combined to make it highly dynamic even in a strong market. Conversely, the Anshan Iron and Steel Company shows how continuing dominance by mandatory planning can stifle initiative and hamper reform. The Shenyang Smelter also was constrained by mandatory planning, which among other things prevented it from engaging in lucrative production of alloys.

The experience of both of these firms suggests that even if enterprises are allowed to market part of their output directly, benefits will be limited unless the share of direct marketing in total output exceeds a certain threshold, probably in the range of 25 to 30 percent. Otherwise, the enterprises remain oriented primarily toward the planning system and administrative supervisory apparatus, with direct marketing perceived only as a sideline. The same situation can obtain if government agencies impose substantial involuntary levies, outside the state plan, of products from enterprises.[8]

Enterprise Objectives and Worker-Oriented Behavior

The case studies shed light on the objectives Chinese firms pursued during the early years of reform. Byrd and Tidrick (1987, pp. 61–67) postulated five main motivations in Chinese state-owned industrial enterprises:

1. *The family motive.* The most ubiquitous objective was to improve the living standards and welfare of employees and their dependents. This was reflected in high bonuses, massive construction of workers' housing and public facilities by enterprises, provision of a full range of welfare benefits, and guaranteed employment of workers and (as they entered the labor force) their children. The enterprise in many respects functioned as a community, responsible for its members.

2. *The expansion drive.* Chinese state enterprises, like those in other centrally planned economies, exhibited a strong drive to expand capacity and production. This was sometimes reinforced by the family motive, when expansion permitted additional hiring of workers' children.

3. *The engineering or technical motive.* Managers of Chinese state enterprises were increasingly selected from the ranks of engineers, and enterprise behavior to some extent reflected their predilections—that is, a concern for obtaining and using the most advanced technology, producing goods of excellent quality, maintaining a clean, orderly production line, and winning prizes for quality and technical excellence.

4. *The desire for a quiet life.* The bureaucratic objective of compliance with the wishes of superiors was still important to many managers, particularly in firms without a high degree of autonomy from their supervisory agencies. This motivation led to a desire for easy plan targets and general (although often superficial) willingness to respond to government policy measures and directives, as long as doing so did not involve strenuous effort.

5. *The profit motive.* Enterprises worked toward making profits to further other objectives such as augmentation of workers' benefits. But the desire to increase profits was rarely unfettered, and the link with other objectives resulted in distortions. Conventional profit maximization was not pursued wholeheartedly.

Most sample firms pursued several or all of these five objectives, which often interacted with each other in complex ways and distorted enterprise decisionmaking and performance. Market conditions and availability of financial resources also constrained the ability of firms to achieve different goals, in particular (2) and (3). All of the enterprises studied manifested worker-oriented behavior, often to a striking degree. Many managers apparently did not internalize workers' interests as their own, however, and instead viewed those interests as a prior constraint that had to be minimally satisfied before pursuing other objectives.

How the Rules of the Game Affect Enterprise Motivation

Another phenomenon noted in some of the case studies is that the administrative or societal constraints imposed on firms can have an important influence on the concrete objectives they pursue (also see Byrd and Tidrick 1987, p. 66). Hence changes in the rules, both formal and informal, to which enterprises are subject can affect their motivation, incentives, and decisionmaking.

A most interesting example of this phenomenon is the shift from direct control over wage rates and employment to indirect control through linkage with the financial performance of enterprises. Under the former regime, an enterprise's total wage bill was determined by the size of its work force, so firms naturally strove to increase employment, particularly by hiring children of existing workers. With the abolition of controls over the size of the work force and average wage rates and the determination of the total wage bill based on profits and tax payments, firms had a strong incentive to economize on labor, usually through attrition. Children of workers could be provided jobs in collective subsidiaries, which were not included in computing the total wage bill in the linkage scheme. Such a strategy could maximize total income of all workers as well as the average wages of regular workers.[9]

Since the new system of determining the wage bill has been widely implemented in China's state-owned industries, there has probably been a significant trend toward higher productivity. It is difficult to disentangle this change from altered demographics and other factors. Nevertheless, real labor productivity in state-owned industrial enterprises increased by 7.9 percent in 1987 and an additional 9.3 percent in 1988, compared with an average annual increase of only 4.2 percent in 1978–86 (State Statistical Bureau 1986, p. 273, 1988, p. 384, and 1989, p. 18).

With widespread overstaffing in Chinese state industry, incentives to economize on labor usage may be beneficial in the short run, but they may exacerbate tendencies toward excessive capital intensity in the long run. Growth in the pool of people state enterprises feel responsible for (mainly workers' children) will slow over time. As the need for enterprises to generate employment declines, firms may well channel their investments into more capital-intensive technologies. A desire to improve working conditions may reinforce such tendencies. Since labor is abundant outside the state sector, stagnation of employment in state enterprises is probably not the optimal pattern.

The Changing Effect of the Soft Budget Constraint

The term "soft budget constraint" has been widely used in the analysis of centrally planned economies to describe the behavior of enterprises in these systems. The term refers to a situation in which the enterprise acts as if its access to financial resources is virtually unlimited or at least does not constrain its activities. As a result, enterprise demand for material resources and investment projects is excessive and financial discipline weak. In contrast, private firms in market economies are considered to face a "hard budget constraint" and hence have to behave more responsibly because their demand is limited by available financial resources. The degree to which the financial environment could be manipulated varied considerably among the firms analyzed in this volume, yet all to one degree or another exhibited manifestations of the soft budget constraint.

The variations in the extent of financial indiscipline are of great interest. Generally, based on the experience of this sample, relatively small, locally controlled firms in remote parts of the country tended to face a softer budget constraint than large, centrally controlled enterprises, especially those that contributed substantial amounts of products or money to the state. There is evidence of hardening of the budget constraint in some enterprises over time, which, in some cases, reflected greater systematization of reforms as well as tighter financial constraints for local governments. The hardening of the Nanning Silk and Ramie Mill's profit target in 1983, after a sharp decline in realized profits in 1982, is a good example. Overall, the degree of softness of the enterprise budget constraint was probably influenced by the financial situation of the enterprise, its previous financial performance, and the resource position of its government owner.

Investment Financing and Bank Loans

Problems in China's investment financing system and with loan financing of fixed investment are evident in several of the case studies. During the reform period grant financing of most investment projects by the government gave way to much heavier reliance on retained profits and other internal sources and, externally, on repayable bank loans. This shift is evident in the changing investment financing patterns of most sample firms (Byrd and Tidrick 1987, table 4-2, pp. 86–87). It is doubtful, however, that the efficiency of investment improved much as a result, and in fact new problems emerged.

The objective of loan financing was to induce enterprises to exercise more caution in their investment decisions and thereby economize on investment resources. Because of unusual (by international standards) provisions for loan repayments, however, demand for investment increased. Most firms repaid bank loans from their before-tax profits, giving them a strong incentive to borrow. The ability to divert depreciation funds, indirect taxes, asset taxes, and so forth to loan repayment further strengthened this incentive. (See chapter 3 for a detailed discussion.) Hence most sample firms financed their expansion primarily through bank loans, using their retained profits to provide workers with additional bonuses, welfare, or housing and other facilities.

The Qinghe Woolen Textile Mill, however, was required to repay loans from after-tax profits. Although it did engage in a large expansion project in 1979–80, it was unenthusiastic about a second project assigned to it in 1981. This reluctance may in part have been the result of the different provisions governing its repayment of bank loans. The Qingdao Forging Machinery Plant also was reluctant to engage in loan-financed fixed investment projects, because its loan repayments were drawn from incremental rather than existing profits, and given the low indirect tax rates on machinery, the scope for diverting taxes to loan repayment was limited. [10]

Beginning in 1984 enterprise loan repayments were further subsidized by allowing additional deductions from profits that otherwise would have been turned over to the government, to help cover enterprise payments for workers' bonuses and welfare. [11] Subsequently attempts were made to force enterprises to make at least a portion of their loan repayments from after-tax profits, but with more success in the nonstate sector than in the state sector. All in all, the specific rules on repayment of bank loans and the extent to which they were enforced had a strong influence on the investment behavior of enterprises.

Coordination between enterprise investment planning and the decision processes of banks, which were heavily influenced by local governments, also presented problems. Projects were often evaluated and approved by the planning system based partially on assumed financing by bank loans that did not materialize or were much delayed. More generally, the planning and coordination of investment and the design and implementation of projects suffered from cumbersome bureaucratic procedures and conflicts among agencies.

Location

Systemic obstacles to land acquisition and relocation by state-owned industrial enterprises can have a severe adverse effect. The Shenyang Smelter stood on an increasingly inappropriate site that exacted high social and economic costs; however, the plant was unable to relocate because of administrative constraints and the prohibitive expenses of moving. Other firms faced less severe problems with space and location. The urban land system in general discouraged transfers of land among enterprises, and the effective price of urban land was highly distorted (see Byrd and Tidrick 1987, pp. 76–78). Hiring additional workers from the community or entity that had previously held custody of the land in question was usually the largest component of acquisition costs. The experience of the Chongqing Clock and Watch Company illustrates how risky and costly such land acquisition could be if market conditions subsequently shifted adversely.

Administrative Demarcation of Enterprise Boundaries

Several of the case studies highlight the effect of administrative delineation of enterprise boundaries, that is, the limits to the scope and types of activities firms were allowed to engage in. The Shenyang Smelter was prevented from moving into production of nonferrous alloys, even though this was often the most rational approach. (Nonferrous metals smelters around the world engage in the production of alloys.) The Anshan Iron and Steel Company faced a situation in which government agencies sometimes acquired facilities that it had established and invested in. Firms were subjected to conflicts among various interested local and central government agencies, and any solutions tended to be temporary and unstable. These problems were exacerbated by the weakness, ambiguity, instability, and fragmentation of property rights in China's public ownership system. In general, such problems were most serious in the large heavy industrial enterprises still subject to mandatory planning.

These examples illustrate the more general tension between integration and fragmentation in centrally planned economies. Enterprises facing a choice between integrating production of needed resources within their own boundaries and relying on allocations through the state plan would overwhelmingly opt for the former. But the state planning apparatus tends to resist integration, because such a trend weakens its control over resource allocation (see Tidrick 1987, p. 195). The result is a series of unsatisfactory, unstable bureaucratic compromises, and solutions tend to be inefficient because market-based allocation is usually not permitted as an alternative.

Decentralization and Administrative Fragmentation

Problems resulting from fragmented, overlapping, and confused administrative jurisdictions are apparent in most of the case studies. The multiheaded leadership system, under which an enterprise answered to two or more levels of government, plagued the Qingdao Forging Machinery Plant, the Shenyang Smelter, and, to a lesser extent, the Anshan Iron and Steel Company. But even for firms nominally under the supervision of only one government entity, there were numerous problems with overlapping jurisdictions and conflicts among government agencies. The Qinghe Woolen Textile Mill is a good example.

These problems stemmed in part from transfers of control and cycles of decentralization and recentralization. Certain administrative functions were more easily carried out by one level of government than by another, and these functions naturally gravitated toward the appropriate level. Because Chinese workers were not geographically mobile, recruitment of workers was most appropriately a local administrative function, and hiring indeed tended to be localized even for larger enterprises under provincial or central control. On the other hand, for sizable enterprises operating in the national market, technical functions and distribution of products tended to remain under centralized government supervision. The result was splintering of administrative responsibilities and consequent inconsistencies and conflicts.

Administrative fragmentation led to atomization of enterprise activities. Coordinated planning and management within firms became difficult. Moreover, this fragmentation contributed to the proliferation of offices and unproductive personnel in enterprises, as each supervisory agency insisted that the enterprise designate staff to handle liaison. Several agencies were often involved in a particular sphere of activity. This led to conflicts and delays, and fostered a situation in which no one organization took any real responsibility for solving a problem. Planning, finance, material supply, labor, and other government departments all had partial jurisdiction over some facets of enterprise activity.

The Problems of Centralization

In light of the experience of sample firms, recentralization clearly is not the answer to the problems of administrative fragmentation. In the first place, it has proven difficult to recentralize effectively in China; hence recentralization has tended to be incomplete, as in the nonferrous metals industry. Decentralization has remained entrenched in some spheres of activity despite efforts to centralize. Recentralization typically required accommodation of the local authorities who lost control over enterprises, which in part defeated the purpose. Centralization does not solve the problems of fragmentation, even though they may be ameliorated and may change in form.

Second, centralized control can hinder efforts to make enterprises more independent and accountable, as happened with the Shenyang Smelter and the Anshan Iron and Steel Company. Although recentralization resulted in modest improvement in the case of the former, the problems did not disappear, and new issues related to centralized control emerged. Certainly recentralization has tended to increase the dependence of enterprises on the central ministry.

Finally, centralization, even when reasonably effective, has not markedly improved efficiency, either at the enterprise level or in the functioning of the administrative supervisory apparatus. Changes in personnel are typically minimal, consisting of reassigning staff under different organizational labels, and little if any reform of administration and management occurs in the new or strengthened central agencies. Reorganization tends to become endemic, with one round of centralization or reorganization generating new problems leading to further administrative changes, and so on. This pattern creates instability in enterprise administration and detracts from the effectiveness of any particular organizational reform.

In any case, centralization has not been pursued vigorously by Chinese authorities. Instead, the government has promulgated a massive decentralization of most state-owned industrial enterprises to municipal control, with an emphasis on the role of large cities in economic management. This strategy may have been intended to weaken central government industrial ministries, but it has strengthened municipal governments and encouraged trends toward the fragmentation of regional markets. Regardless, ownership of state enterprises by central industrial ministries has been largely phased out.

Fundamental Problems of Administrative Control

The case studies suggest that administrative adjustments and reorganizations cannot solve the fundamental problems of Chinese industry.[12] Although some administrative measures resulted in noticeable improvements, they could not fully resolve difficulties. A fundamental problem in the Chinese state-owned industrial sector is the prevalence and continued importance of administrative supervision. Despite all the superficial change, state enterprise reform scarcely affected the relation between firms and supervisory agencies until the late 1980s. The only enterprise studied in this volume that was able substantially to escape the shackles of administrative control was the Second Motor Vehicle Factory; the experience of this firm indicates that weakening government administrative control can have an important bearing on whether reform can fully achieve its goals.

The resistance to breaking the hierarchical ties between firms and the government bureaucracy came in part from the enterprises themselves. Many had a symbiotic patron-client relationship with their immediate supervisory agency, which provided many concrete benefits and protected them from the intrusion of other government agencies.

The effort of the late 1980s to treat the relationship between the firm (as represented by its manager) and the supervisory agency contractually rather than hierarchically may be important in this context. The contractual responsibility systems achieved only mixed success because of numerous distortions and problems with implementation (see chapter 1). Their main goal of equality between enterprise and supervisory agency has been elusive. These systems do indicate, however, that Chinese reformers identified the source of problems correctly.

Distortions Induced by Partial Reform

A conclusion that emerges from the case studies is that partial reform, as practiced in Chinese state industry, led to distortions that reduced efficiency and partly negated the benefits of reform. Certainly, enterprise reform has accomplished a great deal, especially when accompanied by competitive markets. Even where reform persevered and where a buyers' market was sustained long enough to have a lasting effect on enterprise behavior, however, limitations are evident. The soft budget constraint allowed firms to pay less attention to cost reduction than would have been desirable. Administrative ties still hindered independent decisionmaking by enterprises and encouraged a dependent relationship. Within enterprises, workers' pay and benefits still constituted a prior, binding claim on the firm's surplus. A host of administrative restrictions limited the exercise of dynamic entrepreneurship. Where the market environment did not become competitive and centralized administrative controls remained in place, progress was even more limited.

As noted earlier, the evolution of state enterprise reform in 1984–87 indicates that reformers had become aware of the problems of partial reform and were striving to achieve more fundamental changes, albeit with only limited success. The setback suffered by industrial reform in 1988–89, however, meant that there was little prospect for more comprehensive reform, at least in the short run.

Notes

1. These questionnaires, which were completed before interviews were conducted, brought issues and problems to the attention of researchers relatively early in the process.

2. Two enterprises, the Jinling Petrochemical Corporation and the Qingyuan County Economic Commission, refused to allow reinterviews, apparently because their reform experiments had "failed."

3. The seventh case study, the Qinghe Woolen Textile Mill, had exceptionally good quantitative and interview data.

4. The Mindong Electrical Machinery Company, the only firm visited by World Bank researchers that was not included in this volume, had a very interesting history involving successful export development, change of corporate status and supervisory agency, relocation, acquisition of other firms, management changes, and so on. Unfortunately, Mindong failed to complete the quantitative questionnaire adequately, and company representatives sometimes evaded interviewers' questions.

5. The family motive involves enterprise pursuit of objectives related to the material well-being and longer-term interests of workers and their dependents (see Byrd and Tidrick 1987, pp. 62–63).

6. For a detailed review of the Third Front, which clearly shows the magnitude and cost of this defense-based industrialization, see Naughton (1988).

7. The only other sample firm remotely comparable in this respect is the Mindong Electrical Machinery Corporation, which became a highly successful exporter, moved its headquarters from eastern Fujian Province to the provincial capital of Fuzhou in the early 1980s, changed its corporate status and supervisory agency, and acquired several failing factories.

8. The Xiangxiang Cement Plant, for example, was required to sell a large propor-

tion of its above-plan output to such powerful organizations as the railways and power bureaus as well as to local governments (see Byrd 1987, pp. 249–50).

9. Employment in collectives, or in various nonregular categories (such as temporary workers, contract workers, and peasant workers), was a common feature of the prereform system, but its objective then was to circumvent administrative constraints on the size of the labor force.

10. In principle, any loan repayments from enterprise profits were supposed to come from incremental profits attributable to the loan, but this provision seems to have been widely ignored. Calculating such incremental profits would have been a time-consuming task, impossible for many smaller investment projects.

11. This measure was instituted in response to complaints that firms engaging in expansion projects that were financed by loans to be repaid from profits often had to expand their labor force as well, which reduced average retained profits per member of the labor force since total retained profits were unchanged but the size of the labor force had increased.

12. Tidrick (1987, pp. 202–3) notes that such changes have had little salutary effect on planning and material supply.

References

Byrd, William A. 1987. "The Role and Impact of Markets." In Tidrick and Chen.

Byrd, William A., and Gene Tidrick. 1987. "Factor Allocation and Enterprise Incentives." In Tidrick and Chen.

Naughton, Barry. 1988. "The Third Front: Defense Industrialization in the Chinese Interior." *China Quarterly* 115 (September): 351–86.

State Statistical Bureau. 1986. *Statistical Yearbook of China 1986*. Hong Kong: Economic Information and Agency.

———. 1988. *Zhongguo Tongji Nianjian 1988* (Statistical Yearbook of China 1988). Beijing: Zhongguo Tongji Chubanshe.

———. 1989. *Zhongguo Tongji Nianjian 1989* (Statistical Yearbook of China 1989). Beijing: Zhongguo Tongji Chubanshe.

Tidrick, Gene. 1987. "Planning and Supply." In Tidrick and Chen.

Tidrick, Gene, and Chen Jiyuan, eds. 1987. *China's Industrial Reform*. New York: Oxford University Press.

3

The Chongqing Clock and Watch Company

William A. Byrd and Gene Tidrick

THE CHONGQING CLOCK AND WATCH COMPANY (hereafter referred to as Chongqing or as the company) provides an interesting case study of the Chinese government's adjustment and reform policies[1] and the response they elicited from producers of durable consumer goods. This chapter examines how reforms and changing market conditions influenced Chongqing's behavior and affected its performance. It first provides some general background on China's clock and watch industry and a brief survey of Chongqing's prereform history and subsequent developments. The bulk of the chapter examines the main reforms introduced in 1980, analyzes their effects on the company's incentives, reviews enterprise response to the reforms and changing market conditions, and evaluates the broader implications of Chongqing's experience. The final section provides an update on developments after 1983.

Introduction and General Background

Chongqing is of interest for several reasons. As a producer of consumer durable goods, it benefited from policies favoring light industry and the growth of consumption. On the demand side, rapidly growing consumer incomes added to existing unsatisfied demand for watches. On the supply side, the company was encouraged to expand production and was given the means to do so through a variety of reforms. Chongqing is a typical example of how China achieved impressive growth in the production of consumer durables in the late 1970s and early 1980s.[2]

Consumer durables industries all over the world are vulnerable to overexpansion and market saturation. A classic argument for central planning is that it can prevent business cycles and overinvestment by coordinating decisions about production and investment. In planning for consumer durables industries, the Chinese authorities faced a dilemma. They needed to decentralize decisionmaking in order to improve incentives to expand production and upgrade quality, but they feared that decentralization of control over inexperienced enterprises in a highly profitable industry carried the risk of overexpansion and market saturation. In fact, the clock market did become saturated by the end of 1981, competition sharpened in the watch market, and planning authorities intervened to slow the growth of watch production. Chongqing is an example of how planning authorities interpreted the general directive to treat the "planned economy as primary and market regulation as auxiliary" and of how an enterprise responded to increased autonomy. What is interesting about the company's experience is not only how it took advantage of expansion opportunities but also how it responded to subsequent problems and how reforms shaped those responses.

Chongqing participated in several very advanced reforms. The company became responsible for sales, changed into a corporation in charge of several subordinate factories, formed numerous joint ventures and associations with other enterprises, and converted from a system of handing over profits to a system of paying taxes. It supposedly assumed full responsibility for profits and losses and had considerable autonomy in the use of its funds. Chongqing has been held up as a model of reform (see, for example, Ding Jiatiao 1983, Xu Lu 1983, and Yu Zuyao 1983). It was one of initially only 10 and later 456 enterprises nationwide that participated in experiments substituting taxes for profit delivery, and its example undoubtedly influenced the government's decision to introduce a national program of conversion to taxation in 1983–85. In March 1983 Finance Minister Wang Bingqian led a team that investigated experimental firms, including Chongqing, and drew up plans for conversion to a taxation system in Chongqing City (*Renmin Ribao*, May 4, 1983, p. 2). Moreover, unlike many other enterprises, Chongqing underwent reform in a fairly stable manner. The government fixed its tax rate for three years from January 1, 1980, and most other reforms were also stable for three years. Although it is difficult to disentangle the effects of adjustment policies and special circumstances from the effects of reforms, a three-year period is sufficiently long for analysis of the influence of reforms on the company's behavior.

Although Chongqing was a typical beneficiary of national adjustment policies, it was atypical of Chinese enterprises in the advanced degree of its reforms. It provides an interesting example of the effect of adjustment and reform policies and of the interactions between them.

The Chinese Clock and Watch Industry

China began making clocks in 1915 and watches in 1955.[3] Production of both grew rapidly after the 1950s, and output reached 27.7 million clocks and 28.7 million watches in 1981, making China the fifth-largest producer of watches in the world. About 35 percent of clocks produced and nearly 10 percent of watches produced in that year were exported. There were more than 100 factories producing clocks, watches, and parts; only six provinces did not produce any watches as of 1982. The Shanghai Clock and Watch Company has dominated the industry. It produced 9.3 million watches in 1981, one-third of the national total. The largest Shanghai factory alone produced nearly 5 million watches (Shanghai City Clock and Watch Corporation 1981).

Watch production grew rapidly from a very small base in the 1960s (table 3.1). The growth rate fell below 20 percent in the early 1970s but then accelerated again after 1976, despite the much larger base of production. Amid growing signs of overexpansion of production of consumer durables, a national conference in September 1981 drew up production plans for major light industry products through 1985. The 1985 national target for watch production was set at 45 million. This limited the expansion plans of many producers. Although the market for clocks had become much more saturated than the market for watches, no national targets were set because clock production and prices were controlled at the provincial level.

The national ceiling on the output of watches for 1985 was disaggregated to all major producers. Chongqing's 1985 annual production target was set at 1.4 million watches, much lower than the company's own plan to produce 3 million in that year. The plans of thirty-eight state-listed factories called for production totaling nearly 60 million watches by 1985, 33 percent above the national target. Planning targets in China have been enforced to varying degrees. In some industries, such as cigarettes, the target was a firm upper limit; if it was exceeded, the firm was penalized. At the other extreme,

Table 3.1. Production of Wristwatches in China, Selected Years, 1960–82
(millions of units)

Year	Production	Annual growth rate (percent)	Imports	Exports
1960	0.5	n.a.	0.1[a]	0
1970	3.5	21.3	0.5	0
1975	7.8	17.6	0.8	..[b]
1976	9.1	16.5	0.7	..
1977	11.0	21.2	0.9	..
1978	13.5	22.3	2.2	..
1979	17.1	26.3	1.9	..
1980	22.2	29.8	3.1	..
1981	28.7	29.7	5.4	2.8
1982	33.0	14.9	1.0	3.5

n.a. Not applicable.

.. Negligible.

a. The year 1960 was an unusual year. Imports ranged from 58,900 in 1961 to 1,662,100 in 1963. Average annual imports in 1960–69 were 540,000.

b. Watch exports started in 1973 but most probably were very small until the late 1970s.

Source: State Statistical Bureau 1982, 1983.

targets for many products were set so that a moderately competent enterprise could exceed them. This was the position of the watch industry around 1980. The situation after 1982 appears to have been one in which watch producers were not permitted to expand capacity beyond the target level (assuming constant productivity). They could exceed their target, however, if they improved productivity and if they could sell what they produced. It is unclear, however, whether aggregate watch production was effectively controlled through the state plan. Localities had set up twenty-five factories unlisted in the state plan, which would have produced an additional 3 million watches a year by 1985 if their production was unchecked. Central authorities apparently were unsuccessful in controlling these factories.

Watch prices were lowered three times between 1980 and 1983, by a total of more than 20 percent. The price set by the state was the *minimum* price, which was supposed to protect high-cost producers and safeguard budget revenues from high taxes and profit remittances. As of 1983, the minimum retail price for a first-grade men's watch was Y70—still well above the average cost of Y18[4] and the world price of around $10[5] (Y20 at the official exchange rate in the early 1980s).[6] A substantial portion of that price was wholesale and retail markup (Y15.80 for a first-grade watch) and industrial and commercial tax (Y21.70, or 40 percent of the ex-factory price), but the profit margin has still been high (Y13 for a first-grade watch made by Chongqing but only Y3–Y4 for a third-grade watch). The price reductions of the early 1980s in part reflected the national adjustment strategy of expanding consumption and improving living standards, but they were also prompted by changes in market conditions as supply caught up with demand.

The Chinese clock and watch industry has some unusual features. First, Chinese per capita production and consumption are high in relation to income (see table 3.2). India produced fewer than 5 million watches and consumed an estimated 8 million in 1981. In per capita terms, China's annual

Table 3.2. Annual Consumption of Watches in Selected Countries, 1980

Country	Per capita income, 1980 (dollars)	Estimated consumption of watches per capita
India	240	0.011
China	290	0.024
Kenya	420	0.006
Malaysia	1,620	0.033
United Kingdom	7,920	0.288
Japan	9,890	0.491

Source: Per capita income is from World Bank 1982. Estimates of consumption are based on production statistics in United Nations (various years) and on national foreign trade statistics. Chinese figures are based on table 3.1 and an additional assumption that 2 million watches were exported in 1980; Chinese population data are from State Statistical Bureau 1989, p. 87. Indian figures are estimates supplied by industry sources.

consumption was more than twice that of India and production four and one-half times as high. China's per capita consumption was nearly three-fourths that of Malaysia, which had a much higher per capita income.

Demand for watches is affected not only by the average level of income but also by income distribution. As incomes rise beyond a certain threshold, demand for luxury goods such as watches grows very rapidly. In China's urban areas, where incomes are relatively equally distributed, watches have become a mass consumer good. In rural areas demand for watches has grown rapidly as a result of large increases in rural incomes, but watch ownership is still much lower than in cities. Nearly 19 percent of the total Chinese population owned watches in 1982 (10.2 percent of the rural population and 55.8 percent of the urban population). Chinese watch demand may have been higher as a result of both the fairly equal distribution of urban incomes and the unequal distribution between urban and rural areas. At a low level of per capita income the most favorable income distribution as regards demand for consumer durables is one in which as large a percentage of the population as possible has an income only slightly greater than the threshold of demand for consumer durables, subject to a constraint on minimum income for the rest of the population. As average income rises, the optimal distribution from this perspective moves toward greater equality.

A second contrast of the Chinese watch industry with that of other countries is the low level of Chinese labor productivity. Average annual output of watches per worker in China in 1981 was 524 (State Statistical Bureau 1982). In one of the two watch factories in India, labor productivity was 909 watches per person a year, whereas in a certain Japanese factory output per worker was 16,500 watches, over thirty times the Chinese average (industry sources). This does not necessarily mean that the Chinese watch industry was inefficient. The use of labor-intensive production techniques rather than highly automated Japanese methods may be an appropriate response to different relative factor costs. Japan produced electronic quartz watches that had only 55 components, compared with 138 components in the typical Chinese mechanical watch. In the Indian factories 20 percent of output was electronic watches, whereas in China the share of electronic watches was still very low in the early 1980s.

There was, however, considerable variation in labor productivity and costs within the Chinese watch industry. Output per worker in the Shanghai Watch Factory, which produced more watches than the two Indian factories combined, was 1,052 units in 1980 and 1,220 in 1981. The average in the rest of the Chinese watch industry, however, was only 377 watches per worker in 1981. Labor productivity in one Chinese factory was as low as 89 watches per worker in 1980 (State Economic Commission 1983). This was due to diseconomies of scale, to inferior management, and perhaps to other factors.

Part of the Chinese watch industry thus appears to have been highly inefficient. In Chongqing's main production unit, with output per worker similar to the national average, there were a few obvious ways in which labor could have been used more economically.[7]

The large number of producers with great differences in efficiency is a third unusual characteristic of the Chinese watch industry. China in the early 1980s had the largest number of independent, fully integrated watch producing firms in the world.[8] Twenty-one small factories, with output of fewer than 500,000 watches each in 1980, accounted for about 21 percent of total national production in that year. The share of small producers may have increased subsequently. Five medium-size firms with an output of 500,000 to 1 million watches accounted for another 16 percent of total national production. Variation in production costs, labor productivity, and capital-output ratios is striking. Production costs at factories for which data are available varied by a factor of about 4 to 1, nearly 7 to 1 if certain factories not registered in the state plan are included. Labor productivity varied by a factor of 12–13 to 1, and capital productivity by 12 to 1 (State Economic Commission 1983).

In view of the apparent economies of scale in watch production (see "Enterprise Response," in this chapter) and very low transport costs for finished watches and for parts and components, the existing industrial structure was not the most economically rational one. The proliferation of small producers was probably caused by a number of factors: (1) adjustment policies that gave high priority to rapid expansion of production of consumer durables, largely disregarding cost; (2) local authorities' desire to promote local industrialization; (3) a tendency to establish integrated production even in small factories, perhaps in part due to impediments to the free flow of watch parts and components among different areas; and (4) the high price of watches, which enabled even inefficient producers to earn a profit.

A fourth notable feature of the Chinese watch industry has been the continued dominance of mechanical watches. In much of the world, mechanical watches have been displaced by electronic quartz watches. Official Chinese policy in the early 1980s was to continue expanding the production of mechanical watches (Ministry of Light Industry 1982). The main reason given for this policy was consumers' resistance to electronic watches. Digital watches were almost completely unacceptable in China, but even quartz analog watches (with conventional face and hands) have been unpopular because of difficulties in getting service and replacement parts. Chongqing had to cut the price of a trial batch of digital watches from Y100 to Y15; even so, sales were slow.

There are good economic reasons for the preference for mechanical watches in China. The cost of repairing mechanical watches is much lower than in high-wage industrial countries, whereas batteries and other electronic parts are at least as costly as elsewhere. Even if watches were sold at international prices in China, some time would probably elapse before a significant portion of the population would follow the common practice in industrial countries of replacing rather than repairing watches. These same factors lend plausibility to the Chinese assumption that there will continue to be a market for mechanical watches from China in low-income countries for several years to come.

There is a second, policy-related reason for the slow development of electronic watch production. Chinese authorities intended to build a completely self-sufficient watch industry, and they were confident that the domestic market could be insulated from foreign competition if consumer tastes changed—although smuggling has been cited as a problem (State Economic Commission 1983). Furthermore, the authorities wanted to prevent obsolescence of existing investments and the loss of employment that would result from encouraging production of electronic watches. Most important, the quality and price of Chinese electronic components were still internationally uncompetitive in the early 1980s. Although electronic watches could be mass-produced as cheaply as mechanical watches if imported electronic components were used, Chinese authorities did not wish to develop the electronic watch industry on that basis. China's watch industry became self-sufficient in the production of difficult mechanical components such as shock absorbers well before the Indian industry, which also pursued autarchic policies, did. The cost of domestic Chinese shock absorbers, however, was still two and one-half times the cost of imports from Switzerland, and quality was inferior, according to company officials. One of the most important issues of development strategy in China is the role of foreign technology: when to import, when to license, and when to pursue independent development. In the early 1980s foreign licenses were not available for several key electronic components for watches.

Enterprise Development and Constraints

What is now the Chongqing Clock and Watch Company was founded in 1952 as the Chongqing Musical Instrument Factory, which produced violins and accordions. In 1963 the factory was closed down because of declining demand for these products and was split into three different units, one of which became the Chongqing Clock and Watch Factory. Clock production had begun on a modest scale in 1958 and expanded after the establishment of the separate factory to 100,000 clocks a year by 1969 and nearly 500,000 a year by 1975 (table 3.3). In 1970 Chongqing began experimental production of watches, but full-scale production was not approved until 1977. By 1979 production had reached 280,000 watches a year and 700,000 clocks a year. In that year the factory participated in an experimental scheme that allowed it to retain 5 percent of planned profits and 20 percent of above-plan profits.

Before the implementation of full-scale reforms starting in 1980, Chongqing faced two main constraints: the prereform economic system, which limited the discretionary authority of enterprises in important ways, and its lack of access to financial and material resources. Lack of resources was probably a more important constraint than were restrictions on autonomy. In the prereform period Chongqing could not make major investment decisions on its own; those resulting in an increase in floorspace of more than 10 square meters required the approval of supervisory authorities. All financial resources for investment projects were strictly controlled by supervisory authorities, and additional resources were hard to obtain. For example, government capital construction grants totaling Y17 million were provided to Chongqing in the 1970s to build an annual production capacity of 300,000 watches. This phase of investment was essentially completed, however, by 1978–79; state capital construction grants virtually ceased at that time, and without another infusion of investment funds there was no prospect for further expansion.

Lack of capital was not the only constraint. Land was in short supply in Chongqing City, and the enterprise had little room for expansion on its original site. Restrictions against conversion of agricultural land to industrial use were severe, there was no market for land, and firms requesting land for expansion faced formidable bureaucratic difficulties. Chongqing was also tightly restricted in its hiring of new workers to augment the labor force

Table 3.3. Development of Chongqing, Selected Years, 1952–82

Year	Gross value of output (millions of yuan)[a]	Clock production (thousands of units)	Watch production (thousands of units)	Employment (persons)	Gross value of fixed assets (millions of yuan)[b]
1952	0.05	0	0	109	—
1960	4.0	—	0	1,020	—
1969	1.6	100	0	965	—
1975	5.4	481	4	1,515	13.8
1976	5.7	382	9	1,746	16.8
1977	10.8	557	70	1,948	21.6
1978	20.5	654	181	2,501	22.4
1979	27.4	700	280	2,654	27.2
1980	45.9	1,000	502	3,787	31.9
1981	73.6	1,210	800	3,978	39.8
1982	64.9	542	884	4,287	63.7

— Not available.

a. Values for 1952–69 are in current prices. Values for 1975–82 are in constant 1970 prices.
b. Undepreciated value at original purchase price.
Source: Information provided by the company.

(but not in replacing existing workers who retired) and could not discipline or dismiss inefficient or unsuitable workers. These restrictions hindered the enterprise's ability to expand rapidly and improve labor efficiency.

The prereform economic system limited Chongqing's discretionary authority and incentives in important ways and reinforced the constraints that arose from lack of access to resources and from national economic policy. Before the major organizational reform at the beginning of 1980, Chongqing was an ordinary enterprise, with little administrative authority and subject to multiple layers of bureaucratic control. It was directly under the Chongqing Municipal Daily Use Consumer Goods Corporation, which itself was supervised by the Municipal Light Industry Bureau. Other city government and Party organizations were also involved in supervising various spheres of the enterprise's activity. The extent of plan-based control over Chongqing is not clear; the general weakness of China's planning system during the period from the Cultural Revolution to the fall of the Gang of Four (1966–76) would argue against tight control. In general, however, administrative controls over day-to-day operations and strategic decisions appear to have been more limiting in the prereform environment than subsequently. National policy favoring heavy industry may also have limited enterprise discretionary authority and restricted the flow of resources.

Chongqing had very weak formal incentives to increase output and improve efficiency. Material incentives for individual workers were nonexistent before the restoration of the bonus system in 1978. The enterprise as a unit was not allowed to retain profits before 1978. It was not permitted to market its output directly; all production was procured by the commercial system. Nevertheless, it can be assumed that Chongqing operated according to an expansion drive typical of enterprises in centrally planned economies, and would have willingly expanded production and investment if given the opportunity to do so, even in the absence of financial incentives.

On the eve of reforms, therefore, Chongqing had to maneuver within a number of tight constraints: (1) very limited access to capital, land, and labor; (2) little authority to make decisions; and (3) little incentive to expand production or improve efficiency. These constraints, in the absence of reforms, would most likely have prevented it from significant expansion.

Chongqing had certain resources and natural advantages, however, that allowed it to grow rapidly once reform and adjustment policies eased some of the constraints. Perhaps most important, the enterprise had, after many years, attained the capability to mass-produce watches. Technical skills had been mastered by the work force, production was better organized and coordinated, and the required equipment (imported and domestically produced) had been acquired. Clock production had been well established for more than a decade.

Another resource that would prove useful in the period of rapid expansion was existing ties with smaller local firms that processed raw materials and produced components for Chongqing. These trading relationships began in 1969 for clocks and in 1975–76 for watches. Although they were limited to purchases of parts and processing agreements, and no joint investment was involved, these relationships made possible the subsequent use of closer associations with other enterprises to ease resource and market constraints.

Chongqing also had a strong natural advantage in being the only major watch producer in Sichuan, China's most populous province, and the only integrated producer in all of southwest China (Sichuan, Guizhou, Yunnan, and Tibet). Although these areas were relatively poor, the potential demand for watches from 170 million people was great, once incomes started rising as a result of adjustment policies. Chongqing faced very little competition for this market from within southwest China. If it could meet the competition from advanced producers outside the region, its prospects would be favorable. This was one reason the enterprise was chosen to participate in what was at the time the most advanced experimental reform program in China.

The reforms introduced at the beginning of 1980 established Chongqing as a corporation with authority over numerous subsidiary enterprises. The company was also given access to bank loans, allowed to retain a large share of its profits, and made partially responsible for its sales. These reforms eased financial constraints and provided strong incentives to expand production. National adjustment policies begun in 1979 reinforced these effects. On the supply side, the priority given to light industry—particularly consumer durables—gave Chongqing a strong claim on investment resources. On the demand side, the rapid rise in consumption added to existing excess demand for watches and ensured that production would not initially be constrained by the market.

Chongqing's development in 1980–83 can be divided into two distinct phases: a period of rapid expansion in 1980–81, followed by strenuous efforts to cope with emerging market difficulties beginning in 1982. Gross output value nearly tripled in real terms between 1979 and 1981, as the company invested heavily in clocks and watches and organized numerous joint ventures and mergers with other firms. Employment increased by 50 percent, while average wages per worker rose by 26 percent.

At the end of 1981, however, the clock market became saturated, and, in response to signs of imminent overcapacity in the watch industry, national planning authorities reduced the company's future targets for watch production by about half. At the same time, Chongqing began facing difficulties in maintaining the quality of its first-grade watches. Moreover, the price of watches was lowered, and overall market conditions shifted from excess demand to approximate balance or moderate excess supply. As a result, gross output value fell by 12 percent in 1982, and the company was forced to initiate measures to cope with the change in market conditions. Chongqing changed its development strategy from quantity expansion to quality improvement and new product development.

Analysis of Main Reforms

Reforms at Chongqing can be divided into the following categories: (1) organizational changes, including designation as a corporation and establishment of joint ventures and various forms of associations with other enterprises; (2) enterprise-level financial reforms, primarily the experimental system that replaced profit remittances with tax payments; (3) credit financing of fixed investment; (4) greater scope for the company to engage in sales promotion and direct marketing of its products; (5) changes in the planning system; and (6) reforms in the employment and wage system.

Changes in Organization

At the beginning of 1980, Chongqing was transformed from an ordinary firm into an enterprise-type industrial corporation. It retained the characteristics of an enterprise in most respects but was given greater authority in dealing with subordinate units and government supervisory agencies. Although it occurred earlier than in other industries, this change was part of a wholesale reform of industrial administration in Chongqing Municipality that involved combining numerous industrial firms into specialized corporations (see *Renmin Ribao*, January 27, 1983, p. 3).

As a corporation, Chongqing built up a complex network of twenty-five production, processing, and assembly units. Seven firms were merged outright to form the company at the beginning of 1980. In addition, Chongqing developed close links with eight associated enterprises and eight joint ventures. The company maintained a purely commercial relationship with two other enterprises.

The joint ventures and associations were built on trading and processing relationships started as much as a decade earlier. The concrete arrangements differed in each case and were quite complicated, but there were some common features. To varying degrees, all of them involved investment by Chongqing and the other partner or its supervisory unit, with sharing of profits according to respective investment shares. Each associated enterprise and joint venture had a management committee, composed of representatives of the partners concerned, that was to rule by consensus on policy issues. In nearly all cases the chairman of the committee was appointed by Chongqing. The director of the associated enterprise carried out the decisions of the management committee; in daily operations (production, supply, and sales), the company was to exercise primary leadership.

The seven units directly incorporated into the company were controlled much more tightly than were the others. In 1983 the eight associated enterprises were also put directly under Chongqing, and their ties with their former supervisory agencies (the district industrial bureaus) were severed. Although it was related to general shifts in industrial administration in Chongqing

City, this measure reflected the specific desire to further strengthen the company's authority over these firms.

The goals of establishing Chongqing as a corporation were (1) to strengthen its ability to manage production comprehensively, in order to facilitate rapid expansion, and (2) to strengthen its position in relation to supervisory organizations and reduce the "petty tutelage" over its activities exercised by them. The change in organizational form was an important means by which the company's independence was strengthened, more important perhaps than changes in the formal rules of the game under which Chongqing operated. It gave the company greater administrative authority and removed its immediate supervisory unit (the Chongqing Municipal Daily Use Consumer Goods Corporation) from the scene. The Municipal Light Industry Bureau, which then became Chongqing's supervisory unit, was not in a position to monitor Chongqing closely or exercise tight control.

Usually in the shift from a smaller to a larger economic organization there is a tradeoff between the benefits of increased size (economies of scale, ability to pool resources, and so forth) and its costs (need for larger information flows, difficulties in communication and coordination, weakened incentives). In the case of Chongqing, however, there may not have been such a tradeoff, at least not in the short run. Even before the reforms the company was extensively involved with numerous other enterprises. Thus problems of coordination and communication were already present; by increasing its authority, the reforms allowed Chongqing to coordinate production more effectively and did not create significant additional disadvantages.

The company's motives for involvement in associations and joint ventures were complex.[9] It was not motivated in the short run by the profits it expected to earn from its financial investments in these enterprises. Many of the joint ventures were unprofitable, and Chongqing was forced to shore up some of them with interest-free loans or aid in other forms. The company did, however, make considerable profits from shipping components to these enterprises, particularly to those in Yunnan and Guizhou provinces. Watch and clock parts were traded within Chongqing's network at uniform internal prices that were determined and periodically revised by the company.[10] Originally, prices were set high so that relatively inefficient producers could cover their production costs. Until production at the associated enterprises developed fully, Chongqing shipped out more components than it received from them. It was expected that trade would become more balanced, and internal prices would be gradually reduced as production costs decreased. The large profits the company earned from trade in components were thus expected to be only a temporary phenomenon.

A stronger motivation for the formation of associations and joint ventures was to gain access to resources needed for expansion, the most important of which was space. This was a prime consideration in the establishment of the clock factory at a new site that originally belonged to a commune.

It may also have been a reason for the association with a factory in the Beipei suburb of Chongqing City, which acquired a piece of land from a commune, at which a workshop to manufacture shock absorbers was then built.

Chongqing may also have engaged in some associations and joint ventures to obtain financial resources. As a result of its joint venture in Yunnan, it obtained foreign exchange from that province with which to import machinery for its own use. On balance, however, the company probably put more funds into joint ventures and associations than it received directly or recouped through profits. The fact that some factories were already operating may have entered Chongqing's calculations, since it was usually cheaper and faster to build up existing production facilities than to construct entirely new ones.

The associations also were viewed as a means of circumventing restrictions on the hiring of additional regular employees, a shortsighted approach that backfired. New workers were forced to undergo a period of training to learn the specialized skills required for watch manufacturing, regardless of whether the workers were hired immediately after finishing school or were transferred from other factories. Chongqing's vocational school has been its most important source of trained labor. Labor obtained through associations and joint ventures could become fully trained only after a period of time. Moreover, by 1982 the change in market conditions reduced labor requirements. As a result, the company was saddled with excess labor, mainly from the merger with the commune to form the clock factory. The original contract for the merger stipulated that the clock factory should hire 770 commune members as temporary workers, in perpetuity. Because of the collapse of the clock market, however, the hiring of commune members ceased when their number reached 380. None of the workers already hired, however, was laid off. If the situation of the clock factory should ever improve, Chongqing was committed to start hiring additional workers.

An important rationale for Chongqing's links with enterprises in other provinces was to gain access to markets. By shipping components to Yunnan and Guizhou for final assembly there, Chongqing acquired closer ties with the two provincial markets and prevented other producers from making inroads. Commercial departments (CDs) in Yunnan and Guizhou favored local producers in their procurement of watches; this preferential treatment may also have obtained for the company's own products sold in the two provinces, particularly top-quality watches, which were not produced by the Yunnan and Guizhou factories. If Chongqing had not engaged in these joint ventures, the enterprises concerned might instead have cooperated with other watch producers.

The final and perhaps strongest motivation for the associations was to strengthen control over the management of production of parts and components. Many associations and joint ventures were built on earlier trading and processing relationships; such situations did not give Chongqing a great deal of power to coordinate production. Joint ventures, which involved the company providing some investment funds, and which explicitly put the company in charge of production, supply, and marketing, permitted tighter and more comprehensive management. This was especially true of the units directly incorporated into Chongqing.

The joint venture with the Kunming Watch Company provides an interesting illustration of Chongqing's motives and the complex arrangements typically involved in these associations (see Yunnan Economic Research Institute 1981). The terms of the agreement were as follows:

1. Total initial investment cost was Y8.5 million, including some equipment already imported by Kunming; investment costs were to be split 60/40 between Kunming and Chongqing, with profits to be divided in the same proportions.

2. Kunming was to engage in specialized production of ten watch parts and components and eventually reach annual production of 1 million pieces for two of them (700,000 of which were to be supplied to Chongqing) and 2 million pieces for eight of them (1.7 million of which were to be supplied to Chongqing); Kunming by 1985 was to assemble 300,000 complete watches a year, with 127 of the necessary 137 parts and components supplied by Chongqing.

3. The following numbers of complete sets of parts and components were to be supplied to Kunming by Chongqing: 20,000 in 1981, 50,000 in 1982, 100,000 in 1983, 200,000 in 1984, and 300,000 in 1985.

4. Kunming was to obtain a foreign exchange allocation quota from Kunming City and Yunnan Province authorities to import Y1.05 million in equipment it still needed. Chongqing would provide any additional equipment needed by the venture at a fair price.

5. A factory management committee was to be set up jointly by both sides, with its leading member and top factory managers to be appointed by Kunming Municipality; Chongqing was to be responsible for production and technical aspects.

6. A tax exemption was to be requested from the state until Kunming's production reached 300,000 watches a year.

In 1981 the prospects for the new venture appeared favorable, but its ambitious plans must have been affected by the clampdown imposed on the watch industry in 1982. It is doubtful whether Chongqing ever reaped the forecast large amount of untaxed profits from the venture, although it probably made money on sales of parts and components. Moreover, Chongqing complained about management problems at Kunming and conflicts with local authorities.

From Kunming's perspective, doubts were raised about the benefits and costs to the locality. Yunnan Province had to put a considerable amount of foreign exchange into the project. The tax exemption meant the province would forgo substantial revenues as well. There were also concerns about going outside the province to obtain machinery when local machinery producers had underutilized capacity, and about Kunming's reliance on Chongqing possibly relegating Kunming to a position of perpetual dependency.

Since circumstances differed in each case, it is difficult to form an overall assessment of joint ventures and associations. Three main points can, however, be made:

1. During rapid expansion, these relationships probably did ease certain constraints and enabled Chongqing to grow more quickly than would otherwise have been possible. Forming these relationships may not, however, have been the most economically efficient way for the company to expand.

2. Many of these relationships entailed explicit or implicit long-term commitments by Chongqing that it could ill afford after market conditions changed drastically and growth slowed in 1982.

3. Despite the closer links established by joint ventures, associations, and mergers, many at Chongqing believed that the company still did not sufficiently control the activities of subordinate units.

The Tax System

Sichuan Province at the beginning of 1980 chose five state-owned industrial enterprises, of which Chongqing was one, to participate in a new scheme involving substitution of direct tax payments for profit remittances to the government budget. This pushed the company to the forefront of China's industrial reform effort, made it highly visible, and at the same time gave supervisory agencies a considerable stake in its success.

The essence of the new financial incentive scheme was simple. Instead of remitting most of its profits, Chongqing paid a fixed proportion (40 percent in 1980–82) of its total income as tax. Income was defined in a peculiar way: conventionally defined profits plus the total wage bill and collective welfare funds charged to production costs. The tax essentially was levied on value added minus depreciation, or net product at factor cost; we will refer to it as net product tax. The remaining 60 percent of income was kept by Chongqing and used for wages and collective welfare payments, which constituted a prior claim; fixed investment (development of production); individual workers' bonuses; and construction of workers' housing and provision of other benefits and amenities. There were guidelines on the amounts that could be used for each of these purposes. The wage bill was subject to a ceiling, and collective welfare expenditures charged to production costs could not exceed 11 percent of the wage bill—the rest had to be financed from profits retained by the enterprise. At least 60 percent of retained profits (after subtraction of wages and collective welfare expenditures charged to production costs) were to be used for development of production and no more than 40 percent of them for other purposes.

Chongqing also paid industrial-commercial sales tax at a rate of 40 percent of the ex-factory price of watches, 25 percent for clocks, and 5 percent for unassembled parts and components sold outside the company. These taxes had been in effect since long before the reforms. New products at the stage of trial production could be exempted from industrial-commercial tax for two years.[11]

As part of the reforms, Chongqing was allowed to retain for its own use 70 percent of the basic depreciation charge on its fixed assets (compared with only 40 percent previously).[12] Major repair funds had been retained by the company all along, but in 1979 the rate was raised from 2.5 to 2.9 percent a year of the original value of fixed assets. A provision of the reforms in Sichuan was that enterprises were permitted to combine their retained profits, retained depreciation funds, and major repair funds in a single pool for use in fixed investment.

To ameliorate the well-known problems of the ratchet effect,[13] the net product tax rates for the five Sichuan pilot enterprises were fixed in advance and remained unchanged for three years. Chongqing's 40 percent tax rate was levied in 1980, 1981, and 1982. The principle used in setting the tax rate, the crucial variable in the incentive system, was that if performance, as measured by net product, were the same in a particular year as in a stipulated base year, the amount of funds received by the enterprise should be the same as in the base year. With superior performance the enterprise would receive more funds, whereas if performance were inferior, it would receive fewer. This principle was common to most of China's enterprise-level reform programs. In the case of Chongqing the base year chosen was 1979. The sum of 1979 retained profits, wages, collective welfare funds drawn from production costs, and the state grant for development of new products was divided by the sum of total profits, wages, and collective welfare funds, and the resulting ratio was subtracted from one to derive the appropriate income tax rate. (The fund for development of new products had previously been provided as a government grant, but after the reforms it was paid for by the enterprise itself.)

This principle was, however, only loosely applied. The appropriate tax rate with 1979 as the base year would have been 42 percent. To "provide some additional help to the enterprise," as one interviewee said, the rate was set at 40 percent. When the authorities set the 1983–85 tax rate, it would not have made much sense for them to use the original principle and 1982 as the base year because this calculation would result in exactly the same 40 percent tax rate as had been in effect before. All organizations concerned recognized the need to consider Chongqing's greatly expanded production and increased profits in setting the 1983–85 rate. There was disagreement about the exact rate, however, with the Chongqing Municipal Tax

Bureau favoring a rate of 50 percent. Chongqing itself, the Municipal Economic Commission, and the Municipal Light Industry Bureau suggested a rate of 44 percent. The final decision was to be made by municipal authorities, but the company expected that it would be about 44 percent. The tax rate was determined at least in part by negotiations among supervisory agencies, and the outcome often favored Chongqing.

Chongqing also gained substantial benefits from the choice of 1979 as the base year. The company had certain resources and advantages that had not been fully utilized in 1979. Moreover, it had been in an early phase of the learning curve in watch manufacturing; large increases in output and profits could be expected as workers gained experience and management of production became smoother, in the natural course of events. Furthermore, there was much underutilized equipment that could be made more productive quickly with relatively small new investments. Using 1979 as the base year resulted in a low tax rate, which allowed the enterprise to benefit from the rapid expansion that subsequently occurred. In contrast, the financial incentive scheme for a firm that had already achieved most of its potential in production and profitability would have been considerably less attractive. A good example of this situation is the Chongqing Number 3 Printing Factory, one of the other four Sichuan enterprises that participated in the tax experiment. Its income tax rate was set at 60 percent, which indicated greater profitability at the outset, but its subsequent expansion was much slower than that of the company.

Credit Financing of Fixed Investment

This innovation involved both reform and adjustment. Credit financing of investment was to encourage enterprises to economize on their use of capital by making them pay for it. Short- and medium-term equipment loans from the People's Bank of China (which accounted for most of Chongqing's borrowing in 1980–82) were also the main vehicle through which investment resources were channeled into China's light industries and textile industries during the adjustment period.

The interest rate on these loans was relatively low, but their short maturities (generally not exceeding three years) made for a heavy amortization burden, with large payments required shortly after the loan was made. This unattractive feature was offset, however, by the provisions on loan repayment, which imparted to these loans some of the characteristics of grants. Loans were to be repaid from the incremental benefits earned by the investment project they financed. The first source of such funds was incremental profits, but in most cases these would not be sufficient for repayment because of the short maturity. To make up any shortfall, basic depreciation charges on fixed assets created by the loan-financed project and fixed asset taxes on the same could be diverted to loan repayment. If funds were still insufficient for repayment, industrial-commercial tax on the additional goods produced by the project could be diverted to this purpose. In addition, principal and interest repayments on bank loans for fixed investment were deducted from income before net product tax was calculated. This was quite different from normal practice in most other countries.

As part of the reforms, Chongqing was required, starting in 1980, to pay a tax on its fixed assets. The tax rate was 2.52 percent of the original value of fixed assets per year. Starting in 1982, the company began paying a fee on its state-allocated circulating assets as well. Both levies on assets were subtracted from income before net product tax was calculated. This was an unusual feature of Chongqing's pilot program; in most of the other 450-odd enterprises in China experimenting with the substitution of tax payments for profit delivery, asset fees (though not loan repayments) were subtracted from enterprises' after-tax retained funds. This system also obtained for the nationwide income tax scheme implemented in 1983. (In the nationwide system, the tax was based on profits rather than net product.)

Chongqing had all along paid interest on circulating assets financed by bank loans. In 1982 interest rates on this type of loans were raised, and the company participated in an experimental floating interest rate scheme. Excessive use of working capital was to be penalized by higher interest rates, and low levels of inventories and of use of circulating capital were to be rewarded by lower interest charges. In practice, however, penalty interest rates were not charged when circulating capital use rose sharply because of market difficulties.

Sales Promotion and Marketing

Starting in 1980, Chongqing was permitted to market directly part of its total output of clocks and watches. The company set up forty local retail outlets; it also sold some products to lower-level commercial wholesale stations inside and outside of Sichuan Province. This procedure bypassed the official commercial intermediary, the Chongqing municipal branch of the Sichuan provincial second-level wholesale station for general consumer goods, which still handled the bulk of the company's total sales of clocks and watches in the early 1980s. Direct marketing was authorized for all of Chongqing's above-plan output and a stipulated percentage of its within-plan output. In 1982 about 30 percent of watch output was marketed directly by the company, 6.8 percent at retail and the rest to other commercial units.

The goal of direct marketing was to make the company more dependent on and more responsive to market conditions. It was hoped that direct marketing would generate improvements in quality, greater attention to customer needs, better warranties and repair service, greater efforts at sales promotion, and development of new product varieties to meet market needs. It was also hoped that Chongqing would expand rapidly in response to market demand.

There was to be very little reform of the pricing system, however. The extent of improvement depended crucially on the demand-supply situation in the market, as will be shown.

Changes in the Planning System

As an integral part of the reforms, Chongqing was given the power to plan its production and was to let demand determine its output. The company was also permitted to sign sales contracts directly with commercial units at its own discretion. On the supply side, it was permitted to procure inputs directly from suppliers when its needs exceeded its allocation of inputs under the state plan. Chongqing also could make its own investment and financial plans.

The company thus had considerable freedom to plan and arrange its activities, but government supervisory agencies continued meanwhile to grind out plan targets for the company, with little or no change in the way such targets were determined. In the early 1980s Chongqing had four mandatory targets: physical output of main products, product quality, labor productivity, and profit.[14] Labor continued to be allocated by government authorities. In addition, contracts to supply watches and clocks to the commercial system had to be fulfilled. Allocations of inputs were also still assigned, but since the clock and watch industry consumes few scarce materials these input quotas never constrained the company's production. In principle, fulfillment of plan targets was required in order for workers' bonuses to be paid. The output and quality targets must also be fulfilled for workers' bonuses to be paid. Failure to meet the profit target or inability to fulfill supply contracts would lead to a reduction in workers' bonuses.

Planning control over Chongqing was slack, however. Targets were set at low levels or revised downward if the original targets could not be met. Many plan targets were overfulfilled by substantial margins year after year. Plan targets for gross industrial output value at constant prices, for example, were overfulfilled in every year between 1975 and 1982, except 1976. In 1982 the original plan target was not reached, and it was revised downward by more than 20 percent. As a result, the revised target was overfulfilled by nearly 11 percent. In 1975–82, the margin of overfulfillment ranged from 11 to 61 percent; it was less than 20 percent in only two of those years. Only in 1976 were important plan indicators not fulfilled after the fact. In 1980–82 Chongqing fulfilled not only its four mandatory targets but all of its indicative targets as well.

Revision of some targets was easy. For example, in 1982 the criteria originally set for bonus payments included targets for output of clocks and watches. In view of the deteriorating market for clocks, Chongqing asked that 1982 bonuses be determined solely by watch output, a request that was promptly granted. National quality standards for watches had to be met, however, and apparently could not be lowered, which forced the company to make extra efforts to improve quality in 1982.

Aside from the weak link between plan fulfillment and workers' bonuses, there was no formal link between directive plans and enterprise rewards or incentives. The process of determining the plan seems not to have impinged greatly on Chongqing's decisions and activities. Supervisory organizations set only annual plans; short-term plans were determined solely by the company for its own use. Control figures handed down were highly aggregated—there was one target for the number of clocks to be produced and one for watches. Product mix within the two categories was determined by Chongqing in consultation with the commercial unit that purchased its output. The company could arrange its activities in accordance with its own plans and market forecasts, even if they differed greatly from the control figures set by higher levels. In 1983 Chongqing made arrangements to produce 1 million to 1.2 million watches and hoped to make 300,000 clocks, depending on the market; the state control figures handed down for that year were 900,000 watches and 500,000 clocks. Based on its past experience, Chongqing expected that the control figures would be changed in the last quarter of the year to conform with its actual performance. The company was more constrained, however, by its profit target, which was harder to revise. The 1982 clock production target could be lowered easily, in part because the profit target did not have to be changed.

Although Chongqing's annual production planning was only minimally affected by the planning apparatus, after a certain point this was no longer true of its investment decisionmaking. The threat of oversupply in the watch market forced central authorities to set fixed production targets for all watch producers, as a result of which the company had to curtail some investment plans. Nevertheless, it appeared that Chongqing would be permitted to exceed its 1985 production control figure, provided that it did so by improving labor productivity rather than by expanding capacity and provided that it could readily market the additional watches.

Reforms in the Employment and Wage System

Labor allocation remained largely unreformed. Quotas unrelated to the production plan still limited the number of workers Chongqing could hire in the early 1980s. Lazy or inefficient workers were rarely penalized, let alone dismissed. Redundant workers could not be laid off. When several hundred workers were made redundant by the collapse of the clock market in 1982, all the company could do was put groups of 300 workers at a time on study leave with temporary loss of bonus.[15] The company also had little control over selection of workers, although it could give limited preference to children of workers who passed apprenticeship or the company's technical school entrance exams.[16]

Bonuses for individual workers were restored in 1978 and expanded in 1980. Bonuses equivalent to 2.5 months' average basic wages could be paid and charged to production costs if the company met its four mandatory planning targets and fulfilled all economic contracts in accordance with national stipulations. In theory, 10 percent of total retained profits were to have been available for additional bonuses during 1980–82, but the resentment of workers in other factories about Chongqing's workers' high bonuses led municipal authorities to instruct the company to use this bonus fund for collective welfare payments instead. There was also a director's fund (financed from retained profits and equivalent to 3 percent of the wage bill) that could be used for special bonuses such as labor competition, product development, technical innovation, and cost reduction.

Bonuses were not closely linked to the performance of individual workers or of the enterprise as a whole. With slack planning, targets could be easily met or revised; this weakened the link between bonuses and overall performance. Individual incentives were weak because bonuses were distributed on an egalitarian basis. Because targets and related bonuses were handed down to factories, workshops, and small groups, an individual's bonus depended more on his work unit's performance than on his own. There were only small variations between work units in the value of the bonuses they received. Clock Factory workers received an average bonus equal to 2 months' basic wages in 1982, for example, compared with a company average bonus of 2.5 months' wages. Differences within factories were smaller; about 70 percent of workers received bonuses within a narrow range.[17] Only about half of the bonus fund for labor competition was distributed to individual workers in 1982; the rest was paid out equally to all workers at the end of the year. Other bonuses also were shared equally. Management had more authority to differentiate individual bonuses than it actually used in the early 1980s.

Pressure for egalitarianism came mainly from the workers themselves. The unpopularity of sharp differentiation among individuals is illustrated by the failure of a piece-rate wage system tested in 1981. Productivity increased under the system, but it was withdrawn, mainly because workers found that the slight advantage of additional income afforded by piece rates was more than offset by harder work and greater differentiation of incomes among small groups and individual workers. Ceilings on the wage bill (and hence on average pay per worker) remained in place. As a result the earnings of individual workers were subject to limits, no matter how productive the workers were. The contrast with rural nonstate industries, in which piece rates and other types of performance-related pay are ubiquitous, is striking (see Byrd and Lin 1990).

Two other changes in the wage and benefit system had a more significant effect on worker motivation. Both functioned largely as group incentives for all of the company's workers.

The first was a new floating wage system introduced in 1981, under which workers could be temporarily paid a wage rate higher than that stipulated for their wage grade. Under this system, Y1.50 per worker a month could be put into a wage adjustment fund to finance floating wage increases, provided all mandatory targets were met. The fund was increased by Y0.10 per worker a month for every 3 percent overfulfillment of the profit target, up to a limit of Y1.95. At the end of the year, the fund could be used to finance a provisional wage grade increase for a specified percentage of workers.[18] This increase would be confirmed as a permanent increase if company performance was maintained the following year, and it would be revoked if performance worsened. At the end of 1981, 76 percent of Chongqing's workers received a floating increase. In 1982 only 20 percent of the labor force qualified for the increase because company performance worsened; all but seven workers who had received the floating increase in 1981, however, were to be confirmed in their new grade in early 1983. The amounts of money involved may seem small, but, because these were permanent increases and wage grade promotions in China were rare, the benefit was actually quite large. For example, with a 5 percent discount rate and an additional working life of twenty-five years, the present value of a Y4 a month increase (one wage grade promotion) was Y676, compared with the average wage (including bonuses) per permanent worker of Y884 a year in 1982.

The second group incentive provided by the reforms was the collective welfare benefits financed from a share of retained profits. Of total retained profits of Y13.3 million during 1980–82, about 60 percent went to welfare benefits; most of that was used to build apartments for families of 334 workers.[19] Chongqing's labor force suffered from an acute shortage of housing. Only workers who had joined the company in 1970 or before were living in company apartments. In the prereform period, housing (such as there was) for workers had been financed by state capital construction grants. Subsequently, however, firms that retained profits paid for workers' housing construction themselves, and government grants for this purpose were discontinued. Company housing was valued because rents were highly subsidized— they were less than ordinary maintenance costs—and because once allocated to a worker an apartment virtually belonged to him and his heirs for as long as they maintained continuous occupation. Workers' only means of obtaining additional company housing was through Chongqing's retention of large amounts of profits.

The Company's Objective Function

The impact of the new incentive system depended very much on the objectives the company actually pursued.[20] We argue that Chongqing strove to maximize the family income of its workers. Given the company's particular circumstances and constraints, this was roughly equivalent to maximizing the sum of its retained profits and wages (or net product, in other words).

Other possible maximands include personal benefits of managers, fulfillment of company performance targets, profits, and average net product per worker.

It has been commonly assumed in analysis of enterprise management in the Soviet Union and Eastern Europe that managers maximize some narrowly construed function of their present and future earnings, including benefits from future promotions and transfers. This approach is inappropriate for analyzing Chinese management in the early 1980s, for several reasons. Managerial bonuses were small and did not vary much with enterprise or individual performance. Salaries were fixed; promotions were relatively infrequent and were based on many other factors besides individual performance. Finally, turnover was low among managers as well as workers. Although managers may not have stayed their entire working lives in one enterprise as most workers did, many of them spent long periods at a single firm. As a result, they were more likely to identify closely with the long-term performance of their units and the welfare of their workers.

It is difficult to believe that enterprises maximized some function of the performance targets set by outside authorities. If they did, Chongqing would probably not have made so many efforts to manipulate and distort the incentive system in 1980–82. In addition, the planning system was so slack and targets so easily revised that fulfillment of targets had little meaning in practice.

Profit maximization, the conventional motivational assumption in most models of capitalist enterprise behavior, appears at first glance to provide a better explanation of Chongqing's behavior. Reforms gave the company control over large amounts of discretionary funds, and the company made strong efforts to increase retained profits through output expansion, new product development, and manipulation of its administrative and incentive environment. Under Chinese labor market conditions a profit-maximizing firm would probably try to restrict increases in wages, bonuses, and worker amenities. Chongqing, however, often tried to increase worker benefits. Much of the company's effort to manipulate the rules on calculation and use of retained income was motivated by the intention to increase workers' bonuses or collective welfare payments.

Chongqing clearly was concerned about both wages and profits, but the question remains whether the company wished to maximize average net product per worker or total net product. It is normally assumed that the maximand of labor-managed firms, such as those in Yugoslavia, is average net product per worker (Ward 1958, Meade 1972). In this model, firms are concerned only with benefits to existing workers. They will expand employment only if the marginal net product of a new worker exceeds the average net product of existing workers, because only then will expansion raise incomes of existing workers. If completely unconstrained, Chinese firms might conform to this model. Binding upper limits on workers' wages and bonuses were in effect in the early 1980s, however, so firms were effectively prevented from increasing benefits per worker beyond a certain point. This suggests that their interest in expanding output would cease once allowable worker benefits had been attained.

Chongqing had strong reasons for wanting to expand employment and output beyond the point at which workers received the maximum allowable bonus. One important reason was the shortage of highly subsidized company housing, allocated by seniority, which only a minority of workers had received. A large share of retained profits could be used to build housing, so workers had a strong interest in expanding company profits. The motivation was strongest for those workers next on the eligibility list, of course, but even workers who already had housing would be interested in the company's profitability if their own children were working at Chongqing and still living at home. (About 1,500 company workers lived with their parents, half of whom were themselves children of company workers.) In this situation, existing workers did not oppose the hiring of additional laborers, because it would not lower their own incomes and might, through expansion of production and an increase in profits, speed up the allocation of housing to them or to their children living at home.

Two other features of the situation contributed to Chongqing's motivation to expand output. First, the floating wage scheme provided a direct link between wages and profits that was absent in many other firms. Second, because about half of the increment to the company's labor force consisted of dependents of existing workers, existing workers must have looked favorably on new hiring.

This discussion suggests that Chongqing was more concerned with increasing total wages and total profits than with maximizing value added per worker. The relative weights of profits and wages cannot be ascertained with any precision. They would be sensitive to a variety of parameters in the incentive structure. If the weights were equal, however, the company's objective function in the early 1980s would be best approximated by total net product.

A firm's objective function depends on its particular circumstances and on the constraints under which it operates. The desire to obtain workers' housing was a prime force behind Chongqing's expansion drive, but other enterprises in China may have had quite different interests. There is an interaction between the objective function and rules or incentives. If Chongqing were permitted to distribute all profits as bonuses rather than as collective welfare expenditure or investment, or if the company could no longer hire children of existing workers, it might well prefer to maximize average rather than total net product. Changes in rules governing management appointments and rewards, or greater tautness of plans, could also have changed the enterprise's objective function and behavior.

Chongqing's postulated maximand is equivalent to value added net of depreciation, interest payments, and indirect taxes on inputs and outputs. Interestingly, this is the same base used in calculating the company's liability under the proportional income tax system. As a result, the income tax would have had certain neutrality properties and would not have affected company choices with respect to level of production, size of workforce, or capital. Implicit in this analysis is the assumption that all the main components of net product are weighted equally: an extra yuan in retained profits is worth exactly the same to the company as an extra yuan of bonuses or an extra yuan of wages to new workers. This assumption is made only in the interest of simplicity; there is no a priori reason to believe the weights should be fixed or equal.

Incentives Created by Financial Reforms

TAX SYSTEM AND ENTERPRISE OBJECTIVE FUNCTION. Under the new tax system, Chongqing shared in a much higher proportion of its profits, 60 percent at the margin, compared with 20 percent of incremental profits it kept in 1979 under an earlier pilot scheme. It had retained no profits at all before the reforms. The new tax system must have improved incentives to increase profits. One unusual feature of it was that all of net product—both profits and wages—was taxed. The resulting incentives depended on the firm's objective function. Without a tax, or with a conventional profit tax, a profit-maximizing firm will expand employment and output as long as the marginal product of a new worker exceeds the wage rate. With a tax on both wages and profits, however, the firm will seek to substitute capital for labor and will employ new workers only as long as their marginal product exceeds the wage plus tax rate. A labor-managed firm striving to maximize average net product will always be more restrictive in hiring than a profit-maximizing firm. A tax on both wages and profits will not, however, make the labor-managed firm any less willing to expand than otherwise, because the tax reduces existing and incremental net product equally. Finally, a firm with Chongqing's assumed objective function (maximization of net product after deduction of indirect taxes, depreciation, and interest) would have an incentive to hire additional labor up to the point at which its marginal product falls to zero. Such a firm would be more expansionist than a conventional profit-maximizing firm or a traditional labor-managed firm. A profit tax on such a firm would create an incentive to raise wages or employment until profits were reduced to zero. Since only profits are taxed, the firm could expand after-tax net product even by employing labor with negative marginal product. The net product tax would, however, have a neutral incentive effect and would leave enterprise choices on factor mix and level of output unchanged, because the taxable base would be the same as the assumed maximand.

The marginal product of new workers was so high in 1980–81 that Chongqing would have had a strong incentive to expand employment whatever its objective function. The average wage of a regular worker in 1979 was Y706; it rose to Y929 in 1981. After-tax net product per regular worker increased from Y922 in 1979 to Y2,868 in 1981 but fell to Y1,506 in 1982. A decisive test of alternative hypotheses is therefore not possible with data from these years. The company's behavior in 1980–82 was, however, completely consistent with the goal of maximization of total net product.

Since the net product tax has a broader base than does a profit tax, for a given tax yield in the initial year it has a lower tax rate. The incentives generated are too complex to analyze in detail, but two particular effects should be noted. First, the net product tax gives a stronger incentive than a profit tax does to reduce material costs of production, because the retention rate of incremental profits created by savings in material costs is higher. (The net product tax gives no incentive to reduce labor costs, but then a firm maximizing total net product has no incentive to reduce labor costs in any case.) Second, the net product tax implies a higher risk for labor. Under a profit tax, if profits disappear, tax liability is reduced to zero. Under a net product tax, labor in principle would still be taxed even if a firm is experiencing a financial loss.

TREATMENT OF LOAN PAYMENTS. Credit financing of fixed investment was intended to give Chinese enterprises a greater incentive to conserve capital than existed under the old system of grant finance. Unusual tax deduction features (by Western standards), however, caused strange and probably unintended incentive effects. Under grant financing, enterprises were required to hand over to the state not only profits but also a high proportion of depreciation allowances. Moreover, fixed asset fees were introduced to create an incentive to conserve capital provided by the state. Although Chongqing's retention rate for depreciation funds was raised from 40 to 70 percent when grant financing was discontinued under the reforms, the basic principles that it should hand over part of depreciation fees and pay a fixed asset tax continued to apply to new investment as well as to existing grant-financed capital. Both of these provisions taxed capital and hence lowered the rate of return on investment and created an incentive to substitute labor for capital. Perhaps such incentives partly offset existing biases in the system. Because of price distortions, the rate of return on investment in light industry was very high. Similarly, industrial wages may have exceeded the opportunity cost of labor, whereas prices of capital equipment were generally below the shadow cost of production. But there is no evidence that rates of depreciation retention and fixed asset tax bore much relation to distortions in the prices of products and factors.

The effect of capital taxation was largely offset for credit-financed investment by loan repayment provisions that made credit financing much more attractive than self-financing. Because Chongqing was permitted to deduct both principal and interest repayments from incremental profits before paying income tax, 40 percent of the principal amount of a loan was in fact a grant because it consisted of money that would otherwise have been turned over to the government in the form of taxes. The diversion of other funds to loan repayment made loan financing even more attractive. Repayments were to be made from the incremental benefits of the project, in the following order: profits, depreciation charges, fixed asset tax, and industrial-commercial tax. Chongqing retained 70 percent of depreciation funds, so the diversion of these funds to loan repayment did entail a loss for the company. This situation did not obtain for fixed asset taxes and industrial-commercial tax, however. If the company used these sources for loan repayment, in the end it paid considerably less than 60 percent of the cost of loan-financed projects. This was a fairly likely occurrence because the maturity of loans was very short, generally not more than three years, and incremental profits alone were generally insufficient to fully amortize them.

Perhaps more important to the enterprise than the level of benefits was their distribution with respect to uncertain outcomes. This was important because enterprise decisionmakers are risk-averse, with respect to their personal situations as well as to that of the enterprise. Attitudes toward risk are especially important in considering technological innovation and development of new products, which are inherently risky activities.

Because of the mode of repayment, Chongqing bore none of or only a part of the financial risk of loan-financed projects. The vertical axis of figure 3.1 shows benefits accruing to the company as a result of a project, in the form of retained profits and wages, while the horizontal axis measures total incremental benefits of the project, including total profits, depreciation funds, fixed asset fees, and industrial-commercial tax. The line AE gives enterprise benefits as a function of total project benefits. The different segments of the line correspond to different rates at which the enterprise and the government share in the risks and benefits of the project, depending on which funds are used for loan repayment.

The segments AB and A'B correspond to the range in which total project benefits are so low that they are insufficient to repay the loan. The regulations did not state exactly what would happen for Chongqing in this case. If the additional payments came from Chongqing's profits earned from other activities, the segment AB would be the correct one. The enterprise would assume 60 percent of the marginal risk in this case. If the enterprise's supervisory agency undertook to repay the loan with its own funds or to divert other funds to this purpose, the segment A'B would be the correct one; there would be a clear floor, below which enterprise benefits from the project would not fall, that would correspond to the additional wage payments to enterprise employees generated by the project (0A').

Figure 3.1. Benefit Schedule for Loan-Financed Fixed Investment Project

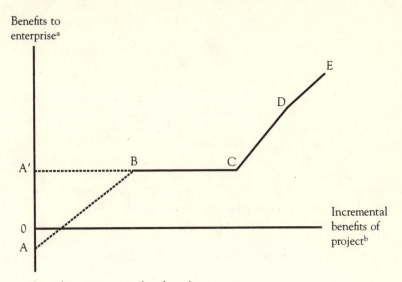

a. Sum of enterprise-retained profits and wage costs.
   b. Sum of incremental profits, depreciation funds, fixed asset fees, and industrial-commercial tax.

The segment BC covers the range of project benefits for which total benefits are sufficient to repay the loan, but for which incremental profits and depreciation funds are not. In this case the marginal loan repayment would come from the fixed asset tax or from industrial-commercial tax (which does not affect what the enterprise receives). The enterprise would not share in the risks of the project at all but would receive project benefits in lump-sum form (additional wages). The segment CD corresponds to the range of benefits in which the marginal repayment comes from depreciation funds. Since the enterprise would otherwise be allowed to keep 70 percent of these funds for its own use, it shares in 70 percent of the marginal benefits and risks of the project. In the range of project benefits corresponding to segment DE, the level of benefits is so high that the entire loan can be repaid from incremental profits, of which the enterprise would otherwise turn over 40 percent to the government and keep 60 percent.

The net effect of the tax payments, depreciation charges, and tax deductions depends on the profitability of the investment, on loan repayment terms, and on the rate of time preference. Broadly, in comparison with typical Western accounting and tax procedures (under which all depreciation funds are retained by the firm, no asset tax is paid, and only interest payments are deductible from taxable income), the system applied to Chongqing generally lowers the net cash flow from self-financed investment and raises the net cash flow from investment financed by loans. Chongqing's self-financed investment was effectively taxed and its loan-financed investment subsidized.

MARKETING AND GROWTH PATTERNS. The new tax system gave the company an incentive to increase net product, and the complicated system of capital taxes and deductions made borrowing more attractive than self-financed investment. A third reform gave Chongqing increased responsibility for marketing and thereby encouraged the company to engage in intensive growth. Extensive growth involves growth of output with equal growth of inputs and little if anything in the way of improvements in quality, development of new products, improvements in efficiency, or reductions in product costs. Intensive growth can imply growth of output without commensurate growth of factor or material inputs, as well as quality improvement, development of new products, and substantial improvement of technology.

The direction of effort toward extensive or intensive growth depends crucially on the demand-supply situation in the market. Since the reforms initially did not affect price determination, prices were generally fixed by the state at neither short-run nor long-run market equilibrium levels. Assuming that an enterprise accepted state-set prices as given and that those prices were high enough for profitable production, with excess demand in the market a profit-maximizing firm and a net-product-maximizing firm would both expand production. There would be little if any incentive to engage in intensive growth or provide better service to customers because the firm could sell whatever it produced without taking such measures. Thus few, if any, of the desired benefits of reliance on the market mechanism can be realized if there is chronic excess demand.

If the market is in rough equilibrium or if there is excess capacity, the enterprise can no longer take for granted its ability to sell all of its output—it must meet competition from other producers. Since the fixed price regime prevents overt price competition, companies resort to various forms of non-price competition. There will be a natural tendency for producers to improve quality, provide better services to customers, develop new products and more stylish varieties, and engage in sales promotion. Thus the benefits desired from greater reliance on the market mechanism can be realized if there is a buyers' market.

The preceding discussion has focused on the short run. In the long run, if the price is fixed at a level that gives producers high profits, new producers will have an incentive to enter the market and existing producers will have an incentive to increase capacity. In the long run there will be a tendency for excess demand to disappear. This process and its effects will be analyzed in the next section. Here the essential point is that giving firms responsibility for sales does not in itself create an incentive for intensive growth. A necessary precondition for such an incentive is elimination of the seller's market.

Enterprise Response, 1980–82

The reforms and policy measures described in the preceding section eliminated the most important constraints on Chongqing's expansion. Adequate financial resources for investment were made available, mainly from retained profits and bank loans. The company was given greater freedom to obtain material inputs directly from suppliers on the open market. Other required resources, such as land and production facilities, could be acquired through associations and mergers. Chongqing was also given considerable authority to determine how resources should be used. In the early stages of reform, the company could make strategic decisions and short-term plans on its own with surprisingly little interference from authorities. Finally, Chongqing was given strong incentives to increase production and profits. The new tax system linked Chongqing's discretionary funds (retained profits) to total earnings. Although bonuses for individual workers were not closely related to individual or group performance, the link between retained profits and construction of workers' housing gave workers a stake in increased company profits. The authority to market part of its output directly may have provided additional incentives.

The Expansion Phase

Chongqing responded quickly to the new opportunities opened up by the reforms. It engaged in a highly ambitious investment program designed to triple annual production of clocks and increase watch production nearly tenfold. In order to finance this massive expansion, the company borrowed heavily—a total of nearly Y27 million in 1980–82, with an additional Y4.5 million planned for 1983 (see table 3.4). This compares with the government's investment of only Y17 million in developing the company's watch production in 1970–77. Retained profits of Y10.3 million were used for fixed investment in 1980–82. Major repair funds and depreciation funds also financed significant amounts of investment. Total fixed investment in 1980–82 amounted to Y38.5 million, including Y5 million invested by Chongqing in associated enterprises. The radical changes in the amount and financing of the company's fixed investment are apparent in table 3.5.

Chongqing made these large investments based on its own long-term plans. These plans were influenced by the company's perception of market demand in southwest China, but they neglected to consider national developments, particularly the growth of older, more efficient producers in Shanghai and Tianjin. In 1980 the company set a very ambitious goal to produce 1 million men's watches, 300,000 women's watches, and 2 million clocks annually by 1982. These targets were never approved by higher-level authorities. In 1981 Chongqing set even higher long-term targets, for production of 2 million men's watches, 1 million women's watches, and 2 million clocks annually

Table 3.4. Total Amount of Fixed Investment Loans, 1980–83
(millions of yuan)

Source of loan	1980	1981	1982	1983 (planned)
People's Bank	3.25	3.25	10.0	2.0
Construction Bank	0	0	6.0	2.5
Bank of China	2.80[a]	0	0	0
Local government	1.47[b]	0	0	0
Total	7.52	3.25	16.0	4.5
Total for 1980–82		26.77		

Note: This table shows loans granted to Chongqing rather than the company's actual invest-ments financed by loans, which are shown in table 3.5.

a. This was a foreign exchange loan of $1 million.

b. Y850,000 of this amount was subsequently changed into a grant.

Source: Information provided by the company.

by 1985. This set of targets was likewise never formally approved by the authorities. Until the drastic change in the market situation in 1981–82, however, the company made large investments and obtained numerous bank loans on the basis of these plans. Bank loans were approved project by proj-ect, without consideration of long-term plans, and investment financed by retained profits did not at that time require higher-level approval.

Another response to the opportunities presented by reforms was the estab-lishment of numerous joint ventures and associations with suppliers of compo-nents and watch assembly points. These ventures and associations would, it was thought, enable the company to expand production more rapidly than if it had set about acquiring the requisite land, facilities, and labor directly. In 1980–82 Chongqing invested Y5 million in joint ventures and associated enterprises, not including assistance to the units incorporated directly into the company. Joint ventures and mergers played an important role in easing resource constraints and circumventing administrative barriers. The most important benefit of these associations, however, was probably the tighter control they allowed Chongqing to exercise over the entire production process for clocks and watches. Thus, at the same time the company was gaining greater discretionary authority in relation to its supervisory organizations, it was tightening up supervision of its numerous, theretofore only loosely related units involved in various stages of production.

Another significant response to reforms was the company's effort to improve the material well-being of employees. Substantial wage increases had been instituted as early as 1978 and continued through 1981, accompanied by rising bonuses. The average income of permanent employees increased by 87 percent between 1977 and 1981 (table 3.6). Average collective welfare spending per employee doubled between 1978 and 1981. These sharp in-creases in workers' incomes were mainly the result of national policies.

Table 3.5. Source of Financing of Fixed Investments, 1975–82
(millions of yuan)

Year	Total fixed investment	State budget appropriations[a]		Depreciation funds		Retained profits		Bank loans[b]		Other[c]	
		Amount	Percent	Amount	Percent	Amount	Percent	Amount	Percent	Amount	Percent
1975	3.19	3.19	100.0	0	0	0	0	0	0	0	0
1976	3.02	3.02	100.0	0	0	0	0	0	0	0	0
1977	4.81	4.81	100.0	0	0	0	0	0	0	0	0
1978	0.92	0.80	87.7	0	0	0	0	0.11	12.3	0	0
1979	2.56	0.08	3.3	2.08	81.3	0	0	0	0	0.39	15.4
1980	4.96	1.00	28.2	0.62	12.4	0.68	13.8	1.39	28.0	1.27	25.7
1981	8.55	1.96	22.9	0.25	3.0	0	0	4.30	50.3	2.04	23.8
1982	25.00	3.29	13.1	1.42	5.7	9.61	38.5	8.73	34.9	1.95	7.8
1975–78	11.94	11.83	99.1	0	0	0	0	0.11	0.9	0	0
1980–82	38.50	6.25	16.2	2.29	5.9	10.30	26.7	14.41	37.4	5.26	13.7

Note: This table shows Chongqing's completed investment rather than its appropriations or expenditures. Percentages may not add up exactly because of rounding.
a. Includes various subsidies from higher levels and funds for trial production of new products as well as budgetary capital construction and renewal investment appropriations.
b. Includes loans from the People's Bank of China, People's Construction Bank of China, and Bank of China.
c. Includes major repair funds and loans from the local government.
Source: Information provided by the company.

Chongqing's profitability and consequent ability to pay for large bonuses and collective welfare expenditures, however, facilitated this trend. Construction of workers' housing was financed entirely by company funds after the implementation of reforms. The average value of nonproductive fixed assets (mainly housing) per employee soared from Y707 in 1979 to Y2,234 in 1982. Even so, only workers who had been hired in 1970 or earlier were provided with apartments by 1982. Continued large investments were still required to satisfy workers' housing needs, so many employees must have had a strong interest in Chongqing's profitability even after 1982.

Adjustment and reform policies allowed the company to engage in an ambitious long-term investment program and eased many of the short-run constraints the company faced. As a result, output of clocks and watches grew rapidly in 1980–81 (see table 3.7). Watch output in 1981 was 186 percent higher than in 1979, and clock production, starting from a much larger base, increased by 73 percent during the same period. Production of watch components to be sold unassembled rose by more than 400 percent between 1979 and 1981.

Although greater reliance on the market mechanism was one of the key objectives of reforms, before 1981–82 the market appears to have only weakly constrained Chongqing's activities. Excess demand for clocks and watches was substantial at the outset of the reforms[21] and was stimulated by the rapid growth of personal incomes and, in the case of watches, by moderate price reductions.[22] Though Chongqing took measures to promote sales even during the early stages of reform, its viability and profitability did not depend

Table 3.6. Wages and Welfare Benefits per Regular Employee, 1979–82
(yuan)

Year	Average wage[a]	Average bonus	Collective welfare expenditures	Increase in non-productive fixed assets[b]
1979	755	164	72	—
1980	950	180	99	383
1981	950	134	144	578
1982	899	146	168	890

— Not available.

Note: All data are for the Chongqing Clock and Watch Company.

a. Includes all bonuses, but not wages of temporary workers. Average wages for earlier years are as follows:

1975	543
1976	514
1977	509
1978	595

b. Refers to original value of fixed assets. The total value of nonproductive fixed assets per regular employee in 1977 was Y707, in 1982 Y2,234.

Source: Information provided by the company.

Table 3.7. Growth of Chongqing's Production, 1979–82
(percent a year)

Year	Clocks	Watches	Watch components (value at current prices)
1979	7.0	54.6	410.7
1980	42.8	79.0	−3.5
1981	21.0	59.6	435.9
1982	−55.3	10.5	11.9

Source: Information provided by the company.

on these measures. The company perceived that it could sell virtually whatever it could produce in the short run.

Chongqing's response to this environment in which the constraint of market demand was relatively weak and the profit margin very high took the form of rapid expansion in output, with little attention to improved quality or technology, and relatively slow development of new products and styles.[23] Cost reductions were small in view of the large increase in production. This strategy was probably optimal as long as the constraint imposed by market demand was weak. In unreformed centrally planned economies, this is a typical behavior pattern for an industry or firm that is given priority in the allocation of resources and is ordered or simply allowed to expand production as rapidly as possible. Reforms may not have significantly affected Chongqing's behavior until the market constraint became stronger.

Market Constraints and Other Problems

By late 1981 market conditions began to change, dramatically for clocks and more gradually for watches. Demand for clocks fell as a result of market saturation. Demand for watches was still growing, but supply was quickly catching up, and rationing was discontinued for many varieties. Stocks of watches held by commercial departments doubled in 1980 and increased by a further 35 percent in 1981. Stocks were said to exceed the "rational" level by 1.7 million watches.

These developments were entirely predictable. If firms or their local government sponsors have some autonomy and are responsive to profit signals, excess demand at a highly profitable fixed price will induce new firms to enter the market and existing firms to expand. As long as the price remains fixed at a level greater than long-run marginal cost, producers will continue to expand production until supply exceeds demand. At this point producers have some choices. They can cut prices to gain an advantage over their rivals, and if prices are allowed to fall the market will balance at a new equilibrium price. Producers can also try to gain a competitive advantage by improving the quality or variety of products; these efforts could shift the demand curve outward and increase total demand at the controlled price.

If the demand curve does not shift far enough to clear the market, however, some producers will be unable to sell all their output and will be forced to accumulate inventories or to cut production.

National planners could do one or more of the following three things in conditions of excess supply: (1) lower the controlled price to increase demand and reduce the incentive for further expansion of supply; (2) restrict the growth of supply through administrative controls; and (3) remove all controls and let the price fall to balance supply and demand.

In the case of watches, the authorities used a combination of (1) and (2). In late 1981 they imposed new production control figures for 1985 for watch producers and forbade investments that would increase supply beyond them. Chongqing's production quota for 1985 was set at 1.4 million watches, less than half the company's own proposed target of 3 million. This restriction was enforced through the project approval process, particularly approval of bank loans. In April 1982 the authorities again reduced the minimum controlled price for most watches by Y10. Neither of these actions was sufficient, however, to prevent a continuing shift toward a buyer's market. Producers still had an incentive to cut price or improve quality and variety. Investments to improve quality and increase variety continued to be encouraged.

Clocks were controlled at the provincial level rather than at the national level. The authorities in Sichuan took no action at all in the clock market despite conditions much more difficult than in the watch market. Producers were left to cope with the situation as best they could. Whereas in the case of watches the authorities controlled supply with standard methods used in planned economies and supplemented them by lowering the regulated price, with clocks they used neither planning—options (1) and (2)—nor the market—option (3)—to correct the situation. Clock producers were left in the worst of both worlds.

The company's slow recognition of the collapse of the clock market exacerbated the problem. The Chongqing Municipal Commercial Department (CD) warned Chongqing at the beginning of 1982 that the clock market had worsened and urged it to revise its production target of 1.15 million clocks. The CD was able to put pressure on the company to reduce production because a reform in 1982 gave it authority to "purchase by selection" rather than by order. Chongqing resisted production cutbacks and questioned the CD's evaluation of the situation, but after a market survey confirmed the CD's gloomy predictions, the company asked for a lower target and cut production sharply beginning in mid-1982. Output of clocks in 1982 was 540,000 (compared with 1.2 million in 1981), of which the CD bought only 220,000. Stocks of materials sharply increased, and Chongqing was left with very high circulating capital costs. The worst problem facing the company was redundant labor that could not be laid off. Under the terms of a merger agreement with a commune in 1980, Chongqing had in fact committed to employ 390 more commune workers in clock production by the end of 1982, in addition to the 380 such workers it already employed. Although the company was able to avoid taking on new workers, it was unable to dismiss any of the existing workers.

Increasing competition in the watch market did not pose an immediate threat, but the authorities' actions to prevent oversupply created problems to which Chongqing must respond. The new production limit left the company holding equipment that it could not use. Investment completed before the ceiling was imposed was unbalanced; in some lines the company had equipment for annual production of 3 million watches, while in others it did not have enough equipment to produce even 1.4 million. Chongqing faced heavy repayment obligations for bank loans it had used to finance equipment purchases. The reduction in watch prices in April 1982 cut profit margins. A further price reduction in January 1983 did not affect the company's own watches directly, but it lowered the price of Shanghai watches and thereby stiffened competition.

In addition to these market-related problems, at the end of 1981 Chongqing suddenly developed a severe problem of quality control with its first-grade (Shancheng brand) watches. It was unable to meet the nationally prescribed quality standard of 88 marks for a sufficient number of these watches.[24] This endangered 1982 bonuses and confirmation of the 1981 floating wage increases. Production of watches was reduced while the company tried to correct the problem.

The result of all these difficulties was that in 1982 watch output increased by only 10 percent; clock production fell by 50 percent; gross output value rose by only 3.9 percent (compared with 66 percent a year in 1980 and 1981); total profits fell from Y17 million to Y11.5 million; and retained profits (after taxes and repayment of bank loans) fell from Y6.6 million to Y2.3 million.

The quality control problem and the changes introduced by planning authorities forced Chongqing to confront earlier the fundamental marketing problem that would have emerged sooner or later. It faced increasingly severe competition from other watch producers, shrinking profit margins, the end of unlimited expansion of production, and most likely a permanent reduction in demand for clocks. Although the company faced a declining market, it was left with strong financial incentives. Its overall reaction was to move from an emphasis on production and expansion of capacity to a focus on marketing and easing sales constraints.

Response to Problems

Although it appeared to stem from lack of quality control during Chongqing's drive to expand production, the problem with watch quality at the end of 1981 was essentially technical. The average quality of first-grade watches fell from 90.35 marks in 1980 to 88.31 in 1981.[25] In January 1982 it dropped to 81.07, far below the required standard of 88. A large number of Shancheng brand watches failed to pass a shock absorption test because of an improper taper on an axle. This problem was caused by machine drift and was not detected because of faulty equipment for testing components. Intensive effort and a great deal of time were required to locate and correct the problem. By June 1982 quality had improved to more than 90 marks, but average quality for the year did not exceed 88 marks until December 1982, after all engineers and technicians had been mobilized to assist with production. During the course of the year procedures for quality control were completely revamped, and in January 1983 three watch factories were merged into a single unit (the Number 1 Watch Factory) to improve technical standards. This essentially technical and organizational response was stimulated in large part by reforms linking bonuses and floating wages to fulfillment of targets. Bonuses were not paid for two months; although these were later made up, final confirmation of bonuses was not assured until the end of the year.[26]

The problem with quality also stimulated an interesting business response: Chongqing used substandard components of the Shancheng watch to produce a new third-grade (Kunlun brand) watch. Development of the new watch started in May 1982; batch production began in June and sales in July. By October full-scale production had been launched. Thus the company was able not only to recover from its production mistakes but also to turn them into a profit. The launching of Kunlun was part of a longer-term effort to diversify production (as will be discussed later), but the main impetus for the new product came from the problems and opportunities the company encountered in maintaining the quality of components.

Chongqing's response to the more general problems with marketing and profitability can be grouped into five categories: manipulation of rules, sales promotion, development of new products and varieties, price reductions, and cost reductions.

MANIPULATION OF RULES. Chongqing tried to mitigate the effect of its marketing problems by manipulating the rules restricting its actions and affecting its incentives. When it became evident that the company would not meet its 1982 clock production target, for example, it applied to remove clock production from the list of targets affecting eligibility for bonuses. Later in the year Chongqing asked for lower output targets for clocks and watches. The Municipal Light Industry Bureau in every case almost immediately permitted the company to organize its production in accordance with the requests. The bureau accepted responsibility should provincial authorities reject the requests, but the possibility of such a rejection was considered very slight. In fact, revision of plan targets appears to have been so commonplace in China that such requests can hardly be characterized as bending the rules.

Manipulation was more clear-cut in Chongqing's 1982 exemption from the tax on all of its fixed assets—not only from the tax on newly created assets—

to help finance its loan repayments. (Retained profits that were to have been used for this purpose had already been diverted to other uses, contrary to regulations.) Municipal authorities appear to have acceded to the company's request because Chongqing Municipality was responsible for its own finances and had already met its annual revenue quota set by Sichuan Province.

In yet another instance of manipulation of rules, the local branch of the People's Bank of China helped Chongqing evade regulations on investment. In 1982 the company wanted to increase its investment in associated enterprises. Only retained profits were permitted to be used for this purpose, but Chongqing shipped component parts to its associated enterprises on credit anyway and counted this transfer as its share of investment in them. The resulting increase in the company's receivables was financed by a circulating capital loan from the People's Bank. Because this arrangement contravened regulations, the People's Bank charged a penalty interest rate 50 percent higher than normal (0.9 percent instead of 0.6 percent a month) and asked Chongqing to work out a schedule for repayment.

Chongqing also managed to spend more than the stipulated share of retained profits on collective welfare and bonuses in 1980–82, and it took advantage of opportunities to pay special bonuses despite the authorities' attempts to restrict such payments. In early 1983, for example, the company was permitted to give a special bonus of Y20 per worker following the visit of the finance minister. Manipulation of the rules reached new heights of ingenuity with the squeeze on profits and the threat to workers' benefits in 1982.

A common thread running through all of these attempts to bend the rules was the willingness of municipal authorities to help out. To what extent was Chongqing given special treatment because of its status as an experimental reformed enterprise or because it was a favored producer of consumer durables? Statements by municipal officials that the reforms should be given "a fair chance" and that the experiments at the company "should not be allowed to fail for lack of resources" suggest that Chongqing indeed received preferential treatment, raising questions about the replicability of reforms at Chongqing. If reforms were effective only because of special treatment, they cannot be expected to work for the economy as a whole, since it is impossible to provide preferential treatment for every firm. Moreover, participation in an experimental reform itself may lead to superficial short-term improvements through the Hawthorne effect.[27]

The extent or effect of the preferential treatment received by the company should not be exaggerated, however. Some of the concessions extended to Chongqing were costless; they were examples of the normal leniency of local authorities toward their enterprises. More generally, it appears that the company's success at manipulation reflected two widespread features of the Chinese incentive system: a "soft" budget constraint (see Kornai 1979) and a slack planning system. These features raise issues that will be explored later. It is sufficient to note here that Chongqing's attempts to manipulate the rules and the municipal authorities' acquiescence are perfectly normal and understandable in such a system. Even though manipulation softened and delayed the effect of market problems, the company still had to take vigorous actions to counter them.

SALES PROMOTION. Direct marketing (self-sales) was originally intended to encourage greater responsiveness to consumer preferences by putting an enterprise in direct contact with the market. According to the changes introduced in 1980, the cd was obliged to buy 70 percent of Chongqing's quota of within-plan watch production and 80 percent of quota clock production; it had previously bought 100 percent of both. The company could sell the remainder of quota output and all above-quota output to anyone it chose, including lower-level wholesale stations in the cd system or even directly to consumers. Prices remained controlled at all stages, but the change enabled Chongqing to capture some of the commercial margins. In a seller's market this provided the company with attractive options: it could choose to make direct sales of particularly profitable products or to particularly lucrative markets and still sell any other output to the cd, which was hungry for consumer durables.

The effect of direct marketing was radically different when excess supply developed. In a softening market the cd could limit its purchases to the minimum required and had a much greater say concerning the variety of products it purchased. The cd thus added to market pressures in forcing Chongqing to produce a product mix more in line with consumer preferences. In the first quarter of 1983, the cd and the company agreed that Chongqing would sell 220,000 of its total planned output of 250,000 watches to the cd, but there was marked disagreement about product mix. The cd wanted to purchase 120,000 Shancheng (first-grade), 20,000 Shanhua (second-grade), and 80,000 Kunlun (third-grade) watches, but the company wished to sell 160,000 Shancheng and 40,000 Kunlun watches to the cd. It wanted to sell more first-grade watches to the cd because it could produce more of them, they earned a higher profit margin, and they were less popular in the market than the Kunlun watches. The bargaining power of the cd and the influence of the market on product mix were greatly enhanced by the introduction of selective procurement for clocks in 1982. This enabled the cd to purchase only the number and varieties of products it wished and assigned more of the risk of declining sales or changes in preferences to the producer. Selective procurement had not yet been implemented for watches, but in practice the cd was able to choose the varieties it wished to purchase if an agreed product mix was not incorporated in the contract with Chongqing.

Since the company could not lower prices to less than the fixed minimum, it made strenuous efforts to promote sales. It increased advertising, stepped up its efforts to sell clocks and watches to third-level wholesalers in Sichuan and second-level wholesalers in other provinces, and expanded its retail outlets. Chongqing would not have tried to bypass the CD if it could have sold all it wanted to that agency. It tried to sell to other wholesalers in order to expand total sales.

The main purpose of Chongqing's retail outlets was not mainly to obtain higher prices for clocks and watches sold directly to customers, but rather to expand sales by providing service centers for cleaning and repair of watches. Chongqing subsidized the retail outlets and repair centers (most of which were cooperatives) by providing cheap spare parts and a flat subsidy for repairs under warranty. As of 1983 the warranty period was one year, but the company was considering increasing it to two years. Chongqing's excellent service network was credited with enhancing the company's strong competitive position in Sichuan. Although parts for Chongqing and Shanghai watches were interchangeable, most customers did not know this and preferred the local Chongqing watches because of convenient repair services.

The company introduced several market surveys in connection with its new product development, to identify shortcomings in functions and design that were harming sales. The surveys were revealing with respect to the tastes of potential growth markets. In a survey of upper-middle-school students, for example, it was found that boys wanted a durable, shock-resistant watch that could be worn while playing basketball. Girls wanted a cheap, stylish watch with a short life span because they expected to be able to purchase another, more durable watch when they started working or to receive a watch as a present from their parents if they went to college.

The most extraordinary sales promotion efforts were undertaken by workers in the Clock Factory. The company was unable to dismiss redundant clock workers and had only limited ability to shift them to producing watch components, so it placed groups of these workers on study leave, at full basic pay but without bonus. In 1983 it introduced targets for the Clock Factory that provided for loss of up to 20 percent of workers' basic wages if it failed to break even.

In early 1983 Chongqing introduced three schemes for sales by Clock Factory workers. In the first, a worker took a voluntary long-term leave of absence to sell clocks on a contract basis. The worker bought clocks at 4 percent below the wholesale price and sold them at whatever price he could. Only eight or nine workers chose this alternative. The second scheme was also voluntary; it involved about 800 workers. They were permitted to sell clocks in their spare time at 0.3–0.4 percent commission. Because of the tiny commission, the primary motivation for participating in this scheme was the collective incentive linking sales and profitability to wages and bonuses. The third and most drastic scheme was involuntary. About 200 workers who had no production tasks were assigned to sell clocks within Chongqing Municipality. If they sold fifty clocks a month they received full salary and travel expenses. If they sold more than fifty clocks they received a bonus. If they sold fewer, their salary was reduced and they received no travel expenses. Although the scheme did not explicitly discriminate against commune workers, the workers who were forced to sell clocks were less skilled and unable to contribute to production or the development of new products; these undoubtedly included a disproportionate number of commune workers.

About 10,000 clocks were sold through these three schemes in March 1983. The schemes were intended to be temporary measures lasting for about six months, but it is remarkable that they could be introduced at all. The third scheme, in particular, must have reduced wages. In Eastern Europe such a scheme would probably have collapsed, because workers easily could find jobs in other factories in the tight labor markets prevailing there. This was not true in China, with its looser overall labor market conditions. Even the reduced income from selling clocks might well have been higher than an individual's potential earnings in agriculture.

DEVELOPMENT OF NEW PRODUCTS AND VARIETIES. For the Clock Factory, the development of new products was intended to provide employment for redundant workers. For its watch operation, Chongqing was attempting to develop new varieties or to improve quality in order to enhance its long-term competitive position. Development of new varieties of watches began before 1982, but market changes gave a much stronger impetus to this effort. On the whole, the company was more successful in diversifying watch production than in finding new products to replace clocks.

The value of clock output peaked at Y10.9 million in 1981 and fell to Y5.9 million in 1982. In 1983 the Clock Factory expected to produce about Y4 million worth of clocks and Y2 million worth of other products, mostly timers for fans and washing machines. One problem was that timers and other obvious lines of diversification were also being pursued by other clock factories. In addition, timers were components of consumer durables that themselves may have faced market saturation.

Three aspects of the situation further encouraged Chongqing to develop new products. First, it still had fairly large retained profits, 60 percent of which were to be used for production development. Since expansion of total production was blocked, the opportunity cost of using these funds for investment in new products, new varieties, or quality improvement was slight. It was also still relatively easy to obtain loans for these purposes. The second stimulus was a state-mandated development fund for new products, amounting to 1–3 percent of total profits. Chongqing spent Y300,000 in 1982 and planned to spend Y400,000 in 1983 for this purpose. (Before 1982 the company's development of new products had been financed largely by state grants, but thereafter most new product development was funded from its own profits.) The third and probably most important incentive was the remission of industrial-commercial tax for two years on approved new products.

Approval was not automatic, but when granted it was a very potent incentive, as tax rates were 40 percent for watches and 25 percent for clocks. One deterrent against diversification into producer goods such as timers has been the low industrial-commercial tax rate on such goods (only 5 percent), too low a margin for tax exemptions to help cover the high initial costs of production.[28]

These financial incentives were augmented by awards given by all levels of government for excellent products. Chongqing won municipal awards for its Kunlun watch, for a timer for washing machines, and for a clock to be used by students. It also received a first-grade provincial prize for a new 17.2-millimeter women's watch. The company has never won a national prize for its products, however. Prizes did not carry monetary awards but were useful in establishing reputation. Moreover, they could sometimes provide an excuse for extra bonuses for workers, as they did for other firms in this study. The company also gave awards to research and design teams for completion of particular projects. The designer of the Kunlun watch, for example, received an award of Y150.

Chongqing developed several new products in the early 1980s. It introduced a second-grade men's watch (the Shanhua brand) in 1981, along with a 20.5-millimeter women's watch, both of which were market successes. A digital watch produced in 1982, however, failed in the marketplace. In 1982 the company brought out its highly successful Kunlun watch and a new 17.2-millimeter women's watch. The women's watch was jointly developed with the Shanghai and Qingdao clock and watch companies. Each partner shared development tasks and expenditures and produced identical watch mechanisms with different appearances. Chongqing also imported Swiss equipment worth Sw F 4 million to produce watch cases of different shapes. As of 1983 the company had thirteen new products under development, financed by its new product development fund: a men's calendar watch, an analog quartz watch with date and day, batch production of the 17.2-millimeter women's watch, sample production of the same watch with a date function added, a students' watch, a 26.5-millimeter men's watch with comprehensive functions, a student clock, a clock with date and day, a quartz wall clock, a timer for fans, a timer for washing machines, a musical toy, and a gold-plated watch case. All of the products other than watches were to be produced by the Clock Factory.

It is difficult to assess the importance of funding mechanisms and financial incentives in new product development. The Shanhua watch was only partially exempted from industrial-commercial tax (which was reduced to 15 percent), and the Kunlun watch received no exemption at all. These products used the same components (sorted by quality) as the Shancheng watch and needed no special incentives. Chongqing received a full two-year tax exemption for both its designs of women's watches, which would have been unprofitable otherwise. The 20.5-millimeter women's watch was, in fact, to be phased out of production in 1983 and may have been developed only to get a tax exemption. Hence the incentives may have encouraged minor modifications of existing products and bogus new product development. For the most part, however, the company's development of new products and varieties seems to have been prompted by the need to meet stiffening market competition in the watch industry and to find new production opportunities for the Clock Factory. Financial incentives merely enhanced the effect of these changes, which resulted from adjustment and reform.

PRICE REDUCTIONS. The change from a sellers' to a buyers' market generated strong pressures for price reductions, but producers were constrained from price competition by controls fixing minimum prices. Chongqing nevertheless found ways to reduce prices.

The company was granted permission by the provincial Price Commission in November 1982 to reduce prices on some of its stockpiled clocks by 18–40 percent. These reductions applied only to inventories, not to new production. In the first three months after the reduction, Chongqing was able to clear 100,000 clocks from inventory, mostly by retail sales. The market for clocks, however, was already saturated, there was great excess production capacity in the industry, and many producers must have been forced to exit. Had price reductions been permitted earlier, expansion would have been curtailed and adjustment would have been more orderly.

Planning authorities intervened in the watch market by restricting supply and reducing regulated prices; they achieved only partial success. The establishment of numerous small watch factories not listed in the state plan caused the State Economic Commission to conclude that "planning is out of control and production is developing unchecked" (State Economic Commission 1983, p. 33). State production plans probably did not prevent larger producers from increasing production. As a result, there were still strong incentives for further price reductions.

Chongqing was able to lower its prices in two ways. The first was the familiar one of evading regulations with the cooperation of municipal authorities. Although the minimum price for a third-grade watch in 1983 was Y50, Chongqing was selling its third-grade Kunlun watch for Y45. The company had applied to both the provincial and municipal price commissions for permission to do this; only the municipal authorities had agreed (no reply was forthcoming from the province), so the company sold these watches at Y45 within Chongqing Municipality but at Y50 in other areas.

The second method of evading price restrictions was disguised price reductions through changes in the product mix. Since all three of its brands of men's watches were made from the same components, Chongqing simply increased the proportion of Shanhua and Kunlun watches it produced. The company often may have put second-grade faces on watches that would qualify for first grade, and it reserved only its highest-quality watches for marketing under the Shancheng brand name. In this way it effectively upgraded the quality of all its watches. The company's strategy was to maintain an excellent reputation for the Shancheng watch and use that reputation to promote sales of all of its watches. Shanghai and other companies also engaged in this method of disguised price reduction and quality improvement.

The extent to which Chongqing could change its product mix was constrained, however, by its profit target. If it produced too many lower-grade watches it would fail to meet its profit target and might be unable to pay bonuses. The company's response to this constraint was to expand total output. The state-set production target in 1983 was 900,000 watches, but the company set an internal target of 1.2 million watches. If it could produce a larger number of watches, it could shift its product mix toward lower-grade (and lower-profit) watches and thereby respond to consumer preferences while still meeting its profit target.

The pressure for price reductions (and tax reductions or exemptions from local authorities) was so strong throughout the watch industry that Xue Muqiao, one of China's leading economists, questioned whether plan targets could influence production without more realistic prices:

> Because our price system is irrational . . . to carry out guidance planning would only lead to greater . . . imbalance as a result of which enterprises are encouraged to organize production in violation of the state plan. If prices are not adjusted, even directive plans cannot be realized. . . . [High-cost] watch producers reduce their prices, some to Y50–60, some to Y30–40, to compete with Shanghai watches. If we let this situation develop, not even indicative planning can fully play its role, not to mention guidance planning (Xue Muqiao 1983, p. 5).

COST REDUCTIONS. Cost reduction is an obvious third stage of response to adjustment and reform. In conditions of excess demand, the first response of producers is naturally to expand output of existing products. As the market moves into excess supply, producers should respond by increasing variety and reducing price. Chongqing responded predictably in these first two stages, but there is no evidence that the company made much effort to move to the third stage, that of cost reduction. Although it reduced its average cost of production of watches by nearly 27 percent from 1979 to 1982, the reduction appears to have been entirely due to expansion in the scale of production rather than special efforts to reduce costs.

One would expect substantial economies of scale in the Chinese watch industry because of the great number of small but comprehensive producers in the country. The unit production costs of some important watch components decline substantially with mass production. Although specialized assembly plants might be able to compete with large integrated producers, small integrated producers would be expected to have very high costs of production. This expectation is confirmed by 1980 data on cost and output for large Chinese watch factories, shown in figure 3.2. The figure shows a scatter diagram of observations and a regression line based on them. The regression estimates of cost as a function of output indicate that for every doubling of output, the cost of production falls by 20.5 percent.[29]

Chongqing's production costs did not fall as fast during 1979–82 as the regression equation would predict for a firm that more than tripled its output. Table 3.8 shows that whereas Chongqing's predicted and actual costs were equal in 1979, when it was producing 280,000 watches, the company's actual costs in 1982 were 7.5 percent above predicted costs at an output of more than 880,000 watches. In figure 3.2, three observations for Chongqing are indicated by solid circles and dated (only 1980 is included in the regression data). The company's failure to lower costs in relation to output expansion appears as a movement away from the regression line. This lag in cost reduction should not be overemphasized. The divergence is not statistically significant, and adjustment for inflation might change the results. Moreover, costs

Figure 3.2. Output and Cost of Production for Watch Factories, 1980

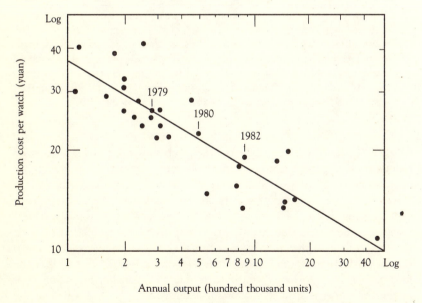

Annual output (hundred thousand units)

Note: This figure shows the relationship between cost and output for large Chinese watch factories. The line drawn through the scatter diagram represents an ordinary least squares regression. The three dated observations relate to Chongqing in different years; only 1980 was included in the regression equation.

and output both might reflect managerial efficiency; they might not be directly linked through economies of scale.[30]

With all of these qualifications, the fact remains that Chongqing's reductions in cost were considerably less than would normally be expected with a large expansion in output. In 1980 the company was the highest-cost producer among eleven Chinese enterprises manufacturing 500,000 or more watches a year. By 1982 it was still the second-highest-cost producer (if its 1982 cost is compared with the 1980 costs of the others), despite an increase in output of more than 75 percent. It thus seems fair to interpret Chongqing's cost reduction as only an incidental result of economies of scale. This is consistent with interview evidence suggesting that as of 1983 company management had only recently begun to pay attention to cost reduction.

Implications of Chongqing's Experience

Basing general conclusions about economic reforms in Chinese state-owned industry on only one or a few case studies is a difficult and risky task. The obvious danger is that the enterprises investigated are atypical or were provided special treatment, so their experiences are radically different from those of other firms and cannot be replicated. Observations may also be unduly influenced by the particular circumstances and problems of the industries in the sample. Nevertheless, this section draws some general implications from Chongqing's experience in the early 1980s. The conclusions presented here should be viewed as tentative ideas and hypotheses that may be supported or refuted by other evidence.

Role of the Market

During the period under study, the dominant influence on Chongqing was the market, not directive plans promulgated by supervisory organizations. The most important reform measure for the company was not the new tax system in 1980 but rather the end of guaranteed purchase by the commercial

Table 3.8. Predicted and Actual Watch Production Costs for Chongqing, 1979, 1980, and 1982

Year	Production (units)	Cost per unit (yuan)		Difference	
		Predicted	Actual	Absolute	Percent
1979	280,000	26.06	26.06	0.00	0.0
1980	501,210	21.49	22.15	0.66	3.1
1982	883,923	17.80	19.14	1.34	7.5

Source: Predicted cost is from the regression equation. Chongqing's costs for 1979 and 1982 are from *Jingji Guanli* (September 1983): 24.

system of all output regardless of market demand. The effect of direct marketing was to remove the buffer between the firm's own sales (and therefore its production decisions) and market demand.

In the case of such consumer durables as clocks and watches, demand is affected primarily by incomes and tastes and by commodity prices. Government adjustment policies stimulated demand by sharply increasing personal incomes in urban as well as rural areas. Demand was further increased by sharp price reductions for clocks and moderate reductions for watches.

Annual and short-term plans for Chongqing and many other enterprises appear to have been based largely on assessments and forecasts of market conditions. Where enterprise plans or actual performance deviated from control figures sent down by authorities, the control figures were invariably adjusted, often retroactively, to be consistent with actual performance. Directive plans were not only flexible; they appear to have been quite slack: they could easily be overfulfilled under normal circumstances.

Market demand also affected Chongqing's longer-term strategic decisions on investment projects and development of new products and varieties. Government pricing policy, through its effects on demand and profitability, was a primary factor in decisionmaking. Government sectoral and subsectoral development policies, which indicated priorities for bank loans financing fixed investment, also played an important role. The central government intervened, finally, to prevent new investment in the watch industry. Nevertheless, the degree of enterprise autonomy in strategic decisionmaking, including initiating projects and obtaining resources to implement them, was surprisingly great. Because the capacity for market forecasting and information gathering in China was still weak, it is not surprising that enterprise evaluations of the market situation were often incorrect, especially when it came to predicting long-term developments or assessing the nationwide (as opposed to the local) situation.

Reliance on the market mechanism has had certain benefits in terms of enterprise behavior: improvement of quality and stricter quality control; alteration of product mix; development of new varieties in response to market demand; and various sales promotion activities. Chongqing undertook a massive expansion in productive capacity and engaged in extensive sales promotion activities. It was also very active in developing new products.

In general, Chongqing's responses to reforms strengthening the role of the market were influenced by a number of industry-specific variables: (1) producer prices in relation to production costs; (2) the overall market situation (excess supply or demand); (3) whether the output was a producer good or a consumer good; (4) the degree to which the product was differentiated; (5) the level of technology required for production; (6) the market situation for the main material inputs; (7) the rate of obsolescence of products and, correspondingly, the degree of importance of development of new products; and (8) the rate of industrial-commercial tax on the product. (See Byrd

1987, pp. 244–53, for a detailed discussion of factors influencing enterprise response to market forces.)

Effect of Manipulation of Rules

One of the main conclusions of this chapter is that, like the planning system in general, financial incentive systems at the enterprise level were weak and manipulable. Firms could change the rules of the game to their financial benefit, and almost every enterprise was made, on one pretext or another, into an exceptional case, entitled to special treatment. The amount of retained profits and workers' bonuses could hold steady or even increase when enterprise performance as measured by total profits deteriorated significantly. Tax exemptions were given freely to Chongqing, and in one case a loan of Y850,000 from the local government was changed into a grant. Chongqing was also able to persuade local authorities to lower the price of one of its products. Much of this manipulability of rules stemmed from the weakness of the planning system. Rewards, to the extent that they depended on fulfillment of directive plans set by supervisory organizations, were only loosely related to actual performance, and there was a tendency toward upward drift in enterprise and individual rewards.

For individual workers, there was somewhat stricter control from outside the enterprise in the early 1980s. The total wage bill and the average level of bonuses were limited by labor and industrial departments and were monitored fairly closely by banks. Firms were able to get around these restrictions, however, by using retained profits to increase welfare benefits and construct more workers' housing. In addition, various special bonuses (above the limits) were awarded in many enterprises, subject to case-by-case approval.

Overall, there is abundant evidence that in China the enterprise budget constraint remained soft despite the market constraint's having become rather tight for many firms. No matter what the circumstances, it was virtually inconceivable that the Chinese government would allow sizable enterprises to go bankrupt. In both China and Yugoslavia at this time, many firms were characterized by a soft budget constraint and a hard market constraint. Public enterprises in many non–centrally planned countries may operate under similar conditions.

The manipulability of the incentive environment and the soft budget constraint did have certain benefits. The system responded with considerable flexibility to adverse situations. In particular, workers' incomes were maintained in the face of a deterioration in enterprise performance, especially when that deterioration could be attributed to factors beyond the enterprise's control. The alternatives of laying off workers or lowering incomes for all employees might have resulted in a decline in morale and productivity. This in turn could cause a further deterioration in performance and start a vicious downward spiral. The soft budget constraint did not, as one might expect, distract Chongqing's attention from improving performance. Although efforts were made to distort the incentive system to benefit the company and its employees, the very ease with which this could be done meant that the system did not interfere greatly with attempts to improve quality, develop new products, and so forth.

There were problems, however. Efforts to reduce costs appear to have been weak and largely unsuccessful. Moreover, the incentive system was unstable and unpredictable from the perspective of the enterprise. The financial incentive system's provisions for many Chinese firms changed nearly every year. For a firm like Chongqing, however, the formal income tax system was fairly stable, so the weakness of the incentive environment reintroduced instability in a disguised form. Also, incentives at the margin were undoubtedly harmed by the loosening of the link between enterprise performance and rewards.

In general, tailoring incentive systems to the needs of individual enterprises is not an appropriate pattern for comprehensive reform. There will always be inequities and objective circumstances that impinge more on some firms than on others, but beyond a certain point the disadvantages of ad hoc corrections and tailor-made schemes far outweigh any of the supposed advantages of improved equity. Indeed, at the extreme, the manipulable environment degenerates into an administered system in which formal rules mean little and each matter is decided on an ad hoc, case-by-case basis. Such a system is probably little better than the prereform system.

Effect of the Labor Allocation System

Labor allocation remained the most unreformed part of China's state-owned industrial system in the early 1980s. Binding quotas set by supervisory agencies determined enterprise employment. Workers were never laid off to economize on costs or to respond to poor market conditions. Conversely, the hiring of additional regular employees was a cumbersome and time-consuming process. The labor system thus affected enterprise decisions both in an upturn and in a downturn.

For many firms, including Chongqing during its expansion phase before 1982, the labor system restricted growth of employment. Enterprises with rapidly increasing output naturally would want to hire additional laborers. Moreover, enterprise decisionmakers may see additional wage payments as a benefit rather than as a cost if they are maximizing income accruing to the enterprise and its employees, rather than merely maximizing retained profits. The ability to hire sons and daughters of existing workers provided a strong incentive to expand the labor force.

To circumvent the perceived labor constraint, Chongqing engaged in a number of activities, including associations and mergers with other enterprises and hiring of temporary workers not subject to state quotas. Other firms may have bought large amounts of new equipment and used an overly capital-intensive production process as a result of the labor constraint. They may also have hoarded labor; that is, they may have retained unneeded workers and even hired more labor to meet future contingencies.

Enterprise response to a downturn, such as that faced by Chongqing in 1982, is also affected by the labor system. Since it cannot and probably does not want to lay off workers, a firm is forced to find ways to keep them occupied. One obvious possibility is for it to divide up tasks so that a given amount of work is spread out among more workers. In situations in which new equipment or improved technology might otherwise cause a sharp rise in labor productivity, retention of the workers rendered redundant would result in stagnant or only slowly rising productivity.

A second kind of response is the channeling of excess labor into auxiliary activities, which often earn low returns. Examples of such activities include provision of additional services to the other employees of the enterprise, utilization of waste materials generated in the production process, additional minor processing of the firm's output, and even involvement in retail commerce. In some cases the private returns to the enterprise are substantial, but the social returns may be insubstantial or even negative, as, for example, when an enterprise uses its excess labor to perform operations that were previously undertaken by other firms. Even if the returns on them are low, these activities are more beneficial than is greater idleness on the job. The opportunity cost of the resources used is near zero, and more important, the damaging effects of work-sharing on morale and work habits are avoided.

Restrictions on laying off workers may also deter a firm from undertaking risky new activities. If an expansion project fails, the enterprise risks carrying a permanently redundant labor force. As a result of its experience with the commune merger to obtain a new site for the clock factory, Chongqing undoubtedly acquired an aversion to such risky, employment-expanding activities. To the extent that greater risk aversion promotes cautious analysis of projects it is beneficial, but a socially suboptimal degree of risk aversion may result.

The most interesting and strategically most important response of a firm with a fixed labor force to deteriorating market conditions is diversification into new lines of products. This response is illustrated most prominently by the effort to develop new products at the company's Clock Factory in the wake of the collapse of the clock market in 1982. Development of new product lines is qualitatively different from production of new varieties or similar products to ease the demand constraint within a single market, such as Chongqing's production of thinner, more stylish men's watches and the low-priced Kunlun brand.

In many respects product diversification is beneficial. Instead of laying off workers, who will presumably, at some later point, be hired by other factories producing for markets in which demand is expanding, firms retain their labor forces and themselves seek new opportunities to produce for expanding markets. Thus there is entrepreneurial behavior by firms seeking to keep their existing work forces employed, instead of search behavior by workers seeking jobs. Search behavior by firms also occurs in market economies; it occurs, for example, among large Japanese firms with a tradition of providing lifetime employment to workers. Product diversification may well be less costly in social terms than laying off workers would be, for a firm that wished to shift activity in response to the changing structure of demand. This is particularly true if the government has obligations to maintain consumption levels of workers during the process of transition.

The relative benefits of diversification also depend on technical conditions: the degree of specialization of the firm's equipment, the levels and kinds of skills in the work force, the nature of the existing product, and its degree of similarity to other products. If a firm diversifies into new product lines in which it has a technical advantage, and if market demand is strong, the effect should be positive. If firms diversify into product lines for which they are not really suited, however, and for which market demand is weak, the effect is probably harmful. Much diversification in Chinese industry during the early 1980s probably occurred in the latter set of circumstances. In the case of Chongqing, the technical base and skills were adequate for diversification. Many of the products into which the company was technically suited to diversify, however, were consumer durables (or parts of consumer durables) characterized at that time by incipient or actual market saturation.

Investment Financing

Chongqing was given significant authority to make investment decisions as part of the reforms; it also obtained financial resources in the form of retained profits and bank loans, which enabled the company to expand rapidly in response to high demand for its products. When the market constraint became tight, however, as it did in 1982, retained profits could no longer be used for expansion of capacity in the same line of products. Chongqing stopped investing in expansion of clock production capacity of its own accord. Capacity-increasing investments for watches were limited by a national policy decision to forestall market saturation. In both cases the company was effectively prevented from undertaking major investments designed only to increase production capacity. Other producers of consumer durables faced a similar situation.

Enterprise discretionary funds that can no longer be used for capacity expansion may first be diverted to construction of workers' housing and provision of other amenities. Funds may also be used for "intensive" investments that do not increase output but result in improved technology, better quality, more attractive styling, and so forth. Some investments may rectify imbalances in the production process or allow internalization of activities previously performed by other firms. There is also the possibility that some enterprise discretionary funds may be used simply to increase capital intensity: although the firm in these circumstances probably has excess labor, the opportunity cost of its funds (which may be earmarked for investment anyway) might be near zero, in which case it will be advantageous for the enterprise to invest in capital-intensive technologies despite the labor surplus. Greater capital intensity may also reduce the amount of arduous work and may be strongly desired on that ground.

There are technical and externally imposed limits to the kinds of investment just described. Simply leaving the funds in the enterprise's bank account, however, renders them vulnerable to confiscation, to freezing by administrative decree, or to the only slightly more palatable alternative of involuntary purchases of treasury bonds.[31] Thus enterprise discretionary funds may sooner or later flow to investments in diversification of product lines. This eventuality reinforces the effect of the labor allocation system discussed earlier.

Chongqing was unusual in that it was engaged in a very profitable line of business and at the same time retained a high proportion (60 percent) of its profits. Incentives to diversify may, however, also have accumulated in other firms that were tightly constrained by market demand for their original line of products and that had ample discretionary funds. Contrary to the labor-resource situation, in which there are significant costs in moving workers from firm to firm, financial resources can be transferred by an efficient financial intermediation system from one enterprise to another at very low cost. (Diversification by a single firm, however, entails significant transition and development costs.) In China, mobility of funds through and within the banking system has been quite limited. Firms generally prefer using their funds in self-financed projects or for investment in joint ventures to depositing them in banks, where they earn only nominal interest. This preference for self-financed investment is similar to patterns in market economies, in which as much as 75 percent of corporate investment expenditure is self-financed. The benefits of an efficient financial system hence may lie more in its provision of appropriate signals on the opportunity cost of capital than in its channeling of financial resources among firms.

A number of measures could ameliorate the problem of excessive liquidity leading to inefficient use of funds or inappropriate diversification. Reductions in the price of outputs may attack the problem from two angles by simultaneously stimulating demand and decreasing enterprise discretionary resources. Reductions in profit retention rates are another possibility. An increase in the industrial-commercial tax rate would accomplish the same purpose. Any of these actions, however, would be resisted by the enterprises concerned.

Chongqing's Performance

In response to the new opportunities presented by the reforms, Chongqing exhibited behavior that can be described as entrepreneurial. It acted aggressively to increase capacity, output, and market share in southwest China. Its preemptive investment strategy and extensive involvement in joint ventures and associations enabled it to become the largest of the six relative newcomers in the Chinese watch industry. Faced with an emerging market demand constraint for watches and with market saturation for clocks, the company responded admirably. Quality improvement, disguised price reductions, development of new brands and more attractive styles, and aggressive sales promotion were the most important measures the company took to ease the market demand constraint for watches. The clock situation was much more serious, requiring more drastic measures, which included reducing prices sharply, forcing about 20 percent of the work force to sell clocks themselves in order to earn their pay, and aggressively pursuing direct commission sales to wholesale and retail commercial units. Chongqing's primary long-term response, however, was a desperate search for new lines of products, in recognition of the fact that clock production alone would probably never fully employ the labor force at the Clock Factory.

The nature of Chongqing's response to reforms depended crucially on the market situation. The company took advantage of initial excess demand to pursue extensive growth. As the market constraint tightened, however, the company could no longer rely on output expansion and turned instead to an intensive growth pattern. This is, of course, much more difficult than simply increasing output, but it is in the end more socially beneficial. Measured performance, particularly growth of output and profits, does not fairly reflect Chongqing's response to reforms. In 1980–81 growth was spectacular but was achieved relatively easily. The true test of Chongqing's capabilities and response to reforms came in 1982. Though profits and other performance indicators declined in 1982, the company became fully engaged in its largely successful intensive response to a very difficult external situation. The weak incentive environment, slack planning system, and relatively loose administrative controls allowed Chongqing to channel some of its energies into manipulating the system but did not prevent it from responding in other, highly effective ways.

The one instance when central authorities and planners intervened directly and constrained Chongqing's activities was the imposition of capacity limits on watch producers in 1982. This intervention meant that the company could no longer depend solely on output growth to maintain or increase its profits, in line with changing market conditions. This episode suggests that some guidance of industrywide development occasionally can play a positive role. Administrative direction is not, however, an adequate substitute for flexible, market-based adjustment.

Chongqing's development during the early 1980s is an illuminating case study of a crucial shift from extensive to intensive growth, brought on by an enterprise's changing response to reform measures and, especially, to market conditions. This shift is the primary goal of Chinese economic reforms. In this context the question of whether Chongqing's success can be replicated throughout Chinese industry looms important. Unquestionably, the company received special help in various forms from different sources because of its prominence in the reform experiments and its status as a producer of consumer durables. Even in the absence of overt aid, the company may have performed better because it was in the limelight. An important determinant of Chongqing's success, however, was its orientation toward market demand, in a situation in which excess demand was rapidly eliminated and replaced by rough equilibrium or excess supply. This orientation could indeed be widely replicated, through a combination of market-oriented reforms and price changes. Overall, the core of Chongqing's experience can provide some guidance for Chinese industrial reforms.

A Postscript on Subsequent Developments

Only fragmentary information is available about Chongqing's situation, behavior, and performance after 1983. Nevertheless, there were some developments that are worthy of notice. Certain changes in the environment and in the rules to which the company was subject appear to have had a significant effect on it.

The incentive system probably became somewhat "harder" than in the past. The income tax rate finally agreed on for the second three-year period of the experimental income tax system (1983–85) was 50 percent. This was the rate proposed by Chongqing municipal finance authorities; the company, its supervisory agency, and the municipal Economic Commission had advocated a rate of only 44 percent. It is not clear, however, whether the numerous channels by which Chongqing had been able to manipulate the incentive environment in the early 1980s were sealed off. In 1986 the company probably dropped its experimental income tax system and implemented the nationwide profit tax system.

There was a substantial further reduction in watch prices and significant changes in relative prices of different grades. In 1984 the price of first-grade watches was cut from Y70 to Y55, that of second-grade watches from Y55 to Y50, and that of third-grade watches from Y40–Y45 to Y39. Most watch producers apparently were affected by these price changes; the changes had two important effects on Chongqing:

1. Along with rising personal incomes and general inflationary pressures in the economy, the price changes stimulated demand, so the company again faced a relatively strong market.

2. The price changes completely reversed Chongqing's incentives with respect to product mix. By 1985 the company apparently was producing almost exclusively first-grade watches, which were most in demand in the marketplace because of their relatively low price.[32] There was still some demand for third-grade watches from urban areas, but most people wanted to buy only first-grade watches.

One indication that market conditions had reverted to a mild sellers' market was a new conflict between Chongqing and the CD over watch procurement. In 1982 the company had striven to have the CD procure as large a number of watches as possible, including as many first-grade watches as possible, but the CD wanted to limit total watch procurement, to purchase mainly third-grade watches, and to avoid procurement of expensive first-grade watches. By 1985 Chongqing wanted to maximize self-sales of watches, whereas the CD, on the basis of government directives, insisted on procuring half of the company's total output of watches, much to the company's resentment. The CD, moreover, now wanted to procure only first-grade watches. Without additional research it is not possible to ascertain whether the return of a mild sellers' market was sustained and whether it had a substantial effect on Chongqing's behavior. The rise in the self-sales ratio from about 30 percent of total output of watches in 1982 to 50 percent in 1985 suggests that Chongqing remained firmly committed to direct marketing of its output, that it had strong incentives to engage in self-sales, and that it was able to resist tendencies for a return to mandatory procurement. In this respect its experience may have been similar to that of the Second Motor Vehicle Factory (see Byrd 1987, p. 266, and chapter 9 of this volume).

In a significant new development, by 1985 Chongqing had almost entirely quit clock production. It produced only 50,000 ordinary alarm clocks in 1985, compared with 542,000 in 1982 and a tentative plan for 300,000 in 1983. Company management also claimed that it had divested its entire "overhang" of clock inventories. It is not clear what happened to clock production workers and facilities, but total employment at Chongqing did not decline and gross industrial output value did not fall even in current prices, which suggests that Clock Factory workers were successfully shifted to other activities.

Some insight into Chongqing's performance in the mid-1980s can be gained from table 3.9. (Figures from 1982 are included in the table to facilitate comparisons.) Output of watches at 1.59 million in 1985 slightly surpassed the target of 1.4 million for 1985 set by planning authorities in 1982. Gross and net output value showed only modest increases between 1982 and 1985, but there was considerable real growth, considering the price decline. The company's increasing employment by 15 percent in 1982–85 may mean that additional commune workers were hired (see "Analysis of Main

Reforms," in this chapter). The total wage bill increased by almost 90 percent during this period, so there were double-digit annual increases in average nominal wages per employee. This phenomenon indicates substantial real wage growth, considering China's moderate inflation.[33] Fixed assets seemed to reach a plateau, suggesting that Chongqing's investment boom ended after 1982. Financial performance, as measured by total profits and taxes, improved only marginally, but this was probably largely because of the price decline.

In 1986 there were some interesting changes. Chongqing's nominal gross industrial output value jumped by more than 27 percent and net output value by 46 percent. In part, this increase may have been the result of higher prices in the stronger market situation, but undoubtedly there was also considerable real growth. The apparent decline in employment in 1986 may be a statistical artifact, if the 1986 figure does not include temporary workers and the 1985 figure does include them. An actual fall in employment, if there was one, suggests a number of possibilities. Perhaps Chongqing eventually terminated its temporary commune workers, even though they were supposedly employed in perpetuity. Alternatively, the possible decline in employment may have been the result of changed incentives resulting from the institution of a new system linking the enterprise total wage bill with financial performance (see chapter 8), and from significantly reduced external administrative control over the size of the labor force. If so, the company probably reduced employment by means of attrition, since a fair number of older work-

Table 3.9. Performance of Chongqing, 1982, 1985, and 1986

Item	1982	1985	1986
Gross value of industrial output (current prices, millions of yuan)	63.97	68.96	87.71
Net value of industrial output (current prices, millions of yuan)	40.00	41.37	60.56
Output of watches (millions of units)	0.89	1.59	—
Output of clocks (millions of units)	0.54	0.05	—
Total employment at year end (persons)	4,287[a]	4,910[b]	4,527[a]
Total wage bill (millions of yuan)	3.34	6.28	5.64
Gross value of fixed assets[c] (millions of yuan)	63.70	72.02	71.76
Value of quota circulating assets (millions of yuan)	27.69	34.06	45.27
Total profits and taxes (millions of yuan)	28.00	31.41	—

— Not available.

a. Average employment during year.

b. It is not clear whether this figure includes temporary workers, whereas the 1982 figure definitely does. It is possible that the apparent sharp decline in employment is spurious, or it may represent shedding of temporary laborers rather than of permanent ones.

c. Valued at original purchase prices.

Source: State Statistical Bureau 1988, p. 412, and information provided by the company.

ers were reaching retirement age. Chongqing may have been no longer striving to take on workers' children as regular employees, possibly because most of them had already been hired at the company or elsewhere.

Notes

1. In late 1978 the Chinese government launched a new economic strategy of adjustment and reform, which emphasized development of agriculture and light industry, raised urban wages and agricultural procurement prices, and introduced experiments with decentralized decisionmaking and greater use of markets to improve producer incentives. See World Bank 1983, 1, pp. 146–71.

2. Between 1978 and 1982 output of light industry grew by 56.6 percent, compared with only 14.4 percent for heavy industry. Among light industries, the growth of consumer durables production was particularly rapid, ranging from 164 percent for sewing machines to 1,044 percent for televisions.

3. Most of the information in this section is from Ministry of Light Industry 1982 and State Economic Commission 1983. Quantitative information is from State Statistical Bureau 1982 and 1983. For a survey of the development of the world clock and watch industry since the sixteenth century, see Landes 1979.

4. Production costs in 1980 ranged from Y11.02 for the Shanghai Watch Factory (output 4.63 million) to Y41.37 for the Yangzhou Watch Factory in Jiangsu (output 0.26 million). Chongqing's unit cost was Y22.15 in 1980 (output 0.5 million). The costs of small factories outside the state plan (not included in the national average) were as high as Y75 and averaged Y43.33. See "Enterprise Response," in this chapter, for analysis of production costs and economies of scale. Data are from State Economic Commission 1983.

5. All dollar amounts in this volume are U.S. dollars.

6. The cost, insurance, and freight (c.i.f.) import price of a Chinese watch into Thailand was $8.81 in 1979. The Chinese unit export value of watches in 1981 (from *Chinese Customs Statistics*, based on first three quarters average) was Y18.04 ($10.62 at the average 1981 exchange rate). The unit export value fell to Y12.01 in 1982 (first three quarters), however, and to Y4.53 in 1983 (first two quarters). These price declines may reflect exports of low-grade mechanical watches or digital watches that could not be sold domestically.

7. One method might have been to increase the number of automatic lathes tended by each worker. Overall efficiency (not necessarily labor productivity) might have been sharply raised by expanding operations from two to three shifts. Output per worker in the main production unit has been generously estimated: in 1982, 1,533 workers produced about 500,000 watches and 300,000 sets of components for assembly by other units.

8. Integrated firms produce the bulk of the parts and components that go into their watches themselves, including the most critical ones. The twelve largest producers in the Chinese watch industry in 1980 probably were fully integrated. The smallest of them, Chongqing, certainly was. A substantial number of smaller producers also may have been largely integrated.

9. Authorities often had their own reasons for promoting associations and joint

ventures. They took the initiative, for example, in arranging closer ties between Chongqing and a component factory in Beipei to rescue the latter from bankruptcy.

10. If a uniform state price existed for a certain good, that price was to be used; there were no unified state prices for watch parts and components, though, so the company itself could set them. Information about the market prices of parts and components as well as the internal prices used by other manufacturers was readily available.

11. A circular from the Ministry of Finance and other central organizations in mid-1982 ordered an end to tax exemptions or reductions for clocks and watches as well as for bicycles and sewing machines. It is not clear whether this applied to new products under trial production. See *Caizheng* (June 1982), p. 10.

12. Depreciation in China was calculated using the straight-line method, with a single, comprehensive depreciation rate for all fixed assets of enterprises, usually established industry by industry. Basic depreciation fees were drawn to provide funds to replenish the stock of fixed assets, and major repair funds were to be used for overhauls and major maintenance. For Chongqing the basic depreciation rate was 4.5 percent of the original value of its fixed assets in use per year. The rate had been set in 1953 and had remained unchanged since then.

13. The ratchet effect occurs when targets are frequently revised in the light of actual performance. It causes enterprises deliberately to perform more poorly than they otherwise would, in order to generate lower, easier-to-achieve targets in the future. For a simple theoretical model, see Weitzman 1980.

14. Other state-owned industrial enterprises in China had eight mandatory targets: the four given to Chongqing, plus varieties or mix of products, consumption of inputs, cost of production, and use of circulating capital. The company also had indicative (nonmandatory) targets, including input consumption, which was used for internal evaluation, and gross value of output, which was derived in part from the mandatory targets for physical output of main products but was no longer itself a mandatory target. Before 1978, gross value of output had been the primary mandatory target for Chinese enterprises.

15. In 1983, however, Chongqing was planning to withhold bonuses for clock workers unless the Clock Factory made a profit. Moreover, 20 percent of their basic wages was to depend on meeting the factory profit target. Some workers were forced to sell a certain number of clocks themselves or lose part of their salary. See "Enterprise Response," in this chapter.

16. About half of all apprentices and entrants to the technical school, set up in 1978 to train skilled workers, were children of workers. A retiring worker's child generally could inherit the retiree's place in a state-owned factory.

17. Managerial bonuses also varied over only a narrow range. The distribution of annual bonuses among the nineteen factory directors and assistant directors in the seven factories directly under the company in 1982 was as follows: the lowest bonus paid was Y50 and the highest more than Y90, with 70 percent of the managers receiving a bonus of Y80. Average bonuses paid to manual workers were 25–35 percent higher than managerial bonuses, but the variability was similar.

18. Chongqing had its own wage grade system with fifteen grades for manual workers instead of the usual eight. Grade increments were smaller (about Y4 a month

at middle-income levels), but the range of wage rates was similar to that of the eight-grade system.

19. Regulations stipulated that only 30 percent of retained profits could be used for collective welfare. The 10 percent share designated for bonuses could also be used for collective welfare when bonus payments were restricted, as they were in Chongqing's case. It is not clear how the company was able to overspend substantially on collective welfare.

20. The objective function is a construct giving the particular combination and weighting of different goals that the enterprise pursues. Sometimes the objective function can be specified mathematically (see Svejnar 1990, p. 246, for an example); more often the term is used in a qualitative sense. See "Enterprise Objectives and Worker-Oriented Behavior," in chapter 2, for a discussion of the general objectives pursued by Chinese state enterprises. Also see Byrd and Tidrick (1987, pp. 62–67).

21. In the prereform period, purchasers of Chongqing's Shancheng brand watch had to present a ration coupon along with their money. Because of their lower price, clocks may have been even more in demand in rural areas than watches initially.

22. These price cuts of Y10 for a top-grade watch in 1980 and a further Y10 in 1982 had the effect of postponing the time at which supply caught up with market demand. The government's primary motivation, especially for the 1980 price reduction, however, was probably to improve the real standard of living and to lower inflation as measured by overall price indexes for consumer goods.

23. Development of women's watches did start during this period, and investments were made to improve the styling of clocks. The changing situation in 1982, however, imparted much greater urgency to these activities.

24. Marks were awarded for accuracy, shock resistance, and water resistance and then aggregated for a composite score. Although the standard was set nationally, Chongqing conducted its own inspections of quality. The CD did some sample tests before taking delivery.

25. The average national quality rating for watches fell from 88.1 marks in 1980 to 84.7 in 1981 and then rose to 90.4 in 1982 (State Statistical Bureau 1982 and 1983).

26. It is not clear how Chongqing could pay any bonuses at all before the end of the year because the quality standard was supposedly a threshold that must be passed before bonuses could be paid.

27. This refers to an experiment conducted in the 1920s in Western Electric's Hawthorne, California, factory. New organizational methods produced spectacular increases in labor productivity, but productivity declined again after the experiment had been running for some time. Moreover, other quite different organizational changes produced similar results. The conclusion was that workers responded positively to any increase in attention, and that the very act of conducting any experiment showed initially favorable but unsustainable results. See Roethlisberger and Dickson 1939.

28. The Qingdao Forging Machinery Plant was far less aggressive in developing new products than was Chongqing (see chapter 4). It was perhaps deterred by the low tax rate (and consequent low value of tax exemption) and the low profit rate

on machinery products. Stricter definition of new products may also have been a deterrent factor.

29. The results are:

$$\text{Log } C = 2.838 \quad - 0.332 \quad (\text{Log } O)$$
$$(.044) \quad (.036)$$
$$\text{Adjusted } R^2 = 0.76$$

where C = cost and O = output. The t-values are 64.6 for the intercept and −9.4 for Log O. Standard errors are shown in parentheses. Data are from State Economic Commission, Investigation and Research Section 1983, tables 1 and 2, p. 36. The regression excludes the Nanjing Watch Factory and the three smallest factories for which data are available. Nanjing produces only cheap watches with few jewels, while the small factories appear to be nonintegrated assembly plants.

30. Such was clearly the case for the two largest producers in 1980, the Shanghai Watch Company (with an output of 4.63 million units) and the Tianjin Watch Company (with an output of 1.63 million units). The Tianjin Company had more fixed assets and nearly as many workers as Shanghai but produced only about one-third as many watches. Shanghai's higher efficiency is reflected in higher output and lower unit cost; its lower costs are not the result of a larger plant (the usual interpretation of economies of scale). Ironically, Shanghai's actual cost was greater than the cost predicted for its scale of output by the regression results, and Tianjin's actual cost was less than its predicted cost. One must be cautious, therefore, in interpreting divergence from the regression line as an indication of inefficiency.

31. Treasury bonds were a revenue-raising device instituted by the Chinese government in 1981. Mandatory targets for treasury bond purchases were passed down through the administrative hierarchy to enterprises. Chongqing was required to buy Y400,000 worth of treasury bonds in 1981 and the same amount in 1982. The bonds carried a 4 percent annual interest rate and a maturity of five to ten years. (Interest rates were subsequently raised.)

32. Chongqing's shifting its product mix to almost exclusive production of top-grade watches in only two to three years suggests that it had completely solved the technical and quality problems that had plagued it in 1982.

33. It is impossible to be more precise in this analysis because of likely differences in definitions between 1982 and 1985 data. Nominal wage increases of this magnitude, however, were not unusual in Chinese state industry during this period.

References

Byrd, William A. 1987. "The Role and Impact of Markets." In Tidrick and Chen.

Byrd, William A., and Lin Qingsong, eds. 1990. *China's Rural Industry: Structure, Development, and Reform*. New York: Oxford University Press.

Byrd, William A., and Gene Tidrick. 1987. "Factor Allocation and Enterprise Incentives." In Tidrick and Chen.

Caizheng (Government Finance). Monthly magazine.

Chinese Customs Statistics. Quarterly magazine.

Ding Jiatiao. 1983. "Shixing Kuashengshi Lianhe, Fahui Zhongxin Chengshi de Zuoyong—Chongqing Zhongbiao Gongye Gongsi de Diaocha" (Experimenting with Cooperation across Provinces and Cities to Develop the Role of Central Cities—An Investigation of the Chongqing Clock and Watch Company). *Jingji Guanli* (Economic Management) (July): 21–25.

Jingji Guanli (Economic Management). Monthly journal.

Kornai, Janos. 1979. "Resource-Constrained versus Demand-Constrained Systems." *Econometrica* 47(4): 801–19.

Landes, David. 1979. "Watchmaking: A Case Study in Enterprise and Change." *Business History Review* 80(1): 1–39.

Meade, James. 1972. "The Theory of the Labor-Managed Firm and of Profit Sharing." *Economic Journal* 82(325S): 402–28.

Ministry of Light Industry. 1982. "Zhongguo Zhongbiao Gongye" (China's Clock and Watch Industry). In China Economic Yearbook Editorial Committee, *Zhongguo Jingji Nianjian 1982* (1982 China Economic Yearbook). Beijing: Jingji Guanli Chubanshe, pp. V/60–V/63.

Renmin Ribao (People's Daily). Daily newspaper.

Roethlisberger, Fritz, and William Dickson. 1939. *Management of the Worker: An Account of a Research Project.* Cambridge, Mass.: Harvard University Press.

Shanghai City Clock and Watch Corporation. 1981. "Women Shi Zeyang Tongguo Hangye Neibu Tiaozheng Zengchan Zhongbiaode" (How We Increased Production of Clocks and Watches Through Internal Adjustment). In *Shanghai Gongye Qiye Jingyan* (The Experience of Shanghai's Industrial Enterprises), vol. 1. Shijiazhuang: Qiye Guanli Chubanshe.

State Economic Commission, Investigation and Research Section. 1983. "Woguo Shoubiao Gongye Jingji Xiaoyi Fenxi" (An Analysis of the Economic Efficiency of the Watch Industry in China). *Jingji Diaocha* (Economic Investigations) 1 (October): 33–36.

State Statistical Bureau. 1982. *Statistical Yearbook of China 1981.* Hong Kong: Economic Information and Agency.

———. 1983. *Statistical Yearbook of China 1983.* Hong Kong: Economic Information and Agency.

———. 1988. *Zhongguo Tongji Nianjian 1988* (Statistical Yearbook of China 1988). Beijing: Zhongguo Tongji Chubanshe.

———. 1989. *Zhongguo Tongji Nianjian 1989* (Statistical Yearbook of China 1989). Beijing: Zhongguo Tongji Chubanshe.

Svejnar, Jan. 1990. "Productive Efficiency and Employment." In Byrd and Lin.

Tidrick, Gene, and Chen Jiyuan, eds. 1987. *China's Industrial Reform.* New York: Oxford University Press.

United Nations. Various years. *Yearbook of Industrial Statistics.* New York.

Ward, Benjamin. 1958. "The Firm in Illyria: Market Syndicalism." *American Economic Review* 58(4): 566–89.

Weitzman, Martin L. 1980. "The 'Ratchet Principle' and Performance Incentives." *Bell Journal of Economics* 11(1): 302–08.

World Bank. 1982. *World Development Report 1982*. New York: Oxford University Press.

————. 1983. *China: Socialist Economic Development* (3 vols.). Washington, D.C.

Xu Lu. 1983. "Chongqing Zhongbiao Gongye Gongsi Diaocha" (An Investigation of the Chongqing Clock and Watch Company). *Jingji Diaocha* (Economic Investigations) 1 (October): 37–40.

Xue Muqiao. 1983. Speech delivered at a conference on the theory of economic system reform, September 25, 1982. *Jingji Yanjiu* (Economic Research) (August): 5.

Yu Zuyao. 1983. "Chongqing Zhongbiao Gongye Gongsi Shixing Yishui Daili Diaocha" (Investigation of the Chongqing Clock and Watch Company's Experiment of Substituting Tax Payments for Profit Remittances). *Caimao Jingji* (Finance and Trade Economics) (June): 41, 51–54.

Yunnan Economic Research Institute. 1981. "Zou Lianhe zhi Lu, Da You Kewei: Kunming Shoubiao Chang yu Chongqing Zhongbiao Gongye Gongsi Xieshang Lianhe Jingying de Qingkuang Diaocha" (The Path of Combination Has Great Possibilities: An Investigation of the Agreement between the Kunming Watch Factory and the Chongqing Clock and Watch Company for Joint Operations). *Gongye Jingji Guanli Congkan* (Selections on Industrial Economic Management) (March): 40–43.

4

The Qingdao Forging Machinery Plant

Chen Jiyuan, Xu Lu, Tang Zongkun, and
Chen Lantong

THE QINGDAO FORGING MACHINERY PLANT (hereafter referred to as Qingdao or the plant) has produced mainly twin-disc friction presses since the 1960s, with an annual output of 250–300 sets in the early 1980s. It has had a checkered history with regard to its output, administrative supervision, management arrangements, supply of inputs, and financial performance.

Qingdao was severely affected by the government's policies of readjustment and reform. After 1979 the government no longer took responsibility for purchasing and selling the plant's products or for supplying raw materials. Nor did it work out the plant's production plans after that year. Production quotas came to be based on sales and were set by a method that combined planned regulation with responsiveness to market forces. These changes forced the plant to revamp its management practices and mode of operations. The plant implemented a system of independent profit-and-loss accounting for selected production shifts and groups. Labor norms were established, and an economic responsibility system based on "small collective piecework awards" was introduced. Controls over inventories and equipment maintenance were strengthened. The plant also expanded repair services for customers. Finally, it instituted programs to train new employees.

This chapter looks at the changes the Qingdao Forging Machinery Plant made, the success it achieved, and the issues and problems that arose. The first section provides some background on the enterprise's evolution and development up to the late 1970s. The next section looks at the plant's supervisory structure (which has evolved over the past several decades), the problems of that structure, and a possible solution. Qindgao's adjustment to changes in the government's role in its production decisions is examined next. The fourth section discusses the plant's economic performance and suggests means for further improvement. The section following that looks at changes in the plant's labor and wage policies. The sixth section discusses constraints on technological transformation and accomplishments in improving old products and developing new ones. The last section provides a brief postscript on subsequent developments and some general observations.

Historical Background

The earliest predecessor of the Qingdao Forging Machinery Plant was a firearms repair shop under the Binbei Military Subdistrict of Shandong Province. Formed in 1946, the shop had a work force of 160 and two crude machine tools; it practiced a system of payments in kind to its workers, in the form of basic consumer goods. In 1948, as the economic situation in the liberated areas of Shandong improved, the shop shifted to production and repair of weaving looms and cotton gins. It was renamed the Dahua Iron Works of the Binbei Prefectural Industrial Company. In 1949 the plant was moved to the seat of Jiao County, at which time it was renamed the Binbei Yinong Iron Works; it produced waterwheels, cotton gins, and other small agricultural implements.

In 1951 the plant was put under the supervision of the Jiaozhou Prefectural Industrial Company and was amalgamated with the Hongda Metal Works to become the Yinong Iron Works. It officially became a state-owned enterprise under local government administration. Annual industrial output value was Y127,000 in 1951; output consisted mainly of cotton gins and waterwheels. In 1952 the government began to assign production plans to the plant and provided Y38,000 of budgetary funds for investment. The value of industrial output jumped to Y546,000 in that year, and profits were Y55,400. Payment in kind was replaced by payment in accordance with work.

In 1954 the plant was renamed the Jiao County Iron Works. In 1956, when Jiao County came under the jurisdiction of Changwei Prefecture, the ironworks was put under the supervision of the Changwei Prefectural Industrial Company. In 1956 this company became an industrial bureau, and Jiao County established an industrial bureau of its own; the plant was put under the supervision of the latter bureau. In 1958 it was renamed the Jiao County Machine Tool Plant. Between 1953 and 1957, the plant introduced piece-rate wages and nonmaterial incentives for workers. It began to produce manual drills and other new products. Although there were virtually no increases in investment, equipment, or labor force, gross industrial output value rose to Y1,978,100 in 1958, 3.6 times what it had been in 1952.

In 1958–60 the plant came under the influence of the Great Leap Forward movement. Unrealistically high output targets resulted in production of some shoddy products such as power machinery for agricultural use, mining transport equipment, and wooden-wheeled motor vehicles. Reported output rose sharply, but most of the products were expensive and of poor quality. Some of them were indeed useless. An investigation in 1961 found rejects valued at Y350,000.

In 1960 the plant was renamed the Jiao County Forging Machinery Plant (a name that would not change again until 1981) and was put under the supervision of the Qingdao Municipal Machine-building Bureau. At that time it began to produce the twin-disc friction presses that have been its most important product up to the present. Between 1961 and 1965 the plant restored and perfected its rules and regulations and emphasized product quality. By the mid-1960s it had established itself as the leading producer of twin-disc friction presses in China, and had a good reputation among its customers. The plants annual output value, which had averaged less than Y1 million a year in 1961–63, reached Y2 million in 1964. Profits rose from Y100,000 annually in 1961–63 to Y220,000 in 1964, Y650,000 in 1965, and Y1,120,000 in 1966. From 1962 until April 1964 the plant was directly under the supervision of the Shandong Provincial Machine-building Bureau; from May 1964 until 1970 it answered to Changwei Prefecture (to whose jurisdiction Jiao County had been shifted).

The plant fared somewhat differently than did most other Chinese state-owned industrial enterprises during the Cultural Revolution period (1967–76). Production was held up because of political problems for only a brief period. Subsequently, with industrial production throughout the country at a virtual standstill, the plant took advantage of the ready availability of funds for investment and organized large-scale capital construction, erecting new workshops and storehouses and making extensive purchases of machinery and equipment. The plant's total value of fixed assets increased sharply from about Y3 million to nearly Y14 million in this time period. Annual gross industrial output value was Y5 million to Y6 million in 1967–70 and then rose to Y7.42 million in 1971, Y10.05 million in 1972, and a peak of Y12 million in 1973. Profits rose commensurately to Y2 million by 1973. Production fell sharply in 1974 because of political interruptions, but then it jumped again, reaching Y17.08 million in 1975. The enterprise came under the control of Jiao County in 1971–73 and then was returned to Changwei Prefecture in 1974.

In 1977–79 the plant carried out a restructuring program with emphasis on quality control and quality improvement. Management standards were returned to pre–Cultural Revolution levels. The enterprise's products regained their national reputation for quality. The plant was certified by the Qingdao Municipal Heavy Industry Bureau. Though gross industrial output value dropped from its 1977 peak of Y25.7 million to Y18.9 million in 1978, it partially recovered and climbed to Y21.1 million in 1979. Other economic indicators reached new highs, and profits peaked at Y3 million in 1979. In that year the plant's operational activities came under the control of Qingdao Municipality. There was a complicated system of "multiheaded leadership," however, involving Jiao County as well. This system is discussed in the following section.

Supervisory Structure

The Qingdao Forging Machinery Plant is a local government enterprise. In the early 1980s it was under the supervision of the Qingdao Machine-building Bureau, which assigned its yearly production and financial plans and was responsible for evaluating its performance. Matters relating to wages, distribution of bonuses, and recruitment, training, and transfer of all staff (except cadres) had to be approved by the bureau; the bureau then sent an aggregated report to the Qingdao Municipal Labor Bureau. Responsibility for appointing and removing factory-level and middle-level cadres and for party organizations within the plant belonged to the Jiao County Party Committee. The Jiao County Finance and Tax Bureau was entrusted by the Qingdao Municipal Finance and Tax Bureau with collecting taxes from the plant and receiving the profits it handed over to the government. The branch office of the People's Bank of China in Jiao County managed the plant's circulating funds, made the loans it needed for production development, and supervised its use of funds. Qingdao hence has been under the authority of various organizations in the municipality and the county. Its output value target was part of the aggregate plan for Jiao County, and the county was responsible for seeing that the plan was fulfilled. Other plan targets were set by Qingdao Municipality.

The supply of various materials to the plant was handled by the Ministry of Machine-building, the Shandong Machine-building Bureau, the Qingdao Materials Bureau, and Jiao County. The central Ministry of Machine-building was responsible for the distribution of raw materials needed to fulfill the production quota it assigned. For principal raw materials (such as pig iron, steel products, nonferrous metal products, coke, fire-resistant materials, and wood) needed to fulfill the production target assigned by the Municipal Machine-building Bureau, however, the plant was required to apply directly to the Provincial Machine-building Bureau; this bureau then assigned a quota to the plant, on the basis of which purchase contracts were signed with designated suppliers. The plant applied to the Qingdao Materials Bureau for a quota for coal, which was supplied by the Municipal Fuel Company.

Jiao County was responsible for supplying petroleum products, electric power, paint, and local building materials such as bricks, tiles, sand, and stones, but there was no guarantee that the plant's needs would be met when these resources were in short supply. (For instance, an electric power shortage in 1983 forced the factory to stop work from 6:10 P.M. to 9:00 P.M. every day, no matter how urgently its output was needed.) The Jiao County Commercial Bureau determined the plant's quotas of gasoline, diesel oil, and lubricating oil, which were then supplied by gas stations under its control.

Few enterprises have such a complex supervisory structure as did Qingdao. (It was the only one of the forty-two enterprises under the Qingdao

Machine-building Bureau with such a structure.) This system caused many management problems for the county and the municipality as well as for the plant itself. As mentioned, the Qingdao Machine-building Bureau supervised the plant's production in the areas of output and varieties produced but not in the area of output value; it handled personnel matters for general staff but not the appointment and removal of managers. It was therefore difficult for the bureau to ensure that the plant was run efficiently. For example, the bureau chose the plant as an experimental reform unit in October 1982 and quickly completed preparation of a management restructuring program for it. The plant's management, however, still reported to Jiao County. Examination and approval of the restructuring proposal therefore did not take place in March 1983 as had been originally foreseen.

The Jiao County Party Committee was responsible for the Qingdao plant's party business and managers. The committee and its agencies were absorbed in agricultural affairs and were in fact unfamiliar with the plant's production and management. These groups therefore had no basis to make suggestions about the plant's organization. The county paid attention only to the plant's output value. It used no objective criteria to assign the plant an output value target but simply calculated it in light of the total output value quota assigned to Jiao County by the Qingdao Planning Commission.

The complex supervisory structure caused several serious difficulties in managing Qingdao and in optimizing production. First, the quotas assigned for the plant often contradicted one another. In 1982 the plan quota for output value assigned by Jiao County was Y19 million, but the output value of the quantity and product variety targets assigned by the Municipal Machine-building Bureau was only Y13 million. With the assigned quantity and product variety quotas, the plant could not possibly have fulfilled the output value target assigned by the county. Although it performed very well and made marked improvements in management, for which it was commended by the Municipal Bureau, the Provincial Bureau, and the Ministry of Machine Building, the plant was criticized by Jiao County for not fulfilling the county's output value quota.

Second, the bifurcated system of personnel management was not conducive to modernization. One reason for the delay in restructuring the plant's management was that the county's Party Committee was overextended in many other areas. The committee was unfamiliar with the plant's production and management situation and therefore could not evaluate the managers affected by the proposed restructuring.

Third, there was no single unit coordinating the plant's production, supply, and sales; each activity was the responsibility of a different agency. Production targets were assigned by both the municipality and the county. Responsibility for the supply of various categories of materials was shared by the central ministry, the province, the municipality, and the county. Domestic sales were handled mostly by the enterprise itself (some products were handled by the municipality), and export sales were handled by the Ministry of Machine Building and the Provincial Export Corporation. With this management system, it was impossible to achieve a balance between production, supply, and sales.

Fourth, because the county's party committee was in charge of party affairs and cadres, it sometimes requested manpower, vehicles, and materials from the plant; managers were usually required to accommodate these demands. The plant at various times assisted in combating drought, harvesting wheat, and repairing roads.

Fifth, difficulties arose because of frequent changes in the supervisory structure. Each new supervisory organization needed to become familiar with conditions in the plant, and the plant needed to adapt itself to its new leadership. Thus there was little continuity or stability of leadership, and long-term planning was severely hampered. Moreover, these frequent changes inevitably affected staff relations adversely.

The problems described above clearly indicated that the multiheaded leadership system needed to be abolished. Employees at all levels advocated that the plant have only one supervisory body, irrespective of its level. The supervisory organizations in Qingdao Municipality and Jiao County agreed that the system, under which each organization had only partial responsibility but could interfere with and delay the other's work, must definitely be changed.

In view of the modernization drive and of the composition of the Qingdao plant's production and sales, it seemed appropriate for the Qingdao Machine-building Bureau to become the plant's sole supervisory body. The production technology used by the plant was complex; its products were sold nationwide, and some were exported; and the supply of important raw materials was handled directly by the Provincial Machine-building Bureau. These characteristics of the plant and its situation suggested that a higher rather than a lower level of government, with broader geographical scope and greater administrative clout and contacts, would be the most suitable supervisory agency.

Jiao County authorities could not rationally arrange the production of forging machinery products or plan future expansion, nor could they guarantee the supply of important raw materials for the plant. They were unfamiliar with market changes and therefore could not handle sales. Jiao County leaders focused on agriculture and had little time for responsibilities in other areas. Their lack of modern scientific and technological knowledge limited their ability to manage a large enterprise in the modern industrial sector.

Central government authorities in China have decided that major cities should gradually take over the supervision of industrial enterprises in their vicinities; reform at the Qingdao plant should align with this policy.

Even if no longer supervised by Jiao County, the plant should still consider the county's interests. The county supplied the plant's electric power, local building materials, and some other materials. The plant also needed the county's support in providing social services (education, medical care, and so forth) for its staff and their families. Therefore, the plant should provide some economic benefits to the county—perhaps it could turn over a portion of its income to the county as taxes or in some other way. This would smooth the plant's transition to management by municipal authorities and would promote good relations with county organizations.

Reforms in Planning and Marketing

In 1979, when readjustment of the national economy was instituted, the Qingdao Forging Machinery Plant, like other enterprises in the machine-building industry, came to suffer from underutilized capacity. Previously the government had assigned the plant annual directive plans with quotas for output, product variety, specifications, and so forth, and governmental departments had been responsible for production, the supply of materials, and marketing. Whether its products sold was a matter of no concern for Qingdao; for several decades its top managers experienced no pressure to make important changes in product quality and variety. After 1979, however, directive plans were replaced by indicative plans supplemented by market regulation: the enterprise's output, product mix, and specifications were now determined by the market and by customers' needs. This new planning system put greater pressure on the plant, forcing it to change its past procedures and practices.

The planning system of the early 1980s differed from the plant's past system in three important ways:

1. Sales determined output: the plant must "find the rice for its pot." It became involved in marketing in addition to production.
2. Previously Qingdao had simply executed plans assigned by authorities; after readjustment it had to draw up plans itself and then submit them to its supervisory agencies for approval.
3. Production plans for workshops were no longer based on assigned output quantities but were drawn up in accordance with dates of delivery to users. Previously the plant could group together production plans for the same product; now that plans were determined by users' needs, production of the same product might occur at several different times during the year.

Marketing management also changed in the late 1970s. Before that time, products had been centrally allocated by the state, and Qingdao made deliveries according to the allocation list it received from its supervisory agencies. In 1980 the plant became responsible for the sale of its own products; it entered into supply and sales contracts with users and made deliveries according to contract provisions.

Enterprise managers found it difficult to come to grips with the new situation and could not immediately come up with appropriate responses. At first they expected that their plant, as an important enterprise under the First Ministry of Machine Building, could easily get assignments during readjustment. Even when production was reduced significantly in 1979, the managers still waited for the government to assign work, allocate materials, and sell its products. They continued to send leading cadres to supervisory departments in the province, the municipality, and the Ministry of Machine Building to await product assignments, but none were forthcoming. Marketing personnel were sent to many cities in other provinces with samples of products, but very few orders were received. Managers sought help through contacts in the State Material Supply Bureau, in the form of a guarantee for the purchase of enough products for the plant to survive; orders for 240 units of machinery were obtained in this way. The problem seemed to have been solved. After only three months, however, these intermediaries found that too large a portion of their circulating funds was being tied up, and 80 percent of the orders were subsequently cancelled.

The Qingdao Forging Machinery Plant's future course of action was discussed frequently. As they reviewed the plant's development over the preceding 30-odd years—its growth from a shop that used pushcarts and belt-driven lathes to an important enterprise equipped with modern machinery—the staff agreed to try to overcome the new market difficulties.

Reforms in Operations and Management

As a first step in this process, reforms were instituted in the management system. Planning functions and marketing functions previously had been performed by two different sections independently of each other. In 1980 the two sections were merged. The new Planning and Marketing Section oversaw the scheduling of production within the plant and kept abreast of the market situation, thus linking production and marketing. The formation of the section represented an attempt to break away from the old management style in which planning had been separated from marketing and production from end users. The new section was geared toward raising product quality, satisfying the needs of customers, and improving efficiency.

In its operations Qingdao began to focus on socioeconomic benefits, on improving quality and increasing variety of products, and on service to users. Before 1980 there had been more than ten factories in China producing friction presses. At the time of the reforms, many of these factories switched to producing other items or stopped production altogether because their products did not meet quality standards. Only two factories—Liaoyang and

Qingdao—continued as state-approved forging machinery plants. Qingdao gained 70 percent of the national market. In the early 1980s the plant undertook to improve quality control, and as a result product quality did improve a great deal.[1] Users' confidence in the quality of Qingdao's products contributed to the plant's increasing market share.

In the past the plant had focused only on production of complete machinery and had neglected production of spare parts. The supply of spare parts had often failed to meet demand; this had caused much difficulty for users. With the reforms, the plant tried harder to produce sufficient supplies of spare parts to meet users' needs.

At this time Qingdao also started providing various customer services, such as technical training. It organized a special seven-member team to assist users in equipment installation, trial runs, and maintenance. For its easy reference, the plant set up product files for all of the 2,759 presses it had produced in the previous twenty-odd years. It also conducted market surveys and forecasts, and it promoted sales by setting up sales and service centers, by visiting users, by organizing user forums, and through advertising and other forms of promotion.

Changes in Product Design

The plant organized user service teams to visit more than 200 of its customers in six industries (cutlery, spanner and plier hardware, bicycles, sewing machines, medical appliances, and fire-resistant materials) in twenty-six provinces, municipalities, and autonomous regions. These teams promoted and serviced the plant's products and at the same time solicited comments and suggestions from customers. Many light industrial users commented that the presses were inefficient, consuming as they did a great deal of energy, and that they were incompatible with other machines involved in production. This process of soliciting suggestions enabled Qingdao's staff to identify areas in which it could be of service. The plant also discovered that its sales had stagnated not because friction presses themselves were obsolete but because Qingdao's product designs had not changed for thirty years, and its products no longer met users' needs.

In the past, presses had mainly been used in heavy industries such as automobile and tractor manufacturing and lathe building. As readjustment of the national economy proceeded, the demand for presses from heavy industry decreased, but demand from fast-growing light industry increased rapidly. In 1980 sales to the spanner and plier industry and the cutlery industry increased by 50 percent and sales to the bicycle industry by 25 percent. Rural enterprises and the fire-resistant materials industry also began to purchase presses. These new customers required different types of products with new designs. Qingdao responded to this need in several ways.

First, Qingdao geared its research and development and production toward users' needs. It learned from market surveys that 60 percent of the new demand for presses came from the spanner and plier industry, with lesser demand coming from the cutlery industry, the medical appliances industry, the bicycle and tractor industries, the fire-resistant materials industry, and other industries. Demand for small, light presses was increasing. China's cutlery industry, as a case in point, was at this time poorly equipped to satisfy the requirements of international markets and urgently needed to replace its outdated equipment in order to expand production capacity. Qingdao organized technical teams to design and manufacture, specifically for the cutlery industry, a 160-ton twin-disc friction press that could be used for cold-pressing and precision forging of tableware and could increase efficiency three to five times. Qingdao also designed and manufactured, for a vacuum bottle factory, a compact and efficient 63-ton extension punch with a long stroke. For the bicycle industry, the plant designed and produced a 630-ton automatic, multiposition, cold-extrusion press. In 1981 alone the plant developed twelve new products, which accounted for 70 percent of all the product varieties it manufactured in that year.

Second, Qingdao organized technical teams to tackle important production problems and expand its range of products. Facing a long-term sales constraint and recognizing that sales now determined output, the plant had to explore all possible channels of market development and take on new business while continuing to produce its existing products.

Third, to take advantage of the technical transformation of light industry, Qingdao abandoned its practice of supplying only single pieces of machinery and started instead to supply complete sets of equipment for production lines. The plant obtained contracts from two factories for machinery for complete production lines, including the design and manufacture of the machinery, its installation, and trial runs. One of these factories was the new Suigang Hardware Plant in Panyu County, Guangdong Province, financed by Overseas Chinese. This plant planned to build three production lines for tableware with an annual capacity of one million dozens, which would require sixty sets of forging equipment. The other factory was the Shanghai Medical Appliances Plant, which invested Y1.6 million in 1982 to build a new production line.

Fourth, Qingdao emphasized the potential market and technical development. It modified and improved existing products, but it did not neglect its long-term development. It made great efforts to develop new product varieties. Because it was driven by friction, the plant's main product, the twin-disc friction press, was inefficient in its consumption of energy, and it had too low a stroke frequency. Design of a new drive mechanism was therefore an important part of the plant's technical development program. In 1982–83 the plant organized technical teams to develop a new spiral press. By 1983 it had designed and manufactured a 10-ton two-way spiral press, a 100-ton high-energy press, and a 160-ton high-efficiency, energy-saving press. These three new products marked an important breakthrough for Qingdao.

All of these measures enabled the plant to improve product quality, expand sales, and increase output value and profits. Because the plant needed to seek its own markets and customers and sell its products on their own merits, there was now much better coordination between production and demand. The variety and quality of products became more suited to the market. Orders were placed in 1982 (some for delivery in 1983) for a record 335 units of machinery (36 percent more than had been placed in 1981), and orders for 1983 again exceeded capacity. There was no new stockpiling in these years. The plant's inventory of finished products—valued at Y879,000 in 1981 and at Y904,000 in 1982—remained within the approved quota. (The inventory had been as high as Y2,874,000 in 1977 and Y2,003,000 in 1980.)

Improving Economic Performance

In 1979–82 Qingdao overcame difficulties and developed itself in the course of readjustment. The plant sought new customers and opened up new markets; it obtained a sufficient number of orders to maintain normal production. Its annual output of presses, which totaled 203 sets in 1978, dropped to 199 in 1979 and to 176 in 1980 but then rose to 199 in 1981 and reached a record 238 in 1982. The plant accumulated a surplus and turned over profits to the government every year. It remitted an average of Y2,649,400 to the government each year during 1979–82, Y742,900 as taxes and Y1,906,500 as profits. During the same period the plant also upgraded old products, developed new ones, and improved the quality of its output. It exported thirteen presses during this period.

These were considerable achievements. Qingdao reoriented its production, expanded its range of products and improved their quality, and strengthened its technical services. Most important, the plant conducted experiments in system reform, and made adjustments in its relationship with the government, and with its staff; it expanded its decisionmaking power in management and operations; and it linked its economic responsibility to its economic performance and benefits. These reforms improved production incentives. In 1979 Qingdao became a pilot firm in the reform that expanded enterprises' decisionmaking power, and in 1981 it became an experimental unit promoting the economic responsibility system in industrial production.

Reforms in the Financial System

Six significant reforms were implemented in Qingdao's financial system. First, in addition to contributions to the plant director's fund (equivalent to 5 percent of total wages) and the collective welfare fund (equivalent to 11 percent of total wages), the plant implemented various profit retention schemes. Profits retained by the plant were as follows:

1979	Y310,300
1980	Y80,800
1981	Y242,500
1982	Y124,000
Total	Y748,600

Second, in 1980 Qingdao's quota for total working capital approved by the People's Bank was fixed at Y9,634,000. Beginning in that year, the plant must borrow its working capital from the People's Bank, except for Y4,305,000, which originally had been allocated to it by the state (from local government resources). By the end of 1982 the plant's loans outstanding totaled Y11,417,000, of which Y5,329,000 was within the fixed quota for working capital, Y3,880,000 was above the fixed quota, Y1,591,000 was above the total quota, and, Y617,000 was for settling accounts.[2] Beginning in 1980 the plant could also apply to the bank for medium- and short-term loans to finance equipment purchases.

Third, beginning in 1979 Qingdao was permitted to retain only 40 percent of the depreciation fund, drawn at the rate of 4.6 percent of the value of fixed assets. Of the remaining 60 percent, 30 percent was turned over to the state, 20 percent to the province, and 10 percent to the municipality. Before 1979 the plant had been permitted to retain 60 percent of the fund in some years and 50 percent of it in others. Despite the lowered share of depreciation funds retained, the plant's fixed assets increased by 30 percent between 1978 and 1982. The year-end gross value of fixed assets was as follows:

1978	Y16,080,400
1979	Y17,523,600
1980	Y19,253,400
1981	Y20,626,700
1982	Y20,890,000

Fourth, Qingdao established a three-level economic accounting system for administrative and managerial offices, workshops, and shifts and work groups. In 1982 it instituted an independent accounting system for its workshops, known as the "five quotas, three guarantees, and three evaluation criteria" (see "The Labor and Wage System," in this chapter). Units and individuals with outstanding performance or contributions (that is, surpassing the quotas for output, quality, and profits by 50 percent or more) were rewarded with additional bonuses. Those who failed to fulfill the quotas would receive no bonuses and might even have up to 20 percent of their basic wages deducted. In this way the plant developed a system whereby the economic responsibilities of the workshop were linked to its performance and benefits.

In 1982 Qingdao also implemented independent accounting systems for its administrative and technical offices; it required separate accounts for management expenses, special funds, and welfare expenses, as well as for working capital. Moreover, certain work groups (about 40 percent of the total number of work groups at the time) were treated as first-level accounting units and were required to account independently for their own profits and losses. Work groups not yet in this system made separate accounting of such major indicators as output, quality, and consumption of inputs.

The economic and technical quotas of the plant were subdivided into smaller quotas at every level and assigned under the responsibility system to each office, workshop, work group, and individual worker (or job). Performance was regularly evaluated against these quotas and was linked with a system of rewards and penalties. These measures to a certain extent succeeded in rewarding those who worked well and penalizing those who did not and thus created effective work incentives.

The effect of these reforms was especially remarkable after mid-1982. Borrowing from the experience of the Capital Iron and Steel Company, Qingdao put new emphasis on the rationalization of management, production, and technical organization, and made further improvements in its various accounting and economic responsibility systems. As a result, the accounting profits of all nine workshops in the plant increased from Y46,000 in the first half of 1982 to Y113,000 in the second half of the year. At the same time the unit production costs of four principal products dropped by 1.7–8.1 percent. In 1982 the turnover of working capital was seventy-four days less than it had been in 1981, and total profits were 37 percent above the planned figure.

Fifth, for staff in production workshops, the enterprise implemented a piece-rate bonus system for the work group (or small collective), for work above the fixed quota. For staff in supporting departments and offices, a system of time-rate bonuses was introduced. For the plant as a whole, total piece-rate bonuses for above-quota work could not exceed 25 percent of total basic wages for the year; the bonus fund under the time-rate wage system could not exceed 12 percent of total basic wages. Thus the total amount of bonuses was limited, but the amount of bonuses given to any workshop or to any worker varied and had no limit.

Finally, the plant was permitted to continue its practice of including in production cost all expenses incurred for research and trial production for modifying and improving existing products. It could not, however, raise the ex-factory price of the modified products, regardless of how much their design, performance, quality, or cost-effectiveness had been improved.

Overall, Qingdao's steps toward reform during these years were small ones. The changes did not affect the basic principle of "everyone eating out of a common pot." There were only limited funds for bonuses, and differences between individuals' bonuses in actual practice were small. As a result, bonuses effectively became additional wages, and the plant was not able to break away from basic egalitarianism in distribution. With regard to its financial relationship with the government, the plant still adhered to the old system of paying an industrial and commercial tax and handing over profits.

Poor Economic Performance

Qingdao improved its economic performance to some extent through its efforts to improve management. Despite the plant's success in matching production to demand, however, its economic performance continued to be poor, as is evidenced by its excessive use of capital (both fixed assets and working capital). Capital used per Y100 of gross or net industrial output value increased between 1979 and 1982 (table 4.1).

Another indicator of poor economic performance is the decrease in taxes and profits turned over to the government, shown in table 4.2. In 1979–82, this figure declined every year until 1982, when it started to rise again, but even at that time it was still lower than the average for the four-year period. Total remitted profits and taxes as a percentage of gross industrial output value were lower in 1979–82 than they were in 1975–78.

Table 4.1. Indicators of Financial Performance for Qingdao, 1978–82
(millions of yuan unless otherwise specified)

Indicator	1978	1979	1980	1981	1982
Year-end gross value of fixed assets[a]	16.080	17.524	19.253	20.627	20.890
Year-end total value of circulating capital[b]	17.534	18.017	17.485	15.535	17.628
Gross value of industrial output (GVIO) (in 1970 prices)	18.903	21.093	20.884	16.555	17.357
Net value of industrial output (NVIO) (in current prices)	4.745	5.280	5.234	4.428	4.353
Total capital used per Y100 of GVIO (yuan)[c]	179	168	176	218	222
Total capital used per Y100 of NVIO (yuan)[c]	708	673	702	817	885

a. Valued at original purchase cost, without subtraction of accumulated depreciation.

b. The year-end total value of circulating capital is calculated as the sum of the following items: (1) year-end within-quota circulating capital, (2) year-end above-quota circulating capital, and (3) year-end accounts receivable less accounts payable.

c. Total capital used per Y100 of output value (net or gross) was calculated by dividing the sum of year-end total circulating capital and gross value of fixed assets by industrial output value for that year and multiplying the result by 100.

Source: Information provided by the plant.

There are several reasons that Qingdao's profitability declined. First, the plant carried unsalable goods on its books and it used working capital far in excess of its quota. It still had a huge inventory of unwanted products remaining from the period in which it had pushed for high output value without regard to customer demand. An audit of fixed assets in 1980 revealed Y7 million of substandard products, half of which were reported to be worthless; even in 1982–83, products worth Y2.2 million were still excluded from the accounts and were thus subject to interest as material in stock. The audit also found that Y1.5 million worth of finished and semifinished products included as goods in process and in the reserve fund had to be discounted or scrapped. More than half of these products had little value, and some had to be sold at much reduced prices.[3] Because of poor management, the total amount of working capital used by the plant at the end of 1982 reached Y17.63 million, a figure Y7.99 million greater than the approved quota. In 1982–83 Qingdao was required to pay more than Y100,000 in fees to the government (for the working capital the government provided in the form of grants) and more than Y600,000 each year in interest to the bank. The increase in interest payments raised production costs and, correspondingly, reduced profits.

Second, the prices of some of Qingdao's principal products were reduced. After 1979 the price of the J53-630B press was reduced from Y200,000 to Y180,000 per set, and the price of the Y83-400 baling press for metal filings was reduced from Y94,000 to Y80,000.

Third, the demand for heavy presses did not grow, whereas the need for

Table 4.2. Taxes and Profit Remittances for Qingdao, 1975–82
(millions of yuan unless otherwise specified)

Item	1975–78	1979–82	1979	1980	1981	1982
GVIO	83.178	75.888	21.093	20.884	16.555	17.357
Taxes remitted to state	2.926	2.972	0.919	0.722	0.529	0.801
Profits remitted to state	9.644	7.626	2.714	2.561	0.968	1.383
Total taxes and remitted profits	12.569	10.598	3.633	3.283	1.497	2.185
Taxes and remitted profits as a percentage of GVIO	15.11	13.96	17.22	15.72	9.04	12.59
Average annual taxes and remitted profits	3.142	2.649	n.a.	n.a.	n.a.	n.a.

GVIO, Gross value of industrial output.
n.a. Not applicable.
Source: Information provided by the plant.

smaller presses used in light industry, brick making, technical transformation, and commune and brigade enterprises increased substantially. This situation led to fundamental changes in Qingdao's product mix. The output of profitable, high-priced large presses was reduced, and that of cheaper, less profitable small presses was increased. As a result, total profits and taxes in relation to output value declined. The plant had no permission to set its own prices to counter the adverse trend in profits. It lost money in producing the J53-160B press, for example, which was priced at Y16,000. (The Provincial Machine-building Bureau approved a temporary price of Y20,000 for this press, beginning in 1983.) The J53-300B press, whose design and quality were improved but whose production cost increased and whose unit profits declined, also lost money because the plant was not permitted to raise its ex-factory price. A third example of this phenomenon was the improved J53-400A press, which was sold at Y60,000 and on which the plant lost Y10,000 a set. Qingdao also lost money on most of its projects for technical cooperation with other units. The plant suggested that its supervisory departments should make reasonable adjustments in the prices of some old products, the prices of improved products, and the prices charged for technical cooperation with other factories. These suggestions had not yielded any results as of 1983.

Fourth, because state allocations of fuel and raw materials to Qingdao decreased, the plant needed to purchase much larger quantities of these on the market, at prices much higher than the state-allocated prices. The prices of materials allocated by the state also increased somewhat.[4] Consequently, production costs rose rapidly. The cost structure of the plant involved six principal items: raw materials, fuel, power, wages, overhead expenses for the workshops, and overhead expenses for the plant itself. In 1982 the plant's total cost of production was Y15.11 million. About Y6 million (or 40 percent) of the cost involved power, wages, and overhead expenses for workshops and the plant itself; these costs did not vary much each year. The other 60 percent of total cost involved raw materials and fuel, which were greatly affected by price increases.[5] As a result, it was difficult for the plant to keep total costs under control, and profitability inevitably declined.

The Labor and Wage System

In general, the labor, wage, and bonus systems in the Qingdao Forging Machinery Plant followed state regulations. Cadres and technical staff were assigned by the state; ordinary workers were recruited and allocated by labor departments. The plant was not permitted to hire workers on its own, and it could not fire workers unless they violated the criminal codes or laws of the state. The plant used the uniform wage scale set by the state. Collective welfare payments and labor insurance payments were levied at national rates.

No factory could promote workers or increase wages without a directive from the State Council. Bonuses were usually awarded to about 99 percent of workers. As was noted earlier, the amount of bonuses was limited, and the difference among bonuses was very small. Thus the bonus system played only a limited role in rewarding diligent workers and punishing lazy ones.

Composition of the Staff

At the end of January 1983, Qingdao had 1,662 staff on its payroll—1,279 staff and workers under the state ownership system, 299 collective workers, 37 contract workers, and 47 peasant workers. There were 1,264 ordinary workers (76 percent of the total); 91 engineers and technical personnel (5.5 percent); 193 managerial and administrative personnel (11.6 percent); 104 service personnel (6.3 percent); and 10 other categories of workers (0.6 percent), including those on sick leave or study leave.

Some explanation is needed of the circumstances that led to this state enterprise employing collective and other nonregular workers. When Qingdao needed to recruit new workers in 1979, there was no state quota, so the plant was permitted to hire 300 collective workers. These new employees worked alongside the regular employees and received the same pay and benefits. The plant was subsequently asked by the goverment to set up a separate factory for collective workers, that would be responsible for its own profits and losses. It planned to assign 100 of them to a new can production line (see "Technical Transformation and Development of New Products," in this chapter) and to sign labor contracts with the remaining 200.

The contract workers had been recruited in 1977. At that time Qingdao was under the jurisdiction of the Changwei Prefectural Machine-building Bureau, which had recruited the workers from the countryside under contracts renewable every three months. These contract workers were included in Qingdao's labor quota under the state plan, but the plant could not recruit any additional contract workers.

Peasant workers had been first employed by the plant in 1975. With the objective of providing technical training for rural workers, Qingdao recruited a total of 360 peasant workers, 100 in 1975, 200 in 1976, and 60 in 1978. Contracts with these workers were signed for five-year periods, at the end of which the peasants were to return to the countryside; Qingdao did not expect to replace them. In 1982 the plant still employed forty-seven peasant workers, who were to be dismissed in August 1983, when their terms ended. The plant did not recruit any more of these workers, who were not included in the state labor quota.

Qingdao had an affiliated factory run by ninety-five dependents of regular workers. The factory was registered with the county's Industrial and Commercial Administration Bureau, held its own business license, and was required to pay taxes. Although it contracted with the Qingdao plant to provide services and products, it also had the right to solicit work from other units.

Problems with Labor

The system of labor recruitment and dismissal gave rise to several problems. First, Qingdao, in recruiting new workers, was allocated a quota by the Municipal Labor Bureau. Recruitment was implemented by the Jiao County Labor Bureau, which tested candidates, arranged for their medical examinations, and arranged placements for them. The plant itself was not permitted to hire better-qualified workers than the ones the county provided. Although the plant's production tasks required a male-female worker ratio of 70 to 30, half of the workers allocated by the county were female, and it was difficult for Qingdao to find jobs for so many women.

Second, the plant had a weak technical staff and too few college graduates. When it applied to the authorities for permission to hire college graduates for the first time in 1982, it had to go through the Municipal Machine-building Bureau and Personnel Bureau up to the Provincial Machine-building Bureau to obtain an allocation of only twelve graduates. The county kept five of them so the plant got only seven. Qingdao planned to request more college graduates in the future. In the meantime, to provide better training for its existing staff, the plant established an educational committee and built a new training center. It arranged for some staff to receive full-time training and ran three courses (each lasting a term) at the workers' spare-time college. Ninety-two staff had graduated from the workers' spare-time college after completing three years of study, and most of them were assigned to technical tasks. To encourage staff to study, however, government recognition for the academic qualifications of those who completed training and appropriate titles and positions for those who acquired technical skills were needed.

Third, Qingdao had only limited power to deal with staff who made serious mistakes. It had the power to suspend them and put them on probation for a year, but it was required to pay each of these workers Y25 a month for living expenses during that year and to reinstate him or her afterward at the original wage level. If Qingdao wanted to release these workers permanently, it had to obtain approval from the Municipal Machine-building Bureau.

The Wage System

The wage system in force at the plant was the eight-grade system generally used in Chinese state-owned factories in the early 1980s. Monthly wages by grade level are shown in table 4.3. As of January 1983, workers under the state-ownership system had an average grade of 3.08 and an average monthly wage of Y42.49. Workers under collective ownership were mostly in the first grade. The daily wage rate for contract workers was Y1.48 for men and Y1.25 for women. Peasant workers received Y39 a month in their first year, Y41 in their second, Y43 in their third, and Y45 in their fourth and fifth years. At the end of their contract they received three months' pay outright. Qingdao paid Y2 a day for each worker in its affiliated factory, and the factory actually paid Y1.2 a day to each of those workers. Workers of different categories generally started with approximately the same wages; there was little difference between grades, and the gap between the highest and the lowest grades was not large.

There were three principal issues concerning the wage system. First, Qingdao used a time-rate wage system with a modified piece-rate bonus for some workers. The plant had achieved good results with a full-fledged piece-rate wage system before the Cultural Revolution, but its supervisory bureau did not allow such a system in the early 1980s. Plant managers believed that restoration of full piece rates would increase labor efficiency and would double output value without additional equipment.

Second, Qingdao also considered instituting a floating wage system, in which 20 percent of total basic wages would be floating wages. This system would conflict, however, with labor insurance regulations under which staff who were on sick leave for less than six months and who had completed at least eight years of service were to receive 100 percent of their wages. According to the floating wage system under consideration, they would receive only 80 percent of their basic wages. Similarly, workers who fulfilled production quotas based on working hours would receive only 80 percent of their basic wages under the floating wage system. It would also have been difficult for the plant to implement a floating wage system for staff in its administrative offices, which did not have fixed quotas. Setting aside 20 percent of basic wages for floating wages would have created hardship for some staff, because existing wages were generally low. Thus a floating wage system had not yet been implemented at the time of this study. The plant

Table 4.3. Base Monthly Wages by Employee Grade, Early 1980s (yuan)

Grade	State-ownership system	Collective system
1	30	31
2	35	36
3	41	42
4	48	49
5	56	58
6	66	68
7	77	79
8	90	93

Source: Information provided by the plant.

was also considering an experiment with a contract system for service work.

Third, Qingdao had no power to demote or promote staff, even though such actions, if they involved less than 1 percent of the wage bill, were theoretically at the discretion of the plant director, according to the regulations governing factory directors. The State Council decided whether wage adjustments would be made and issued directives accordingly, whereas the actual amounts allocated for this purpose were determined by the supervisory bureau.

The Economic Responsibility System

In order to provide a sound basis for evaluating performance, on July 1, 1982, Qingdao introduced an economic responsibility system—the "five quotas, three guarantees, and three evaluation criteria"—in its workshops and offices.

There was a set of five quotas for both workshops and offices. In workshops, quotas existed for number of people, number of machines, output, quality standards, and profits. In offices, quotas covered number of people, number of posts, quality of work, amount of work, and expenses.

The three guarantees referred to output, quality, and profit, the three principal indicators that Qingdao had undertaken to fulfill as part of its economic responsibility to the government. These indicators were subdivided into quotas for workshops, offices, work groups, and individuals. The workshops had to meet the annual profit, output, and quality targets set by the plant's management. Depending on the nature of their work, the plant's offices usually had to meet targets for amount of work, profit, and overhead expenses.

The three evaluation criteria referred to the three aspects of performance examined by the plant. The first criterion was the three guarantees against which the performance of workshops and offices was evaluated every month. The second consisted of ten standards of work expressed in percentage terms, including attendance, condition of equipment, safety and tidiness, cost of managing production processes, and so forth. The third criterion was the working relationships between the various units.

Aside from checking the indicators of output, quality, and input consumption, the workshop also evaluated the performance of work shifts and groups against a number of lesser targets, such as attendance, record keeping, equipment maintenance, safety, and spare-time study. Each of these targets had specific contents, requirements, and methods of evaluation.

In 1982 Qingdao established labor requirements or norms for its subunits. Workshops set norms for the numbers of people and machines required based on the workshop's production task. As a result, the workshops dismissed twenty temporary workers and transferred thirty-three technical staff to a special workshop to develop new products. Despite these staff reductions another twenty-three pieces of equipment were put into operation. The offices also made staff adjustments, and twenty of their workers returned to first-line production tasks.

In 1982 Qingdao also revised the norms for the number of hours of work required to produce its principal products. The hours-norm for the 160-ton press was reduced by 2.5 percent; for the 300-ton press by 3.23 percent; for the 400-ton press by 1.32 percent; for the 630-ton press by 1.6 percent; for the 1,000-ton press by 0.7 percent; and for the 1,600-ton press by 0.9 percent. The revised norms were advanced by the industry's general standards in China. The plant planned subsequently to revise these norms regularly, once or twice a year.

Bonus Systems

As mentioned in the previous section, Qingdao implemented two bonus systems, one based on piece rates for staff in the production workshops, the other on time rates for staff in its supporting departments and offices. In 1982 there were 422 office employees and 1,147 workshop employees in the bonus system. The average annual bonus was Y135.2.

The piece-rate bonus system was introduced in 1981. Under this system, production quotas were set on the basis of hours of work per task (at an average level at that time of 204 working hours per person per month), and Y0.22 was paid for each hour's worth of work done above the quota. In 1982 the highest bonus paid under this system was Y550. The plant evaluated the performance of its workshops, which in turn evaluated the performance of their work shifts or groups.

Distribution coefficients for bonuses were set according to the economic contribution, importance of the job, technical complexity, labor intensity, and magnitude of the economic responsibility of the unit or individual. The plant's units and cadres were divided into nine grades, each with its own coefficient. A coefficient of 1.0 was equivalent to a monthly bonus of Y10. The lowest coefficient gave a bonus of Y7 and the highest Y14. The distribution coefficients for the director and deputy directors were 1.4 and 1.3, respectively. The coefficient for first-line production workshops (such as hot processing) was 1.2; for second-line workshops (such as cold processing) it was 1.1; and for third-line workshops it was 0.9. Offices directly related to production had a coefficient of 0.9; for other offices it was 0.8. Heads of workshops and offices had coefficients 0.2 higher than those for their units, deputy heads 0.1 higher. If one of the three targets for output, quality, and profit was not reached, the monthly bonus was reduced. The factory director and deputy directors had their bonuses reduced in 1982 on this account. Implementation of the system of coefficients improved production and management. In 1982 fewer than fifty employees did not receive bonuses, some because they took more than five days of sick leave or failed to complete production tasks.

An amount equivalent to 1 percent of total wages was drawn from the enterprise fund at the end of each year for awards to workers. In 1982 more than 270 people (15 percent of the total staff) received such awards. Four employees cited as "pacesetters" received Y150 each, and six cited as "production experts" received Y70 each. The remaining 260-odd were cited as outstanding workers; some of them received awards of Y7, and some received certificates and prizes.

Other Workers' Benefits

Qingdao has done much to improve collective welfare and labor insurance for its workers and staff. In 1979–82, the plant built about 8,000 square meters of new workers' housing. As a result, all workers were allocated housing. Those who had been hired before 1962 were allocated three-room apartments, each with a total floor space of 50 square meters (plus a kitchen); newlyweds received a living space of 14 square meters (plus a kitchen); college graduates recently allocated to Qingdao shared one room between two; and other unmarried persons shared one room between four. Average per capita living space was 6.5 square meters. Rents were quite low, about Y0.06 per square meter per month.

Qingdao's collective welfare facilities included a canteen, a nursery, a hospital, a public bathhouse, a cold-storage room, and a cultural club. The plant gave its staff subsidies for haircuts, baths, and transport each month, and for heating costs in the winter. In 1982, Y20,000 of subsidies were distributed to workers in financial difficulties.

State regulations guaranteed workers free medical care and covered half of their dependents' medical fees. Workers on sick leave received full pay for the first six months and 60 percent of basic wages afterward, paid out of the labor insurance fund. In case of death, labor insurance regulations required the plant to pay out a lump sum equivalent to six, nine, or twelve months of basic wages to directly related dependents. This amount was so small, however, that the family of the deceased often found itself in financial difficulty. In such cases the plant preferred to follow the more generous regulations for government agencies, which required that aged parents be supported until they died and young children until they reached adulthood.

Technical Transformation and Development of New Products

In 1982, Qingdao possessed 507 sets of machines and equipment, with a gross value of Y12.77 million. It attached great importance to the management and maintenance of this equipment. A team of workers and managers worked full-time to keep the equipment in good condition, improve its performance, reduce downtime, and extend its useful life.

Much equipment was technically out of date, however, and urgently needed to be remodeled and updated. The plant made great progress in this area after 1979, remodeling and updating 108 pieces of equipment between 1980 and 1982. The Shandong Provincial Machine-building Bureau ranked Qingdao ahead of fifty-two other machine-building enterprises in the province for its success in technical transformation. Ninety percent of Qingdao's small equipment was remodeled at this time, but, partly because of a shortage of funds, technical transformation of large equipment had to be postponed.

Much of Qingdao's large equipment had been made by the plant itself and was ten to twenty years old. The double-housing planer, the principal item of equipment used in manufacturing the frames and bodies of presses, was the key to technological modernization. Because some parts of the planer were higher than its crossbeam, its efficiency was very low. Using these planers, more than 40,000 work hours were spent each year in manufacturing frames and bodies of presses (this figure represents one-seventh of the total number of annual work hours in the plant). Fitting milling-cutters onto the planers would increase efficiency by 20–30 percent; this would also save energy and reduce power requirements from 120 kilowatts to 30 kilowatts. Remodeling one planer would cost an estimated Y60,000 to Y70,000, of which Y50,000 would buy the milling-cutter; a new double-housing milling machine would cost about Y200,000. By remodeling the planer, the plant could increase its income by Y20,000 to Y30,000 each year through savings resulting from improved efficiency and energy conservation, and the total cost of converting the planer could be recovered within three years. Shortage of funds for technical transformation, however, prevented this improvement.

Other obstacles to technical transformation were the lack of technical information, especially about foreign technology, and shortages of technical staff. The plant had fewer than thirty workers assigned to technological development, or about 2 percent of its total work force.

Managers thought that if they could solve problems of funding, information, and technical training of staff, they could carry out technical transformation of equipment effectively, develop new products, increase production capacity, and reduce consumption of raw materials. They thought that through such intensive growth, the plant could quadruple its output value by 1987, and require no increase in staff and equipment.

Developing new products was another urgent task. Although there was still a domestic market for Qingdao's friction presses in the early 1980s, they were obsolete and their designs no longer met users' needs. Qingdao had been producing twin-disc friction presses for more than two decades. Before the late 1970s it had no incentive to improve or upgrade its products, so the presses became outdated and were inefficient in their use of energy and materials. As in the area of technical transformation, the plant's efforts in this area were hampered by shortages of funds and technical personnel.

Qingdao programmed its research and new-product development to suit the demand for technical transformation in light industry. It designed and manufactured a 160-ton twin-disc friction press for the cutlery industry, which was used for cold pressing and precision forging in tableware production. The new press was efficient, safe, and labor-saving. The plant developed a 630-ton horizontal, multiposition, cold-extrusion press for the bicycle industry, which was used in making such parts as mudguards and brake shoes. This press reduced raw material requirements by 20 percent, improved efficiency by 50 percent, increased the precision of manufactured parts, reduced wear on cutters, and helped improve working conditions. Qingdao also designed and manufactured a 63-ton punch for a vacuum bottle factory, which was compact and efficient and had a long stroke. As mentioned earlier, the plant also began to provide complete production lines rather than single machines.

Qingdao used various means to elicit the views of customers on the adaptability, reliability, and durability of its products. It remodeled light friction presses such as the 160-ton, 300-ton, and 400-ton models; they became lighter, quieter, better-designed, and easier to operate. The plant also improved the quality and technical performance of its heavy presses.

Qingdao concentrated on the design of a new drive mechanism for the twin-disc friction press. This effort led to some initial success in designing a 10-ton two-way spiral press, a 100-ton high-energy press, and a 160-ton high-efficiency energy-saving press. These new products marked a breakthrough in the press's mode of transmission; this breakthrough eliminated the two friction discs and used an electric motor to move the drive wheel. The new presses were compact, lightweight, highly efficient, versatile, and energy-saving. Qingdao hoped that these technical innovations would ensure continuity of production after demand for the twin-disc friction press declined.

The plant encountered difficulties in developing new products, mainly because of shortage of funds. Except for projects directly assigned by the central government, for which the plant was allocated sufficient funds and assured of profits, it did not have adequate financing to develop new products or to conduct technical research. Funds for research and trial production allocated by authorities and payments made by customers fell short of actual expenses.[6] Moreover, it cost more to produce the better-quality new products than the existing models. Price increases for raw materials also added to production costs. Prices of improved products could not be increased, however, and were sometimes even reduced. Under these conditions, the more new products the plant developed, the higher the losses it incurred.

Qingdao also had difficulty in obtaining bank loans for developing new products. For example, in early 1982 it learned from the Ministry of Light Industry that the export of beer and other beverages was adversely affected by the backward technology that had been used to make their containers, three-piece welded tin cans, since the 1950s. In response, the plant decided to develop a production line for high-frequency resistance-welded cans, which required thirteen sets of equipment. Design work was well under way, and the plant planned to complete the first production line shortly; with this line it would make test runs to prepare for additional production. At the same time, the plant would produce the new beer cans itself. Qingdao estimated that in two years this plant could more than double its output value and almost triple its profits. The project was approved by the packaging committee of the Ministry of Machine Building, which agreed to allocate Qingdao a loan of Y1.2 million from the ministry's 1982 loan quota. An objection from the provincial People's Bank prevented the plant from receiving this loan, however, after it had already spent more than Y100,000 in designing the new production line. At the time of the present study, the plant planned to continue discussing this matter with the provincial People's Bank. This example shows that in the new system of loan financing, disagreements between the supervisory agency and the bank could hinder the granting of loans and hence prevent the start of urgently needed projects.

In sum, Qingdao made some progress, through its own efforts, in developing new products, but it faced many difficulties. For the plant to cover the cost of developing new products, the products must be reasonably priced and the plant must receive a reasonable share of profits. Neither of these conditions was met in the early 1980s.

Editor's Supplementary Observations and Postscript

Very little information is available about the Qingdao Forging Machinery Plant's situation or performance after 1983. Nevertheless, some new developments that shed light on the earlier analysis can be reported. In addition, certain aspects of the plant's experience in the late 1970s and early 1980s deserve a closer look.

Self-Made Machinery

Qingdao's extensive use of equipment that it had made itself had adverse implications for the plant's performance. Other machine-building plants in China also have relied heavily on self-made equipment, so Qingdao's experience in this context probably has wide relevance.

During the prereform period, when the plant made large amounts of equipment for its own use, there was little concern for quality control, and much substandard or even useless output was produced. This affected the plant's performance over the long term, contributing to inefficiency in capital utilization as well as in energy consumption. In fact, heavy reliance on self-made equipment "internalized" the demand side within the plant; in an environment in which demand was in any case neglected, this circumstance probably further weakened the effect of demand. The plant as user probably would have found it even more difficult than would outside users to reject some of its products on grounds of poor quality. Even the minimal (in a sellers' market) sanction of acceptance by material supply authorities or by outside users was not available.

While it was being manufactured and before it was actually put into operation, self-made machinery was financed as working capital (goods-in-process or finished product inventory). Working capital financing has generally been virtually automatic in China, so production of machinery for a plant's own use may have escaped some of the bureaucratic scrutiny normally applied to fixed investment projects. Once built, if the equipment was deemed unsuitable for use, it could remain in the finished product inventory for years. As noted earlier in this chapter, an audit in 1980 found Y7 million worth of unacceptable equipment in inventory, about half of which was reported to be completely useless; in 1982–83 Y2.2 million of such equipment remained on the books, still financed by working capital loans.[7]

Once created, these assets also generated significant accounting and financial problems in writing off those that were useless. Generally, fiscal and banking constraints prevented full write-offs (which had to be financed largely from outside, because the enterprise had no real equity). The central government set ceilings on the amount of grant-financed working capital assets that could be written off; the local government sometimes allowed additional write-offs by diverting for this purpose profits that would otherwise be remitted to it. The rules and procedures governing write-offs were rather rigid. Only fully depreciated assets originally worth less than Y10,000 could be written off on the plant's own authority. Write-offs of small assets not yet fully depreciated and of all assets worth more than Y10,000 required government approval, in some cases by the central Ministry of Machine-building. Failure to clear accounts of these assets tied up capital and built in higher interest costs.

Bank Loans

The Qingdao plant's reluctance to take on bank loans to finance investments in modernization or development of new presses was alluded to earlier. This attitude seems to have been related in part to the accounting treatment of its loan repayments, but in larger part to the very low profit margins and indirect tax rates on the plant's products. Given low value added, there was little room for diversion of profits or taxes to loan repayment, which may have made bank loans much less attractive to the plant.

The provisions affecting Qingdao's loan repayments seem to have been something of a hybrid of repayment from before-tax profits, as allowed for the Chongqing Clock and Watch Company and most other Chinese state-owned industrial enterprises in the early 1980s (see chapter 3 in this volume), and repayment from after-tax profits, as was practiced by the Qinghe Woolen Textile Mill (see chapter 6 in this volume). The Qingdao plant was to repay loans from "above-quota profits," which presumably meant that only after it remitted the stipulated quota of profits to the government could it use additional profits for loan repayments. It appears, however, that loan repayments could be made from above-quota profits before tax was levied on them. The plant's profits were low and relatively stagnant, so that not much money was available to be diverted to loan repayments, whether before taxes or after taxes.

The plant was eager to obtain a bank loan for a project to produce machinery for manufacture of beer cans and to manufacture the cans themselves, which shows how important financial profitability was in decisions on loan financing. Beer cans as a new product would have been exempt from indirect tax for three years, they would be a profitable product for the plant, and it was understood (at least by the plant) that repayments for loans related to this project would come from total profits, not from above-quota profits. In fact, Qingdao's management was anticipating that the loan for the entire project would be repaid with profits from the manufacture of beer cans alone.

Development of New Products

Low profitability also seems to have seriously affected Qingdao's incentives to engage in new product development, although management recognized that developing new products embodying more modern technology was crucial to the plant's long-term survival. Low profits and low indirect tax rates made the value of tax exemptions low; hence the exemptions provided a weak incentive for development. Moreover, strict criteria must be satisfied before any product could be considered new—quite the opposite of the situations that obtained for many producers of consumer durables.

The plant's claim that research and new product development were money-losing propositions, reported earlier in this chapter, can be documented with some limited quantitative data. For fifteen new products developed by the plant over several years, the total research and development cost was Y1.506 million, whereas revenues generated for the same time period were only Y1.385 million and the state grant for new product development was only Y100,000. This left a gap of Y20,000 that the plant must absorb. Management attributed this problem to inadequate research and development funding[8] and to the plant's inability to pass on the costs of research and development, quality improvements, and more modern and generally better products to customers in the form of higher prices.

The Scope for Manipulation

As a locally administered state-owned enterprise, Qingdao to a considerable extent was, like other enterprises in the sample, subject to a soft budget constraint. Rules were bent in its favor, with the approval of local authorities.

One example is the diversion in 1980 of *all* retained profits to pay workers' bonuses, an action that flouted central government guidelines but was at least tacitly approved by local supervisory agencies. In 1982 the plant would have failed to meet the target set by Jiao County for gross industrial output value, but the target was revised downward, so that in the end it was achieved.

Low profit margins and low tax rates limited the scope for manipulation of the incentive environment and hence in a peculiar way hardened the enterprise budget constraint. There was simply very little surplus for the plant and its various supervisory agencies to bargain over. The consequent reduced flexibility undoubtedly was an important factor in Qingdao's perception of severe administrative and financial constraints hindering its activities, particularly its modernization and new product development. The lack of scope for manipulation may conceivably have had some positive incentive implications, but, from the perspective of the enterprise, these were dominated by the adverse effects.

Postscript

The most important post-1983 development in the story of the Qingdao Forging Machinery Plant that has come to light was an important readjustment in the plant's relations with supervisory agencies. The supervision of the plant's managers, including appointment and dismissal of the plant's top leadership, was shifted from Jiao County to Qingdao Municipality, whereas the supervision of work-force size, the hiring and firing of workers, and so forth, was transferred from the municipality to the county. This reversal probably resulted in a more rational set-up for the plant, but the continuing supervisory role of Jiao County indicated that the multiheaded leadership system had not been completely abolished. In 1985 Qingdao complained that it had been given a mandatory plan target for a specific product that it was not able to produce, but it feared offending its superiors if it refused.

As of 1985, Qingdao was still directly marketing most of its output; only a few special items were procured by government material supply departments. Sales were booming; the plant reported that its output was now constrained by the supply of steel and zinc. On specific product lines, however, Qingdao was almost certainly still market-constrained. That planning and material supply authorities made no strong attempts to regain control over the distribution of Qingdao's products suggested that the products' obsolete technology and high energy consumption made them unattractive to users in the state sector of the economy. Demand continued to emanate primarily from urban collectives and from rural industries, which were experiencing extraordinarily rapid growth and had little or no access to other, more efficient technologies.

It was not clear how much progress the Qingdao Forging Machinery Plant had been able to make toward resolving its long-term problems of backward technology, high energy consumption of products, obsolete equipment, and wasteful manufacturing techniques. Despite significant improvements in internal management, these fundamental issues clouded the plant's long-term prospects.

Notes

1. The enterprise's 300-ton press, for example, won the state silver medal, its 160-ton press met the "high-quality product" standard set by the province and the Ministry of Machine Building, and all of its other presses were raised to higher-quality grades.

2. The monthly interest rate was 0.21 percent for the capital allocated by the state and for bank loans within the fixed quota, 0.6 percent for bank loans above the fixed quota, 0.78 percent for loans above the total quota, and 0.6 percent for loans to settle accounts.

3. Among them were a double-housing planer valued at Y500,000; Y50,000 of unsalable, poor-quality presses for manufacturing tableware; Y400,000 of new products unsuccessfully trial-produced; and unusable purchased inputs such as steel bars, worth many thousands of yuan.

4. The price of a ton of coke delivered to the factory increased, for example, from Y90 to Y200; one cubic meter of timber that cost Y160 at the state-allocated price came to be sold on the market at Y600; and one ton of tin, which previously had cost only Y9,000, had a negotiated price of Y29,000.

5. Because of price increases, an extra Y400,000 was reportedly spent by Qingdao in 1982 in purchasing coke, pig iron, rolled steel, nonferrous metals, timber, ancillary machinery, and electrical products.

6. For instance, Qingdao spent Y94,100 in developing the 100-ton high-energy press and the 10-ton two-way forging press, but it was only allocated Y30,000 by authorities for these tasks, so it incurred a loss of Y64,100.

7. The single most important item was a huge double-housing planer nominally valued at Y500,000. There were also five presses for making cutlery (total value Y50,000), new products that were odd lots for complete sets of equipment (value Y600,000), and new products that could not be finished (Y400,000).

8. In one instance the government apparently had promised funding of Y94,000, but only Y30,000 was actually disbursed.

5

中国企业改革

The Shenyang Smelter

William A. Byrd

THE SHENYANG SMELTER was much less affected by reforms after 1978 than were many other Chinese state-owned industrial enterprises. It faced increasingly severe, often interrelated, and mutually reinforcing problems in the late 1970s and the early 1980s. These problems severely limited the smelter's freedom of action and dominated its attention; they made many reforms largely irrelevant from its point of view. This chapter examines these problems: how they arose and how the enterprise responded to them. It also treats the nationwide reorganization and centralization of administrative control in the nonferrous metals industry in 1983, which had a considerable effect on the Shenyang Smelter. Overall, the role of the smelter and its management appears to have been relatively passive, so the essence of the story is what happened to the enterprise, not how it manipulated its environment. The smelter adapted as best it could and focused on day-to-day survival, marginal improvements, and avoiding deterioration.

The first, introductory section of this chapter provides some background information on the world nonferrous metals industry and on that of China and briefly reviews the history of the Shenyang Smelter. The next section looks at the main problems the smelter faced in the late 1970s and the early 1980s. The following section analyzes the enterprise's responses to these problems. The systemwide response of reorganization and recentralization is the subject of the next section, followed by some general observations and conclusions about the Shenyang Smelter's experience. The last section is a postscript on developments after 1983–84.

Industrial and Historical Perspective

An international perspective sheds light on issues and choices in the development of China's nonferrous metals industry and on the experiences of the Shenyang Smelter. This section first reviews the development of the nonferrous metals industry worldwide, emphasizing lessons from international experience that may be relevant for China. It then discusses China's nonferrous metals industry, primarily focusing on the so-called heavy nonferrous metals (lead, copper, zinc, and tin) because these include the Shenyang Smelter's main products. The section ends with a brief history of the smelter.

The Nonferrous Metals Industry Worldwide

Demand for and consumption of nonferrous metals tend to rise rapidly in the process of industrialization and economic development.[1] Per capita consumption of nonferrous metals correlates closely with a country's gross national product (GNP) per capita, and it is also related to level of industrialization, subsectoral structure of industry, infrastructure, substitution possibilities, and national endowment of mineral resources. The elasticity of nonferrous metals consumption with respect to growth of average per capita national income is typically great at low income levels and during the early stages of industrialization. At higher levels of per capita income, consumption elasticities tend to fall below one; the pattern varies, however, for different countries and metals. (Aluminum, for example, has a high consumption elasticity at all income levels, which shows up in both cross-section analysis and time-series analysis.)

Table 5.1 shows that world consumption of nonferrous metals has increased steadily except in times of large-scale wars.[2] World consumption of copper

Table 5.1. World Consumption of Selected Nonferrous Metals, Selected Years, 1890–1983
(thousands of metric tons)

Year	Aluminum	Copper[a]	Lead[b]	Zinc	Tin	Nickel	Total
1890	..	289	567	347	56	—	1,258
1900	7	513	871	475	82	—	1,948
1910	44	922	1,123	825	119	—	3,033
1920	132	929	974	689	127	—	2,850
1930	206	1,639	1,523	1,233	167	—	4,762
1940	823	2,711	1,653	1,741	167	—	7,094
1950	1,584	3,009	1,868	2,075	170	158	8,888
1960	4,177	4,756	2,617	3,082	201	293	15,125
1970	10,028	7,291	3,914	5,042	226	577	27,077
1979	16,017	9,883	5,481	6,332	234	777	38,725
1983	15,466	9,116	5,285	6,355	206	691	37,119

.. Negligible.

— Not available.

a. Figures for 1890–1920 are for unrefined copper; those for 1930–83 are for refined copper.

b. Figures for 1890–1950 are for pig lead; those for 1960–83 are for refined lead.

Source: Muller-Ohlsen 1981, p. 92; Metallgesellschaft AG 1984, pp. 4–5. Some figures for earlier years are based on three-year averages.

grew thirty-three-fold between 1890 and 1979, when it stood at 9.9 million tons. Growth of zinc and lead consumption in this period was slower: seventeenfold for zinc and ninefold for lead. The structure of consumption of nonferrous metals has changed over time because of discoveries of new metals and new uses for metals and because of consumers' substitutions among different metals. Substitution of other materials for certain nonferrous metals (for example, plastic for copper pipes) has also contributed to the changing structure of consumption. The rapid growth of consumption of aluminum and other light nonferrous metals has been especially noteworthy. The share of copper in consumption of heavy nonferrous metals has held steady; the shares of lead and, to a lesser extent, of zinc have fallen.

The growth of demand for nonferrous metals has stimulated increases in production, worldwide exploration and exploitation of untapped mineral resources, and improvements in the technology of mining and smelting. The nonferrous metals industry has increasingly taken advantage of economies of scale by creating larger production units. Advances in technology have stimulated the mining of ores with very low metal content. Great advances have also been made in the recovery of by-products and impurities generated in the smelting process. Copper, lead, zinc, and nickel smelters have long produced sulfuric acid. (Roasting of sulfide ores generates metal oxides and sulfur dioxide, which are harmful pollutants if they are not converted into sulfuric acid.) The industry is increasingly relying on secondary recovery of nonferrous metals from scrap metal. In 1979, for example, secondary recovery accounted for nearly 40 percent of total world production of copper, 36 percent of lead, and 21 percent of zinc.[3]

Some interesting historical trends are evident in the location of different stages of production (mining, ore preparation, metal extraction and refining, and metal fabrication). In the early stages of industrialization, mining and smelting operations tended to be located close together (in industrializing countries in which demand was increasing sharply) and were usually integrated under the management of a single company. As local sources of raw materials dwindled, ore mining tended to move away from the sites of smelting operations. The more distant mines were generally autonomous; they supplied ores to smelters in market transactions. Many ores were dressed and concentrated near the mines, however, in order to reduce the weight of impurities transported. Copper ore, for example, is commonly smelted into an unrefined product, or blister, that is then sold and transported for refining. In developing countries, where mining was increasingly concentrated, any smelting industry that did arise tended to be integrated with mining and located near mines—a rational arrangement in view of transport costs.

Mining of most nonferrous metals today is concentrated in a few countries, whereas production of refined metals and metal fabrication tend to be located near sources of demand in industrial countries. This split between mining and processing can to some extent be attributed to historical reasons. The pattern of location that emerged in the early period of industrialization was reinforced by colonization or economic subjugation in the primary mining areas. More recently, cascading tariff rates in many industrial countries have protected the later stages of processing and fabrication.

Transport costs and weight reduction at different stages in the production process can also be very important in influencing patterns of location. The metal content of most copper ores, for example, is so low that they have to be concentrated before they are shipped any distance from the mine site. Bauxite, however, generally has a relatively high aluminum content, so the extra costs involved in shipping it over long distances before further processing are relatively small. Availability of cheap energy is the primary criterion for location of aluminum smelting, which requires large amounts of electricity; it is also an important consideration in the smelting of other metals. Availability of infrastructure in mining areas also affects the choice of location.

Another factor that affects location is ability to respond to the needs of users. Many, if not most, users of nonferrous metals require specific alloys rather than pure metals. It is most economical for smelters themselves to produce these alloys because users would otherwise need to remelt pure metals and then mix them with the appropriate adulterants (some of which would have been present in the original ores). This process would waste a considerable amount of energy. Most nonferrous metals smelters hence produce alloys as well as pure metals. Many alloys must meet user specifications and quality standards exactly, however, and must be customized for different users or for the same user at different times. The need for close ties between smelters and users provides an economic argument for locating smelters near sources of demand rather than sources of supply.

Because of the location of natural resources and the aforementioned structure of production, there is large-scale international trade in most nonferrous metals ores. There is also a considerable amount of international trade in pure metals. World exports of nonferrous metals rose from $3.6 billion in 1955 to $21.7 billion in 1976, an average annual nominal increase of nearly 9 percent. This growth has been accompanied by an increase in the share of industrial countries in total exports from 55 to 60 percent and a decrease in the share of developing countries from 34 to 25 percent (Muller-Ohlsen 1981, p. 193).

Short-term inelasticities on both the demand side and the supply side mean that prices of nonferrous metals on the world market are highly volatile. For the most part, price competition is fierce, and cartel-like pricing arrangements by producers usually raise or stabilize prices only temporarily. Because of the homogeneity of the products in their pure forms with precise grading, marketing and sales promotion are relatively unimportant, and it is relatively easy for a new exporter to gain a foothold in the world market.

China's Nonferrous Metals Industry

China has large deposits of many nonferrous metals (see Sun 1983, p. 193). Its exploitable reserves of tungsten, antimony, rare earths, lithium, and magnesium are the largest of any country in the world; its reserves of tin, mercury, zinc, molybdenum, copper, lead, nickel, and titanium also are large. Ores of the most important industrial metals, such as copper, lead, and zinc, are found in most of China's provinces; fairly concentrated reserves of copper are found in thirteen provinces, and heavy lead and zinc mining activity occurs in six provinces. China's deposits of metals for which the world's total verified reserves are relatively small, such as tin, tungsten, antimony, molybdenum, and magnesium, are concentrated in a few localities. This is also true of China's uniquely high deposits of rare earths, niobium, vanadium, and titanium.

Most of China's reserves of nonferrous metals are located near abundant sources of energy (hydroelectric power, petroleum, or coal), convenient for energy-intensive smelting activities. These reserves are located in remote regions with difficult mining conditions and poor transport, however, and this has slowed exploitation considerably. The potential advantages of abundant energy near mineral reserves have not been exploited much, except in Gansu and Yunnan provinces. Most smelters are located in coastal provinces far from mineral reserves and energy sources.[4]

This pattern of location is inefficient, and it is not clear how or why it emerged. The nonferrous metals industry in China was very small before 1949, so the situation was not a legacy from the past. Existing small smelters in places such as Shanghai and Liaoning may have undergone massive expansion (that perhaps initially depended on imported raw materials) and then continued their lucrative activities even after mining developed in the interior of China. This suggests that national planning in the nonferrous metals industry was inadequate. The country does not reap the benefits of its smelters' locations close to users because Chinese smelters produce only pure metals, not customized alloys. (See "Response to Problems," in this chapter, for details.)

Output of the main nonferrous metals has grown rapidly. Ten metals (copper, aluminum, lead, zinc, nickel, tin, antimony, mercury, magnesium, and titanium) account for nearly all physical output of nonferrous metals, and China's total production of them ranks sixth in the world.[5] From 1952 to 1979, production of these ten metals increased at an average annual rate of 10.6 percent (China Economic Yearbook Editorial Committee 1981, p. IV-84). During the same period, the gross value of output of the nonferrous metals industry grew at 12 percent a year in real terms, compared with 11.1 percent for China's gross value of industrial output and 13.4 percent for the value of output of heavy industries (State Statistical Bureau 1983, p.

17). Output growth has fluctuated greatly. Total output of copper, lead, zinc, and aluminum increased at an average annual rate of 23.7 percent during the First Five-Year Plan (1953–57), 4 percent during the Second Five-Year Plan (1958–62), 21.2 percent in the readjustment period (1963–65), and only 2.4 percent in 1967–76 (Li 1983, p. 271).

Despite rapid long-term growth, it is often claimed in China that both investment in and output of nonferrous metals have been unduly low. For instance, the ratio of China's output of copper, aluminum, lead, and zinc to its output of steel in a recent year was 1 to 33, compared with a world average of 1 to 19 (Sun 1983, p. 160). In the early 1980s, nonferrous metals accounted for only about 2 percent of China's total capital construction investment (State Statistical Bureau 1983, p. 330). It is probably true that China has underinvested in mining of nonferrous metals, particularly in the mining of those with rich deposits and good export markets. Because of the imbalances among countries of endowments of minerals and the extensive world trade in most of them, however, an investment strategy geared toward complete self-sufficiency would not be effective.

Copper, lead, and zinc, the main products of the Shenyang Smelter, are of particular interest for this case study. Estimates of Chinese production of these three metals, along with that of aluminum, are shown in table 5.2. Because China does not publish statistics on output of individual nonferrous metals, these figures are subject to error. Nevertheless, they do clearly indicate that China's output of copper, lead, and zinc grew rapidly from a small base in 1949 until growth slowed in the 1970s and virtually stopped in the early 1980s. Growth of aluminum production was very rapid, beginning in the late 1950s, and it also slowed down in the early 1980s. The main Chinese copper smelters in the early 1980s were located in Shenyang, Kunming, Baiyin, Luoyang, and Shanghai; the Shanghai smelter primarily used scrap copper and imported blister. Lead and zinc smelters were located in Zhuzhou and Shaoguan; Huludao (in Liaoning) had a large zinc smelter; and a lead smelter was located in Kunming (Sun 1983, p. 163).

The central plan has in principle controlled the production and distribution of nonferrous metals in China. As in the cases of other important producer goods, actual control over production and allocation was, however, considerably decentralized. One-fourth of China's total mining output came from small mines under the supervision of local governments (China Encyclopedia Editorial Committee 1983, p. 372). Moreover, scrap metals were not subject to allocation by the plan (as was scrap steel before 1987). Thus a considerable share of total output of nonferrous metals was allocated outside the central plan. It is therefore not surprising that Shanghai Municipality, a large user of nonferrous metals, reported in the early 1980s that 40 percent of the supplies it received were outside the state plan (Hu and Liu 1984, p. 67).

Prices of the main nonferrous metals in China have been fixed administra-

Table 5.2. China's Production of Selected Metals, Selected Years, 1949–83
(thousands of metric tons)

Year	Aluminum[a]			Copper			Lead			Zinc	
	Bauxite[b]	Aluminum oxide	Aluminum	Mine production[c]	Smelter production[d]	Refined production	Mine production[c]	Smelter production[d]	Refined production	Mine production[c]	Smelter production
1949	—	—	—	—	2.2	—	—	—	—	..	..
1952	—	—	—	—	—	—	—	—	—	1	1
1953	—	—	—	8	—	—	9	—	—	—	—
1955	—	—	—	—	—	—	17	—	18	13	15
1957	50	—	10	15	15	—	30	—	45	37	37
1965	400	—	90	87[e]	87[e]	110[e]	100	—	100	90	90
1970	500	270	135	120[e]	120[e]	130[e]	110	—	110	100	100
1975	1000	500	300	140	150	230	140	125	140	135	140
1978	1400	700	360	160	170	290	150	140	160	150	160
1979	1500	700	360	160	170	290	155	150	170	155	160
1980	1700	700	350	165	175	295	160	145	175	150	155
1981	1800	700	350	170	190	300	160	150	175	160	160
1982	1950	800	370	175	205	300	160	155	175	160	175
1983	1900	800	400	175	195	310	160	160	195	160	185

.. Negligible.
— Not available.
Note: All data are rough estimates.
a. Estimates for 1970 and earlier years are suspect because those for later years were raised substantially after the data for earlier years were published.
b. Total weight, not weight of metal content.
c. Weight of metal content.
d. Not including secondary recovery.
e. Including production by the Democratic People's Republic of Korea.
Source: Metal Statistics various years; Schmitz 1979.

Table 5.3. Prices of Chinese Nonferrous Ores and Metals, 1981

Ore or metal	Ex-factory price (yuan per ton)[a]	Converted price (dollars per ton)[b]	International price (dollars per ton)[c]	Domestic-international price ratio (yuan to dollars)
Ores				
Tungsten				
(65 percent metal content)	9,685	3,459	5,277[d]	1.84
Molybdenum				
(51 percent metal content)	16,320	5,829	8,863[d]	1.84
Metals				
Electrolytic copper	5,500	1,964	1,755	3.13
Zinc ingot	1,900	679	862	2.20
Aluminum ingot	2,760	986	1,264	2.18
Tin (before 1981)[e]	12,650	4,518	14,375	0.88
Tin (after 1981)[e]	18,500	6,607	14,375	1.29
Lead[f]	2,300	821	737	3.12
Antimony	3,470	1,239	2,011[d]	1.73
Cadmium	19,000	6,786	3,117	6.10

a. Price paid by Chinese customers (including commercial and foreign trade procurement agencies) to producers.

b. Converted at the rate of Y2.8 to $1.00.

c. Unless otherwise indicated, these are the average cash prices at the London Metals Exchange in 1981. Figures are converted from pounds sterling into dollars at the average exchange rate for 1981.

d. It is not clear whether these figures are comparable with the London Metals Exchange prices.

e. The price of tin was raised in 1981.

f. Estimated figures based on a reported price ratio for tin to lead of 5 to 1 and a reported price for tin of Y11,500 a ton.

Source: Shanghai Means of Production Service Company 1982, p. 56; Hu and Liu, 1984, p. 67; Wu 1982, pp. 41–43; Metallgesellschaft AG 1984, pp. 385–416; World Bureau of Metal Statistics 1984, p. 64; *International Financial Statistics* 38 (August 1985): 111.

tively by the central government and changed only at rare intervals. The price of electrolytic copper has remained the same since 1962 and that of electrolytic aluminum has not changed since 1966. There were significant increases, however, in the prices set by the state for certain other nonferrous metals in the early 1980s, including a 27 percent increase for molybdenum and a 79 percent increase for tin (Hu and Liu 1984, p. 67).

Prices of goods traded outside the central material supply plan have been flexible, with sales offers and transaction prices widely posted in specialized newspapers since 1984. In the early 1980s the negotiated price of molybdenum was reportedly 31 percent higher than the state price (which had itself been sharply raised). The negotiated price of tin was 75 percent above the state price and that of copper as much as 24 percent higher than the state wholesale price (table 5.3 and Hu and Liu 1984, p. 67). The price of lead on the open market may, however, have been slightly less than the state price in the mid-1980s (see *Shanghai Wuzi Shichang*, no. 176 [July 7, 1984], and no. 180 [August 4, 1984]). Strict price controls were applied only to that part of supply allocated by the central material supply plan. At the opposite extreme, some transactions in nonferrous metals seemed to occur at prices determined by the market. In between, there were many transactions for which prices may have been administratively controlled to some degree (often by provincial and local authorities) but were considerably higher than the state plan price. These transactions often included barter deals or exchange arrangements.

Information on the administratively fixed prices of some nonferrous metals and ores is presented in table 5.3. Comparison with world prices is difficult because of their volatility and because world prices in 1981 (the year shown in the table) tended to be high. The exchange rate used for these data (the former internal settlement rate of Y2.8 to $1.00) results in lower dollar-equivalent Chinese domestic prices than would result if the official exchange rate in 1981 had been used. The choice of the internal settlement rate and the use of 1981 world market prices therefore make Chinese prices appear low in relation to world prices.

In view of this bias, the comparisons in table 5.3 are all the more striking. Only in one case, that of tin, was the Chinese domestic price of a refined metal less than half the world price. (The domestic price of antimony also was considerably lower than the world price.) In some cases, such as those of copper and lead, Chinese prices exceeded world prices by considerable margins.[6] Where world prices slightly exceeded Chinese domestic dollar-equivalent prices (the cases of zinc and aluminum), use of a different exchange rate or another year's international prices would probably change the results. Chinese domestic ore prices, however, were low in relation to world prices, in line with the general pattern in which mining earns very low profits in China relative to smelting and refining profits.

Because of administrative controls over foreign trade and significant price distortions, the aforementioned price comparisons do not accurately reflect relative scarcities or the supply situation in China. For example, the domestic price of copper was slightly higher than the world price, but, with controls over imports, the relative scarcity of copper was, in large part, a result of the relatively poor quality of China's resources. Copper itself was significantly underpriced in relation to the prices of fabricated copper products. The Shenyang Smelter's profit per ton of copper smelted in the early 1980s was about Y700, including some indirect taxes. But the profit from fabricating one ton of aluminum-copper alloy rods (which involved little extra effort) was over Y1,300 a ton; the profit from producing copper tubes or sections was more than Y3,000 a ton.

Historical data on China's exports and imports of nonferrous metals are

Table 5.4. China's Exports and Imports of Nonferrous Metals, Selected Years, 1950–83
(metric tons)

Year	Exports				Imports		
	Tungsten ore	Tin	Antimony	Mercury	Copper	Aluminum	Lead
1950	8,800	4,800	4,900	2	13,900	3,000	800
1952	21,800	7,900	10,000	13	8,400	1,900	400
1955	31,900	20,400	9,900	326	11,500	3,400	10,200
1957	35,400	25,700	5,800	499	17,700	3,700	6,100
1960	25,200	26,200	7,400	1,697	73,900	22,000	2,900
1962	25,400	20,000	7,300	1,720	8,100	9,300	3,000
1965	20,900	10,100	5,100	347	67,000	4,200	24,000
1967	16,300	5,800	7,900	153	96,300	53,800	16,300
1970	8,200	7,700	2,400	118	132,000	91,600	51,200
1972	16,300	11,600	10,600	169	101,200	111,700	11,900
1975	14,300	15,200	8,100	357	112,500	287,100	52,300
1976	20,500	7,800	6,600	557	67,300	300,100	28,800
1977	13,600	5,600	7,700	795	91,200	150,500	14,000
1978	18,200	5,500	11,500	659	134,100	211,800	28,600
1979	21,300	4,600	12,500	492	134,200	146,100	35,200
1980	20,400	4,200	8,900	985	128,200	110,200	33,800
1981	22,100	3,400	7,200	946	46,600	46,100	35,100
1982	10,600	2,900	10,100	476	152,400	209,300	13,800
1983	23,900	3,200	10,000	496	522,700	301,400	12,300

Note: Data are for exports and imports handled by foreign trade departments. Since the late 1970s, an increasing share of trade in nonferrous metals has been arranged by ministries and by provincial or local government.
Source: State Statistical Bureau 1984, pp. 407, 409.

shown in table 5.4. Imports have generally fluctuated more than exports, which is not surprising if exports were used to meet targets for foreign exchange earnings and imports were used to fill gaps in volatile domestic supplies. One interesting development was a sharp increase in copper imports in the early 1980s. This may in part reflect a government decision to give lower priority to development of copper mining, in view of the relatively poor quality and high cost of extraction of China's copper resources.[7] In general, because of the scale of China's economy and its administrative controls over foreign trade, there has not been a close relation between domestic development and international trade in the short run.

China's long-term plans for development of the nonferrous metals industry called for total output of the ten most important metals to rise by 180 percent between 1980 and 2000, an average annual increase of 5.3 percent (Li 1983, p. 272). This growth rate would be somewhat lower than past long-term trends, but considerably higher than the average rate of growth in the early 1980s. The ambitious goal of quadrupling China's gross output value of industry and agriculture between 1980 and 2000 implies that consumption of non-ferrous metals may well rise faster than production, necessitating increased imports. Top priority evidently was to be given to developing aluminum production, despite problems of high electricity consumption in smelting. Lead and zinc were also to be developed, but copper would receive lower priority because investment requirements per ton of annual copper production capacity are reported to be four times those of aluminum and twice those of zinc or lead. It is not clear, however, whether a careful evaluation has been made of the choice between domestic mining and importing for each main metal.

Brief History of the Shenyang Smelter

The Shenyang Smelter is in Shenyang City, the capital of Liaoning Province and the largest city in northeast China. It was established in the 1930s during the Japanese occupation of Manchuria, and it was then known as the Fengtian Metal Smelter. It first smelted lead in 1936 and began producing copper in 1939. Unsuccessful attempts to smelt zinc were made in 1944–45. During the period of Japanese occupation, technology was backward and production was very low; only 2,160 tons of electrolytic copper, 180 tons of copper sulfate, and 6,800 tons of lead were produced in the peak year. The plant was taken over by the Kuomintang government in March 1946 and renamed the Shenyang Smelter. Production did not revive; in 1948 output of copper was only 70 tons.

Shenyang City was brought under Communist control in November 1948, and two months later production resumed at the Shenyang Smelter, which became the first major nonferrous smelting plant in the People's Republic of China. Electrolytic lead and copper were the first products; in 1951 hydrosmelting of zinc occurred on an experimental basis, and in 1952 more than 2,000 tons of electrolytic zinc were produced. Copper, lead, and zinc continued to be the mainstays of the smelter's production in the three decades that followed. By 1953 the pre-1949 peak output had already been surpassed.

Production continued to grow rapidly; from 1949 to 1982 the smelter's gross industrial output value increased at an average annual rate of almost 12 percent in real terms; it reached Y684 million in 1982. The capacity of the main production lines was greatly increased and the level of mechanization was raised, resulting in improved working conditions. Annual production capacity in the early 1980s was more than 50,000 tons of copper, more than 50,000 tons of lead, and 20,000 tons of zinc. In 1982 the Shenyang Smelter apparently accounted for about 24 percent of total national production of copper, 29 percent of that of lead, and 9 percent of that of zinc.[8] Quality of output also improved considerably.

In line with the growth of production, employment at the Shenyang Smelter rose to 6,770 in 1982. In addition, there were 5,768 workers employed under the collective ownership system, primarily children of smelter employees. Of these, about half worked alongside regular state employees in the plant's main production facilities, and the other half were engaged in various services and construction activities organized by two subsidiary collective enterprises. The gross value of the smelter's fixed assets reached nearly Y178 million by 1982 (up from Y109 million in 1975); the depreciated net value of fixed assets was only Y72 million because a large proportion of the capital stock was very old. Annual profits were more than Y50 million in 1980–82; this implies a relatively high financial rate of return on capital.[9]

Recovery of by-products in the smelting process gradually assumed greater importance, starting in the 1950s with the recovery of certain metals from ores, such as bismuth (1952), cadmium (1953), indium and selenium (1956), and tellurium, palladium, and platinum (1958). By 1980 a total of fourteen by-products were being recovered, including gold, silver, nickel, sulfur, antimony, and germanium in addition to those already mentioned. Sulfuric acid, the production of which started in 1969, has become a major product of the plant, with annual production capacity of about 110,000 tons. Although they accounted for only about 8 percent of the Shenyang Smelter's gross value of industrial output, by-products and subsidiary metals recovered from ores made an important contribution to profits, accounting for more than 40 percent of the total (see State Economic Commission 1983a, p. 338). Indeed, increased output of gold, of which 428,000 troy ounces was produced in 1980, or a sharply higher price for gold, or both of these factors, may have contributed to the tripling of the smelter's profits between 1978 and 1981 (see table 5.7).[10] One article in an industry publication listed gold and silver as leading products of the Shenyang Smelter, in addition to copper, lead, zinc, and sulfuric acid (State Economic Commission 1983a, p. 337).

From 1949 until the late 1960s the smelter was under the direct control of the central government, first under the Ministry of Heavy Industry (which was soon abolished), later under the Ministry of Metallurgy. (It also operated for a time under the Northeast Nonferrous Metals Administration, which also was abolished.) Although production was under the jurisdiction of the central government, the plant's Communist Party affiliation was with the Shenyang Municipal Party Committee. Appointment of the plant's leadership, however, was subject to final approval by the Organization Department of the Central Committee of the Chinese Communist Party.

During the Cultural Revolution period, as part of a national decentralization campaign, the Shenyang Smelter was transferred from central control to local control. In 1970 it was put under Liaoning Province, in 1971 under Shenyang Municipality. Thus its direct supervisory unit (which had previously been the bureau responsible for nonferrous metals in the Ministry of Metallurgy) became the Shenyang Metallurgy Bureau. This decentralization was very uneven across different spheres of activity, as it was for many other Chinese enterprises, and it created the problem of so-called multiheaded leadership. The municipality did take control over finances and labor, but supply of the main raw materials (which came from all over China) and production planning remained under the control of the central ministry. Distribution of output also remained largely under the control of central authorities. Supplies of certain materials and energy were handled by Liaoning Province. Multiheaded leadership became an important feature of the enterprise's management system and generated severe difficulties in planning, incentives, and control. Although this problem has been very common in China (see, for example, chapter 4 of this volume), the two stages of decentralization through which the Shenyang Smelter went and its national orientation in production and supply made it an extreme example of the problem.

By the mid-1970s the smelter had apparently reached a plateau in its main production activities (see table 5.5). Output of copper and lead in 1982 was only slightly higher than the levels reached in 1975–76, and there was some decrease in zinc output. Production of sulfuric acid depended to a large extent on the sulfur content of the ores smelted, but here too the limits of what could economically be recovered may already have been approached in the early 1980s.

A final point worth noting is that the Shenyang Smelter developed on one site in increasingly urbanized surroundings. Expansion in the immediate area eventually became impossible because of nearby industrial development. Thus the smelter faced a severe space constraint, and its heavy polluting had very high social costs in its urban location.

Main Problems

The Shenyang Smelter suffered from a number of problems of growing severity starting in the late 1970s. These so dominated the plant's environment that its evolution in the early 1980s is best understood as a set of responses to problems rather than as a function of the reforms, policy changes, or organizational changes it underwent. The smelter tried to adapt to increasingly ad-

Table 5.5. Shenyang Smelter's Output of Copper, Lead, and Zinc, 1975–82 (metric tons)

Year	Electrolytic copper	Electrolytic lead	Electrolytic zinc
1975	45,616	48,200	20,026
1976	47,285	51,433	17,612
1977	36,315	50,563	16,134
1978	46,154	47,808	20,727
1979	50,242	47,377	21,513
1980	56,547	51,489	17,691
1981	51,938	55,024	17,723
1982	48,654	57,255	17,235

Source: Information provided by the smelter.

verse circumstances and a difficult external environment; it could not remake or sharply change that environment. Thus its stance was fundamentally passive and focused on survival rather than on expansion. This defensive approach was a response to the external environment and outside constraints, rather than a result of managerial attitudes or capabilities.[11]

The smelter had already gone a long way toward developing its potential on its existing site with its existing facilities; this situation made the smelter's problems all the more difficult to deal with. Production of lead, copper, and zinc had reached a plateau by the mid-1970s. Profits continued to rise until 1980 but then stabilized at slightly more than Y50 million annually, before they declined sharply in 1983. The plant may have exhausted the potential for developing new products through recovery of by-products from ores. Slack and waste in the system that could easily be eliminated probably were addressed in the initial years of reform (1979–81). Another factor at work in the early 1980s was inflation in the prices of various inputs. Overall, the enterprise had little room to maneuver in responding to its worsening situation, particularly after 1981.

The problem of pollution was a long-standing one, and it was aggravated by changes in the attitudes of authorities, by organizational changes, and by increased urbanization in the smelter's vicinity. Other problems, such as the location itself, could be solved only by drastic measures that were beyond the ability of the enterprise to institute on its own. Still other problems, such as energy consumption, were more amenable to technical solutions. Finally, some problems, such as the multiheaded leadership system, the burden of employing a large number of workers' children, the shortage of investment funds, and the smelter's inability to produce alloys, were directly related to the economic system or to the policies of central or local authorities.

Location

In a certain sense, the fundamental problem faced by the Shenyang Smelter was its location, which may have been an advantageous one when the factory was established but which became a serious liability over time. The plant was hemmed in on all sides by other industrial establishments that had grown up since the 1950s; its restricted site left little room for expansion and exacerbated problems with storage and sorting of ores. Furthermore, the smelter was located in a region in which output of electric power was growing relatively slowly and one which faced a growing energy shortage. Finally, the Shenyang Smelter was by far the worst polluter in Shenyang, which itself is one of the largest, most heavily industrialized cities in China.

The problem that impinged most directly on the smelter's decision making and prospects was the space constraint at the existing (or any nearby) site. Many other factories in China faced a similar constraint; some responded by acquiring additional land elsewhere, often through associating or merging with other enterprises or rural collectives and transferring some of their own production activities there (see, for example, chapter 3 of this volume). This option appears not to have been available to the Shenyang Smelter, however. The vertically integrated production process, its capital intensity, and the immobility of the large capital structures involved most likely made it inappropriate to move facilities unless large new investments were made. Hence space constraints may have interacted with shortages of funds for investment. Financial constraints may also have made land acquisition more difficult.[12] Moving only one of the three main production lines to another site may not have been economical for the smelter because the sulfuric acid facility served all three.

Other factors may also have been at work. Management may not have explored the possibility of associations with rural collective firms, which were at that time recycling large amounts of scrap copper in small, inefficient operations. More than thirty small copper smelters were reported to be recycling scrap in Liaoning Province alone in the early 1980s. Their products often had a copper content of only 80–90 percent, and copper losses in production were as high as 20 percent. It is also possible that associations and mergers may not have been accepted ways of doing business in Liaoning Province or in northeast China as a whole, as they were elsewhere.[13] Moreover, associations and mergers generally entail a commitment to provide employment for a certain number of people in the partner unit. This would have been difficult for the smelter, since it already had its hands full taking care of the employment needs of its own workers' children.

Other disadvantages of the Shenyang Smelter's location may have been more costly from a social perspective than was the space constraint, but as immediate problems they were less threatening to the enterprise. The smelter did not bear the full burden of these costs itself. Other than pollution, which is discussed later, the main problems were raw material and energy supplies.

Liaoning Province's copper, lead, and zinc mines could satisfy only 30 percent of the province's smelting capacity (Zhu 1983, p. 56). The Shenyang Smelter, which accounted for the bulk of smelting of these metals in the province, had to obtain most of its raw materials from distant sources. It is not clear what part of the costs of long-distance transport of raw materials the smelter paid. Although railway freight costs are normally factored into prices of raw materials bought by Chinese enterprises, tariffs were far below market clearing levels, and there was a severe shortage of railway transport capacity. The location of the plant was not an ideal one for a user of imported raw materials, either; imports accounted for about 27 percent of total supplies of copper ore and for 40 percent of blister in 1984.

Originally the smelter's needs for energy and electricity must have been well met, because coal and hydroelectric power were developed in Liaoning during the period of Japanese occupation. Liaoning subsequently became a large net importer of coal, however, and electricity supplies grew much more slowly there than they did in other parts of China.[14] Between 1957 and 1982, total output of electricity in China grew at an average annual rate of 12 percent; in Liaoning it grew by slightly more than 7 percent; for the period 1978–82 the figures were more than 6 percent for China and less than 2 percent for Liaoning (State Statistical Bureau 1983, p. 244, and Zhu 1983, p. 380). With the development of electricity production in interior provinces with more abundant ore reserves, the siting of the Shenyang Smelter became less advantageous.

Although smelting of nonferrous metals is highly energy intensive and electrolysis requires large amounts of electricity, the smelter was not forced to bear the brunt of Liaoning's severe shortages of coal and electricity. (Both of these inputs were to a large extent subject to provincial allocation.) The Shenyang Smelter appears to have benefited from the diversion of power supplies from the Fushun Aluminum Plant, which was an even bigger consumer of electricity. The total allocation of electricity to the nonferrous metals industry in Liaoning declined, but the share of the Shenyang Smelter in this reduced flow increased and allowed it to maintain a constant absolute volume of electricity usage. As a large and prominent local enterprise, the plant undoubtedly also received help from local authorities in arranging supplies of energy and especially electricity.

Pollution

Perhaps the most serious problem with the smelter's location was the microgeographical one of pollution. The Shenyang Smelter accounted for 45 percent of all the sulfur dioxide discharged in Shenyang Municipality, 50–80 percent of the heavy metals in waste water, and 95 percent of all arsenic released. Highly toxic cadmium in the factory's waste water had contaminated large areas of farmland in Shenyang's suburbs. The effect of pollution on the people of Shenyang was exacerbated by the lack of urban zoning in China and by the responsibility of enterprises to provide housing for their workers, which resulted in the intermingling of factories and apartment buildings. The pollution problem had been recognized as early as 1953, and the smelter was frequently criticized on this account by local governments and representative assemblies. Until 1978, pollution was worsening rather than improving, although recovery of by-products such as cadmium and sulfuric acid must have helped limit pollution. The very fact that sulfuric acid recovery, a universal practice in nonferrous metals smelters worldwide, was not developed until the 1970s indicates that the pollution problem was not taken seriously.

The smelter could avoid taking extraordinary and costly measures to control pollution in part because of laxity in national policies. Another reason for its not responding to pollution problems may have been the assignment of the factory to municipal jurisdiction; as a result, the local government of the area that suffered from the pollution at the same time benefited directly from the profits and other contributions (especially employment) made by the smelter. Conversely, when the plant was returned to the control of the central government in 1983, local authorities started levying heavy fines for water pollution and generally increased their vigilance.[15] Demands for more aggressive pollution control also became stronger as national antipollution policies hardened and local government concern for popular welfare increased.

Supply of Raw Materials and Energy

The Shenyang Smelter's problems with supply of raw materials had many causes aside from the smelter's location at a great distance from mines. The plant's sources of lead and copper ores were widely scattered. Concentrated copper ore came from thirty-three mines in nine provinces, and lead came from fifty-one mines in twelve provinces. In its zinc supplies, the plant was more fortunate: all of its prime processed zinc ore came from a single supplier in Liaoning Province. It was difficult for the smelter to regulate the incoming flow of copper and lead ores because the shortage of railway transport capacity made delivery schedules unreliable. Moreover, mines were unable to maintain steady production; this problem was exacerbated by the effects of weather.

Because raw materials were allocated by the Ministry of Metallurgy (and later by the Nonferrous Metals Industry General Corporation), the decisions of the central government sometimes led to interruptions in supply, as possibly did obstruction by local authorities in the mining areas. It appears that in 1983, when there was a conflict between central authorities and Shenyang Municipality over putting the smelter under central jurisdiction, ore supplies and imported raw materials were held back; this made it difficult for the smelter to fulfill its plans.

Irregular delivery of raw materials and lack of space at the production site combined to create serious problems in storage and sorting. Because shipments of concentrated ore from different mines were of varying degrees of purity and would yield different by-products, they ideally should have been kept separate so that they could be processed separately. Due to space restrictions, however, the smelter could at best store copper ore from thirty-three mines in only four different piles, at some cost in production efficiency. Similar problems obtained for lead ores.

The supply situation for copper was complicated by imbalances in the smelter's capacity at different stages of the production process. Its capacity for smelting ore into unrefined copper, or blister, was 25,000 tons a year, but its capacity for refining and electrolysis (the final stages in producing pure copper) was 60,000 tons a year. Thus it could not use additional concentrated ore beyond a certain point but required instead either blister or scrap copper. Although relative prices made smelting ore more profitable than processing blister, the former operation required more energy than the latter. The smelter typically operated at or very near production capacity in processing ore into unrefined copper but operated considerably below capacity in transforming unrefined copper into pure electrolytic copper.

The Shenyang Smelter's reliance on imported raw materials added further to uncertainty in supplies. The quantity of the imported ore and especially of the blister the smelter was to receive was not determined until relatively late each year. It appears that imports, particularly imports of blister, were used as a balancing item to fill or at least partially to cover the gap between needs and allocations from domestic sources. This situation was confused, however, by the multiple output and supply plans to which the smelter was subject as a result of the multiheaded leadership system. The state plan for output was essentially covered by allocations of raw materials, but the local plan (which was set by the Shenyang Metallurgy Bureau and which was considerably higher than the state plan) was not so covered. Supplies of domestically produced blister were also highly uncertain, and the allocations tended not to be set until late in the year.

The most important source of supply for production outside the state plan was scrap copper for recycling. Scrap copper was not subject to state plan allocation, however, so no input quota was provided to the smelter as part of the plan. Different organizations vied to procure scrap, and the market was tight; this situation resulted in price escalation to the point at which some scrap sold for Y5,500 a ton (the state price of pure copper) or more. The smelter was at a severe disadvantage in procuring scrap for several reasons. The need to earn a profit prevented it from bidding too high for scrap copper.[16] Small rural scrap reprocessors, however, apparently were less constrained by price controls on the output side. Moreover, enterprises that made highly profitable copper products (such as copper wire) could afford to pay higher prices for scrap than could the smelter. The chaotic market for scrap copper was perhaps the worst supply problem the plant faced in the short run.

Problems with energy supply were exacerbated by the Shenyang Smelter's location and by the multiheaded leadership system. Even without these added difficulties, however, the smelter, as a large consumer of energy, faced problems as China's supply of energy tightened. Its annual energy consumption was 210,000 tons of standard coal-equivalent (7,000 kilocalories per ton); its consumption represented more than 0.03 percent of total commercial consumption of primary energy in China in 1982 and about 0.4 percent of total energy consumption in Liaoning Province in that year (State Statistical Bureau 1983, p. 250; Zhu 1983, p. 402). The plant's share in the energy consumption of Shenyang Municipality must have been substantial.

The smelter's unit energy consumption was probably better than average in China, but it fell well below international standards. Consumption of coal-equivalent per ton of copper smelted, for example, was 900 kilograms, compared with only 400 kilograms at an efficient Japanese plant. Part of this difference may stem from Shenyang's using backward technologies, part from its smelting of lower-grade ores, and part from its inefficient use of techniques.

Multiheaded Leadership

As location can be considered the fundamental technical and physical constraint the Shenyang Smelter faced, the multiheaded leadership system was the critical organizational problem it suffered from in the 1970s and early 1980s; this problem manifested itself in nearly all spheres of the smelter's activity. The basic problem was that in its different functional aspects, the plant was supervised by different government organizations at the central, provincial, and municipal levels. As a result, the smelter was commonly given inconsistent targets and directives.

The multiheaded leadership system at the Shenyang Smelter was a direct result of the massive decentralization of industrial administration, government finance, and material supply that occurred in China in 1970–71 (see Xing 1983 and Zhou 1984, pp. 134–47). Numerous Chinese enterprises were transferred to the control of lower levels of government at that time; the problems the smelter faced were by no means unique. Because it was transferred downward not once but twice (from the central government to Liaoning Province in 1970 and to Shenyang Municipality in 1971) and because of its nationwide economic orientation in the areas of supply and distribution of output, the plant's multiheaded leadership problem was, however, probably among the worst faced by Chinese enterprises.

The original idea of the 1970–71 decentralization was that control over all aspects of an enterprise's operations would be handed down to lower levels of government. It was soon found that local authorities and even provincial authorities could not handle raw material supplies for enterprises such as the Shenyang Smelter. Moreover, they often had little knowledge about the technical side of production. Finally, these firms produced important goods that the central government wanted to continue to distribute in line with national priorities. As a result, central organizations continued to be responsible for allocation of supplies of the main raw materials and for allocation of output. That the Shenyang Smelter's sources of ores were scattered all over China made such an arrangement all the more necessary. The central government also continued to set an annual production plan, but in the case of the smelter this plan was simply the amount of output that could be produced from the raw materials allocated by the central government on the basis of technical input-output relationships.

The situation with regard to finances was quite different. Local authorities generally could monitor the financial situation of their enterprises and collect taxes and profit remittances from them.[17] The decentralization of government finance in 1970–71 gave provincial governments an incentive to increase revenues and therefore to accept financial responsibility for profitable enterprises that were handed down to them. Since formal administrative jurisdiction over an enterprise generally carried with it the right to collect that enterprise's profits, this part of the decentralization was relatively easy to accomplish, and it tended to "stick." Moreover, local authorities losing "their" plants strongly resisted subsequent recentralization of formal jurisdiction and control over enterprise finances.

In the case of investment financing, decentralization appears to have been less extensive than it was in enterprise administration; large numbers of decentralized enterprises must have continued to rely at least in part on budget grants from the central government to finance investment projects. Central authorities were willing to make investments in enterprises not under their direct control because they could allocate the output generated; they operated on the principle that the organization that provided the investment funds had the right to allocate the resulting output.

Authority over hiring and size of labor force tended to gravitate to the lowest level of government, as did authority over finances. This was a natural tendency given the interest of municipalities and counties in providing employment to persons entering the labor force. Decentralization of authority to appoint and remove enterprise directors and party secretaries was uneven. In the case of the Shenyang Smelter, the Organization Department of the Central Committee of the Chinese Communist Party retained the right to formally approve changes in factory leadership. In other firms the pattern was sometimes quite different, and this authority devolved to the lowest level of government.

Three serious problems resulted directly from the multiheaded leadership system: (1) inconsistency between output targets (and corresponding allocations of raw materials) and profit targets; (2) the constant need to bypass the organization in nominal charge of the smelter (the Shenyang Metallurgy Bureau), which did not have the expertise or ability to help the smelter but which made many demands on it; and (3) a confused supply system with numerous gaps and the involvement of agencies at three levels of government (central, provincial, and municipal) in allocating materials.

The Shenyang Smelter had at least three different output plans and two different profit (and profit-remittance) targets. The Ministry of Metallurgy gave the factory output targets that were based primarily on the amounts of raw materials the ministry allocated to the factory according to the central plan. These output targets implied a certain level of profits. The Shenyang Metallurgy Bureau gave the smelter output targets and profit targets, all of which were considerably higher than were those the ministry set and none of which were backed up by allocations of materials. Moreover, the profit targets and profit-remittance targets given by the Shenyang Metallurgy Bureau were excessively high even in relation to the output targets given by the same organization. For electrolytic copper, output targets were generally more than twice as high as those assigned by the ministry,[18] whereas for lead and zinc discrepancies were smaller. In 1983 profit and profit-remittance targets set by the Shenyang Metallurgy Bureau were more than 30 percent higher than what the enterprise thought it could attain on the basis of its past performance. The third set of output targets was the enterprise's own forecast of what it could actually produce; these forecasts were rather higher than the targets given by the ministry but often less than those set by the bureau, and in any case below what would have been needed to fulfill the bureau's profit target.

The explanation of these conflicting targets was very simple: the output targets set by the Ministry of Metallurgy were based primarily on balancing of centrally controlled supplies of raw material at the national level, and the profit target set by the Shenyang Metallurgy Bureau was based on a total profit-remittance target given to it by Shenyang Municipality, which in turn reflected revenue-remittance targets set for the municipality by Liaoning Province. There was no reason for these targets to be consistent in the first place and no built-in mechanism by which they could be reconciled.

Although these inconsistencies may have been present all along, they were probably to a large extent submerged when the Shenyang Smelter's realized profits rose sharply in 1979 and 1980 and held stable in 1981 and 1982. Remittance targets in the public finance system tended to increase more slowly than did aggregate production and profits, but they would still tend to increase even when production or profits were falling. The problem, then, became acute when profits fell drastically in 1983, as a result of the conflict over recentralization of the smelter. This aspect of the multiheaded leadership system became a severe problem only when attempts were made to change the system.

The multiheaded leadership system placed the Shenyang Metallurgy Bureau, an organization without the necessary geographical scope or technical expertise, in charge of the Shenyang Smelter. The enterprise constantly had to bypass the bureau and deal directly with the ministry on problems of production, supply, technical transformation, investment financing, and so forth. The bureau had certain administrative procedures, however, that the smelter must follow even if it preferred to handle matters on its own. The local government also made repeated demands on the plant, requiring it, for example, to construct public facilities and even bus stations when it built apartments for its workers. Although these social responsibilities have been a common problem for Chinese enterprises, the multiheaded leadership system may have aggravated them by giving local authorities a greater implicit claim on the smelter's resources. Finally, the Shenyang Metallurgy Bureau exploited the smelter by transferring supplies nominally allocated to the smelter by higher levels of authority to smaller local factories also under its jurisdiction. This kind of favoritism may also partly explain the excessively high profit targets set for the smelter.[19]

The complexities and contradictions of the multiheaded leadership system were most obvious in the area of material supply. The most serious problems were severe gaps in the supply of certain important inputs; these gaps were aggravated by the multilevel planning system described earlier and by the allocation of different types of materials by different organizations and different levels of government, with little, if any, coordination among them.

Domestic and imported supplies of the three main ores (lead, copper, and zinc) as well as unrefined copper (blister) in principle were subject to unified allocation by the Ministry of Metallurgy.[20] Suppliers were generally fixed for multiyear periods. There were often large gaps, however, between allocated supplies and the smelter's production capacity for copper and lead. These gaps were to be covered by supplies obtained outside the central government plan, from small local mines and, particularly in the case of copper, from recycling scrap. These alternative sources of supply were abundant for lead, and indeed the plant was offered more than it needed by local sources. In the case of copper, however, resources from small local mines were limited, and they accounted for only about 3 percent of total copper production in 1984. Scrap supplies were uncertain and increasingly subject to bidding wars.

Allocations of coke and fuel oil were provided by the ministry, but there were gaps in both allocations, and, moreover, contracts to supply coke often went unfulfilled. To make up the difference between total annual requirements of about 26,000 tons of oil and the state allocation of only 20,000 tons, the smelter relied on high-priced purchases from Liaoning Province, on barter with the province of sulfuric acid for fuel oil, and on purchase of oil skimmed from fields by peasants. There were basically no sources outside of the state plan for coke; all the plant could do was press suppliers for more and rely on its good long-term relationship with its main supplier in Beijing.[21]

The gap between coal requirements and the allocated quota was even more extreme: 40,000 to 45,000 tons were needed each year, but the state allocation was only 20,000 tons. A considerable proportion of total coal usage, however, was for nonproductive operations or for collective enterprises employing children of factory employees. Supplies within the quota were provided by the Liaoning Provincial Metallurgy Bureau, which probably also had a hand in determining the quotas. The rest had to be obtained from small or distant mines at high prices and often with high transport costs.

Electricity supplies were allocated by the Liaoning Economic Commission, still another important actor on the list of organizations that determined the smelter's production in the short run. Because there were no alternative sources of electricity, the plant could only make repeated requests for extra supplies to the commission and to power authorities. Two staff members of the smelter were engaged full-time in this task. These requests were often effective in obtaining additional supplies, but there was a great deal of day-to-day uncertainty.

Overall, although problems with the supply of each kind of input can be attributed to specific factors and shortages, the multiheaded leadership system compounded them. The large number of agencies at different levels of government that were responsible for allocation of important material inputs invited conflicts and certainly had an adverse effect on the smelter's production and morale.

Shortage of Investment Funds

The Shenyang Smelter was plagued by old and deteriorating equipment, backward technology, and consequent high production costs and high energy consumption. The plant faced severe difficulties, however, in obtaining funds for investment projects to ameliorate the situation. Although average annual fixed investment almost tripled between 1975–77 and 1980–82 (see table 5.6), it was still far from sufficient to renovate and modernize aging equipment and to invest in pollution control and energy conservation. Indeed, managers at the smelter cited shortage of funds as the primary constraint on their investment activities, not availability of construction materials and equipment or approval of projects by planning authorities.

A number of projects suffered severely from the shortage of investment funds, although they had received final approval from central government authorities. The most important was a project for comprehensive utilization of slag from the lead smelter, approved by the State Economic Commission in November 1982. The approved investment cost for the project was Y11.5 million, of which Y3 million was to be financed by a state grant and the rest by bank loans. The state grant was to come from depreciation funds generated in Shenyang Municipality but remitted to the central government. Because of a policy change that allowed Shenyang Municipality to retain for its own use the depreciation funds previously remitted to the central government, the state grant was effectively cancelled. Shenyang Municipality, which now had additional financial resources for investment, was supposed to cover the gap, but it appears to have instead allocated these funds for other purposes.

After a delay of eight months, Shenyang Municipality gave the smelter a "quota" to borrow Y4 million from the local bank, but the bank at first refused to lend any money until grant funds were forthcoming as originally stipulated. Finally, the bank grudgingly provided an initial loan of Y1.3 million in October 1983. The enterprise then started work on the project, spending Y1 million on civil construction and Y1.4 million on equipment.

Table 5.6. Shenyang Smelter's Sources of Investment Financing, 1975–82
(millions of yuan and percentage of total)

Source	1975–77 Amount	Share	1978 Amount	Share	1979 Amount	Share	1980 Amount	Share	1981 Amount	Share	1982 Amount	Share	1978–82 Amount	Share
State grants	4.28	15.6	0.00	0.0	3.60	24.3	2.81	11.0	1.7	6.1	0.00	0.0	8.11	7.8
Local government grants	0.00	0.0	0.00	0.0	0.00	0.0	0.00	0.0	0.00	0.0	0.50	1.9	0.50	0.5
Retained profits	0.00	0.0	0.00	0.0	0.00	0.0	0.82	3.3	3.20[a]	11.8	4.61	17.8	8.72	8.4
Basic depreciation funds	12.57	45.8	5.60	58.6	3.25	21.9	11.68	46.6	10.9[a]	39.0	7.74	29.9	39.17	37.9
Major repair funds	8.77	32.0	3.96	41.4	4.92	33.2	4.96	19.8	7.69	27.5	4.41	17.0	25.94	25.1
Pollution control funds[b]	1.80	6.6	0.00	0.0	3.07	20.7	4.80	19.1	3.93	14.1	7.43	28.7	19.23	18.6
Bank loans[c]	0.00	0.0	0.00	0.0	0.00	0.0	0.00	0.0	0.45	1.6	1.20	4.6	1.65	1.6
Total fixed investment	27.42	100.0	9.56	100.0	14.84	100.0	25.07	100.0	27.96	100.0	25.89	100.0	103.32	100.0

Note: Data are for total fixed investment by source of financing, including both capital construction and investment and modernization investment.

a. Assumes that half of the Y1.5 million in capital construction investment financed by "self-raised funds" in 1981 consisted of retained profits and that the other half consisted of basic depreciation funds.

b. Profits from production of sulfuric acid earmarked for use in pollution control projects, plus 80 percent of pollution charges levied on the smelter, which were also earmarked for investment in pollution control.

c. All from the People's Construction Bank of China.

Source: Information provided by the smelter.

The equipment was still sitting in the warehouse as of late 1984; it was financed by short-term bank credit and treated as receivables in the smelter's working capital accounts.

Meanwhile, it was discovered that some complementary work would be required on other parts of the lead production line and would cause further delays in the project. There was also a conflict with the Number 3 Metallurgical Construction Company which had been assigned the project. In August 1983 this company made exorbitant demands for extra compensation for its construction workers, on the ground that they would be exposed to lead poisoning. Specifically, it demanded that an extra health insurance fee be paid (at the rate of Y0.24 per worker per day) and that workers receive one month's extra pay (for "vacation") every four months. The smelter refused this request, so work halted for a number of months. The cost of this delay was reported to have been Y15,000 a day.

By late 1984 the conflict with the construction company had been resolved, and work was to be resumed shortly. The Ministry of Metallurgy had verbally agreed to provide the smelter a grant of Y2 million (through the Nonferrous Metals Industry General Corporation) and a loan quota for Y3 million in 1985. The costs of construction and materials had increased 18 percent, since the project originally had been approved, however, and, in any case, sufficient funding for completing the project still had not been arranged. Although there were a number of specific problems affecting this project, their fundamental source was the shortage of funds and conflicts about who should provide financing. It is particularly striking that the enterprise faced such problems and delays for a project that was in the state plan and had priority status. The project appears to have been fundamentally sound; it was expected to bring in additional profits of Y3 million to Y4 million annually and to reduce environmental pollution significantly.

Another project adversely affected by the shortage of funds was enriched-oxygen smelting in the copper blast furnace. For an estimated total investment cost of Y8.3 million, the project would have increased production of electrolytic copper by 3,100 tons and that of sulfuric acid by 25,000 tons and would have generated additional profits of more than Y8 million annually. This project also was approved by the State Economic Commission; it was to be financed by Y4.5 million in bank loans and Y3.8 million from the plant's own funds. Only Y1.3 million in loans had been provided as of late 1983, however, and there was no assurance that the rest of the money would be forthcoming. An oxygen generator the smelter had purchased in 1975 was inefficient; it used large amounts of energy, and it did not meet new noise standards. The generator should have been traded in to its producer for upgrading at an additional cost of Y2 million, but it was not, because of a shortage of funds. Funding problems also appear to have delayed renovation and replacement of some old lead sinterers that smoked badly and adversely affected the health of workers.

The Shenyang Smelter's internal financing sources were likewise viewed as inadequate. The factory believed that the depreciation rate on its fixed assets (5.62 percent a year) was too low, in view of their age and because 50 percent of depreciation funds had to be turned over to government supervisory authorities (as was the case for most Chinese state enterprises in the early 1980s). Moreover, the smelter had to use some of its retained profits and depreciation funds to buy its assigned target of Y700,000 to Y800,000 worth of national treasury bonds each year starting in 1981, and a stiff tax on retained profits and depreciation funds, the levy for energy and transport, was instituted in 1983, initially at a rate of 10 percent, later raised to 15 percent and then to 18 percent. Subsequently, a 10 percent tax on construction projects outside the state plan also was imposed.

The shortage of funds for investment was in part a symptom of the underlying problems discussed earlier. It may have been related to location: high-level authorities may have decided that the smelter should not undertake major capacity-increasing investments because of pollution, its congested site, and related difficulties. The lower priority given to copper mining in development plans for the nonferrous metals industry may also have had an influence. The multiheaded leadership system undoubtedly played a rôle as well; various government agencies would have tried to avoid providing funds and instead to shift funding responsibilities to other agencies. Overall, there were severe organizational problems, as can be seen from the following comments by the smelter's management in an interview:

> Sources and channels of funds for technical measures in the plant are numerous. Some are small loans approved by central authorities; some are provided by the Ministry of Metallurgy; and some are provided by the Provincial Department of Metallurgy or the Municipal Metallurgy Bureau, or are provided by the enterprise itself. In principle, whoever provides the money exercises control, though statistical information is given to the Municipal Metallurgy Bureau. Many funds are decided upon without reference to the Municipal Metallurgy Bureau or the Provincial Department of Metallurgy, with the result that channels for these kinds of funds are fairly chaotic, there is no assurance of corresponding materials, and management is also chaotic. For example, some items are decided on by the State Economic Commission; however, since these are numerous it cannot exercise control. The Provincial Department of Metallurgy and the Municipal Metallurgy Bureau do not exercise control, nor are they able to do so. They only figure in the disbursement of funds, but when it comes to procedures, actually no one is in charge.

Despite shortages of investment funding, there is no evidence that the Shenyang Smelter diverted funds for workers' bonuses or welfare to productive investment. Instead, the plant overspent on collective welfare in 1982 and 1983 and compensated for this in part by underspending on productive investment.[22] Thus its complaints about the shortage of investment funds must be seen in the context of an apparently overriding commitment to maintain workers' benefits in the face of falling profits. Moreover, as will be seen in the next section, "Response to Problems," the absolute amount of investment spending by the smelter was not small, even though it may have fallen short of perceived needs.

Employment of Workers' Children

For an enterprise like the Shenyang Smelter, finding employment opportunities for workers' children was exceedingly important and difficult. Large numbers of workers who joined the factory in the 1950s had many children since there was no strict family planning at the time; these individuals entered the labor force in the late 1970s or the early 1980s. Moreover, expansion of the smelter's main production activities, which would have been a potential source of jobs, was minimal after the mid-1970s. The magnitude of the problem can be seen from the number of workers' children who were eventually placed in the factory or in subordinate collective enterprises. By 1982 the total number of workers' children employed reached nearly 6,000, or about half of the enterprise's work force. It is not known how many children of employees were still awaiting work assignments at that time.

The smelter's difficulties in finding employment for workers' children were perhaps unusual in the degree of their severity, but they were similar in nature to the difficulties of other enterprises, particularly of enterprises in the older industrial base of Liaoning. In many parts of the country each enterprise was responsible for finding employment for its own workers' children. Under regulations, when a worker (but not a cadre) retired, his or her child was ensured a job in the enterprise. Many workers who were hired in the 1950s had more than one child, however. Moreover, timing problems often did not permit such replacements. As of 1982, only 279 children of smelter workers had replaced their parents.

The Shenyang Smelter and many other factories in northeast China responded to the employment problem of the late 1970s in two ways: they hired children as collective workers in positions alongside state workers (in the same workshop), and they created subordinate collective enterprises that could undertake various production and service activities. The first of these practices could breed tensions among the workers; it was criticized by China's State Council. Subsequent attempts to separate state workers and collective workers were only partly successful. In the case of the smelter, more than 2,000 collective workers remained in "mixed" positions in state-owned work units of the plant in 1983, compared with nearly 4,000 such workers in 1981.

Two collective enterprises were established as divisions of the Shenyang Smelter in March 1979, one handling repairs and construction work, the other handling personal services for employees. They were combined into a comprehensive services company in 1981, then again split at the beginning of 1982, into the Repair and Construction Services Company and the Labor Services Company. Both enterprises were dependent on the parent factory for financial assistance and for a guaranteed market; neither was successful in obtaining much work outside the smelter. In 1982 outside work accounted for only 37 percent of the revenues of the Labor Services Company (some of this work may have represented sales to smelter employees); virtually all of the construction company's work was for the parent factory. As of 1982, 62 percent of the fixed assets of the construction company and 21 percent of those of the Labor Services Company were leased or rented from the smelter, probably at low rates covering only depreciation of the equipment and facilities concerned. Both collective enterprises owed considerable sums of money to the smelter, which permitted indefinite delays in payments and apparently financed them as receivables in its accounts. Despite measures in 1984 to strengthen incentives for the collectives and to make them more responsible for their economic performance, they apparently still remained a drain on the Shenyang Smelter's finances.

Response to Problems

This section looks at the ways in which the Shenyang Smelter dealt with the problems described earlier. The creation of a national nonferrous metals corporation and the recentralization of administrative jurisdiction over the plant at the end of 1983 constituted a response of the system as a whole rather than a response of the enterprise itself, so it is discussed in detail separately. The response to the problem of employing workers' children also was a systemwide response and is described briefly in the previous section.

Production Management

In this area the Shenyang Smelter took relatively simple yet effective measures to ameliorate problems with the shortage of electricity, with irregular supply of copper and lead ores, and with a highly congested site with limited storage space. In arranging production over the short run, the smelter basically let production of zinc be the residual; as a result, zinc production showed greater year-to-year fluctuations than did output of lead or copper. This method was adopted for three reasons: (1) zinc production was relatively electricity intensive, requiring seventeen times as much power per ton as copper and twenty-four times as much as lead; (2) all prime processed zinc ore was obtained from one nearby plant, and that supplier could expedite or delay shipments as necessary; and (3) the highly irregular shipments of copper and lead ore to the plant could not be regulated in this manner.

The smelter gave first priority to smelting copper and lead ores as they arrived, diverting electricity supplies from zinc production if necessary. This procedure allowed it to minimize inventories because shipments of zinc ore could be delayed if they were not needed and because inventories of copper and lead ore were run down as quickly as possible. Lower inventories meant less congestion and lower circulating capital costs. This method also ensured that if there was a shortage of electricity, the adverse effect on production and profits would be minimized because production of only the most electricity-intensive product would be affected.

This technique for managing production may seem elementary, and, in any case, it merely ameliorated but did not solve any important problems, but it shows a certain ingenuity that might have been missing in many other state enterprises. It represented precisely the kind of incremental, marginal improvement that could generate substantial gains in efficiency if it were applied by many enterprises.

Because of the external environment the Shenyang Smelter faced and the optimizing measures it took in the short run, binding constraints on immediate increases in production were different for each of its main products. In copper smelting (producing blister from concentrated copper ore), the binding constraint most likely was capacity; this constraint was related to the plant's inability to expand at its existing site. Any significant expansion in capacity, however, might well have engendered a raw material supply constraint.[23] In copper refining (transforming blister or scrap into pure copper), the binding constraint was clearly availability of raw materials. Capacity was 60,000 tons a year; production was considerably lower. The binding constraint on zinc production was electricity. This constraint, as has been seen, was a rational one because of zinc's higher electricity intensiveness and the raw material supply situation. In lead production, the binding constraint was probably market demand. Prices were soft nationally, and the smelter did not accept all concentrated lead ore made available to it, presumably because of weak demand for lead on the market.[24] Finally, for sulfuric acid, the binding constraint had previously been capacity, but with expansion it may have become the sulfur content of the ores the plant received, over which it had no control.

Comprehensive Utilization of By-products

The comprehensive utilization of by-products was a long-term response to problems of pollution, limited capacity and supplies of raw materials, and financial constraints (because many of the by-products were highly profitable). Recovery of rare metals from ores started as early as the 1950s; sulfuric acid production began in the early 1970s and greatly expanded thereafter; and it appears that there were substantial increases in gold and silver production in the late 1970s.

The most important impurity recovered was sulfur, common in most ores, which was used to make sulfuric acid. The smelter and the authorities first discussed producing sulfuric acid in 1969. Production was expected to be profitable and at the same time to reduce sulfur pollution, for which heavy fines were then apparently being introduced. The Ministry of Metallurgy and Liaoning Province provided grants for the needed investment. Facilities apparently were put in place very rapidly, and production started in 1970. From the outset this activity earned a profit (at the state price, which was used all along). By 1973, output was substantial and stable enough to be included in the state plan; most sulfuric acid was turned over to the State Material Supply Bureau for allocation, but some was turned over to Liaoning Province and some was sold by the smelter directly.

A question naturally arises: because production of sulfuric acid is a near-universal activity of nonferrous metals smelters worldwide, because Shen-yang's investment requirements apparently were manageable, and because the gestation period of this operation was short, why was it not developed in the 1950s instead of in the 1970s? There may be some reasonable explanation, but most likely the late development of sulfuric acid production reflected a lack of concern about profits and an insensitivity to the problems created by pollution.

The smelter was forced to pay copper mines a fee of Y50 for each ton of sulfur it recovered; this ate into its profits substantially because the price of sulfuric acid before November 1983 was only Y110 a ton. (It was later raised to Y155 a ton.) The fee was even paid for sulfur recovered from imported copper concentrate (in this case it was paid to the China Metals and Ores Import-Export Corporation). The fee was set by the Ministry of Metallurgy; because all mines and smelters were under the control of the ministry, the ministry only redistributed income among mining and processing activities. This redistribution could have been better accomplished by raising the price of ore (which would not have dampened incentives for smelters to recover sulfur).

Efforts to utilize by-products and recover valuable metals from waste appear to have increased in the 1980s. The large investment project to recover lead and zinc from slag produced by the lead smelter was one example (see the discussion in the previous section). Intensified recovery of sulfur dioxide from flue gases and conversion to sulfuric acid was another example. These efforts may well have encountered diminishing returns, however, as the easy and highly rewarding investment opportunities were exploited.

Pollution Control

The importance attached to controlling pollution by the Shenyang Smelter is evidenced by its slogan, "Using environmental protection to remain in existence, energy conservation to develop." A significant commitment to reduce pollution was made only in 1978, however. The smelter's energetic program of pollution control, which started in that year, included establish-

ing an environmental protection office under the leadership of the plant director (with a total of 160 personnel), establishing a monitoring network and
penalties for noncompliance by workshops, and investing in a number of
pollution control projects. In 1978 smokestacks were consolidated (and perhaps increased in height) to decrease local air pollution. In 1979, facilities
to recover sulfuric acid from sulfur dioxide flue gases generated in copper
smelting were completed; these facilities reduced the amount of sulfur dioxide
gas discharged by more than half and increased annual output of sulfuric
acid from 60,000 tons to 127,000 tons. In 1980, water recycling was improved; this reduced the amount of waste water discharged by two-thirds.
In 1981 the plant began to recover sulfuric acid from sulfur dioxide flue
gases in the lead production system. Other pollution control projects were
in the process of planning and construction at the time of this study.

Overall, the smelter spent Y23.9 million on pollution control in 1978–82;
this was equivalent to 29 percent of its total fixed investment in that period.
All but Y2 million of this amount came from the plant's own resources.
The bulk of the money (Y16 million) came from profits the plant derived
from production of sulfuric acid that it then plowed into reinvestment.[25] The
rest came from profits earned by utilizing by-products and from "returned
fines" for pollution. The system of charges for pollution was a nationwide
one designed to make the charges more palatable to polluters and to encourage investments in pollution control. Eighty percent of pollution fees levied
were returned to the polluting enterprises and earmarked for use in pollution
control projects.

Pollution control efforts by the smelter were greatly aided by their profitability: recovery of valuable impurities in ores and by-products of the smelting
process typically was involved. Most pollution control projects were financially
lucrative; this suggests that in the prereform period the smelter must have
paid little attention to profits or to environmental pollution, or at least that
it had little or no voice in investment decisions.

Energy Conservation

Lax energy management and poor control of energy consumption in the past
meant that improved organization and management of energy use by the
Shenyang Smelter would have high payoffs. In 1979 an energy office was
established; its staff grew from three to twenty-one. Full-time energy personnel were placed in each workshop, and part-time energy workers and inspec-
tors were designated in work sections and teams. Norms established for energy
consumption in production of important products were slightly tougher than
those handed down by the Shenyang Metallurgy Bureau. These norms were
passed down to the work units and, in some cases, even to individuals,
and bonuses were issued for superior performance in energy conservation.
A considerable amount of work was done to monitor energy consumption

and heat balances. In 1980–81 a plantwide exercise in energy testing was conducted, and the smelter was certified by authorities as meeting standards.

The smelter also made investments in energy-saving projects. In 1981 a total of thirty such projects were started, including utilization of hot cooling water for heating in winter, better utilization of waste heat, and use of cooling towers to recycle waste water. In 1980–82 a total of Y4.5 million was spent on these projects; this resulted, according to the enterprise's calculations, in a saving of 10,000 tons of standard coal-equivalent. Assuming a cost of about Y50 a ton for standard coal (the state price), the profits generated by these projects would total about Y500,000 a year; this would imply a financial rate of return of more than 10 percent. Although respectable, this return is much less than the returns on pollution control projects discussed earlier.

Although considerable attention was paid to energy conservation in operations, investments were rather small compared with investments in pollution control. Indexes of unit energy consumption generally showed a moderate downward trend, although there were considerable year-to-year fluctuations. Electricity consumption per unit of electrolytic copper produced dropped by 14 percent from 1975 to 1982, but the 1981 figure was slightly higher even than 1975–77 levels. The corresponding index for lead declined more steadily, whereas consumption of heavy oil in lead and zinc smelting showed little tendency to fall. Unit total energy consumption rose somewhat in the first eight months of 1983, but this was apparently due to factors beyond the smelter's control (see "General Observations," in this chapter).

Pursuing energy conservation became more difficult after some obvious opportunities had been exploited and the worst forms of waste eliminated. Further improvements probably required more substantial investments and therefore may have been hindered by the Shenyang Smelter's shortage of funds and also by the generally low financial returns on energy conservation. Finally, because nonferrous metals smelting is inherently energy intensive, if energy conservation in the Shenyang area or in Liaoning Province were deemed to be an overriding priority, the option of shutting down the plant and relocating operations elsewhere or relying more on imports of nonferrous metals should have been considered.

Improvements in Quality

Purity was used as the primary indicator of quality for the Shenyang Smelter's main products. Measured by this standard, the smelter's output was of exceptionally high quality. It won a gold medal for electrolytic lead in 1980 and a silver medal for electrolytic copper in 1984.[26] Five other products were certified as high-quality by the Ministry of Metallurgy.

Quality control work was under the leadership of a quality control committee headed by the plant director and including all workshop heads and several other top managers. Implementation and inspection were handled by a quality control section and a technical inspection station; there were also quality control teams in each workshop. If quality was not up to standard, workshop bonuses could be cut. In addition to internal quality control, there were random quality checks by the Shenyang Municipal Bureau of Standards and (before 1984) by the Shenyang Metallurgy Bureau.

One-time bonuses could be awarded to the work force when the smelter won a national quality prize. (In 1980 the bonus was Y60 per worker, in 1984 Y20.) These bonuses were drawn from production costs, so retained profits that otherwise would be used for bonuses could be diverted to workers' welfare or to productive investment.[27] Aside from this, the main benefit from winning prizes for quality or, more generally, for maintaining high-quality output appears to have been a better reputation for the firm and its products. This benefit did not have an effect on sales because the smelter's products were in short supply anyway. A good reputation for quality might, however, have helped the plant when the authorities were making decisions about possible shutdown, relocation, or recentralization of control.

There is some evidence that the Shenyang Smelter's concern for quality went well beyond the needs of its customers. The national quality standard for top-grade electrolytic copper was 99.95 percent purity. This level of purity was more than sufficient for the needs of nearly all users. But the smelter surpassed even this, sometimes achieving 99.97 percent or 99.98 percent purity. Because of fluctuations in quality, it might have been necessary to produce copper of a purity greater than 99.95 percent to ensure that this standard was always met, but the desire to win a quality prize and gain a good reputation may have been a more important motivation.

The quality of zinc also exceeded customers' needs, but the reason for this was strictly financial. The production costs for zinc of different grades were very nearly the same, but the prices were different: Y1,930 a ton for first-grade, Y1,900 a ton for second-grade, and Y1,850 a ton for third-grade. Customers preferred second- or third-grade zinc; the smelter's output plans and supply contracts, however, called only for first- or second-grade zinc, and it always produced first-grade. Earlier, it had been specified that the smelter should produce 70 percent first-grade zinc and 30 percent second-grade zinc, but this rule was subsequently dropped.[28]

Thus the smelter's concentration on quality control and its success in improving quality appear to have been in part dysfunctional. How much extra it cost the plant to maintain excessively high quality and what payoff it might have seen from reducing quality slightly cannot be determined without further study. If much of the extra cost lay in unrewarded additional efforts of workers and managers, it might well have been worthwhile for the smelter to maintain high quality standards as a means of improving the organization of production and of instilling pride and discipline in the labor force.

Investment Financing

Although the Shenyang Smelter faced shortages of investment funds, its investment was not insignificant. In 1978–82, total fixed investment by the plant (not including its subordinate collective enterprises) was Y103.32 million (table 5.6). Investment in physical working capital during the same period was Y12.55 million. Total investment was therefore Y115.87 million, equivalent to 53 percent of total administrative profits earned in 1978–82 or to 63 percent of total capital at the end of 1982. This was a respectable reinvestment rate for an aging, highly profitable enterprise such as the Shenyang Smelter. The perceived shortage of investment funds may have become acute only when authorities were attempting to recentralize jurisdiction over the smelter, and government agencies allocating investment resources were not certain about which of them would eventually gain administrative control.

Viewed from another perspective, however, the smelter's complaints about shortage of funds appear more reasonable. If investment financed by depreciation funds and major repair funds were subtracted from total investment, the ratio of net investment to profits would be only 18 percent. This would indicate that relatively little new investment money flowed in to the smelter. Moreover, the enterprise was permitted to retain only 50 percent of total depreciation charges on its fixed assets in the early 1980s, and some retained depreciation funds appear to have been diverted to purposes other than fixed investment. There was, then, probably a shortfall in replacement investment as well as a lack of new investment.

The financing of the Shenyang Smelter's fixed investment is shown in table 5.6. Contrary to trends for many other firms, the sources of investment finance were not too different before and after the late 1970s. In particular, reliance on bank loans and on local government grants remained minimal. Depreciation funds and major repair funds were the main sources, and profits from sulfuric acid production earmarked for pollution control investment and pollution fees returned to the factory became increasingly important. State grants were relatively small, accounting for less than 16 percent of total fixed investment in 1975–77 and for less than 8 percent in 1978–82.

Except for the earmarking of profits from sulfuric acid production for investment in pollution control, the use of returned pollution fees for the same purpose, and an increase in the depreciation rate from 5.62 percent to 6.62 percent in 1984, all of which factors might have been national policy measures that were not specific to the enterprise, the smelter was unsuccessful in tapping new sources of investment funds. This may reflect the low priority given to the smelter's investments by the authorities or their lack of receptivity to innovative investment practices. The plant might also have been hindered by its lack of control over the marketing of the vast bulk of its products. Such control would have been a strong bargaining chip in obtaining funds.

Should the Shenyang Smelter have spent more on investment in renovating and modernizing facilities at its present site, or, if eventually shutting down the facility were the best option, should it have invested even less than it did? A strong case can be made for the appropriateness of the smelter's not being permitted to spend all it would have liked to spend on investment. In its situation, it was only natural that the smelter perceived a severe shortage of investment funds.

Financial Manipulation

The unexceptional history of profit-sharing schemes at the Shenyang Smelter conformed to the broad trends followed by Chinese state industry as a whole. In 1978 the enterprise fund scheme was restored after a lapse of more than a decade; the plant retained the equivalent of 5 percent of its total wage bill. (This fund was drawn from profits and was used for collective welfare expenses.) In 1979 the smelter was put under the national pilot program of enterprise-level reform and was permitted to retain 5.74 percent of within-quota profits and 10 percent of above-quota profits. Retained profits were to be used in specified proportions for productive investment, collective welfare, and workers' bonuses. In 1980 the rate for above-quota profit retention was raised to 20 percent, but there were no other changes in 1980 or 1981. During this period, profit quotas appear to have been substantially raised in response to the sharp increase in realized profits (see table 5.7), so as a result there was little change in the average rate of profit retention between 1979 and 1981. (The profit quotas used in the profit-retention scheme had no discernible relationship to plan targets for total profits or for profit remittances to the government.)

In 1982 the system was changed; the smelter retained no within-quota profits but 40 percent of above-quota profits. The profit quota was reduced, and the new average rate of profit retention was slightly higher than it had been in 1981. In 1983 the plant was included in the nationwide profit tax system; it had to pay a 55 percent profit tax and a 36.2 percent adjustment tax, so it retained only 8.8 percent of total profits. This new tax system was reported to have made no distinction between within-quota and above-quota profits. The smelter, however, was apparently allowed to retain more than 8.8 percent of its total profits in 1983.[29] Possibly there was provision for a higher retention rate from above-quota profits (as was common in other firms).

As it did in other state-owned industrial enterprises in China, a soft financial incentive system cushioned the effect of declining profits on the Shenyang Smelter's retained profits and workers' living standards. Total profits dropped by more than 40 percent in 1983, but retained profits fell by only 16 percent; the share of the plant's retained profits in its total profits increased from 7.7 percent in 1982 to 11.2 percent in 1983 (table 5.7). Bonuses were not

Table 5.7. Shenyang Smelter's Profit Sharing, 1978–83
(millions of yuan, unless otherwise specified)

Year	Total profits[a]	Retained profits	Implied profit quota[b]	Share of profits retained (percent)
1978	18.76	0.28	n.a.	1.5
1979	43.05	3.00	30.6	7.0
1980	53.32	4.28	44.8	8.0
1981	54.16	3.91	48.5	7.2
1982	50.35	3.90	40.6	7.7
1983	29.20	3.27	11.2[c]	11.2

n.a. Not applicable.

a. Data are administrative profit, that is, profits from commodity sales net of profits and losses on nonbusiness activities.

b. Data are derived from within-quota and above-quota profit retention rates provided by the smelter and calculations that determined what the quotas should have been, considering actual total profits and retained profits. These estimates are subject to error.

c. The 1983 profit retention rate was given as 8.8 percent. Actual retained profits, however, were 11.2 percent of total profits; this signifies that the smelter was given special consideration in 1983 or else that there was a provision for retention at a higher rate from above-quota profits.

Source: Information provided by the smelter.

much affected by the decline in profits or the shift to the profit tax system, contrary to the smelter's initial fears.

In 1984 a sharp rise in the price of sulfuric acid helped boost profits. The scheme whereby the smelter was permitted to retain a substantial proportion of profits earned from sulfuric acid production, completely separate from the regular profit-sharing system, may have involved special consideration not afforded to other smelters and producers of sulfuric acid. According to very rough estimates, total production of sulfuric acid in 1978–82 was about 500,000 tons. At the state price of Y110 a ton, this production was worth Y55 million, of which Y16 million was used for pollution control investments. Such investments hence may have accounted for nearly all profits from sulfuric acid production.

The smelter was permitted to finance a long-term loan to the Benxi County Cement Plant through its circulating capital accounts, an arrangement that also might have involved special treatment. This loan, part of a compensation trade deal, was for Y1.7 million interest free with a maturity of fifteen years (repayable in equal yearly installments). In return the Benxi County Cement Plant agreed to provide the smelter with 10,000 tons of cement a year, at the price of Y92 a ton.[30] Another part of the deal required the smelter to convert an old rotary kiln that had been used in zinc production into a cement kiln and provide it to the cement plant, apparently free of charge. The loan was carried in the smelter's accounts as a receivable. It is not clear whether the bank knew of or consented to this practice.

In 1983 the Shenyang Smelter gained substantial benefits from its designation as an experimental unit in wage reform. It could raise wages by an average of Y1.5 per worker a month, in addition to increasing them by Y7 per worker a month in line with a general wage adjustment instituted at the time. The extra money was used to simplify a complicated and inequitable wage-grade system while ensuring that no workers suffered wage reductions in the process. In addition, wages of certain deserving employees, such as intellectuals and workers in the lead production system, were raised by one-half grade. These large wage increases diminished any worker discontent in response to a slight reduction in bonuses in 1983. Total bonuses drawn from retained profits fell by about 12 percent in 1983; this decline was far less than the proportional declines in total profits and in total retained profits. Based on the average number of employees in 1982, the reduction in bonuses was about Y24 per worker. The increase in wages, however, averaged more than Y100 per worker. Moreover, special bonuses drawn from production costs jumped by 86 percent in 1982 and may have further increased in 1983.

Despite these machinations, the Shenyang Smelter, compared with many other Chinese enterprises, appears not to have been especially active or successful in manipulating the incentive system. For example, there was no great increase in the average rate of profit retention in 1981 or 1982, years in which other enterprises were taking advantage of the campaign to promote economic responsibility systems to sharply increase their own retained profits. The smelter also had great difficulties in getting its profit target reduced in 1983, when it had valid reasons for expecting lower profits, and in the end the actual increase in the profit-retention rate was relatively modest. The plant's inability to manipulate the incentive system more than it did probably was due to its awkward position in relation to the Ministry of Metallurgy and Shenyang Municipality; its requests may not have been supported by the municipality, which believed it was losing its stake in the enterprise, or by the ministry, which may not have been able to give the smelter special treatment under the circumstances. This lack of a suitable patron at the local or the central level may also partly account for the severity of some of the other problems the smelter faced.

Direct Marketing

To a large extent direct marketing was the Shenyang Smelter's passive response to the refusal of material supply authorities to purchase certain by-products and, more rarely, part of the output of its main products. Direct marketing predated the economic reforms of the late 1970s and was largely unrelated to them. Four situations involving sales outside the state plan can be distinguished: (1) material supply authorities forced the plant itself to market certain by-products that were in excess supply; (2) sales of sulfuric acid by the smelter were a lucrative exception to the general pattern mentioned above; (3) mines that supplied ores to the smelter outside the central plan often demanded that the resulting metal output be sold back to their localities, and similar processing arrangements might have applied when the plant purchased scrap for recycling; and (4) as a result of the sharp cutback in investment in early 1981, some customers assigned allocations of copper via the plan cancelled their purchase contracts, leaving the smelter with inventories to divest.

One of the most telling complaints of management was that the enterprise was forced to market goods that were in excess supply, whereas material supply authorities insisted on distributing all production of goods in short supply. This practice may have had certain benefits in cases in which producers could respond to market demand, but the smelter had little, if any, ability to change its output of most by-products. Reducing production would have indirectly exacerbated pollution, and maximum output was determined by the mineral composition of the raw materials shipped in. The smelter was therefore in the unenviable position of being responsible for selling goods over whose production it had no control.

Cadmium is a good example of this situation. Cadmium had previously been used to make plastic sheeting for agricultural use, but this had resulted in food contamination and had been discontinued. Inventories accumulated, and the smelter was made responsible for marketing. The market price of cadmium tumbled to less than Y10,000 a ton, compared with the official price of Y19,000 a ton. Even so, the only way the plant could divest of inventories was to tie sales of cadmium to some sales of zinc to its within-plan customers. Because cadmium was a by-product of zinc smelting (equivalent to 5–8 percent of zinc output), the smelter received approval from the State Material Supply Bureau to tie sales at the rate of one ton of cadmium per ten tons of zinc, for 12 percent of its total zinc output.

Other examples of goods in excess supply that the smelter was forced to market on its own were indium and palladium. One exception to the general pattern seems to have been platinum, which had brisk sales but which apparently was nevertheless marketed directly by the plant. Starting in 1980 certain products previously allocated by the Ministry of Metallurgy were also directly marketed by the smelter; these included copper sulfate, nickel sulfate, and zinc oxide. The plant itself preferred to engage in no self-sales at all for any of these products.

The smelter did gain considerable benefits from self-sales of sulfuric acid, which until the mid-1980s was in short supply. All along, some output of sulfuric acid (about 25–30 percent) was subject to provincial allocation and some (5–10 percent) was under the control of the plant itself. After 1980 the unwritten but apparently quite stable arrangement was as follows: The annual state plan was fixed at 80,000 tons, all of which was allocated by the State Material Supply Bureau. Liaoning Province received 20,000–30,000 tons, and the smelter retained about 5,000 tons for its own use and in addition could sell 5,000–10,000 tons directly. Some of the sulfuric acid earmarked for the plant's own use was actually exchanged in rural areas for rice for smelter employees, and some of the self-sales portion was sold in accordance with the requests of government authorities and other units. Most important, the sale of sulfuric acid to Liaoning Province was informally tied to the plant's purchase of 3,000 tons of fuel oil a year from the province at the state price. (All sales of sulfuric acid also occurred at the state price.) This arrangement went a long way toward alleviating the smelter's chronic shortage of fuel oil.

Direct marketing of the aforementioned products was not insignificant in aggregate; it amounted to Y9.23 million in 1978, before nationwide policy promoted self-sales. In 1982 the figure reached Y12.37 million; thus reforms had no significant effect in increasing direct marketing of this type. The share of these self-sales in total sales was very small, less than 2 percent in 1978 and only slightly more than 2 percent in 1982.

Inadequate and contradictory information prevents a full understanding of the Shenyang Smelter's direct marketing of copper, lead, and zinc. According to one account, there was no direct marketing of lead or zinc by the plant. Another smelter representative stated that at least until 1983, zinc recovered in the recycling of scrap lead could be directly marketed. Elsewhere it was stated that self-sales of lead accounted for no more than about 7 percent of total output; they consisted of above-plan supplies from ore mines and recycling of scrap. (Because lead became readily available on the market, very little was sold back to mining areas in tied transactions.)

Comments on direct marketing of copper showed the most serious discrepancies. According to one account, no more than about 5,000 tons of copper was produced from concentrated ore supplies obtained from domestic mines outside the central plan, and about 3,000 tons of this was marketed directly by the smelter. (The rest was sold back to producing areas in tied transactions.) Self-sales of copper amounted to about 7 percent of total output; in addition a certain proportion of copper recycled from scrap, which in total accounted for 30 percent of copper output in 1983 and 1984, also presumably was directly marketed. Until 1983 the smelter reportedly had the right to market all copper produced from scrap it purchased on its own. At a later point in interviews at the smelter it was denied that there was ever any significant direct marketing of copper. Self-sales controlled by the smelter were said to be minuscule, no more than 250 tons a year. Nearly all copper produced from outside-of-plan supplies of ore was "returned" to the mining areas, and copper recycled from scrap was either returned to suppliers of the scrap or allocated by authorities.

At least part of this discrepancy may be explained by the role of the Shenyang Smelter's provincial-level supervisory agency (now the Shenyang Nonferrous Metals Corporation, previously the Liaoning Provincial Metallurgical Bureau) in arranging procurements from small local ore mines and possibly also from scrap suppliers. The resulting output was not subject to unified allocation by the State Material Supply Bureau; it was probably allocated mainly by provincial authorities and hence was probably not really under the smelter's control. A reliable understanding of the smelter's direct marketing of copper would require further inquiry.

In 1981 some enterprises that had already been allocated copper produced by the plant under the central plan and that had already signed supply contracts had their production and investment targets sharply reduced and some of their funds in bank accounts frozen. As a result they were unable to fulfill their contracts and left the smelter with rising inventories that reached 2,000 tons by May 1981. The plant asked the State Material Supply Bureau and the State Economic Commission to deal with the problem. In the end the Northeast Procurement Station of the State Material Supply Bureau did purchase the excess inventories, some of them on credit. By July 1981 the inventory problem was solved; apparently conflicts over self-sales of copper continued during the next several years, however.[31]

Despite the confusion, a number of common themes about direct marketing emerge. Except in the case of sulfuric acid, the Shenyang Smelter had no interest in self-sales and appeared not to gain any significant benefits from those in which it did engage. In fact, the smelter would have greatly preferred unified central allocation of all products to the hybrid situation it faced, partly because price controls were stringent even for directly marketed output but mainly because the plant was commonly forced to market directly items in excess supply and was not permitted to market directly goods in short supply.

It is doubtful whether heavier reliance on direct marketing would have encouraged the enterprise to be more active in developing new products, improving quality, reducing costs, or otherwise better serving customers' needs. The nature of the smelter's products and production process was not conducive to such responses, and the smelter had already achieved high quality standards in the absence of direct marketing. Finally, copper and zinc were in chronic short supply, so sales were assured. Overall, the role and benefits of direct marketing were much diminished compared with the case of differentiated products in excess supply (see, for example, chapter 3).

Development of Alloy Production

The Shenyang Smelter strongly preferred to produce alloys rather than pure metals because alloys were overpriced relative to pure metals and therefore much more profitable. Alloy production might also have allowed the smelter to take over lucrative business handled inefficiently by small enterprises. (Lead alloys for typesetting, for example, were being produced by 400–500 collectives and individual households in Shenyang Municipality alone.)

The smelter all along was required to provide the State Material Supply

Bureau with pure metals, which many users then had to resmelt into alloys for use in production. The quality and durability of alloys produced by users was reported to be poor. For instance, underwater cables produced in China lasted only three or four years because of poor alloy quality, compared with twenty to thirty years in other countries. Furthermore, because smelting is a process of purification and because alloy production reintroduces certain impurities in fixed amounts, some of which may have been present in the original ores, separating the two activities generally increases costs, energy consumption, and pollution. In other countries, most nonferrous metals smelters are also involved in alloy production (this is the case in more than three-quarters of smelters in the United States, for example), but in China this was not so, and there was no government organization responsible for developing alloy production.

The smelter argued cogently that it was better equipped than most users to produce high-quality alloys and could do so at lower cost because it could operate on a larger scale. Users and their ministries opposed this idea, however, because it would have eroded lucrative profits and employment provided by alloy production. Users might also have feared that they could not rely on outside suppliers for timely shipments of alloys of the right specifications. The smelter could produce alloys on a large scale only with the approval of central authorities, who would have to impose this change in industry norms on users. In the absence of such a change, Shenyang produced only small amounts of alloys experimentally, using materials obtained outside the plan. Its intention to produce several thousand tons of alloys in 1984 apparently did not materialize (see "Later Developments," in this chapter).

There were some signs of progress in alloy production elsewhere in China. In Shanghai certain aluminum smelting plants were already producing aluminum alloys in 1983. This new situation adversely affected aluminum processing factories, one of whose functions had been to resmelt pure aluminum into alloys. Nevertheless, because direct smelting of alloys conserved energy, processing factories were urged to adapt to the new situation (*Shanghai Wuzi Shichang*, no. 146 [December 17, 1983], p. 1).

Relocation

There was no effective response to the smelter's fundamental and increasingly severe problems related to its location. The smelter was constrained from farming out parts of the production process as a means of downsizing (see "Main Problems," in this chapter). The alternative of completely stopping production at the smelter's existing site and either building new capacity elsewhere in China or relying more on imports to meet China's needs for nonferrous metals is examined here. The Shenyang Smelter had considered moving production to a mountain ravine beyond the suburbs when attention was focused on pollution problems in 1978. This alternative was rejected, however, because it would be more costly than on-site pollution control and because it would not solve the fundamental problem but merely relocate pollution nearby.

A number of factors biased the choices of government authorities and diminished the smelter's own incentives to relocate. In the first place, the smelter was not paying the full social costs of the pollution it generated, and it was paying artificially low prices for the energy it consumed.[32] As a result, any financial advantages to the enterprise from possible relocation were severely eroded. The social responsibilities of Chinese enterprises, which were a feature of the economic and political system, were probably an even more important obstacle to relocation. In the state sector of the economy, workers were very closely tied to their enterprises; they were virtually guaranteed lifetime employment, and their enterprises were responsible for providing jobs for their children. Hence it was administratively and politically extremely difficult to shut down a firm, probably almost impossible in the case of a large employer such as the Shenyang Smelter. Moreover, if a factory was relocated the workers had to be moved along with the facilities. The enterprise would also most likely have to pay for housing and other facilities for workers at the new site, and it would have to pay for any production-related infrastructure needed. Finally, a Chinese enterprise could not sell its existing site, facilities, and workers' housing at full market values, which, in a large city such as Shenyang, would be high. Hence an important social benefit of moving, the freeing of land and facilities for other use, would not be translated into private financial benefit for the enterprise concerned.

All of these factors sharply raised the costs (financial and otherwise) to the smelter of relocation and hence militated against this alternative. To the extent that supervisory agencies were responsive to the same considerations as the smelter, their decisions would be similarly biased.

The government's choice between continuing production at the smelter's present site and importing the same metals that the smelter produced is in principle relatively simple, although the difficulty of shutting down an existing state enterprise undoubtedly would bias the decision against importing. The domestic unit cost of production, with all inputs evaluated at economic prices, should be compared with the (expected) international price. The use of existing production facilities should not be charged to the cost of domestic production except to the extent that these assets can be productively employed in other activities. The optimal choice may well be different for different metals and dependent on China's resource endowment, on pollution, on energy requirements and other aspects of cost structure, and on international prices. Strategic considerations may affect the choice, but these should be made explicit and their economic costs evaluated.

In the case of electricity-intensive products, such as zinc and especially aluminum, importing can be viewed as a means of importing electricity from parts of the world where it is relatively cheap. Electricity itself cannot economically be transmitted over long distances or preserved over time. Electricity can be "embodied," however, in an electricity-intensive commodity, such as aluminum. Because of the severe shortage of electric power in China, an import strategy for electricity-intensive goods may be desirable.

The Fushun Aluminum Plant, a large aluminum smelter in Liaoning Province, furnishes an example of the systemic obstacles to relocation. Production of aluminum requires more than five times as much electricity per unit of output as does zinc and close to 100 times as much as does copper. In electricity-deficient northeast China the case for stopping aluminum production at Fushun was therefore even stronger than was the case for shutting down the Shenyang Smelter. In the early 1980s Fushun was operating at far below capacity, producing only about 35,000 tons of aluminum a year compared with a previous high of 100,000 tons. Provincial authorities consciously and systematically diverted power supplies from Fushun to the Shenyang Smelter and other users whose operations were less electricity-intensive.[33]

At one point Liaoning provincial authorities suggested that the Fushun Aluminum Plant be moved to another part of China where electricity supplies were more plentiful, such as Gansu Province.[34] This issue was debated at length, and a final decision was made only by China's State Council. In the end it was decided not to move the factory, because the existing facilities and equipment would have had to be written off and because Gansu did not want the plant. (Gansu itself would soon be short of electricity.) The first of these justifications had no validity, because the existing capital assets represented sunk costs. The second may have been more reasonable, but what mattered was the relative shortage of electricity, or, in other words, differences in the economic price of electricity across regions. Finally, the alternative of importing the aluminum required apparently was not even considered, although this had been recommended as a suitable temporary measure for China as a whole (Li 1983, pp. 274–75).

The course of action eventually agreed on was to keep Fushun in operation and build new thermal power plants (presumably to be financed by the central government) in the local area to meet its needs. This, of course, was just as economically inefficient from a national perspective as would have been allowing Fushun to run at full capacity by diverting supplies from other users, because at the margin the tradeoff between using electricity for aluminum production and for other purposes remained the same. Moreover, if the cost of building the new power plants were higher than that of adding new electricity capacity elsewhere in China or if there were transport bottlenecks that hindered an increase in coal shipments into Liaoning, this decision might have reduced overall economic efficiency.

Organizational Reforms

The problems faced by China's nonferrous metals industry elicited a system-wide response in 1983, the core of which was organizational reform and recentralization of administrative control over the larger and more important enterprises in the industry. For the Shenyang Smelter, recentralization was seen as a fundamental solution to the problems of the multiheaded leadership system. This section first touches on some of the industrywide problems that hindered efficient exploitation of China's nonferrous mineral resources and slowed growth of production. The establishment of the China Nonferrous Metals Industry General Corporation in April 1983 and the subsequent transfer of large nonferrous metals mines and factories to its jurisdiction is discussed next. Regional branch corporations, one of which became the supervisory agency of the Shenyang Smelter, also were set up. The process by which the smelter was transferred from municipal to central control provides an interesting example of how difficult recentralization can be when it must be based on consensus among different levels of government. The last part of this section looks at the benefits and problems of the new system from the point of view of the smelter and then at the system's effect on China's nonferrous metals industry as a whole.

Problems in China's Nonferrous Metals Industry

The State Economic Commission circular that set up the China Nonferrous Metals Industry General Corporation highlighted six features of China's nonferrous metals industry: (1) because mineral resources were scattered in remote, mountainous areas, exploitation and production were difficult and working conditions were poor; (2) the gestation period for mine development was long, about ten years in the case of a medium-size mine; (3) mining output was uneven; (4) investment requirements were much higher than in most manufacturing industries, and profits from mining were low, so localities were generally unwilling to invest in mines; (5) the production stages of mining, concentration, smelting, and processing of finished metals required cooperation of enterprises across the country; and (6) most ores were shipped out of the mining area and not refined locally, so localities again had little incentive to develop production. Nonferrous metals were important not only economically but also strategically (State Economic Commission 1983b, pp. 435–36). All of these characteristics were seen as dictating a centralized form of industrial organization.

Some of the problems the industry faced were largely the result of past government policies. These aspects included the administrative structure and location pattern, the structure of relative prices (particularly the prices of mining products and metals), and the supply system. An underlying basic problem was the geographical separation of mines, smelters, and processing facilities; this problem also stemmed at least in part from past policies and systemic problems. China's nonferrous metals industry seems to have suffered more than most industries from the multiheaded leadership system that evolved after the Cultural Revolution. Even the largest smelters were put under provincial or lower-level jurisdiction, yet their production, input supply, and marketing of output remained under tight central control.

Nonferrous mines faced a different, even worse set of problems, including, most prominently, difficult mining conditions, poor transport, and lack of investment funds. Low prices for ores adversely affected incentives to invest in mine development.[35] Under a more centralized regime it would have been possible, at least in principle, to transfer investment resources from high-profit downstream activities to mines. Under the existing decentralized regime, however, local authorities in charge of smelters as well as the smelters themselves resisted price increases for ores, and other means of transferring investment resources were cumbersome.[36]

Whereas a number of problems in the nonferrous metals industry were long-standing, at least one was new; it did represent the culmination of the trend of administrative decentralization, however. Before 1980, control over foreign trade transactions had remained a monopoly of the Ministry of Foreign Trade, despite decentralization in other spheres of economic activity. With the end of this monopoly, ministries and provinces could export independently and retain part of their foreign exchange earnings for their own use. Because of the value of foreign exchange in an economy characterized by chronic domestic shortages, these organizations had strong incentives to increase exports. The ready marketability of nonferrous metals internationally led to a situation in which organizations at different levels heavily promoted exports in order to earn and retain more foreign exchange. Some of these exports probably were excessive in view of domestic requirements. In a few cases, such as tungsten, competing localities and organizations bid down prices by competing for export markets (see *China Business Review*, March–April 1983, pp. 38–40). Finally, some localities and units may have been forced to import metals and products that were being exported by others. A concrete example of the problems to which administrative decentralization and fragmentation combined with export incentives could lead is the case of the magnesium needed by the Anshan Iron and Steel Company for refractory materials (see chapter 8 of this volume).

The China Nonferrous Metals Industry General Corporation

Recentralization of control over China's nonferrous metals industry was decreed, as was the establishment of the China Nonferrous Metals Industry General Corporation, in April 1983 (State Economic Commission 1983b). More than 100 nonferrous metals enterprises were transferred from local to central control in 1983, and more were expected to be transferred in 1984.

There were to be more than 200 enterprises under the national corporation; these enterprises accounted for 70 percent of total physical output of nonferrous metals, for 71 percent of output value, and for 82 percent of profits (China Economic Yearbook Editorial Committee 1984, p. V-152).

The nucleus of the new corporation as regarded personnel and organization was the Nonferrous Metals Industry Bureau of the Ministry of Metallurgy, which had previously been responsible for the industry. The corporation was established as an independent accounting unit reporting directly to China's State Council. In administrative terms, its rank was nominally equivalent to that of a ministry, and it was responsible for overall planning and centralized leadership of China's nonferrous metals industry and imports and exports. The 30 percent of depreciation funds nonferrous metals enterprises had previously turned over to government financial authorities was now turned over to the headquarters of the national corporation for reinvestment in nonferrous metals. A national tungsten company that was set up under the corporation was to take control of fifteen tungsten enterprises that had previously been transferred by the central government to local jurisdiction. Gold and silver production was subject to a more complicated arrangement. The national gold company was still managed by the Ministry of Metallurgy, but investment funds to develop gold and silver production by the nonferrous metals enterprises that produced them as by-products were given directly to the China Nonferrous Metals Industry General Corporation by the People's Bank of China. Finally, all large and medium-size nonferrous metals enterprises that were established thereafter were to be under the control of the corporation, but local governments that provided investment funds could receive profits in accordance with investment shares.

The ability of the new corporation effectively to centralize administrative control was compromised by at least two important provisions. First, transfers of enterprises from local to central jurisdiction were to be voluntary on the part of both levels of government, and the financial interests of the local governments losing their enterprises were to be safeguarded, leading to protracted negotiations and delays. Second, the corporation was to exercise direct administrative control over only some twenty especially large and important plants. The rest of the centralized enterprises, including the Shenyang Smelter, were to be divorced from local governments as regarded their financial relationships but were to be supervised by newly established regional branch corporations. The exact status of these branch corporations was vague; in some respects they appeared to be provincial-level units and hence may have been responsive to provincial rather than to national priorities, especially because they were formed from and largely staffed from nonferrous metals departments in provincial metallurgy bureaus.

The net effect of these provisions weakening direct central control and of other forms of bureaucratic inertia may have been greater movement toward centralization in the financial sphere than in the nexus of planning, production, and supply. (The financial sphere had been more decentralized than planning, production, and supply under the previous regime.) Perhaps even more important, systemic obstacles to promoting a more efficient industrial structure and a more rational pattern of location may not have been significantly weakened by recentralization. Hence one of the main advantages of administrative centralization, the ability to make large-scale reallocations of resources that have inevitable, detrimental effects on some regions and enterprises, may have been lost.

The functions of regional branch corporations were spelled out in the State Council circular that established the national corporation (State Economic Commission 1983b, p. 437). Twelve branch corporations were set up; although they were named after cities rather than after provinces, their territorial jurisdictions were demarcated along provincial lines. They were to supervise those centralized enterprises located in their areas of jurisdiction that were not directly managed by the national corporation. If deputed by provincial authorities, they could also coordinate the activities of small local nonferrous metals firms that had not been transferred to central control.

The regional branch corporations were given financial incentives in the form of quotas for profits to be turned over to the national corporation; the branch corporations in turn disaggregated these quotas to enterprises. Above-quota profits were divided between the branch corporation and the enterprise, usually 30–70 or 40–60, with the lower share going to the enterprise. Apparently no above-quota profits were turned over to the national corporation. Financial arrangements for the regional branch corporations, however, were provisional and subject to change.

Issues about the institutional nature of the regional corporations had not been settled as of late 1984. The corporations were formally administrative branches of the national corporation, although they had some autonomy and financial incentives; their rank was similar to that of provincial metallurgy bureaus. Because they were formed from and largely staffed from provincial metallurgy bureaus, however, they must have retained informal ties with provincial authorities. The regional branch corporations preferred to be independent, enterprise-type units, since this status would increase their financial autonomy. Most nonferrous metals enterprises, however, apparently preferred the 1984 arrangement. (The Shenyang Smelter itself preferred to be directly managed by the national corporation and to have no relationship with its immediate superior, the Shenyang regional corporation.) The larger enterprises feared that establishing regional branch corporations as economic entities would result in a reduction in their own independence. The attitude of the national corporation was probably ambivalent.

The Shenyang Regional Nonferrous Metals Industry Branch Corporation was formally established only in December 1983, less than a month before the Shenyang Smelter was transferred to its jurisdiction. Its organizational nucleus and 80 percent of its staff came from the unit of the Liaoning Provincial Metallurgy Bureau that previously had been responsible for nonferrous metals. The remaining 20 percent of its staff came from enterprises, about 7 percent from the Shenyang Smelter. The regional corporation had three deputy managers: one was previously director of the Fushun Aluminum Plant, another was a deputy director of the Anshan Iron and Steel Company Economic Research Institute, and the third was the deputy director of the Liaoning Metallurgy Bureau who had been responsible for nonferrous metals. That a general manager had not been chosen by October 1984 probably reflected continuing uncertainty about the corporation's exact position and role.

Transfer of Control over the Shenyang Smelter

It is not surprising that the Shenyang Metallurgy Bureau strongly resisted losing its largest and most profitable enterprise (the Shenyang Smelter accounted for 55 percent of the gross industrial output value and for 60 percent of the profits of the bureau). The Shenyang Municipal Finance Bureau also was concerned about this loss, because the smelter accounted for nearly 13 percent of the municipality's profits from industry. The sharp drop in profits the plant suffered in 1983 aggravated the situation. Arguments about the distribution of the smelter's products were not, however, a significant source of contention.

Apparently, by May 1983 a list of factories to be transferred from local to central control, including the Shenyang Smelter, had been promulgated. A serious dispute about financial aspects, however, held up consummation of the smelter's transfer until the end of the year. The main disagreement concerned the profit base that would be used in adjusting Shenyang Municipality's quota for remittance of revenue to Liaoning Province. Shenyang Municipality naturally wanted to use the 1983 initial enterprise profit-remittance target of Y46.2 million as the base; it would benefit from this because its target would then be adjusted downward by a relatively large amount.[37] The smelter thought that it could remit only Y35.2 million, an estimate that it later lowered to Y29 million, and provincial and national authorities naturally wanted to use one of these lower figures as the base.

The problem was eventually solved partly through the initiative of the smelter itself. It consulted with the Liaoning Metallurgy Bureau, which then went to the national corporation to discuss the matter. The corporation in turn went to the Ministry of Finance. Eventually the ministry decided that Y29 million should be used as the base. Apparently Shenyang Municipality's 1983 revenue target was adjusted downward retroactively to reflect the enterprise's lower profits, and, under this condition, the city readily agreed to use Y29 million as the base. Liaoning Province probably also had an appropriate adjustment made in its target for revenue remittance in relation to the central government. With this adjustment the entire burden of the smelter's 1983 decline in profits effectively was borne by the central government.

Benefits of Recentralization

The transfer of the Shenyang Smelter from the control of the Shenyang Metallurgy Bureau to that of the Shenyang regional corporation and the ending of the plant's administrative and financial relationship with Shenyang Municipality had considerable benefits for the smelter. The Shenyang Metallurgy Bureau had been a poor patron from the smelter's point of view: it made demands, diverted resources from the factory to other enterprises under its jurisdiction, and set excessively high targets. The bureau was unable to provide much help to the plant in the crucial area of supply, and it had no expertise on technical aspects of production. It gave no assistance in the area of marketing, either. Overall, the Shenyang Metallurgy Bureau must have been seen as a superfluous organization, whose interference far outweighed any help it could provide.

Recentralization eliminated one of the "heads" of the multiheaded leadership system and was therefore highly beneficial for the smelter. Any small problems that arose from severing its connection with Shenyang Municipality were minuscule in comparison with the benefits. In this respect the smelter's situation was probably different from that of most other factories, in that they derived concrete benefits from their relationships with local governments.

One of the specific improvements resulting from recentralization was a better situation for the smelter with respect to supply of important construction materials. These materials were the responsibility of Liaoning Province, but they previously had been in part diverted by the Shenyang Metallurgy Bureau to other factories under its jurisdiction. The market for steel, cement, and timber tightened considerably after 1982, but the smelter believed that the situation had been improved by recentralization. It also appears that the conflict between output targets and profit targets was ameliorated, though by no means eliminated, by recentralization. In 1983 the gap between the initial target for profit remittance set by the Shenyang Metallurgy Bureau and what the Shenyang Smelter thought it could achieve was 30 percent. In 1984 the gap between the initial target set by the Shenyang regional corporation and what the smelter thought it could reach was only 15 percent, and, moreover, the plant did not ask for a revision of the target; this suggests that the putative 15 percent gap was to a large extent related to bargaining. In 1983, by contrast, the real gap had been larger than 30 percent because the smelter fell short of its own initial predictions.

New and Continuing Problems

The main unanswered question about recentralization in 1984 concerned the role of the Shenyang regional corporation. The smelter increasingly viewed the corporation as an obstacle similar to what the Shenyang Metallurgy Bureau had been in the past. There were important matters with which the smelter could deal only by going directly to the national corporation, such as the transfer of extra supplies of blister from a plant in Hebei and the acquisition of imported raw materials. Moreover, the Shenyang regional corporation forced the smelter, in one case, to buy lead that it did not need from a small local mine, and as a result the smelter had to refuse shipments from suppliers designated in the central plan.[38] Such responsiveness to the needs of small mines illustrated the problems an economically independent regional corporation with considerable decision-making authority might cause for the national corporation as well as for the smelter itself.

The problematic situation of the regional branch corporations in China's nonferrous metals industry has broader implications for the structure and role of corporations in Chinese industry as a whole. In the mid-1980s it was stressed that regional branch corporations should be true economic entities rather than administrative agencies that differed only in name from industrial bureaus. Enterprises may well have preferred the supervision of a relatively weak administrative bureau, however, to that of a more powerful business corporation oriented toward increasing its own profits. Some economically independent corporations used their supervisory relation with firms to levy fees unrelated to any services provided to those firms. Thus the financial position and role of corporations could adversely affect the autonomy and incentives of enterprises.

Certain concrete problems emerged from the estrangement of the smelter from Shenyang Municipality, but these were probably small in relation to the benefits of the separation. The most important problem was more careful monitoring of the plant's pollution by local authorities and the imposition of progressively larger pollution charges. In 1980–82 the smelter paid no fees for waste water. In 1983 a fee of Y5 million was levied; the fee was increased to Y6.2 million in 1984. Eighty percent of these charges was still returned to the factory for investment in pollution control projects. The smelter also faced greater difficulties in obtaining locally controlled building materials and other supplies. In some cases price increases were imposed, and some prices may have been higher than those paid by other customers. For example, the local price for a roof tile made of refractory materials was Y6.7, but the smelter was forced to pay Y8. In most cases, however, tighter supplies and price increases reflected general market trends that would have been experienced even in the absence of recentralization.

The creation of the China Nonferrous Metals Industry General Corporation and the recentralization of control over the smelter did not resolve the smelter's fundamental problems despite undoubted improvements. There was no significant effect on the location issue. Irrationalities in the supply system remained, and it is not clear to what extent the allocation of investment funds was improved. Difficult questions regarding production of alloys were not addressed. The chaotic market for scrap copper and the inefficient recycling of scrap by small enterprises seem to have been unaffected by the recentralization.

Broader Issues

In the Chinese nonferrous metals industry as a whole, a number of issues arose from the 1983 recentralization. The multiheaded leadership system was the result of differing degrees of administrative decentralization in different spheres of operations. It is therefore not surprising that the 1983 organizational reforms involved differing degrees of recentralization. Recentralization in the financial sphere, that is, control over profit remittances, was greater than it was in other spheres, such as the supply of raw materials. Whereas large and medium-size enterprises came to hand over their profits to the central government, mostly through the regional branch corporations, there appears to have been no change in the supply of raw materials, since ores from larger mines had been centrally allocated all along. Nor did recentralization affect distribution and utilization of scrap copper. To a large extent, uneven recentralization merely redressed the earlier imbalance, in which financial control had been quite decentralized but production and supply had remained under central control.

One problem area was supplies of raw materials outside the plan. Financial recentralization decreased the financial stake of provinces in the nonferrous metals industry; this change harmed incentives for them and for lower levels of government to arrange supplies of ores to large smelters. Because ores from small mines accounted for one-fourth of China's total output of nonferrous metals ores, this was a severe problem. Prices of ores were much lower than those of pure metals, so small mines were generally willing to supply ore to smelters only if the mines or their local governments had control over the output generated. A similar pattern was emerging in the arranging of supplies of scrap copper. The rigidity of barter and of processing arrangements certainly hindered flexible adjustment of supply to demand. The position of the local organizations that maintained de facto control over the allocation of scrap copper was strengthened, which went against the intent of recentralization.

The role of regional branch corporations was problematic, as was already mentioned. The most important question was to whom would these corporations respond: to the provinces in which they were located or to the China Nonferrous Metals Industry General Corporation in Beijing. Another issue was the degree of control the corporations would exercise over enterprises. A related question concerned the extent to which the national corporation gained the ability through recentralization to make necessary adjustments in prices, to redistribute resources between mines and smelters, to shut down plants where appropriate, and so forth. The national corporation was not able to act much in these crucial areas; one of the main advantages of centralization was thus lost. The corporation's capability to do coordinated long-term planning for the nonferrous metals subsector also was in question.

A final set of questions concerned aspects which were largely out of the control of the national corporation and of enterprises. Production of alloys was the most obvious issue. It was irrational to prohibit smelters from producing alloys, but users had to be assured that they would receive timely supplies of alloys of appropriate specifications before they would give up their own production, and even then they might not do so voluntarily. Something also needed to be done about the distribution and inefficient recycling of scrap copper. A way had to be found to ensure that scrap was reprocessed at highest efficiency by larger smelters with good quality control. If small scrap reprocessors were ordered to close down and if copper scrap were ordered to be delivered to a specified government organization, however, supplies of scrap copper would probably dry up.

General Observations

This section distills some general conclusions based on the experience of the Shenyang Smelter. It starts with an evaluation of the smelter's performance, first in narrow technical and financial terms, taking as a given the limitations on the smelter's freedom of action. Then the discussion turns to industrywide considerations, in particular to the efficiency of the administrative structure and the pattern of location in China's nonferrous metals industry as a whole. Finally, some tentative comments applicable to Chinese state-owned industry in general are put forward.

The Shenyang Smelter's Performance

As is discussed in "Response to Problems," in this chapter, the smelter made great efforts to reduce energy consumption, raise quality standards, recover more by-products from ores, increase profits, and reduce pollution. Measured performance (changes in production costs, profits, input consumption, and so forth) did not fairly reflect these measures, as can be seen in table 5.8. Unit production costs for copper and zinc reached peaks in 1982, whereas 1982 lead production costs were only five percent below those of 1975. The average rate of profit on sales declined in 1976–78, then rose sharply in 1979–80, and finally fell again somewhat in 1981–82; the net result was a modest rise of one percentage point between 1975 and 1982. There was undoubtedly a severe drop in profitability and a rise in costs in 1983.

Material input consumption and electricity usage per unit of output show only modest declines amid considerable year-to-year variation. Lead wastage in smelting (that is, loss of recoverable metal during the smelting process) declined from 9.0 percent in 1975 to 5.5 percent in 1982; for zinc the drop was from 5.5 percent to 3.7 percent; and for copper it was from 3.3 percent to 2.9 percent. Compared with the national average loss rate for large nonferrous metals enterprises in 1982, the smelter's loss rate was somewhat lower for zinc, exactly the same for copper, and slightly higher for lead (State Statistical Bureau 1983, p. 281). Electricity consumption in copper production (electrolysis) fell unevenly, that for lead declined more steadily, and for zinc production it stayed about the same.

There were a number of reasons for the smelter's superficially poor performance in lowering production costs. First, wage costs rose considerably after 1977; average income per worker increased at an average annual rate of 6.1 percent in 1977–82. This increase in average wages was fully translated into unit wage costs, because real gross output value per worker was almost the same in 1982 as in 1975.[39] More important, prices of many material inputs the smelter used rose substantially, although no figures are available on the effect on costs. The main reason for less than dramatic improvements in indicators of efficiency was simply the restricted, deteriorating environment in which the Shenyang Smelter had to function. In certain spheres, reform implementation was minimal, further limiting the smelter's options. As a mature enterprise, the plant had less potential for making efficiency improvements by moving along the learning curve and for expanding output with declining marginal costs.

An example of how the operating environment adversely affected the enterprise's performance despite the smelter's best efforts is the plant's energy consumption in the first eight months of 1983. Average energy consumption rose from 2.94 tons of standard coal-equivalent (7,000 kilocalories of heat content per ton) for each Y10,000 of gross industrial output value generated in the first eight months of 1982 to 3.43 tons in the same period in 1983. This increase of 16.7 percent is more than explained, however, by various external factors, according to the smelter's calculations. These factors included (1) a rise in the share of concentrated copper ore (which required energy-intensive smelting) in total raw material supplies (this contributed an increase of 0.1 tons per Y10,000 of energy consumed); (2) the use of more adulterated scrap, which required longer refining to eliminate impurities (0.054 tons per Y10,000); (3) an overall shortage of raw materials, which caused stoppages and waste of energy at the furnaces (0.052 tons per Y10,000); (4) a deterioration in the quality of concentrated copper and lead ores received, which required more energy in smelting (0.033 tons per Y10,000); (5) the full burning of flue gas from the more adulterated ores, which required more energy (0.092 tons per Y10,000); and (6) an increase in energy consumption because of expansion by subordinate collective enterprises (0.189 tons per Y10,000). (It is debatable whether this last factor should be considered as having been out of the enterprise's control.) The combined effect of these factors as calculated by the smelter was slightly greater than the actual increase in energy consumption, which implies that the smelter had somewhat improved the technical efficiency of energy utiliza-

Table 5.8. Shenyang Smelter's Indicators of Efficiency, 1975–82

Indicator	1975	1976	1977	1978	1979	1980	1981	1982
Production costs (yuan per ton)								
Copper[a]	4,722	4,729	4,827	4,768	4,170	4,792	4,811	4,836
Lead[a]	1,886	1,899	1,925	1,882	1,852	1,884	1,829	1,793
Zinc	1,531	1,575	1,571	1,528	1,478	1,589	1,569	1,652
Loss of metal content in production (percent)[b]								
Copper	3.3	3.2	3.2	3.0	3.0	3.0	2.9	2.9
Lead	9.0	8.6	9.3	6.8	5.9	5.8	5.7	5.5
Zinc	5.5	5.5	5.5	4.3	4.1	3.9	3.8	3.7
Unit electricity consumption (kilowatt-hours per ton)[c]								
Electrolytic copper	259	260	259	251	257	269	265	224
Electrolytic lead	193	195	206	191	183	174	152	145
Electrolytic zinc	3,715	3,793	3,879	3,680	3,650	3,670	3,680	3,733
Labor productivity (yuan)[d]								
Gross output value per employee (in current prices)	—	77,239	69,304	80,448	86,161	106,002	108,256	101,092
Net output value per employee (in current prices)	—	11,218	9,104	10,819	13,408	15,494	14,977	13,870
Gross output value per employee (in 1970 constant prices)	77,733	77,239	65,242	75,966	80,537	88,547	83,566	78,061

Capital productivity (percent)ᵉ								
Gross value of output at current prices/original value of fixed assets	—	414.4	310.0	316.9	345.1	389.3	399.5	385.0
Gross value of output at constant prices/original value of fixed assets	423.9	414.4	291.8	299.3	322.6	325.2	308.4	297.3
Circulating capital/sales	29.4	24.6	25.3	20.8	23.9	25.8	21.1	18.6
Financial indicators (percent)ᶠ								
Profit rate on sales	7.4	6.9	5.8	4.0	8.7	9.9	9.5	8.4
Tax rate on sales	6.5	6.3	6.5	6.1	6.0	5.7	5.7	5.7
Profit rate on fixed assets	29.6	27.7	16.4	11.7	27.6	31.3	31.0	28.3

— Not available.

a. Data are unit costs for producing metal from concentrated ore (including prices paid for concentrates).

b. Data are ratios of final metal output to total metal content of raw materials, minus one and converted to percentages. Corresponding figures in national statistical publications indicate that data refer to the loss rate in coversion of unrefined metal (or of blister, in the case of copper) to pure metal, rather than to losses in smelting ores, which can be substantial (see State Statistical Bureau 1983, p. 281).

c. It is not clear whether these figures refer only to electricity consumption in electrolysis. In any case, they do not include electricity consumption in mining or concentrating ores.

d. Data are the total number of state employees. If collective workers in "mixed" positions were included, the productivity figures would be somewhat lower.

e. Constant-price gross value of output figures are at 1970 prices. Fixed assets are value at original purchase price, without adjustment for depreciation or revaluation. Figures for circulating capital are total "quota" circulating assets.

f. Profit figures are for administrative profits; tax figures are for indirect taxes only.

Source: Information provided by the smelter.

tion. The precise methodology and quantitative results of this exercise can be questioned, however.

In view of the difficult and deteriorating situation the Shenyang Smelter faced, a tentative evaluation—based more on qualitative impressions than on quantitative evidence—of its performance and certainly of its efforts to improve efficiency would be positive. Such an assessment is based on the given external environment and the smelter's lack of freedom of action and ignores possibilities for improving industrywide efficiency through more radical changes. It should also be noted that the smelter did not strive to meet the needs of customers; this was only to be expected because most of its products were in chronic short supply. The smelter's actions appear to have been motivated by a desire to increase profits and to maintain a good reputation with government authorities.

Industrywide Considerations

It is paradoxical but nevertheless probable that the Shenyang Smelter's attempts to improve efficiency at the micro level may actually have hindered efforts to improve industrywide performance. A fundamental solution to the smelter's problems required drastic measures involving relocation to a better site elsewhere in China or perhaps more reliance on imports. The smelter's good performance improved its standing and reputation and might have made it more difficult for authorities to contemplate taking any drastic action.

In China relatively advanced and rapidly growing firms commonly have been held back from fully exploiting their potential because of protection of backward enterprises. The case of the Shenyang Smelter is somewhat different; it was an enterprise that did well, considering its limited resources and restricted environment. A careful analysis from the national perspective might well conclude, however, that the smelter's production should be phased out and replaced by increased production elsewhere in China (or by imports, particularly in the case of copper). Because of the difficulties in closing down even inefficient, poorly managed, and small state-owned industrial enterprises in China, the prospects for such action or even for a careful consideration of the alternatives in the case of the smelter were bleak. The smelter was highly profitable in purely financial terms as a result of the distorted structure of relative prices, making it even more difficult to consider drastic solutions.

In principle, administrative centralization should have made it easier to implement drastic changes in industrial structure and location patterns, including, if necessary, shutting down or moving large enterprises. In practice this seems not to have been the case. The central government's inability to relocate the Fushun Aluminum Plant, the energy consumption problems of which were much more serious than were those of the Shenyang Smelter, suggests that recentralization had not really changed the situation (see "Response to Problems," in this chapter). It is particularly striking that, in this case, provincial authorities advocated what was probably the appropriate course of action—relocation—and the central government refused to go along.

The Choice between Imports and Domestic Production

The China Nonferrous Metals Industry General Corporation could have played an important role in evaluating the relative economic costs and benefits of importing nonferrous metals compared with continuing or expanding domestic production. The choice between importing and domestic production tended, however, to be ad hoc, haphazard, and based primarily on short-run pressures, on local interests, on distorted measures of financial profitability, and, in some cases, on strong incentives for and biases toward exporting. Central authority appears to have been relatively weak and largely unable to offset distortions through administrative intervention. As a result, some obvious irrationalities in foreign trade patterns and practices for nonferrous metals emerged.

Drastic changes in foreign trade patterns, particularly importing rather than producing domestically, would have required significant adjustments in production structure. The national corporation appears to have been unable to contemplate changes of this magnitude. The same was true of the possible consequences of foreign trade decisions for China's energy situation. As is mentioned in "Response to Problems," in this chapter, importation of electricity-intensive products, such as aluminum, is a means of importing cheap electricity indirectly. The corporation may not have considered these options, or it may have been overwhelmed by parochial concerns, such as the need to maintain employment in the industry.

Implementing Reforms in the Face of Chronic Shortages

Implementation of reforms at the Shenyang Smelter lagged far behind implementation in certain other enterprises, although the plant appears on the whole to have been about average in this respect in relation to Chinese state-owned industry as a whole. There were a number of reasons for the slow progress of reform implementation, some of them specific to particular areas of operations. The economic and strategic importance of the plant's main products, however, and the fact that they were in chronic short supply undoubtedly were important factors.

Because of shortages, government authorities had no reason to relinquish their control over the distribution of output and to allow direct marketing. On the contrary, the perceived need for rationing to ensure that available supplies were allocated to high-priority users reinforced the tendency not to release control. The contrast of this situation with one of excess supply is striking. (Commercial departments were only too happy to put the burden of responsibility for sales on enterprises as means of dealing with a weak market and stemming the rise in their own inventories.)

Material supply authorities forced the Shenyang Smelter to market directly certain by-products that were in excess supply; this was particularly damaging because the plant had virtually no control over the amounts of these it produced. By-products that were in short supply, however, were generally tightly controlled. Sulfuric acid was the only major exception, for several possible reasons. Sulfuric acid is a chemical, so it fell in a different category from the smelter's other products. Production of it was developed comparatively late in the plant's history, when the central plan's control might have been relatively weak and the role of Liaoning Province, which allocated part of the enterprise's output of sulfuric acid, stronger.

Aside from the difficulties of implementing reforms amid chronic shortages, the effectiveness of reforms, once implemented, is also questionable under such circumstances. Even with substantial direct marketing by enterprises, the incentives for producers to respond to customer needs are minimal, because the producers can always sell the goods concerned without any trouble. Certainly the Shenyang Smelter was not oriented toward responding to nonquantitative aspects of demand, although this was in part because it produced rather homogeneous products. In a situation of excess supply or of rough market equilibrium, however, producers may respond strongly to customer needs even if the share of direct marketing in total sales is relatively small.

Incentives for Backward Integration

This case study provides some interesting examples of how chronic shortages generate tendencies toward backward integration; these tendencies can be strengthened or weakened by administrative demarcation of enterprises, goods, and activities. A fundamental solution to the problem, however, requires eliminating the shortage itself; once this has been done, incentives for backward integration become weaker and administrative distinctions less important.

Production of alloys is a clear case of backward integration by users; such backward integration may have been rational if suppliers (smelters) could not be relied on to meet user specifications exactly and in a timely manner, a common problem in chronic shortage situations. A pure metal could be held to a simple yardstick to ensure quality, whereas ensuring quality would be difficult and complicated in the case of a customized alloy. Backward integration by users was legitimized and entrenched by administrative demarcation of products, which assigned production of alloys to users and allowed smelters to produce only pure metals. The relative price structure made independent production of alloys highly profitable, even though this activity must have added little economic value, as smelters could do the same job at minimal extra cost. Users strove to hold on to their alloy production activities, and the end result was that even firms willing and able to meet exacting user specifications were prevented from producing alloys. The adverse effects of these artificial barriers to entry are obvious.

The opposite extreme from backward integration is administrative separation of upstream activities, for example, the transfer of the magnesium mines away from the control of the Anshan Iron and Steel Company (see chapter 8 of this volume). This case also illustrates the harmful effect of biased incentives to export. Anshan would certainly have been better off if it had been allowed to retain its control over the magnesium mines; such a situation might also have been better than establishment of administratively separate magnesium mines from a national perspective, provided that the magnesium products could still be exported as an alternative to their captive use by Anshan. The best approach, however, would involve decontrol of prices and liberalization of the exchange rate system to the point at which tradeoffs between domestic sales and exports reflect underlying economic conditions.

Problematic Aspects of Upgrading Existing Enterprises

The Shenyang Smelter's experience raises questions about the wisdom of following an indiscriminate policy of technical renovation in existing enterprises, as opposed to building entirely new production facilities. It is widely assumed that upgrading existing enterprises is more economically efficient than is building new plants, and this is often true. A crucial prerequisite for this assumption to hold is that the enterprise receiving the new investment and technology should be in a fundamentally sound position with respect to location, scale, material supplies, energy, and so forth. If the enterprise is not in such a position, upgrading may be counterproductive, and economic costs (including those of externalities, such as pollution) may be far higher than would be those of shutting down the existing facilities and building entirely new ones.

In the case of the smelter, it appears to have been recognized that significant new investments to increase capacity at the existing site would not be appropriate. So the real question concerned smaller investments to conserve energy, to reduce pollution, to increase recovery of by-products from ores, and to modernize technology. The aggregate value of investment at the smelter in the late 1970s and early 1980s was substantial, as can be seen in table 5.6. Thus, in planning ahead over the medium term (five to ten years), the choice between building new facilities and upgrading existing facilities was relevant.

The systemic obstacles to making drastic changes in existing large and medium-size firms in China made initial decisions about setting up new enterprises all the more crucial. If a factory could not be moved or closed, it was essential that it be well sited. The best initial choices might, however, have become inappropriate after a long time. The Shenyang Smelter and even the Fushun Aluminum Plant might well have been optimally located when they were first set up (fifty-odd years ago in the case of the smelter), but their locations were clearly no longer optimal in the 1980s. The initial investment in the smelter was relatively small. Over the years, however, building up capacity at the same location became counterproductive. Thus upgrading and expansion of existing enterprises often may be less preferable than starting from scratch and building entirely new facilities.

Limitations of Organizational Reshuffling

In any process of organizational reform, there is the danger that it will degenerate into mere reshuffling of organizations and their titles and will bring little in the way of real change. It is also possible that organizational reform will leave the relation between government agencies and the enterprises they supervise largely unchanged. This second problem seems to have been avoided in the case of the Shenyang Smelter: removing the Shenyang Metallurgy Bureau as its immediate superior undoubtedly was an important and beneficial change.

There were signs, however, that some organizational changes involved mere reshuffling. The China Nonferrous Metals Industry General Corporation was formed from the old bureau in charge of nonferrous metals in the Ministry of Metallurgy. Similarly, the regional branch corporations were formed largely from parts of provincial metallurgy bureaus. Under these circumstances, old organizational and personal ties probably hindered the adoption of new and independent roles by these new agencies. The continuing need of enterprises to rely on provinces and lower levels of government for significant portions of material supplies might have reinforced this tendency, especially at the regional level.

More generally, a strong organization is required to implement needed changes in China's nonferrous metals industry. To close down or relocate large enterprises in a socialist economy, considerable administrative clout and a willingness to use it are necessary. (This is even true in some of the industrial market economies that have successfully adjusted their industrial structures in response to changing circumstances, such as Korea and Japan.) Although the Chinese government's original intention may have been to create a new national corporation that would be strong enough to carry out drastic changes, the corporation turned out to be weak in practice.

In any case, administrative centralization alone cannot solve the fundamental problems China's nonferrous metals industry faces. The ideal administrative organizational form has yet to be designed; it is a chimera. None can escape the deficiencies in information and incentives that occur when government agencies direct industrial production.

Table 5.9. Performance of the Shenyang Smelter, 1982 and 1985
(millions of yuan, unless otherwise specified)

Indicator	1982	1985
Gross value of industrial output (current prices)	684.39	813.63
Net value of industrial output (current prices)	93.90	112.75
Output of copper (tons)	48,654	56,574
Output of lead (tons)	57,255	51,489
Output of zinc (tons)	17,235	19,521
Total employment at year end (persons)	6,507[a]	8,127[b]
Gross value of fixed assets[c]	177.77	209.58
Net value of fixed assets[d]	71.74	78.83
Value of quota circulating assets	112.21	169.46
Total profits and taxes	84.56	74.67
Profits before tax	50.35	48.00

a. Average employment for the year, not including apprentices, persons on long-term sick leave and on study leave, and those engaged in agricultural production. These adjustments were made in order to render the 1982 figure and 1985 figure more closely comparable.

b. Regular and permanent contract employees only.

c. Valued at original purchase prices.

d. After depreciation.

Source: Information provided by the smelter.

Later Developments

Much is known about developments at the Shenyang Smelter after 1983, although gaps in knowledge remain. New perspectives on the smelter's various supervisory agencies also have emerged.

Stagnant Performance and Continuing Difficulties

In the mid-1980s the smelter continued to stagnate at the level of production it had reached in the late 1970s. As can be seen in table 5.9, physical output of copper, lead, and zinc stayed within the range established earlier, with no significant rising or falling trend. The 19 percent increase in nominal gross industrial output value between 1982 and 1985 may in part reflect increases in output prices and in part increased output of by-products. There was a 12 percent decline in total profits and taxes between 1982 and 1985, most of which was accounted for by indirect taxes. Indirect tax payments by the smelter declined from more than Y34 million in 1982 to about Y28 million in 1985–86.[40] The smelter's profits fell precipitously in 1983 but rebounded in 1984–85. The recovery of profits after 1983 was striking: they totaled Y50.35 million in 1982, Y29.2 million in 1983, Y38 million in 1984, Y48 million in 1985, and Y58.2 million in 1986. Figures on assets reveal substantial gross and net investment between 1982 and 1985. The 25 percent rise in employment between 1982 and 1985 shown in the table may be a statistical artifact, reflecting different definitions used in the two years. Otherwise it suggests that the enterprise created substantial new employment, at the expense of labor productivity and financial performance.

The Shenyang Smelter made little progress toward solving its most severe problems in the mid-1980s. The enterprise still believed it faced virtually insurmountable difficulties, exacerbated (even, in some cases, created) by the new superstructure of industrial administration. Thus its overall strategy, a defensive one of day-to-day survival and marginal improvements, most probably remained unchanged. The smelter continued to face severe problems in investment financing. It believed that it was being given low priority in national plans, because it had no key project in either the Sixth or the Seventh Five-Year Plan. Starting in 1987, the smelter, like other state enterprises, was permitted to retain all of its depreciation funds; this must have provided some help with regard to investment financing.

The cost of the lead smelting renovation project, which had earlier been a source of problems (see "Main Problems," in this chapter), apparently had further escalated from less than Y20 million as of 1984 to Y80 million by the time the project was completed. This project had become a big money-loser; more than Y40 million in loans financing it was still outstanding as of 1987. Undoubtedly, the cost escalated in part because of the expanded scope of the project, but this in turn consisted in part of necessary facilities that the original project design had neglected to include.

Mandatory planning has continued to account for more than 90 percent of the smelter's output, and price controls have remained tight. In the inflationary environment of 1987–88 some modest adjustments were made in state plan prices by setting higher temporary prices. The price of copper was raised by 20 percent (from Y5,500 a ton to Y6,600 a ton) on June 15, 1988.[41] It was specified, however, that the controlled price of concentrated copper ore was to be increased disproportionately, so the measure provided more relief to mines than it did to smelters. Moreover, the Shenyang Smelter had already been allowed to charge a higher price of Y6,050 a ton (10 percent more than the state price) because of its silver medal, and it is not clear whether it was subsequently allowed to charge a price 10 percent more than the new temporary price.

Management continued to complain about the plant's low rate of profit retention. On the surface at least this complaint would appear unwarranted. The base profit quota of Y29.66 million was set according to actual profits in 1983. The enterprise was allowed to retain 13.02 percent of base profits, after paying profit tax at the rate of 55 percent and an additional adjustment tax of nearly 32 percent. (Apparently another 6.68 percent of within-quota profits, representing bonuses that had previously been charged to production costs, was separately retained by the enterprise.) For profits above the quota, the 55 percent profit tax was still paid, but 70 percent of the adjustment tax was kept by the enterprise and only 30 percent of it paid to the government. In other words, the marginal profit retention rate reached about 35.4 percent. This was a considerable improvement over past rates of profit retention, but it is not clear whether and to what extent the 1983 base was progressively raised over time. (In principle it was to remain constant until 1990.)

The smelter continued to be prevented from engaging in large-scale production of alloys. In fact, there appears to have been some deterioration in that situation after 1984. The state plan still required delivery of pure metals; although the smelter was free to produce alloys outside the plan, it has not done so because of the small amounts of above-plan output and the large share of such output it exchanges for raw materials in various ways. The smelter hoped to attack the alloy problem through its new "enterprise group" (to be discussed later) but has achieved no success.

Management criticized the system of enterprise ranks and state prizes for superior quality. It was thought that part of the reason for the Shenyang Smelter's inadequate administrative authority was its administrative rank, which was lower than those of some other large enterprises. Rather than suggesting that the smelter be promoted to higher rank, management recommended that the whole system of ranks for state enterprises be abolished. It criticized state prizes for quality on the ground that they distorted incentives and required a great deal of unnecessary work for the plant to maintain eligibility for the awards after they were won. Management contended that the awards also affected the thinking of managers, who may have believed that as long as the enterprise won quality prizes everything was fine. In management's view the awards improved the reputation of the enterprise director, but this was an insufficient justification for the awards. Hence management strongly recommended that state quality prizes be abolished.

Subordinate Collective Enterprises

The basic situation of the Shenyang Smelter's collective employees and firms remained unchanged. There were still large numbers of collective workers in state work units who could not be shifted to the status of state workers but who also could not be terminated because of their technical skills and their importance on the production line. Thus, unlike the Anshan Iron and Steel Company (see chapter 8 in this volume), the Shenyang Smelter was making no progress toward separating out collective workers. The continued mixing of state and collective workers did not appear to be generating any problems, however. Collective workers were put into a special category, long-term workers outside the plan, and they received essentially the same benefits as did state workers. The workers themselves did not seem to care about the difference in status, and many of them were not even aware of their own status. Thus, in the absence of renewed demands from the authorities for an imposed solution to the situation, there was no real problem.

The smelter claimed that the performance of the subordinate collective enterprises had improved somewhat, although no evidence is available to back up this claim. Perhaps more interestingly, the relative fortunes of the two collective corporations had become reversed. In the mid-1980s the Repair and Construction Services Company found itself in bad shape financially, but the Labor Services Company was doing better than it had been. The declining volume of investment in renovation at the smelter was the proximate cause of the Repair and Construction Services Company's business and financial problems. Inadequate and probably overspecialized technical capabilities made diversification a difficult task for the company. The Labor Services Company, on the contrary, had improved incentives for work units and had a more stable demand for its services from within the enterprise, as well as from outside.

A poignant story illustrates the problems of the subordinate collectives. In October 1984 the Shenyang Smelter had arranged for the combining of the Labor Services Company with two small local factories, one that produced transformers and another that produced fiberglass. Both of these factories were collective firms; one was under the control of Shenyang Municipality and the other was under the control of the local district. The two factories had been operating at a loss and had a combined debt of Y700,000, which the Labor Services Company undertook to repay over a four-year period. The Labor Services Company was also to invest Y300,000 in the factories and provide equipment and technical personnel. The main objective of the combination was to provide employment for 400 children of smelter workers. In the heady proreform atmosphere of that time (just as the Third Plenum of the Twelfth Communist Party Central Committee was meeting and issuing its important declaration on urban economic reforms), the combination was speedily approved by municipal authorities with a minimum of red tape.

This haste may have been ill considered. Although the investment cost per job created (about Y2,500, including repayment of debts but not including the value of equipment provided gratis by the Labor Services Company) superficially appeared relatively low, the original lines of business of the two factories were unviable and hence shifts to new products were needed, all of which made the venture highly risky for the company. The transformer factory appears to have run into trouble fairly soon after the combination. In 1987 it was leased to three individuals as a desperate measure to stem continuing losses. The source of the factory's problems was not clear, but it was saddled from the start with obsolete equipment and aged workers from the original collective enterprise.[42]

The leasing of the transformer factory was part of a general trend of increased managerial incentives and incentives for work units at the Labor Services Company and the construction company. The mechanisms used to establish these incentives included economic responsibility systems for construction projects; management contracts for some service entities, such as an underground restaurant; leasing schemes; and possibly also sale of certain productive assets to individuals. These mechanisms were meant to improve financial performance and reduce the dependence of the collective companies on the smelter. They seem to have achieved some success, although the collectives remain dependent on the smelter, and it is not clear how redundancy of labor is dealt with in the new arrangement.

The Enterprise Group

One significant new event since 1983 was the formation of a large enterprise group under the Shenyang Smelter's leadership.[43] The Northern Nonferrous Metals and Gold Associated Group was formed on October 15, 1986. It consisted of twenty-eight enterprises, including the Shenyang Smelter, Shenyang Cable Plant, Shenyang Nonferrous Metals Processing Plant, Fushun Aluminum Plant, and Hongtou Copper Mine. The group encompassed eight provinces (from Liaoning to Jiangsu) and five industries: nonferrous metals, nonferrous metals processing, cables and wires, chemicals, and gold.

The goals of establishing the new entity, from the perspective of the smelter, were the following:

1. To integrate the fragmented vertical stages of production for nonferrous metals in a loosely coordinated framework
2. To improve the allocation of funds for production, and to compensate for the smelter's shortage of funds and lack of land for development
3. To solve the problems of chaotic procurement, bidding up of prices, and inefficient processing of scrap copper.

The group was sponsored by a large enterprise (the smelter), but its other members included some firms that were at least equal to the smelter in size and status. This was an unusual feature; it created a structure and a dynamic very different from those of the typical group consisting of one main firm and a number of smaller, clearly subordinate units. The Northern Nonferrous Metals and Gold Associated Group hence necessarily involved a very loose association, under whose auspices most enterprises included only a small proportion of their activities.

The formal structure of the group was relatively simple. Each of the twenty-eight participating firms had one representative on the board of directors, which was to meet twice a year. Voting was by show of hands. The director of the Shenyang Smelter served as chairman of the board, but the post of deputy chairman remained vacant for at least eight months because of the inability to choose among the leaders of the other large and powerful enterprises involved. Each functional unit in the smelter also served as the corresponding unit in the group and carried a second title for this purpose.

The basic problems of the group have been its lack of administrative authority and lack of control over funds and goods, according to smelter representatives. When the group was registered, the capital of the smelter stood for the capital of the enterprise group as a whole; no other enterprise put in any capital directly. Since the membership of the group spanned a number of provinces and localities, and since China's banking system is divided into territorial branches, it was difficult for the group to obtain bank loans. Moreover, the requirement set by banks that 30 percent of the cost of a project to be financed by a loan must be covered by the loan applicant itself was difficult to meet because of the group's paucity of funds. Much to the Shenyang Smelter's disappointment, the group was not given an independent status under China's state plan, so the enterprises participating in it still had to meet all of their plan targets as separate units. The amounts of goods produced and traded outside the plan that the group conceivably could allocate were minuscule.

One example of the problems the group faced with the planning system was the mandated flow of copper from Yunnan Province to the Shenyang Cable Factory and from the Shenyang Smelter to the Northeast Light Alloy Processing Factory in Heilongjiang. In 1985 the Shenyang Cable Factory consumed 24,000 tons of copper, a mere 240 tons of which came directly from the smelter, whereas 9,800 tons of copper was transported to the factory over a very long distance from Yunnan Province in southwest China. This was the kind of irrationality that the new group hoped to dispense with, but nothing could be done about it as long as allocation of intermediate goods in the production chain was subject to control by the planning system.[44] Hence the smelter's plea for independent status for its enterprise group under the state plan, with input allocations and planned delivery requirements only at the two ends of the production chain, is understandable.

A second set of problems that the group faced related to taxation. The local governments in charge of the firms participating in the group strove to avoid any loss of local tax revenues on account of group activities. (Corporate profit tax as well as indirect taxes are collected by localities and often figure in their schemes for retention of revenue.) The fragmentation of the tax system has been one of the most important obstacles to the development of cross-locality enterprise groups. Although their concerns about revenue losses may have been justified, the result of local governments' attitudes and defensive measures has been an environment inimical to new activities or to rationalization of activities among a set of enterprises. Moreover, localities tend to make exorbitant demands when an enterprise group wants to take over a local firm; this discourages the evolution of closer links within a group.

A third, related problem of the group has been the difficulty of starting initiatives in an atmosphere in which bargaining over division of benefits is the primary concern of its participants. The enterprises other than the Shenyang Smelter seem to have striven primarily to achieve short-run gains and to minimize their own costs and contributions of materials. This situation made for a system dominated by caution and consensus-building, as a result of which many profit opportunities must have been lost.

Still another problem cited by the smelter was that its group had no supervisory agency or "mother-in-law." The Shenyang Regional Nonferrous Metals Industry Branch Corporation opposed the establishment of the smelter's enterprise group, most likely because it saw the new group as a rival that might usurp its own position as a coordinating body. The national nonferrous metals corporation, though generally supportive, did not in any way directly sponsor the group. Thus there was no government agency willing to help the group get past the numerous administrative hurdles it inevitably faced. The smelter believed that independent status for the group under the state plan would resolve this problem, because the group would then directly answer to the State Planning Commission.

Overall, the Shenyang Smelter's enterprise group has not made much progress in fulfilling the high hopes that led to its creation. The group's experience provides an interesting case study of how even a significant innovation can be stymied by an existing fragmented administrative and fiscal system and by mandatory planning and government demarcation of responsibility for different stages of production. There was, however, one area in which the group seems to have been effective, the reform of scrap copper procurement.

Changes in Scrap Copper Procurement

The most important venture of the Shenyang Smelter's enterprise group was the Revival Metallurgical Associated Corporation. The corporation was set up under the auspices of the group, of various material supply bureaus, and of commercial departments (including rural supply and marketing corporations). The basic objectives of the new entity were to monopsonize the procurement of scrap copper, which had been subject to conflicts and bidding wars among various agencies (see "Main Problems," in this chapter), and to rationalize the processing of scrap copper, which had increasingly been diverted to small rural collective enterprises that wasted large amounts of energy and recoverable metal. A related objective was to utilize fully the smelter's capacity for processing scrap into electrolytic copper. (As is noted in "Response to Problems," in this chapter, the smelter had considerably higher capacity for production of copper from blister or scrap than it did for smelting concentrated copper ore.)

The main sources of profits for the new corporation were envisioned to be (1) savings in consumption of input (scrap copper) relative to norms and relative to the consumption of other processors, because of the Shenyang Smelter's greater production efficiency, and (2) extra profits from downstream fabricating of recycled copper scrap into various products. In 1987 the corporation was to produce 15,000 tons of copper recycled from scrap, and it was hoped that in 1988 production would rise to 20,000 to 30,000 tons.

The basic operating arrangement of the corporation was unified procurement of scrap copper; the agencies previously competing in this regard, now members of the new corporation, gave up their independent procurement activities and instead procured only on behalf of the corporation. Reprocessing of scrap was to be done by the Shenyang Smelter. The proceeds from scrap reprocessing were split among the corporation's members; only 5 percent of these profits were kept by the corporation itself.

The new corporation seems to have succeeded in stopping the competition among different agencies in procuring scrap and in preventing bidding wars, which apparently still raged in other parts of the country. If production forecasts materialized, they would indicate considerable success in diverting scrap from inefficient small processors to the smelter. Although the new monopsony was not used to push scrap procurement prices downward, the prices apparently stabilized, and the need to return copper recycled from scrap to scrap suppliers might have been reduced.

The main problems the new corporation faced mirrored those of its sponsor, the smelter's enterprise group. There was a severe shortage of circulating funds, which were to be provided by the participants of the group in accordance with their investment shares but for the most part were not forthcoming. Smelter management was considering turning the corporation into a joint stock company as a means of raising more capital. The other main issue was division of profits among corporation members. Profits had to be divided among all the entities that had previously been involved in scrap procurement and processing, that is, those that handled procurement, collection, sorting, refining, electrolysis, and manufacture of copper products. Division of profits was both the subject of extensive bargaining and a source of rigidity.

In 1987 it was too early to tell whether the Revival Metallurgical Associated Corporation would achieve lasting success, although, according to the smelter, much progress had been made. Monopsony procurement could lead to attempts to bypass it, particularly in rural areas, if suppliers were exploited excessively by holding down procurement prices. In view of continued price controls affecting electrolytic copper and the strong inflationary pressures in Chinese industry, this danger was a real one.

The National Corporation and the Subsector Responsibility System

Additional information about the China Nonferrous Metals Industry General Corporation has become available. The share of China's nonferrous metals industry under the corporation's control turned out to be somewhat smaller than had been originally envisaged. In the late 1980s the corporation was in charge of 134 nonferrous metals production enterprises, accounting for 68 percent of total physical output, 60 percent of gross industrial output value, 76 percent of employment, and nearly 70 percent of total profits and taxes of the nonferrous metals industry. The corporation's earlier forecast had been that it would control 200 or more enterprises, accounting for 70 percent of output value and 82 percent of profits (see "Organizational Reforms," in this chapter). The corporation also supervised some ninety nonproduction units (scientific research institutes, schools, and so forth). In addition to the eleven regional corporations it supervised (down from twelve in 1984—one of them apparently was abolished), a number of specialized companies were established by the corporation and were responsible for handling foreign trade, foreign construction projects, equipment sales, and tungsten production, among other activities.

The concrete functions of the corporation, as they evolved in practice, included (1) influencing the development plans of subordinate enterprises, (2) setting their annual mandatory plans, (3) approving all large capital construction and renovation projects, (4) fixing profit-sharing schemes with subordinate firms and regional corporations, (5) appointing directors for all large and medium-size nonferrous metals enterprises, (6) monitoring firms' wage bills, and (7) allocating controlled materials not handled by the State Planning Commission and the State Material Supply Bureau.[45]

The corporation believed that it had made progress in a number of areas of reform. The director responsibility system and fixed terms for directors had been instituted in a large proportion of its subordinate firms. There was also considerable development of horizontal investment relationships, particularly of those involving mine development. The corporation itself participated in many of these projects as an investor. A number of enterprise groups were formed.

The corporation made no progress, however, in weaning enterprises away from mandatory planning, which still accounted for more than 90 percent of their output in the mid- to late 1980s. In contrast, virtually all production by locally owned firms was outside the mandatory plan. Overall, the share of mandatory planning in total industry output was only about 55 percent in 1987. This highly dualistic structure must have led to distortions and inequities between different enterprises.

The corporation acknowledged that it was unable to do a good job of sector management because local interests were involved in the part of the industry outside of its direct control. It even had trouble getting accurate information on local production, imports, and exports. (Although licenses were required to import or export nonferrous metals, provinces apparently could issue them.)

As in other heavy industries, a multiyear responsibility system was instituted in the nonferrous metals industry starting in 1984. This arrangement took the form of a scheme for profit-sharing between the corporation and the state; the scheme was replicated in the financial relationships between the national corporation, the regional branch corporations, and the enterprises. Unlike other subsectoral responsibility systems (see, for example, chapter 8 of this volume), only the financial targets and flows were included in the scheme; production and allocation of inputs and outputs remained largely subject to mandatory planning as before.

The central provision of the responsibility system was a fixed rate of profit sharing between the national corporation and the central government, according to which the corporation remitted 38 percent of total profits and retained 62 percent. This sharing rate was fixed for the seven years from 1984 to 1990. The corporation itself used various methods of profit sharing with its subordinate branch corporations and enterprises:

1. Fixed proportional remittance from a base level of profits and a lower rate for profits above the base level. This was the method used by the Shenyang Smelter and 26 of the other 133 enterprises.
2. Fixed sharing rate for total profits, with no distinction related to a base figure. This method applied to thirty-eight enterprises.
3. One hundred percent retention of all profits, but no subsidy for losses (twelve enterprises).
4. Fixed amount of profits to be remitted, with 100 percent retention of above-quota profits (four enterprises).
5. Targets for losses, involving progressive yearly reductions, with corresponding subsidies (four enterprises).
6. Fixed loss targets, with the enterprise retaining all or part of the proceeds from loss reductions (thirty-six enterprises, mostly mines).

It was claimed that these methods enhanced incentives for nonferrous metals mines and smelters and resulted in improved financial performance. Fragmentary information appears to indicate that output and profits of the nonferrous metals industry have risen considerably. Between 1983 and 1986, total national production of the ten most important nonferrous metals rose by 29.4 percent, and gross output value of the nonferrous metals industry rose by 40 percent. In 1987 there were further real increases of 13.8 percent in the output value of nonferrous metals mines and 8.8 percent for smelting and processing (State Statistical Bureau 1988, pp. 314, 317). In 1988, physical output of the ten main nonferrous metals surpassed 1987 output by 10 percent (*Beijing Review*, January 23–29, 1989, p. 38).

For the 134 production units under the national corporation, remitted profits and taxes rose by only 7.5 percent between 1983 and 1986, whereas profits retained by enterprises were reported to have risen by more than 100 percent. Thus financial performance improved only modestly, and the greatest share of proceeds went to firms rather than to the government. The effective marginal rate of taxation of enterprise profits during this period must have been extremely low. It would require further research to ascertain which parts of the nonferrous metals industry reaped these rewards; mines were chronic loss-makers because of low output prices and they obviously deserved some relief. Because retained profits rose sharply and most mines continued to lose money, however, profitable enterprises most likely also saw large increases in retained profits.

The Role of the Shenyang Regional Corporation

Whereas in 1984 it had still been uncertain what precise form the Shenyang Regional Nonferrous Metals Industry Branch Corporation and similar entities would take, shortly afterward authorities decided that they would be economic entities and have rights to retain profits and to take on business activities. This decision was much resented by the Shenyang Smelter, which had opposed such an arrangement in 1984. It found most objectionable the regional corporation's use of part of the smelter's profits to subsidize the other, weaker enterprises under the corporation's jurisdiction. This objection was strikingly similar to the smelter's earlier complaint about the Shenyang Metallurgy Bureau, although the subsidized enterprises in question were different ones. The smelter also perceived that its own power to make decisions was more circumscribed in this new situation.

The problematic position of the regional branch corporations was also evident to the national corporation, which in 1987 was considering transforming them into branch offices of headquarters, with no business or financial role. Particularly after several large nonferrous metals smelters formed enterprise groups, the justification for regional corporations was weakened. The original reason for the establishment of the regional corporations—the impossibility of the national corporation's supervising all of its more than 100 subordinate enterprises directly—lost most of its relevance under these circumstances.

Views of the Shenyang Metallurgy Bureau

The Shenyang Metallurgy Bureau had strongly opposed the recentralization of the Shenyang Smelter and the creation of the Shenyang regional corporation. It believed that the local agency previously in charge (itself) could do a good job in integrating the activities of large and small nonferrous metals enterprises in the locality. The bureau claimed that before the national corporation was formed the nonferrous metals industry in Shenyang had been integrated and balanced but that the new system had led to a number of severe problems.

Flows of goods within the area were reported to have been disrupted, and, moreover, an additional 4.5 percent service charge was now levied for transactions through the material supply system. Procedures were lengthy, and they interfered with production by local processors. Cooperative relations between large and small local nonferrous metals enterprises were weakened under the new arrangements. The bureau still had under its jurisdiction some nonferrous metals enterprises, small processing firms that the Shenyang regional corporation was not willing to take over. Thus the control of the nonferrous metals industry in the Shenyang area continued to be split between central and local sectors. The bureau also cited some administrative problems, which were perceived by the smelter as the bureau's petty forms of revenge for its loss of a valuable local enterprise. The bureau still had nominal control over the smelter's party affairs, but it believed this control was meaningless because it did not appoint the enterprise's party secretary.

Although the Shenyang Metallurgy Bureau's complaints were related to its loss of control over an important enterprise, they do have a certain validity. Even if, overall, the administrative changes of 1983 represented an improvement over the highly decentralized system of the past, there were costs and tradeoffs attendant to them, some of which may have involved economic losses rather than mere redistribution of profits between the locality and the central government.

Future Strategy

The China Nonferrous Metals Industry General Corporation in 1987 expressed strong views about the future of the Shenyang Smelter; these views indicated that the corporation understood the enterprise's fundamental problem of location. At the same time, the implicit strategy underlying the corporation's remarks reflected the constraints on relocation and shutdown that were present in China's industrial system. The corporation believed that the smelter should not try to expand production capacity on its present site, but rather should increase recovery of by-products and improve pollution control. The corporation asserted, moreover, that the smelter should gradually disperse its production, particularly lead production, to other localities. The mechanism for dispersal of production, in the corporation's view, was to be horizontal associations of the smelter with other factories. In such arrangements the smelter could share investment funds and technology with the other factories involved. It was hoped that the Northern Nonferrous Metals and Gold Associated Corporation would serve as a suitable vehicle for these associations.

A number of questions about this strategy naturally arise. The most important one concerns the transfer of investment funds—whether this flow would occur efficiently and in a way that protected the interests of the smelter. Because of the efforts of other localities to ensure that no loss of local revenue would result from their enterprises' dealings with outside concerns, the costs of these associations could become high and the returns to the smelter unacceptably low. The other problems of the smelter's enterprise group cited earlier also hindered dispersal of production.

The increasing rate of profit retention by the smelter and 100 percent retention of depreciation funds, combined with the difficulties and uncertainties involved in its investing elsewhere, suggest that the level of investment at the present site may continue to be too high and may partly defeat the objective of gradually shifting production elsewhere. Continued survival and a high level of activity for the Shenyang Smelter on its present site seem almost assured over the medium term. This, to some extent, represents failure of the dispersal strategy as well as inability to implement more drastic relocation options discussed earlier. As is noted in "General Observations," in this chapter, by performing well at the micro level, the Shenyang Smelter may have hindered or even have prevented the most rational mode of adjustment from the perspective of the nonferrous metals industry as a whole.

Notes

1. This discussion is based mainly on Muller-Ohlsen 1981, particularly pp. 18, 82–92. Another book on the world nonferrous metals industry is United Nations 1972. Useful sources of quantitative information include Schmitz 1979 and *Metal Statistics*. Still another handy reference is Robbins 1982.

2. Table 5.1 presents estimates starting from the late nineteenth century. Average annual growth of world consumption of nonferrous metals was 3.7 percent in 1800–90 (starting from a small base) and 3.9 percent in 1890–1979. The growth rate rose largely because of the spectacular growth of aluminum consumption (Muller-Ohlsen 1981, p. 92).

3. The figure for lead is biased downward because it excludes some scrap recycling that is part of refinery production. See Muller-Ohlsen 1981, table 37, p. 170.

4. Shanghai and Liaoning, the two provinces engaged in the most nonferrous metals smelting, account for 35 percent of total national output of electrolytic copper, which is striking in view of the lack of mineral reserves in these provinces. See table 5.2 and Shanghai Academy of Social Sciences 1983, p. 293.

5. Just four of these, aluminum, copper, lead, and zinc, account for more than 90 percent of China's total output of nonferrous metals (Sun 1983, p. 160; Li 1983, p. 273).

6. The official Chinese domestic price of cadmium, more than six times the international price, may not have been used in many transactions. The Shenyang Smelter reported that the market price of cadmium had fallen below Y10,000 a ton, only slightly higher than the world price.

7. Li 1983, p. 273, argues that developing production of aluminum, lead, and zinc is more economically efficient than developing production of copper.

8. These figures are based on the information in tables 5.2 and 5.5. As mentioned, national figures are unreliable and in particular may understate copper production.

9. The total value of quota circulating assets (inventories of inputs and outputs and goods in process) was Y112 million in 1982. Using the original value of fixed assets plus quota circulating assets as the denominator, the financial rate of return was more than 17 percent; if the net depreciated value of fixed assets is used instead, the financial rate of return was 27 percent.

10. The price paid for gold by China's banking system was raised from Y95 per liang (Y125.66 per troy ounce) to Y406.25 per liang (Y537.38 per troy ounce) on March 1, 1980. At the same time, the procurement price of silver was doubled.

See *Zhongguo Jinrong*, no. 3 (March 1980), p. 40; and Shanghai Municipal Radio Service, June 11, 1980 (in *jprs China Report: Economic Affairs*, no. 67 [July 2, 1980], p. 42). It is not clear whether this sharp increase applied to enterprises producing gold as well as to individuals and rural collectives offering gold for sale. Even if the Shenyang Smelter were selling its gold at the relatively low procurement price for newly produced gold of the late 1950s (Y130 per liang, or Y171.96 per troy ounce), its gold would bring substantial revenues at the reported volume of production.

11. The Shenyang Smelter had some very capable managers. One of its leading cadres rose from deputy director in charge of production to director (through election by the workers) and then to deputy mayor of Shenyang Municipality within a period of one year.

12. Although there is no market for urban land in China, enterprises that wish to acquire land must provide compensation in various forms to the unit that gives up the land. The costs of such compensation rose sharply in the 1980s.

13. Neither of the other two sample firms in northeast China became extensively involved in associations and mergers, although both of them set up collective enterprises of their own to employ workers' children, as did the smelter.

14. Shipments of coal into Liaoning under the central plan in 1981 were 19.94 million tons, compared with total provincial production of 33.7 million tons and shipments out of the province of only 920,000 tons. See Ministry of Coal Industry 1983, pp. 17, 24.

15. Before 1983 no fines for water pollution were levied on the smelter, even though regulations called for such fines. In 1983 a fine of Y5 million was levied, in 1984 Y6.2 million.

16. This is a clear case of a Chinese enterprise constrained by the need at least to break even in activities and transactions at the margin. The smelter's behavior in this respect was consistent with profit maximization, but it does not necessarily demonstrate that the Shenyang Smelter or other Chinese enterprises actually maximized profits.

17. In the Chinese financial system, taxes and profit remittances are generally collected by local organs of public finance (finance and tax bureaus), regardless of the level of government to which the revenues accrue. Similarly, an enterprise's bank of account would not change when it was transferred from one level of government supervision to another.

18. In 1978 the copper output target set by the ministry was 22,000 tons, and the target assigned by the Shenyang Metallurgy Bureau was 50,000 tons. In 1979 the ministry's target was 25,000 tons, the bureau's target still 50,000 tons.

19. The Shenyang Finance Bureau passed down a total profit-remittance target to the Shenyang Metallurgy Bureau. The bureau may have put an extra burden on the smelter because of this, in order to support its smaller enterprises, which may have had more difficulty in meeting targets. This was certainly the Shenyang Smelter's impression, but it would require data about the other factories under the bureau to determine whether this indeed occurred.

20. Although copper blister was imported by the state, it appears not to have been included in the smelter's supply allocations from the ministry at the beginning of each year. Instead it may have been used to cover gaps that remained after the smelter had acquired on its own as many supplies as possible.

21. One reason coke supplies were short of requirements was that the Shenyang Smelter's allocation for coke was not raised when a technical renovation project increased copper smelting capacity in 1982. Because of the severe shortage of coke in China, new users and users with increased requirements tended not to be accommodated with additional allocations.

22. Specified percentages of retained profits went into each of the following three funds: production development fund, workers' bonus fund, and workers' collective welfare fund. These percentages were set for the factory by higher levels but could be changed from year to year. In 1979–83 the smelter overspent from its collective welfare fund by a cumulative total of Y540,000 and underspent on production development by Y500,000 and on bonuses by Y340,000. Extra bonus funds were accumulated in part to pay for a 1983–84 wage adjustment, which was to be partly paid out of the bonus fund. Running surpluses and deficits in the different funds did not require approval by higher-level authorities but must be reported in year-end statistics and carried over from year to year.

23. The 1982 expansion of copper smelting capacity from 21,000 tons annually to 25,000 tons was apparently accommodated without significant difficulties with raw materials. The supply of coke did become problematic, however.

24. If the binding constraint on lead production had been energy, the smelter would have had a further incentive to shift production from zinc to lead, to the point at which some other (nonenergy) constraint became binding.

25. At least some profits from sulfuric acid production could be retained by the smelter for investment in pollution control. These were separate from the enterprise's normal profit-retention scheme. This may have been a factory-specific arrangement or a general policy applied to the industry. It apparently predated the profit-retention schemes instituted in the late 1970s.

26. These medals were awarded by the state for high-quality products. A gold medal was given for meeting advanced international standards, a silver medal for top quality by domestic standards, and a bronze medal for slightly lower quality. The Shenyang Smelter was the only enterprise to win a gold medal for lead in 1980; three other factories also won silver medals for copper in 1984.

27. The smelter claimed that these bonuses could not result in an increase in the total amount of bonuses paid to workers, but in 1980 control over bonuses was very lax anyway, and in 1984 ceilings on bonuses were being phased out.

28. This is a very concrete example of how weakening control over product mix in a situation of chronic shortage hurts the interests of users. Montias (1977) has shown that, in general, aggregation of targets will result in an inferior composition of output from the viewpoint of central planners.

29. Dividing 1983 retained profits by 8.8 percent yields Y37.2 million, considerably more than actual 1983 profits of Y29.2 million. The smelter may have been permitted to retain profits in accordance with its revised profit target of Y35.2 million rather than with actual profits.

30. This was the official price set by Liaoning Province for cement subject to its jurisdiction. In fact, the smelter sometimes received more cement than it actually needed. The extra amount it either exchanged with peasants of Panjin Prefecture for natural gas to meet employees' cooking needs or simply did not purchase.

31. In the difficult situation of 1981 the director of the State Material Supply

Bureau was reported to have given oral instructions for the smelter to market excess inventories of copper directly, and these instructions were never formally rescinded. They appear never to have been implemented, either.

32. The smelter paid only Y0.05 per kilowatt-hour (Y0.035 per kilowatt-hour before June 1983), compared with an average of more than Y0.065 per kilowatt-hour in China as a whole. This lower price appears to be a historical legacy, set at a time when electricity supplies in northeast China were abundant in relation to demand and to the situation in other parts of the country.

33. Central authorities apparently had to go along with provincial decisions on electricity allocation; they cut back shipments of raw materials to Fushun accordingly. This is a striking example of the effect of provincial control over distribution of an important input, such as power. Production at Fushun appears to have been effectively determined by the Liaoning Economic Commission.

34. This is a rare example of a regional government authority wanting to get rid of a large, profitable enterprise under its jurisdiction, but it is entirely understandable in view of the power supply situation in northeast China. Liaoning probably expected that factory and workers would be removed together, so it would not have to deal with any unemployment.

35. Since prices of ores were nominally set by the Ministry of Metallurgy, all the prices did was redistribute a given amount of surplus (determined by the price set by the state for pure metals) between mines and smelters. The inability of the ministry to raise ore prices even under these circumstances provides strong evidence of paralysis induced by the scattering of administrative jurisdiction and control.

36. Some voluntary investment resource transfer mechanisms evolved after the late 1970s, including joint ventures and compensation trade between regions. These mechanisms appear to have been less important in the nonferrous metals industry than they were in certain other subsectors, such as the coal and cement industries. Compensation trade was, however, for a time widely used to acquire tin from Yunnan Province.

37. This, of course, provided an important incentive for Shenyang Municipality and the Shenyang Metallurgy Bureau to set an unrealistically high profit target for the smelter.

38. This course of action may well have been the best alternative in economic terms, if the economic cost of producing lead ore of comparable quality locally were less than the cost of mining it elsewhere and transporting it to the smelter.

39. If collective workers employed in mixed positions were included, there might even have been a decline in output per worker. This stagnation in labor productivity should not be blamed on the enterprise, however, because the smelter had little discretion in hiring and was forced to employ workers' children.

40. The nonferrous metals industry may have received some relief in the form of lower indirect taxes; otherwise the trend of declining indirect tax payments is hard to explain.

41. See *Jiage Lilun yu Shijian* (July 1988), pp. 53–54. Temporary prices were differentiated across large copper smelters. Shenyang and one other factory (in Shanghai) received the lowest price increases. The maximum price increase was 27 percent (to Y7,000 a ton).

42. In China, when industrial enterprises are transferred from one owner to another, the employees typically move with the productive assets and become the responsibility of the new owner.

43. Enterprise groups became a centerpiece of industrial reforms in 1987, based on the success of some enterprises, such as the Second Motor Vehicle Factory, in establishing associations of firms to better coordinate production (see chapter 9 of this volume).

44. From the perspective of central authorities, the existing allocation pattern distributed transport costs more fairly among different users, whereas direct shipments from the smelter to the Shenyang Cable Factory would have given the factory a great cost advantage compared with those of other processors because of lower transport costs. This perspective neglected to consider the proper role of prices in guiding decisions about location, and, moreover, efficiency gains from on-site transfer of materials and on-site production of alloys were lost.

45. Of the fifty-six goods subject to control by the State Planning Commission and the national corporation, the commission handled eleven and the corporation was responsible for the remaining forty-five. Over time, government authorities substantially reduced the number of goods subject to central allocation, but, since the founding of the corporation, the number of products under the control of the Planning Commission increased from seven to eleven.

References

Beijing Review. Weekly magazine.

China Business Review. Bimonthly magazine.

China Economic Yearbook Editorial Committee. 1981. *Zhongguo Jingji Nianjian 1981* (1981 China Economic Yearbook). Beijing: Jingji Guanli Zazhishe.

———. 1984. *Zhongguo Jingji Nianjian 1984* (1984 China Economic Yearbook). Beijing: Jingji Guanli Zazhishe.

China Encyclopedia Editorial Committee. 1981. *Zhongguo Baike Nianjian 1981* (1981 China Encyclopedia Yearbook). Beijing and Shanghai: Zhongguo Da Baike Quanshu Chubanshe.

———. 1983. *Zhongguo Baike Nianjian 1983* (1983 China Encyclopedia Yearbook). Beijing and Shanghai: Zhongguo Da Baike Quanshu Chubanshe.

Hu Changyuan and Liu Fengqian. 1984. "Jiagong Gongye Chanpin Chengben, Jiage Wenti Diaocha" (An Investigation of Production Costs and Prices for Products of Processing Industries). *Jingji Diaocha* (Economic Investigations) 3: 66–78.

International Financial Statistics. Monthly.

Jiage Lilun yu Shijian. Monthly journal.

Li Rui, ed. 1983. *Zhongguo Gongye Bumen Jiegou* (The Subsectoral Structure of Chinese Industry). Beijing: Zhongguo Renmin Daxue Chubanshe.

Metallgesellschaft AG. 1984. *Metallstatistik 1973–83* (Metal Statistics, 1973–83). Frankfurt.

Metal Statistics. Annual.

Ministry of Coal Industry. 1983. *1982 Zhongguo Meitan Gongye Nianjian* (1982 China Coal Industry Yearbook). Beijing: Meitan Gongye Chubanshe.

Montias, J. M. 1977. "The Aggregation of Controls and the Autonomy of Subordinates." *Journal of Economic Theory* 15(2): 123–34.

Muller-Ohlsen, Lotte. 1981. *Nonferrous Metals: Their Role in Industrial Development.* Cambridge, U.K.: Woodhead-Faulkner and Metallgesellschaft AG.

Robbins, Peter. 1982. *Guide to Nonferrous Metals and Their Markets.* London: Kogan Page.

Schmitz, Christopher. 1979. *World Nonferrous Metal Production and Prices, 1700– 1976.* London: Frank Cass.

Shanghai Academy of Social Sciences. 1983. *Shanghai Jingji 1949–1982* (Shanghai's Economy 1949–1982). Shanghai: Shanghai Renmin Chubanshe.

Shanghai Means of Production Service Company. 1982. "Shanghai Shengchan Ziliao Jiaoyi Shichang Qingkuang Huibao" (A Report on Conditions at the Shanghai Market for the Means of Production). In China Enterprise Management Association, ed. *Shanghai Gongye Qiye Jingyan* (The Experiences of Shanghai's Industrial Enterprises), vol. 1. Shijiazhuang: Qiye Guanli Chubanshe.

Shanghai Wuzi Shichang (Shanghai Materials Market). Weekly newspaper.

The Sixth Five-Year Plan of the People's Republic of China for Economic and Social Development (1981–1985). 1984. Beijing: Foreign Languages Press.

State Economic Commission, Enterprise Management Department. 1983a. *Gongye Jingying Guanli Jingyan Xuanbian, 1982* (Selections on Experience in Industrial Administration and Management, 1982). Beijing: Renmin Chubanshe.

State Economic Commission. 1983b. "Guojia Jingji Weiyuanhui Guanyu Chengli Zhongguo Youse Jinshu Gongye Zong Gongsi de Baogao (Zhaiyo)" (The State Economic Commission's Report on Establishment of the China Nonferrous Metals Industry General Corporation (Draft)). In *Zhonghua Renmin Gonghe Guo Guowuyuan Gongbao* (Bulletin of the State Council of the People's Republic of China) 10 (June 20): 435–39.

State Statistical Bureau. 1983. *Zhongguo Tongji Nianjian 1983* (Statistical Yearbook of China 1983). Beijing: Zhongguo Tongji Chubanshe.

———. 1984. *Zhongguo Tongji Nianjian 1984* (Statistical Yearbook of China 1984). Beijing: Zhongguo Tongji Chubanshe.

———. 1988. *Zhongguo Tongji Nianjian 1988* (Statistical Yearbook of China 1988). Beijing: Zhongguo Tongji Chubanshe.

Sun Jingzhi. 1983. *Zhongguo Jingji Dili Gaikuanglun* (A General Economic Geography of China). Beijing: Shangwu Yinshuguan.

United Nations. 1972. *Nonferrous Metals: A Survey of Their Production and Potential in Developing Countries.* New York.

World Bureau of Metal Statistics. 1984. *World Metal Statistics Yearbook 1984.* London.

Wu Yin. 1982. "Lun Woguo Xi Chanpin de Jiage Wenti" (On the Problem of Our Country's Tin Price). *Jingji Wenti Tansuo* (Explorations on Economic Questions) 3 (March): 41–43.

Xing Hua. 1983. "Shinian Dongluan Shiqi Caizheng Tizhi Biandong Pinfan" (Frequent Changes in the Government Finance System during the Ten Years of Turmoil). *Caizheng* (Government Finance) 8 (August): 22–24 and 9 (September): 8–10.

Zhongguo Jinrong (China's Finance). Monthly journal.

Zhou Taihe, ed. 1984. *Dangdai Zhongguo de Jingji Tizhi Gaige* (Economic System Reform in Contemporary China). Beijing: Zhongguo Shehui Kexue Chubanshe.

Zhu Chuan, ed. 1983. *Liaoning Jingji Tongji Nianjian 1983* (Liaoning Economic and Statistical Yearbook 1983). Shenyang: Liaoning Renmin Chubanshe.

6

The Qinghe Woolen Textile Mill

Lora Sabin

THE QINGHE WOOLEN TEXTILE MILL in Beijing provides an interesting case study of the ways in which Chinese economic reforms affected a particular enterprise, the new problems they engendered, and the old constraints they left unresolved. As a microcosm of the changes that have occurred in much of China's industrial economy since the late 1970s, Qinghe's recent history provides valuable insights.

Qinghe's experiences during the early years of reform are noteworthy in several respects. As a producer of high-quality woolen fabrics and as one of the first enterprises chosen to participate in the national pilot reform program in industry, Qinghe was in a position to benefit simultaneously from adjustment policies favoring light industry over heavy industry and from measures granting enterprises more autonomy. Stimulated on the demand side by rising incomes and domestic consumption and on the supply side by easier access to investment funds and greater responsibility for output, Qinghe's management quickly expanded production after 1979. The mill also took advantage of its status as a reformed enterprise to improve internal management and experiment with planning and production.

The responses of Qinghe's management to certain problems encountered in the course of reform also are relevant. By 1982 the supply of domestically produced textile goods had begun to surpass demand, and the Chinese market for woolen products shifted from a sellers' to a buyers' market. In this new environment, Qinghe sought to reorient production toward market demand, particularly demand for high-quality goods and a wider range of products. The mill's success in responding to market signals has been held up as a model for other firms.[1]

Another problem with which Qinghe grappled was the persistence of bureaucratic controls and restrictions. These constraints were often longstanding ones that had previously posed no distinct threats to the enterprise. With the new incentives created by profit sharing and supposed responsibility for profits and losses, however, the inability of the mill's management to free itself from dealings with slow, incompetent, or obstructive bureaucrats severely hindered its development. The persistence of bureaucratic restrictions and Qinghe's attempts to maneuver around them suggest that, in significant ways, the reforms failed to achieve their goals.

This chapter is divided into three main sections. The first section provides background information on China's textile industry and its woolen textile industry, along with a brief description of the Qinghe mill. The next section analyzes the effect of reforms on the mill and focuses on changes in Qinghe's behavior and the constraints it continued to confront. The final section steps away from consideration of specific reforms and examines the mill's response to changes in its economic environment. The chapter concludes with an outline of some broader implications of Qinghe's experience.

An Introduction to the Industry and Enterprise

Background information on China's textile industry and especially on its woolen textile industry provides a broader context for detailed analysis of particular enterprises. This section also includes a brief history of the Qinghe Woolen Textile Mill.

China's Textile Industry

From a small, regionally concentrated base in 1949, the Chinese textile industry has grown steadily, to become one of the world's largest.[2] The gross value of industrial output (GVIO) of China's textile factories in 1952 amounted to only Y9.43 billion, compared with more than Y50 billion in 1978 and nearly Y110 billion in 1984 (see table 6.1). Diversification of China's economy in the 1950s and 1960s and the deliberate stress on investment in heavy industry resulted in a gradual decline in the share of textile production in total national GVIO from more than 25 percent in the early 1950s to roughly 15 percent in 1984. Largely as a result of consolidation, the total number of Chinese textile mills fell in the 1950s and 1960s, but by the late 1970s more than 1,000 new enterprises were beginning production each year. The total labor force in state textile factories has enjoyed steady growth, rising from just under 1 million in 1952 to 4.1 million in 1982.

There are ten large subsectors within China's textile industry, among them cotton, woolen, flax, and silk textiles; chemical fibers; and textile machinery. Approximately one-third of the 17,100 firms producing textile goods in 1981 were under the direct administration of the Ministry of Textile Industry and its subordinate textile bureaus in local governments; they produced nearly 90 percent of total national textile GVIO (Ministry of Textile Industry 1983a, p. 158). As shown in table 6.2, state enterprises and urban collective enterprises accounted for the bulk of the total output value of firms under the ministry's jurisdiction. The approximately 11,500 producers outside the min-

Table 6.1. China's Textile Industry, Selected Years, 1952–84

Indicator	1952	1957	1965	1978	1980	1982	1984
GVIO (billions of yuan)[a]	9.4[b]	14.4[b]	22.1[c]	52.9[d]	73.5[d]	86.7[e]	108.3[e]
As percentage of total national GVIO	26.9	20.5	15.8	13.0	14.7	15.5	15.4
Investment in capital construction (billions of yuan)[f]	0.3	0.3	0.4	1.3	1.1	0.3	—
As percentage of total industrial investment in capital construction	6.7	2.5	2.3	3.4	3.9	1.0	—
Number of enterprises (thousands)	—	13.9	8.4	12.1	15.3	18.1	19.7
As percentage of total number of industrial enterprises	—	8.2	5.3	3.5	4.1	4.7	4.5
Number of employees (millions)[f]	1.0	1.3	1.5	2.7	3.4	4.1	4.1
As percentage of total industrial employees	19.9	17.7	12.3	8.9	10.5	11.8	11.5
Value of exports (billions of dollars)[a]	0.04	0.28	0.45	2.15	3.24	3.59	4.63
As percentage of total exports	5.2	17.7	20.3	22.1	17.7	16.5	17.7
Taxes and profits remitted to government (billions of yuan)[a]	0.7	1.8	4.7	11.0	—	14.9	—
As percentage of state budget income	3.8	5.7	9.8	9.8	—	16.4	—

GVIO, gross value of industrial output.

— Not available.

Note: Data exclude the garment and leather industries, which in 1984 had GVIO of Y17.8 billion and Y6.2 billion, respectively.

a. Data are for all enterprises under the administration of central and local government agencies, except those run by villages and individuals.

b. In 1952 prices.

c. In 1957 prices.

d. In 1970 prices.

e. In 1980 prices.

f. Data cover only state enterprises under the supervision of the Ministry of Textile Industry.

Source: State Statistical Bureau 1985, 1986; Ministry of Textile Industry 1983b, 1984; China Economic Yearbook Editorial Committee 1984, 1985.

istry's jurisdiction included smaller firms under the supervision of other branches of government as well as collectives operated by rural townships and urban neighborhood organizations.

Despite the official supervisory role of the ministry, central control over textile firms in China was relaxed. As part of the massive decentralization of Chinese industry during the Great Leap Forward movement in 1958, the ministry transferred direct supervision of most textile enterprises, with the exception of textile equipment manufacturing plants and large chemical fiber factories, to provincial and city authorities. Although the central government regained control over investments in large projects in the early 1960s, the vast majority of textile firms remained largely free from control by the ministry, whose role was generally restricted to overall planning, coordination, and technical guidance. Remaining central control was exercised through

Table 6.2. Enterprise Ownership under the Ministry of Textile Industry, 1981

Ownership type	Number of enterprises	Share of total enterprises (percent)	Output value (billions of yuan)	Share of total output value (percent)
State	3,261	57.8	68.2	90.0
Urban collective	2,314	41.0	7.0	9.2
State-collective jointly run	62	1.0	0.6	0.8
State–Hong Kong jointly run	4	..	0.02	0.02

.. Negligible.
Source: Ministry of Textile Industry 1983b.

quotas for the allocation of raw materials and equipment, as well as through ceilings on investment in capital construction (see Zhou 1984, p. 376).

The quick expansion of the textile industry in the early years of the People's Republic of China was driven mostly by the need to clothe a large and growing population and by the need for export earnings with which to pay for imports of foreign equipment and technology. The development of the textile industry was also guided by China's policy of regional self-sufficiency and its desire to locate textile mills near sources of raw materials. In 1949, China's textile production was heavily concentrated along the eastern seaboard, with Shanghai City and several coastal provinces accounting for 87 percent of the cotton textile manufacturing capacity and 90 percent of the woolen textile manufacturing capacity.

At least ten inland provinces each lacked even a single textile plant. In the 1950s and 1960s, new textile mills were opened in the hinterland, especially in cotton- and wool-producing provinces such as Shanxi, Hebei, Hunan, and Nei Monggol. By 1982, despite the continuing dominance of the eastern provinces, every province had established a textile industry base.[3] An estimated 43 percent of the nation's capacity for producing cotton cloth and 34 percent of its capacity for producing woolen cloth were located in interior provinces (Qian 1984, pp. 15–16).

China's textile development strategy also stressed the supply of textile equipment and raw material resources. To reduce the need for imported machinery and to develop heavy industry in the western part of the country, complete textile equipment factories were built in Shanxi, Henan, and other inland locations. As regards raw materials, priority was given to increasing cotton production during the 1950s and 1960s. A full 62 percent of total investment in the textile industry between 1952 and 1970 went to the cotton textile subsector (Qian 1984, p. 118). By 1982, China was growing 3.6 million tons of cotton, more than five times the amount it had cultivated in 1949 and 24.5 percent of the world's cotton output. Other subsectors, such as silk and woolen textiles, absorbed far less investment and produced largely for export markets. Still, silkworm and wool production in 1982 exceeded the levels of 1949 by fifteen and eleven times, respectively (Qian 1984, pp. 17–27). By the early 1980s the cotton textile industry's rate of self-sufficiency for raw material had risen to 84 percent from 50 percent in 1949, and the woolen textile industry's rate had increased from 20 percent to roughly 60 percent.

China has also emphasized development of the domestic chemical fiber industry. As a result of the expansion of the petrochemical industry, annual production of chemical fibers skyrocketed from 50,100 tons in 1957 to nearly 300,000 tons in 1978 and more than 500,000 tons by the early 1980s. The share of investment in the cotton textile industry in total national investment in textiles plummeted to about 30 percent by 1982; investment in the chemical fiber industry claimed over half of total investment in textiles in the 1970s (Qian 1984, pp. 118, 287).

Adjustment and reform policies of the late 1970s injected new dynamism into the Chinese textile industry. With the new stress on light industry, textile firms gained favored access to raw materials, fuel, electricity, transport facilities, investment loans, and hard currency for equipment imports. The sharp rise in personal incomes boosted demand for all consumer goods. The average annual growth rate of the value of textile output shot up from 6.9 percent in 1953–78 to 13.6 percent in 1979–85 (State Statistical Bureau 1985, p. 226). In the six years after 1978, the number of textile firms and employees expanded by well over 50 percent. By 1984 nearly 5 million workers were engaged in textile manufacturing. The share of profits and taxes remitted by textile firms in total budget revenues rose from 9.8 percent in 1978 to 16.4 percent in 1982. Textile exports more than doubled from $2 billion in 1978 to nearly $5 billion in 1984.

By the early 1980s this rapid growth had begun to generate new problems, which were compounded by structural imbalances within the textile industry. As a result of distortions in relative prices that encouraged the production of polyester and cotton-polyester blends at the expense of pure cotton fabrics, the market for polyester fabrics and blends became saturated. The Chinese government adjusted the prices of different types of cloth in late 1981 and again in 1983 and applied more restrictive production ceilings for goods in excess supply. By 1982 a more general buyers' market for a wide range of textile goods was emerging and intensifying competition among producers. The new challenge textile firms faced was to improve the quality and variety of products in order to match more closely the demands of domestic and foreign customers.

The Woolen Textile Industry

Although the first Chinese woolen textile mill, the Gansu General Bureau of Woolen Piece Goods, was established in 1876, well before its first cotton textile counterpart, the subsequent development of the woolen textile industry was far slower than was that of the cotton textile industry. By 1949 only 130,000 spindles for woolen textile production had been installed, compared with 5 million cotton spindles. Pre-1949 output of cotton cloth reached a high of nearly 3 billion meters a year, but output of the main woolen textiles—woolen fabrics, woolen yarn, and wool blankets—was only 7.5 million meters a year, 3,000 tons a year, and 84,000 blankets a year, respectively (Qian 1984, pp. 175–76, 193).

Since 1949, investment in woolen textiles has generally been less than in cotton cloth and chemical fibers; woolen textiles accounted for a mere 6.5 percent of total capital construction investment in the textile industry between 1953 and 1982; chemical fibers accounted for 42 percent and cotton cloth, printing, dyeing, and knitted goods for 38.7 percent (Qian 1984, p. 118). Woolen textiles have also trailed behind cotton textiles, silk, and—since the late 1960s—chemical fibers in share of textile industry GVIO, although the share of woolen textiles rose steadily from 1.5 percent in 1952 to more than 8 percent in 1984 (see table 6.3). Woolen textiles has consistently been one of the fastest growing subsectors of China's textile industry; its GVIO increased at an average annual rate of 23.6 percent between 1953 and 1982.[4] Woolen fabrics have consistently made up an important share of Chinese textile exports.

Woolen textile mills were concentrated in the eastern provinces in 1949. Shanghai and Tianjin produced 82 percent of the GVIO of woolen textiles. New woolen textile mills were built in the inland provinces in ensuing years. Nei Monggol, Qinghai, Gansu, Xinjiang, Ningxia, and Shanxi were the main beneficiaries of early investment; by 1966 even Tibet could boast of its own woolen textile mill. The share of Shanghai and Tianjin in total production capacity of woolen textiles gradually fell, to 23 percent by the early 1980s. Roughly 34 percent of total production capacity was located in the interior, and every province had established a woolen textile industry (Qian 1984, pp. 197–98).

Development of woolen textiles was hampered by inadequate equipment and raw materials. Production capacity actually fell after 1949, before beginning to rise again in 1953. With the exception of a spurt of growth between 1958 and 1962, increases in production capacity were sluggish until the 1970s, when nearly 290,000 spindles were added, almost twice the number added in the preceding twenty-one years. Despite pressures to rely only on domestically produced equipment, machinery was imported from Japan and Italy in 1956 and 1962 in order to equip several new or expanding woolen textile mills in Beijing and Tianjin. (Qinghe was one of the lucky recipients of imported equipment in 1956.)

Lack of wool was a far more serious obstacle to development. Although sheep wool, cashmere, goat wool, rabbit hair, camel wool, and yak hair are all used in the production of woolen textile goods, sheep wool is by far

Table 6.3. Growth of China's Woolen Textile Industry, Selected Years, 1952–84

Indicator	1952	1957	1965	1978	1980	1982	1984
GVIO (billions of yuan)[a]	0.1	0.6	0.9	2.7	3.5	5.1	7.3
As percentage of total output value of textiles[a]	1.5	4.2	4.2	5.7	5.2	6.7	8.6
Number of employees (thousands)	21.0	—	8.3	15.3	20.4	29.7	—
As percentage of total employees in textiles	2.2	—	5.6	4.9	5.3	6.4	—
Production of woolen yarns (thousands of tons)	2.0	5.7	11.0	37.8	57.3	92.5	110.0
Production of woolen fabrics (millions of meters)	4.2	18.2	42.4	88.9	101.0	127.0	180.5
Production of woolen blankets (billions)	0.7	0.9	2.4	6.3	8.8	13.8	17.5
Production capacity (thousands of spindles)	123.1	156.2	279.3	478.0	600.5	889.0	1,205.2
Sales of woolen fabrics (millions of meters)	3.6	7.1	24.4	81.0	142.2	184.1	264.2
Average per capita consumption of woolen fabrics (one-third meters)[b]	0.02	0.03	0.10	0.25	0.43	0.55	0.77
Exports of woolen fabrics (millions of meters)[c]	..[d]	—	7.5	6.4	15.6	12.2	9.7

GVIO, gross value of industrial output.

— Not available.

.. Negligible.

a. GVIO figures are in constant prices by decade (see table 6.1). Data cover only enterprises under the supervision of the Ministry of Textile Industry.

b. Data include sales of woolen clothing.

c. Data are from State Statistical Bureau, various years. Data in various sources differ substantially.

d. Exports for 1952 were 4,000 meters.

Source: State Statistical Bureau 1984, 1985, 1986; Ministry of Textile Industry 1984; China Economic Yearbook Editorial Committee 1985.

the most important, accounting for approximately 70 percent of total raw materials. The domestic supply of raw materials was so low in 1949 that 80 percent of the wool used in production had to be imported (Ministry of Textile Industry 1983b, p. 12). To help alleviate the problem, the Chinese government in 1950 imported more than 30,000 high-quality sheep and began to stress improvements in sheep breeding. Efforts to boost wool production have gradually borne fruit. The amount of sheep wool purchased by the government from domestic producers in 1978 was triple that of 1957, and the amount of cashmere purchased doubled in that period (see table

6.4). By 1982, China had become the world's fourth-largest producer of raw wool, after Australia, the U.S.S.R., and New Zealand.

The poor quality of Chinese natural wool has also been a persistent problem. In the 1950s most wool produced in China was too coarse for fine textiles, such as worsted wool products. In the 1960s the breeding of fine-haired sheep was promoted, and, by the 1980s, about three-fourths of all domestically produced wool was fine or partially fine wool. Despite this progress, substantial purchases of high-quality foreign wool have been necessary over the years; more than 50 percent of the natural wool used in woolen textiles was still being imported in the early 1980s (Qian 1984, pp. 202–3).

Expanded use of chemical fibers has been a significant development. Since the 1960s, wool has been blended with polyamide, acrylic, polyester, and other chemical fibers to produce a variety of woolen fabrics that have become extremely popular among Chinese consumers. By the early 1980s, overall use of chemical fibers in the production of woolen textiles was nearly 50 percent. Given the insufficient domestic supply of wool and constraints on imports, these trends will undoubtedly continue (see Woolen Textiles Group 1984, p. 222).

The woolen textile industry expanded especially quickly starting in the late 1970s (table 6.3). Production of woolen textiles benefited from preferential treatment under the readjustment policies, and it was also stimulated by the dramatic rise in domestic and foreign demand for high-quality fabrics. Per capita consumption of woolen cloth rose by 72 percent in China in the two years after 1978 and by another 80 percent in the following four years. Exports of woolen fabrics also jumped, from 6.4 million meters in 1978 to nearly 16 million meters in 1980.[5] Spurred by the increase in demand, both production capacity and the number of employees in the woolen textile industry nearly doubled between 1978 and 1982. The relative position

Table 6.4. *Domestic Production of Raw Materials for Woolen Textiles, Selected Years, 1952–84*

Item	1952	1957	1965	1978	1980	1982	1984
Sheep raised (millions)	36.9	53.4	78.3	96.4	106.6	106.6	95.2
Sheep wool purchased (thousands of tons)	31.0	46.0	—	138.0	—	180.0	183.0
Goats raised (millions)	24.9	45.2	60.8	73.5	80.7	75.2	63.2
Goat wool purchased (thousands of tons)	1.0	4.0	—	8.0	—	8.0	11.0

— Not available.

Source: State Statistical Bureau 1985, 1986; China Economic Yearbook Editorial Committee 1984.

of woolen textiles within the textile industry as a whole improved after the late 1970s. Woolen textiles absorbed almost 12 percent of total investment in the textile industry in 1981–82 and accounted for a record high 8.6 percent share of the total output of textiles (Qian 1984, p. 118).

In spite of this success, woolen textiles came to suffer from many of the problems besetting the Chinese textile industry as a whole. The greatest challenge for producers was meeting the demands of domestic and foreign markets. As it did in other textile subsectors, this challenge called for improved quality, variety, designs, and colors in products. Measures promoted in the early 1980s included increased market research, trial production of new products, and experimentation with raw materials and dyes. Producers appear to have responded well to the new environment; a large number of woolen fabrics have been named "famous brand products" and have won national quality awards (Woolen Textiles Group 1984, pp. 222–24). Domestic retail sales of woolen fabrics rose a full 50 percent between 1983 and 1985, and there were some indications of a shift back to a sellers' market starting in 1984.[6] Chinese producers of woolen textiles thus seem to have risen to the challenges of the market, at least in the mid-1980s.

Brief History of the Qinghe Woolen Textile Mill

Located on the Qing River in the northern suburbs of Beijing, the Qinghe Woolen Textile Mill was established by the Chinese imperial government during its twilight years. The mill began operations in 1908, equipped with textile machinery imported from Great Britain that gave it a production apparatus of 4,800 spindles. In the years that followed, Qinghe was controlled by a series of governments—warlord, Republican, and Japanese—that militarily occupied Beijing. The mill continued to use its original equipment throughout this period and almost exclusively produced coarse varieties of woolen cloth. It served as an army supply factory for the Japanese and then for the Kuomintang. By the late 1940s, Qinghe was operating with only several hundred employees—a fraction of its earlier labor force—and production had virtually ground to a halt.

As the sole woolen textile mill in Beijing and as a newly designated state enterprise under the supervision of the Beijing Municipal Communist Party Committee, Qinghe, in the early years of the People's Republic of China, continued to produce heavy woolen fabrics for military use. In 1951 the mill's facilities were expanded and new equipment was added to increase total capacity to 7,200 spindles. The mill gradually began to produce finer woolens for domestic consumption, particularly after 1956, when it was one of a few recipients of modern textile manufacturing equipment imported from abroad (see Tung 1982). Approximately 10 percent of Qinghe's output, however, was for the military even in the early 1980s.

Qinghe underwent further expansion in 1958. By the early 1960s, it employed a labor force of more than 7,000 and produced five products: worsted woolen cloth, heavy woolen cloth, woolen blankets, plush, and knitting wool. In mid-1962 the mill was divided into three enterprises to improve management and facilitate the conducting of foreign trade; the plant that kept the parent factory's name is the subject of this study.[7] Qinghe retained production of worsted woolen products, knitting wool, and artificial woolen slivers (also called tops).

In the 1970s Qinghe expanded gradually (see table 6.5). The mill had a total work force of 2,340 in 1972 and GVIO of slightly more than Y42 million (in constant 1970 prices). Six years later, Qinghe's employees numbered 2,514, and its GVIO topped Y60 million. Domestic sales revenues rose by nearly 50 percent to more than Y46 million. Despite a slight drop in Qinghe's exports during the same period, Qinghe's products were available in a number of foreign countries throughout the 1970s, and total exports of worsted woolen cloth and woolen yarn amounted to nearly Y10 million in 1978. Production of worsted woolen fabrics and artificial slivers rose gradu-

Table 6.5. Development of the Qinghe Woolen Textile Mill, 1972 and 1977–82

Item	1972	1977	1978	1979	1980	1981	1982
GVIO, current prices (millions of yuan)	43.1	52.8	63.4	55.4	55.0	71.2	78.5
GVIO, 1970 constant prices (millions of yuan)	42.2	57.6	60.8	52.4	53.5	71.7	77.0
Sales revenue, excluding sales of slivers (millions of yuan)[a]	42.2	52.9	55.9	43.6	42.9	59.9	60.6
Total sales revenue (millions of yuan)[ab]	42.2	52.9	62.8	54.1	54.8	70.9	75.1
Realized profits (millions of yuan)	9.1	14.4	15.3	13.6	13.0	17.6	18.6
Average number of employees (thousands)	2.34	2.47	2.51	2.44	2.72	3.11	3.32
Production of worsted woolen cloth (millions of meters)	1.60	2.00	2.20	2.33	2.77	3.46	3.50
Production of woolen yarn (thousands of tons)	0.96	1.05	1.08	0.53	..	..	..
Production of artificial slivers (thousands of tons)	0.60	1.23	1.39	1.51	1.56	1.33	1.51
Exports of worsted woolen fabrics (thousands of meters)	52.4	38.1	43.2	56.1	81.3	113.6	140.4
Value of exports (millions of yuan)	10.7	8.6	9.2	10.3	13.6	19.9	26.5

GVIO, gross value of industrial output.

.. Negligible.

a. Data are in current prices.

b. Even though production of slivers is included in GVIO, according to government regulations total sales revenue should exclude sales of slivers, and therefore Qinghe's own accounts do not include its sales of slivers to other mills. The actual values of total sales revenue are presented here to avoid confusion. (The ratio of sales to output value would appear unnaturally low if sales of slivers were excluded from sales revenue.)

Source: Information provided by the mill.

ally between 1972 and 1978, from 1.6 million meters to 2.2 million meters and from 600 tons to 1,390 tons, respectively. Output of woolen yarns rose only slightly, however, from 960 tons to 1,080 tons, and then was sharply curtailed the following year because production was reorganized in several of Beijing's woolen textile plants. By 1980 the Qinghe mill produced worsted woolen fabrics and artificial woolen slivers almost exclusively.

Qinghe's Response to the Changing Economic Environment

In 1979, Qinghe was one of eight enterprises selected by the State Economic Commission to participate in a nationwide experiment to "confer greater decisionmaking power on enterprises."[8] The mill was allowed to retain part of its profits, granted easier access to financial resources for investment, given greater authority over internal management and planning, and made partially responsible for marketing products and purchasing inputs. These reforms were later duplicated in some 6,600 state industrial firms throughout China during the first half of 1980.

The mill's operating environment was immediately affected by these changes. With the approval of its supervisory agencies, Qinghe took out large bank loans in 1979 to finance an important expansion project that included purchase of the most advanced textile manufacturing equipment from abroad. As a result, output of woolen cloth jumped from 2.33 million meters in 1979 to 2.77 million meters in 1980 and then to 3.46 million meters in 1981. The mill's output in 1981 represented more than 27 percent of Beijing's output of woolen fabric and 3 percent of total national production. Average annual growth in these two years was 22 percent, compared with an annual growth rate of roughly 6 percent between 1972 and 1979. Qinghe's exports of worsted cloth doubled between 1979 and 1981 and accounted for more than one-third of the mill's total production in 1981. Output of the mill's other main product, artificial woolen slivers, was comparatively stable. The mill's work force grew by 27 percent between 1979 and 1981 to well over 3,000 employees. Barely a year after completion of the first expansion project, the mill undertook another one in late 1981, again financed by bank loans.

By the end of 1982 the Chinese market for woolen fabrics was becoming saturated. As a result of increased output in existing plants as well as establishment of a number of new mills, total national output of woolen fabrics grew by more than 40 percent between 1979 and 1982.[9] Although Qinghe's production of worsted woolen cloth rose only slightly between 1981 and 1982, its inventory of finished products increased greatly. Output of artificial woolen slivers, however, grew sharply during 1982 to more than 1,500 tons, without creating any backlog. Profits continued to rise, and Qinghe's overall performance was still strong in 1982, despite incipient market problems.

A confluence of additional problems beset the mill in 1983, including a price adjustment for chemical fiber products and a reduction in domestic procurement prices of woolen goods for export. Production was further disrupted by the transfer of Qinghe's sliver manufacturing equipment to other Beijing mills. Qinghe barely met its own production target of 3.5 million meters for worsted woolen cloth; factory GVIO increased by only 2.9 percent in real terms. Profits declined to Y15.5 million in 1983, and the mill was compelled to reduce its own retained profits for the first time since 1979, in order to maintain the level of funds turned over to the government.

To cope with these difficulties, the mill had to change in a number of ways. Even though its management had initiated internal reforms as early as 1979, efforts to improve the mill's performance were redoubled after 1981 in light of the new situation. Consistent with an overall emphasis on directing production to meet market demand and despite continuing constraints, bureaucratic and otherwise, the mill's leadership explored a variety of methods to forecast demand, maintain high quality standards, and develop new and popular products. This section examines the industrial reforms affecting Qinghe, the mill's response to these changes, and the obstacles that continued to impede progress, in the following spheres: organization and leadership, finance, planning and supply, marketing, investment in fixed assets, and the labor and wage system.

Organization and Leadership

The initial reforms affecting Qinghe included some changes in its formal supervisory structure. In substance these changes were insignificant in comparison with the efforts of the mill itself to revitalize its internal management. Qinghe continued to be plagued by government intrusions into virtually every important aspect of its operations throughout the early- and mid-1980s. The mill's experiences suggest that the reluctance of government agencies to relinquish their time-honored supervisory roles has often thwarted the goal of increased autonomy for enterprises.

Qinghe had been put under the jurisdiction of the Beijing Municipal Textile Industry Bureau, a subordinate branch of the Ministry of Textile Industry, in the early stages of the Cultural Revolution. (Previously it had been under the Beijing Municipal Communist Party Committee.) In 1974 the Beijing Municipal Textile Industry Bureau was renamed the Beijing Municipal Textile Industry Corporation (it is, however, referred to as the Beijing Textile Bureau, or as the bureau, in this chapter). At the same time, the bureau established the Beijing Wool, Flax, and Silk Textiles Industry Corporation (referred to here as the Textiles Corporation) to supervise Qinghe and three other mills.[10] Qinghe was supervised through a single chain of command, unlike several other enterprises studied in this volume. In practice, of course, the Beijing City government could also exercise considerable influence over decisions about labor, land use, and other local aspects of the mill's operations.

When the State Economic Commission designated Qinghe an experimental enterprise in 1979, the Beijing Municipal Economic Commission was granted general authority over the reforms at the mill and at the other two Beijing participants in the program, probably in order to temper the strong influence of the Textiles Corporation and its parent bureau. Qinghe's day-to-day operations, however, remained under the jurisdiction of the latter two agencies.

As part of the reforms, Qinghe also gained some control over its middle management. The Beijing Economic Commission had the power to appoint and dismiss the mill's director and the bureau continued to appoint deputy directors, but top management at the mill was given the right to choose, subject to the approval of the Textiles Corporation, the mill's middle- and lower-level cadres. Figure 6.1 shows the mill's formal supervisory structure after the 1979 reforms. Changes in Qinghe's supervisory structure were relatively superficial.

The mill's internal leadership system underwent considerably more change and experimentation. Qinghe in 1979 reinstituted a version of the director leadership system that had been popular in the 1950s, under which the factory director and one deputy director sat on the party committee, together

Figure 6.1. Qinghe's Formal Supervisory Structure, after 1979

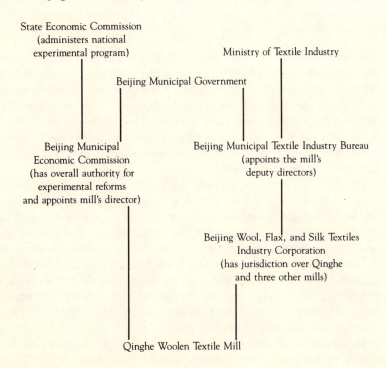

State Economic Commission
(administers national
experimental program)

Ministry of Textile Industry

Beijing Municipal Government

Beijing Municipal
Economic Commission
(has overall authority for
experimental reforms
and appoints mill's director)

Beijing Municipal Textile Industry Bureau
(appoints the mill's
deputy directors)

Beijing Wool, Flax, and Silk Textiles
Industry Corporation
(has jurisdiction over Qinghe
and three other mills)

Qinghe Woolen Textile Mill

with the party secretary, deputy party secretary, and several other party members. Important issues were discussed by the full party committee, but the director was responsible for implementing decisions concerning production and administration. The four deputy directors in charge of the production workshops and functional sections reported to the director rather than, as previously, to the mill's party secretary. The party committee was to provide general enterprise leadership, without interfering in production management.

In spite of these changes, party branches in the workshops proved recalcitrant and often prevented deputy directors from carrying out the director's instructions. Pressures for further reform led to the introduction of the "director responsibility system and Workers' Congress system under the leadership of the party committee" in 1980. This new internal reorganization extended down to the workshop and section levels the limitations on party control already in place at the top. Party branches in the workshops were officially restricted to ideological and political activities. At enterprise and branch levels, the judgments of management held official sway over the party. When disagreements arose between the director and the party committee, the director was allowed to proceed as he saw fit, and a final determination would be made later by supervisory authorities. Qinghe's Workers' Congress—restored in 1978 or 1979—was also enjoined to participate in decisionmaking and management. The mill's director was to present work reports to the congress on a regular basis. It was envisaged that the mill's employees eventually would play a role in the appointment of top managers, but as of 1984, this plan seemed destined to take effect only in the distant future. Chinese press reports on the importance of workers' congresses notwithstanding, at Qinghe the congress was largely confined to discussing labor problems and serving as a conduit for communications between employees and management.[11]

The quality of Qinghe's top management was improved by the promotion of younger, better-educated cadres. In 1981 a forty-five-year-old intellectual with a technical background was appointed from within the mill to a three-year term as director.[12] Three other managers with training in engineering were promoted to the second-tier positions of deputy director, and one such manager was prmoted to deputy chief engineer. The following year, older cadres on the party committee were replaced by younger party members with higher academic qualifications, thus reducing the average age of members of the party committee from fifty-one to forty-one. The new director and deputy directors sought to reinvigorate Qinghe's middle management. A number of older managers were retired or demoted to make way for younger persons with better technical skills. By early 1984 the mill's middle managers had been reduced from ninety-two to eighty in number, thirty-one of whom had been promoted since 1979. The proportion of middle managers who were graduates of senior middle school or higher-level educational institutions rose from 39 percent in 1979 to 50 percent in 1984, and their average age decreased from forty-seven to forty-four.

The new leadership moved aggressively to transform Qinghe's management style. Because of new freedom in planning as well as greater responsibility for marketing output, the mill's traditional objective of simply meeting production targets was clearly obsolete. The mill adopted a "production-operation" approach to internal organization, an approach designed to reorient management toward a more highly coordinated system integrating the concerns of planning, supply, and marketing. Weekly meetings of the heads of functional sections were held to resolve factorywide problems. Efforts were also made to expand the scope of deputy directors' responsibility for day-to-day operations, to reduce the number of layers in the mill's administration, and to free the director's time for strategic planning.

By early 1984 two critical organizational issues were impeding the mill's management from further improving performance. One set of problems revolved around the respective roles of the director and his deputy directors, the party secretary, the party committee and its workshop and section branches, and the Workers' Congress. Despite the constraints placed on the party committee, tension concerning its powers relative to those of the director continued. For instance, the committee could thwart the express wishes of the director by withholding approval of his recommendations for appointments and dismissals of middle- and lower-level cadres. To maneuver around the rule that no more than 30 percent of the party committee consist of administrators, when important proposals concerning production matters were to be presented, the mill's director convened enlarged meetings with section and department heads attending as well as formal committee members.

There was also confusion about the powers of the Workers' Congress. Protesting that the workers were of low quality, that they were primarily interested in bonuses, housing, and other factory subsidies rather than in operational problems, and that including the congress in important decisions would create needless delays, Qinghe's managers resisted increased participation by the Workers' Congress in management. The debate over allocation of living quarters in 1983 was cited to support the administrators' belief that "if any major issues on production and operation which need to be solved immediately are submitted to the Workers' Congress, it would be very difficult for us to get good results . . . and the director would have still another mother-in-law." Subsequent clarification of the rights and responsibilities of directors and workers within factories apparently increased internal control by Qinghe's director. In 1986, state enterprises were authorized to establish management committees, consisting only of top management personnel, to assist directors (see Xinhua 1987, pp. K9–30).

Qinghe's most serious problems, however, stemmed from the extensive array of governmental interventions that continued to constrain the mill. The

Textiles Corporation and its parent bureau maintained tight control over many facets of the mill's operations, such as retained profits and production targets. The ministry and the Beijing Labor Bureau continued to control most aspects relating to the mill's labor force. The mill was still subject to confusing procedures and rules stemming from multilayered supervision. For example, the annual bonus quota was issued by the bureau, but the bank would not release the funds without the seal of the Textiles Corporation.

In certain respects the reforms actually created an additional layer of bureaucracy by placing the Beijing Economic Commission in charge of the mill's experimental reforms. A case in point is the fractured system of appointment for Qinghe's top managers. Another example is the roundabout way in which permission to invest in projects for technical transformation had to be obtained: the mill was required to gain approval not only from the ministry and from each of its two subordinate agencies, but from the Beijing Economic Commission as well.

Additional complications arose from the lack of close coordination between the bureau and the Beijing Economic Commission. They disagreed, for example, over the response to special requests from the mill. Qinghe's management sought to raise bonuses in 1983 as a reward to employees for particularly hard work that year. The Beijing Economic Commission granted permission for the increase, but the Textile Bureau's denial of the request ultimately prevailed. The exclusion of the mill from an in-house experiment with floating wages conducted by the bureau in seven other enterprises under its supervision is another illustration of poor bureaucratic coordination. Qinghe's leadership reacted bitterly to this exclusion, which it viewed as proof of the bureau's unwillingness to extend the preferential treatment the mill deserved as an experimental enterprise.

The persistence of government controls suggests that in Qinghe's case the reform goal of substantially increasing enterprise autonomy had met with considerable impediments. One layer of external supervision was removed, however, when the Beijing Municipal Textile Industry Corporation was dissolved in 1985, and its swollen staff of some 200 was parceled out to Qinghe and to other firms.

Tax and Economic Responsibility Systems

At the very heart of the program for enterprise reform lay profit retention. Building on 1978 experiments in Sichuan Province, Qinghe instituted two successive profit retention schemes in 1979 and 1980. In mid-1980 the mill became one of ten enterprises in Beijing chosen to take part in an advanced program involving substitution of tax payments for profit remittances.[13] Qinghe's strongest response to the financial incentives created by profit retention and by the tax scheme was an immediate expansion of production and, consequently, of profits. The mill also experimented with new styles of financial management, primarily the much-vaunted internal "economic responsibility system." The mill's response to financial incentives is examined in detail after the two profit retention schemes and the new tax system are briefly described.

The first scheme was relatively simple, at least on paper. Together with members of Qinghe's finance section, officials from the State Economic Commission and from the Ministry of Finance calculated a profit retention rate of 10.64 percent. This rate was reported to be based on the ratio of the sum of the following five items to total profits in an earlier, unspecified base year: (1) welfare expenditures charged to production costs (fixed at 11 percent of the total wage bill); (2) bonuses (reinstated in 1978, initially restricted to 11 percent of yearly wages); (3) the enterprise fund (restored in 1978, set at 5 percent of total wages); (4) product development costs (2 percent of profits handed over to the government); and (5) payments for research and technical training of employees. Because this ratio essentially represented the proportion of profits previously used by Qinghe, the mill's retained profits in principle would rise only if total realized profits increased.

No particular base year for this calculation was mentioned by Qinghe, but figures for the 1970s suggest that this ratio had typically been in the range of 6–8 percent. The higher rate actually assigned therefore appears generous and was no doubt largely the outcome of negotiations between the mill and supervisory officials. This should not be surprising, because plan targets and allocations of supplies have also traditionally been set through bargaining. The profits retained by Qinghe were to be divided three ways between the production development fund (37 percent), the bonus fund (35 percent), and the welfare fund, used for housing, welfare, and other subsidies (28 percent). Qinghe was also responsible for supplying funds for neighborhood improvement and upkeep activities, such as road repairs and construction (estimated at more than Y100,000 each year).

In the first half of 1980 the mill briefly implemented a second profit-sharing method. Under this scheme Qinghe was permitted to retain a base rate of 10.64 percent from profits up to the amount realized in 1979. For profits above that figure, a higher retention rate of 20 percent was allowed; this rate created a stronger incentive to increase profits. The uses of retained profits were stipulated, this time as 40 percent for production development, 30 percent for bonuses, and 30 percent for the welfare fund.

In mid-1980 the mill was designated an independent accounting firm, responsible for its profits and losses, and it was switched from profit retention to a system of direct tax payment. This scheme involved slightly more complex calculations. A base income was derived by first adding 20 percent of total standard wages to realized profits and then subtracting a so-called adjustment tax.[14] The mill paid to the state a 40 percent tax on income, as well as a city construction tax equal to an additional 5 percent of income. These two taxes were standard for all ten Beijing enterprises in the program, but the amount of the adjustment tax—designed to equalize the burden between firms with different operating conditions (including prices, location, and endowment of natural resources)—was unique to each enterprise. Qinghe's adjustment tax rate was set at 5.2 percent of total sales revenue (not profits), including income from sales of artificial slivers. The mill continued to remit the 18 percent industrial-commercial sales tax that had been in effect all along.

The mill also had to pay two fees that were critical to the meaningful implementation of the new tax system. It was charged a 4.2 percent yearly fee for its state-assigned circulating funds and a 5 percent yearly fee on fixed assets. These fees provided an incentive for enterprises to economize on their use of fixed and working capital. Like other enterprises in Beijing, Shanghai, and Tianjin, but unlike enterprises in other cities, Qinghe was required to pay these fees out of retained profits rather than before the calculation of the income base for tax purposes.

Qinghe's use of funds remaining after payment of taxes and fees was tightly controlled. Forty percent was designated for production development, 30 percent for the welfare fund, 20 percent for bonuses, and 10 percent for the enterprise reserve fund, created chiefly in order to provide funds for bonuses in lean years. Qinghe was also subject to a ceiling that restricted yearly bonuses to the equivalent of 3.3 months of average wages. (Most enterprises were supposed to limit bonuses to three months of average wages, but higher payments were common.)

Qinghe was also given permission to keep for its own use a higher proportion of depreciation funds than previously. In the early 1970s the mill had retained 70 percent of depreciation funds, but by the middle of the decade this had declined to slightly less than 40 percent. Under the first two profit retention schemes, the mill reverted briefly to a 70 percent share; beginning in 1981, it was allowed to keep all depreciation funds. The rate at which depreciation funds were drawn also rose somewhat, from 3.6–4.1 percent before 1980 to 4.7 percent in 1981.

In contrast to the first two experiments in profit retention, the tax system involved an important measure of security for the enterprise. No doubt largely in order to ameliorate the well-known disincentives of the ratchet effect, Qinghe's rates for taxes and fees and stipulated uses of retained profits were fixed in July 1980 for the next three years and were later extended through 1986.[15] The principle of set rates offered straightforward and stable incentives to the mill.

As noted earlier, Qinghe's strongest response to the new financial incentives was immediate expansion of production. Output of worsted woolen cloth grew at a particularly rapid pace, increasing by 50 percent in the three-year period after 1979 (see table 6.5). As is shown in table 6.6, GVIO in constant prices grew by 21 percent a year on average between 1978 and 1982; average annual growth had been only 6 percent between 1972 and 1978. After the brief decline in 1978–80 that followed the sharp curtailment of yarn production, total profits grew by 35.4 percent in 1981 and by 5.4 percent in 1982. By 1983, however, problems relating to market demand and price changes had a deleterious effect on profits. Total profits fell by 17 percent in 1983 but stabilized in 1984 as market conditions improved.

Evaluation of Qinghe's ratios of profits to sales and profits to fixed assets suggests that profitability did not appreciably improve over this period (table 6.6). The ratio of profits to fixed assets was unusually high in the late 1970s and declined over the next few years mainly as a result of the large expansion projects of 1979–80 and 1981–84, which significantly added to the mill's stock of fixed capital. Despite this drop, Qinghe's profit rate on fixed assets (63 percent in 1980–83) was still relatively high.[16]

The new tax system allowed the mill to keep substantial amounts of profits for its own use. After remitting the three main taxes and the two fees, Qinghe retained 37 percent of its total realized profits in 1981 and 1982 (but only about 17 percent after deducting loan repayments). This figure compares with retention rates of 8.2 percent in 1979 and 17.9 percent in 1980.[17]

Table 6.6. Qinghe's Profit Performance, 1978–82
(millions of yuan, unless otherwise specified)

Item	1978	1979	1980	1981	1982
GVIO in 1980 constant prices	34.1	38.3	51.5	69.9	74.3
GVIO in current prices	63.4	55.4	55.0	71.2	78.5
Total profits	15.3	13.6	13.0	17.6	18.6
Net profits remitted[a]	8.5[b]	9.4[b]	9.8[c]	10.8[d]	12.0[d]
Gross profits remitted[e]	15.0	12.5	9.7	11.1	11.8
Profits retained[f]	..	1.1	3.3	6.5	6.8
Loan repayments	..	..	1.0	3.5	3.7
Ratio of profits to total sales revenues (percent)[g]	24.3	25.1	23.8	24.9	24.8
Ratio of profits to fixed assets (percent)[h]	100.0	95.3	85.8	58.0	60.3

GVIO, gross value of industrial output.

.. Negligible.

a. Figures are presumably net of various grants from the state.

b. Profits remitted to the state.

c. Profits, taxes, and fees remitted to the state.

d. Taxes and fees paid to the state.

e. State grants (which became negligible after the late 1970s) presumably have not been subtracted from these figures.

f. Including retained profits used for loan repayments.

g. Sales revenues include sales of artificial woolen slivers.

h. Fixed assets valued at original purchase prices.

Source: Information provided by the mill.

Conversely, the proportion of profits turned over to the state declined significantly, although this decline was at least partly offset by the simultaneous reduction in state grants to the mill.

Qinghe also responded to the new incentives by attempting to improve management of internal finances, particularly cost management, at all levels. First, beginning in mid-1981, monthly meetings of the "five examiners" were held, at which responsible managers from planning, technical, supply and marketing, product design, and finance sections met to discuss predictions of annual, quarterly, and monthly costs and profits. Second, the mill promoted new efforts to cut costs, assigning personnel to watch over use of raw materials and energy. Third, the mill performed annual, quarterly, and even monthly cost analyses, with an emphasis on reducing consumption of raw materials.

More significantly, Qinghe was reported to be the first state enterprise in Beijing to extend economic responsibility systems down to the workshop and section levels. In early 1979 the mill instituted an independent accounting system for its administrative and technical sections, involving separate accounts for costs, profits, circulating funds, and fixed assets. Monthly meetings to analyze workshop costs produced accounts of consumption (raw materials, dyes, and so forth), wages, and fees, for review by the finance section. The mill's targets for costs and profits were broken down and assigned to lower levels, following rough guidelines provided by the ministry. Midway through the year, the mill went still further and instituted a scheme for profit retention by workshops, whereby bonuses for workers were linked to the profit performance of workshops.

In 1982 Qinghe implemented a more extensive economic responsibility system on the model of the Shoudu (Capital) Iron and Steel Company. Introduced in mid-1981, the system's "contract, guarantee, and examine" principles—according to which economic tasks were contracted out to workshops, cooperation and assistance were guaranteed, and rewards were distributed on the basis of economic performance—were cited (by Shoudu itself, at least) as the reason behind the steel company's improved performance during the second half of 1981.[18] Following Shoudu's lead, Qinghe contracted out specific tasks to sections and workshops. Moreover, it began charging its workshops a 2 percent fee for use of fixed assets and circulating funds, to be remitted from their retained profits. An in-house bank was also established; it offered a 1.8 percent annual return on deposit accounts, as well as loans to workshops and sections at a 4.2 percent interest rate. Workshops also further subdivided their quotas by allocating them to work groups. At this lower level, targets for output, quality, attendance rate, accident incidence, and consumption of raw materials, other materials, and mechanical parts were converted into financial quotas for accounting and evaluation.

According to mill officials, adoption of the new system produced at least some of the desired results. Workshop requests for "critically necessary" equipment that subsequently sat unused came to a halt; surplus equipment was even returned. The positive gains in utilization of energy during this period also were probably related to the new accounting and economic responsibility systems. Although electricity consumption per unit of woolen cloth produced rose slightly (by 10 percent) between 1979 and 1982, use of coal fell by one-fifth and oil consumption declined by rather more than 50 percent. Changes in use of circulating funds were more complex. Stocks of inputs fell by 44 percent in nominal terms between 1978 and 1982, but this decline was offset by a rise in goods in process and in final product inventory, particularly after 1981. This rise was a reflection of marketing problems in the face of excess supply. Total circulating funds declined sharply for a brief period after 1978 but then gradually rose again; the net decline between 1978 and 1982 was only 2 percent.

After several years of Qinghe's participation in the tax system, two problems concerning financial management seemed especially acute. First, the mill's management lacked meaningful control over the use of retained profits. Because this restricted management's ability to promise employees higher financial rewards for harder work, its significance as a barrier to further improvements in economic performance should not be underestimated.[19] The 1983 "bonus incident" mentioned earlier apparently proved embarrassing for the mill's director, possibly because the bonus increase had been promised to the workers before permission was sought from authorities.

It should also be noted, however, that the mill frequently succeeded in making larger bonus payments than official stipulations and its own complaints would suggest. According to official policy, yearly bonuses were not to exceed 3.3 months' average wages. The bonus payments Qinghe actually distributed, however, were consistently higher than this state-set ceiling and higher than the guidelines for profit retention, which, after mid-1981 restricted bonuses to 20 percent of retained profits. In 1981, for instance, the 3.3-month cap would have limited bonuses to Y555,000, and, under the guidelines for profit retention, bonuses should not have surpassed Y599,000. A total of Y694,000 was actually paid out in bonuses that year. Between 1980 and 1982, mill employees received a total of Y397,000 in extra bonuses, nearly 25 percent more than the amount stipulated by state regulations.

Qinghe was able to maneuver around the rules because of a convenient loophole permitting enterprises to grant supplementary awards out of retained funds for labor competition, overfulfillment of piecework, new product design, and advances in quality. Bonus payments above the ceilings occurred because the mill received state awards for various quality prizes, overfulfillment of profit targets, and new product development. These extra payments suggest that a certain degree of flexibility was at least implicitly permitted.

A second problem was inherent in the tax scheme. The focus on profits meant that an otherwise impressive performance might be obscured because of the influence of factors beyond the enterprise's control. This was Qinghe's predicament in 1983. That year witnessed several events that reduced the mill's profits by more than Y2 million. Of this total loss, nearly Y900,000 was the result of an adjustment in prices for products using chemical fibers, and more than Y600,000 stemmed from a 15 percent reduction in the prices at which the government procured woolen textiles for export. Enterprises have often appealed to "objective conditions" as justification for lenient treatment; requiring firms to take full responsibility for profits and losses and at the same time maintaining government control over prices is nonetheless a significant flaw of partial reform in China.

Planning and Supply

As part of the effort to increase the autonomy of enterprises, Qinghe was to be given greater authority over planning. Substantial central control persisted, however, in the form of mandatory production targets. Moreover, inadequate supplies of necessary inputs—a problem related primarily but not exclusively to allocation of raw materials by the government—proved to be a formidable barrier to effective production planning, particularly when the mill sought to reorient production to meet market demand. Thus Qinghe remained significantly constrained in the areas of planning and supply.

After 1979 the state plan continued to be the major determinant of Qinghe's production: each December the mill submitted to the Textiles Corporation a draft plan for the coming year. The corporation then issued GVIO targets that Qinghe used to finalize internal plans. For production under the state plan, inputs were supplied chiefly by the supply section of the Beijing Textile Bureau through the materials sections of the Textiles Corporation. As a growing number of inputs were freed from state control, Qinghe was allowed to order items such as textile equipment directly from manufacturers and to obtain domestic dyes, bearings, and valves through commercial wholesale stations. Allocation of imported materials, including wool and dyes, however, remained the exclusive domain of the state. Qinghe was free to produce goods above the plan, but the mill had to obtain supplies needed for this production itself.

In the early 1980s Qinghe was subject to twenty economic and technical targets assigned by the Beijing Textile Bureau, through the Textiles Corporation, in accordance with ministry guidelines. Ten of these targets were mandatory comprehensive targets used by the Beijing Economic Commission to evaluate the performance of Beijing enterprises in the areas of gross output value, sales revenue, total profits, profits (taxes and fees) remitted to the state, quality of products, unit production costs, reduction in variable costs, turnover of circulating funds, productivity, and safety. Failure to fulfill any target would result in a 10 percent reduction in workers' bonuses. The other ten targets were indicative (nonmandatory) only. Whereas some of these were formulated by the mill itself and were basically higher versions of the mandatory targets, others of them covered quantity of output, exports, variety of products, and condition of equipment. Qinghe was subject to an unusually large number of binding targets. In the course of reform, targets for most enterprises were reduced to four: gross output value, physical output, profits, and quality of products.

Qinghe has never had any problems meeting its targets. As is shown in table 6.7, the mill consistently overfulfilled the gross output value and quantity targets even before the reforms; this indicates that there was little if any ratchet effect. The extent of overfulfillment did, however, rise dramatically after 1979, as the mill expanded production rapidly in response to new incentives. This pattern was typical of producers of textiles and consumer durables who were interviewed for this study (see chapters 3 and 7 of this volume and Granick 1987). Some targets may have been revised downward, but this probably occurred rarely. On the contrary, the Textiles Corporation tended to underestimate the mill's productive capacity, particularly after the first expansion project.

Beginning in 1982, Qinghe and other textile mills had their annual performance with respect to the twenty targets evaluated on a three-category scale. Depending on its overall score, a mill could be classified as a "qualified enterprise" or "an enterprise good in six respects." A firm could rate lowest-category in one to three minor target areas and still be designated "qualified," but to achieve the title of "six goods" it had to rate first-category in all its targets with the exception of one or two minor ones (in which it had to rate second-category).[20] In addition to conferring prestige, the title "quali-

Table 6.7. *Qinghe's Production Targets and Performance, Selected Years, 1972–82*

Item	1972	1976	1978	1979	1980	1981	1982
GVIO *(millions of yuan)*[a]							
Target	40.0	52.5	58.0	50.0	47.0	64.0	74.0
Actual	42.2	53.7	60.8	52.4	53.5	71.7	79.7
Overfulfillment (percent)	5.5	2.3	4.8	4.8	13.8	12.0	7.7
Worsted cloth (millions of meters)							
Target	1.60	2.00	2.15	2.20	2.50	2.90	3.25
Actual	1.60	2.00	2.20	2.33	2.77	3.46	3.50
Overfulfillment (percent)	0.0	0.0	2.3	5.9	10.8	19.3	7.7
Artificial wool slivers (tons)							
Target	600	1,050	1,230	1,350	1,450	1,250	1,350
Actual	603	1,083	1,387	1,515	1,559	1,332	1,514
Overfulfillment (percent)	0.5	3.1	12.8	12.2	7.5	6.6	12.1

GVIO, gross value of industrial output.
a. In 1970 constant prices.
Source: Information provided by the mill.

fied enterprise," according to Beijing Economic Commission regulations based on Document 65 of the State Council in 1983, entitled an enterprise to raise wages and grant its workers a substantial bonus increase. In 1982 Qinghe rated first-category in all but two targets and thus became one of the first enterprises designated "qualified." Wages and bonuses were promptly raised in 1983. An important goal of the mill's management in mid-1984 was to achieve the status of a "six goods" enterprise as quickly as possible.

Qinghe's management in the early 1980s strove to strengthen internal planning in several ways. The mill adopted a "production-operation" approach to internal organization (as discussed earlier) and made planning more integrated through meetings of the "five examiners" and other newly formalized inter-section channels of communication. The finance section, for example, analyzed cost prediction and control with other sections; the design section cooperated more closely with the finance, technical, and marketing sections to ensure the feasibility and marketability of new products. A computer, reported to have been the first ever purchased by a Chinese textile mill, was applied to analysis of costs, quality control, and other aspects of production in order to improve planning and coordination.

In this more integrated planning environment, Qinghe focused on responding to market demand, particularly in the wake of the emergence of a buyers' market for woolen textiles in 1982. The mill relied on its own predictions of market demand and also took into account its productive capacity in planning. Since 1982, however, market demand has been the decisive factor in making production plans.

The economic responsibility system (which was discussed earlier with reference to financial management) also played an important role in efforts to improve planning. Once enterprise-level targets were formulated, the functional sections of the mill disaggregated them into workshop targets. Workshop personnel further subdivided these targets to work groups, teams, and individuals. Performance criteria and rewards were similarly developed at two levels: the intermediate level of sections and workshops and the individual level. At most factories, ministry "work norms" served as yardsticks in drawing up lower-level targets. These targets, however, were based on production using domestic equipment; since Qinghe benefited from more productive imported equipment, the mill was charged with developing its own norms. After initially adjusting norms upward in incremental fashion, the mill in 1982 carried out an extensive survey of workshop processes. On the basis of this study, which revealed surprisingly low labor productivity in some sections, new work norms—increased by an average of 48 percent—were established and used in setting lower-level production targets.

On the supply side, Qinghe's behavior was dominated by the need to secure important raw materials, primarily wool and artificial fibers. In theory the government was still responsible for supplying inputs for production under the state plan. In practice, however, allocation of raw materials by government authorities proved increasingly inadequate to meet output plan targets. Moreover, even in years when the mill's supply of wool was sufficient in quantity, it was frequently inadequate in type and specification. Supply problems persisted despite quarterly meetings with the Textiles Corporation to resolve these issues.

From 1982–83 onward, Qinghe faced extremely tight supplies of wool. As a producer of high-quality fabrics, the mill depended on imported wool for 70–80 percent of its inputs of raw materials, but in 1984 foreign wool provided by the state met only 60 percent of Qinghe's production needs.[21] Although the mill acquired all domestically produced wool on its own, greater reliance on Chinese wool was not a realistic long-term option. The most accessible domestic wool was from Nei Monggol, where wind, dust, and dryness combined to produce wool of exceedingly low quality. Moreover, pervasive hoarding of raw materials by factories exacerbated chronic shortfalls in wool supply. The negotiated price of domestic wool consequently jumped to 30–40 percent more than the state price in the early 1980s. Increased use of Chinese wool thus not only exposed Qinghe to the risk of failing to meet the ministry's quality standards for worsted fabrics but also brought with it lower profits. Cloth produced with domestic wool reportedly brought a 26–27 percent profit margin on sales, compared with a 36–37 percent margin for fabrics produced with imported wool.

In addition to engaging in lengthy negotiations with higher-level authorities about this problem,[22] Qinghe responded to it primarily in two ways. First, to avoid the high cost of domestic wool, it established links with "brother factories" (other textile mills) in neighboring provinces, from which it obtained artificial yarns in exchange for its own surplus (domestically produced) raw materials. Although it was not a particularly efficient method of solving supply problems, this cooperation clearly eased some of the mill's supply constraints. These exchanges tended to be based on state prices rather than on higher negotiated prices. The proportion of artificial yarns in Qinghe's worsted fabrics rose noticeably in 1979–83 as a result.

Second, because the government guaranteed the supply of imported wool needed to produce export goods, the mill signed contracts with the Beijing Import-Export Corporation for Textile Products to produce substantial quantities of products for export. Between 1981 and 1983 an average of 36.4 percent of Qinghe's worsted fabrics were sold overseas. Even after export procurement prices were adjusted downward in 1983, the mill continued to rely on export contracts as a means of obtaining foreign wool supplies. It also attempted unsuccessfully in 1985 to form a joint venture with a garment factory that had its own allocation quota for imported wool.

A host of other planning and supply problems also plagued the mill in the mid-1980s. These problems reflected the inherent inefficiencies of directive planning. In spite of the reforms, the mill's scope of production was still not determined by enterprise managers, but rather, in the traditional, top-down fashion, by outside authorities. Qinghe's managers were particularly resentful of automatic increases in output targets. Though it consistently achieved its targets, the mill complained that "the practice of 'whipping the fast ox' forces the enterprise to hold back a trick or two."

Additional problems were generated by inconsistencies between targets, for example, between targets for output or profits on the one hand and those for quality on the other. To meet certain mandatory targets, such as that for capacity utilization, Qinghe often had little choice but to produce fabrics that it later had serious difficulties selling. This situation led to tensions between the planning and marketing sections. Moreover, plans tended to reach the mill quite late in the year. The final annual plan, which was supposed to be issued in February, rarely reached Qinghe before April. This often necessitated disruptive adjustments. At the end of 1982 the Beijing Textile Bureau revised the mill's target for gross output value upward by Y300,000 when it became clear that the bureau's own target otherwise would not be fulfilled. Compelling Qinghe to increase output of high-quality products that it subsequently was unable to market, this late intervention contributed to the mill's burgeoning inventory of finished goods.

With respect to supply of inputs other than raw materials, the mill had a long list of complaints stemming chiefly from the inadequacies of continued state allocation. One persistent problem concerned electricity. The Beijing Power Supply Bureau randomly shut off power in the mill's neighborhood several times a month without notifying consumers in advance. After extensive consultations, the bureau in 1983 agreed to maintain a fixed schedule of power outages, but after a short period of time the schedule was simply ignored. Other problems were created by bureaucratic procedures for purchase of materials regulated by the state. For example, the mill was required to submit its requisition for its entire year's supply of imported dyes each February, long before it had formulated its quarterly and monthly plans for the second half of the year. Special-purpose textile equipment and materials similarly could be ordered only once a year and then had to be stockpiled.

Increased flows of goods outside plan channels in the early 1980s offered enterprises alternative sources of supplies. For a range of items from wire hooks to coal, Qinghe could turn directly to manufacturers. This freedom, however, brought new challenges. First, the necessary good had to be located. For instance, steel was provided to the mill by the Textiles Corporation, but only in the form of steel bars. The thin steel strips the mill actually required were apparently available only in Shanghai. Suitable wire hooks were likewise impossible to obtain in Beijing. If the mill was fortunate, it might procure them in Shanghai; otherwise it was forced to buy imported hooks at ten times the domestic price. Second, as in the case of wool, the tight domestic supply situation was exacerbated by hoarding, and, in response to this, the floating prices of many important industrial goods rose. Qinghe could buy substantial amounts of coal, for example, but only at high prices.

Product Marketing

Under the reform program initiated in 1979, Qinghe was allowed to market its above-plan output independently. The mill was relatively slow, however, in taking on its new marketing responsibility. Not until 1982 did its share of direct sales surpass 5 percent of total sales (see table 6.8). In 1983, however, this figure rose to roughly 30 percent, and in 1984 self-marketing accounted for one-half of total sales. By 1985–86 Qinghe was responsible for virtually all domestic sales. It established sales links in Beijing and in other cities and began marketing its products to clothing factories, shops, and wholesale departments throughout China. Within a few years the mill had sixteen permanent sales locations and another seventy-four liaison points in Beijing alone.

The dramatic rise in self-sales after 1982 related more to adjustment policies than it did to enterprise reforms. Its warehouses bursting with textile products, the wholesale department of the Beijing Textile Products Corporation was authorized to sharply reduce its purchases of Qinghe's output. This abdication by the government of much of the responsibility for procurement of outputs probably did more to further many of the goals of enterprise reform than did the reforms themselves. Despite the difficulties of suddenly refocusing planning and production and the further aggravation of persistent supply constraints, Qinghe by the mid-1980s had clearly made the shift toward market-oriented growth. This conversion was spurred by the emerging buyers' market for the mill's products.

As mentioned earlier, the mill's management sought to put market demand at the very heart of the planning and production process. In order to make appropriate changes in the mix, quality, and style of products, Qinghe established an extensive information-gathering network to forecast market demand. This network's activities included conducting collaborative investigations with nearby Qinghe University; carrying out market surveys; discussing market trends with foreign counterparts and with Chinese commercial de-

Table 6.8. Sales of Qinghe's Products, 1979–84
(percent, unless otherwise specified)

Item	1979	1980	1981	1982	1983	1984
Sales revenue (millions of yuan)[a]	54.0	54.8	70.9	75.1	72.5[b]	67.0[b]
Exported	19.0	24.9	28.1	35.3	26.6	20.0
Purchased by state	81.0	72.7	71.3	58.5	51.4	40.0
Sold by enterprise	0.0	2.4	0.6	6.2	22.0	40.0
Share of direct marketing in total domestic sales	0.0	3.2	0.8	9.6	30.0	50.0

a. Data include income from sales of artificial woolen slivers.
b. Data are estimates provided by Qinghe.
Source: Information provided by the mill.

partments; soliciting customer suggestions; holding sales fairs and exhibitions; and visiting sales locations, other cities, and even the Guangzhou Export Commodity Fair, whenever possible. The mill's director himself was involved in much of this intelligence gathering. Market forecasts considered changes in consumers' purchasing power as well as life cycles of products. Information was also obtained on relative preferences of consumers in different parts of China. Market surveys revealed, for example, that the mill's darker fabrics were more popular in the north than in the south and that thin gabardine was particularly favored in Guangzhou, Wuhan, and Shanghai.

As early as 1979 Qinghe began incorporating market projections into its planning of product mix. For example, it experimented with a new kind of "sparkling suiting" that used reverse twisting and blended gold and silver artificial woolen threads. This new item was inexpensive enough to appeal to a broad market, and it proved immensely popular. Acting on predictions of future domestic buying power, however, the mill after 1979 shifted production in the opposite direction, toward medium- and high-grade goods containing higher quantities of sheep wool, angora, camel hair, yak hair, and rabbit hair. Within one year the share of high-grade pure fiber fabrics in total production increased from 18 percent to 28 percent, and the share of medium-quality blended fabrics rose from 42 percent to 58 percent.

The mill also placed more emphasis on quality for all of its goods beginning in the late 1970s. In this endeavor, Qinghe was responding to several incentives. First, with its modern imported equipment, the mill probably enjoyed a comparative advantage in the production of quality textiles relative to the production of more inexpensive varieties. Increasing the share of first-rate fabrics produced thus added to its competitive edge. Second, firms with exacting quality standards for their products enjoyed high prestige in the public eye. The mill's top management was clearly eager to nurture a strong association between Qinghe's name and excellence in order to maintain its secure niche in the market for high-quality woolen fabrics. Third, sizable awards were granted by various state agencies for improvements in quality as well as for specific outstanding products. These awards could be passed on to workers in the form of bonuses. Fourth, high-quality worsted fabrics were more marketable abroad. Fifth, in the mill's view, supervisory agencies treated firms known to have high quality standards more leniently. The concentration on quality may also have been linked to the increasingly important role of engineers in the mill's top management (see Byrd and Tidrick 1987, p. 64).

A pilot system of factorywide quality control, reportedly the earliest of its kind in China, was first instituted in 1978 and subsequently expanded. A drive toward "total quality control" was begun in 1979. This effort included the formulation of quality standards for functional sections, workshops, and work groups and teams, as well as the integration of quality control measures with the economic responsibility system (State Economic Commission, Enterprise Management Department 1982).

The policy of improving and maintaining quality proved to be one of the most effective internal changes implemented at the mill. In 1979 the title "reliable quality mill" was conferred on Qinghe by the Beijing Textile Bureau. By 1982, twelve varieties of Qinghe's cloth had won regional prizes for excellence and five had been designated by the ministry as "popular name brands." This designation for product superiority and popularity entitled the mill to float the price of each such product upward by 10 percent. One of these products, cashmere suiting, was awarded a national silver medal.[23] All of these awards improved Qinghe's reputation for producing high-quality fabrics and added substantially to the funds it could distribute as workers' bonuses.

Another important element in Qinghe's effort to produce for the market involved product development. Through intensive efforts Qinghe had developed ten new fabric varieties by 1981. Because of the constrained supply of pure wool, most of these were blended fabrics, such as wool-dacron fancy suiting, wool filament–dacron fabrics, and wool-linen-dacron cloth. The mill also produced 633 different patterns and almost 6,000 new color varieties between 1979 and 1981 (Zhu and others 1984, p. 233). Between 1978 and 1982 Qinghe was awarded more than Y100,000 by the state for new product development. Two new products, polyester-wool blended fabric and cashmere suiting, were among the five Qinghe products designated as "popular name brands."

Market forecasting and trial production played an important role in the design of new products. Between January 1980 and September 1980, more than 300 new patterns were manufactured on a trial basis; the vast majority of them were then incorporated into regular production after positive public response. The mill's personnel themselves were often called on to participate in trial usage. In 1981, for instance, mill employees observed that a certain lightweight blended suiting developed excessive fluff when worn; further technical improvements were then made before the suiting was produced on a large scale.

Qinghe apparently also enjoyed a certain degree of flexibility in setting prices for its own domestic sales. The government purchased the mill's fabrics at ex-factory prices (10 percent less than wholesale prices) and then resold them to factories and retail shops at wholesale prices. The state-set retail price was 14 percent higher than the wholesale price. Theoretically, Qinghe's self-sales were to be made at the wholesale price in order to avoid undercutting government purchasing agencies. The mill was occasionally permitted to reduce its prices for certain products to the producer price, however, when excess supplies led to unacceptably slow sales. Such a reduction occurred, for example, when changing demand made Qinghe's spindle-dyed fabrics unmarketable. (Other enterprises similarly received permission from local authorities to reduce prices in times of excess supply.) Moreover, many of Qinghe's improvements in quality can be viewed as a form of price competition, through sale of a superior product at the same price.

The mill was also keenly aware of opportunities to charge prices higher than wholesale prices, particularly in the atmosphere created by the resurgence of domestic demand after 1983. "Popular name brand" fabrics, for instance, were sold at higher negotiated prices within the 10 percent price float permitted for such products. After a State Council decision in May 1984 permitted enterprises to float prices of self-marketed products 20 percent higher or lower than the controlled prices, Qinghe raised prices for a range of its fabrics. Because demand was booming in late 1984, the mill apparently was able to charge some of its buyers prices close to the retail price.

Qinghe's efforts to compete through quality, product development, and price changes were augmented by sales promotion, although, unlike many other firms, it did not make sales promotion an important part of its marketing strategy until after 1982. Sales promotion basically took place within the framework of the economic responsibility system, but, in 1983, extra bonuses were awarded to personnel in the sales section to encourage them to overfulfill their monthly sales targets. Facing swollen inventories of finished goods, Qinghe redoubled efforts to promote sales in 1984. These efforts evidently played a significant role in reducing the mill's stock of finished products by two-thirds within a period of three months in early 1984.

Exports also featured prominently in Qinghe's overall sales strategy. Although exports remained a state monopoly, Qinghe was aggressive in signing contracts with the Beijing Import-Export Corporation for Textile Products after 1979. The quantity of the mill's worsted cloth sold abroad more than tripled in the three years after 1979 and accounted for 40 percent of its total output of worsted cloth in 1982. In part the mill was motivated by the need to ensure a steady supply of high-quality imported wool. Another strong incentive to expand export production may have been the priority given to large exporters in the allocation of foreign exchange for imported equipment. After 1983, however, the mill began to focus on production for the domestic market. This shift was no doubt prompted mainly by a 15 percent reduction in the prices at which the Beijing Import-Export Corporation purchased the mill's output in 1983; this reduction was reported to have caused a Y653,000 decline in profits. Despite its new eagerness to market at home, Qinghe's exports accounted for nearly one-fourth of its total sales in 1984–85, because of high externally imposed targets for exports and because of the mill's continuing need to obtain foreign wool.

Qinghe's direct marketing faced several serious problems in the early 1980s: lack of information about foreign markets, uncertainty about domestic sales, and persistent constraints on planning and supply. Although impressive efforts were made to predict domestic demand accurately, lack of reliable information about foreign markets remained a frustration. This lack primarily stemmed from the state monopoly on export contracts, which resulted in little direct contact between the mill and its foreign buyers. Because they had no opportunity to go abroad, Qinghe's planners and designers relied principally on information they obtained at the Guangzhou Export Commodity Fair to assess foreign demand. Even this avenue was cut off for them when the Beijing Textile Bureau and the Textiles Corporation decided to send their own officials to the fair instead. The mill believed this decision hampered its ability to fulfill export contracts efficiently and handicapped its design of new products.

Uncertainty for the mill resulted from certain actions of the government and of other purchasers of the mill's products. The Beijing Textile Products Corporation occasionally cancelled contracts if it became clear that the products involved would not find ready markets. Such a cancellation occurred in 1983 after the price adjustment for chemical fiber products. The corporation in November 1982 had signed a large order for pure wool fabrics, but when the market responded to price changes by shifting demand toward less expensive blended fabrics, the corporation refused to honor its contract and the mill was left with a large stock of finished woolen fabrics. Perhaps even more frustrating for the mill were experiences with its sales contracts with other businesses, which included no guarantees of eventual payment. The Shenzhen Development Corporation in January 1984 signed a contract for 50,000 meters of gabardine. Well over a year later, despite several visits from Qinghe sales representatives, the Shenzhen company had still not settled its account. The mill vowed it would no longer make sales to warehouses or to supply and marketing cooperatives, because these entities were likely to repudiate their debts.

The general inflexibility imposed by the Chinese system of planning and supply was discussed earlier. Supply shortages and the need to achieve output plan targets inhibited the mill from producing those goods it believed best suited to market demand. In early 1983, for example, Qinghe sought to increase production of strip-dyed fabrics, which it predicted would find a strong domestic market. Limited by bottlenecks in supplies of raw materials and anxious to meet its target for capacity utilization, the mill had no choice but to produce instead a larger quantity of spindle-dyed fabrics, which were then stockpiled because of lack of demand for them. Qinghe was eventually allowed to sell the spindle-dyed fabrics at the ex-factory price rather than at the wholesale price in order to clear its inventories. Together with general bureaucratic interference, the lack of flexibility in planning and supply probably represented the most serious problem the mill faced throughout the early 1980s.

Investment System

Changes in the way Qinghe financed fixed investment resulted from China's adjustment policies as well as from enterprise reforms. On the one hand, Qinghe received favored access to investment funds from the People's Bank of China as part of the nationwide promotion of light industries and textile industries. On the other hand, as a participant in the pilot reforms, the mill was given more authority over production planning and was freer to expand facilities and operations. The government hoped that the switch from grant financing to credit financing of capital investment would create an incentive to economize on the use of fixed capital. A new tax on fixed assets was designed to reinforce this incentive. As is shown in table 6.9, the overall result of these changes was a major shift in Qinghe's chief source of fixed investment financing from basic depreciation funds to bank credit.

Immediately after the mill was selected to participate in the pilot reform program in 1979, it invested in a large expansion project. The project comprised part of an extensive readjustment plan carried out by the Beijing Textile Bureau, so it is safe to assume that at least part of the impetus for it came from above rather than from the mill's own initiative. The plan called for transferring Qinghe's woolen yarn equipment to two nearby textile mills and concentrating Qinghe's own production on worsted woolen cloth. Completed within thirteen months, the project increased the floor space of the mill's operating facilities by 4,600 square meters (not including space made available by the renovation of the former yarn workshop) and boosted productive capacity of worsted woolen fabrics from 7,100 spindles to more than 10,700 spindles. Modern equipment from Japan, the Federal Republic of Germany, and Switzerland was installed; this equipment was the most important reason for the dramatic increase in the mill's production of worsted woolen cloth after 1979.

Altogether, outlays for the project amounted to more than Y16 million. Of this total, only Y0.94 million was provided by the mill itself, mainly

Table 6.9. Sources of Funding for Qinghe's Fixed Investment, Selected Years, 1975–82
(percent, unless otherwise specified)

Source	1975–77	1979	1980	1981	1982	1979–82
Total fixed investment						
(millions of yuan)	1.58	13.66	1.43	15.89	1.75	32.73
Government grants[a]	10.1	0.0	0.0	11.6	28.0	7.1
Depreciation funds	75.7	4.7	32.7	0.0	15.1	4.3
Major repair funds	11.0	1.3	40.2	0.0	0.0	2.3
Retained profits	0.0[b]	0.0	0.0	9.7	19.0	5.7
Bank loans[c]	0.0	94.0	27.1	78.5	38.0	80.5

Note: Percentages may not add to 100 because of rounding and residuals.

a. Data include budgetary capital construction and renewal investment appropriations.

b. Other funds belonging to the enterprise (not necessarily retained profits) accounted for 3.2 percent of total fixed investment financing in 1975–77.

c. Loans were made by Bank of China (88.1 percent), People's Construction Bank of China (9.0 percent), and People's Bank of China (2.9 percent).

Source: Information provided by the mill.

from retained depreciation funds. The balance was supplied by bank loans and included a foreign exchange allocation of $4.24 million (Y7.17 million, valued at the official exchange rate of the time). Although interest rates were not high, the loans' short amortization period of three years placed a relatively heavy repayment burden on the mill immediately. Moreover, Qinghe had to make loan repayments out of after-tax retained profits, unlike most other firms.

Other features of the loan repayment system, however, helped to counterbalance these burdens. Enterprises were generally expected to repay loans from the incremental profits earned on investments. If these profits were insufficient, depreciation charges, then taxes on fixed asset, then finally the industrial-commercial sales tax generated by the newly created assets could be diverted to loan repayment. In Qinghe's case, funds from all these sources, except the tax on fixed assets, were used to repay loans, though not in the stipulated order. Repayments of interest and principal between 1980 and 1982 totaled Y15.72 million, but only 52 percent of this amount (Y8.21 million) was paid out of retained profits.[24] As is shown in table 6.10, the vast bulk of the difference (35.6 percent of total repayments) consisted of funds diverted from the industrial-commercial tax. Depreciation and other enterprise funds supplied the rest. The mill repaid all of the loans within two years and three months.

Before the expansion, Qinghe's equipment section and a small repair team had been responsible for maintenance and repair work. In 1979 a separate capital construction section and an extension project office were established to oversee large investment projects and the maintenance of workshop buildings and living quarters. Most of the building materials for the expansion project were supplied by the government, but the mill itself hired the con-

Table 6.10. Funding of Qinghe's Expansion Project of 1979–80

Item	Amount (millions of yuan)	Proportion of total (percent)
Total investment	16.66	100.0
Enterprise funds	0.94	5.6
Borrowed bank funds[a]	15.72	94.4
Repaid from		
Retained profits	8.21	52.2[b]
Industrial-commercial tax	5.60	35.6[b]
Depreciation funds	1.43	9.1[b]
Other enterprise funds[c]	0.48	3.1[b]

a. Loans were made by Bank of China, People's Construction Bank of China, and People's Bank of China. Figures include principal and interest.

b. Proportion of total bank borrowing.

c. Precise source of funds was not indicated, but these may have been major repair funds.

Source: Information provided by the mill.

struction workers. For the 1979–80 job, it contracted with a building team from Dazhuangke Commune in nearby Yanqing County; Qinghe chose to award a second expansion project to another Beijing building company, however, perhaps as a result of difficulties encountered with the commune team.

Although the mill viewed the 1979–80 expansion as an unqualified success, it was not interested in further expansion of production facilities. This lack of interest may have stemmed in part from crowded operating conditions at Qinghe's site, but management also believed that the 1979–80 expansion had left the mill "unbalanced" with regard to its productive and nonproductive facilities. Management consequently planned in 1981 to invest only in nonproductive facilities—living quarters, a nursery, dining halls, and a warehouse. The Beijing Economic Commission and Beijing Textile Bureau refused to approve this plan, however, unless the mill undertook further investment in productive assets as well. The commission and the bureau apparently sweetened the deal with another foreign exchange allocation for import of modern machinery. The second expansion project was thus born of a compromise: the mill undertook a 4,800-spindle investment and in return received permission to build the auxiliary facilities. Begun in November 1981, this Y25 million project involved physical expansion of the mill's covered buildings by nearly 40 percent. Funding was once more provided primarily by bank loans.

In sharp contrast to the initial expansion, this second project was plagued with problems. From the outset its sheer scope led to planning and construction delays. These were aggravated by the cancellation of a joint venture with Dazhuangke Commune, which left the mill with an unexpected 100 additional weaving machines for which it had to find space. Slackening demand for woolen fabrics and a drop in profits during 1983 compelled Qinghe to extend its loan repayments beyond the stipulated maturity of three to five years. Moreover, because of inadequate government allocations of steel and cement, extra quantities of these materials at high negotiated prices were required, pushing project costs well over budget. Originally scheduled to be completed by mid-1984, the project was ultimately delayed by at least a year.

Frustrated by these developments, the mill's management intended thenceforth to concentrate its efforts on updating and technical transformation of equipment rather than further expansions. Even after the large purchases of imported machinery in connection with the 1979–80 and 1981–85 investment projects, shoddy equipment still constrained the mill. More than half of its machinery had been fabricated in the 1950s and 1960s, and a small amount of it even predated the founding of the People's Republic of China. Qinghe was motivated to update equipment not only in order to increase capacity and raise quality, but also in order to improve working conditions. Under pressure from its employees and its supervisory agencies, the mill used wall padding to reduce excessive noise levels caused by older equipment, but noise-reduction standards were still not being satisfied. In addition, decades-old power machinery continuously exposed workers to black smoke.

The second expansion project shows that Qinghe's main constraint in the area of investment lay in the tension between state control and enterprise autonomy. Permission from supervisory agencies for important investment projects was far from automatic. The role of government agencies in this was a manifestation of continued central control in general, and also of government concern over excessive investment. In this instance, however, the authorities used their power to push for expansion of productive facilities; the mill, in contrast, was keenly aware of capacity limits and preferred to concentrate on improving existing equipment through technical updating and transformation.

With respect to this latter goal, the mill was subject to a number of restrictions. First, it had to obtain permission from no fewer than four government agencies in order to invest in technical transformation: the Beijing Textiles Corporation, the Textile Bureau, the Ministry of Textile Industry, and the Beijing Economic Commission. Requests for foreign exchange were subject to additional bureaucratic procedures and were rarely approved in less than two years. Second, funds for technical transformation were limited; only 30 percent of Qinghe's production development fund could be channeled in this direction. Third, domestically produced equipment was often of notoriously poor quality. The mill complained that during the second expansion, 100 Chinese looms were purchased which then required nine months of modification before they were suitable for use. Fourth, obtaining spare parts for imported equipment was a persistent problem, and Chinese substitutes were generally inadequate. In sum, efforts to update equipment were handicapped by the same administrative and supply constraints that affected the mill in planning and production.

Employment and Wage System

In the early 1980s the labor system was undoubtedly the least reformed sphere of the Chinese economy.[25] Whereas state enterprises had increased their authority over planning, purchasing of inputs, marketing, and investment, they had virtually no control over perhaps the most fundamental factor of all: labor. Qinghe was no exception to this general pattern. Both before and after 1979 the size of its labor force was limited to the total number of employees fixed by the ministry. In choosing new workers the mill theoretically enjoyed a degree of latitude. As soon as the Beijing Labor Bureau had distributed its yearly quota for labor, Qinghe could attempt to recruit those applicants who scored highest on its examination for prospective employees. The vast majority of new staff, however, were children of retiring employees.[26] Once employed, workers essentially became Qinghe's employees for life; they were rarely disciplined and could not be dismissed without the approval of the Textiles Corporation. Wages were set by the government and rarely adjusted; the mill "dared not" penalize a lazy worker with a salary decrease because such a decision would likely be overturned by authorities. Controls over bonuses further restricted the use of financial incentives. Subsidies for health care, transportation, heating, and even summer refreshments were standardized and generally considered part of the basic compensation package. Table 6.11 provides data on Qinghe's average worker wage, bonus, and subsidy.

Despite the restrictions on hiring, firing, wages, bonuses, and other labor incentives, the mill attempted to push beyond the boundaries of control. Its attempts can be grouped into three broad categories: use of incentives to increase productivity, efforts to raise skill levels to improve performance of workers, and limited experimentation with contractual labor arrangements.

The reintroduction of bonuses in 1978 at first glance would appear to have provided an important incentive to improve performance at enterprise and individual levels. Qinghe routinely surpassed its targets by such a wide margin, however, that at the factory level, at least, bonuses probably served only as a relatively mild form of group financial incentive. The flexibility to increase wages and bonuses that accompanied "qualified enterprise" status may have been a more important incentive. This designation resulted in an average wage increase of Y8.1 per worker per month (17.6 percent) and in extra bonuses equal to 5 percent of total wages in 1983.

Another group incentive to improve performance was created by shifting the burden of financing of the mill's welfare fund primarily onto retained profits. The bulk of the increase in the welfare fund after 1978 was spent on workers' housing. Qinghe had a chronically short supply of housing; virtually no housing had been built in the 1970s. Workers highly valued factory housing, not only because it was heavily subsidized, but also because it eliminated the burden of long commutes to work. Although to a certain degree the mill was fulfilling an enterprise duty by investing in housing, mill managers could also use housing as a reward for strong labor performance. Between 1979 and 1982 a full 70 percent of retained profits designated for the welfare fund was channeled into housing; more than 10,000 square meters of living

Table 6.11. Qinghe's Average Wages and Bonuses, 1977–82
(yuan per worker per month)

Item	1977	1978	1979	1980	1981	1982
Total wages	56.63	65.44	74.08	80.05	74.60	74.33
Basic wage	48.40	51.45	52.14	47.87	45.31	46.03
Bonus	0.00	6.00	13.50	14.85	14.85	14.85
Subsidy[a]	8.23	7.49	10.44	17.33	14.44	13.45

a. Includes payments for overtime work.

Source: Information provided by the mill.

space were added to the 15,000-odd square meters already existing in 1979. By 1984 the mill could claim that its basic housing needs had been largely met.

At the level of the individual worker, government restrictions limited bonuses to 3.3 months of average wages.[27] Moreover, Qinghe was required to obtain approval from the Beijing Textiles Corporation each month before distributing bonuses. A constraint that was perhaps even greater resulted from egalitarian pressures within the mill itself. Chinese workers tended to view differentiation in wages and bonuses as leading to harder work and heightened competition, but not necessarily to higher pay. Claiming that to do so would "lead to contradictions among workers," the mill's director as of mid-1984 had never used his right to raise the wages of 1 percent of staff and workers each year by one wage grade. Nonetheless, it was recognized that breaking the "iron rice bowl" was a precondition for effective use of bonuses as an incentive to increase labor productivity. This recognition seems to have been a primary motivation in the early implementation of the mill's economic responsibility system. When an extensive examination in 1982 revealed low productivity in certain areas, many work norms were raised sharply.

By 1982 a fairly complex method using sliding point scales to assess workshop, section, and individual performance had been developed.[28] This method succeeded to some degree in overcoming wage egalitarianism; by mid-1984 the mill claimed that top workers were receiving monthly bonuses of Y40, whereas those who showed little improvement in productivity were receiving only Y0.1. Bonus differentiation was reinforced by the mill's control over distribution of prizes for new product development, quality control, innovations, and labor competition; the prizes were in turn supplemented by government awards for similar factorywide achievements. As noted earlier, these various forms of bonuses actually far surpassed the limit imposed by state regulations.

Financial incentives to boost productivity were also created through special contracts the mill made with particular workshops or sections. For instance, to overcome a production bottleneck in one weaving workshop, extra bonuses of Y13 per month were guaranteed for above-target output, whereas below-target output would result in a financial penalty. In 1983, rising inventories of worsted cloth focused attention on the marketing section; additional bonuses were to be awarded if the annual Y6 million sales plan were overfulfilled. This incentive was apparently responsible for reducing the mill's stock of worsted fabrics from 180,000 meters to 70,000 meters between January and March in 1984.

Further incentives for hard work may have been provided through overtime pay, particularly between 1979 and 1982, when there was virtually no government control over such payments. In 1983, however, the Beijing Textile Bureau established a limit on overtime pay that restricted such awards to

Y13 per worker per year. Overtime payments declined markedly after 1982 as a result of the new restriction.

In 1983 the mill experimented with yet another form of financial incentive: a floating wage system (see also chapter 3 in this volume). Under this system, Y5 per worker was withheld from wages each month and "floated" until the end of the year, as were workers' bonuses, which were calculated according to the extent of overfulfillment of targets. Implemented on a trial basis in the mending section of the dyeing workshop, this system had a significant effect on motivation. Workers who had earlier completed an average of only 85–90 bolts a day—rather less than the mill's standard of 110 bolts a day— became capable of finishing an average of 110–120 bolts a day. In the light of this success, the mill was planning to institute the floating wage system factorywide in 1984.

Qinghe's management also attempted to address in a systematic fashion the problem of low labor skills, which it claimed was aggravated by the practice of allowing children to replace a retiring parent, because workers often selected their least talented child to take their positions. In addition to requiring all workers under the age of thirty-five to take a training course, the mill developed several training programs that used television and outside lecturers. Especially promising staff members were encouraged to pursue college or graduate studies. In 1984 Qinghe also launched an on-the-job training program for the thirty cadres newly assigned out of universities and vocational schools, in which they worked on the production line for a full year in order to familiarize themselves with the mill's frontline operations, before they took up their permanent positions. Persistent complaints about low labor skills suggested that, despite these efforts, additional measures in the area of worker training were still necessary.

The third way in which Qinghe sought to maneuver around the constraints of the labor allocation system was contractual labor arrangements. First, the mill in 1980 undertook the aforementioned joint venture with Dazhuangke Commune near Beijing. The commune supplied buildings, transportation, and labor, and Qinghe provided 100 weaving machines, colored yarn, and finishing. This arrangement was essentially a way for the mill to find labor to utilize its outmoded equipment. After problems relating to the technical competence of the commune's laborers and to sharing of profits emerged, the joint venture was canceled in 1982 or 1983. Second, in 1983 the mill recruited 100 contract workers for what was to be a three-year period. In contrast to the contractual system for state employees instituted by the July 1986 labor reforms, this arrangement involved temporary contract labor outside the state plan. Once recruited, the workers apparently disputed the terms of the contract, and the agreement was never finalized. Although these contractual arrangements were not as substantial as those made by many other firms, they nonetheless reflect the mill's efforts to introduce flexibility into an extremely rigid labor system.

Two problems relating to labor plagued Qinghe in mid-1984. First, although the mill was subject to a fixed total labor quota, several hundred workers were not physically present at the mill. Qinghe was required by its supervisory agencies to supply a large number of workers for various government activities, including construction of power plants, militia training, and citywide arts performances and sports contests. In some cases, such as that of a power plant project in 1983–85, workers might be absent from the mill for years. A large proportion of the mill's labor force consisted of young women, hence maternity leave further added to worker absences. These diversions of labor frequently put a serious strain on production. Moreover, absent workers were included in calculations of productivity; this no doubt contributed to the mill's failure to meet its productivity targets in some years.

The second labor problem stemmed from new constraints the mill experienced in recruiting even its allocated supply of labor. As opportunities increased for lucrative collective employment and self-employment in the early and mid-1980s, once sought-after jobs at state enterprises became less attractive. Moreover, the nature of work in textile mills—repetitive, physically taxing, unhealthy, and financially unrewarding—became less alluring to the average Chinese worker. This trend was reflected at Qinghe in declining morale and rising requests from workers for transfer to other work units. The mill was prohibited, however, from increasing wages and bonuses to attract and retain employees. The rigidity of the Chinese labor system posed an increasingly pressing problem for Qinghe and other industrial enterprises as they moved into the mid-1980s. Qinghe responded to the 1986 labor reforms by seeking to recruit workers in nearby rural areas; their reservation wage presumably was much lower than was that of urban residents.

Conclusions and Implications

Qinghe's experiences in the late 1970s and early 1980s provide insights into how China's industrial system functioned during this period, how it changed, and how enterprises responded and changed. This section looks at firms' objectives and motivation, at their responses to changes in the business environment they faced, and at broader implications of the mill's experience.

Objectives and Motivation

Chinese state enterprises may have sought to maximize any one of a number of variables, including personal benefits of managers, profits, fulfillment of production targets, average net product per worker, and total net product—or profits plus wages (see Byrd and Tidrick 1987, p. 61). It appears that the objective functions of many firms encompassed not only profits but worker benefits as well (see chapter 3 of this volume for a fuller discussion). Although Chinese enterprises, like their labor-managed counterparts in Yugoslavia, might have sought to maximize average net product per worker, the state-set ceiling on wages and bonuses in the early 1980s prevented firms from increasing average benefits per worker beyond a certain limit. If an enterprise continued to expand employment and output once this ceiling was reached, its maximand was more likely total net product.

Qinghe's behavior up to the mid-1980s conforms to this hypothesis. The mill took advantage of every opportunity to raise wages and distribute extra bonuses to its employees, suggesting an objective function that included both the discretionary funds available to managers and workers' income. As a total net product maximand would imply, Qinghe was eager to expand production and increase profits even though its labor force had already received the maximum financial benefits permitted by the government. At least part of the motivation for Qinghe's expansion was no doubt its need to provide jobs for workers' children. Such expansion also held out the prospect of financing new housing construction with retained profits.

Qinghe's objective function, the interaction of the various reforms with one another and with the external economic environment, and the constraints that limited the mill's decisions and operations, together determined the incentive effects of the industrial reforms. The principal incentive affecting the mill was created by the new tax system, under which Qinghe retained a high proportion of its profits. Because of government restrictions on labor utilization, Qinghe's assumed maximand (profits and wages) led the mill to focus on increasing profits. This focus in turn fueled the mill's desire to expand production and employment, because any positive marginal product of labor added to the total profit-wage pool (or to profits alone, if wage costs were fixed).[29]

Another important incentive was created by the marketing reforms that granted Qinghe more responsibility for product sales. Government price controls and the emergence of a buyers' market for woolen fabrics largely determined the effect of this incentive on Qinghe. Prevented as it was from engaging in open price competition, the mill pursued an intensive growth strategy that entailed improving quality, developing new products, reducing costs, and making managerial and technological improvements. Without the competitive pressure generated by excess supply, marketing reforms probably would not have had such a strong effect on the mill.

Policies encouraging credit financing of fixed investment created a third significant incentive. Chinese factories were generally eager to invest in fixed assets, not only in order to increase their profits but also in order to expand capacity, improve working conditions, and provide employment for workers' children. Although the goal of credit financing was to encourage firms to use capital more efficiently, loan repayment provisions permitting diversion of funds from sources other than retained profits made loan financing extremely attractive. Hence firms ultimately bore none or only a part of the financial risk of fixed investment loans (see chapter 3 of this volume). (In cases in which both principal and interest were repaid from pretax profits, credit financing was heavily subsidized and was an even more attractive alternative to self-financing.)

A final incentive seems to have been created by the combined effect of financial and marketing policies. Although a certain amount of bartering outside the state plan had occurred in China even before the late 1970s, the impetus for inter-factory cooperation was evidently strengthened by enterprises' greater responsibility for inputs and marketing. Such cooperation was also closely related to the dynamics of supply and demand in relevant markets. In Qinghe's case, cooperation was driven primarily by the mill's need to obtain supplies in great demand. Alliances with factories that produced critical inputs not only were instrumental in providing Qinghe access to the required goods, but they also frequently allowed the mill to buy at more favorable prices than otherwise would have been possible. Qinghe's associations with other economic entities were motivated in addition by the goals of increasing sales and of utilizing outmoded equipment more effectively. These needs and objectives will likely persist as the Chinese economy continues to develop, so links between factories will probably multiply in the future.

Enterprise Response to a Changing Environment

The preceding discussion of incentives helps elucidate the mill's responses to its changing business environment. As expected, Qinghe's most striking reaction to the new policies was swift expansion of both production and employment, beginning in 1979 and continuing through 1982. By 1983, however, weakening market demand led to an abrupt slowdown in growth that continued through 1984.

Two other important responses of the mill to its changing environment can be identified. Again, these responses conformed to predictions based on the incentives created by the reforms. First, Qinghe made considerable progress in the direction of intensive growth. As is mentioned in "Qinghe's Response to the Changing Economic Environment," in this chapter, the effort to reorient production to better meet market demand entailed the establishment of an extensive information-gathering network, a shift in product mix toward higher-grade fabrics, a factorywide emphasis on quality control, and the development of new products. The mill made sales promotion an increasingly important part of its marketing strategy, particularly after 1982. More significantly, it experimented with what it perceived to be the most modern factory management techniques available, centered around the economic responsibility system. The mill's use of labor incentives, such as bonuses and new housing, may be viewed as an integral part of this attempt to improve productivity and maintain high worker morale. The mill also endeavored to promote young managers with strong technical skills.

Second, Qinghe took advantage of greater access to credit financing to invest borrowed funds in large expansion projects. Although the second expansion project in 1981–85 was undertaken with a measure of ambivalence, the manner in which it was financed was still highly favorable. Because the mill was able to use depreciation charges as well as industrial-commercial tax to repay funds borrowed for the 1979–80 expansion, retained profits accounted for only half of the total repayment. Physical constraints at the plant site appear to have redirected investment goals after that. There is no indication, however, that the new investment priorities signified a disinclination to rely on bank credit.

Qinghe also made some modest attempts to increase and improve ties with other factories. The most successful collaborations were those developed to circumvent constraints on vital raw material inputs. Qinghe also explored joint ventures. Though they were not entirely successful, these efforts indicate an openness to new forms of inter-factory cooperation.

Qinghe's actions comprise a generally positive behavioral response to the reforms. At first blush, the mill's rapid increase in production between 1979 and 1982 may appear particularly significant, but considering the ample investment funds the mill obtained from bank loans and considering the strong market demand for woolen textiles, such growth was predictable—it was in fact accomplished relatively easily. Of greater interest is the mill's response to the adverse conditions that emerged after 1982. In the face of stiff competition, an enterprise ideally attempts to better gauge market demand, cut prices, differentiate its product line through quality improvements and product development, promote sales, and reduce costs. Qinghe's actions essentially conformed to this pattern, although price setting was restricted. In view of the array of supply, labor, and other constraints it confronted, Qinghe's success was laudable. The mill's single most obvious failure was its inability to boost labor productivity and substantially reduce production costs.[30] Rising prices for input supplies, however, mean that it is difficult to judge the true extent of this failure. The scope for increasing labor productivity may also have been diminished because Qinghe's labor productivity was already considerably higher than was the case in most state textile factories.[31] In any case, neither this failure nor the slight deterioration in profit performance in 1983 should obscure the fact that, in most respects, Qinghe's response conformed to the goals of Chinese economic reformers.

Implications of Qinghe's Experience

One pervasive theme of this case study is the partial nature of the reform program. Many of the new difficulties with which the mill had to cope after 1979 were direct results of what was essentially an inconsistent loosening of a rigid economic system. At the same time that enterprises were given more autonomy in planning, marketing, and investment decisions, the state continued to play an important role in determining the use of retained profits, the kind and extent of production, investment, prices, export sales, and the use of and compensation for labor inputs.

A wholesale relaxation of state control would undoubtedly have caused considerable confusion and turmoil, at least at the outset, and certain government restrictions may have been necessary in the face of the strong urge of Chinese state enterprises to expand output and employment. Fragmented reforms, however, bred their own complications, including severe supply shortages as factories hoarded scarce materials no longer allocated by the state, imbalances stemming from an irrational price system, enterprises' increased desire and ability to overexpand, and relative overpayment of workers because firms were able to distribute bonuses unrelated to improvement in performance. As one observer noted, the fact that most of these problems existed to a certain extent even before the introduction of reforms lends strong support to the theory that partial reform included in its effects an exacerbation of the inherent weaknesses of a command economy.[32]

A second implication of this case study, closely related to the effects of partial reform, concerns the importance of an enterprise's relationship with its supervisory agencies. The role played by the Textiles Corporation and its parent bureau in imposing restraints on the mill's activities was particularly conspicuous. Although many directives were merely passed down from higher-level authorities, other directives, such as target assignments, approval for plant expansions, and supply allocations, were in large part left to the discretion of the corporation and the bureau. As a result, enterprises could manipulate rules to their advantage with the support and assistance of their supervisory agencies. In Qinghe's case, this phenomenon is seen in the supervisory agencies' assignment of lax production targets to the mill, in the limited price flexibility Qinghe gained, and in the extensive negotiations and compromises that ensued when disagreements arose (as they did over the second expansion project). This aspect of the interaction between an enterprise and the government reflected the slack planning system and soft budget constraint that characterized the Chinese economy in the early and mid-1980s. The underlying attitude of "we're all in this together" will no doubt continue to distort the effect of reforms as long as firms and their supervisory agencies recognize that the state will generally keep even inefficient firms in operation (Walder 1986, pp. 642–643).

Finally, Qinghe's experiences in the years after 1979 underscore the critical part the market has played in shaping the behavior of enterprises during the course of reform. Two elements of the reforms set the stage for the mill to experience the full effect of the marketplace. First, responsibility for marketing its own products removed the buffer between output and sales that had long numbed Qinghe to market signals. Second, new financial incentives impelled the mill to respond to these signals in order to improve performance and increase retained profits. Whereas these reforms significantly altered Qinghe's economic milieu, it was the dynamics of supply and demand that proved instrumental in prompting many of the positive changes in the mill's planning and production. The intense competition that resulted from excess supply was what led Qinghe to pursue a strategy of intensive growth. Chinese consumers in turn benefited from the mill's concentration on quality and development of new varieties of cloth. In short, many of the goals of China's reformers have been achieved more effectively through market interactions than through specific reforms.

Notes

1. See, for example, Zhu and others 1984 and State Economic Commission, Enterprise Management Department, 1982, pp. 319–24, and 1983, pp. 179–88.

2. China has ranked first among the world's producers of cotton cloth for many years. In 1984 the country produced 137 million meters of cotton and blended cloth, compared with 86 million meters, 75 million meters, and 24 million meters for India, the U.S.S.R., and the United States, respectively. At 730,000 tons, Chinese chemical fiber output was the fifth largest in that year, after those of the United States (3.6 million tons), Japan (1.8 million tons), the U.S.S.R. (1.4 million tons) and the Federal Republic of Germany (930,000 tons). See State Statistical Bureau 1986, p. 72.

3. In 1984, Shanghai alone still accounted for 15.3 percent of the nation's total textile GVIO. Shanghai, Jiangsu, Zhejiang, and Shandong together accounted for more than 47 percent of China's total textile GVIO (State Statistical Bureau 1985, p. 325).

4. Cotton textiles, printing, and dyeing grew at an average annual rate of 6.7 percent during this period; knitted textiles at a rate of 20.3 percent; flax textiles at 6.7 percent; and silk textiles at 19.9 percent. Chemical fibers grew at average annual rates of 15.1 percent in 1966–70, 4.4 percent in 1971–75, and 37.2 percent in 1976–80 (Qian 1984, p. 639).

5. In 1981, exports of Chinese woolen textile products amounted to $276 million and represented 1.3 percent of China's total export earnings (Zheng 1983, p. 12). Between 1980 and 1985, however, the volume of woolen textile exports gradually fell (State Statistical Bureau 1983, p. 405; and 1986, p. 488).

6. Mention of a reemerging sellers' market for woolen textiles in 1984 is made by Qinghe management and by Zhu and others 1984, p. 233.

7. The other two factories are the Beijing Woolen Textile Mill and the Beijing Woolen Goods and Blankets Mill. Both are located close to Qinghe.

8. Of the eight firms in this experiment, three each were located in Beijing and Shanghai, two in Tianjin (Tung 1982, p. 188).

9. There were approximately 600 woolen textile plants in 1980 and 900 in 1984 (State Statistical Bureau 1986, p. 191).

10. Like most other such corporations, the Textiles Corporation seems to have operated as a branch of the bureau above it. In a few places, such as Nanjing, such

corporations evolved into independent enterprise-type units, and they provided extensive planning and coordination services for the enterprises under their administration (Zhou 1984, pp. 384–85).

11. This conclusion is supported by other research findings such as those of Fischer 1986.

12. In 1984 this person was promoted to a position in the ministry. The replacement director was appointed by the Beijing Economic Commission for a four-year term and later signed a contract to continue until early 1990.

13. The tax-for-profit scheme had been introduced experimentally in 1979 in Hubei province. In 1980 it was expanded to include 191 enterprises; within two years 456 factories had converted to the program. In 1983 a simplified income tax system was implemented nationwide (see Naughton 1985, pp. 240–44).

14. This scheme was different from the Chongqing Clock and Watch Company's tax system, under which income was defined as the sum total of profits, wages, and welfare fund, or value added minus depreciation (see chapter 3 of this volume).

15. The ratchet effect has been extensively discussed in the literature on planned economies. Weitzman 1980 presents a theoretical model; also see chapter 3 of this volume.

16. Qinghe's ratio of profits to assets in 1980–82 ranked fourth in the twenty-firm sample (third among the five textile enterprises in the sample). The enterprises in the sample were generally more profitable than the average for Chinese state industry. Qinghe's ratio of profits to sales during the same period ranked somewhere in the middle of the sample.

17. It is not clear why Qinghe failed to retain the specified 10.64 percent share of profits in 1979. The 1980 figure is for profits retained after loan repayments, hence there was not a sharp increase in the profit retention rate in 1981–82. Qinghe's profit retention rate ranked in the middle of those of the twenty firms in the sample.

18. Shoudu's profits rose by 9 percent after it implemented the new economic responsibility system in mid-1981. See Shoudu Iron and Steel Company 1982, pp. III-10–14.

19. At the same time, however, workers' total incomes had already risen significantly because of wage increases and reinstitution of bonuses. That this rise occurred during a period of little improvement in labor productivity supports the argument in favor of continued state regulation of bonuses.

20. According to State Economic Commission stipulations, an enterprise undergoing reorganization had to pass through these two stages ("qualified enterprise" and "enterprise good in six respects") before it could be classified as a "modernized enterprise." A factory that failed to meet the standards of a "qualified enterprise" was designated a "second-rate enterprise." An enterprise with still lower performance levels was classified as a "third-rate enterprise."

21. The Chinese government often deliberately underallocated materials to state enterprises, but, in Qinghe's case, supply agencies were evidently squeezed by import restrictions. In 1984, for example, imports of wool dropped by 20 percent and distribution of foreign wool to textile plants fell from more than 5,000 tons to less than 3,000 tons.

22. The mill estimated that 30–40 percent of total managerial time was spent on discussions with authorities concerning supplies and prices.

23. Chinese products that were judged as meeting top international standards were awarded gold medals; products of top domestic quality that did not meet top international standards won silver medals; and other high-quality products were awarded bronze medals.

24. Qinghe's retained profits between 1980 and 1982 totaled Y16.63 million, of which loan repayments claimed 49.4 percent.

25. Recognizing the imperative for labor reform, the State Council on July 12, 1986, issued four regulations mandating contract employment and providing standards for recruitment, termination of contracts, employment benefits, and other matters relating to labor. For an overview of labor law in China, see Zheng 1987.

26. It was a general practice to permit children to replace their retiring parents. In Qinghe's case the proportion of new staff represented by children of retired workers was probably unusually high: of the 517 workers who retired between 1979 and mid-1984, 430 (83 percent) were replaced by their children.

27. The average wage figure used in this calculation was set by the Beijing Textile Bureau and was not enterprise-specific. The wage used in 1980–82 was Y54 a month; hence average bonuses per worker could not exceed Y15 a month.

28. Performance was assessed in three distinct areas: achievement of economic targets, management, and political work. For most workshops these three categories were worth totals of 90, 25, and 15 points, respectively, for a grand total of 130 points. For functional sections, the respective point totals were 85, 35, and 10. Bonuses were calculated for each section and workshop according to the point totals, the fixed value of each point, the coefficient related to type of work, and the number of workers. Individual workers were evaluated on a 100-point scale.

29. Indeed, because of the tax on profits, a firm maximizing the sum of wages and retained profits would have an incentive to expand employment beyond the point at which the marginal product of labor becomes negative.

30. Labor productivity remained basically constant at about Y22,000 per worker per year between 1979 and 1983. Production costs fell by a total of 14 percent between 1978 and 1982, but the greatest decline in a single year came in 1979 (12 percent). They were virtually constant after that, with the exception of a slight increase in 1981.

31. In 1984, average labor productivity in state-owned independent accounting industrial enterprises in the textile sector was Y18,970 per worker per year. The figure for Qinghe was Y22,000 (State Statistical Bureau 1986, p. 273).

32. See Shirk 1985, p. 203. Shirk also mentions another disruption caused by partial reform—inflation—which she claims has resulted primarily from the bidding up of prices of producer goods as local leaders and factory managers rushed to expand industrial output.

References

Byrd, William, and Gene Tidrick. 1987. "Factor Allocation and Enterprise Incentives." In Tidrick and Chen 1987b.

China Economic Yearbook Editorial Committee. Various years. *Zhongguo Jingji Nianjian* (China Economic Yearbook). Beijing: Zhongguo Jingji Guanli Zazhishe.

Fischer, William A. 1986. "Chinese Industrial Management: Outlook for the Eighties." In United States Congress, Joint Economic Committee.

Granick, David. 1987. "The Industrial Environment in China and the CMEA Countries." In Tidrick and Chen 1987b.

Ministry of Textile Industry. 1983a. "Fangzhi Gongye Guanli Tizhi de Yange, Xianzhuang, he Gaige Shexiang" (Thoughts on the Evolution, Present Situation, and Reform of the Management System of the Textile Industry). In Ministry of Textile Industry 1983b.

———. 1983b. *Zhongguo Fangzhi Gongye Nianjian 1982* (China Textile Industry Yearbook 1982). Beijing: Fangzhi Gongye Chubanshe.

———. 1984. *Zhongguo Fangzhi Gongye Nianjian 1983* (China Textile Industry Yearbook 1983). Beijing: Fangzhi Gongye Chubanshe.

Naughton, Barry. 1985. "False Starts and Second Wind: Financial Reforms in China's Industrial System." In Perry and Wong.

Perry, Elizabeth J., and Christine Wong, eds. 1985. *The Political Economy of Reform in Post-Mao China*. Cambridge, Mass.: Harvard University Press.

Qian Zhiguang and others, eds. 1984. *Dangdai Zhongguo de Fangzhi Gongye* (The Textile Industry in Contemporary China). Beijing: Zhongguo Shehui Kexue Chubanshe.

Shirk, Susan. 1985. "The Politics of Industrial Reform." In Perry and Wong.

Shoudu Iron and Steel Company. 1982. "Shixing Jingji Zeren Zhi Shi Yitiao Banhao Qiye de Xin Luzi" (Implementing Economic Responsibility Systems Is a New Path to Running Enterprises Well). *Jingji Guanli* (Economic Management) 3(March):10–15.

State Economic Commission, Enterprise Management Department. 1982. "Beijing Qinghe Mao Fangzhi Chang Zhuahao Jingying Juece, Jiangqiu Jingji Xiaoguo" (The Beijing Qinghe Woolen Textile Mill Concentrates on Operational Decisions and Stresses Economic Benefits). In *Gongye Jingying Guanli Jingyan Xuanbian 1981* (Selections on Experience in Industrial Business Management 1981). Beijing: Renmin Chubanshe.

———. 1983. "Beijing Qinghe Mao Fangzhi Chang Jiaqiang Quanmian Zhiliang Guanli, Tigao Jingji Xiaoguo" (The Beijing Qinghe Woolen Textile Mill Strengthens Total Quality Control and Improves Economic Benefits). In *Gongye Jingying Guanli Jingyan Xuanbian 1982* (Selections on Experience in Industrial Business Management 1982). Beijing: Renmin Chubanshe.

State Statistical Bureau. Various years. *Statistical Yearbook of China*. Hong Kong: Economic Information and Agency.

Tidrick, Gene, and Chen Jiyuan. 1987a. "Characteristics of the Twenty Enterprises." In Tidrick and Chen 1987b.

———, eds. 1987b. *China's Industrial Reform*. New York: Oxford University Press.

Tung, Rosalie L. 1982. *Chinese Industrial Society after Mao*. Lexington, Mass.: D. C. Heath.

United States Congress, Joint Economic Committee. 1986. *China's Economy Looks toward the Year 2000. Vol. 1, The Four Modernizations.* Washington, D.C.: U.S. Government Printing Office.

Walder, Andrew G. 1986. "The Informal Dimension of Enterprise Financial Reforms." In United States Congress, Joint Economic Committee.

Weitzman, Martin L. 1980. "The 'Ratchet Principle' and Performance Incentives." *Bell Journal of Economics* 11(1): 302–8.

Woolen Textiles Group, National Conference on Development of New Textile Products. 1984. "Mao Fangzhi Chanpin de Fazhan Fangxiang" (The Direction of Development of Woolen Textile Products). In Ministry of Textile Industry 1984.

Xinhua News Agency. 1987. "Regulations on Detailed Work of Factory Directors of State-Owned Enterprises" and "Work Regulations for Grass-roots Organizations of the Chinese Communist Party in State-Owned Industrial Enterprises (September 15, 1986)." January 11, 1987. Reprinted in *Foreign Broadcast Information Service, Daily Report: China*, February 5, 1987.

Zheng Conglie. 1983. "Mao Fangzhi Gongye Gaikuang" (A Survey of the Woolen Textile Industry). In Ministry of Textile Industry 1983b.

Zheng, Henry R. 1987. "An Introduction to the Labor Law of the People's Republic of China." *Harvard International Law Journal* 28(2).

Zhou Taihe, ed. 1984. *Dangdai Zhongguo de Jingji Tizhi Gaige* (Economic System Reform in Contemporary China). Beijing: Zhongguo Shehui Kexue Chubanshe.

Zhu Li, Chen Baohua Zhang Heng, and Tang Yongzeng. 1984. "Beijing Qinghe Mao Fangzhi Chang Kaizhan Shichang Yuce de Diaocha" (The Beijing Qinghe Woolen Textile Mill Develops Market Surveys). In Ministry of Textile Industry 1984.

7

The Nanning Silk and Ramie Textile Mill

Josephine Woo

THE NANNING SILK AND RAMIE TEXTILE MILL (hereafter referred to as Nanning or as the Nanning mill) offers an interesting case study of a state enterprise undergoing reform.[1] The Chinese textile industry went through a turbulent period starting in the late 1970s. Like other textile plants, Nanning had to cope with rapid changes in the textile market as government controls and planning began to disintegrate. It was also affected by economic reforms in various spheres. This chapter explores Nanning's behavior in this changing environment and the effect of reforms on its performance.

The first section, after a brief introduction to the Nanning mill, describes the ramie textile industry in China as a whole and the textile industry of the Guangxi Autonomous Region in which the mill was located.[2] It then discusses the Nanning mill's relationships with government supervisory agencies before 1979. The next section looks at the main reforms carried out in the mill starting in 1979 and at changes in the mill's environment that affected performance. The third section analyzes the effects of reforms and of other changes on the Nanning mill's behavior and performance. The final section discusses outstanding issues in Nanning's experience.

General Background

The Nanning mill, located in Nanning City, the capital of the Guangxi Autonomous Region, was established in the mid-1960s as a silk spinning and weaving mill. Part of a plan of the Guangxi regional government to build five textile mills to process the cassava cocoons produced in the region, it was completed in 1966, with 5,200 silk spindles, 160 looms, and 7 million meters of printing and dyeing capacity. At that time it was called the Nanning Silk Mill.

In 1965 Guangxi produced about 2,500 metric tons of cassava cocoons, but output decreased sharply in subsequent years, which forced the regional

276

government to abort its plan after three of the silk factories had been built. By 1968 the Nanning mill already faced problems with cocoon supplies.[3] The fabric it produced was of such poor quality, moreover, that the commercial departments in charge of selling its products complained. In the meantime, however, construction for a project to expand the mill's capacity by another 5,200 spindles and 160 looms had begun. Shortly after the project was completed in 1971, the mill had to stop producing silk altogether because of the shortage of cocoons. Fortunately, as China's chemical fiber production grew in the 1970s, the mill was provided with new raw materials, such as acrylic and polyester fibers. It started to produce ramie-polyester fine cloth for export in 1973. By 1977 it was producing mainly ramie-polyester and acrylic-polyester fabrics. In 1983 the mill changed its name to the Nanning Silk and Ramie Textile Mill.

Compared with other firms in Guangxi, a relatively undeveloped region, the Nanning mill was a large enterprise with better than average performance. In relation to the textile industry in China as a whole, however, it was at best an average medium-size enterprise.[4] Table 7.1 makes some comparisons of the Nanning mill with another major ramie textile producer, the Zhuzhou Ramie Mill in Hunan, and with regional and national textile industry averages.

Development of Ramie Textiles

Ramie falls in the general category of *ma* textile fibers in China.[5] It is a natural fiber that resembles flax but is longer and finer, and it can be bleached to extreme whiteness. When combed, it is half the weight of linen but is much stronger and more absorbent. It has a permanent luster and a good affinity for dyes, and it is little affected by moisture. Ramie can be processed into pure fabric or blended with cotton, silk, wool, or chemical fibers. It is also used to make ropes and nets (see Corbman 1975, p. 520; Fan 1981, pp. 20–23). Ramie was used in ancient China but was never developed as widely as was cotton because its difficult retting process prohibited its transport over long distances and its manufacture by households (Wu 1985, pp. 196–207). Even in the twentieth century, the cost of processing ramie fiber into textile yarn made it unprofitable for general use. Until the 1970s, ramie was used mostly to make ropes and fishing nets.

Mechanized processing of ramie in China in the early 1950s was mostly restricted to two small factories in Shanghai and Guangdong, that together had 7,700 spindles. They produced mainly ramie yarn for industrial use. In 1956 a complete set of equipment for processing ramie was imported from Japan for a new mill in Hunan Province, the Zhuzhou Ramie Textile Mill. Although there were problems with the technology for retting and carding, a number of ramie factories using domestic equipment were established in

Table 7.1. Profiles of Nanning Mill and Other Enterprises

Indicator	Nanning mill[a]	Zhuzhou Ramie Factory[b]	State textile enterprises in Guangxi[b]	State textile enterprises in China[a]
GVIO (millions of yuan)[c]	53.59	52.93	—	—
Total staff and workers	3,159	4,805	—	—
Gross output/fixed assets (percent)	204.8	138.2	81.9	275.0
Profit+tax/fixed assets (percent)[d]	42.3	49.5	26.1	55.1
Profit+tax/total capital (percent)[e]	26.0	48.3	17.7	43.5
Profit+tax/sales revenue (percent)	30.4	37.9	—	—
Turnover of working capital (days)	149[f]	84	154[f]	94[f]

GVIO, gross value of industrial output.

— Not available.

a. Data are for 1982.

b. Data are for 1984.

c. In 1980 constant prices.

d. Data are based on gross value of fixed assets, valued at original purchase prices.

e. Total capital includes gross value of fixed assets as well as quota and nonquota working capital.

f. Data refer only to quota working capital.

Source: Information provided by the mill; State Statistical Bureau 1983, 1985b.

Guangzhou, Chongqing, and Duyun (Guizhou) in subsequent years. By 1959 there were 19,000 ramie spindles and 300 looms in China. During the next two decades, however, the output of raw ramie did not support further investment in capacity for ramie processing. It was only in the late 1970s that demand for ramie products for export prompted a new wave of investments. Table 7.2 shows the dramatic increase in capacity for ramie processing in 1980–84.

The total output of ramie in China increased from 24,500 metric tons in 1950 to 40,500 metric tons in 1952. After 1959 there was a drastic decline in production. As demand for ramie increased in the late 1970s, the government raised the procurement price to improve incentives for ramie producers. The price rose from Y164.6 per 100 kilograms in 1965 to Y183.2 per 100 kilograms in 1978 and to Y234.2 per 100 kilograms in 1980 (State Statistical Bureau 1985a, 1986). Also in the late 1970s, rural reforms released farmers from strict adherence to quotas for grain output and thus allowed more production of profitable cash crops, such as ramie. By 1982, total output of ramie reached 55,000 metric tons. In 1980–83 the development of capacity for ramie processing lagged behind the growth of output of raw ramie; this situation resulted in excess supply, which, however, was quickly absorbed as new facilities began operating. The price of ramie, which dropped slightly in 1980–83, began to rise again in 1984; it almost tripled to Y797.5 per 100 kilograms in 1985.

Most of China's ramie is grown south of the Yangtze River, mainly in

Hunan, Hubei, and Sichuan; all ramie textile mills are located south of the river. Hunan, which produced 40 percent of the country's ramie, had by far the largest share of capacity for processing ramie, with 42.6 percent of the total number of ramie spindles in China in 1982. Another 35.3 percent of the ramie spindles were distributed among Hubei, Sichuan, Guangxi, Anhui, and Jiangsu, all of which also produced some raw ramie. Shanghai and Guangdong did not produce raw ramie but were close to ramie-growing areas and had a comparative advantage with regard to technology and to access to export markets; together they had 14 percent of the ramie spindles in China (Qian and others 1984, p. 211).

Although the Ministry of Textile Industry organized several national conferences to promote the development of ramie textile technology after 1973, significant efforts in this area started only in the late 1970s. At that time the Nanning mill had fully established itself as a producer of ramie textiles and could reap the benefits of the national attention to this subsector. The fifth national conference on ramie textiles was held in Nanning at the end of 1980. In 1981 the mill won a national silver award for one of its ramie-polyester products.

Guangxi's Textile Industry

The Guangxi autonomous region lies—except for Hainan and other islands in the South China Sea—in the southernmost part of China. Nanning, its capital, is barely 220 kilometers away from the Vietnamese border. Guangxi is classifed as an autonomous region because a sizable proportion of its population (38.6 percent in 1984) consists of ethnic minorities. Most of this minority population (89 percent of it) belongs to the Zhuang ethnic group.[6] As an autonomous region, Guangxi has the same rank as a province in China's administrative structure. Compared with other provinces, it is relatively undeveloped. In 1984 the region had 3.7 percent of China's total

Table 7.2. Capacity for Processing Ramie in China, 1980–84

Item	1980	1981	1982	1983	1984
Ramie spindles[a]					
Long fiber	45,930	45,930	53,240	60,020	72,252
Short fiber	13,660	13,660	18,556	30,080	50,500
Medium-length fiber	—	—	—	12,624	19,344
Ramie looms	1,182	1,604	2,211	2,854	2,886
Output of ramie fabric (millions of meters)	19.7	29.6	44.9	28.6	42.0

— Not available.

a. Data exclude ramie spindles in cotton textile plants.

Source: China Economic Yearbook Editorial Committee 1985, pp. V/46–47; Ministry of Textile Industry 1986, p. 391.

population, but its gross value of industrial and agricultural output was only 1.8 percent of the country's total; industry's share (1.5 percent) was slightly lower than was agriculture's. Guangxi benefits from the central government's preferential policies toward national minorities. The region keeps all taxes it collects from local enterprises and also receives a small budgetary transfer from the central government to help cover its expenditures.

Because of its remote geographical location, its relatively backward industry, and its poor endowment of textile fibers, Guangxi has not played a central role in China's textile industry. It produces a little raw cotton, a small quantity of silkworms, some jute, and some ramie. The central government's development strategy for the textile industry since the 1950s has focused mainly on the nation's important cotton-producing areas and on the technological upgrading of traditional textile centers that produced for export markets. Although the strategy favored the dispersion of textile development and encouraged the creation of local textile bases, it relied mostly on the initiative of provincial and local governments. It supported local efforts by contributing all or part of the financing for development and by providing technical assistance.

Guangxi's contribution to China's textile sector has been relatively small. The gross value of industrial output (GVIO) of its textile industry in 1984 was Y1.2 billion, barely 1.1 percent of the Chinese textile industry's total. None of its outputs of the important textile products exceeded 1 percent of the industry's total in that year. Guangxi's exports accounted for only 0.4 percent of China's total textile exports in 1981 and 1982. The value of its exports jumped from $5.7 million in 1983 to $14.6 million in 1984, however. Guangxi's textile industrial output value grew by only 2.4 percent in 1984; its profits dropped by 52 percent and its tax contribution by 6 percent. In 1984 there were 141 textile enterprises in Guangxi, with a total employment of 82,000. Of these, 75 were state enterprises under the supervision of the Guangxi Textile Bureau. Textile development in Guangxi has been concentrated around the four cities of Liuzhou, Nanning, Guilin, and Wuzhou. Together these cities accounted for 86 percent of the region's total GVIO for textiles in 1984. The largest center was Liuzhou, about 400 kilometers northeast of Nanning; it accounted for 46 percent of the region's total (Guangxi Economic Yearbook Editorial Committee 1985, pp. 197–202).

In 1984 the GVIO of Nanning Municipality's textile industry accounted for 13 percent of the municipality's total GVIO of Y1.8 billion. There were fifty-two textile firms, with total gross fixed assets amounting to Y123 million (Guangxi Economic Yearbook Editorial Committee 1985, p. 414). The gross value of fixed assets of the Nanning mill in 1982 was Y26 million, but with the completion of the 4,800-spindle project in 1984–85 the value must have increased substantially. The mill is undoubtedly a leading enterprise in the municipality's textile sector. The mill's GVIO in 1982 was Y54 million in 1980 constant prices, or Y43 million in current prices. Its performance in

1984 was outstanding among state enterprises in the Guangxi region. Because of large increases in exports, the Nanning mill's foreign exchange earnings increased by 70 percent in 1984; its profits rose by 69 percent—although its GVIO grew by only 2 percent (Guangxi Economic Yearbook Editorial Committee 1985, p. 199). Export volume of ramie and cotton-ramie cloth increased by 83 percent in 1984; that of ramie yarn increased by 270 percent. Exports accounted for 47.5 percent of the mill's total output value in that year.

The Nanning Mill's Administrative Environment

The Guangxi government's proposal to establish the Nanning mill was approved by the State Planning Commission in 1964. A grant of Y8.85 million was then allocated by the central government to build the factory. The 1971 expansion project was also approved and financed by the central government. The central government did not directly supervise the enterprise, however. Once established, the mill was governed by the same pattern of relationships that generally applied to all state textile plants under the supervision of provincial or municipal governments.

Until the second half of 1981, the Nanning mill received annual production targets from the Guangxi Textile Bureau. These included targets for output value, output volume, principal varieties, quality, profit, and cost. Quotas for material inputs were allocated in accordance with production plans by the Textile Supply and Marketing Corporation under the Guangxi Textile Bureau, although allocations sometimes fell short of requirements for both quantity and variety. Output was procured entirely by a second-level wholesale station of the Commercial Department in Nanning, according to contracts based on the production plan. Procurement for export was conducted through the Guangdong Textile Import-Export Corporation before 1982.

Working capital for the mill's routine operations was provided by the Nanning branch of the People's Bank of China, according to quotas based on production plans. The Nanning Finance Bureau was in charge of monitoring the factory's financial performance. In the prereform period all fixed investments were financed by government grants, and all profits were handed over to the bureau. The enterprise functioned as a production branch of the local government, with little independent decisionmaking authority and with no responsibility for profit or loss.

Control over the Nanning mill's personnel matters resided mainly with the Nanning municipal government. Until 1978, appointments of high-level staff, including chiefs of workshops and of functional divisions, were made by the Nanning Economic Commission. Appointments of cadres at lower levels had to be approved by the Nanning Textile Bureau. Recruitment of workers was handled by the Nanning Labor Bureau. The mill applied for labor quotas when it submitted project proposals to the Guangxi Planning Commission. If approved, the quotas were passed down from the Guangxi Labor Bureau through the Nanning Labor Bureau to the factory. Labor management was governed by industry norms for the various categories of work and by state regulations concerning wage scales, promotions, leaves, and transfers. Nearly all workers, except for a few hired to do odd janitorial jobs, were recruited on a permanent basis, remained on the mill's payroll until retirement, and received pensions from the mill after retirement.

Like other state enterprises in China, the Nanning mill provided a complete range of facilities for its staff, including housing, cafeterias, clinics, nurseries, day-care centers, and schools. Regulations imposed by various government agencies determined the allocation of factory staff to perform these functions; for example, 0.3 percent of the total labor force had to be assigned to education, 0.3 percent to public security, and so forth. The mill also had to handle such matters as household registration and the issuing of grain coupons and other coupons. Hence the mill operated not only as a government production unit but also as an administrative branch of various government departments.

Reforms and Changes in the Nanning Mill's Environment

In 1979, the Chinese government introduced a series of reforms to improve the efficiency of the country's economic system. An important objective of these reforms was raising the productivity of state enterprises. Ministries and local governments were asked to select enterprises to experiment with various reform programs. The Nanning mill was chosen as one of ten enterprises for Nanning Municipality's experimental program in 1979. The choice was made by the Nanning municipal government, but how it was made or what criteria were used is not clear. The mill had won an award as a "Daqing model" enterprise in 1978, which perhaps carried some weight in the decisionmaking process (see "Effects of Reform on Nanning's Behavior," in this chapter).

For the mill, participation in the pilot program brought several changes. First, it was allowed to retain a percentage of its profits. Second, the mill's managers (rather than the Nanning Economic Commission) were given the authority to appoint or remove middle management staff in the mill. Third, the Nanning mill was allowed to sell on its own any output above the plan target. As reforms proceeded during the next few years, these arrangements were adjusted, and, in general, the discretionary power of the enterprise's management was expanded. National changes in the economic system—including greater enterprise control over wages and bonuses, labor management, planning, performance evaluation, and the allocation of inputs and distribution of outputs, as well as reforms in taxation and finance—also affected the mill's operations. These changes and reforms are grouped into three categories in the following discussion: financial reforms, labor reforms, and management reforms.

Financial Reforms

Some financial reforms at the Nanning mill—for example, profit retention— were part of the experimental program implemented there; others, such as the profit tax system and bonus tax, were part of national economic reforms.

PROFIT RETENTION. The profit retention scheme devised for the Nanning mill in 1979 and fixed for the three years following allowed the mill to retain 12.14 percent of its total profits. This rate was based on actual profits in 1978, when profits were relatively low. With total profits rising rapidly, from Y4.8 million in 1978 to Y7.9 million in 1979 and to Y13.5 million in 1981, the amount of profits retained by the enterprise was quite substantial, especially because the percentage of profits actually retained was higher than the stipulated figure. (As is shown in table 7.6, retained profits as a share of total profits actually were 14.5 percent in 1979 and 19.9 percent in 1982.) An objective of profit retention was to encourage improved performance, but, in actual practice, retained profits were not closely linked to total profits. For example, although the mill's total profits dropped by 54 percent in 1982, it was allowed to retain almost 20 percent of total profits, the highest share (though not the highest absolute amount) it retained in the period 1979–82.

Retained profits were intended to be used partly for reinvestment and partly for bonuses and welfare benefits for employees. There were state guidelines governing the distribution of retained profits, but actual percentages were set by local authorities. In the case of the mill, the Nanning Textile Bureau stipulated that 20.6 percent of retained profits should be used for production development, 47.9 percent for collective welfare, and 31.5 percent for bonuses. A much higher proportion could thus be used for collective welfare and bonuses than could be used for production development. Elsewhere in China the regulations usually required that 60 percent of the retained profits be used for production development and only 20 percent each for collective welfare and bonuses. The mill's use of retained profits was not closely supervised. The Nanning Finance Bureau stated that it was only concerned about how much profit its firms turned over to the government, not about how they used retained profits. Moreover, the bureau considered the mill to be in a special category as a reformed enterprise, exempt from most restrictions.

Some of the mill's retained profits were used for productive investment, but more than half of them were distributed to employees as bonuses and subsidies or were used for other benefits, such as housing. In 1979–82 Y1.74 million (31 percent of the mill's retained profits) were used for bonuses. Average total bonuses per worker per year were equivalent to almost 3.5 times average monthly basic wages in 1979, almost 5 times in 1980, 4.2 times in 1981, and 3.2 times in 1982.[7] Bonuses pushed up the average monthly total income per worker from Y40 in 1978 to Y51.7 in 1979, Y59 in 1980, and Y54.8 in 1981. Although the mill's total profits dropped sharply in 1982, the average monthly bonus per worker at about Y11 maintained the average monthly total income per worker at more than Y50. Another large expenditure from the mill's retained profits was for collective welfare. The bulk of collective welfare spending went into construction of housing and other facilities for workers. In 1980–83 the mill built 14,767 square meters of family housing; another 2,496 square meters were under construction in 1983. Nanning had about 1,000 family housing units by the end of that year.

PROFIT TAXATION. The central government introduced a new profit tax system to replace profit remittances in June 1983; the new system required state enterprises to pay a profit tax plus an adjustment tax whose rate was set by their supervisory departments. The Nanning mill had to pay profit tax at the rate of 55 percent starting in July 1983. From within-plan profits, the mill was to pay an additional 21 percent as adjustment tax and was to retain 24 percent. The plan quota for profits was approved by the Nanning Finance Bureau. If actual profits exceeded the plan target, adjustment tax would be reduced by 60 percent for the portion above the target.[8] In 1984 the system was made somewhat more favorable: the mill still retained 24 percent of planned profits, but the adjustment tax was reduced by 70 percent for above-plan profits.

Nanning's actual percentage of retained profits could be even higher. In November 1984 an official from the Nanning Finance Bureau said that the final decision on the tax rate for 1984 had not yet been made, but that initial calculations indicated that the adjustment tax for the mill would be 19.08 percent of within-quota profits (based on actual profits earned in 1983) and would be reduced (by 70 percent) to about 6 percent for profits above the 1983 level. Since profits in 1983 were unusually low, this assessment would constitute highly favorable treatment.

BONUS TAXATION. In an effort to divert more of enterprises' retained profits to productive investment, the central government introduced a bonus tax in 1984 that was levied on firms whose total yearly bonuses per worker exceeded 2.5 months of workers' average basic wages. Resistance to the bonus tax was quite strong, and, in 1985, the regulations were relaxed, and no tax was charged on bonuses equivalent to less than four months of basic wages (table 7.3). Most state enterprises in China had come to treat bonuses as part of the regular income of their workers and to pay bonuses as long as minimum performance standards (such as attendance) were met. To avoid the bonus tax, many firms gave their employees noncash subsidies, such as clothing. Most local government departments were sympathetic to firms and their workers; they considered bonuses to be essential because wage levels were so low. The Nanning mill apparently did not pay any bonus tax, although its total bonuses in 1984 did exceed 2.5 months of average basic wages.

Labor Reforms

Although the mill's labor recruitment continued to be handled by the Nanning Labor Bureau, a contract system was introduced in 1980—much earlier than it was in most other state enterprises. High school graduates waiting for job assignments took examinations given by a labor service corporation set up by the bureau. Those who passed were assigned to firms with approved labor quotas but were not offered permanent positions; instead they signed contracts for two or three years. This new system was designed to weaken the "iron rice bowl" of workers in state enterprises and to raise labor productivity. All workers recruited by the Nanning mill from 1980 were subject to this contract labor system.

Between 1980 and 1983 the mill took on about 700 contract workers, each of whom was given three months of training. By 1984 it had terminated twenty to thirty workers because they had not appeared for work for an extended period of time. More than 100 workers had left the mill of their own volition; some of these were continuing their studies, and others had found jobs in other factories or had gone into private business. The mill's director complained about the effort wasted in training these workers. In the short run the contract system did not seem to make much difference in labor management, particularly because it was widely expected that renewal of contracts would be virtually automatic. In the long run, contracts might have introduced some flexibility into an extremely rigid system of labor management and might have paved the way for increased labor mobility.

Management Reforms

When the Nanning mill became a pilot enterprise in 1979, part of the reform program gave the mill's top management authority to appoint or to remove

Table 7.3. State Bonus Tax Regulations, 1984 and 1985
(months of average basic wages)

Percentage tax rate	1984	1985
0	0.0–2.5	0.0–4.0
30	2.5–4.0	4.0–5.0
100	4.0–6.0	5.0–6.0
300	6.0+	6.0+

Source: *Jingji Ribao*, July 5, 1984; BBC, July 17, 1985, FE/W1347, p. C1.

middle-level personnel. In practice, however, the mill's director did not have much authority until the trial implementation of the factory-director responsibility system in August 1984. This new system gave the director the power (1) to make decisions on all production-related matters; (2) to appoint or dismiss any employee; (3) to transfer employees across units within the mill; (4) to determine bonuses for individual workers; and (5) to promote 3 percent of the firm's employees every year. A factory committee consisting of seven to nine people headed by the director was set up. The authority of the enterprise's Communist Party branch was severely curtailed.

At the time interviews for this study were conducted in November 1984, it was too early to assess how far the director had gone in implementing the new system or the effect of the system on the mill's performance. The director himself was in favor of the system and cited several examples where improved performance resulted. For instance, because the director could make prompt decisions on shifting output mix, the mill could meet export demand for pure ramie and could more than double its profits in September 1984. The director could also replace the head of the retting workshop, an issue that had deadlocked the party branch for many months. The director asserted that after the change in personnel, output of the retting workshop doubled. The factory committee seemed to be more representative of the mill's production operations than was the party branch, and it gave the director increased authority to implement various incentive schemes.

In principle, bonuses for each workshop were determined on the basis of performance, evaluated against targets for output, quality, profit, and safety. These criteria were not rigorously applied, however, until an economic contract responsibility system was initiated in 1984. Under this system, each workshop was given quotas for its number of workers and norms for quanity of output, based on standards issued by the Ministry of Textile Industry. Contracts between top management and the workshops were then signed. The workshops in their turn disaggregated targets to their subordinate work units and to individual workers. Total bonuses for each workshop consisted of a bonus fund equivalent to 50 percent of basic wages, plus 15 percent deducted from basic wages. No workers would receive less than 85 percent of the average basic wage, but those who exceeded their targets could receive larger bonuses. According to the director, implementation of this system helped boost the mill's profits by 92 percent in the first ten months of 1984 from the profit level of the equivalent period in 1983. In one of the weaving workshops in which the contract system was implemented in June 1984, output increased from 570,000 meters in June to 850,000 meters in September; the average monthly bonus per weaver rose from Y6.5 to Y25. In September the highest individual bonus in the weaving workshop was Y62, and about thirty workers did not even receive their full basic wage.

Changes in Government Supervisory Structure

In 1981 the Nanning Textile Bureau, which was to become a corporation in 1984, began to play a more active role than did the Guangxi Textile Bureau in directing the mill's operations. This change was in line with a national shift of emphasis to cities as the centers of economic administration. There was confusion at first as to which government department was in charge of which of the mill's targets. Gradually the mill came to receive all of its production targets from the Nanning Textile Bureau and its profit target from the Nanning Finance Bureau. Its profit retention rate was set jointly by the Nanning Economic Commission, the Finance Bureau, and the Textile Bureau. Supply of raw materials and other inputs continued to be controlled by the Supply and Marketing Corporation under the Guangxi Textile Bureau. Distribution of the mill's output was in principle the responsibility of the commercial departments of the municipality until 1981, when, partly as a result of reforms in the commercial system but mostly because of a deteriorating market situation (which is described later), the commercial departments were no longer obligated to purchase all of the mill's output.

The Nanning mill itself preferred to receive its targets from Nanning government agencies rather than from Guangxi regional departments. Municipal agencies were closer to the operations of the mill and could respond to its changing needs more promptly than could the regional departments. Subjecting the mill to Nanning authorities may have had the effect of increasing its dependence on them, however. Municipal agencies were likely to defend the interests of the enterprise at the expense of the interests of the regional or central government; profit targets would be adhered to more loosely, tax exemptions would be given more indiscriminately, and delays in loan repayments would be pardoned more easily. These tendencies are discussed further in "Limitations of Enterprise Reforms," in this chapter.

Changes in the Domestic Textile Market

Toward the end of 1981 and through 1982 and 1983, developments in the domestic market led to drastic changes in the business environment of the Nanning mill. First, excess supply of polyester fabric and polyester blends forced the government to adjust prices in late 1981 and again in early 1983. Second, commercial departments abandoned the system of unified procurement of textile goods, thus forcing Nanning to take more responsibility for the sale of its own products. Third, as the market situation worsened, plan targets prescribed by supervisory agencies became meaningless.

Excess supply was the result of rapid growth of output, fueled partly by policy changes and partly by an irrational pricing system. Light industries and textile industries were given priority in the allocation of raw materials, fuel and electricity, transport, bank loans, and foreign exchange. Rural reforms provided the textile industry with an abundant supply of natural fibers, and the completion of several large chemical fiber plants begun in the mid-1970s increased the supply of artificial fibers. On the demand side, rising personal incomes boosted domestic retail sales of textile products by 67 percent between 1978 and 1982 (Qian and others 1984, p. 514).

From the 1950s until early 1983 the price of cotton cloth remained essentially constant, although the price of raw cotton was raised several times in the late 1970s and the early 1980s. Polyester and cotton-polyester fabrics, however, were priced on the basis of the high cost of imported polyester fiber in the 1960s, and their prices were not adjusted when domestic production costs fell in the 1970s. Hence it became profitable for mills to produce polyester and cotton-polyester blends rather than pure cotton cloth. In 1980–81 output of cotton-polyester blends far exceeded plan targets, the market became saturated, and stocks began piling up from the second half of 1981.

In November 1981, the government lowered the prices of cotton-polyester fabrics by an average of Y0.66 a meter (Qian and others 1984, pp. 531–32). That decision apparently was made too late, however, and the price decline was too mild to have any effect. Nanning's output of cotton-polyester blends in 1981 exceeded its plan target of 2.8 billion meters by 660 million meters (State Economic Commission 1983, p. 3). The government in February 1982 called for a reduction of plan output of polyester blends for the year from 3.2 billion meters to 2.6 billion meters. Local governments were slow to react to the change in the market, however, and some, including Guangxi, actually requested an increase in output targets during the year. By the end of June 1982 the national inventory of polyester blends reached 1.9 billion meters, and output continued to exceed plan targets. Finally, in January 1983 the government reduced the prices of chemical fiber products by 10–30 percent and raised the prices of cotton textiles by 16–20 percent (Ministry of Textile Industry 1984, p. 108).

The drastic changes in the textile market and the price adjustments that followed profoundly affected the business environment of textile firms. Commercial departments abandoned unified procurement, thus forcing enterprises to take responsibility for the sale of their own output. Plan targets became meaningless. Textile mills and their supervisory agencies were forced to concentrate on improving quality and on developing new products.

General market trends in the textile industry and consequent systemic changes were felt by the Nanning mill, although the ramie subsector had distinct features and markets as compared with the cotton-synthetic subsector. Commercial departments had sometimes rejected the Nanning mill's output before 1979 because of poor quality, but procurement always resumed after quality was improved. In principle, commercial departments were in charge of the distribution of all of the mill's output until 1979. When the mill became a pilot enterprise in that year, it was given authority to market its above-plan production itself. This authority was considered a "window" by the mill's director—a channel whereby Nanning could receive direct feedback from the market and thereby respond more quickly and effectively to changes in demand. The director was not keen to take over more responsibility for sales than this, partly because of the mill's lack of adequate market information and adequate sales staff and partly because it was simpler to run the factory as a production unit and not worry about sales. The subsequent drastic changes in the market situation, however, forced the mill to take over the marketing function almost completely. Nanning had to find its own market channels for 50 percent of its domestic sales in 1982 and for 78 percent of them in 1983.

Another effect of the deteriorating market situation was the change it helped to bring about in the planning system. Beginning in the second half of 1981, output targets handed down by the Guangxi Textile Bureau became "guidance" targets rather than mandatory ones. Although there was some confusion as to the roles of the Nanning Textile Bureau and the Guangxi Textile Bureau, neither bureau seriously evaluated the mill's performance. In any case, the profit target set by the Finance Bureau was the only target that really mattered for the Nanning mill. As the market situation worsened, other plan targets lost all importance. Supervisory agencies did not even bother to revise targets to reflect the changes in the market situation, but all concerned understood that the mill was not expected to meet those targets and would not be penalized for failing to do so.

Changes in the Export Market

The export environment for textiles came to have an important effect on Nanning's performance because of the increasing share of exports in the mill's total sales (up from about 19 percent in 1978 to about 30 percent in 1979 and 1980). One new development was the establishment of the Guangxi Textile Import-Export Corporation toward the end of 1981.[9] From the beginning of 1982, the mill's exports went through the Guangxi corporation rather than through the Guangdong corporation. The mill complained that the new corporation was not giving it the favorable prices or the assistance it had received from Guangdong. The primary factor affecting the Nanning mill's exports, however, was not domestic administration but rather changes in export demand.

In 1978–82 China's foreign exchange earnings from textile exports totaled $15.4 billion, an amount equal to the aggregate value of China's textile exports in 1950–78 (Qian and others 1984, pp. 538–39). As protectionist barriers erected by industrial countries began to impose restrictions on textile imports from China, competition among Chinese textile exporters increased. Fortunately for the Nanning mill, demand by export corporations for pure ramie products or those with a high percentage of ramie was increasing.

Surging demand for ramie products was due partly to the growing preference of Western consumers for natural fibers and partly to the workings of the quota system in textile trade with the United States. The Sino-U.S. Agreement on Textile Trade, which came into effect on January 1, 1980, imposed restrictions only on products that contained more than 50 percent wool, cotton, and artificial fibers. Products with more than 50 percent of other fibers by value and by weight were not subject to import quotas. As the quotas for restricted fibers were quickly filled up, demand for the unrestricted fibers increased.

Ramie, hardly known to U.S. trade representatives until 1984 or 1985, was not mentioned in the Sino-U.S. agreement, leaving a loophole for enterprises to circumvent quota restrictions. In 1982 and 1983, demand for ramie textile products increased sharply. Before new investments in facilities for processing ramie were completed (see table 7.2), existing producers were called upon to meet the needs of the export market. Thus new market potentials opened up for the Nanning mill just as the domestic market for its ramie-polyester products deteriorated.

Effects of Reform on Nanning's Behavior

The factors that affected the behavior of the Nanning mill may be divided into two groups: endogenous and exogenous. The former group included the various enterprise reforms carried out as part of the national reform programs or as experiments by the mill itself. The latter group primarily included the changes in domestic and foreign markets for textiles. In 1979–84 the exogenous factors had a greater effect on enterprise performance than did the endogenous ones, and the changing market situation in some respects helped push forward reforms in enterprise management.

As mentioned earlier, the mill encountered problems with raw material supply almost immediately after it started production in March 1966. It then switched from silk to acrylic, polyester, and ramie in the early 1970s. From that time until the end of 1984 the mill went through four distinct phases of development. The first phase covered the period up to 1979, when the mill became a pilot enterprise in reforms. The second phase, during which Nanning enjoyed rapid growth and expansion, stretched from 1979 to 1981. The third phase began toward the end of 1981, when the market situation started to deteriorate; this phase lasted until the third quarter of 1983. The fourth phase started with the mill's subsequent recovery. Table 7.4 shows the main trends in the mill's performance from 1979 to 1983.

Before 1979

Until the late 1970s the Nanning mill had serious problems with the quality of its output. When its first silk products appeared on the market, commercial departments complained that they could not sell them. Problems with quality continued after the enterprise switched to polyester and ramie production. The percentage of first-grade products was only about 50–60 percent of Nanning's total output; the industry standard was more than 80 percent.[10] In the first half of 1978 the commercial department refused to buy any of the mill's output because of its low quality. This refusal forced the enterprise to concentrate on upgrading quality and increasing varieties.

Exports had been important in the mill's activities since the early 1970s. Demand for ramie-polyester blends on the export market offered Nanning an incentive to produce a new product just at the time when the mill faced a severe shortage of raw silk. In 1973 it started to export some of its output through the Guangdong Textile Import-Export Corporation. By the end of 1978, ramie-polyester products comprised half of the mill's total output and fully occupied one of its two spinning and weaving workshops. Exports accounted for 18.8 percent of total sales in 1978.

In 1978 the mill won the title "Daqing-style" model enterprise. As part of a national campaign, the Ministry of Textile Industry at that time urged textile mills to emulate the model of the Daqing petroleum complex, one of whose features was the combination of agricultural and industrial activities. As part of this emulation campaign, the Nanning mill acquired some farmland from a nearby commune with the help of the municipal government. The investment cost was Y120,000, of which Y20,000 was used to build a factory for the commune. Although the farm was closed down after three

Table 7.4. Growth Rates of Nanning Mill's Performance Indicators, 1979–83 (percent)

Indicator	1979	1980	1981	1982	1983
GVIO in 1970 constant prices	9.2	22.3	22.8	7.2	—
GVIO in current prices	9.7	28.9	36.0	−14.4	6.8
Sales revenue	10.9	30.9	12.5	−15.9	−11.9
Domestic	−8.3	38.3	14.5	−15.5	−4.7
Export	93.4	15.6	7.8	−16.9	−31.1
Total gross profit[a]	64.2	44.6	17.5	−53.5	−50.8
Productive fixed assets	0.8	3.1	44.6	8.7	—
Working capital	−2.7	4.1	48.1	14.6	—

GVIO, gross value of industrial output.

— Not available.

a. Estimated growth rate for total gross profit in 1984 was 61.8 percent.

Source: Information provided by the mill.

years because of poor soil conditions, inadequate water supply, and transport difficulties, there were benefits. Some mill workers who had dependents with rural registration were able to move their families to the farm and subsequently obtained work for them in the mill or in Nanning City and had their registration changed to urban.[11] The mill became better known locally and nationally; this recognition had some significant advantages. Nanning was chosen in 1979 to be a pilot in enterprise reforms, despite the poor quality of its products in the previous year, suggesting that noneconomic considerations may have played an important role in the selection process. The mill's party secretary was promoted to the position of deputy mayor of Nanning Municipality in 1980—but this promotion may not have been directly linked to the enterprise's Daqing title.

1979–81

The mill considered this period to be the golden era of its development. It was able to make great improvements in quality; it increased the percentage of first-grade products in its total output from 67 percent in 1978 to 86 percent in 1979 and 89 percent in 1980. The mill's total sales increased by 10.9 percent in 1979, by 30.9 percent in 1980, and by 12.5 percent in 1981. Total profits rose by 64 percent in 1979 and continued to grow rapidly—by 45 percent in 1980 and by 18 percent in 1981. The mill's 1980 profits of Y11.5 million were more than double the profits of 1978, and, in 1981, profits reached a record Y13.5 million. The mill met all targets set by the government, and in 1981 it won a silver medal for its ramie-polyester "palace" fabric.

How much effect the mill's status as a pilot firm in experimental reforms had on its performance is difficult to assess. The reform most significant for the mill's staff was profit retention. Retained profits allowed managers to increase the income and welfare benefits of employees with bonuses and other subsidies and with new housing. Other changes brought by the reform program in 1979 did not seem to have as much effect as retention of profits. The director's authority to appoint middle-level managers was not fully implemented in the early 1980s. Direct marketing on the part of the mill was perceived not as a significant change but rather as a small window that permitted some direct contact with the market. The mill was not prepared and did not want to handle a large volume of sales on its own.

Although reforms of internal management had some positive effects on the mill's performance, the market played a greater role in this. There was a sharp increase in demand in domestic and export markets in 1979–81. Although domestic sales declined by 8.3 percent in 1979—this decline may represent the lagged effect of the problems with quality the mill reported in 1978—in 1980 and 1981 domestic sales increased by 38.3 percent and 14.5 percent respectively. The increase in exports was even more remarkable.

Export sales almost doubled in 1979 and continued to grow—by 15.6 percent in 1980 and by 7.8 percent in 1981. The share of exports in total sales jumped to 32.9 percent in 1979 and remained high in 1980 and 1981 (table 7.5).

Government policies favoring investment in the textile sector prompted Nanning and its supervisory agencies to embark on a project in 1980 to expand the mill's printing and dyeing capacity by 10 million meters. The project was designed to improve finishing capacity, partly to cater to the increased demand for printing and dyeing processing work that resulted when a 50,000-spindle project at another enterprise in Nanning City (the Nanning Cotton Mill) came on stream. The estimated total cost of the printing and dyeing project was Y7.44 million, of which Y5.61 million would be financed by a loan from the People's Bank of China, Y0.25 million by a grant from the Nanning municipal government, and Y1.56 million from the enterprise's own funds. As this project came on stream, however, over-investment in the textile sector as a whole pushed output growth far beyond increasing demand; this situation resulted in growing surpluses on the domestic market.

1982–83

As a result of the weak market situation and of price reductions in 1981–83, Nanning's total sales revenue dropped by 15.9 percent in 1982 and by 11.9 percent in 1983. In early 1983 the ex-factory prices of ramie-polyester and acrylic-polyester fabric were reduced by 35 percent on average, and it became unprofitable for the mill to produce some of its main products, including the award-winning ramie-polyester palace fabric. The mill's total profits dropped by 53.5 percent in 1982 and by another 50.8 percent in 1983.

The Nanning mill was forced to handle an increasing share of its domestic sales after commercial departments abandoned unified procurement. It took some time, however, for the mill to turn the situation around. At the end of 1982 its inventory reached 2.55 million meters, the equivalent of 1.8 months' output. Faced with this grave situation, the mill started to organize

Table 7.5. Nanning Mill's Domestic Sales and Exports, 1978–84
(millions of yuan, unless otherwise specified)

Item	1978	1979	1980	1981	1982	1983	1984[a]
Total sales revenue	26.5	29.4	38.5	43.3	36.4	32.1	26.0
Domestic sales	21.5	19.7	27.3	31.2	36.4	25.2	14.4
Export sales	5.0	9.7	11.2	12.0	10.0	6.9	11.7
Exports as percentage of total sales	18.8	32.9	29.1	27.8	27.5	21.5	44.9

a. Data are for first ten months only.
Source: Information provided by the mill.

its own marketing staff. It engaged in market research and new product development and established sales outlets. Nanning's ultimate savior, however, was the export market.

At the suggestion of the foreign trade corporations in charge of textile exports, in the fall of 1982 the mill began on a trial basis to produce cotton-ramie fabric woven with pure cotton and pure ramie yarn prepared separately as warp and weft. The product, however, was not attractive, quality was poor, and sales were unsatisfactory. In early 1983 the mill managed to master the technique of producing yarn from blended cotton and ramie fibers; it then used the blended yarn to weave cotton-ramie fabric. This new product was popular at a trade fair held in Guangdong in April, and export orders began to flow in, beginning in the second half of 1983. By the end of 1983 the mill had begun to recover from the adverse situation, and sales and profits increased again.

After 1983

In the first ten months of 1984, total profits of the Nanning mill rose by 92 percent in relation to its profits in the first ten months of 1983. Total output increased by 8.3 percent, sales revenue by 14 percent, and output of ramie blends for export and total exports each by more than 99 percent. The huge increase in profits was partly the result of favorable market conditions, partly the result of cost reductions through savings on consumption of inputs. Faster turnover of working capital, improvements in product quality, and lowering of the tax rate also played a role. The mill's ability to respond promptly to changes in market demand, for example by shifting from ramie-cotton blends to pure ramie products in the second half of 1984, contributed greatly to the increase in profits.

One reason for this quick response was the factory-director responsibility system, which increased the director's flexibility in operating the mill. He came to have expanded powers in determining bonus levels for workshops and in making personnel decisions. These changes improved the efficiency of the mill's internal management.

It became possible at this time for the mill to establish links with other enterprises. (In 1984 the central government encouraged associations between enterprises across administrative and geographical barriers to improve efficiency through combining resources.) The Nanning mill had been built for silk spinning and weaving; hence the capacity of its equipment was not well balanced for production of other textile fibers. With changes in market demand, however, the mill had to be prepared to change output mix quickly. Nanning was able to overcome this obstacle by making processing or cooperative arrangements with several small local firms. Some of these firms retted the raw ramie, some spun blended ramie-cotton yarn, and some wove other kinds of fabric for specific orders.

Tax rates for ramie textiles were adjusted in March 1984. Previously rates had been the same for cotton and ramie textiles, and taxes had been levied at each stage of processing: yarn, cloth, and printed and dyed cloth. The aggregated tax rate for all three stages was 18–20 percent. Because the production cost for ramie was higher than was that for cotton, equal taxation left ramie textiles at a competitive disadvantage in terms of costs and prices. To encourage development of ramie textiles, the tax rules were changed in favor of integrated ramie-linen or silk-ramie-linen plants; only the end products of these plants would be taxed, at rates of 3 percent for ramie-polyester blends, 5 percent for pure ramie, and 8 percent for ramie-cotton blends. Because these reduced rates were not applicable to cotton textile factories producing ramie blends, the Nanning mill gained an advantage over its competitors.[12]

Unfortunately data on the Nanning mill after 1984 are lacking. The mill's director estimated at that time that Nanning's exports would increase by another 30 percent in 1985. The mill gained approval from the municipal government to engage in direct export trading in 1985. If reforms continued to give support to the authority of the enterprise director in making business decisions, the mill probably continued to do well in the years after 1984. It must have been increasingly subjected to the fluctuations in the export market, however, and its performance must have depended a great deal on its ability to respond to changes in market demand.

Limitations of Enterprise Reforms

The Nanning mill's experience in the late 1970s and the early 1980s highlights the importance of exogenous as opposed to endogenous factors as influences on an enterprise's behavior and performance. Changing market conditions and the mill's increasing responsibility for marketing its own products led to greater orientation toward customers, important changes in product mix, development of new products and production processes, improved quality, sharply increased exports, ties with other firms, and, by 1984, improved financial performance. Market forces stimulated the Nanning mill to improve its performance in most respects during the reform period.

The partial and incomplete nature of the reforms, however, led to many problems and contradictions. Incentives were weakened by the lack of correlation between performance and rewards. The mill, like other Chinese state enterprises, was subject to a soft budget constraint that further weakened incentives and generated an unstable environment. Although the mill was not subject to a fragmented or multiheaded leadership system (see chapters 4 and 5 in this volume), blurred lines of responsibility between the enterprise and its government supervisory agencies did lead to problems. This section discusses these issues and then ends with a summary of the main lessons and implications of the Nanning mill's experience.

Lack of Correlation between Performance and Rewards

Performance at the Nanning mill deteriorated in 1982 as a result of changes in the market and of price reductions for the mill's outputs; total profits fell by more than 50 percent. Retained profits, however, fell by only 27 percent. As a result, retained profits as a share of total profits increased from 12.8 percent in 1981 to 19.9 percent in 1982 (table 7.6). A closer look at the enterprise's accounts suggests that the percentages of retained profits were subject to renegotiation after they were set. For example, the mill's accounts showed that its retained profits were Y1.15 million in 1979, Y1.58 million in 1980, and Y1.72 million in 1981. These amounts represented 14.5 percent of total profits in 1979, 13.7 percent in 1980 and 12.8 percent in 1981—not the 12.14 percent retention rate fixed at the outset. The mill's accounts also showed that in 1979 the level of total profits was adjusted from Y7.67 million to Y7.94 million with the consent of its supervisory departments. The reason given for this adjustment was simply that the scheme for profit retention started in that year. The adjustment implied that the mill would have been allowed to retain Y964,400 rather than Y930,530 (if the 12.14 percent retention rate had been applied), but even the higher figure was less than the actual amount retained in that year (Y1.15 million).

Of total profits retained by the Nanning mill in 1979–82, about 31 percent was distributed to employees as bonuses and about 26 percent was used for collective welfare. When profits plummeted in 1982, workers still received bonuses, although the amount of the bonuses was slightly less than it had been in 1981, and collective welfare expenditures more than doubled. Such behavior was defended on the ground that poor performance in 1982 was

Table 7.6. Nanning Mill's Retained Profits and Bonuses, 1979–82
(millions of yuan, unless otherwise specified)

Item	1979	1980[a]	1981	1982	1979–82
Total administrative profits	7.944	11.490	13.505	6.279	39.218
Retained profits	1.150	1.576	1.724	1.249	5.699
Retained profits as percentage of total administrative profits	14.5	13.7	12.8	19.9	14.5
Retained profits paid as employee bonuses	0.329	0.506	0.482	0.425	1.742
Share of retained profits paid as bonuses (percent)	28.6	32.1	28.0	34.0	30.6
Retained profits used for collective welfare	0.149	0.373	0.296	0.651	1.469
Share of retained profits used for collective welfare (percent)	13.0	23.7	17.2	52.1	25.8

a. Calculations exclude a special bonus of Y36,000 granted by the Nanning Finance Bureau.
Source: Information provided by the mill.

the result of market changes and price reductions—circumstances beyond the control of the mill—and hence employees should not be penalized. This behavior shows that the mill was not truly an independent economic entity and did not have to abide by a tight budget.

The Soft Budget Constraint

The budget of the Nanning mill had several components that were negotiable, including the amount of profits it should remit to the Finance Bureau, the amount of taxes it should pay to the Tax Bureau, and the amount of loan repayments it should make to banks. Negotiations occurred not only at the beginning of each year, at which time targets were handed down by supervisory agencies, but also during and even at the end of the year. Targets agreed on at the beginning of the year could be drastically changed later. One important element in the enterprise budget, however, was not negotiable, or was negotiable only above a certain floor: wages and bonuses for employees. Before the late 1970s, basic wages were guaranteed to each worker regardless of performance. Bonuses also came to be perceived as part of the basic income of workers rather than as extra income that could be withheld if performance were poor. As a result, incomes of staff and workers would not be affected by poor performance in any significant way; instead the amounts remitted to the government would be reduced.

The management of the mill's loan repayments illustrates how the soft budget constraint worked in practice. The mill borrowed Y5.61 million from the Nanning branch of the People's Bank of China in 1980 for an investment project to expand its printing and dyeing line. The loan was to be repaid within three years after the project started operation in 1981. At the end of 1984, however, there was still an outstanding balance of Y3.7 million on the loan. Negotiations with the People's Bank and the Nanning Finance Bureau resulted in extending the repayment period for another three years, without any penalty. There was a conflict of interest between the Finance Bureau and the People's Bank because the mill's loan repayments came in part from the profits and industrial and commercial taxes generated by the project financed by the loan. For example, in 1983 the mill's total loan repayment of Y620,000 was drawn mostly from industrial and commercial taxes (Y350,000), partly from profits (Y170,000), and partly from depreciation funds (Y100,000). Any loan repayment the mill made would reduce the amount of revenue collected by the Finance and Tax bureaus. Thus it was in the interest of the Finance Bureau to defer the mill's loan repayments.[13]

A similarly lax attitude can be observed in the case of another loan agreement made two years later. At the end of 1982 the Nanning mill borrowed Y10 million from the People's Construction Bank for its 4,800-spindle project (Y8 million from the head office of the Construction Bank and Y2 million from its Nanning branch). This project was approved by the Ministry of Textile Industry and was included in the Sixth Five-Year Plan. Because it was considered a "ministry-approved" project, the local branch of the Construction Bank did not conduct a detailed appraisal. The terms of the agreement were drawn up very loosely: repayment was to be made within five years after signing (by the end of 1987), but it could be extended another two years if the enterprise had difficulty generating sufficient industrial and commercial taxes from the new project to cover loan repayments. Because of a nationwide freeze on textile investments in 1983, the Nanning project was suspended for half a year and was not expected to come on stream until late 1985. The mill estimated that under the most favorable circumstances it would be able to repay the full amount of the loan only three to four years after completion of the project. If everything went smoothly, the mill would be able to repay the loan by the end of 1989 but not by the end of 1987.

The terms of the loan agreements were largely immaterial in any case. Government agencies did not expect the terms to be fully observed, and the Nanning mill did not anticipate any problems if it failed to honor its obligations. The banks did not operate as independent commercial banks that took full responsibility for loan appraisal and recovery. The local government, represented in a fragmented manner by the Finance Bureau, by the Textile Bureau, or by the Economic Commission, acted as intermediary and final arbitrator between Nanning and the lending institutions. As long as an investment project was endorsed by the local government, the mill did not have to worry about ability to repay the loan.

In the case of the 4,800-spindle project, the mill itself initially drew up the proposal. While waiting for approval from the government, however, management became hesitant about the prospects for the project, partly because of the downturn in the textile market. The Nanning Textile Bureau, with the support of the Nanning Economic Commission, then convinced the mill's management to continue with the project. With the help of the local government, land required for the project was allocated, equipment specifications were revised to respond to changing market demand, and financing was secured. In the end, although the project was still considered to be the mill's own, the investment decision was made by concerned government agencies, with the consent of the mill's management.

Blurred Lines of Responsibility

The lack of clear lines of responsibility for the mill and its supervisory agencies is one reason that reforms were ineffective in some spheres. State enterprises in China are invariably directly supervised by an agency or department at one of three levels of government: central, provincial, or county-municipal. Usually the size and importance of a firm's output in the national, regional, or local economy determines what level of government directly supervises the firm, but often other factors come into play (see, for example, chapter 5 in this volume). Policy changes also lead to shifts in the level of government supervising an enterprise. The Nanning mill gradually shifted from regional (provincial) management to municipal management in 1981.

In the prereform period, an enterprise's supervisory agency was responsible for determining or approving enterprise output and performance targets, investment plans, appointment of managers, and labor recruitment. The enterprise was like a production unit that delivers output according to plan. It relied on the supervisory agency to ensure the provision of inputs, including raw materials, labor, and financing, for its investments and operations. Any profits the enterprise made were remitted to the government through the supervisory agency. Compensation of staff and workers was drawn from the wage bill approved by the supervisory agency. The supervisory agency had an obligation to ensure not only the enterprise's smooth operations and delivery of output but also the welfare of its employees. This interdependence between enterprise and supervisory agency helps explain the behavior patterns of managers and government officials, which had become such established norms that the reforms of the early 1980s did not affect them in a significant way.

The close interdependence between supervisory agency and enterprise was such that it would have been difficult to make the enterprise responsible for its profits or losses. The history of the Nanning mill in 1979–84 shows that although the rules of the game might have changed somewhat with the implementation of reforms, the nature and role of the firm remained largely the same. Because rules were not clearly established and were constantly shifting, there was naturally a great deal of bargaining between the enterprise and its supervisory agencies. In the end, the balance sheet of the enterprise bore little relationship to its true performance.

Lessons and Implications

The Nanning mill may be a fairly typical example of a locally controlled enterprise in a remote, less industrial part of China. One implication of this particular pattern of location and administrative supervision appears to be a tendency toward extreme softness in the enterprise budget constraint, at least up to the point at which resource constraints of the local government become truly binding (as they apparently did at Nanning in 1983). Geographical isolation and local control nurtured an open alliance between Nanning and the local government to manipulate the mill's financial arrangements at the expense of higher levels of government. Even the local bank branches participated in this alliance, at least implicitly.

Nanning's experience suggests that efforts to make Chinese state enterprises truly independent from government supervisory agencies may be even more difficult in the cases of locally controlled firms than they are for larger enterprises under central or provincial jurisdiction. Both enterprise and local government gain concrete benefits from their association; hence neither may be willing to give up the relationship under many circumstances. Because China has been moving toward an economic structure in which most medium-size and even many large enterprises are under the control of municipal governments, further progress toward the separating of enterprises and local governments may become more difficult.

The Nanning mill's experience also shows the need for enterprises to respond quickly to domestic and international market trends. Only with the implementation of the factory-director responsibility system in 1984 was it possible for the mill to speed up its decisionmaking and to break away from its old pattern of long party branch (committee) deliberations on any important decision. In this context, the right to deal directly with foreign customers that the mill reportedly gained was important, because it allowed greater and quicker responsiveness to demand.

The Nanning mill was one of the first enterprises in China to institute the contract labor system for regular state employees. Nanning's experience with this reform suggests that the new system was ineffective in meeting reform objectives. It seems to have provided greater flexibility only to workers and to have provided no great improvement in incentives for them. Employees became freer to quit their jobs when their contracts expired (or even earlier), but managers appeared to have had little option but to renew the contracts of all workers who wished to remain employed. It was claimed that some workers quit their jobs at the mill to seek better-paying work elsewhere or to go into private business, after they had received training at the mill's expense.

Overall, the Nanning mill operated in the mold of a family firm, in that it took responsibility for the welfare of its employees and their dependents and cooperated with "close relatives" in the local government to protect the local economy from the impositions of the central government. Although the factory-director responsibility system apparently improved the position of the director in relation to the rest of the management team and allowed him to impose greater discipline on the workers, it did not, at least as of 1984, change this basic "family firm" pattern.

Notes

1. The enterprise's full name is the Nanning Silk and Ramie Spinning, Weaving, Printing, and Dyeing Mill.

2. See chapter 5 of this volume for a review of China's textile industry as a whole.

3. The other two factories that were built likewise never obtained sufficient silk cocoons and, like Nanning, switched to other kinds of production. The Guilin Silk Factory came to use ramie and chemical fiber for raw material (as did Nanning),

and the Tianyang Silk Factory started producing blends of chemical fiber, wool, and cotton. See Guangxi Economic Yearbook Editorial Committee 1985, p. 201.

4. The Nanning mill had 10,400 silk spindles, 1,920 woolen spindles, and more than 3,000 workers in 1982. Of the 6,000-odd textile enterprises under the administration of the Ministry of Textile Industry and its subordinate branches in 1982, there were 138 large, 390 medium-size, and 5,532 small enterprises. An average large cotton textile mill had more than 100,000 spindles and 7,000 to 10,000 employees; a medium-size firm had 50,000 to 90,000 spindles and 3,000 to 5,000 workers; and a small enterprise had 300 to 1,000 workers (Zhou 1984, p. 365).

5. *Ma* is a general term for jute (*huangma*), flax (*yama*), and ramie (*zhuma*). Of these three, jute (the raw material for ropes, bags, and cloth for industrial use) was the most important in 1982; 20 percent of jute output was exported in that year.

6. The Zhuang ethnic group is China's largest minority, with a population of more than 13 million in 1984; that year more than 92 percent of the Zhuang lived in Guangxi (State Statistical Bureau 1985a, p. 19; Guangxi Economic Yearbook Editorial Committee 1985, p. 93).

7. Bonuses in 1980 were higher than in the other years because they included a special bonus granted by the municipality for savings in coal and electricity consumption in 1979 and a special award for the mill's exceptional increase in profits in 1980. Both of these bonuses were approved by the Nanning Finance Bureau.

8. That is, the mill would retain 24 percent of profits up to the planned target plus 24 percent + (21 percent × 0.6), or 36.6 percent of profits above the planned target.

9. The establishment of the corporation might have been triggered by the central government's incentive scheme to promote textile exports. From 1979 the Ministry of Textile Industry had been given foreign exchange retention quotas, which it could allocate to provincial and regional textile bureaus as appropriate. The total amount of these quotas in 1979–82 was more than $100 million. Because Guangxi's textile exports had been going through the Guangdong Textile Import-Export Corporation, Guangxi was not receiving any benefits from the foreign exchange retention system (see Qian and others 1984, pp. 547–48).

10. In 1978 the average percentage of first-grade products in total output of the principal textile mills was 87.6 percent for printed and dyed cloth (State Statistical Bureau 1985b, p. 134).

11. Under China's system of household registration, persons holding rural registration status were not allowed to permanently migrate to the cities, obtain regular employment or public housing, or gain access to low-price rationed commodities and various public services. Living standards and levels of amenities were on average far higher in urban areas than in rural areas, so urban residency was much sought by rural residents. With registration status inherited from the mother rather than the father, complications such as split registration status within households sometimes emerged.

12. See Ministry of Textile Industry 1986, p. 163. According to mill personnel, rates were reduced after Zhang Jingfu, a senior central government leader, discovered during his visit to Nanning in early 1983 that the mill had stopped producing its silver-prizewinner (ramie-polyester palace) because the tax rate on the fabric was

so high that the mill was losing money on it. This story is probably somewhat exaggerated; it would seem more likely that the government's decision to adjust tax rates was based on industrywide considerations.

13. A Finance Bureau representative stated that in 1984 other enterprises in Nanning were also given permission to delay loan repayments in order to maintain the municipality's revenues at an acceptable level.

References

BBC. *Summary of World Broadcasts: The Far East* (daily translation series).

China Economic Yearbook Editorial Committee. 1985. *Zhongguo Jingji Nianjian 1985* (China Economic Yearbook 1985). Beijing: Jingji Guanli Chubanshe.

Corbman, Bernard B. 1975. *Textiles: Fiber to Fabric.* 5th ed. New York: McGraw-Hill.

Fan Jiapu, ed. 1981. *Fangzhi Yiliao Zhishi* (Knowledge of Textile Fabrics). Shenyang: Liaoning Renmin Chubanshe.

Guangxi Economic Yearbook Editorial Committee. 1985. *Guangxi Jingji Nianjian 1985* (Guangxi Economic Yearbook 1985). Nanning: Guangxi Renmin Chubanshe.

Jingji Ribao (Economic Daily). Daily newspaper.

Ministry of Textile Industry. 1984. *Zhongguo Fangzhi Gongye Nianjian 1983* (China Textile Industry Yearbook 1983). Beijing: Fangzhi Gongye Chubanshe.

————. 1986. *Zhongguo Fangzhi Gongye Nianjian 1984–1985* (China Textile Industry Yearbook 1984–1985). Beijing: Fangzhi Gongye Chubanshe.

Qian Zhiguang and others, eds. 1984. *Dangdai Zhongguo de Fangzhi Gongye* (The Textile Industry in Contemporary China). Beijing: Zhongguo Shehui Kexue Chubanshe.

State Economic Commission, Investigations and Research Section. 1983. "Woguo Wuge Gongye Hangye Jingji Xiaoyi Fenshi" (An Analysis of the Economic Performance of Five Industries in China). *Jingji Diaocha* (Economic Investigations) 2 (December): 1–21.

State Statistical Bureau. 1983, 1985a, 1986. *Statistical Yearbook of China.* Hong Kong: Economic Information and Agency.

————. 1985b. *Zhongguo Gongye Jingji Tongji Ziliao 1949–1984* (Statistical Materials on China's Industrial Economy 1949–1984). Beijing: Zhongguo Tongji Chubanshe.

Wu Chengming. 1985. "Lun Nan Geng Nu Zhi" (On Men Farming and Women Weaving). In *Zhongguo Ziben Zhuyi yu Guonei Shichang* (On Chinese Capitalism and Domestic Markets). Beijing: Zhongguo Shehui Kexue Chubanshe.

Zhou Taihe, ed. 1984. *Dangdai Zhongguo de Jingji Tizhi Gaige* (Economic System Reform in Contemporary China). Beijing: Zhongguo Shehui Kexue Chubanshe.

8

The Anshan Iron and Steel Company

William A. Byrd

THIS IS A STUDY of the largest employer among Chinese state enterprises, the Anshan Iron and Steel Company (Anshan for short), a huge, integrated complex in the northeastern province of Liaoning. The first section of the chapter suggests reasons why Anshan makes an interesting case study and reviews Anshan's history and its role in China's iron and steel industry. The second section looks at Anshan's relationship with its government supervisory agencies, particularly the so-called multiheaded leadership system that emerged in the early 1970s and the subsectoral responsibility system in China's iron and steel industry that was implemented in the mid-1980s. Anshan's financial system and financial incentives are covered in the third section, which analyzes profit retention, taxation, and the uneven and changing degree to which Anshan was "compensated" for price changes that affected its financial performance. In the fourth section mandatory planning and marketing controls are examined; mandatory planning dominated Anshan's production activities, and direct marketing did not achieve desired results. The fifth section looks at the critical choice between integration and administrative fragmentation in Anshan's various production activities, using some case studies from Anshan's experience to illustrate the conflicts and problems that arise. Internal organization and management are covered in the sixth section, which focuses on the trend of internal decentralization within Anshan and on the related topic of internal transfer pricing. Labor and wage issues are analyzed in the seventh section, which discusses the interaction between employees' goals and enterprise objectives, wage systems, trends in employment and wages, and subordinate collective enterprises set up by Anshan to employ workers' children. The eighth section looks at issues related to the overall design of Anshan's modernization program, at the program's coordination with ongoing production activities, and at the constraints hindering modernization. The last section presents some generalizations from Anshan's experience that may be relevant to Chinese industrial reforms.

Issues and History

Anshan is of great interest for a number of reasons. It is in many ways a typical large, integrated iron and steel complex that reflects the problems of China's iron and steel industry. Anshan is also representative more generally of very large Chinese state-owned industrial enterprises under the supervision of central ministries. The sheer size of Anshan—220,000 regular employees, more than 170,000 additional personnel in subsidiary enterprises under collective ownership, total fixed and circulating assets of Y4.9 billion, gross value of industrial output (GVIO) of Y4.15 billion (in 1980 constant prices), and annual steel production of 7.26 million tons—raises a number of interesting organizational and economic issues.[1]

Anshan is an old enterprise; much of its equipment and facilities dated from the 1930s. Its modernization presented enormous technical, financial, organizational, and economic problems. The enterprise faced a number of critical strategic issues involving how to conduct its modernization program, how to finance it, and indeed whether its existing plant should be modernized at all. Modernization at Anshan has been adversely affected by the whole gamut of systemic and institutional features of Chinese industry.

Anshan's complicated relationships with its supervisory agencies form another important part of the picture. Its multiheaded leadership system, a legacy of partial and uneven administrative decentralization, affected Anshan to some extent. Anshan is by far the most important source of budgetary revenue for Liaoning Province, so the provincial government was deeply concerned about its finances and profit remittances. Anshan was one of ten large iron and steel plants put under the subsectoral responsibility system involving the Ministry of Metallurgy and the national government; the system affected Anshan's relationship with the ministry and limited the enterprise's freedom of action.

Mandatory planning continued to exert a strong influence on Anshan and on similar firms in the late 1980s, imposing restrictions on decisionmaking that had a serious effect on short-run performance. Mandatory planning and the related objective of maximizing production in the short run affected Anshan's modernization, for instance by rendering impossible the stopping of production during a full-scale renovation program.

As part of the reforms, Anshan was given the right to market some of its output directly. This self-sales authority appears, however, not to have greatly influenced Anshan's behavior or its incentives to respond to customer needs. Facing as it did chronic sellers' markets for steel and for its main production inputs, Anshan remained strongly oriented toward production and technology. Problems with supply, although they were perhaps not as severe as were those many other firms faced, constrained Anshan's freedom of action and adversely affected its performance.

Opposing tendencies to integrate and to administratively fragment

Anshan's many activities led to constant tension among the enterprise, the Ministry of Metallurgy, and other government supervisory agencies. In market economies the choice between the market mechanism and hierarchical, or intrafirm, modes of organization determines the size and shape of firms (see Williamson 1975). In China, for an entity such as Anshan, the choice was not between hierarchical organization and the market mechanism but rather between integration of activities within the firm and reliance on planned allocation from outside. Enterprises generally prefer integration because it creates more reliable, stable sources of supply. Such integration reduces the government's ability to allocate goods to high-priority uses; thus there are pressures from above for fragmentation of activities across firms. This issue, and the inefficiencies that can result from it regardless of the choices made, is one of the main themes of this study.

The internal organization and management of a huge enterprise such as Anshan are worthy topics of research. The most critical issues in this area include: (1) the level at which separate accounting and profit-sharing systems are efficacious; (2) the appropriate degree of autonomy for lower-level units in the complex; (3) the different forms of wage systems and reward systems for workers; and (4) the hiring of workers' children and their employment in subsidiary collective firms. Generally Anshan has moved in the direction of internal decentralization in decisionmaking and finances.

Finally, Anshan is of interest because it provides insights into enterprise behavior in China. For instance, Anshan's actions reflect the effects of the chronic sellers' market it usually faced on both output and input sides. Similarly, the pressure to provide benefits to workers and job opportunities in collective subsidiaries for workers' dependents is evident. Pervasive bargaining, bureaucratic compromises, and exploitive behavior by some government agencies are exemplified by a number of episodes related in the chapter.

Historically, Anshan played an important role in the pre-1949 industrialization of northeast China (see Jiao and Zhang 1984 for details). From the time of its establishment until 1945, Anshan was under Japanese control. Construction of the company's facilities began in 1916, and the first blast furnace went into operation in 1919. In 1931 Anshan expanded to become an integrated complex with mining, ore-processing, sintering, coke-making, iron-smelting, steelmaking, and steel-rolling capabilities, and with a host of subsidiary activities. In 1943, its peak year in the period before 1949, Anshan produced 1.3 million metric tons of pig iron, 843,000 tons of steel, and 495,000 tons of rolled steel. By the end of World War II the company was in poor condition, however, and during Kuomintang rule (1945–48) there was little recovery.

Anshan came under the control of the new Communist government in February 1948. During the next four years it largely recovered from the destruction and scattering of resources that had occurred at the end of World War II and in the civil war. By 1952, output of steel and rolled steel approached peak 1943 levels, but pig iron production remained relatively low (see table 8.1). During this period Anshan had a relatively simple, decentralized management structure, the main goal of which was restoring production and regaining control over dispersed resources. Requirements for product quality were low, and the company's managers had little experience in steelmaking operations.

During the First Five-Year Plan (1953–57) Anshan expanded greatly, and its management system was remolded along highly centralized, Soviet lines. Anshan's expansion was one of the key projects of the First Five-Year Plan, with a total investment of nearly Y1.8 billion. Production increased sharply, with output of steel rising at an average annual rate of 30 percent and that of rolled steel at 33 percent (table 8.1). Anshan's main facilities and site layout were established during this period.

The centralization of Anshan's management structure in 1953–57 was evident in a number of aspects: (1) the company's internal accounting system, which previously had involved money transfers through bank settlement, switched to internal cost accounting and nonmonetary transfers; (2) all procurement of supplies from external units was centralized; (3) subordinate production units of Anshan no longer had the authority to sell outputs di-

Table 8.1. Output of Main Products at Anshan, Selected Years, 1943–86 (millions of metric tons)

Year	Pig iron	Steel	Rolled steel	Iron ore	Coke
1943	1.30	0.84	0.50	—	—
1949	0.10	0.10	0.08	—	—
1952	0.83	0.79	0.47	2.10	—
1957	3.36	2.91	1.92	8.76	—
1965	4.07	4.42	2.61	—	3.31
1973	5.81	6.04	3.61	—	4.01
1975	5.30	5.53	2.85	—	3.76
1976	5.33	5.53	3.07	—	3.71
1977	5.37	5.81	3.22	—	3.59
1978	6.40	6.86	3.86	—	4.02
1979	6.67	6.89	4.06	—	4.18
1980	6.70	6.97	4.21	—	4.18
1981	6.10	6.72	4.15	—	3.99
1982	6.10	6.76	4.43	—	4.10
1983	—	—	4.50	—	—
1984	6.44	7.01	4.83	25.12	4.04
1985	6.61	7.26	5.04	24.12	4.15
1986	7.10	7.49	5.20	24.33	4.46

— Not available.

Source: Liaoning Economic and Statistical Yearbook Editorial Committee 1983, pp. 58, 59. State Statistical Bureau 1985b, p. 271; 1986, p. 285; 1987a, p. 286. Ministry of Metallurgy 1985, pp. 279, 754; 1986a, p. 84. Information provided by the company.

rectly to outside units; (4) appointment and dismissal of managers was controlled by headquarters; (5) a centralized production-dispatch system was established; (6) supervision of product quality was centralized; and (7) a central testing system was established.

In 1957–58, as part of the Great Leap Forward movement and related currents, some internal management functions, including technical supervision, financial accounting, personnel management, and materials procurement, were decentralized; this action led to immediate declines in efficiency indicators. Anshan also suffered from the national campaign to send management personnel to the countryside. Like other state enterprises, Anshan changed its leadership system from the Soviet-type system that vested final authority in the enterprise director to one of director responsibility under the supervision of the enterprise party committee.

After 1959, recentralization occurred, and in the early 1960s Anshan began moving toward a management structure that did not slavishly imitate the Soviet system but did recognize the essential integration of the enterprise's technical production processes. Output growth slowed considerably in 1957–65 (table 8.1), with steel production increasing at an average annual rate of 5.4 percent and rolled steel production at only 3.9 percent a year.

During the Cultural Revolution period (1966–76), Anshan's activities suffered temporarily from political unrest, but more important was the decentralization of administrative supervision of the company to Liaoning Province and Anshan Municipality, an arrangement that lasted through the 1980s (see "The Supervisory System," in this chapter). No important new investments or renovation projects seem to have been undertaken in the decade after 1966; Anshan's production largely stagnated. Between 1965 and 1973 (a peak prereform year), steel output grew by only 4.0 percent a year and rolled steel output by 4.1 percent. Anshan was unable to maintain its record 1973 production levels in 1974–77.

Reforms and structural changes since 1978 are discussed in detail in the rest of this chapter. In many respects Anshan's experience has been similar to those of other large iron and steel plants and to those of large state enterprises in general. Output growth during the reform period has been unimpressive (table 8.1). In 1977–85 steel output increased at an average annual rate of 2.8 percent, rolled steel output at 5.8 percent, pig iron output at 2.6 percent, and coke output at only 1.8 percent. Anshan's product mix shifted toward downstream products, with the share of rolled steel output in crude steel output rising from 55 percent in 1978 to 69 percent in 1985. This shift reflected Anshan's greater profit orientation, as profits from steel rolling were much higher than those from making pig iron and crude steel. The shift toward rolled steel resulted in more balanced capacity for the different stages of production, but it reduced Anshan's ability to supply crude steel to other rolling mills.

Table 8.2 provides summary statistics on financial performance. Profitability shows marked year-to-year fluctuations. Inflation and failure to revalue existing assets probably distort the reported figures. The ratio of output to capital appears to have risen modestly. Growth of labor productivity, however, has been relatively slow in every year since the early 1980s except 1986.

Despite its age and the preponderance of obsolete equipment and old facilities, Anshan's performance was by no means below average among China's large, integrated iron and steel producers. In fact, Anshan in 1985 performed better than average for all of the performance indicators shown in table 8.3, with the bare exception of labor productivity. For certain indicators, Anshan reported figures close to the highest ones, particularly if enterprises that do not produce much of their own pig iron are excluded from the reckoning. Anshan's physical indicators of technical efficiency also were generally above the average for large complexes; this superiority probably reflects the human skills the enterprise built up over its long history and its more efficient use of facilities, their age notwithstanding.

Anshan played a critical role in the development of China's iron and steel industry throughout the twentieth century, although the company's relative importance has declined over the past thirty-five years (table 8.4). The enterprise accounted for more than 63 percent of total national steel output in 1949 but for only 16 percent in 1985. Similar declines in its shares of pig iron, rolled steel, coke, and iron ore occurred. Nevertheless, Anshan re-

Table 8.2. Financial Indicators for Anshan, 1975–86
(percent, unless otherwise specified)

Year	Profit rate on sales	Profit rate on total capital	Output-capital ratio	NVIO-GVIO ratio	Labor productivity (yuan per worker)
1975	29.7	20.5	69.1	—	12,480
1976	30.9	22.7	74.0	45.2	13,360
1977	32.2	23.1	70.0	47.5	13,230
1978	37.8	29.7	76.4	54.5	15,580
1979	36.9	29.7	79.2	43.4	16,630
1980	37.9	34.1	83.1	47.3	18,900
1981	35.4	29.5	76.6	47.8	17,930
1982	32.1	28.8	80.5	47.5	18,080
1983	—	24.0	—	—	—
1984	34.7	29.1	84.0	52.0	18,616
1985	—	—	—	49.3	20,114
1986	—	24.1	—	—	23,451

NVIO, net value of industrial output.

GVIO, gross value of industrial output.

— Not available.

Source: Ministry of Metallurgy 1985, pp. 751–52; 1986b, p. 539. State Statistical Bureau 1985a, p. 171; 1987a, pp. 208–9; 1987b, p. 331. Information provided by the company.

Table 8.3. Financial Indicators for Key Iron and Steel Firms, 1985
(percent, unless otherwise specified)

Company	Ratio of gross output to capital	Ratio of net output to capital	Ratio of profits and taxes to capital	Ratio of profits and taxes to gross output	Labor productivity (yuan per worker)
Average	77.1	31.7	27.3	33.4	20,662
Anshan	85.5	49.8	40.2	44.9	20,114
Baotou	36.6	16.8	11.5	31.3	12,767
Benxi	56.4	20.6	14.2	28.7	12,884
Capital	90.1	59.5	54.2	53.8	23,082
Maanshan	66.3	33.4	29.8	42.9	16,227
Panzhihua	54.3	21.9	21.7	38.7	17,508
Shanghai	223.3	63.9	59.0	25.5	47,669
Taiyuan	72.0	23.5	21.2	24.3	23,240
Tangshan	128.6	49.1	43.6	30.4	22,772
Tianjin	203.7	54.0	49.4	24.8	29,871
Wuhan	52.2	24.5	23.4	53.5	25,331

Note: Data are for large, mostly integrated iron and steel complexes.
Source: Ministry of Metallurgy 1986b, pp. 537–40.

mained one of the handful of large steel producers in China, and it continued to account for more than 20 percent of rolled steel allocated through the state plan (see "Mandatory Planning and Marketing Controls," in this chapter).

The Supervisory System

Like all state enterprises in China, Anshan was subject to administrative supervision by government line agencies, in its case the Ministry of Metallurgy and (only in a nominal sense) the Liaoning Provincial Metallurgy Bureau. Anshan's relationship with its supervisory agencies was complicated by its size, complexity, and importance in China's central plan, as well as by the multiheaded leadership system that emerged in the 1970s and, more recently, by the subsectoral responsibility system. Numerous other government entities were involved in supervising various aspects of Anshan's activities, including the State Planning Commission, tax authorities, banks, the material supply system, labor and personnel departments, and important customers such as the Ministry of Railways. Thus Anshan functioned in a complex administrative environment and interacted with numerous bureaucratic agencies that often had conflicting goals.

Historical Background and Situation in the 1980s

From the 1950s to the late 1960s, Anshan was directly under the supervision of the Ministry of Metallurgy. In 1969, as part of a general territorial decentralization of administrative control over state industrial enterprises, authority over Anshan was transferred to the Anshan Municipal Revolutionary Committee.[2] When the Communist Party structure was restored, the municipal party committee simultaneously functioned as the enterprise party committee, and the steel company was effectively merged with Anshan Municipality. In 1975 the State Council stipulated that Anshan was to be under the dual leadership of Liaoning Province and the ministry, with the province playing the predominant role, an arrangement that lasted through the late 1980s. Liaoning delegated supervision of Anshan's party and government administrative work to Anshan Municipality.

Because of Anshan's size and its dominant role in the economy of Anshan Municipality (which is something like a company town), delegation of supervisory authority to the municipal level was problematic. Total employment in the company (including subsidiary collective firms) accounted for nearly 80 percent of total employment in Anshan Municipality. In many respects the company exerted a dominant influence over the town rather than vice versa.[3] Even Liaoning Province was unable to supervise the company.[4] Thus, by default, operational supervision of Anshan was left to the Ministry of Metallurgy and, because of the dominance of central planning in the company's production, to the State Planning Commission and the State Economic Commission.

The fundamental bifurcation in Anshan's administrative supervision was between production planning, allocation of inputs, and procurement of outputs on the one hand and finances and taxation on the other. The planning, allocation, and procurement activities were supervised by the Ministry of Metallurgy and by central government planning authorities, finances and

Table 8.4. Anshan's Share in National Output, Selected Years, 1949–86
(percent)

Year	Pig iron	Steel	Rolled steel	Coke	Iron ore
1949	40.6	63.1	55.4	—	—
1952	42.8	58.4	41.6	—	49.0
1957	56.6	54.4	44.0	—	45.2
1965	37.8	36.2	29.1	24.8	—
1973	23.3	24.0	21.4	11.6	—
1975	21.6	23.1	17.6	10.2	—
1978	18.4	21.6	17.5	8.6	—
1980	17.6	18.8	15.5	9.6	—
1982	17.2	18.2	15.3	10.2	—
1985	15.1	15.5	13.6	8.6	17.6
1986	14.9	14.2	10.1	12.5	15.3

— Not available.

Source: Ministry of Metallurgy 1986a, p. 33; 1986b, p. 540; 1987, pp. 505, 535. Table 8.1. Information provided by the company.

taxation by Liaoning Province. Most of Anshan's products went to the central government, whereas its profit remittances and tax payments went to Liaoning Province. Whenever there was a conflict between high output and high profits, Anshan was torn by contradictory imperatives from different superiors. The enterprise's own increasing profit orientation, however, reinforced the tendency to limit or stop production of low-profit items and to shift product mix toward highly profitable goods. The province also put increasing pressure on Anshan to raise profits. After Shenyang and Dalian cities were made into independent economic entities directly under the central government, Anshan became the largest "taxpayer" under Liaoning's jurisdiction.

The allocation of material inputs to Anshan was complicated; provincial and local government authorities played an important role in it. Raw materials, coal, heavy oil, and major equipment were handled by the Ministry of Metallurgy. Electricity and natural gas supplies were handled by Liaoning Province. Building materials, such as cement, timber, and steel for construction, were allocated by Anshan Municipality. This system led to numerous conflicts (see "Mandatory Planning and Marketing Controls," in this chapter).

Personnel and labor decisions have also been subject to the multiheaded leadership system. The top managers of the enterprise were appointed by the full Central Committee of the Chinese Communist Party. Deputy directors and deputy party secretaries were appointed by the Organization Department of the Central Committee. The company's party committee, however, was formally subordinate to that of Anshan Municipality (presumably affecting only ideological work and not operations). Directors of lower-level factories within the company were approved by Anshan's general manager, after discussion with the party committee, whereas top party officials of these factories were approved by the company party committee. Thus Anshan did not suffer from the problem, common in other enterprises, of different levels of government appointing managers and party leaders below the top level. Labor allocation was nominally handled by the Anshan Municipal Labor Office, but this agency only followed the instructions of the ministry.

Another sphere in which the effect of the multiheaded leadership system is evident is investment planning and decisionmaking (see "Renovation and Modernization," in this chapter). Numerous central and provincial agencies were involved in these activities, but none wanted to take responsibility for funding or for the returns earned by investments. There was also a great deal of fragmentation in investment financing.

Multiheaded Leadership

It should be recognized that in most respects Anshan was basically a centrally run enterprise whose main administrative contacts were with central government agencies rather than with provincial or local authorities. The company was large in relation to the local and provincial economies, and even to some extent in relation to the portion of the national economy that was subject to central planning; its size might to some degree have insulated Anshan from petty interference by local government. Nevertheless, multiheaded leadership had some important implications for enterprise management.

One of these implications is administrative complexity. Anshan was forced to operate in a complicated administrative environment characterized by chronic instability and by changing bureaucratic compromises among various agencies. For example, Anshan faced difficulties with its modernization program (see "Renovation and Modernization," in this chapter), including uncertainty, conflicts, delays, frequent reversals of decisions, and waste. Although Anshan's modernization program was approved by the central government, much of it had to be financed by bank loans, which were determined primarily at provincial and local levels. As a result, modernization loans chronically fell short of plan stipulations.

Closely related to administrative complexity in this regard is instability. Tugs and conflicts between different levels of government and various supervisory organizations resulted in considerable uncertainty and mutability in Anshan's administrative environment. This situation was most evident in the chronic instability of the administrative boundaries within which Anshan operated, that is, which activities the enterprise was allowed to undertake and which it was not (see "Vertical Integration versus Administrative Fragmentation," in this chapter). Another manifestation of instability, common to other state enterprises, was in the distribution of profits.

The diverse, often conflicting goals of different supervisory agencies diverted the enterprise's attention from improving economic efficiency and, more generally, sapped its ability to accomplish any particular goal. Anshan's best interests tended to become submerged in this environment, and there was confusion about what its goals and priorities should be.

The most serious problem directly resulting from the multiheaded leadership system, however, was the aforementioned chronic conflict between production targets and profit targets. Central authorities not only desired that Anshan should produce more steel, pig iron, and steel products; they wanted particular varieties that suited users' needs, as did users themselves. These varieties frequently were low-profit items or even lossmaking items that Anshan was not willing to produce. Liaoning Province, for its part, relied heavily on the enterprise for fiscal revenue. Hence the province preferred that Anshan should shift product mix toward high-profit items and should reduce or eliminate production of low-profit items. In the 1980s Anshan discontinued production of many low-profit or lossmaking products.

Another problem related to Anshan's status as a centrally run enterprise in a local economic environment was chronic difficulties in obtaining approvals or help from municipal authorities for mundane matters such as hooking up utilities, obtaining food supplies for workers, obtaining local construction materials, and so forth. There were also conflicts with local authorities over a range of other matters. Most of these conflicts stemmed from Anshan's social responsibilities toward its employees and their dependents, as a result of which the enterprise became involved in a host of administrative matters that took up a great deal of the time of senior managers and led to friction with local authorities.

The foregoing discussion shows that Anshan's problems with the administrative supervisory system were not caused primarily by the multiheaded leadership system, the effects of which were less serious for Anshan than they were for many other state enterprises. The fundamental problem in this area was the system of centralized government administration itself, which involved a pattern of excessive government involvement in the day-to-day affairs of firms.

The Steel Industry Subsectoral Responsibility System

In late 1984 a multiyear "input-output responsibility system" for the iron and steel industry was proposed by the Ministry of Metallurgy and was accepted by China's State Council and Communist Party Central Committee.[5] Although the system was billed as a subsectoral one, it affected only large iron and steel plants that had substantial compulsory delivery quotas for steel products under the central plan. The system was lauded as an important but admittedly partial reform that was meant to improve the functioning of planning rather than to abolish it. Although it was approved in principle almost immediately, the system was formally ratified by China's State Council only in 1986; this delay suggests that there was considerable bargaining over its provisions. Nevertheless, the system went into effect in 1985 and was to remain in place for six years, until 1990.

Under the subsectoral responsibility system, the Ministry of Metallurgy was given various physical targets for production and for delivery of goods to the state, as well as certain allocation quotas for inputs provided through the state plan and investment quotas. The ministry then disaggregated these targets and allocations and passed them down to the thirty-odd large iron and steel plants that participated in the system. Targets for the ministry and for subordinate firms were fixed at the outset for each year during the period 1985–90. Financial targets (profit remittances, taxation, and so forth) were not part of the system for the iron and steel industry, as they were for other industries. Most large iron and steel plants, like Anshan, were under the dual leadership of central and provincial governments and had taxation and profit remittances handled by the provincial government. Hence the inclusion of profits or of other financial flows in the scheme would have been difficult.

The system involved five "responsibilities" (or "contracted items") and three "guarantees." The ministry had to achieve five targets:

1. Total crude steel output was to increase at an average annual rate of 2 million tons (starting from a base of 38 million tons in 1984), and rolled steel delivered to the state plan was to increase by 1 million tons a year (from a base of 19.8 million tons in 1984). In addition, 1.8 million tons of casting-quality pig iron and 2.65 million tons of coke were to be delivered to the state annually.

2. Output of rolled steel that met international quality standards was to rise from 2.5 million tons in 1984 to 10 million tons in 1990.

3. Energy consumption per ton of steel produced was to be reduced from 1.78 tons of standard coal in 1984 to 1.6 tons in 1990, for total energy savings of at least 1 million tons of standard coal-equivalent a year.

4. Targets for investment in capital construction and modernization were to be achieved; these targets included total investment amount, progress of construction, and creation of new capacity. By 1990, new capacity for annual production of 15 million tons of steel, 14 million tons of pig iron, and 50 million tons of iron ore was to be created.

5. Total profits and taxes earned by enterprises under the system were to rise from Y9.4 billion in 1984 to Y13.3 billion in 1990.

The central government undertook to provide three items to the Ministry of Metallurgy.

1. The main raw materials required for production within the mandatory plan were to be allocated to enterprises through the plan; these raw materials included iron ore, coal, power, alloys, scrap steel, and transport.

2. The ministry was to be provided with a total quota, or approved ceiling, for fixed asset investments of Y40 billion for 1986–90. Although initially it may have been intended that funding would also be provided (through a combination of loans and government grants), such funding did not materialize. Hence the quota merely represented authority to undertake these investments.

3. The ministry was to be allocated through the plan cement, steel, and timber required for fixed asset investment within the Y40 billion ceiling.

The system was actually much weaker and more malleable than the foregoing list would imply. In the first place, most of the ministry's targets were subject to bargaining. Only those for delivery of rolled steel, pig iron, and coke for central plan distribution were effectively fixed. The investment quota also was fixed (in nominal terms). There was considerable bargaining, however, among enterprises, the ministry, and the State Planning Commission over norms for input consumption per unit of output, as well as perhaps over norms for construction materials used in investment projects. The financing of the Y40 billion investment quota and its allocation over time were sources of severe conflicts. Shortage of funds resulted in underspending during the earlier years of the Seventh Five-Year Plan, although plans for renovation and expansion called for heavier spending near the beginning. This underspending led to a severe financial squeeze and to high demand for investment in the late 1980s, and modernization and capacity expansion most likely fell considerably short of targets.

The most serious adverse implications of the subsectoral responsibility system relate to the entrenchment and perpetuation of mandatory planning and to the consequent lack of enterprise autonomy. Compulsory delivery targets for rolled steel produced by China's largest iron and steel complexes were programmed to rise steadily in absolute amounts at least until 1990. Although the share of total national output of rolled steel that was subject to allocation by the state plan continually declined, under the subsectoral responsibility system a large part of national output continued to be subject to mandatory planning.

More generally, the system generated inappropriate tendencies in the Ministry of Metallurgy. The large iron and steel complexes became, if anything, more closely bound to the ministry, and reformers' attempts to loosen these hierarchical ties met with more obstacles. Moreover, the confusion of ownership, regulatory, and management roles in the ministry was perpetuated, if not exacerbated. Finally, the power and coordinating role vested in the Ministry of Metallurgy may make it difficult to abolish or to consolidate the ministry in the future.

Because the subsectoral responsibility system for iron and steel did not involve indicators of financial performance or profit distribution (as did those for other heavy industries), some problems were avoided. For instance, it was not likely that the Ministry of Metallurgy would engage in monopolistic behavior to increase total profits of the firms under the system. There were numerous inconsistencies between financial and physical planning processes and targets, however, that had been present all along but that may have been exacerbated by the subsectoral responsibility system.

To the extent that the system generated credible commitments for the future, it created rigidities akin to those involved in earmarking funds for particular uses; these rigidities weakened the enterprise's responsiveness to the needs of reform. Rigidity was evident in flows of financing and of materials, in enterprise-ministry relations, and in overlapping, conflicting roles within the ministry. If there were considerable "give" in the system, and if there were room for renegotiation, however, the instability of incentives was perpetuated.

Anshan itself considered the high and rising physical targets for delivery of rolled steel to the state to be the main problem it faced as a result of the subsectoral responsibility system. The enterprise saw few, if any, benefits from the system, because there were no financial incentives associated with it. Although it was undoubtedly well intentioned, the system appears to have negatively affected the autonomy of the enterprise and the incentives available to it.

The Financial System and Incentives

Financial matters were at the heart of the state enterprise reforms that were instituted in the late 1970s. Anshan lagged somewhat in implementing these reforms. Because of its size and its importance as a revenue generator, the government was reluctant to allow large increases in its retained profits. Anshan gained greater access to depreciation funds, however, and to other internally generated funds to facilitate its modernization. One contentious issue concerned whether and to what extent Anshan should be compensated for the effect of changes in administratively controlled prices or of other financial parameters on its finances.

Profit Retention and Other Financial Incentives

Before the late 1970s, Anshan, like other state industrial firms, had virtually no discretionary financial resources under its own control. All profits were remitted to the government, as were depreciation funds and major repair funds.[6] In December 1978 the "enterprise fund" system, which had been defunct since the 1960s, was revived. By its terms, Anshan could keep a sum equivalent to 5 percent of its total wage bill, plus 10 percent of any profits it earned above a set quota, and this money could be used for reinvestment, employee welfare, and bonuses.

In April 1980 Anshan instituted a new profit retention scheme based on principles of enterprise reform enunciated at the national level in 1979. The company was permitted to retain for its own use 4.22 percent of base-year profits and 20 percent of profits that exceeded the base level. For 1980, the base year chosen was 1979. Moreover, the enterprise was allowed to retain 50 percent of its depreciation fund and 100 percent of its major repair fund.[7] The actual rate of profit retention in 1980 was 4.44 percent of total profits; this rate was only slightly higher than the within-quota retention rate, implying that total realized profits barely exceeded the quota.

Starting in 1981 Anshan was put under a new system that involved retention of 7 percent of base-year (1980) profits. The enterprise was allowed to keep all above-quota profits in 1981 and in 1982 but only 20 percent of them in 1983–85. This advance stipulation of a large decline in marginal profit retention rates was unusual; moreover, the stipulation seems to have been largely adhered to, in striking contrast to the sharp increases in profit retention rates seen in many other enterprises during this period. The shares of retained profits to be used for reinvestment in production development, for workers' collective welfare, and for bonuses were stipulated in advance.

The enterprise was to use 3.12 percent of base profits for productive investment, 1.92 percent for workers' collective welfare, and 1.96 percent for bonuses (a 45-27-28 division of the 7 percent of base profits retained by the enterprise). Sixty percent of above-quota retained profits were to be used for productive investment, 20 percent for collective welfare, and 20 percent for bonuses. Anshan's accounts for 1981 and 1982 indicate that these guidelines seem to have been roughly, if not exactly, followed. The share of retained profits Anshan used for productive investment was considerably higher in 1981–82 than it had been in 1980; this increase ran counter to trends in many other state enterprises.

Anshan's greater access to other internally generated funds was quantitatively much more important than was profit retention. The company was permitted to keep all of its depreciation funds starting in 1981. In that year, the depreciation rate was raised to 4 percent (from 2.9 percent) and the major repair fund to 3 percent (from 2 percent). These changes caused a jump of about Y130 million in the investment funds available to Anshan in 1981 and a further rise of Y63 million in 1982, for a total increase of nearly Y200 million in the two-year period.[8] Total retained profits used for productive investment in 1982 were only Y129 million, an increase of Y104 million over the amount for 1980.

The new package of incentives introduced in 1980–81 seems to have given Anshan a more stable financial relationship with the government and greater capacity for self-financed development. During 1981–85 Anshan's retained profits accounted for 13.5 percent of total profits; this share was substantially more than it had been in 1979 and 1980. The 1981–85 period saw the real start of Anshan's most critical task: wholesale replacement and modernization of production facilities.

In 1985 Anshan was brought under the new profit tax system instituted for all state industrial enterprises. It had to pay a profit tax of 55 percent, and, like other large, high-profit plants, it was required to pay adjustment tax, at an initial rate of 19 percent; this rate was gradually lowered to 14 percent by 1987. Unlike many other state industrial enterprises, in which various kinds of contractual responsibility systems superseded the profit tax system in 1986–87, Anshan continued to operate under the latter.

Overall, the history of profit retention at Anshan was in line with trends in Chinese state industry as a whole. Profit retention rates were low, because of Anshan's size and its large absolute volume of profits (see table 8.5). Anshan did benefit, however, from concessions on depreciation funds and on the major repair fund; these concessions were instituted earlier at Anshan than they were elsewhere. There were adjustments in profit retention rates to offset the financial effect of changes in "objective circumstances," most notably changes in price adjustments (see the ensuing discussion). The sharp jumps in retained profits seen in many other firms, however, did not occur at Anshan.

Even with the gradual lowering of the adjustment tax, as of 1987 Anshan still faced a 69 percent average profit tax rate; the marginal tax rate also must have been high. Moreover, the "energy and transport development fund levy" took an additional 18 percent of most of the company's retained funds. High taxation obviously weakened Anshan's profit motive and encouraged its hiding of profits and various tax avoidance measures. Anshan's size and its well-established accounting system, however, prevented these leakages from becoming as serious as they were in smaller firms.

Despite limited formal profit incentives, Anshan clearly became more profit oriented. Enterprise managers admitted this and noted that they minimized or even stopped production of low-profit varieties of steel products and increased output of high-profit varieties. The shift in Anshan's output mix toward rolled steel and away from less profitable intermediate products also reflected an increasing profit orientation. The bulk of Anshan's directly marketed output was sold for cash rather than exchanged for other goods (see "Mandatory Planning and Marketing Controls," in this chapter), suggesting that the company was concerned about maximizing earnings and improving financial performance. One factor behind Anshan's increased profit orientation was pressure from the Liaoning provincial government, which was said to have demanded a 10 percent increase in Anshan's profit remittances and tax payments in 1987. Another factor was the interest of workers in high pay and in benefits such as housing.

Compensation for Price Changes

The ad hoc character of profit retention at Anshan shows most vividly in the issue of compensation. The enterprise complained that it was not fully compensated through adjustments in the base profit delivery quota for in-

Table 8.5. Profit Retention for Anshan, 1978–84

Year	Gross profits (millions of yuan)	Retained profits (A)		Retained profits (B)	
		Amount (millions of yuan)	Rate (percent)	Amount (millions of yuan)	Rate (percent)
1978	1,300.61	8.85	0.7	8.85	0.7
1979	1,336.57	15.39	1.2	38.74	2.9
1980	1,449.65	75.33	5.2	94.14	6.5
1981	1,299.46	95.85	7.4	110.53	8.5
1982	1,258.51	203.91	16.2	220.94	17.6
1984	1,314.07	238.46	18.1	238.46	18.1

Note: Two somewhat different data series for retained profits during the period 1979–82 were provided by Anshan. It is not clear exactly why they differ, but the most likely explanation is that certain expenditures from profits were subtracted before calculating retained profits in series A but not in series B.

Source: Ministry of Metallurgy 1985, p. 751; information provided by the company.

creases in prices of raw materials and for changes in tax rates. In 1982 it was calculated that Anshan's total profits declined by Y115 million because of these factors, but the government agreed to reduce Anshan's base target for profit remittance by only Y92 million and left the remaining Y22 million to be absorbed by the enterprise itself. In 1983 it was estimated that the same factors would cause profits to decline by Y253 million, but the Liaoning Provincial Finance Bureau agreed to reduce the profit remittance quota by only Y139 million and left Y114 million (45 percent of the total) to be absorbed by Anshan.

Although there were provisions in the profit retention schemes and in the national profit tax system for adjustments to offset the financial effect of significant changes in administratively set prices, tax rates, and so forth, this compensation appears not to have worked well at Anshan. Tighter fiscal constraints and strong local government interest in Anshan's profit remittances must have exacerbated the problem of inadequate compensation after the early 1980s. Whether a system of full compensation should be used in the first place is another issue. Although changes in administratively set prices and in tax rates are in principle clearly distinct from other changes in the economic environment (changes whose effects should be borne by the enterprise), in practice it may be difficult to separate the two kinds of changes or even to measure them precisely.

The Experimental Stock System

A much-heralded reform at Anshan was the institution of a stock system and of various improved management practices at Anshan's new steel-rolling plant. The equipment for this plant was a secondhand production line imported from the United States that went into operation in April 1987. Two-thirds of the capital for this factory was provided by Anshan headquarters, and the remaining one-third consisted of stock shares sold to Anshan's employees at large (not only to employees of the new production line). Each Anshan worker was permitted to purchase a maximum of three shares at Y50 each. No shares were sold outside the Anshan community. Shares carried an interest payment of 10 percent and a dividend payment whose amount varied but whose maximum level was an additional 10 percent. Stocks could be inherited but were not otherwise transferable. They carried with them neither voting rights nor the other accoutrements of shares as they are commonly understood in industrial market economies.

The stock experiment was deemed a success, and Anshan considered using it more widely. The size of Anshan's labor force and of its wage bill meant that large sums of money conceivably could be raised in this way. Moreover, because Anshan's ability to obtain funds from the banking system was limited and uncertain, an innovation that resulted in the company's employees removing some of their bank deposits for investment in Anshan shares would benefit the company.[9] Anshan even considered setting up an in-house "stock market," in which only Anshan employees would be eligible to participate.

The new production line performed well in its initial year of operation, but this may have been more a result of the quality of the imported equipment and of improved management practices than of the stock scheme. For example, according to Chinese norms, the total work force of the production line should have been about 800, but, with careful economies and with the use of existing ancillary units (not counted as part of this new facility's work force), actual labor required was only 300 workers.

The governance structure of the new production line included a board of directors, whose chairman was the general manager of Anshan. The board had not been fully constituted, however, and had not yet met as of mid-1987. It is not clear whether the new factory's degree of management autonomy differed significantly from that of other subordinate units of Anshan. Overall, Anshan's stock experiment was an entity rather unlike a joint-stock company in an industrial market economy.

Mandatory Planning and Marketing Controls

Mandatory production planning and associated administrative allocation of inputs and outputs form the heart of a traditional centrally planned economic system. Anshan remained in most respects tightly bound by mandatory planning, although it used various means to circumvent the system and to ameliorate the system's adverse effects. Mandatory planning and the chronic sellers' market for steel products also had a significant negative effect on Anshan's direct marketing activities.

The Continued Dominance of Mandatory Planning

Contrary to trends in most Chinese state industrial enterprises, the share of mandatory planning in Anshan's total output of important products remained high (table 8.6). As late as 1987 mandatory planning still accounted for 84 percent of total rolled steel output, whereas at the national level, the share of the central plan in total supply of rolled steel declined from 74.3 percent in 1980 to 47.1 percent in 1987 (Zhong 1987, p. 25). The share of Anshan's direct marketing rose sharply during the "readjustment" years of 1980 and 1981, when demand for steel through plan channels fell off, but the share of direct marketing fell in 1982–83 and fluctuated in 1984–85. There was only the beginning of a trend toward a lower share of mandatory planning in 1986–87.[10]

Another indicator of the importance of mandatory planning is the number of Anshan's products that were subject to compulsory delivery targets (table 8.7). Products were added to Anshan's mandatory production and compulsory delivery plans each year, beginning in 1983. Moreover, the data in the table

Table 8.6. *Plan and Market Shares in Anshan's Output of Rolled Steel, 1979–87*
(percentage of total output)

Year	Share of mandatory planning	Share of direct marketing
1979	94	6
1980	89	11
1981	86	14
1982	89	11
1983	91	9
1984	87	13
1985	89	11
1986	86	14
1987[a]	84	16

a. Data are estimates.
Source: Information provided by the company.

understate the degree of specificity and detail of mandatory planning, because they do not take into account Anshan's compulsory "sales-resources" plan, which served as the basis for contracts signed with users for within-plan delivery of products and included 300 to 400 varieties of rolled steel. (The data in table 8.7 most probably include only the fourteen main categories of steel products.) Allocations of inputs to users under the state plan were based on these 300 to 400 varieties, but the actual contracts were even more detailed, based as they were on discussions between Anshan and plan-designated users. Anshan produced as many as 60,000 different technical varieties and specifications of rolled steel.

Anshan complained about delayed announcement of plan targets, insufficient deliveries of plan-allocated inputs needed to meet output plan targets, and problems with disaggregation of targets in accordance with Anshan's own capabilities and with users' needs. These are typical problems faced by enterprises in any system characterized by administrative determination of flows of goods. Anshan's problems stood out, however, because of the company's size and importance and because of the central government's continued heavy reliance on Anshan to provide steel to the state plan.

Specific contracts for supply to users through the state plan were agreed on and signed at various "ordering conferences" organized by national, provincial, and local planning authorities, by supply departments, and by metallurgical bureaus. Ordering conferences had served as the primary means of disaggregating plan targets to enterprises and to specific product varieties since the 1960s. They represent a unique Chinese adaptation to the problems of plan disaggregation (see Reynolds 1975 and Byrd 1981). There were, however, numerous problems associated with these conferences that led to inconsistencies and problems for Anshan. In the 1960s there were only two large national ordering conferences each year, organized by the State Material Supply Bureau. About 1974, provinces began to run their own twice-yearly ordering conferences to handle the allocation of goods under their control. In addition, a national "fixed-point fixed-amount" ordering conference came to be held every three to five years. Disproportionate amounts of certain steel varieties tended to be contracted for at the provincial ordering conferences, which were typically held twenty days to one month before the national ones; as a result, insufficient amounts of those varieties were left for provision to plan-designated users at the national ordering conference. Handling individual contracts (more than 100,000 of them a year, with 6,000 different users) was a headache for Anshan.

The high share of mandatory planning and the detailed control over product mix exercised through mandatory planning were a great hindrance to the exercise of independent, profit-oriented decisionmaking by enterprise management. Anshan's attempt to produce a new, better variety of steel rails provides a good example. Anshan had traditionally produced manganese alloy rails for the Ministry of Railways. Subsequently it developed a new tin alloy rail, which won a national gold medal in 1983. The new rail had superior anticorrosive welding properties and greater strength, and its lifetime was double that of the older rail. Its production cost, however, was considerably higher. Initially the Ministry of Railways refused to pay a higher price for the new rail, arguing that it had not been informed when Anshan began test-producing it. Although the ministry recognized that the new rail was more economical, it was short of funds at the time. The issue developed into a significant controversy, and the Ministry of Metallurgy also became involved. In early 1983 the Ministry of Railways agreed to pay Y50 a ton more for the new tin rails. Anshan continued to produce both kinds of rails. Output of the tin alloy rail was constrained by a shortage of tin in 1984.

Even with its significant share of direct marketing at the margin (more than 15 percent in 1987, including 2 percent of within-plan output), Anshan was probably not able to determine freely its total output of many products. This inability calls into question the view that mandatory planning should—if at least a small part of the output of every product of an enterprise is directly marketed—have no effect on total output of each product, because

Table 8.7. Products in Anshan's Mandatory Plan, 1981–86

Year	Product varieties
1981	62
1982	52
1983	66
1984	71
1985	75
1986	83

Source: Information provided by the company.

the amount of above-plan output produced is determined solely by market prices (see Byrd 1987a, p. 298; 1989, pp. 196–97).[11] Although this model may be a reasonably accurate depiction of reality if the share of mandatory planning is not too high and if targets are not too detailed as regards product mix, it seems not to hold in a situation such as that of Anshan. When the share of mandatory planning is very high (80 to 90 percent) and output targets are highly disaggregated, an enterprise may be severely constrained in its short-run decisions concerning above-plan production. Hence the benefits associated with well-functioning product markets are largely lost.

Reasons for the Continued High Share of Mandatory Planning

The "stickiness" of Anshan's high share of mandatory planning and the company's inability to lower it significantly even after 1984 are striking, especially because the share of the state plan in total national output of rolled steel declined substantially, from 74 percent in 1980 to 57 percent in 1985, 53 percent in 1986, and 47 percent in 1987 (Ling 1986, p. 2; State Statistical Bureau 1988, p. VI).

The chronic sellers' market for rolled steel, only briefly interrupted in the early 1980s, undoubtedly was a significant factor in Anshan's continuing high share of mandatory planning. In Chinese industry the share of direct marketing by firms has generally varied systematically with market conditions (Byrd 1987c). A buyers' market has been associated with higher shares of direct marketing, a sellers' market with only limited direct marketing. The situation was actually more complicated than this, however, as is shown by the declining share of mandatory planning for rolled steel at the national level.

Anshan was an important supplier of steel for large, centrally run enterprises and for "key" state investment projects. According to crude estimates, Anshan accounted for 21 percent of total rolled steel allocated through the state plan in 1985.[12] The declining share of the central plan in rolled steel allocation at the national level reflects administrative decentralization to provinces and municipalities, the rising share of local steel-rolling mills in total output, and, to some extent, attempts to reduce the share of mandatory planning as part of economic reforms. As the central government saw its control over distribution of this crucial good weakening, it maintained a tight grasp on the allocation of the products of Anshan and of those of other large complexes in order to assure supplies to meet its own needs. Centrally allocated steel carrying an artificially low price also served as a potent reward or as a bargaining chip for the central government in its dealings with provinces and ministries; thus the center had an added incentive to maintain tight control over Anshan's output.

With rolled steel available through numerous channels, ranging from the central plan to open markets in many cities, price differentials became more important than availability per se. The low price carried by rolled steel allocated through the central plan made it very attractive to users and hence valuable to the central government agencies responsible for its distribution. The market price of some varieties of rolled steel was at times more than double the state plan price; this price differential generated large "rents" carried by plan-allocated goods (see Byrd 1987b, chap. 5). Naturally Anshan tried to capture some of these rents, but central government planning and material supply authorities as well as users with state plan allocations held onto them, and the state mandatory plan for Anshan rose substantially in absolute terms.

The role of the subsectoral responsibility system in facilitating continuing tight control over Anshan's production by central planning authorities and by the Ministry of Metallurgy should not be underestimated. The ministry and Anshan were locked into multiyear commitments to provide increasing volumes of rolled steel products to the state plan. The system may even have forced a tautening of Anshan's production planning, because the compulsory delivery target appears to have been relatively firm, whereas commensurate supplies of inputs were not always forthcoming via the plan.[13]

Responses to Mandatory Planning

Anshan tried in various ways to avoid some of the worst problems and rigidities of central planning and to gain some effective decisionmaking capability. For example, the chronic shortages of many plan-allocated inputs served as Anshan's excuse for its failure to fulfill certain output plans. The company failed to meet its targets for delivery of pig iron to the state nearly every year. From the enterprise's perspective, this problem was directly related to chronic shortfalls in provision of scrap steel supplies through the plan. In 1983 the state plan quota for scrap steel was 670,000 tons, but only 560,000 tons were delivered to Anshan; in 1984 only 530,000 tons were provided out of a plan quota of 730,000 tons. In 1985 the plan quota was 610,000 tons, of which only 360,000 tons reached Anshan. These shortfalls had a disproportionate effect on Anshan's sales, because most of its pig iron output was used internally in steel making. In the early 1980s Anshan's annual state plan target for sales of pig iron to other entities was in the range of 100,000 tons. In 1985 the initial target of 120,000 tons was reduced to 60,000 tons because of the lower supply of scrap steel; Anshan actually delivered only 40,000 tons of pig iron in 1985. By 1987 scrap steel was largely decontrolled; Anshan had to purchase what it required on the market, but it could sell the resulting output on the market as well. Anshan always met its own needs for pig iron first, and deliveries through the state plan were a residual. This understandable practice on the part of Anshan suggests a broader observation: It is unrealistic to expect a firm to give top priority to meeting a plan target when the product concerned is both an output and an important input in the firm's production process.

Sufficient quantities of the other main raw materials needed for production of steel to meet mandatory plan output targets were generally supplied through the plan. There were severe problems, however, with a few other inputs—electric power, fuel oil, and, sometimes, certain nonferrous metals for alloys. Between 1981 and 1987, the amount of electricity provided to Anshan through the state plan remained constant in absolute terms; this situation forced the enterprise to use electricity more efficiently and, in 1987, to buy about 20 percent of its power needs at higher, negotiated prices. Coal supplies, which were cited as having been a problem in the early 1980s, appeared to improve subsequently. Only in the case of scrap steel were the shortfalls in input allocations so glaring as to justify chronic failure to meet delivery targets.

The input-output norms used in calculating input requirements for production within the plan appear to have been another source of flexibility for the company. Because of the considerable slack in the system, left over from the immediate prereform period, even a process of gradual tightening of norms over time would have allowed the enterprise to keep ahead by improving efficiency and cutting waste. Bargaining over input-output norms, to the extent that it occurred, appears not to have had serious adverse effects on the enterprise. More problematic were shortfalls in actual deliveries of inputs in relation to amounts allocated; these shortfalls were often the result of bottlenecks in the railway system.

A method of circumventing the financial constraints imposed by planning was adjusting product mix toward high-profit items and away from low-profit or lossmaking ones; such adjustments could be made within plan categories, or targets that would be financially painful to fulfill could be ignored. Shifts in product mix were facilitated by somewhat greater aggregation in production planning and by pressures to increase profits. By the late 1980s, Anshan had stopped or had cut back production of many unprofitable goods and varieties.

Evolution of Direct Marketing, 1979–87

Still another source of flexibility for Anshan was exchange of outputs for needed inputs, as part of direct marketing (self-sales). In the chronic sellers' market, direct marketing was for Anshan an important means of gaining financial or other benefits. Exchanging products for inputs and shifting high-profit items to self-sales are two examples of Anshan's use of direct marketing. In sharp contrast, direct marketing in a buyers' market is a burden that an enterprise is initially reluctant to take on but one that state planning and distribution systems are only too willing to shed (see Byrd 1987c).

The evolution of Anshan's direct marketing authority was related to changing market conditions for steel and, because of steel's pervasive role as an intermediate product and investment good, to the macroeconomic situation. Before July 1979 all of Anshan's products were subject to state monopoly procurement. Subsequently, because national readjustment policies cut investment sharply in 1979–81, a number of rolled steel products became difficult to sell. As in the cases of other industrial goods, the government's response to the marketing problem was to decontrol (in fact, refuse to procure) the products in excess supply and let producers fend for themselves. Thus the varieties of rolled steel that remained in short supply continued to be allocated through mandatory planning, whereas those that were in excess supply had to be marketed directly by producers. Anshan's share of rolled steel output that was directly marketed rose sharply, although not as sharply as the corresponding share of national rolled steel output, and Anshan's share was somewhat below the average share for China's key iron and steel plants (see table 8.8). In 1981 especially, Anshan made aggressive and successful attempts to market its products nationwide, through the use of sales agents. A "retail shop" catering mainly to small rural factories and workshops was set up.

After 1981, however, as national investment demand began to increase rapidly again, the share of Anshan's direct marketing declined. The planning system retook control over the portion of Anshan's output that for a brief period had been released from compulsory procurement because of excess supply. In 1983, guidelines on the amount of rolled steel Anshan and other large iron and steel complexes could market directly were promulgated: self-sales were limited to 2 percent of within-plan output plus all above-plan output.[14] The 2 percent allowance applied to each major variety of rolled

Table 8.8. Share of Direct Marketing in Total Output of Rolled Steel for Chinese Firms, 1979–87
(percent)

Year	All firms	Key plants[a]	Anshan
1979	3.6	—	6
1980	10.6	15.7	11
1981	19.9	22.2	14
1982	14.4	18.4	11
1983	3.5	5.9	9
1984	—	9.6	13
1985	—	—	11
1986	—	—	14
1987	—	—	16[b]

— Not available.
a. Data are for certain large, mostly integrated iron and steel complexes.
b. Datum is an estimate.
Source: Byrd 1987a, table 3.3, p. 295. Table 8.6.

steel, but material supply bureaus sometimes requisitioned more of varieties that were in especially short supply.

Initially, prices of directly marketed steel were constrained to remain at their official levels, but progressive relaxation occurred as part of industrial price liberalization. In April 1984 most state enterprises were authorized to float prices of above-plan output upward by as much as 20 percent, but implementation of this reform may have been late and somewhat uneven in the iron and steel industry. In early 1985 prices of above-plan output of most industrial producer goods were freed to find their own levels in the market.

During the early to mid-1980s, a large part of Anshan's self-sales was siphoned away, outside the formal plan, by government supervisory agencies. Of 500,000 tons of rolled steel marketed by the enterprise itself in 1985, 80,000 tons was reported to have gone to the Ministry of Metallurgy, 120,000 tons to Liaoning Province, and 100,000 tons to Anshan Municipality. All of these transactions occurred at low official ex-factory prices. Only 200,000 tons of rolled steel were left under Anshan's own control, and they were mostly exchanged for needed inputs.

Subsequently, most of Anshan's directly marketed steel output came to be sold for negotiated prices, with no explicit exchange for other goods involved. That the prices at which transactions occurred were often somewhat lower than the market price suggests that the transactions might have involved some informal side-deals or other relationships not directly reflected in prices. Moreover, more than one-third of self-sold output was still directly exchanged for various needed inputs, including coal, iron ore, railway transport, petroleum, timber, construction materials, machinery, investment funds (through compensation trade), and foreign exchange. Undoubtedly, such exchanges provided important, even essential, benefits to Anshan. Because of the pressure to increase profits, however, the enterprise tried to avoid using too much of its directly marketed output for exchanges at low prices.

Despite the tightening of market conditions in 1982–83, Anshan's share of direct marketing remained substantial (table 8.8). It fell much less than did the corresponding shares at the national level and those for other important iron and steel plants. Perhaps to some extent reflecting reform initiatives, Anshan's share of self-sales rose in 1986 and 1987. Because of the strong sellers' market, however, aggressive marketing by Anshan virtually ceased. The retail shop for steel goods was closed, and sales agents no longer went out to seek new markets.

Implications of Direct Marketing

The role of self-sales and their effect on enterprise behavior and performance were quite different at Anshan than they were at firms facing a buyers' market for their output. Direct marketing was not a lasting stimulant for improved competitiveness, as it was in the case of the Second Motor Vehicle Factory (see chapter 9 in this volume). It did not push ahead reforms at Anshan or provide strong pressure to improve efficiency and enhance competitiveness. Direct marketing does, however, appear to have increased the enterprise's flexibility in responding to the planning system and in improving financial performance.

Although direct marketing in principle could be completely separated from within-plan activities, with only market-purchased inputs used for directly marketed output and only plan-allocated inputs for within-plan production, such was not the case in reality. In some instances Anshan had to purchase inputs on the market in order to meet its plan output targets, and in others it used surplus inputs allocated through the plan in above-plan production. At a more fundamental level, Anshan's capital facilities formed a unified whole that was established largely with plan-based or government-allocated sources of finance. Another input for which it was extremely difficult to distinguish within-plan and outside-of-plan uses was electric power. Nor were distinctions made between within-plan and outside-of-plan uses of labor. There were some workers at Anshan, as there were elsewhere, who were outside the state employment quotas, but there was no segregation of the production of these workers from that of regular employees.

Because of Anshan's inability to clearly separate within-plan and above-plan inputs, direct marketing by the company in the face of a chronic sellers' market appears to have involved a kind of rent seeking.[15] Anshan strove to minimize its state plan output targets and its deliveries of output within the state plan, and at the same time to maximize the low-price inputs it received through the plan. Above-plan output was used to maximize enterprise benefits, through direct cash sales or through exchange arrangements. Anshan had considerable flexibility in allocating the benefits from above-plan output, because it could assign this output a price ranging anywhere from just above the state plan price to the genuine market price. Anshan management claimed that most above-plan output was sold at prices greater than the state price but rather less than the "high" market price. The company thus enjoyed great scope for trading part or all of the embodied rent (the difference between selling price and market price) in its products for other goods or services that usually carried similar price concessions. Because of Anshan's market power as a supplier (particularly as a supplier that could offer below-market prices), the company could extract concessions from customers and did not need to concern itself to a great degree with product quality, new product development, marketing, customer service, and so forth.

One example of Anshan's rent seeking was a deal the company made with a steel-rolling mill in Shenyang, according to the terms of which Anshan supplied steel at a price somewhat higher than the state price but much lower than the market price, and the Shenyang mill turned over half of the profits from its resulting output of rolled steel to Anshan. Although the mill complained about exploitation on the part of Anshan, the transaction merely involved monetary appropriation of rents embodied in Anshan's steel output. Anshan's exchange of its above-plan steel output for natural gas for its employees' cooking can also be understood as rent seeking (in that case as rent seeking on behalf of employees).

Although rent seeking can, under certain circumstances, improve the efficiency of resource allocation in the economy (Bhagwati 1982), in China it appears to have distracted managerial attention and effort from improving efficiency and financial performance through market-oriented behavior and instead encouraged a focus on capturing administratively determined rents in the system. Rents were embodied in plan-allocated goods that become objects of rent seeking, but firms also could embody some rents in above-plan output by charging prices less than the market price. Such rent seeking, although it was rational from the enterprise's viewpoint, resulted in most of the dynamic benefits normally associated with market-based allocation of resources not being realized.

Vertical Integration versus Administrative Fragmentation

Like any large iron and steel complex, Anshan was characterized by extensive vertical integration, including mining, ore preparation, coke production, iron smelting, steel production, steel rolling, and finishing. In addition, many ancillary activities, such as power generation, oxygen manufacture, and petroleum refining, were handled by Anshan itself. Subordinate collective units engaged in many other lines of production. Anshan was forced at various times, however, to give up certain activities and to turn the assets for those activities over to other firms or to government agencies.

The Chinese economic system has faced a more general choice between integrating activities within large enterprises and fragmenting them across distinct firms. This choice is quite different from the "markets versus hierarchies" choice in market economies (see Williamson 1975). In China, the alternative to integration is not the market but rather planning and administrative allocation of flows of goods between separate entities. Second, the choice is not a natural one, although there may be empirical regularities in decisionmaking processes and outcomes. It is subject to administrative fiat, and outcomes are influenced by bureaucratic conflicts and by administrative power, including sometimes the power of large firms. For these reasons, inefficient outcomes are only to be expected.

Administrative Demarcation of Enterprise Boundaries

In contrast to the situation in market economies, the boundaries of state enterprises in China—the set of activities in which they can engage and the assets they can hold—were administratively determined by government agencies. Administrative controls hindered or prevented large enterprises such as Anshan from developing new products and activities. By the same token, some firms were forced to stay in certain lines of business or to continue to produce certain goods, more or less involuntarily.

Institutional and territorial fragmentation in the Chinese system of industrial administration meant that the situation for Anshan was complicated. The Ministry of Metallurgy and other agencies disagreed among themselves on the appropriate scope of activities of Anshan, which gave the enterprise a certain leeway. Moreover, although Anshan itself was prevented from involvement in certain activities, its subordinate collective units could sometimes engage in them. The boundaries of Anshan shifted over time, determined as they were by unstable compromises among different bureaucratic forces. As the relative strengths of various government supervisory agencies and the enterprise itself changed, adjustments and new compromises emerged and added an element of instability to Anshan's situation.

Determining the boundaries of Anshan was often contentious. Sometimes the company made investments and started new activities, only to have the assets it had created stripped away from it later. In other cases assets and activities remained under Anshan's control, but large parts of the output generated were subjected to state plan allocation. The degree to which Anshan could circumvent administratively imposed constraints on its boundaries also varied across different activities and over time.

Incentives for Vertical Integration

Anshan had strong incentives to integrate, under its own control, as much as possible of its main production process and many of its ancillary activities. Backward integration for Anshan was a means of avoiding the uncertainties about supply that inevitably arise in a central planning system. Because the company needed to rely on plan allocations rather than on a well-functioning market for inputs, its incentives were overwhelmingly skewed in favor of backward integration. For Anshan, the need to obtain stable sources of supply reinforced other factors that encourage vertical integration in the iron and steel industry anywhere. The strong tendency toward backward integration is evident in the enterprise's "captive" electric power generation facility, in its attempts to integrate petroleum refining, and in its integration of production of certain investment goods, such as cement.

The profit motive also sometimes encouraged integration. The most notable example of this was Anshan's forward integration into steel rolling, which represented an attempt to capture some of the rents embodied in the crude steel the company produced. The structure of state-set prices in the iron and steel industry was such that the profitability of activities tended to increase, the farther an enterprise moved down the chain of production, from iron ore mining to iron smelting to steel production to rolling. Because of this pattern of relative prices and because Anshan's initial production structure involved sale of a large proportion of its steel output to other firms for processing, it would be rational for the enterprise to engage in forward integration into steel rolling to the extent possible.

A final motivation for integration was the creation of jobs for "surplus" workers as well as for the large numbers of children of existing workers who needed to be placed. The development of subordinate collective units was motivated by the need to find jobs for employees' children, although the profit motive may also have played a lesser role. (It is interesting to note that Anshan Municipality voiced concern about the company's tendency to integrate within the enterprise provision of a whole range of services for workers; this tendency made it difficult for the city to find viable activities for its young residents who were not part of the Anshan complex.)

Countertendencies

What constraints prevented Anshan from integrating all closely related activities under its own control? Physical and technical constraints and the high costs of managing a wider range of activities undoubtedly played a role, but these considerations were not sufficient to explain Anshan's failure to integrate certain activities and especially the instances in which activities were taken away from the company.

The most significant external factor militating against integration was the loss of control for the planning system such integration often implied. For example, Anshan's "ownership" of the iron ore mines that produced about 85 percent of the ore it needed reduced the amount of iron ore under the control of the Ministry of Metallurgy and possibly impaired the ministry's ability to reallocate raw materials among users. At the other end of the production chain, Anshan's active measures to increase rolling capacity and to process more crude steel in-house threatened the stable flow of steel from Anshan to rolling mills that were designated for plan allocations. Certain ancillary production activities fell under the purviews of other industrial ministries that may have wanted to maintain tight control over those activities.

Financial motives probably also played a role in preventing integration. Anshan's forward vertical integration to capture profits from steel rolling, for example, reduced the scope for profitable steel rolling by smaller mills that previously relied on crude steel supplies from Anshan allocated through the plan. The planning system might to some extent have resisted Anshan's forward integration for the benefit of such users.

That Anshan itself sometimes resisted integration of certain activities is not surprising, because the aforementioned three objectives served by integration often conflict. In the prereform period, Anshan's desire for stable supplies may have dominated its other goals, but, once the company became more profit oriented, this objective no longer necessarily took priority over other considerations. The tug-of-war over the iron ore mines (which is discussed next) well illustrates what can happen when an enterprise's own objectives concerning integration, namely gaining access to assured supplies on the one hand and maximizing profits on the other, conflict.

Iron Ore Mines

Anshan's iron ore mines, which are under the management of the Anshan Mining Company, comprise China's largest iron ore production base; they include a center for mining research and development. As of the end of 1985, the mining company had more than 96,000 employees (59,000 state workers and 37,000 collective workers); GVIO (in 1980 prices) was Y630 million; and 1985 iron ore output was 23.1 million metric tons (Ministry of Metallurgy 1986b, pp. 237–38). The mines could satisfy about 85 percent of Anshan's demand for iron ore in the mid-1980s, although the quality (iron content) of the ore was relatively low. They also produced a variety of by-products and other raw materials. The history of the mining company well illustrates the conflicting tendencies of integration and fragmentation and consequent problems.

In 1949 a mining department was set up under Anshan headquarters to manage the enterprise's mining activities. This arrangement continued until 1964, when, with the approval of the Ministry of Metallurgy, the Anshan Mining Company was established. The mining company remained, however, under the direct supervision of Anshan headquarters. In 1978 an ambitious national plan to double iron ore output and steel output by 1985 was put forward. Because half of the mining company's production of iron ore was to go to other iron and steel plants in eastern China according to this plan, it was suggested that the mines be separated administratively from the Anshan Iron and Steel Company. This change was consistent with the desire of central authorities to maintain or to expand their control over the allocation of important industrial producer goods. But the separation was also attributed to other reasons: (1) it would allow Anshan to concentrate its attention on technical renovation and on improvement of the core iron and steel processes and (2) mining and steel making required very different management methods, whose working would be facilitated by administrative separation.

Regardless of the precise motivation, the separation did not work well in practice. The 1978 growth targets were later sharply scaled back, so the iron ore mines still produced exclusively for Anshan; hence the first justification for the separation no longer applied. Moreover, the coordination of supply of raw material with iron and steel production was unsatisfactory, and the mining company and the iron and steel company made duplicate investments in employees' public facilities and in ancillary production facilities. In 1982 Anshan requested that the iron ore mines be returned to its control, and in September 1982 this request was granted, although the mining company kept its name. The Ministry of Metallurgy made the decision; although approval from the State Economic Commission also was required, this was considered merely a formality.

There was a long-standing debate within the ministry on the issue of separation versus integration of iron ore mines within important iron and steel complexes, with the majority opinion favoring integration.[16] Because iron ore does not have uses other than iron making, keeping iron ore mines "captive" is consistent with tight central control, as long as the mines' production capacity is less than the demand of the complexes to which they are tied.

Although the resistance of the Ministry of Metallurgy and the planning system to integration of the iron ore mines appears to have been limited, for Anshan itself, financial considerations conflicted with supply-based tendencies toward integration. The iron ore mines faced long-term declining profits because of low government-set transfer prices for iron ore and because of the need to exploit poorer resources as the richer ore deposits were exhausted. The mines' profits fell from about Y190 million in 1980 to Y140 million in 1981 and Y80 million in 1982. (The profit target in 1983 was less than Y100 million.) Government agencies as well as Anshan itself were leery about taking over financial responsibility for an entity with such poor profit-making prospects.[17]

When the iron ore mines were separated from Anshan in 1980, Liaoning Province, nominally the primary supervisory agency for Anshan, refused to take over ownership of them precisely because of declining profits. As a result, the mining company was then supervised directly by the Ministry of Metallurgy. In 1982 the operations of the mining company were reintegrated into Anshan. The province again refused to take responsibility for the finances of the mining company, so its finances remained the responsibility of the ministry. This awkward arrangement could eventually change, if a contract system for distribution of the profits of the mining company were implemented. Until the mid-1980s, however, the conflict between financial considerations and the need for stable sources of supply (and for close coordination of raw materials production with downstream activities) created a bifurcation between operational and financial control.

Magnesium Mines

Magnesium was used in making refractory bricks to line Anshan's steelmaking furnaces. Liaoning Province's extremely rich magnesium reserves accounted for about 90 percent of the national total. Numerous small magnesium mines were scattered throughout the province; before 1980 they operated under local jurisdictions, with little, if any, coordination among them. Anshan itself was in charge of two of the larger mines.

Like the iron ore mines, Anshan's two magnesium mines were separated from the enterprise in 1980 by a decision of the State Economic Commission and the Ministry of Metallurgy. The mines were transferred to the newly created Liaoning Magnesium Company rather than put under the Anshan Mining Company. The operations and the finances of the Magnesium Company were directly under the ministry. The company was amalgamated from the two magnesium mines that had belonged to Anshan and a local mine in Yingkou County.

The establishment of the new company appears to have had several objectives. It was seen as a means of speeding the development of southern Liaoning's rich magnesium resources. The new company, it was hoped, would also improve management and exploitation of magnesium resources. Magnesium had considerable export potential, and the new company was viewed as an appropriate vehicle for rapid expansion of exports—its export earnings in 1985 were $19 million (Ministry of Metallurgy 1986b, p. 253). Other, unstated goals of the centralization may have related to the ministry's desire to control a growing, profitable foreign-exchange-earning activity.

The separation of the magnesium mines from Anshan led to financial pressures and to a supply squeeze on the enterprise. The combination of domestic monopoly, a degree of continuing central control over domestic prices, a foreign exchange retention system for exporters alongside the lack of an open market for foreign exchange, and import controls naturally created problems. For instance, Anshan needed a large number of high-quality magnesium refractory bricks for a new converter in its Number 3 Steel Mill. These bricks had not been provided for in the central plan (magnesium bricks were designated as products subject to allocation by the ministry). Anshan first negotiated with the Liaoning Magnesium Company directly for the extra supplies, but the Magnesium Company made exorbitant demands. In return for its providing the bricks, the company required that Anshan provide it with a fifteen-year interest-free loan of Y3 million, with 2,000 tons of crude oil a year (in perpetuity, apparently), and with the structural steel, timber, and cement needed to construct a new kiln.

Anshan rejected these demands and made some counterproposals to the Ministry of Metallurgy. One suggestion was that the ministry guarantee supplies of magnesium materials to Anshan (presumably these would come from the Liaoning Magnesium Company), and Anshan would then produce the magnesium bricks itself. A second alternative was that Anshan purchase the magnesium bricks directly from the Magnesium Company, paying in foreign exchange at the international price. A final alternative was that Anshan be permitted to import the magnesium bricks it needed; such a course of action would have been ridiculous, given the rich magnesium reserves and the brick-producing facilities in southern Liaoning.

The ministry rejected the third alternative, and in the end Anshan apparently purchased the bricks from the Liaoning Magnesium Company, without any of the onerous conditions the company originally attached, but at an extra-high price. This was certainly the most attractive of the three alternatives, but the long and acrimonious dispute about the bricks was costly and debilitating. It took three years from the time that Anshan first planned the investment project for the new converter (1981–82) and at least two years from the time that the brick problem emerged (late 1982) to reach a final resolution (late 1984 or early 1985).

What is most striking about this conflict is that it arose at all, because Anshan and the Liaoning Magnesium Company were under the same supervisory agency—the Ministry of Metallurgy. Some in Anshan believed that the ministry took the side of the Magnesium Company, and that the episode represented the ministry's attempt to extract extra profits from one of its "rich" enterprises, Anshan. This view is supported by the fact that the major investment project in the Number 3 Steel Mill was approved by the ministry in the spring of 1982 and was part of China's Sixth Five-Year Plan for modernization investment projects. Anshan's demand for magnesium bricks clearly was not unsanctioned, nor was it outside the state investment plan.

As it did in the case of the iron ore mines, the ministry seems to have had authority over transfer of assets, creation of new entities, and related matters, although, interestingly, magnesium is a nonferrous metal, and most nonferrous metals were put under the control of the China National Nonferrous Metals Industry General Corporation in 1983. Moreover, the ministry somehow had the de facto authority to transfer magnesium mining assets from Anshan to the Liaoning Magnesium Company, although Anshan itself was at least nominally under provincial control. The transfer hence provides a vivid illustration of the vague and ambiguous nature of property rights in China's state sector.

The story of the magnesium mines is also a striking example of how administrative fragmentation can lead to supply problems. The strong incentive to export generated by foreign exchange retention led to a bias against providing supplies to the domestic market; the Liaoning Magnesium Company did, however, provide 90 percent of the needs of China's iron and steel mills for magnesium bricks between 1981 and 1985 (Ministry of Metallurgy 1986b, p. 253). Problems were exacerbated by the Magnesium Company's monopoly position and by the difficulty of importing magnesium bricks.

Other Activities

Severe conflicts over the appropriate boundaries of Anshan arose in several other activities. A common pattern involved Anshan's building a production facility for some urgently needed good, only to have it later taken over by the government agency officially designated to supervise that good's production. Sometimes these facilities were later returned to Anshan as part of subsequent administrative shake-ups, but, needless to say, Anshan's incentives to invest in integration were dampened, and irrational flows of goods sometimes resulted.

THE CEMENT PLANT. A medium-size cement plant built in the 1950s on Anshan's site had an annual production capacity of about 200,000 tons. It was originally an independent plant under the Ministry of Building Materials. At one point in its early history it was put under Anshan but then taken back by the ministry. In the early 1970s the plant was decentralized to Anshan Municipality's control. Then, in 1974, it was again put under Anshan, and was not subsequently transferred.

Given Anshan's voracious demand for cement (about 300,000 tons a year), as well as the company's use of some of the by-products of the steel-making process as raw materials for cement production, it was convenient for Anshan to have its own cement plant. This advantage was vitiated, however, because the cement plant's output was largely allocated through the state plan; only a small proportion (50,000 tons a year in the early 1980s) was kept by Anshan.[18] Shipping out the bulk of the plant's output and bringing in cement from other plants to meet Anshan's needs resulted in wasteful higher transport costs, from Anshan's perspective.

The original motivation for putting the cement plant under Anshan in 1974 was to enable Anshan (once the plant was under its jurisdiction) to invest in doubling the plant's production capacity to 400,000 tons a year, in order to meet its own rising demand for cement. For various reasons, however, the expansion project was never implemented. There were a number of other expansion projects that used land near the cement plant's site, so no one at Anshan was enthusiastic about the cement plant's expansion because that it would compete with these other projects for space. Moreover, it was feared that the cement plant might be taken away from Anshan again in the future; this concern discouraged Anshan from putting resources into the plant's expansion.

This case study is of interest because, in many respects, the most inefficient possible outcome occurred. The cement plant was integrated under Anshan operationally, but most of its output was subject to state plan allocation and was shipped out; hence the main advantage of integration was lost. Moreover, uncertainty about the plant's future ownership made Anshan leery about investing in its expansion.

ELECTRIC POWER STATIONS. Anshan had a small electric power plant with a capacity of 40 megawatts for emergency backup in case of power failure. There was also a much larger power station (with two 110-megawatt generating units) on Anshan's site that had belonged to Anshan Municipality. The central government at one point had wanted to transform this larger facility from a coal-burning one to an oil-burning one. Anshan, whose electricity consumption was enormous (more than 6 million kilowatt-hours daily), wanted to take over the power station and to invest in its expansion, in return for which it wanted to obtain the additional supplies of power that would be generated as a result. Its conflict with Anshan Municipality over this matter apparently was resolved only after a visit by then-Premier Zhao Ziyang to Anshan. In the end it was agreed that Anshan would take over the power station and would invest in its expansion. It was not clear, however, whether Anshan would indeed obtain additional power supplies in this way, and, in any case, the enterprise would still face severe power supply problems. Anshan was planning to build another power plant of its own at the time of this study.

THE OIL REFINERY. As Anshan's energy consumption shifted toward oil products, it was decided to construct an oil refinery under the company's control. Anshan provided investment funds and managed the construction of the refinery; it was to have access to the refinery's output and to share in its profits. These ground rules changed, however, when the central government set up the national Petrochemical General Corporation in 1983. The corporation took over the refinery at the beginning of 1984, and Anshan retained only a commercial relationship with it. The refinery still supplied Anshan's heavy oil needs, but some Anshan managers complained that they had to scrounge for diesel oil even as large amounts of it were shipped out from the refinery.

In the case of the refinery, reorganization and centralization of an important industry resulted in fragmentation. Although Anshan's target for profit remittance was adjusted downward after the oil refinery was taken over by the national corporation, the transfer might have hurt Anshan's financial prospects.[19] It undoubtedly exacerbated the company's supply problems. The initial decision to construct the refinery under Anshan's jurisdiction was a sign of the strength of tendencies toward backward integration.

THE NEW CONSTRUCTION COMPANY. Modernization at Anshan generated great demand for construction work. Anshan kept the Number 3 Metallurgical Construction Company, which was subordinate to the Ministry of Metallurgy, fully occupied. In order to meet its additional demand, Anshan was given approval by the ministry and by the People's Liberation Army to take over an existing army construction unit, which was converted into Anshan's own construction company in May 1983. This integration also served as a convenient means of creating jobs for workers' children, because it was agreed that Anshan could add 3,000 new employees to this unit, thus doubling its strength.

Because of Anshan's need for large-scale renovation and modernization, there appears to have been no conflict between the new in-house construction firm and the Number 3 Metallurgical Construction Company. Most likely the Construction Company engaged in specialized tasks related to building iron and steel production facilities, and the in-house firm did much simpler construction work on ancillary facilities, housing, public buildings, and so forth. Nevertheless, if Anshan's demand for construction work should slacken, conflicts over allocation of jobs may emerge, in which case Anshan probably would favor its in-house unit and the ministry would try to protect the Construction Company.

COLLECTIVE FACTORIES FOR WORKERS' CHILDREN. A huge group of collective firms and workshops, with a labor force of about 160,000, was sometimes used by Anshan as a means for obtaining needed inputs, sometimes as a means of forward integration into activities such as steel rolling, and sometimes as a means of spreading into ancillary activities.[20] (There was a small collective cement plant, for example.) A large number of children's collectives were organized to provide various services to Anshan employees (shops, restaurants, and so forth). The most important objective of the collective units, however, was to create jobs for workers' children; this motive usually superseded the profit motive (although transfer pricing might sometimes have been used to manipulate accounting profits). The collectives were not really autonomous; they depended on the parent enterprise for inputs, financing, and technical assistance.

Another possibly important objective of establishing the collectives was to provide additional jobs for middle managers. The top management of subordinate collective firms consisted almost entirely of Anshan's own managerial personnel. This arrangement allowed Anshan to cut down the size of its managerial staff in the main enterprise without terminating or demoting anyone, to expand its total number of managers beyond what otherwise would have been possible, or both. Managers and other Anshan personnel who were transferred to the collectives retained their status, pay, and perquisites as state employees.

The proliferation of Anshan's subordinate collectives led to severe conflicts with Anshan Municipality. Municipal officials complained that goods and services that had previously been provided by municipal firms were increasingly handled by Anshan's own collectives, depriving the municipal firms of their livelihood. This conflict was most striking in the sphere of services. Anshan Municipality could do little about the situation; central ministries, by comparison, could protect their interests much better in similar situations that involved important products. Anshan's freedom to adjust its own boundaries was probably greatest in the activities of its subordinate collective enterprises.

Fundamental Problems

Common themes in these stories point toward the fundamental problems underlying conflicts over delineation of enterprise boundaries. The immediate cause of Anshan's problems was, of course, administrative determination of enterprise activities by government agencies, but why was the government so concerned about this matter? Behind the administrative determination of enterprise boundaries lies the system of administrative allocation of flows of goods in the economy. This system precludes the market alternative (available in the markets-versus-hierarchies framework) and leads to issues of control over which activities occur inside and which outside the enterprise. Hence, as long as there is a primary or dominant role for mandatory planning in the economic system, conflicts and problems involving administrative delineation of firms' boundaries will be common.

The aforementioned episodes also highlight other problematic aspects of the Chinese economy. Property rights were vague and unstable, although not entirely nonexistent in a de facto sense. A great deal of uncertainty for enterprises resulted. Assets that enterprises considered their own could be taken away by government agencies. Adjustments were made in profit remittance targets when such transfers occurred, but these were probably not sufficient to compensate firms for their loss of control over physical commodities. The weakness of property rights exacerbated problems because enterprise choices and bureaucratic decisions were always subject to revision or cancellation. Anshan was unwilling to invest in expansion of certain facilities for fear that they might be taken away.

Ambiguous property rights and consequent uncertainty notwithstanding, there appears to have been a general pattern in which the entity that had provided the investment funds for a facility had a presumptive right to control the allocation of the facility's output. This pattern was probably less pronounced in Anshan's activities than it was in those of other Chinese industrial enterprises, particularly enterprises not under central control. Nevertheless, the pattern was evident in some cases and it added further complexity to an already uncertain situation.

The effect of the profit motive could be problematic in this context, as could that of foreign exchange retention and similar export incentives. The removal of the oil refinery from Anshan's control may be an example of the intrusion of the profit motive.[21] The Liaoning Magnesium Company episode is a convincing illustration of the intrusion of export incentives. The profit motive can also lead to a situation in which no entity wants to control an unprofitable activity. More generally, the profit motive, although it is desirable, even essential in a market economy, may be a source of problems in a bureaucratic system.[22]

The close relationship between administrative controls and monopolistic behavior is also evident in this context. Controls, by their very nature, open the door for monopolies to develop; sometimes they even create monopolies where none would otherwise have existed. The combination of administrative controls and the profit motive can easily lead to monopolistic behavior, although this behavior may be tempered somewhat by the administrative controls (for instance, by price controls) themselves.

Finally, like the market-versus-hierarchy choice, the integration-versus-fragmentation choice is not entirely clear-cut, and more than two outcomes are possible. Ownership can be separated from control over the allocation of products, as it was in the case of the cement plant. Administratively separate entities can serve as captive suppliers, as did the iron ore mines before their reintegration in 1982. Administrative jurisdiction can be separated from financial responsibility, as it was in the case of the iron ore mines after 1982. These choices make for a complex, unstable system, in which outcomes tend to be inefficient.

Internal Organization and Management

Given Anshan's size and complexity, internal organization and management was an immense task. Anshan was more like a minisociety than a business firm in many ways. It had a population exceeding half a million.[23] It produced a wide range of products and total GVIO of rather more than Y5 billion. It generated massive flows of funds and goods and dominated the local economy. Anshan owned two-thirds of the housing in Anshan Municipality, the rents of which covered only 40 to 50 percent of routine maintenance costs. The complexity of Anshan's internal management is illustrated by its serious problem of distorted internal transfer prices and the comprehensive internal "price reform" it undertook in 1985.

Anshan had an organizational structure that was at once functional and multidivisional. A total of 106 second-level factories and mines reported to Anshan Headquarters in the mid-1980s. Many of these entities, such as the mining and construction companies, were themselves large organizations with numerous subordinate sections and workshops. Anshan Headquarters had in addition more than forty departments responsible for functions such as planning, finances, material supplies, labor, and so forth. There was evolution toward a more multidivisional structure at Anshan. Some functional units and responsibilities were "decentralized" from headquarters to subordinate factories. Perhaps most important, custody and control over some of Anshan's retained profits, depreciation funds, and major repair funds were decentralized to lower-level units in 1987.

It can be questioned whether a multidivisional structure was really the most appropriate one for a highly integrated complex such as Anshan. A conglomerate structure did not suit the core iron and steel production process, although it might have been appropriate for some of Anshan's ancillary activities and for most of the services provided by the company's subordinate collectives. Nevertheless, the internal decentralization and widespread internal "contracting" that occurred at Anshan (as is discussed later) were very much in line with nationwide trends in enterprise reform in 1986–87. Decentralization of authority over operations virtually requires a multidivisional structure.

The Leadership System

At Anshan Headquarters the leadership system in force in 1987 was the director responsibility system under the leadership of the party committee. Nominally this was exactly the same system that prevailed in Chinese state industry in the immediate prereform period. Within this unchanged framework, however, the position of the company general manager became stronger. This strengthening started as early as 1980, when Anshan began to implement a division of labor between party and management. The party committee still deliberated on important questions, however, and, unlike most other state enterprises, Anshan established no Enterprise Management Committee composed of the director, deputy directors, and technical managers. The party committee in 1987 consisted of the following people: (1) the party secretary and his two deputies, (2) the general manager and his two deputies, (3) the Organization Department head, (4) the Administrative Office head, (5) the union chairman, (6) the chief of the party disciplinary unit, and (7) the chief engineer. Whereas previously the party committee had met once a week, it now met biweekly; this change perhaps signified some decline in its role in day-to-day decisionmaking.

The leadership systems of Anshan's subordinate units underwent more significant changes. In the early 1980s factories had a leadership system roughly similar to that of headquarters. For important production and business decisions, the process worked thus: first, several options assembled by the factory director were discussed at the director's administrative meeting (at which were present the director, deputy directors, the chief engineer, and others). This meeting chose one of the options, and then the factory party committee deliberated and made a final decision. In 1984 Anshan began experiments with the factory-director responsibility system in four of its subordinate factories.[24] By the end of 1985 this system had been implemented in ninety-four subunits of Anshan, more than 60 percent of the total number of subunits. Anshan planned in 1987 to implement the factory-director responsibility system in all of its subordinate factories and other units. Thus the leadership system of subunits became similar to the norm for state enterprises, although reforms at headquarters lagged.

The structure of appointments at Anshan was all-important. Three top headquarters staff were appointed by the Central Committee of the Chinese Communist Party.[25] The Organization Department of the central committee made other appointments at this level. Appointments of directors of factories under Anshan Headquarters were discussed by the headquarters party committee and approved by the general manager; deputy directors were suggested by the general manager, discussed at the Manager's Office meeting, and then approved by the general manager. Top party officials of the factories were approved by the headquarters party committee. Thus appointment authority was complex and involved both general manager and party committee, but there appears to have been no role for outside organizations in selection of managers of subordinate units.

In the early 1980s Anshan made some moves toward worker participation in management, through its establishment of Employees' Representative Assemblies at several levels. In 1980–83 Anshan's assembly was convened four times, and subordinate units altogether held 287 assemblies. Union chairmen served as secretaries-general of their units' assemblies, and it was claimed that the functioning of unions was also strengthened. All of this organizational development, however, meant little in practice. There were also experiments with so-called democratic appraisal and election of managers in the early 1980s. By 1983, sixteen units had engaged in the appraisal experiment and nine in the election experiment. The elections, however, mostly affected work team leaders and shop stewards; only in two cases was there democratic election of a factory director. One of the problems encountered in this experiment was how to proceed should the manager in place lose the election.

Internal Decentralization

Anshan went through several episodes of internal centralization and decentralization after 1949, as is noted in "Issues and History," in this chapter. In the early 1950s management was decentralized and ad hoc. Subunits practiced independent accounting and carried out transactions through bank settlement. In 1953 Anshan's management system was centralized along Soviet lines. Subunits lost independent accounting status, bank accounts, and the ability to engage directly in transactions with outside units. Appointment authority and various functions, such as quality control, technical management, and equipment management, were centralized. During the Great Leap Forward movement Anshan decentralized certain management functions and replaced its one-man leadership system with the system of factory-director responsibility under the leadership of the enterprise party committee. By early 1959, however, there was a call for restoring rules and regulations, which Anshan followed; considerable recentralization then took place. During the Cultural Revolution period internal management was disrupted by political mobilizations, but Anshan's formal internal organizational structure remained unchanged. Probably the greatest effect on internal management resulted from the temporary "merger" of the company with Anshan Municipality, which diverted managerial attention from production to municipal services, social welfare, and related governmental activities. (Anshan's tendency to act as a social welfare agency may have come to the fore during this period.)

In the late 1970s and the early 1980s Anshan maintained a relatively centralized system of internal management and finances. Movement toward a more centralized, functional system culminated in the creation of new departments of science and technology, energy, electric power, education and training, health care, and services. Subordinate factories carried out only cost accounting, and only minuscule cash expenditures were allowed on a discretionary basis. These factories did, however, have their bank accounts restored to them, along with some authority over miscellaneous expenditures such as administration, travel, and so forth.

Limited reforms in internal management took place in the early 1980s. One of these was the institution of profit accounting at lower levels, which required setting transfer prices for all materials moving from one subordinate factory to another. Perhaps more important, factories were allowed to allocate certain retained funds, for production development, for welfare, and for bonuses, with approval from headquarters. Factories' bank accounts were changed from deposit accounts to settlement accounts, so direct financial dealings with outside units were possible. Nevertheless, Anshan's financial system remained rather centralized. Depreciation funds were entirely controlled by headquarters. Subordinate factories had no authority with respect to fixed asset investments. Expenditures and circulating funds were closely monitored by headquarters.

Substantial internal financial and nonfinancial decentralization at Anshan started after the mid-1980s, in response to the widespread perception that financial management within the company was overcentralized (see *Renmin Ribao*, October 14, 1987, pp. 1–2). A large share of the additional financial resources that accrued to Anshan from higher profit retention rates, depreciation fund retention, and other sources was passed down to lower-level factories. The effects of decentralization were especially striking when, in 1987, factories were reported to have been permitted to retain all of their depreciation funds and major repair funds, as well as a portion of their accounting profits, for reinvestment in their own facilities. Factories also instituted the system of linkage between their total wage bills and their measured financial performance (see "Labor and Wages," in this chapter). More generally, strong financial incentives for lower-level units appear to have been instituted; these incentives were of an almost contractual nature, similar in many respects to the arrangements between other state enterprises and their supervisory agencies.

Although internal financial decentralization undoubtedly improved incentives for subordinate units to improve performance, it must also have been problematic. In the first place, transfer pricing acquired great importance and became a headache for company management (as is discussed later).

Second, there was the potential danger that headquarters' flexibility in its use of funds would become impaired, and that the internal distribution of funds and investments would be inefficient.

There is no detailed information about the decentralization of control over operational decisionmaking that occurred in tandem with internal financial decentralization at Anshan. It is clear, however, that subordinate factories became responsible for business as well as for production. They could sell some of their products directly to units outside the Anshan complex, provided their contributions to the achievement of Anshan's state plan targets were guaranteed. Subunits were also given some authority over production organization, material procurement, construction work, machinery maintenance, and so forth (*Renmin Ribao*, October 14, 1987, pp. 1–2).

Perhaps most important, internal decentralization at Anshan came to affect investment decisionmaking as well as production, procurement, and marketing. Along with the control they gained over certain financial resources, subordinate factories appear to have gained some authority to decide on smaller investment projects. Partial decentralization of investment authority became entwined with financial incentives related to the implementation of investment projects. For example, a substantial part of the proceeds from savings on construction projects could go to the project authority (often the subordinate factory itself) and to the construction team involved. The segmentation of some important flows of investment funds within Anshan and the partial delegation of control over the use of these funds to subunits were potentially important changes, whose consequences are discussed at the end of this section.

Internal Transfer Pricing

When an enterprise institutes internal decentralization of decisionmaking authority and meaningful financial incentives for lower-level units, internal transfer pricing becomes important. If factories and workshops calculate accounting costs and profits and if these indicators are used to determine financial rewards, subunits as well as headquarters become concerned about internal transfer prices and about how these prices are determined.

Internal transfer prices apparently had been in effect for a long time at Anshan, but, until 1985, they remained largely fixed. They were mainly an accounting device and had little, if any, effect on financial flows and rewards. In the 1980s this changed, however, and irrationalities in the structure of internal transfer prices began to have more serious adverse consequences. Headquarters believed that these prices did not put enough pressure on many of Anshan's factories to perform well, because accounting profits could be made even from rather inefficient operations. Headquarters was also concerned that, because they remained fixed, prices did not reflect changes in market conditions outside Anshan. Finally, because of significant inflation in the producer goods sector, Anshan Headquarters bore the burden of rising market prices for inputs by subsidizing its internal transfer pricing system, with Y300 million in 1986.[26]

In 1985, after a year of hard effort, Anshan accomplished a wholesale readjustment of transfer prices. This exercise was deemed successful, and it resulted in a more rational price structure, which presumably improved incentives for efficient operations in the company. Because of the large numbers of goods transacted within Anshan, readjusting prices was an onerous task, in some respects akin to a comprehensive readjustment of administratively controlled prices in the national economy or a large subset of it. Even if Anshan could determine rational prices, these became out-of-date rapidly; hence the new set of prices most likely soon harbored significant irrationalities. It had been planned that internal transfer prices would be adjusted once a year, in line with changes in market conditions. The magnitude of the 1985 effort, however, convinced management that this was not feasible, and no comprehensive adjustments occurred subsequently.

There is a case for price flexibility (or at least a case for no external price controls) in market relationships between independent firms. Within an enterprise (or a hierarchy, in Williamson's terminology), there is a presumption that hierarchical directives and controls maximize flexibility and efficiency. This presumption clashes with internal decentralization and with financial incentives based on transfer prices, so any outcome is an uneasy compromise, with tradeoffs and inefficiencies. Overemphasis on price-based incentives, in the absence of a market mechanism, creates problems within a large enterprise, as it does in the economy as a whole.

Implications of Internal Decentralization

Decentralization can have important implications for an enterprise's decisionmaking and performance, including (1) greater attention to profits at lower levels, which may result in a stronger profit orientation in the enterprise as a whole; (2) improved incentives for efficient operations; (3) tendencies toward fragmentation and toward loss of central control as decentralization proceeds beyond a certain point; and (4) possibly inappropriate investment patterns. Substantial internal decentralization measures were implemented at Anshan starting in 1987; their full effects would be experienced only over a period of several years.

Internal decentralization, especially improved financial incentives at lower levels in Anshan's hierarchy, might have contributed to the company's increasing profit orientation. The importance of internal decentralization relative to that of other changes is hard to gauge, however, especially changes in the financial incentives of Anshan Headquarters in relation to its government supervisory agencies. Part of the modest improvement in various indicators of efficiency at Anshan in the 1980s perhaps could be attributed to internal decentralization.

Strong financial incentives for subunits might have been the only mechanism available to Anshan to encourage improvements in productive efficiency. Without these incentives, it appears to have been difficult for the company to ensure hard work and adequate quality of work from its subordinate units and its employees. Many firms resorted to large and, in many cases, continually increasing bonuses for individual workers; this tactic, of course, required passing financial resources through intermediate levels in the enterprise hierarchy. Incentives at the subunit level also have increasingly been used as a means of eliciting greater effort and productivity from workers. The contracting of construction projects to the implementing unit is an important example of such incentives.

The possibility that internal decentralization at Anshan could lead to fragmentation of the decisionmaking structure and to significant loss of control for headquarters should not be discounted, although such effects were not apparent in 1987. The problems and tradeoffs of internal decentralization are akin to those involved in territorial decentralization of authority within the government hierarchy. Autonomous decisionmaking at lower levels simply could not go beyond a certain point without serious adverse consequences ensuing for Anshan's core activities; some delegation of authority, however, might have been beneficial for motivation as well as for efficient decisionmaking.

Decentralization of investment decisionmaking authority can unleash much stronger centrifugal forces than decentralization of control over production operations. Indeed, in large corporations in other countries, control over important investment decisions and allocation of available investment funds is typically centralized, even if the corporation's command structure is multidivisional, with a large degree of lower-level autonomy in production operations, procurement, marketing, and so forth. When investment authority is decentralized, the future shape of an enterprise can be affected. Moreover, lower levels are likely to make some investment decisions that are inappropriate and wasteful from the perspective of the enterprise as a whole. The ability to take advantage of economies of scale in ancillary activities and workers' welfare facilities may be threatened.

It was not clear in 1987 what the internal decentralization measures then being implemented would really mean in practice, but they appear to have involved a genuine attempt to increase discretionary authority, incentives, and financial resources of lower-level units. Anshan's decentralization, particularly in the investment sphere, may have gone too far. Performance-based financial incentives for a subordinate steel production facility or workshop may be highly beneficial, but such a unit probably should not be allowed to reinvest a large part of the surplus it generates.

Labor and Wages

Labor in Chinese state enterprises is much more than a mere input into production: it also plays an important role in determining firms' objectives. The family motive has been very powerful in influencing, and even determining, enterprise behavior (see Byrd and Tidrick 1987, pp. 62–63). Anshan's experience provides some vivid illustrations of how labor-oriented behavior can distort decisionmaking and affect performance; the most striking example is the company's development of a huge subordinate collective sector, primarily to employ children of Anshan workers. This section cannot do justice to the vast topic of labor and wages, so it covers only a few issues and themes.

Employees' Goals and Enterprise Objectives

A most striking feature of labor recruitment at Anshan was its inward orientation. The great bulk of all new employees hired in the early 1980s were children of Anshan's existing workers. In 1981–83, about 27,000 new regular state employees were taken on by the company. Of these, 17,000 were workers' children replacing their parents, 5,400 were demobilized soldiers from the People's Liberation Army (a large proportion of whom also were children of Anshan employees), and 4,500 were people hired "from society" (these people were actually all children of Anshan employees also). Thus, as regards labor flows, Anshan was a largely closed community. The supply of new labor from within the Anshan community was much greater than was the demand for new state employees, so large numbers of workers' children had to be taken on by Anshan's subordinate collective units. Anshan clearly felt a strong obligation to provide some kind of job for every worker's child.

In the early 1980s Anshan perceived a severe shortage of qualified and skilled workers. The enterprise reportedly needed an additional 25,000–30,000 construction workers for its modernization program. It was also short of about 6,000 frontline production workers; this gap was being filled with collective employees working in state workshops and units. The proximate cause of the perceived labor shortage was administrative controls over the size of Anshan's state labor force by municipal and provincial labor authorities and by the Ministry of Labor and Personnel. Anshan's request for an additional 12,000 construction laborers was eventually turned down by the ministry. The enterprise also believed it was stuck with a large number of unskilled and underqualified employees, including many newly hired workers' children and retired soldiers Anshan had been forced to take on.

By the late 1980s the company's labor situation had changed dramatically. A new system of linkage between Anshan's total wage bill and its total profits and taxes was instituted in 1986; under this system the ceiling on the total wage bill was abolished, and, instead, the wage bill was allowed to rise in a stipulated proportional ratio to the increase in total profits and taxes. Because of this linkage, better enterprise financial performance would result directly in higher total pay for employees. At the same time, the total wage bill was "de-linked" from the size of the labor force, so reductions in the labor force would raise the average pay of remaining workers. (These two reforms were widely implemented in Chinese state industry in 1986–87.) Under the new system, Anshan could maximize average wages by holding down the size of its state labor force; hence it became reluctant to hire additional labor. Although outright layoffs or firings of workers were still impossible, natural attrition permitted the enterprise to reduce total employment. Moreover, total financial rewards to all members of the Anshan community could be maximized by holding down state employment to raise average pay per regular worker and by taking on excess new labor as collective employees, who would not be subject to the performance-based ceiling for the total wage bill. In interviews held in 1987, Anshan managers confirmed their reluctance to expand employment, in a complete turnabout from managerial attitudes in the early 1980s.

This is a striking example of how rules governing the total wage bill and its distribution can drastically affect enterprise objectives. Under the previous system of more-or-less effective ceilings on average compensation (including bonuses) per worker and control over the total wage bill that was achieved primarily through control over the number of employees, Anshan had an incentive to increase employment to the extent possible. Hence the enterprise actively lobbied with responsible government agencies for an increase in labor quotas. Once average wages were largely freed and remaining control was solely related to the total wage bill, however, Anshan's incentives changed dramatically. It strove thenceforth to economize on employment of state workers and absorbed the continuing influx of workers' children into the community labor force in subordinate collective units. This important change in Anshan's orientation was facilitated by demographic trends: because of implementation of effective family planning in China's urban areas starting in the early 1970s, the number of children of Anshan employees entering the labor force would decline sharply in the late 1980s and the early 1990s. Moreover, outflow of labor due to retirements must have increased, as the large cohorts of workers Anshan had taken on in the 1950s began to retire.

Wage Systems

The main change in wage systems at Anshan was the aforementioned shift in 1986 to linkage between the total wage bill and financial performance. Before then there had been only a few experiments in wage reform. (The restoration of workers' bonuses in 1978 was a significant development, however.) Most workers received basic wages plus bonuses under a system that had been in place since 1956. (Bonuses were converted to fixed wage payments during the Cultural Revolution period.)

There was some experimentation with piece rates, mainly the payment of limited piece-rate wages for above-quota production. About 12 percent of Anshan's total work force was under some form of the piece-rate system in 1983. Often piece rates were instituted for "bottleneck" tasks that were constraining Anshan's production and for activities such as transportation and loading and unloading that were naturally conducive to such a system of payment. The use and effectiveness of piece rates, however, was limited by external controls and by administratively imposed ceilings on total compensation per worker. Most workers could be paid no more than 30 percent more than the base wage in extra rewards for piecework; this restriction severely limited work incentives.

Before the mid-1980s Anshan's discretionary authority in the areas of promotions, demotions, and wage adjustments for individual workers was very limited. Similarly, the bonuses it could pay were subject to a ceiling, specified in terms of average bonus as number of months of average base wage (typically three months in the early 1980s). Anshan's flexibility with regard to paying bonuses was increased somewhat by the replacement of bonus ceilings with a bonus tax starting in 1984, but the tax rate was steeply progressive, and it discouraged the granting of bonuses above levels not too much higher than the old ceilings. Overall, Anshan did not have a great deal of independence in decisionmaking on employment, wages, and bonuses before the mid-1980s. As they did in other state enterprises, reforms in Anshan's labor and wage system tended to lag behind reforms in other spheres.

Starting in 1986, different wage systems related to the new wage and labor force policies proliferated in Anshan's subordinate factories and units. Anshan Headquarters passed much of its increased discretionary authority under the new system down to lower levels, instituting among them similar linkages between labor compensation and financial performance. Many factories instituted a "floating wage system with grade increases," under which, if targets were met, 20 percent of the workers could receive a one-grade promotion each year. There were also various versions of a "wage content of output" scheme, itself a variant of the piece-rate system. These schemes could stipulate, for instance, the wage content per ton of steel produced, the wage content per Y100 output value of construction work, or the wage content in savings on production costs. Work units were paid wages in accordance with these rates and with the output produced. Another wage system in use after 1986 was linkage between increments in wages and progress in improving technical indicators of production. Still another system was used for construction workers: if the length of the construction period turned out to be less than was budgeted in advance for a project, some of the resulting savings could be distributed to workers.

Under the more flexible and decentralized wage system, some new problems emerged. There was extensive bargaining between Anshan Headquarters and its subordinate factories over their respective targets and wage bill norms. Similarly, the determination of "hardship coefficients" for different kinds of work was the subject of disputes between headquarters and factories. Despite these problems, Anshan's subordinate units gained a great deal of flexibility in choosing the wage system most appropriate for them. Headquarters stopped intervening in wage determination except to the extent that it maintained some degree of control over subordinate units' total wage bills.

Employment and Wage Trends

The size of Anshan's state labor force fluctuated but showed no marked rising or declining trend; it averaged slightly more than 200,000 in 1978–86 (table 8.9).[27] The fairly sharp (5 percent) decline in total employment in 1986 might have been a result of changed incentives related to linking the wage bill to financial performance. In 1980 there was also a sharp decline in employment; this decline perhaps was related to Anshan's loss of its magnesium mines (workers in the company's iron ore mines continued to be counted in the employment total) and possibly to the removal of the oil refinery from Anshan's jurisdiction. The apparent sharp jump in total employment in 1983 may be spurious because data for 1982 and the years before it and data for 1983 and the years after it are from different sources; moreover, the former data refer to average employment during the year, the latter data to year-end employment.

Anshan's total wage bill grew only very slowly in the 1970s and the early 1980s; there were substantial declines in 1980 and 1981. There were sharp increases, however, in 1984–86, in line with trends in Chinese state industry as a whole. Average nominal wages actually declined through 1977, reflecting the retirement of high-wage employees who had started work before 1949, the influx of low-wage new workers, and the virtual freezing of average wage levels and the moratorium on promotions during the Cultural Revolution period. Average wages rose sharply in 1979, as a result of the promotion of a large number of workers in that year, but otherwise average wages did not increase substantially until 1984–86. The large increases in average wages and in labor productivity in 1986, along with the previously noted decline in employment in that year, may indicate that the new linkage system indeed encouraged higher labor productivity, rapid increases in average wages, and attrition-based declines in employment, as would be expected.

The Enterprise as Social Service and Welfare Agency

Anshan's social responsibilities were generally similar to those of other state enterprises. Its sheer size, however, required that the staff and other resources

Table 8.9. Employment and Wages at Anshan, Selected Years, 1965–86

Year	Labor force		Wage bill		Average wage		Labor productivity	
	Persons	Growth rate (percent)	Amount (millions of yuan)	Growth rate (percent)	Amount (yuan)	Growth rate (percent)	Amount (yuan per worker)	Growth rate (percent)
1965	140,145	n.a.	126.56	n.a.	903	n.a.	15,450	n.a.
1973	201,746	44.0	161.76	27.8	802	-11.2	15,100	-2.3
1975	208,148	3.2	163.99	1.4	788	-1.7	12,480	-17.4
1976	211,202	1.5	164.61	0.4	779	-1.1	13,360	7.1
1977	216,380	2.5	166.40	1.1	769	-1.3	13,230	-1.0
1978	214,983	-0.6	177.03	6.4	823	7.1	15,580	17.8
1979	214,438	-0.3	212.98	20.3	993	20.6	16,630	6.7
1980	187,237	-12.7	195.48	-8.2	1,044	5.1	18,900	13.7
1981	188,241	0.5	190.29	-2.7	1,011	-3.2	17,930	-5.1
1982	194,638	3.4	197.29	3.7	1,014	0.3	18,080	0.8
1983	218,256	12.1	—	—	—	—	17,400	-3.8
1984	221,177	13.6	260.97	32.3	1,180	16.4	18,616	7.0
1985	219,892	-0.6	301.00	15.3	1,369	16.0	20,114	8.0
1986	208,588	-5.1	356.51	18.4	1,709	24.9	23,451	16.6

n.a. Not applicable.
— Not available.
Source: State Statistical Bureau 1985a, p. 271. Ministry of Metallurgy 1985, p. 752; 1986b, p. 752; 1987, p. 534. Information provided by the company.

devoted to employee welfare be considerable. In the early 1980s there were more than 8,000 people in the enterprise's welfare system, including providers of food service, education, housing, medical care, storage and transport, and so forth. Headquarters welfare facilities had total fixed assets of more than Y40 million; annual expenditures were about Y6.5 million and revenues less than Y500,000; the difference was subsidized with proceeds from Anshan's business operations. These figures represent only the tip of the social service and welfare iceberg, however, because they do not include the operations of collectives that provided services for Anshan employees or the welfare facilities and personnel that were attached to subordinate factories. Anshan's central education and housing departments also are excluded from these figures; the housing department employed more than 2,000 state workers and 4,000 collective workers.

Obviously, Anshan's most important social obligation was to provide employment and livelihood to its workers and their adult dependents. Another important (and costly) social service it provided to its employees was housing. In the early 1980s, 70 percent of Anshan's employees lived in company-owned apartments. The enterprise had nearly 4 million square meters of employees' living space and nearly half a million square meters of ancillary facilities (kitchens, bathrooms, and the like). The value of housing assets (in terms of construction cost) was more than Y570 million and accounted for 8 to 9 percent of the total value of Anshan's fixed assets. More than 6,000 people at Anshan were involved in housing management, preparing newly completed housing units for use, undertaking major repairs, and engaging in routine maintenance and upkeep. Annual spending on maintenance and upkeep was more than Y10 million.

In the early 1980s Anshan faced a severe housing shortage. Twenty thousand households lacked company housing, and another 30,000 households were living in overcrowded units; parents, adult children, and grandchildren were often living together. Moreover, the quality of the housing left much to be desired. As was the case throughout China's urban economy, rents were extremely low—only Y0.12 a square meter on average—so there was inadequate funding for maintenance. More than half of Anshan's depreciation and major repair funds generated by housing assets, which totaled nearly Y23 million a year, were diverted by the company to other uses, leaving only Y11 million for housing repair and renewal.[28] There were also problems with the numbers and quality of the staff engaged in housing work.

These same problems of underfunding and inadequate quantity and quality were evident in the other social welfare services provided by Anshan. Top management appears to have viewed the enterprise's social obligations as a burden and as a constraint on its business operations rather than as a positive goal. Thus social objectives actively furthered by enterprises such as Anshan may well be seen as constraints by most managers, binding on them because of workers' attitudes and because of the lack of alternative means of provision. Anshan's management also appears to have taken a jaundiced view of the near-universal hiring of workers' children. The subordinate collectives for workers' children were viewed by management as a financial burden.

This discussion raises questions about Anshan's worker orientation or family motive. Company management seems not to have internalized worker goals, despite generally acting as if increasing workers' incomes and improving housing and other benefits were an overriding priority. Hence worker-oriented behavior exhibited by large firms such as Anshan may be based on precarious foundations and may be unstable. Analysis of managerial actions as opposed to their attitudes, however, reveals no sign of a diminished worker orientation in Anshan up to 1987.

Collective Workers and the Collective Economy

The most striking manifestation of Anshan's worker orientation was the emergence of a whole society of "second-class" employees and of a large group of subordinate firms in the collective sector. These employees and firms made up a large part of Anshan's total work force and a substantial part of its total economic activity. Subsidiary collective firms and their employees are interesting not only in themselves but also as a management problem for Anshan and in relation to issues of vertical integration (see "Vertical Integration versus Administrative Fragmentation," in this chapter). Anshan's interactions with its subordinate collectives also shed light on the enterprise's pursuit of multiple objectives in a constrained environment.

Anshan's collectives dated back to the 1950s. At that time the enterprise began to organize family members into production teams to provide some basic services for employees and to engage in processing, transport, and other simple manual labor. By 1966 there were more than 46,000 people in family production teams; Anshan's total force of regular state workers was 140,000 in 1965 (table 8.9). In 1975 the Liaoning provincial government called for a reorganization of these family teams, so Anshan put 33,000 collective workers into two collective companies. The rest were incorporated into the Welfare Management Department and into the other units in which they had already been working.

In 1979, with the change in the policy of sending youth out to the countryside, Anshan had to set up collectives on a large scale to provide jobs for workers' children returning from the countryside and for new entrants to the labor market who were no longer being sent away. The Anshan Subsidiary Enterprise Corporation, responsible for supervision of the collectives, was established around this time. Growth was extremely rapid, and, by 1982, there were more than 160,000 collective employees.[29] The value of the collectives' fixed assets reached Y66 million, their circulating assets Y39 million. In 1986, total collective employment was still only 160,000-plus, whereas fixed assets had grown to Y578 million and circulating assets to Y349 million (Ministry of Metallurgy 1987, p. 399). Total sales revenue of the collectives in 1986 was Y530 million, of which Y290 million consisted of industrial output. Total profits were Y70 million.

More detailed information on the subset of collective enterprises directly supervised by the Subsidiary Enterprise Corporation is presented in table 8.10. These figures do not include collectives of the Anshan Mining Company and roughly fifty-four collective firms established by Anshan's subordinate factories and units. Nevertheless, this table tells an interesting story about developments in the 1980s, following the tremendous increase in collective employment in the late 1970s. In the 1980s, employment did not rise but rather declined somewhat from the peak reached in 1982. Total sales revenue, GVIO, and profits all increased rapidly, at 22.6 percent, 22.1 percent, and 13.9 percent a year respectively between 1981 and 1986. Fixed assets grew by 23.5 percent a year and circulating assets by 20.7 percent a year during the same period. The wage bill also rose sharply, by 13.1 percent a year, which, with the moderate decline in employment, translated into a 15.6 percent annual rise in average nominal wages per employee. Average wages more than doubled, from Y582 to Y1,203, between 1981 and 1986. Since capital grew no more rapidly than output and the labor force declined, economic performance of the collectives must have improved markedly, probably reflecting greater efficiency in operations. In particular, labor productivity more than tripled in nominal terms between 1981 and 1986.

These trends suggest a number of interesting conclusions. First, by the mid-1980s, massive employment creation was no longer a primary concern for Anshan, because the influx of new entrants into the labor force appears to have been offset by the outflow of retiring workers.[30] Second, Anshan improved the lot of collective workers, as is shown by the rapid growth of their average wages (15.6 percent a year, compared with 11.1 percent a year for state employees). This improvement also was facilitated by demographic trends, but undoubtedly it required productivity-increasing investments as well as favorable treatment of collectives with regard to input and output pricing. Finally, although output increased sharply and productivity improved, financial performance was still a problem in the mid-1980s. Profits grew much more slowly than did output and capital, suggesting that incremental surplus was siphoned off for wages and employee benefits.

In the light of subsequent developments, some of the problems Anshan's subordinate collectives faced in the early 1980s would appear to have been resolved or at least ameliorated. The large increase in collective employment predicted in 1983 (to 200,000 by 1985 and 250,000 by 1990) did not materialize, greatly easing the task of employment creation. The sharp rise in wages must have at least in part addressed collective workers' complaints about

Table 8.10. Profile of Anshan's Subordinate Collectives, 1981–86
(millions of yuan, unless otherwise specified)

Indicator	1981	1982	1983	1984	1985	1986
Gross value of output	191.76	224.10	303.39	383.29	439.72	530.11
GVIO	106.62	119.71	173.29	209.88	243.78	289.92
Total profits	36.39	36.92	53.06	70.26	82.25	69.65
Fixed assets	42.58	61.41	78.70	88.80	114.92	122.47
Circulating assets	31.08	39.52	47.01	57.81	61.88	79.77
Total wage bill	68.15	77.98	70.46	81.88	100.56	126.01
Year-end employment (persons)	117,151	127,640	114,271	116,832	107,167	104,704
Children hired (no. per year)[a]	13,316	15,007	10,102	9,819	5,777	5,217

GVIO, gross value of industrial output.

Note: Data do not consider dependents' collective enterprises set up by the Anshan Mining Company, which had more than 37,000 collective employees as of the end of 1985. Certain other categories of collective employees (for instance, those working on the front line of production in state factories under Anshan) also may not be considered in the data. Total employment in subordinate collectives was more than 160,000 in 1986.

a. Children of Anshan workers.

Source: Ministry of Metallurgy 1987, p. 399.

low incomes and living standards. Anshan in the early 1980s was concerned about how to handle the 8,000 collective employees who were working alongside state employees in state work units.[31] Their number fell to less than 5,000 by 1987, through attrition as well as perhaps through some shifting of workers from collective- to state-employee status. In the early 1980s, Anshan management was concerned that profit tax rates for subordinate collectives would rise sharply as the collectives' initial exemptions expired.[32] Management also feared that it would be difficult to relocate and restructure collective firms on Anshan's crowded site in accordance with the enterprise's modernization program. In actuality, these problems seem not to have hindered production in the collective sector. Similarly, input supplies and marketing did not become binding constraints.

The principal unresolved issue with respect to Anshan's collectives was their inability to become financially independent from the parent company. A large part of their activities and profits was still accounted for by captive markets at Anshan. Construction work for Anshan was the single most important activity of these firms, and in such work they probably faced little, if any, competition from outside the enterprise. It would require additional research to ascertain the precise degree to which Anshan's collective sector depended on the parent enterprise and to ascertain the total financial burden this dependence imposed on Anshan. Both were almost certainly substantial, and they may not have declined significantly in the 1980s, despite superficial improvements in the collectives' performance.

Renovation and Modernization

Anshan is by far China's oldest iron and steel complex; some of its facilities date back to the 1930s, most to the 1940s or the 1950s. By the early 1980s the bulk of Anshan's production technology was outdated, inefficient, and severely aging, and its site, which had been built up haphazardly over six decades, was very crowded. Thus the issue of modernization was a salient one. Although they were extreme in their complexity and difficulty, Anshan's problems were similar to those faced by China's iron and steel industry as a whole. Massive investments over a number of years were required if the industry was to improve efficiency and to supply the bulk of domestic demand on a more internationally competitive basis than it had in the past.

Anshan put together two five-year plans for technological renovation (one covered 1981–85, the other 1986–90), another, overlapping plan (covering 1983–90), and longer-term plans for 1990–2000. Anshan combined replacement of old facilities and technological modernization with investments to increase capacity utilization and, more generally, to expand production without building complete new facilities. There were many problems, however, some physical and technical in nature, others financial and systemic. As a result, progress in modernization was slow, uneven, and costly.

Overall Design

The most important choice in designing the overall strategy for modernization at Anshan was whether the existing plant should be modernized at all. One option was to construct an entirely new facility on a different site and to let the existing plant depreciate itself out of existence, that is, continue production there until that became uneconomic. This option would involve either a shutdown of Anshan or a transfer of the enterprise (including most or all of its personnel) to a new, probably nearby site. Although construction of an entirely new facility would be costly and would not make use of Anshan's existing assets and infrastructure, it does not automatically follow that this should not be the option chosen. As is seen in the ensuing discussion, the costs of "modernization in place" could also be very high.

In any case, this option was rejected, ostensibly because of the high cost of a new plant. Shortage of land also was cited as an obstacle. The administrative problems of shutting down a gigantic enterprise, including moving employees to the new site or finding other jobs for them and arranging housing and other services, would have been enormous and most likely constituted the strongest deterrent to building a complete new plant.

Anshan's decision to modernize rather than to shut down engendered several important strategic choices concerning the modernization program: at the micro level, for instance, should modernization occur on the existing plant site, or should there be some small moves (for example, moves of several kilometers) within the locality? Anshan made an initial decision to modernize entirely on the existing site and implemented this decision, despite serious difficulties, during 1981–85 (see the ensuing discussion). There appears, however, to have been a shift in strategy after the mid-1980s; extensive construction began then at a new site roughly 10 kilometers away from the old one, and it was recognized that additional large-scale construction at the old site would be impractical.

Another important strategic issue concerned whether to maintain current production while the enterprise engaged in renovation and modernization. Maintaining production would have presented no problems if an entirely new plant were being constructed, but it would generate problems and conflicts during modernization of the existing plant. China's tight steel supply situation and Anshan's large share in the total national supply of steel provided strong arguments for maintaining, if not increasing, production. This interfered, however, with the enterprise's efficient and timely implementation of its investment projects; the difficulties were aggravated by Anshan's crowded site conditions. Thus the option of closing down the plant or large parts of it while modernization work was going on at least deserved consideration. The debate within Anshan and within the Ministry of Metallurgy over this issue was lengthy and heated. It was only resolved during a visit to Anshan by then-Premier Zhao Ziyang, at which time a decision was made to undertake comprehensive modernization in place while maintaining full-capacity production. There seems to have been no change in this basic approach subsequently.

In sum, decisions on broader strategic issues gave heavy emphasis to maintaining current production, minimizing additional use of land, and avoiding any threat to the existence or to the continued viability of Anshan. Systemic features of the Chinese economy limited the scope of Anshan's choice in designing a modernization program, leading to substantial delays, greater physical and technical difficulties, higher costs, and inefficiency.

Problems and Constraints

Some of the difficulties Anshan encountered in the detailed design and implementation of its modernization program were inherent in such a massive undertaking and were almost impossible to avoid. Other difficulties were direct results of the aforementioned broader strategic choices. Finally, some problems were created or aggravated by the institutions and the administrative mechanisms for investment planning and control in China.

The sheer physical and technical problems of modernization were emphasized by enterprise managers. Anshan's site presented tremendous difficulties for the execution of a large-scale program of modernization in place. Workshops and plants had been built haphazardly over the course of fifty years, and the site had become increasingly crowded. Almost any large job required moving other units to make room and could indeed set off chain reactions of such costly moves. Construction of a coal powder plant, for example, required moving Anshan's civil engineering team office to the educational facility of the coal gas plant. As a result of this move, the educational facility also was forced to move. In many projects, moving costs accounted for 40 to 50 percent of total investment costs, and timetables for project completion were not met as a result of moves.

Anshan's crowded site also made construction operations extremely delicate and difficult. It was hard to store construction materials on-site or to bring in heavy construction equipment. The dense network of underground pipelines and cables required that digging and demolition work be done with great care. Often construction teams unearthed pipes of whose existence they had not been aware and whose function was unclear, yet these pipes had to be bypassed, for fear that they might be essential for some part of the production process. The extra work and caution required in construction must have raised investment costs substantially.

These problems were aggravated by the decision to maintain full-capacity production while construction was proceeding. Utilities could not be cut off during construction, for example, and, more generally, construction work had to be planned around production activities. Simultaneous production and construction to a considerable degree limited the scope for choice in designing and planning construction work and undoubtedly had adverse effects on efficiency.

Modernization in place severely taxed the infrastructure of Anshan's existing site and required that new ancillary and infrastructural facilities be built. Hence one of the primary advantages usually ascribed to modernization of existing facilities—the ready availability of utilities and of other infrastructural services—did not fully apply. In fact, building entirely new infrastructural facilities on a new site might have been cheaper than augmenting infrastructure on the crowded existing site.

A second set of problems related to the planning and organization of the modernization program. A large number of actors outside the enterprise were involved, often in unproductive and conflicting ways.[33] This situation, from Anshan's perspective, resulted not only in inefficient decisionmaking but also in considerable instability and consequent debilitating uncertainty. Fragmented decisionmaking led to great delays and red tape, preventing quick reactions to problems and resulting in built-in technological backwardness in many projects. Anshan reported that, as a general rule, it took four years for a modernization project to pass through all the preimplementation (that is, preconstruction) stages.

An example of the problems that arose from disjointed bureaucratic decisionmaking and from instability in project design was the modernization of the Number 3 Steel Mill. This facility had both open hearth furnaces and oxygen converters; the furnaces were old and costly to operate and to maintain. The combination of the two technologies resulted in technical and management problems. Therefore a new converter was built and an old furnace was torn down, making room for a continuous casting line. After much debate, however, the Ministry of Metallurgy decided, apparently despite the objections of Anshan's technical personnel, to install two large continuous casting lines. As a result, downstream steel-rolling capacity at the site became inadequate, and new oxygen-making facilities and more electric power were needed as well. The total cost of the project thus escalated from Y170 million to more than Y500 million.

Financing Modernization

The biggest problems and bottlenecks of modernization concerned its financing, which called for huge amounts of resources. The plan for 1981–85 originally specified a total investment of Y1.246 billion and comprised 159 modernization projects. This investment figure was revised upward in the 1983–90 modernization plan, which had 187 projects and a total investment cost of Y3.05 billion. Because of further cost escalation and possibly subsequent expansion of the program, its total projected investment cost over the Seventh Five-Year Plan alone (1986–90) was more than Y3 billion. The financing of such large expenditures would have been a headache under any circumstances, but Anshan's problems were aggravated by rigidities and distortions in China's investment financing system. Shortfalls of financial resources allocated were a serious problem for the enterprise, but there were also gaps between funds committed and those actually forthcoming. As part of the subsectoral responsibility system (see "The Supervisory System," in this chapter), Anshan was assigned a target, or quota, of investment funds for the period 1985–90, but this quota was not accompanied by financing in any form; instead the enterprise was forced to obtain the money required on its own.

The main sources of finance for Anshan's modernization were its own retained profits and other discretionary funds on the one hand and bank loans on the other. Grants from the Ministry of Metallurgy or from other government agencies had dwindled to insignificant amounts by the mid-1980s, although they might have been important sources of funding for Anshan in earlier years. In 1985 Anshan's modernization investment totaled Y439.8 million, of which only 0.4 percent was financed by state grants. The bulk (90 percent) of total investment came from the enterprise's own funds, and only a small proportion (8.7 percent) of it was financed by bank loans (Ministry of Metallurgy 1986a, p. 133). In fact, Anshan's share of bank loans in total modernization investment financing was far lower than was the average share for large iron and steel plants in 1985 (24.2 percent). Anshan's investment financing picture did not change greatly in 1986.

Financing problems were aggravated by the way in which bank loans for modernization were allocated. The company received annual quotas for such loans from the headquarters of the Industrial and Commercial Bank of China; these quotas were set in consultation with the ministry. The loan funds themselves, however, had to come from the "autonomous" deposits of the local branch of the Industrial and Commercial Bank, which was under the supervision of the bank's provincial branch. Local and provincial bank branches, responding to demands from local and provincial governments, did not accept Anshan's centrally determined loan quotas as binding targets. Hence there were chronic shortfalls in loans forthcoming in relation to quotas for loans. For the Seventh Five-Year Plan as a whole, Anshan was given a total quota of Y600 million for modernization investment loans; this quota would imply average annual lending of Y120 million. Actual lending during the early years of the plan, however, was only about Y70 million a year. Making up these shortfalls in the latter part of the plan probably turned out to be extremely difficult.

The severity of Anshan's financing problems is illustrated by the enterprise's situation in the middle of 1987. Anshan's total modernization investment plan for 1987 was originally set at Y650 million. It was envisioned that the enterprise's own retained profits and other funds would provide Y370 million of that total. An additional Y120 million was to come from bank loans, although management doubted whether these funds would indeed be forthcoming. Finally, the enterprise was trying to raise some additional funds through compensation trade. There was great pessimism at Anshan about its ability to fund its approved modernization investment program for 1987.

Preliminary Assessment

Anshan's experience through 1987 indicates that some of the strategic decisions on the design of the company's modernization program were apparently flawed. Careful technical research and a great deal of data would be required to shed more light on the relative merits of modernization in place and greenfield construction (that is, building entirely new facilities). The problems, delays, and cost escalation Anshan encountered do suggest that the former alternative was not necessarily less costly and more effective than the latter. The requirement that Anshan's modernization occur without any halt in current production was intimately related to systemic features of the Chinese economy—the quantity orientation of planning, chronic shortages, and the lack of free resort to imports. More generally, systemic aspects combined with Anshan's strategic choices to make its task of modernization much more difficult, costly, and slow.

Anshan's experience with modernization also constitutes a serious indictment of the Chinese system of planning, organizing, and controlling investment in large state enterprises. There was great fragmentation in supervision and control of investments, and financing became increasingly uncertain as government budgetary grants dried up and local banks gained greater independence. Financial shortfalls almost certainly prevented Anshan from implementing its approved program on schedule. Given Anshan's huge size and work force, there was no danger of the enterprise's being left to depreciate itself out of existence, much less of its being shut down in the short run. The severe problems in Anshan's modernization program, however, undoubtedly raised its costs sharply, delayed implementation by several years, and hindered efforts to improve efficiency.

Conclusions

Rather than summarize the contents of this case study, this section distills some general themes from Anshan's experiences and shows how they are relevant to Chinese state industry as a whole.

Mandatory Planning, Sellers' Markets, and Reforms

A theme that pervades Anshan's experience in the late 1970s and the early to mid-1980s is the extreme difficulty of achieving meaningful results with enterprise reform in an environment characterized by continuing dominance of mandatory planning in production, procurement, and marketing and by chronic sellers' markets. Anshan was involved in most reforms implemented in the state industrial sector, not as a pioneer in most cases but as a mainstream participant. The effect of these reforms in improving the enterprise's performance was limited.

Anshan became more profit oriented as a result of the reforms, but, because of the enduring sellers' market for steel and steel products, this increasing profit orientation did not result in strong efforts to respond to customer needs or to cut costs. Anshan exhibited many of the characteristics of a technically oriented firm (see Byrd and Tidrick 1987, p. 64). It was well run and was clearly concerned about productivity and efficiency. Distortions resulted, however, because the enterprise was not responding to well-functioning markets but rather was operating in a context of perceived unlimited demand for its main products. The period in 1981 in which Anshan faced excess supply was not long enough to engender lasting changes in its behavior.

The continuing dominance of mandatory planning and the chronic sellers' market were closely related. The sellers' market justified mandatory planning, at least in the minds of planning authorities, and mandatory planning in turn helped perpetuate the sellers' market. At Anshan the share of total output subject to mandatory planning and administrative allocation remained very high, even as it was declining in the steel industry and in Chinese industry as a whole.

Mandatory planning prevented autonomous decisionmaking by firms. At Anshan planning was so dominant and detailed that the "marginal" view of the role of markets and direct marketing (Byrd 1987a, p. 298) did not apply. Anshan does not appear to have acted as if its output of most goods at the margin (and hence total production) were determined by the market. This behavior suggests the more general point that the share of direct marketing in total output must exceed a certain threshold before an enterprise becomes genuinely market oriented.

In this context, the adverse effect of low plan prices was probably not felt primarily through distorted incentives and resource allocation (although these might well have been severe problems). Rather, the existence of plan prices far different from underlying market equilibrium levels created artificial embodied rents and allowed enterprises to maintain a sellers' market for their output, simply by charging a price somewhat lower than the free market price, thereby gaining access to other goods in short supply through exchange. As a result it was difficult to induce market-oriented behavior in enterprises, and the existing free market remained thin; those purchasing goods at high market prices primarily were entities without any product of their own in short supply for use in exchanges.

Wage and Employment Systems and Enterprise Objectives

It has been postulated that the rules affecting wage determination and size of work force can have a significant effect on the concrete objectives firms pursue (Byrd and Tidrick 1987, p. 66). Anshan's experience provides a striking example of this phenomenon. In 1986 there was an important change in Anshan's wage system: its switch to linkage between the total wage bill and profits and taxes. Government control over labor force size and average wages also was relaxed. Anshan subsequently strove to hold down the size of its labor force and even to reduce it to the extent possible through attrition. There is some evidence of Anshan's greater efforts to increase labor productivity as well. The company's behavior in this context contrasts sharply with its emphasis in the early 1980s on increasing employment of regular workers. Anshan's immediate goal seems to have shifted from maximization of employment (including both state workers and collective workers) to maximization of average pay per state worker.

The underlying family orientation at Anshan (whether it is viewed as an objective or as a constraint) might not have changed appreciably in the course of reform. There was, however, a sharp reversal in Anshan's outward behavior from 1986 onward. This reversal suggests that changes in the rules governing enterprise behavior can have a powerful influence, even if the fundamental goals firms pursue are not affected. The 1986 wage and employment reforms at Anshan were also implemented in the bulk of Chinese state industrial firms, so they could lead to a massive shift in the orientation of enterprises from maximization of total employee benefits to maximization of average pay per worker. This could result in sharply reduced new hiring, in declining employment through attrition, and in higher labor productivity.

The short-term, microeconomic effects of this change in the orientation of state enterprises seem to have been positive, although the new system did not generate an incentive to hold down total labor costs. Questions can be raised, however, about the long-term, economywide implications of this change in orientation. Enterprise investment decisions may become skewed in the direction of increasing capital intensity, and labor mobility in the state sector of the economy, limited in the first place, may be further obstructed. The need to generate productive employment opportunities for the huge numbers of people who will be entering China's labor force in the next several decades means that such incentives are highly inappropriate.

Worker Orientation as a Constraint

Anshan management's complaints about various aspects of the labor system suggest that it had not internalized workers' objectives but rather perceived them as binding constraints that must be met before management's own objectives could be freely pursued. Creating jobs for workers' children was considered an onerous burden, and the financial dependence of the collectives on the parent enterprise was a matter of concern. More generally, the numerous family ties among workers generated by the enterprise's employment obligations were perceived as an obstacle to efficient management.

To the extent that workers' goals were perceived by management as a constraint rather than an objective, Anshan's worker orientation was somewhat different in character from that of firms more thoroughly imbued with the family motive, such as the Chongqing Clock and Watch Company and the Nanning Silk and Ramie Textile Mill (see chapters 3 and 7 in this volume). Anshan may have been more typical of Chinese state industry as a whole in this respect, especially of very large firms. Hence the strong worker orientation that has been a hallmark of Chinese state industry since the late 1970s may be more precarious and unstable than is suggested by the experiences of enterprises such as Chongqing and Nanning. If, at some point, management should perceive that workers' ability to further their interests (or to threaten the enterprise, should their demands not be met) is weakened, many firms might shed their worker orientation surprisingly quickly.

Problems of Internal Decentralization

Starting in 1987 a major package of decentralization measures was implemented at Anshan; these measures, at least in principle, gave subunits more discretionary authority, access to substantial financial resources, and strong financial incentives to improve performance. More broadly, internal decentralization, to some extent at Anshan and to a greater extent in other large enterprises, appears to have taken on some of the characteristics of the contractual arrangements that have become a popular means of governing the relationships between firms and supervisory agencies.

Internal decentralization has problematic aspects, including, most importantly, possible loss of control by headquarters and fragmentation of decisionmaking. Decentralization of investment decisionmaking and of control over flows of investment resources is more problematic than is decentralization of control over production operations and marketing. (The former can eventually affect the shape, size, and orientation of the enterprise as a whole.)

The contractual approach to internal organization carries with it tradeoffs and difficulties, although it may generate strong incentives for improved financial performance in the short run. Most of the criteria used to distinguish situations in which hierarchical organization of activities within a firm is more advantageous than is reliance on the market mechanism would seem to apply.[34] More specifically, the situation is one of bilateral-monopoly bargaining, with asymmetric information and with incentives for either side to break contracts to its own advantage. Hence the internal contracting method that is becoming increasingly popular in Chinese state industry will likely prove unstable and will be a source of continuing conflicts.

Delineation of Enterprise Boundaries

Government administrative intervention in the determination of enterprise boundaries was a significant source of problems for a large, multifaceted enterprise such as Anshan. The most important consequences included instability, loss of control for the enterprise, supply problems, and disincentives to investment and to new product development. Administrative delineation of enterprise boundaries inevitably involves varying degrees of inefficiency. In the first place, the choice is between planning and integration rather than between market and integration. Second, severe problems are created by instability and by lack of enterprise control, irrespective of the particular choice of boundaries. A final point worthy of note is that the intrusion of the profit motive in this situation can be problematic.

Government authorities face a dilemma in setting policy on integration of activities within firms. If they wish to create appropriate incentives and encourage smooth operations, allowing firms themselves to determine which activities they should incorporate within their boundaries is probably the best strategy. Chronic supply problems associated with mandatory planning, however, overwhelmingly skew the choice for enterprises in favor of integration. Hence for government authorities to give firms more freedom would result in a great increase in vertical integration in Chinese industry as a whole. Such integration would result not only in loss of control for planning authorities but also in waste of capital because of overinvestment in duplicate, underutilized facilities by different firms. There is no easy solution to this dilemma; only the emergence of well-functioning markets as a viable alternative to both planning and integration will lead to efficient results.

Problems of the Subsectoral Responsibility System

The problematic nature and the consequences of the subsectoral responsibility system for the iron and steel industry are clearly shown in Anshan's experience. Perhaps most important, the system seems to have strengthened and entrenched mandatory planning and administrative control over flows of goods, at a time when their role in industry as a whole was declining. It is doubtful whether the long-term commitments embedded in the system were credible. The subsectoral responsibility system perpetuated the supervisory role of the ministry and probably made future reforms more difficult. Moreover, giving the ministry an economic role to supplement and partially to replace its administrative authority most likely generated major distortions. The subsectoral responsibility system for the iron and steel industry appears to have resulted in retrogression rather than in advancement; the same is probably true of the systems introduced in other heavy industries.

Fundamental Difficulties of Administrative Control

The problems with administrative delineation of enterprise boundaries, with the multiheaded leadership system, and with the subsectoral responsibility system can all be traced to the basic pattern of government administrative determination of the production and flow of goods in the economy. As long as mandatory planning remains in place and accounts for the bulk of production and supply, these and other similar problems will arise. Thus Anshan's experience provides a strong case for weakening and eventually abolishing mandatory production planning and administrative allocation of industrial producer goods. Although Anshan may be exceptional in the extent to which mandatory planning retained a dominant influence on it, a considerable number of other large Chinese industrial firms may be in similar situations.

Notes

1. Steel production figures are for 1985 (Ministry of Metallurgy 1986a, pp. 14–16, 84).

2. Party committees were abolished for a time during the Cultural Revolution, and so-called revolutionary committees were established to take over their functions.

3. Nevertheless, managers believed that when the company was merged with Anshan Municipality, noneconomic goals were emphasized and there was greater waste.

4. A representative of the Liaoning Provincial Metallurgy Bureau stated that the

bureau received no benefits from Anshan and, moreover, that it basically had nothing to do with Anshan, except under rare and extraordinary circumstances. Although some of Anshan's steel output was turned over to Liaoning Province, this went to the provincial material supply bureau rather than the Metallurgy Bureau.

5. The initial form of this system is discussed in *Renmin Ribao* (People's Daily), November 11, 1984, reprinted in Ministry of Metallurgy 1985, p. 21.

6. Depreciation is funded in the Chinese accounting system—money is drawn from income at specified rates and put in a depreciation fund. There is also a major repair fund, for which money is drawn in the same way. In the prereform period, Anshan's depreciation rate (which applied uniformly to all kinds of fixed assets) was 2.9 percent computed with the straight line method. The major repair fund was drawn at 2 percent of the original value of fixed assets per year.

7. Immediately before this change, Anshan had not been permitted to retain any of these funds. During the Cultural Revolution and its aftermath, however, the enterprise may have been allowed to keep a portion of the depreciation fund. Different persons' accounts of this matter varied.

8. These figures were derived by multiplying the original value of productive fixed assets by the stipulated rate for drawing major repair funds and then adding to that product Anshan's own reported figures for retained depreciation funds. Because major repair funds were also drawn for nonproductive assets, and because it is quite possible that some of these funds were diverted to productive investments, the figures in the text probably understate the increase in Anshan's investment funds other than retained profits.

9. A decline in deposits would reduce the local bank's lending capacity, because of the Chinese practice of linkage between deposit levels and lending levels at local bank branches, but if Anshan was not getting very much in the way of bank loans anyway, it probably would gain on a net basis from sales of shares. Moreover, raising money by issuing stock involved much less red tape than did raising it through bank loans.

10. The increase in Anshan's share of self-sales in 1987 was at least partly related to the opening of the market for scrap steel. Steel producers could exchange rolled steel for scrap steel supplies; this portion of their output was considered part of self-sales.

11. For profit-maximizing firms operating under decreasing returns to scale, output responds to the price faced for output at the margin, which is the market price for above-plan output, unless the plan quota is so high that the enterprise chooses to produce no output at all above the plan.

12. Based on the aforementioned 57 percent state plan share and on output figures for the industry as a whole and for Anshan (Ministry of Metallurgy 1986a, pp. 2, 84).

13. Anshan may have been forced to purchase some inputs it needed for production within the state plan on the market, or through exchanging its own above-plan products for them. As a result of higher prices for inputs purchased on the market, production costs rose, and Anshan's financial performance suffered.

14. For a brief period, planning authorities apparently tried to require enterprises such as Anshan to turn over 70 percent of above-plan output for unified distribution, but this requirement seems never to have been implemented.

15. There is extensive literature on rent seeking. See Krueger 1974 and Buchanan, Tollison, and Tullock 1980, among others. Byrd 1987b, chap. 5, discusses the concept of rents embodied in plan-allocated goods.

16. This issue is not unknown in the publicly owned steel sectors of other countries. In late 1988 the Steel Authority of India decided to divest its steel plants of their captive mines for iron ore and other raw materials and instead combine the mines under a Central Raw Materials Directorate. It was expected that this change would allow the steel plants to concentrate exclusively on management of steel production operations and that shortages and surpluses of raw materials affecting different plants would be eliminated. It was also expected that expansion and modernization of the mines would be facilitated. See *The Hindu*, October 22, 1988, p. 10.

17. Since base-year profits would be reflected in adjustments in profit targets when transfer of financial authority occurred, what mattered in the transfer was the expected change in profits over time. If profits declined or stagnated, the mines would become a drag on the aggregate financial performance and on the retained profits of their "owner."

18. Most of the rest of Anshan's needs were filled by other cement plants in Liaoning. Because Anshan's own facility did not produce all the varieties of cement it needed, some of these flows may have been rational. Anshan managers believed, however, that much more of the plant's output could have been used in-house.

19. Two factors contributed to a decline in Anshan's profitability: (1) the oil refinery had made large profits for the company and (2) lacking supplies of oil products at the state price, Anshan might have been forced to pay much higher prices for such products, raising Anshan's production costs.

20. See "Labor and Wages," in this chapter, for a detailed discussion of dependents' collectives.

21. The precise motives of the Petrochemical General Corporation were not clear.

22. Perkins 1988, p. 616, argues that the significance of profit maximization depends on whether it is oriented toward market activities or toward obtaining government favors and manipulating the bureaucracy.

23. Anshan's state labor force totaled 208,588 at the end of 1986 (Ministry of Metallurgy 1987, p. 534), employment in collectives under Anshan Headquarters was 104,704 (Ministry of Metallurgy 1987, p. 399), and estimated total employment in collective firms under Anshan's subunits was 60,000, including 37,336 collective workers in the Mining Company at the end of 1985 (Ministry of Metallurgy 1986b, p. 237). It is conservatively assumed that the average ratio of dependents not employed by Anshan to Anshan employees was 0.33; hence Anshan's total population was about 500,000.

24. The factory-director responsibility system at that time was being implemented fairly widely but still experimentally in state industrial enterprises. It is not to be confused with the director responsibility system under the leadership of the party committee; the new system gave final authority over operational matters to the director.

25. These presumably included the general manager and party secretary; it is unclear who the third person was.

26. This situation must have developed because of a relative price squeeze between inputs and outputs that Anshan experienced. Fixed transfer prices prevented

Anshan's subordinate factories from experiencing the squeeze. The Y300 million inflation subsidy in 1986 was the result of only a year of market price rises. (Internal transfer prices had been comprehensively readjusted in 1985, as is discussed later.)

27. For purposes of comparison, employment and wage data for the Anshan Mining Company have been included, even for those years in which the Mining Company was separated from Anshan.

28. Because revenues generated by housing were tiny, the depreciation fund and major repair fund for housing must have been drawn from operating revenues. Hence their diversion to other uses was in a certain sense justified.

29. Of these, 135,000 were workers' children who had had no other jobs, 15,000 were state workers and managers who had been transferred to the collectives (but who retained their status and perquisites), 10,000 were family members of collective workers, more than 2,000 were retired workers, and 1,000 were in other categories.

30. There may have been flows between the state sector and the collective sector, but these did not affect the total, because the number of state employees also declined (table 8.9).

31. The practice of using such "mixed-position" workers had been criticized by the central government, which ordered state enterprises to phase it out. The Shenyang Smelter, like many other enterprises in northeast China, faced a similar problem (see chapter 5 in this volume).

32. Collective firms that were set up to provide employment for educated youth in urban areas typically could be exempted from profit tax for up to three years.

33. Organizations that had interests in Anshan's modernization program included the Ministry of Metallurgy, Liaoning Province, the State Economic Commission, the State Planning Commission, and even the State Council itself. Within the Ministry of Metallurgy, a number of different offices were involved in the program.

34. See Williamson 1975 and 1985. Williamson also provides a strong critique of the "inside contracting" arrangements that were widely used by U.S. corporations in the late nineteenth century. It should be noted, however, that in China before 1949 similar contractual arrangements were a widespread mechanism for handling internal management of firms too large for proprietor-based management. Hence, for various social and cultural reasons, internal contracting may be more viable in China than it was in the presently industrialized countries.

References

Beijing Review. Weekly magazine.

Bhagwati, Jagdish N. 1982. "Directly Unproductive, Profit-seeking (DUP) Activities." *Journal of Political Economy* 90(5): 988–1001.

Buchanan, James M., Robert D. Tollison, and Gordon Tullock. 1980. *Toward a Theory of the Rent-Seeking Society*. College Station: Texas A&M University Press.

Byrd, William A. 1981. "Material Allocation Conferences in China's Industrial Supply System: A Significant Departure from the Soviet Pattern." Unpublished. Harvard University, Cambridge, Mass.

———. 1987a. "The Impact of the Two-Tier Plan/Market System in Chinese Industry." *Journal of Comparative Economics* 11(3): 295–308.

————. 1987b. *The Market Mechanism and Economic Reforms in Chinese Industry.* Ph.D. diss. Department of Economics, Harvard University, Cambridge, Mass.

————. 1987c. "The Role and Impact of Markets." In Tidrick and Chen.

————. 1989. "Plan and Market in the Chinese Economy: A Simple General Equilibrium Model." *Journal of Comparative Economics* 13(2): 177–204.

Byrd, William A., and Gene Tidrick. 1987. "Factor Allocation and Enterprise Incentives." In Tidrick and Chen.

The Hindu. Daily newspaper.

Jiao Xueshi and Zhang Keliang, eds. 1984. *An Gang Shi (1909–1948)* (A History of Anshan (1909–1948)). Beijing: Yejin Gongye Chubanshe.

Krueger, Anne O. 1974. "The Political Economy of the Rent-Seeking Society." *American Economic Review* 64(3): 291–303.

Liaoning Economic and Statistical Yearbook Editorial Committee. 1983. *Liaoning Jingji Tongji Nianjian 1983* (Liaoning Economic and Statistical Yearbook 1983). Shenyang: Liaoning Renmin Chubanshe.

Ling Yuxun. 1986. "Duanzheng Dangfeng, Jianchi Gaige, Fazhan you Jihua de Shengchan Ziliao Shichang" (Rectify Party Methods, Support Reform, Develop a Planned Market for the Means of Production). *Wuzi Guanli* (Materials Management) (April): 2–11.

Ministry of Metallurgy. 1985. *Zhongguo Gangtie Gongye Nianjian 1985* (China Iron and Steel Industry Yearbook 1985). Beijing: Yejin Gongye Chubanshe.

————. 1986a. *Statistics of Iron and Steel Industry of China 1986.* Hong Kong: Economic Information and Agency.

————. 1986b. *Zhongguo Gangtie Gongye Nianjian 1986* (China Iron and Steel Industry Yearbook 1986). Beijing: Yejin Gongye Chubanshe.

————. 1987. *Zhongguo Gangtie Gongye Nianjian 1987* (China Iron and Steel Industry Yearbook 1987). Beijing: Yejin Gongye Chubanshe.

Perkins, Dwight H. 1988. "Reforming China's Economic System." *Journal of Economic Literature* 26(2): 601–45.

Renmin Ribao (People's Daily). Daily newspaper.

Reynolds, Bruce L. 1975. "Central Planning in China: The Significance of Material Allocation Conferences." ACES *Bulletin* 17(1): 3–14.

State Statistical Bureau. 1985a. *1949–1984 Zhongguo Gongye de Fazhan Tongji Ziliao* (Statistical Materials on China's Industrial Development, 1949–1984). Beijing: Zhongguo Tongji Chubanshe.

————. 1985b. *Zhongguo Gongye Jingji Tongji Ziliao 1949–1984* (Statistical Materials on China's Industrial Economy 1949–1984). Beijing: Zhongguo Tongji Chubanshe.

————. 1986. *Statistical Yearbook of China 1986.* Hong Kong: Economic Information and Agency.

————. 1987a. *Zhongguo Gongye Jingji Tongji Ziliao 1987* (Statistical Materials on China's Industrial Economy 1987). Beijing: Zhongguo Tongji Chubanshe.

————. 1987b. *Zhongguo Tongji Nianjian 1987* (Statistical Yearbook of China 1987). Beijing: Zhongguo Tongji Chubanshe.

———. 1988. "Statistics for 1987 Socio-Economic Development." *Beijing Review* 3(10): I–VIII.

Tidrick, Gene, and Chen Jiyuan, eds. 1987. *China's Industrial Reform*. New York: Oxford University Press.

Williamson, Oliver E. 1975. *Markets and Hierarchies: Analysis and Antitrust Implications*. New York: Free Press.

———. 1985. *The Economic Institutions of Capitalism*. Cambridge, Mass.: Harvard University Press.

Zhong Huiran. 1987. "Shilun Wuzi Guanli Bumen Zhineng de Zhuanbian" (A Discussion on the Transformation of the Functions of Materials Management Units). *Wuzi Guanli* (Materials Management) (July): 25–26.

9

The Second Motor Vehicle Manufacturing Plant

William A. Byrd

RELATIVELY NEW among China's handful of truly large industrial firms, the Second Motor Vehicle Manufacturing Plant (hereafter referred to as Number Two) became the nation's largest truck producer in the 1980s, after a long period of preparation (1965–69), construction (1969–75), and initial trial production (1975–78). By 1987 it had become China's eighth-largest industrial enterprise in output value, sales revenue, and total profits and taxes; twenty-third in employment; and thirty-ninth in value of fixed assets (State Statistical Bureau 1989b, pp. 351–55). Number Two was a pioneer in various aspects of reform, and it set up a highly successful and widely acclaimed enterprise group, the Dongfeng (East Wind) Motor Vehicle Industry Associated Corporation (Dongfeng for short), which promoted partial rationalization of the Chinese truck industry.

Number Two's rise to the top of China's motor vehicle industry and its emergence as a model enterprise at the forefront of reforms are of great interest. Even more important, Number Two evolved into a largely autonomous, dynamic, commercially oriented business entity with a strategic vision and long-term perspective.[1] It engaged in extensive, largely self-determined expansion projects; entered into collaboration agreements with foreign truck and component manufacturers; aggressively increased market share, both directly and indirectly through the Dongfeng corporation; modernized technology and designs; partially relocated its production activities; and built up thriving associations with more than 200 smaller manufacturers of vehicles and components.

Overall, Number Two represents one of the most clear-cut success stories of Chinese state enterprise reform. Hence it is important to distill and to analyze the essential ingredients in that success, in order to ascertain whether and to what extent Number Two's experience can be replicated widely in Chinese industry. Although these questions may be impossible to answer definitively, this case study may suggest fruitful directions for future reform.

This chapter cannot hope to be comprehensive but rather centers around this main theme: how, from its unpromising, remote, and military-related beginnings, Number Two was able to become not only a principal actor in its industry but also an autonomous, business-oriented, and highly competitive entity that exhibited dynamism rarely seen in Chinese state industry. The first section of the chapter provides some general background on China's motor vehicle industry and a historical account of Number Two's development. The next section looks at the crucial area of administrative supervision—how the enterprise, gradually, over a period of time, and not without struggle, was able largely to cast off its administrative and financial ties to the government bureaucracy. The third section covers the related topic of planning and marketing controls, focusing on the freeing of a large part of Number Two's activity from mandatory planning and on the expansion of direct marketing by the enterprise. The fourth section analyzes Number Two's business orientation and strategy as well as the changing economic environment in which it operated. The Dongfeng corporation is discussed in detail in the following section. The last section returns to the chapter's central question and addresses the issue of the replicability of Number Two's evolution elsewhere in Chinese industry.

China's Motor Vehicle Industry and Number Two's Development

Number Two's emergence and subsequent highly successful evolution need to be understood in the context of the development and reform of the Chinese motor vehicle industry, to which it was a relative latecomer. The enterprise had a complex history in the 1970s and 1980s, which is also reviewed in this section.

The Motor Vehicle Industry in China

The history of motor vehicle production in China consists of the establishment and expansion of a few large manufacturers, along with several waves of proliferation of small plants, scattered throughout the country.[2] The industry concentrated mainly on production of trucks and, to a lesser extent, of other commercial vehicles; automobile production was negligible until the 1980s.

Truck manufacturing started in China in 1955. The First Motor Vehicle Manufacturing Plant, built in the 1950s with Soviet assistance in the northeastern city of Changchun, for a long time accounted for most of total national production. In the Great Leap Forward of 1958 and later, in the early 1970s, significant efforts were made to develop truck production on a provincial, even local basis. Localities set up numerous tiny assembly plants, many of which made no more than a few hundred units a year, and the industry spread to all provinces except Xizang (Tibet). By the end of 1978 there were 138 plants producing motor vehicles in China (Jiang 1986, p. 58).

Average production per factory was only slightly more than 1,000 units, well below that if the two largest producers are excluded from the calculations.

Growth of output, shown in table 9.1, was not unimpressive. Average annual growth of total national motor vehicle production between 1957 and 1988 was more than 15 percent; the growth rate in the 1980s (more than 14 percent a year) was hardly below long-term trends, although the base of existing production had become large by the 1980s. Since the mid-1980s the focus of development in the industry has been on automobiles and light trucks, as opposed to the traditionally emphasized medium-size (4- or 5-ton-capacity) trucks. Moreover, the mode of development has shifted from the prereform emphasis on self-reliance to aggressive acquisition of foreign technology through licensing, joint ventures, and other collaborative arrangements with foreign producers.

The main characteristics of the industry that Number Two joined in the late 1970s were the following:

1. *Excessively small scale of production and consequent high costs and inefficiency.* Average output per factory was far below minimum efficient scale. Many plants produced only a handful of vehicles per year, hardly any plants more than a few thousand. Diseconomies due to small scale were severe, and production costs were extremely high.

2. *Poor quality and backward technology.* The main product of the industry, the Jiefang, or Liberation, brand 4-ton truck, was based on a 1950s Soviet design that in turn followed the model of the American-made International of the 1930s. Other products (with the exception of those of Number Two, starting in the mid-1970s) seem to have been, if anything, even more backward in technology and even poorer in quality.[3] Until 1986 there was no significant modernization of the Jiefang design. Trucks used obsolete, energy-inefficient gasoline engines, and vehicles were subject to frequent breakdowns and to high maintenance costs.

3. *A highly dispersed location pattern.* All provinces except Xizang carried on some truck manufacturing activity by the mid-1970s. In 1981 all but four provinces in China were still producing motor vehicles, most of them in tiny amounts of several hundred to several thousand (State Statistical Bureau 1982, p. 245). The four relatively large producers (the Beijing-Tianjin and the Shanghai-Nanjing areas and the First and Second Motor Vehicle Manufacturing Plants in Changchun and Shiyan, respectively) were scattered among four different regions.

4. *Excessive integration of production within plants.* The tendency for factories to become "large and comprehensive" or "small and comprehensive" was pervasive in the Chinese industrial sector, and the motor vehicle industry was no exception. This tendency was particularly at odds with the technical requirements of production of motor vehicles because of the numerous different parts and components that go into a truck or a car. Lack of

Table 9.1. Number Two's Share in Total Output of Motor Vehicles in China, Selected Years, 1955–88
(units and percent)

Year	Total national output		Number Two's share of output[c]	
	All motor vehicles[a]	Trucks[b]	All motor vehicles	Trucks
1955	1,000	1,000	n.a.	n.a.
1957	7,900	6,200	n.a.	n.a.
1962	9,700	7,800	n.a.	n.a.
1965	40,500	26,500	n.a.	n.a.
1970	87,200	47,100	n.a.	n.a.
1975	139,800	77,600	1.1	1.9
1976	135,200	74,500	1.6	2.9
1977	125,400	75,900	1.2	1.9
1978	149,100	96,100	3.4	5.3
1979	185,700	116,700	7.8	12.5
1980	222,300	135,500	14.2	23.2
1981	175,600	108,300	21.4	34.6
1982	196,300	121,800	26.1	42.0
1983	239,800	137,100	25.1	43.8
1984	316,400	181,800	22.2	38.6
1985	437,200	269,000	19.1	31.0
1986	369,800	229,100	23.7	38.2
1987	471,800	298,400	22.7	35.9
1988	646,700	—	—	—

n.a. Not applicable.
— Not available.

a. Excludes motorcycles, scooters, mopeds, and so forth.

b. Complete trucks only. Data exclude truck chassis on which superstructures for various specialized vehicles were built.

c. Data are for completed trucks and trucks without superstructure that were sold to other factories. Hence the appropriate comparator is neither total national motor vehicle output nor total national truck output, but rather total national output of trucks plus truck chassis without superstructure. Because national statistics on the combination of items for the appropriate comparator are not available, ratios of Number Two's output to national motor vehicle output and to national truck output are given separately.

Source: State Statistical Bureau 1985b, p. 56; 1987b, p. 151; 1989a, p. III; 1989b, p. 350. Table 9.3.

specialization led to very small production runs for parts and components, which further raised costs. Most motor vehicle factories in China used craft rather than mass production techniques.

5. *Tight control over product distribution by the planning system.* Motor vehicles were highly prized commodities in prereform China. Their distribution was tightly controlled by central plans and, to a lesser extent, by ministerial and local plans. Output of large firms was in its entirety part of the

central plan promulgated by the State Planning Commission.[4] The smaller producers were dispersed as regards ownership and location, so a significant proportion of total national output was not allocated centrally. About three-quarters of total national output in 1978 was distributed under the central plan (see Lyons 1986b, p. 88, who cites a Chinese source). The remaining one-quarter, however, undoubtedly was tightly controlled by ministries, provinces, and localities.

In sum, the Chinese motor vehicle industry, despite its rapid growth, faced severe economic and administrative problems in the late 1970s. Large investments scattered over space and time had not yielded desired returns. The industry was left with a legacy of small (except for the First Motor Vehicle Manufacturing Plant), backward, overly integrated, and high-cost producers. The industry survived with automatic protection from imports, and it had virtually no export prospects. Efforts to reform, to rationalize, and to modernize the motor vehicle industry were high on the policy agenda.

Reform of the Motor Vehicle Industry

Much of the story of reforms in China's motor vehicle industry is told as part of the analysis of Number Two's experience. A few highlights can be mentioned here, however.

The main administrative reform in the motor vehicle industry was the creation of the national China Automobile Industry General Corporation (AGC) in 1982, to supervise centrally run enterprises and to undertake guidance and long-term planning for the industry as a whole. AGC was to play a commercial role as well as an administrative role, and this duality led to conflicts between AGC and the enterprises under its jurisdiction, such as Number Two. In early 1987 the central government decided to abolish AGC and to replace it with an industry association that would no longer exercise administrative supervision or function as an independent business entity. This policy change was a clear sign that AGC was considered to have failed.

Motor vehicle producers participated in state enterprise reforms of a more-or-less standard variety: profit retention, increased autonomy, bonuses for workers, and so forth. Reform implementation proceeded at about the same pace as it did in the rest of state industry. Number Two, which by the time of the reforms accounted for a substantial share of industry output, was given especially favorable treatment as regards profit retention starting from 1983 (see "Administrative Supervision," in this chapter).

Marketing reforms in the Chinese motor vehicle industry were first spurred by widespread excess supply in the aftermath of the investment cutbacks of 1981; subsequently they were pushed forward by conscious reform efforts, despite the return of a strong market situation. Direct marketing of trucks by their producers outside the plan grew substantially as a share of total output. This growth was in part related to a dramatic shift in the pattern of truck ownership after rural individuals were permitted to enter the transport trade and to buy trucks on their own accounts.[5] In the mid-1980s, trading centers for motor vehicles were set up in several large cities, at which trucks could be freely bought and sold at flexible, largely market-determined prices. By 1987, 53 percent of all motor vehicles and 58 percent of trucks produced in China were marketed by their producers outside the plan (State Statistical Bureau 1988, p. 471).

Opening up to the outside world was another conspicuous part of reforms in the motor vehicle industry, especially in the mid-1980s. Firms were encouraged to collaborate in various ways with foreign companies. Virtually all of the large producers and many of the smaller ones entered into such arrangements, for acquisition of technology, new designs, assembly of imported parts with indigenization of production over time, and so forth. In the area of foreign trade, exports of motor vehicles peaked at a very low level in 1981, when excess supply in the domestic market must have provided strong pressure to increase exports (see table 9.2). Exports of parts showed some tendency to increase, however. The tremendous boom of motor vehicle imports in 1984–86 is evident in table 9.2. In 1985, imports of motor vehicles more than doubled, reaching more than 350,000, and imports of fully assembled trucks increased by nearly 300 percent to more than 110,000. This surge of imports depressed the domestic market in 1986. Subsequently there was a sharp decline, but in the late 1980s imports were still much larger in absolute terms and as a share of national output than they had been in the early 1980s.

Significant efforts were made to rationalize industrial structure and the organization of production of parts and components. Attempts to accomplish this by closing down small, inefficient producers were half-hearted and unsuccessful. The more fruitful strategy involved specialization across firms as a means of improving efficiency, accomplished through the establishment of corporations such as Dongfeng that brought together numerous small producers and encouraged specialization of parts production, resulting in longer production runs and realizing economies of scale. Although dispersion of production remained a characteristic of China's motor vehicle industry, the emergence of Number Two meant that the large producers, who undoubtedly attained minimum efficient scale for truck production, still dominated the industry as regards output generated.

History of Number Two

Decisions on the construction and location of Number Two were intimately related to military considerations and to the difficult strategic situation China perceived itself to be facing in the late 1960s. The establishment of the enterprise was part of the Third Front strategy designed to render Chinese

Table 9.2. Automotive Imports and Exports in China, 1981–87

| | Motor vehicles and chassis | | Complete | Motor vehicle parts[b] | |
Year	Imports (units)	Exports (units)	trucks imported (units)[a]	Imports (millions of dollars)	Exports (millions of dollars)
1981	41,587	1,800	20,770	35.22[c]	10.85[c]
1982	16,077	522	7,730	58.65[c]	5.90[c]
1983	25,156	50	8,445	135.52[c]	0.37[c]
1984	148,743	285	28,047	166.52	13.94
1985	353,992	95	111,492	288.48	5.45
1986	150,052	315	64,570	277.08	31.54
1987	90,239	—	19,216	259.62	—

— Not available.

a. Data for 1981–87 are customs statistics. Data for selected years, 1950–80, reported by the Ministry of Foreign Trade, are as follows:

1950	2,000	1975	18,600
1952	1,800	1976	14,100
1955	12,800	1977	14,900
1957	1,600	1978	21,900
1962	2,400	1979	24,800
1965	6,200	1980	22,000
1970	10,500		

b. Not including vehicle batteries, for which exports were sometimes substantial.

c. Value in domestic currency, converted into dollars at the average exchange rate for the year.

Source: State Statistical Bureau 1983, pp. 416, 419, 435; 1984, pp. 392, 394; 1985a, pp. 505, 507, 516; 1986, pp. 489, 491; 1987a, pp. 527, 529; 1988, pp. 729, 731.

industry less vulnerable to military attack by either the United States from the south (from southeast Asia) or by the Soviet Union from the north.[6] The basic idea of this strategy was to set up a strong industrial base in remote areas that would be the last ones to be invaded and that also would presumably be hard to destroy from the air. The choice of the site for Number Two, Shiyan Town, in a remote, mountainous part of northern Hubei Province that was initially inaccessible by rail, is otherwise inexplicable. Because of the mountainous terrain and in view of strategic considerations, Number Two's production facilities were scattered across different valleys and caves, thus creating serious problems in production coordination and in the flow of materials. Number Two's location and siting resulted in sharply higher investment costs and in serious delays in construction. Another indication of Number Two's initial military orientation was that its first product—a 2.5-ton truck suitable for difficult terrain—was designed for military use.

Although Mao Zedong was reported to have raised the idea of building a second large motor vehicle producer in 1953 and again in 1958, Number Two's establishment was formally approved by the Central Committee of the Chinese Communist Party only in 1965.[7] It had been planned to start construction in 1967, but this schedule was interrupted by the Cultural Revolution, and work actually started only in 1969. In June 1971 the first assembly line was completed and began to produce trucks on a trial basis. Facilities with a designed annual capacity of 25,000 2.5-ton military trucks went into operation in June 1975. It was soon found that military demand was limited, and that Number Two would never erase its operating losses if it continued to rely solely on production for the military. In late 1977 top management decided to develop rapidly production of a 5-ton truck for civilian use; this truck was to become the enterprise's main product. After extensive preparations during the first half of 1978, the new model went into regular production in July of that year.[8]

Difficult site conditions explain much of the delay in construction. For example, the railway line leading to Number Two was completed only in 1975. The initial emphasis on production for the military, followed by the switch to a larger-model truck for civilian use, also must have contributed to delays. Poor project management, uneven timing of approvals and funding, and political uncertainties also slowed the progress of construction. Thirteen years passed between the time that construction of Number Two began in 1969 and the time that the plant reached the originally envisaged production capacity of 50,000 vehicles a year in 1982; the period between project approval and full-capacity production was seventeen years.

An example of policy-related difficulties that hindered Number Two's construction was Lin Biao's number 1 order of 1969, which stipulated that installations be completed urgently (presumably because of military considerations) and hence that equipment for these facilities be shipped out by their manufacturers as quickly as possible, regardless of whether it was in working order. One thousand eight hundred and fifteen pieces of equipment that had been sent to Number Two were subsequently discovered to be unusable and in need of further repair or renovation. Some of this equipment was still unusable in the early 1980s.

Number Two's construction drew on resources from all over China. Technology and manpower from the First Motor Vehicle Manufacturing Plant, especially managerial and technical personnel, were critical. Vehicle design came partly from this source as well, although there was also some incorporation of foreign designs. Number Two was a quintessential example of national self-reliance—only 2 percent of its equipment was imported. Overall, the enterprise's equipment and technology were broadly equivalent to world standards of the 1960s and hence represented a great advance over the 1930s-vintage technology then prevalent in the Chinese truck industry. This achievement came, however, at a very high cost in investment and time.

Once established, Number Two faced production and quality problems with its Dongfeng brand 5-ton truck. Because of high costs, the initial price of the truck had to be set somewhat higher than that of its main competitor, the Jiefang brand. In this environment, Number Two's early efforts focused on quality control and improvement and on rapid expansion of production. Both of these efforts were successful. Growth of production is shown in table 9.3. Between 1978, the first year of regular production, and 1980, Number Two's total vehicle output increased more than fivefold, and the value of spare parts production rose by 280 percent. Number Two devoted considerable attention to quality control during this period (State Economic Commission 1983, pp. 198–208). By the early 1980s Number Two's reputation for quality had improved so much that management asserted that its trucks were more accepted by users than were the vehicles produced by the First Motor Vehicle Manufacturing Plant. Substantial cost reductions allowed the enterprise to reduce its output price to a competitive level.

The next stage of development of Number Two encompassed the market difficulties of 1981–82 and the establishment of the Dongfeng corporation. The enterprise dealt with the problem of weak demand by seeking out new markets, most notably among rural individuals; by aggressively promoting sales through measures such as the granting of installment credit; and by further strengthening its customer orientation. Output continued to increase

Table 9.3. Physical Output of Number Two, 1975–87
(units, unless otherwise specified)

Year	All motor vehicles[a]	Engines sold commercially	Spare parts (millions of yuan)	Vehicles for associated units[b]
1975	1,502	250	3.54	n.a.
1976	2,185	162	4.52	n.a.
1977	1,452	50	5.13	n.a.
1978	5,120	50	13.75	n.a.
1979	14,541	100	21.71	n.a.
1980	31,500	543	38.93	n.a.
1981	37,503	480	47.26	1,525
1982	51,171	580	52.26	2,430
1983	60,106	—	—	3,000+
1984	70,173	—	—	—
1985	83,431	—	—	—
1986	87,592	—	—	—
1987	107,000[c]	—	—	—

n.a. Not applicable.

— Not available.

a. Data include drivable undercarriages (chassis and engines) to which superstructures were added elsewhere. Number Two's production of such vehicles totaled 2,040 in 1980 and 29,432 in 1985.

b. Data are for production by the Second Motor Vehicle Factory in association with the Dongfeng corporation.

c. Datum is an estimate.

Source: State Statistical Bureau 1985b, p. 141; 1985c, p. 307. Hubei Statistical Bureau 1988, p. 357. Information provided by the enterprise.

rapidly, from 31,500 vehicles in 1980 to 51,171 in 1982 (table 9.3). In April 1981 Number Two established the Dongfeng corporation, initially involving eight associated enterprises. Dongfeng rapidly increased its membership and economic activity, serving as a vehicle for expanding of Number Two's market share and also as a means of promoting partial rationalization of the industry (see "The Dongfeng Corporation," in this chapter).

The subsequent period (1982–85) was one of strengthening market conditions and, partly as a consequence, serious conflicts between Number Two and the planning and administrative hierarchies. The establishment of AGC in May 1982 led to frictions, because AGC was more a rival to Number Two (and to Dongfeng) than it was a purely administrative supervisory agency. During this period Number Two reversed a sharp decline in its share of directly marketed vehicles that had occurred in 1983. Even more important, Number Two gained considerable de facto autonomy from its government supervisors during this period. Its independence was officially acknowledged by its designation as an entity directly under the central plan in September 1984 and by a similar designation for the Dongfeng corporation in 1986. Number Two's "victory" over AGC was formally consummated by AGC's demise in early 1987. Output growth continued at rapid rates through 1985, reaching more than 83,000 vehicles in that year (table 9.3).

Market difficulties returned in 1986, because of a tremendous increase in imports in the previous year (see table 9.2). Number Two dealt with market problems more successfully than did other producers and achieved some growth (about 5 percent). Rapid growth resumed as market conditions improved in 1987. In the mid- to late 1980s Number Two aggressively pursued foreign collaborations and began to locate substantial production facilities, including a new diesel engine plant, at Xiangfan City, also in northern Hubei but much better situated than was Shiyan as regards terrain, accessibility, and transport. These developments were part of a more general and highly ambitious effort by Number Two to position itself at the forefront of China's motor vehicle industry, to outmaneuver the First Motor Vehicle Manufacturing Plant (which had come out with a new design of its own in 1986), and to become internationally competitive.

Number Two's financial performance improved dramatically over time. The enterprise ran large operating losses, in addition to its huge investment costs, until 1978. Losses peaked at more than Y50 million in 1976 but were erased by 1978 as a result of the rapid growth of production. Profits rose sharply thereafter, reaching Y620 million by 1985. The ratio of profits to total assets surpassed 10 percent in 1982 and was more than 20 percent in the mid-1980s (table 9.4). As can be seen in table 9.5, Number Two's financial indicators were not outstanding in relation to those of other important motor vehicle producers; if anything they fell a bit below average. Most of the other enterprises shown in the table, however, produced highly profitable light trucks.

Producers more comparable to Number Two were the First Motor Vehicle Manufacturing Plant and, to a lesser extent, the Nanjing Motor Vehicle Factory; Number One's financial indicators benefited from its old, low-value capital stock. Comparisons of labor productivity are distorted by differing degrees of vertical integration. Overall, Number Two has distinguished itself from the rest of the Chinese motor vehicle industry more by its rapid expansion than by its financial performance.

This expansion is reflected in the growth of Number Two's assets, as is shown in table 9.6. Fixed assets were already substantial by 1975, and, with further investment, largely financed by enterprise retained funds and bank loans, they more than tripled (in terms of original value) by 1986. The enterprise's labor force did not increase nearly as rapidly as did fixed assets (table 9.7), in part because large numbers of people employed as construction workers, most of whom stayed on and became production workers, apparently were counted in the total in 1975.

Overall, Number Two's history after the mid-1970s represents an almost unmitigated success story. It is important to understand the key elements in this success and in particular the extent to which they were specific to Number Two or replicable in other firms.

Table 9.4. Financial and Productivity Indicators for Number Two, 1975–86

Year	Profit and tax rate on total assets (percent)	Profit rate on total assets (percent)	Rate of GVIO to fixed assets (percent)[a]	GVIO per employee (yuan)[bc]	Output of motor vehicles per employee (units)[b]
1975	−2.6	−2.8	6.8	1,248	0.04
1976	14.3	−4.7	7.0	1,467	0.05
1977	−3.0	−3.1	4.2	979	0.03
1978	0.7	0.1	13.9	3,761	0.12
1979	6.4	5.0	31.5	8,970	0.33
1980	12.5	9.9	58.2	17,491	0.66
1981	9.6	7.6	65.9	19,799	0.74
1982	17.0	13.3	84.9	25,553	0.96
1983	20.0	16.5	96.7	29,700[d]	1.09[d]
1984	23.7	19.1	109.3	35,000[d]	1.18[d]
1985	34.6	28.0	151.0	37,422	1.31
1986	27.8	21.0	109.2	38,122[d]	1.33[d]

GVIO, gross value of industrial output.

a. GVIO in current prices.

b. Data are based on year-end employment figures unless otherwise indicated.

c. GVIO in 1980 constant prices.

d. Data are most likely based on average employment figures for the year.

Source: State Statistical Bureau 1985b, p. 141; 1985c, p. 307; 1988, p. 410. Tables 9.3, 9.6, 9.7. Information provided by the enterprise.

Table 9.5. Performance Indicators for Large Motor Vehicle Factories, 1985

Factory	Output of motor vehicles (units)	Employment (persons)	GVIO per employee (yuan)[a]	Ratio of profits to total capital (percent)[b]	Ratio of export value to total output value (percent)	Ratio of net output value to capital (percent)[bc]
First	85,003	64,075	23,618	66.7	0.03	107.0
Second	83,431	61,266	38,767	30.6	1.80	47.3
Beijing Second	19,000	6,304	41,289	79.7	0.02	126.0
Tianjin	17,326	3,085	98,353	94.8	0.00	122.4
Nanjing	15,539	14,594	21,274	23.3	1.00	39.1
Shenyang	11,847	7,441	30,771	53.8	0.00	70.9
Jilin City	9,012	4,256	24,488	40.5	0.00	71.4
Beijing	9,000	6,955	28,351	87.4	1.40	89.2

GVIO, gross value of industrial output.

a. GVIO in 1980 constant prices.

b. Total capital consists of year-end net depreciated value of fixed assets plus average value of quota circulating assets (physical inventories and goods in process) during the year.

c. Net output value in current prices.

Source: Industrial census data. Information provided by the enterprise.

Administrative Supervision

Number Two's escape from the administrative shackles that tied it to the government bureaucracy was a gradual process, hard to pin down as regards precise timing or particular episodes. Number Two exhibited an independent orientation and a considerable degree of autonomy in decisionmaking relatively early; its 1980 initiative to continue on its own, after state investment was cut off, is one example. In the early 1980s the enterprise complained, however, about cumbersome, time-consuming procedures it had to go through in order to secure administrative approvals for investment projects and in order to obtain foreign exchange. The enterprise experienced numerous conflicts with supervisory agencies, which were often costly, time consuming, and debilitating in the short run. For the most part, however, Number Two came out ahead in these disputes, and increased its autonomy. Then, in the strongly proreform atmosphere of 1984–86, Number Two gained a large measure of independence from the government bureaucracy.

Number Two's Supervisory System

The construction of Number Two was initially under the supervision of a construction command established for that purpose in 1969. Earlier, a preparatory office had been set up in 1965, as had preparatory sections for Number Two's main subordinate plants. In 1972 a field leadership group was formed. In 1975, the year in which regular production started, management

Table 9.6. Year-end Assets of Number Two, 1975–87
(millions of yuan)

Year	Original value of fixed assets	Net value of fixed assets	Value of quota circulating assets
1975	721.06	710.10	213.69
1976	855.07	835.30	253.94
1977	969.30	945.16	265.89
1978	1146.46	1111.67	226.90
1979	1268.84	1211.27	255.07
1980	1439.40	1334.91	290.29
1981	1528.85	1368.89	309.26
1982	1596.69	1380.35	261.47
1983	—	—	—
1984	—	—	—
1985	2013.24	1572.77	633.73[a]
1986	2208.60	—	604.82
1987	2413.70	—	—

— Not available.

a. Average value during the year.

Source: State Statistical Bureau 1988, p. 410; 1989b, p. 352. Information provided by the enterprise.

of the enterprise was merged with the administration of Shiyan Town. The director of Number Two concurrently served as mayor of Shiyan. This arrangement apparently was changed only in 1981, when Number Two was placed under the supervision of the Motor Vehicles General Bureau under the Ministry of Machine Building.

The merger with Shiyan and other evidence indicate that in certain respects Number Two was subordinate to Hubei Province during the 1970s. For example, it was Hubei Province that designated Number Two as a participant in the experimental pilot program for expanded enterprise autonomy in 1979. Labor recruitment was under the supervision of the Hubei Provincial Labor Department. As one of the most important projects in the Third Front defense construction program, however, Number Two undoubtedly had close ties to the Third Front command as well as to the central government itself. Central government funds financed Number Two's construction, and its output was subject to distribution via the central plan. Although it was apparently not formally designated as Number Two's supervisory agency until 1981, the Ministry of Machine Building had played an important role before then.

Given this multifaceted structure of administrative control, it would appear superficially that Number Two functioned under a multiheaded leadership system. Management, however, voiced few complaints about this subject.[9] The large number of agencies whose approval was required for projects was resented, but these were mostly different central organizations rather than

Table 9.7. Employment and Wages for Number Two, 1975–87

Year	Year-end employment (persons)	Total wage bill (millions of yuan)	Average wage per worker (yuan)
1975	39,664	23.41	590
1976	40,719	24.06	591
1977	41,595	24.53	590
1978	42,503	27.19	640
1979	44,536	34.84	782
1980	47,885	39.07	816
1981	50,875	41.33	812
1982	53,062	45.24	853
1983	55,354	—	—
1984	59,605	—	—
1985	63,469	89.69	1,413
1986	65,810	111.52	1,695
1987	70,798	—	—

— Not available.

Source: State Statistical Bureau 1985b, p. 141; 1985c, p. 307; 1988, p. 410; 1989b, p. 351. Information provided by the enterprise.

local governments. Perhaps Number Two's lack of concern about multiheaded leadership was the result of the centralization that occurred in 1981, or perhaps the enterprise had, in most respects, been effectively under central supervision all along (as was implied by a deputy director of Number Two in late 1984). It is also possible that the lack of multiheaded leadership problems was simply a reflection of Number Two's relative independence from the government bureaucracy at all levels. Regardless of the cause, for all practical purposes Number Two was a centrally run enterprise after 1981, and multiheaded leadership was not a significant concern for it.

An extensive reform of the administrative supervisory structure for the motor vehicle industry occurred in May 1982 with the creation of the China Automobile Industry General Corporation (AGC). Carved out from the part of the Ministry of Machine Building that had previously been responsible for motor vehicles, AGC replaced that agency as Number Two's immediate bureaucratic supervisor and had jurisdiction over the other large, centrally run enterprises in the industry as well. AGC's dual role—it also served as a business-oriented economic entity—generated severe conflicts of interest. Contrary to the intentions of reformers, AGC behaved more like an administrative and business rival to Number Two than like a provider of advice and guidance to the enterprise. Moreover, AGC tried to use its administrative authority to derive financial and other benefits from Number Two's activities. Number Two did not need AGC for administrative help or protection, and the Dongfeng corporation served many of the functions that AGC ostensibly was to take on with respect to smaller firms.

AGC at least nominally had considerable administrative authority over Number Two. It determined the enterprise's mandatory plan output targets and related input allocations, based on aggregate targets and allocations for large truck producers handed down to it by the State Planning Commission. AGC also promulgated labor and wage plans for Number Two. Appointments to top leadership positions in the enterprise apparently were suggested by AGC, but final approval rested with the highest levels of the central government and Communist Party. Deputy directors and deputy party secretaries of Number Two were appointed by AGC. For a time, AGC also even asserted the right to appoint functional department heads; Number Two fought hard to have this authority rescinded. Profit distribution was handled directly by Number Two and the central government, so AGC was not involved. AGC, however, appropriated some of Number Two's funds in order to cover its own expenditures; these levies included 10 percent of depreciation funds, 3 to 5 percent of enterprise retained profits, and 0.05 percent of sales revenue (the last as a so-called management fee). Retained profits of Number Two accruing to AGC in 1985 were reported to have amounted to only Y500,000, and the management fee probably gathered an additional Y1.1 million. Although the amounts involved were relatively small, Number Two resented these levies.

Far more troublesome were AGC's intervention in Number Two's business affairs and its attempts to take lucrative business away from the enterprise. Another source of conflict was AGC's responsibilities toward other truck producers. For example, when the truck market was weak and enterprises were striving for higher rather than for lower mandatory plan targets in 1983, AGC apparently assigned the First Motor Vehicle Manufacturing Plant a higher target than it gave to Number Two.

Number Two saw AGC's involvement in the plant's affairs as counterproductive, with no redeeming features. Number Two's reaction to AGC was similar to that of other enterprises in the sample to supervisory government corporations that combined administrative, advisory, and business functions (see chapter 5 in this volume). The difference between Number Two's experience and that of the other enterprises is that Number Two was able gradually to overcome its supervisor (AGC) and gain greater independence as a result.

Within a period of about two years, Number Two won its struggle for independence from AGC in business decisionmaking. In September 1984, as a result of Number Two's repeated requests and of discussions between the State Planning Commission and AGC, Number Two was given a separate line item in the state plan, and AGC no longer served as an intermediary in the planning process. (The First Motor Vehicle Manufacturing Plant was given a similar status at that time.) In 1986 the Dongfeng corporation also was granted independent status under the state plan, which improved Dongfeng's organizational cohesiveness. Finally, in March 1987, it was announced that AGC was to be abolished and replaced by an industry association for the motor vehicle industry. The new entity would not exercise administrative supervision or function as an economic actor in its own right; instead it was to provide an information network, guidance on development planning, and related services.

After March 1987 Number Two and the Dongfeng corporation were left without any immediate administrative supervisory agency. The State Planning Commission of course determined mandatory plan targets, and there was still some vague relationship with the Ministry of Machine Building. Number Two was free from interventionist administrative supervision, however, and it achieved the autonomy in business decisionmaking that was one of the primary goals of state enterprise reforms. From well before 1987, Number Two had exercised a growing degree of independence in its operations.

Financial Self-Reliance and the Profit-Increase Responsibility System

The evolution of Number Two's financial relationship with the state reflected its growing autonomy. In particular, the central government's decision to discontinue investing in Number Two in 1979 and the enterprise's counter-proposal for self-financed development, which was accepted by the State Council in March 1980, must have had important effects, both psychological and actual, in weaning Number Two away from administrative supervision.

The government's refusal to continue funding construction was probably based on a number of factors, including sharp cutbacks in fiscal spending at the time, a possible desire to limit production of trucks to hold down energy consumption, and the general policy of switching from state grant financing to enterprise self-financing and loan financing of investment in existing firms. Number Two was in an awkward position, having already started regular production but still falling far short of capacity and needing substantial additional investments just to reach the designed output level of 55,000 vehicles a year. There is even some possibility that the central government considered Number Two to be unviable without additional investment and hence possibly subject to closure, although the option of closing the plant appears never to have been seriously considered.

The enterprise responded to the government's refusal to continue funding its investment with a series of counterproposals for completing its construction with self-financing. First, Number Two suggested that the unfinished investments be completed using the enterprise's operating profits. Although it was approved by the State Planning Commission, the State Economic Commission, and the State Capital Construction Commission, this proposal was rejected by the Ministry of Finance, presumably because of the forgone government revenue it would entail. Number Two's second suggestion, that half of the profits retained by the enterprise be used to finance construction, also was rejected. Finally, Number Two proposed to pool 40 percent of its retained profits, 70 percent of its retained depreciation funds, and 50 percent of its major repair fund in an "enterprise self-raised fund" for use in financing the remaining construction. Energy conservation loans and equipment loans from the People's Bank of China also were to be used. Number Two guaranteed that it would eliminate financial losses and would remit the stipulated amounts of profits and depreciation funds to the government. The State Council accepted this proposal and gave permission for Number Two to operate on this basis in 1980–85.

In 1979, like many other state enterprises, Number Two participated in an experimental profit retention scheme, under which the enterprise was to retain 22.7 percent of profits. This arrangement apparently continued until 1981.[10] The upward creep in the actual profit retention rate, from 20.9 percent in 1979 to 21.8 percent in 1980 and 27.1 percent in 1981, perhaps reflected higher retention rates from above-quota profits. Because total profits were increasing rapidly in line with growth of production (table 9.8), retained profits also jumped sharply.

In November 1982, following a visit by Wan Li and other government leaders the previous month, Number Two was put under a profit-increase responsibility system similar to that of the Capital Iron and Steel Company. Starting in 1983, Number Two was required to increase the absolute amount

Table 9.8. Profits and Taxes for Number Two, 1975–87
(millions of yuan)

Year	Total profits and taxes	Gross profits before income tax	Indirect taxes
1975	−24.26	−25.44	1.18
1976	−47.14	−50.66	3.52
1977	−36.01	−37.50	1.49
1978	8.95	1.31	7.64
1979	94.53	73.24	21.29
1980	202.91	161.47	41.44
1981	160.27	126.77	33.50
1982	279.72	219.13	60.59
1983	—	—	—
1984	—	—	—
1985	762.53	620.91	141.62
1986	617.86	—	—
1987	864.54	—	—

— Not available.

Source: State Statistical Bureau 1985b, p. 141; 1985c, p. 301; 1988, p. 410; 1989b, p. 355. Information provided by the enterprise.

of its profit remittance to the state by 7 percent a year, from a 1982 base of Y140 million.[11] In 1983, following a visit by then-Premier Zhao Ziyang, the profit-increase responsibility system was extended to 1990. Because output and total profits were growing much more rapidly than 7 percent a year, the system built in a rising profit retention rate and a sharply increasing absolute volume of retained profits for Number Two. (Total profits increased at an average annual rate of 41.5 percent between 1982 and 1985—see table 9.8.) Rough calculations indicate that the profit retention rate rose from 23.6 percent in 1982 to 72.4 percent in 1985; a large portion of retained profits, however, may have been used for loan repayments. If the system functioned as stipulated in late 1982, retained profits increased from Y51.65 million in that year to nearly Y450 million in 1985. The base for profit remittances was increased by 16 percent to Y200 million in 1986. Its rate of increase in 1986–90 was, however, to remain the same as in 1983–85, at 7 percent a year.

The post-1982 profit retention scheme was very lucrative for Number Two. Many other state enterprises wanted to be put under similar arrangements, but few were granted permission to use the profit-increase responsibility system. Because of the higher and increasing rate of inflation in the mid-1980s and because of greater freedom from price controls, the targeted 7 percent annual rate of increase in profit remittances continued to be highly beneficial to Number Two.

Thus, overall, Number Two gained the fortuitous combination of financial independence and a high level and share of retained profits. The greatest part of retained profits Number Two used for investment in expansion, improving the enterprise's development potential and further increasing its financial resources. The profit-increase responsibility scheme reflected favorable treatment of the enterprise by central government authorities. By 1982–83, however, Number Two clearly was already embarked on the path of progressively increasing independence from the government supervisory system. Although the profit distribution arrangement undoubtedly facilitated Number Two's movement down this path, it did not have a determining influence in this regard.

Planning, Supply, and Marketing Controls

The weakening of mandatory planning and Number Two's increasing control over the distribution of its own output formed a crucial part of the enterprise's more general evolution toward independence from administrative supervision. Although mandatory planning continued to account for a substantial share of Number Two's total output in the late 1980s, that share was declining rapidly in the face of rising production. Ingenious methods of obtaining material inputs that could not be supplied by the planning system also increased Number Two's autonomy.

Evolution of Direct Marketing, 1981–87

Before 1981 all of Number Two's output was subject to mandatory plan allocation. Although the supply of trucks fell far short of demand, Number Two
initially faced problems in gaining acceptance with users, because of problems
with quality, high prices, and lack of recognition of its Dongfeng brand name.
Nevertheless, because all output before 1981 was centrally allocated, the main
hurdle Number Two had to overcome was certification of its product by the
authorities.

Market conditions changed drastically in 1981. A sharp cutback in state
investment reduced funding for users with plan allocations for trucks. Moreover, the perceived energy shortage in the early 1980s led to an attempt
to hold down truck production, and limits were imposed on the number
of trucks enterprises could buy.[12] Originally, central government planning
and material supply agencies had intended to procure Number Two's entire
targeted 1981 output of 39,000 units as part of the plan, but cutbacks in
funding and difficulties in the market induced them to reduce their procurement to less than half the original level. In some cases users had to refuse
plan allocations for lack of funds.

In the end Number Two was forced to market on its own 20,000 of its
1981 realized total output of 37,500 vehicles. The enterprise engaged in
aggressive sales promotion and sought out new customers; through extraordinary efforts it was able to sell all 20,000 units, 7,000-odd of them on credit.
(Number Two apparently was provided additional circulating capital loans
by the banking system to cover these sales.) Thus, within one year, the
share of directly marketed output at Number Two jumped from zero to 53
percent (see table 9.9).

In early 1982 market conditions remained weak: although Number Two's
mandatory plan output target was 50,000 vehicles, assured procurement by
the State Material Supply Bureau (MSB) through the central plan was initially
only 20,000 units. Consequently, Number Two continued its aggressive sales
promotion efforts. After the first quarter of the year, however, plan-sanc-
tioned demand firmed up, and orders were received for all output within
the mandatory plan.[13] In the meantime Number Two had signed other sales
contracts for some of this output.

Total orders in 1982 (plan and nonplan) hence exceeded total output,
and 8,679 vehicles allocated as part of the central plan could not be delivered. Because these vehicles had been produced with raw materials supplied
through the plan, MSB asserted that Number Two owed a "debt" of 8,600-odd
vehicles to the state material supply system that it must pay out of 1983
above-plan production. Number Two, for its own part, argued with some
justification that it had contracted the outside-of-plan sales at a time when
the central planning system was not guaranteeing procurement of production
under the mandatory plan. This dispute dragged on for a period of time

Table 9.9. Direct Marketing for Number Two, 1980–87

Year	Total output (units)	Directly marketed output (units)	Share of directly marketed output in total output (percent)
1980	31,500	0	0.0
1981	37,503	20,000	53.3
1982	51,171	30,000	58.6
1983	60,106	10,000	16.6
1984	70,173	15,000	21.4
1985	83,431	28,500[a]	34.2
1986	87,592	32,500[a]	37.1
1987[b]	107,000	56,000[c]	52.3

a. The mandatory plan target for Number Two was reported to have remained constant at the 1984 level of 55,000 motor vehicles in 1985 and 1986.

b. Data are estimated.

c. In the middle of 1987, enterprise management reported that the mandatory plan quota was being reduced to 51,000 motor vehicles.

Source: Table 9.3; information provided by the enterprise; author's estimates.

and provides an indication of the strength of conflicts over distribution in the Chinese system; it also illustrates Number Two's tenacity. The disagreement was finally resolved in October 1983. Number Two was forced to make up only 2,000 units of the backlog; the central planning system in effect recognized the remaining 6,600-odd vehicles as within-plan sales of 1982.

In 1983 and 1984 market demand was very strong. A State Economic Commission circular of early 1983 stated that direct marketing of trucks by Number Two would be limited to 10,000 vehicles of within-plan production. (All vehicles produced outside the mandatory plan presumably could be directly marketed.) Actual direct marketing in 1983 was only about 10,000 units. In 1984 total output increased by 10,000 vehicles, but the mandatory plan was raised by only 5,000; hence directly marketed output rose by 50 percent. The strong proreform atmosphere in 1984 probably played some role in the expansion of direct marketing. Moreover, from 1984 onward, the increase in direct marketing was officially sanctioned, whereas it had been ad hoc and dependent on weak demand in 1981–82.

Number Two's direct marketing after 1984 seems to have grown by the same absolute amounts as did total production, given constancy or near-constancy in the absolute amount of output subject to mandatory planning. By 1987 the share of direct marketing was more than 52 percent (table 9.9), compared with 53 percent for the motor vehicle industry as a whole. Number Two's direct marketing share was probably higher than were those of other large, centrally run motor vehicle producers, such as the First Motor Vehicle Manufacturing Plant.

Conflicts with Material Supply Authorities

The expansion of direct marketing and the sharp decline in the share of mandatory planning were not frictionless for Number Two. The conflict over the debt of trucks owed from 1982 is discussed earlier; its resolution largely in favor of the enterprise's position seems to have been the typical pattern. There were a number of other disputes between Number Two and government authorities over distribution of output, some of which are discussed below. Unlike similar conflicts affecting other large enterprises in our sample (see chapters 5 and 8 in this volume), these seem to have strengthened Number Two's position as well as its desire for increased autonomy. The reasons behind these outcomes are obscure, but Number Two's perception that it was fighting rival entities rather than superiors, none of which had developed a true patron-client relationship with the enterprise, might have played a role, as might possibly have political support for the enterprise from the central government leadership.

As mentioned earlier, both sides in the conflict over the debt of trucks owed to MSB put forward logical arguments from their own points of view. Number Two would seem to have had the stronger case on substance, however, as it had sold off trucks produced within the mandatory plan only because procurement by the material supply system was not guaranteed. It was clearly unfair of MSB to demand that these trucks be repaid afterward, when it had not been willing to procure them beforehand. Since the trucks concerned were already gone, there was little that MSB could do to enforce its demand, short of taking drastic measures that inevitably would have affected Number Two's entire production under the mandatory plan. Supplies of inputs were severely constrained in 1982–83, and MSB itself undoubtedly faced an awkward situation with regard to users that had been allocated trucks through the central plan in 1982 but had not received them.

In the dispute between AGC and MSB over dump trucks, Number Two was the victim of a struggle between government agencies. Perceiving dump trucks to be in short supply, Number Two had made an exception to its usual practice and produced about 1,000 of these specialized vehicles. They were originally intended to be part of the mandatory plan, but MSB, fearing it would be unable to sell the dump trucks, was initially reluctant to procure them. In this situation AGC made a bid to control their distribution. When it came out that demand for dump trucks was in fact ample, MSB insisted on procuring them under the mandatory plan. The trucks stood idle in Number Two's lot for months while the argument went on. Eventually the conflict was resolved in MSB's favor: AGC was not allowed to control distribution of any trucks produced under the mandatory plan. Perhaps as a result of this experience, Number Two did not again produce dump trucks or other specialized vehicles, instead leaving this activity entirely to other members of its Dongfeng corporation.

In 1983 AGC tried to take control over distribution of all spare parts produced by Number Two. Enterprise management strongly resisted this, because production of spare parts was profitable—profit margins were often as much as 10 percent higher than were those on complete vehicles—and because it was trying to promote sales and to improve its reputation with customers by providing spare parts and servicing at its own service centers. The interim resolution of this conflict was that AGC would control distribution of two-thirds of Number Two's output of spare parts, and the enterprise itself would distribute the remaining one-third. Number Two was not happy with this arrangement and expected further changes as part of reforms in 1984.

There were some common themes in these conflicts. Supervisory authorities acted largely as self-interested entities promoting their own benefits and protecting their own interests, with little regard for Number Two. MSB in particular seems to have acted primarily to protect itself from losses that might result from its inability to sell the output it procured. Not surprisingly, after market conditions firmed up in 1982–83, MSB became an advocate of a high share of mandatory planning. The behavior the supervisory agencies exhibited must have brought them down to Number Two's level, in the enterprise's own perceptions. As a result these disputes seemed to Number Two more like administrative rivalries among equals than like conflicts between different levels in a well-defined hierarchy.

Another striking feature of these conflicts is that in the end Number Two came out on top. Although its initial position was not confirmed in every case, compromises were generally closer to Number Two's stand than they were to that of the other disputant in the conflict. The extent to which such outcomes stemmed from the inherent strength of Number Two's case, the plant's increasing autonomy and administrative power, or intervention by patrons at the higher, political level is hard to ascertain and probably varied in each instance. Although they were costly and time consuming in the short run, these conflicts were not seriously harmful to Number Two; indeed, they reinforced its independent tendencies.

Acquisition of Supplies

Number Two faced shortages of some inputs it needed for production under the mandatory plan, and it had to obtain inputs for above-plan production on its own. Given China's highly imperfect, administratively restricted producer goods markets in the early 1980s, Number Two had to use special methods to obtain supplies. These methods can be divided into several categories.

Exchange of above-plan output for needed inputs was sometimes called "processing of materials on behalf of customers," but in actuality it involved tying sales of trucks produced outside the plan to purchases of stipulated amounts of inputs in short supply, most commonly rolled steel. Especially because Number Two did not let the prices of its trucks produced outside the plan rise by a large margin, such exchanges helped maintain profits by holding down the cost of inputs. Exchanges started in 1983, when Number Two's trucks were in such demand that they commanded scarce raw materials in return.

Exchange did not, however, account for a very large proportion of directly marketed output. The total number of trucks exchanged for raw materials was 2,895 in 1983 (29 percent of total directly marketed output) and about 5,300 in 1984 (35 percent of directly marketed output). Exchanges in 1984 were not limited by supply of trucks or willing purchasers; they were stopped when Number Two obtained all the materials it needed through exchange and instead preferred to earn higher profits through untied cash sales at higher prices.[14]

Trucks were most commonly exchanged for rolled steel, which was expensive on the market. In 1983, 2,895 vehicles were exchanged for the following amounts of various materials: 22,100 tons of rolled steel, 20 tons of tin, 969 tons of zinc, and 19,000 tons of coal. It was reported that a truck would trade for 15 to 25 tons of rolled steel, depending on the specifications of the steel. Rolled steel consumed for each motor vehicle produced at Number Two in 1982 was only 3.6 tons.[15] Hence far more of the material than was needed in production would be exchanged for each truck. Because of this slack, some of the materials Number Two needed for production within the mandatory plan but not supplied through the plan also could be arranged through exchange of above-plan output.

In another form of exchange, Number Two was able to swap one of the by-products of its operations, scrap steel, for a needed input, pig iron. The enterprise was allocated through the plan a sufficient quantity of pig iron for within-plan production, but the quality of about half of it was too poor to use in motor vehicle production. Hence Number Two simply refused to purchase that part of its allocation (produced by the Wuhan Iron and Steel Company and by the Chongqing Iron and Steel Plant). Number Two apparently did not or could not barter these plan quotas for something of value— other needed inputs, financial benefits, and so forth. The remaining half of Number Two's state plan allocation of pig iron, from the Linxian Steel Plant, was of superior quality and was suitable for production of motor vehicles. Number Two also had an exchange arrangement with Linxian outside the plan, through which it exchanged its scrap steel for additional pig iron. Although Number Two had a mandatory target for scrap steel that it had to deliver to the state, this target was stagnant in absolute terms even while production was growing rapidly; hence the enterprise was left with large quantities of surplus scrap steel that it could provide to Linxian.

Purchase of inputs at high market prices occurred on an ad hoc basis, especially when only a small quantity of some item was required. Mindful of its profit performance, however, and of the need to meet profit remittance targets, Number Two avoided excessive use of this channel, particularly if the market price exceeded the plan price by a large margin (in the case of rolled steel, for example). Sometimes inputs could also be purchased from state material supply agencies outside the plan, but the purchases carried additional "handling charges."

Number Two resorted to compensation trade most prominently in the case of tin from Yunnan Province in 1984. After some experience, Number Two's management came to consider compensation trade as a cumbersome method, without any assurance of returns. Hence, unlike some other firms, Number Two did not use compensation trade as a primary means of acquiring needed inputs.

Number Two's severely limited foreign exchange resources dictated that it could make substantial purchases of imported materials only with the release of foreign exchange by Hubei Province or by some other government entity, which did occur from time to time. (Indeed, explicit or implicit exchange of vehicles for foreign exchange quotas sometimes was involved.) Moreover, in the early 1980s Number Two could borrow foreign exchange from the China International Trust and Investment Corporation to pay for imported inputs. These loans could be repaid in domestic currency, at the then-current internal settlement rate of Y2.8 to $1.

It is interesting that Number Two did not extensively utilize various other channels for obtaining inputs outside the plan, most notably backward integration. With the exception of its construction of an electric power plant in 1985, Number Two made no efforts to integrate production of important raw materials, of other inputs, or of investment goods. It did not construct a steel-rolling mill, a cement plant, or other similar facilities. Instead, Number Two built up an extensive network of suppliers of parts and components, although the critical parts of its vehicle were all produced in-house. The Dongfeng corporation provided a convenient mechanism for coordinating production of parts and components without full integration (see "The Dongfeng Corporation," in this chapter). It is possible that through Dongfeng, Number Two gained some of the advantages other Chinese state enterprises sought through integration.

The Decline of Mandatory Planning

The sharp fall in the share of Number Two's output that was subject to mandatory plan allocation after 1983 (see table 9.9) reflects near-constancy in the absolute level of mandatory plan targets in the face of sharp increases in Number Two's total production. These trends were related partly to inherent tendencies of the planning process in Chinese industry, in particular to the tendency to "plan from the achieved level." Targets tended to be maintained at constant levels or were adjusted upward only slightly over time, resulting in sharp increases in above-plan output for fast-growing enterprises such as Number Two. Shortages of raw materials accessible to the planning system made it difficult to increase mandatory plan targets of downstream producers, because these producers would reject plan output targets not accompanied by allocations of inputs. From 1984 onward, conscious reform efforts also played a role in holding down mandatory plan targets.

Among industry-specific factors in the decline of mandatory planning, the shift in the pattern of truck ownership toward rural individuals may have been important. Moreover, motor vehicles were singled out, as was rolled steel, for development of the market mechanism in 1985 (Xia 1985, p. 4). A number of truck trading centers were established in major cities, at which trucks could be freely bought and sold at flexible prices. Producers such as Number Two were allowed to sell their above-plan output at these centers and to reap at least part of the benefits from higher market prices.

General or industry-specific factors are insufficient in themselves, however, to explain Number Two's escape from the shackles of mandatory planning. Number Two's aggressive pursuit of greater independence from the plan and possible support from the Chinese political leadership also contributed, as did Number Two's size and rivalrous rather than hierarchical relationships with bureaucratic superiors. As noted in the preceding section, Number Two's increasing freedom from mandatory planning was paradoxically related to the enterprise's designation as an entity directly under the state plan in 1984.

Business Environment, Strategy, and Practices

Previous sections of this chapter concentrate on the administrative environment Number Two faced and on how the enterprise freed itself from bureaucratic subordination to supervisory agencies. During that process, Number Two was also evolving highly competitive business practices and a forward-looking strategy that enabled it to expand rapidly and to occupy a large share of the domestic truck market. This section looks at the business side of Number Two's success—its market environment, its competitive strategy, its internal management, its personnel practices, and so on. (The associations with other enterprises Number Two organized through the Dongfeng corporation and the use of the corporation as a vehicle for furthering Number Two's long-term strategic goals are discussed in "The Dongfeng Corporation," in this chapter.)

Changing Market Conditions

The domestic market for trucks was the single most important part of the business environment Number Two faced. Trucks are durable investment goods for which there is considerable flexibility as regards precise timing of purchases, especially in the case of replacement demand, so cyclical and other fluctuations in demand are only natural in any country, and these can have severe effects on producers. In China natural sources of instability from the demand side were augmented by administrative interventions on both demand and supply sides. On the demand side, sudden cutbacks in administratively sanctioned investment demand, such as the one that occurred in 1981, were followed by relaxations and by investment booms. Administrative restrictions on purchases of vehicles or on access to fuel sometimes also affected demand.

Government interventions also seriously affected the supply side. Administrative controls may have had some effect on expansion of production as well as on investment by domestic motor vehicle producers. Provision of inputs through the plan also affected supply. The most destabilizing factor affecting the Chinese motor vehicle industry in the mid-1980s, however, was changing government policy toward imports. Administrative restrictions on imports of cars and trucks were relaxed in late 1984; combined with increases in foreign exchange resources in the hands of local governments and, to a lesser extent, of enterprises, this relaxation generated a tremendous import boom. Balance of payments problems led to a severe tightening of import controls in 1985–86. Because users preferred imported vehicles to domestic products, fluctuations in imports caused great instability in residual demand for domestically produced motor vehicles.

The destabilizing effect of imports on domestic supply is shown in table 9.10.[16] Net imports varied between 7 percent and 45 percent as a share of total domestic supply of motor vehicles, and fluctuations in imports were a leading determinant of fluctuations in domestic supply. Domestic production did not respond quickly to changing domestic demand, so fluctuations in imports tended to have drastic effects on the domestic demand-supply balance. The sharp cutback in imports of motor vehicles in 1982, for example, reinforced the effect of rebounding demand by generating a slight decrease in domestic supply despite rapidly rising domestic production. The 1984–85 import boom expanded domestic supply so much that it exceeded demand by a large margin in 1985. In response, domestic production declined, with a lag, in 1986, at which time, together with the drastic cutback in imports in that year, it caused a great tightening of domestic supply. In sum, changes in imports exacerbated rather than ameliorated domestic demand-supply imbalances.

Number Two faced a changing, unstable market for its products. It faced a weak market at least three times before 1987: (1) in the late 1970s, when it tried to establish itself as a mass producer; (2) in 1981–82, during the period of readjustment and significant investment cutbacks; and (3) in 1986, when it faced a flood of imported trucks. The uncertain and unstable market seems to have stimulated positive responses by Number Two. The enterprise clearly did not act as if it faced a chronic sellers' market. In fact, the unstable

Table 9.10. China's Domestic Supply of Motor Vehicles, 1980–87

Year	Domestic production (units)	Imports (units)[a]	Exports (units)[a]	Domestic supply (units)[b]	Share of domestic supply (percent) Domestic production	Net imports	Number Two
1980	222,300	40,000[c]	1,000[c]	261,300	85.1	14.9	12.1
1981	175,600	41,587	1,800	215,387	81.5	18.5	17.4
1982	196,300	16,077	522	211,855	92.7	7.3	24.2
1983	239,800	25,156	50	264,906	90.5	9.5	22.7
1984	316,400	148,743	285	464,858	68.1	31.9	15.1
1985	437,200	353,992	95	790,877	55.3	44.7	10.5
1986	369,800	150,052	315	519,537	71.2	28.8	16.9
1987	471,800	90,239	300[c]	561,739	84.0	16.0	19.0

Note: Data ignore the contribution of changes in inventories of motor vehicles to domestic supply, substantial in certain years, because of a lack of information about these changes.

a. The foreign trade figures most comparable with figures for domestic production of motor vehicles are those for imports and exports of motor vehicles and chassis.

b. Domestic supply equals domestic production plus imports less exports.

c. Estimated by author.

Source: Tables 9.1, 9.2, 9.3.

market and Number Two's aggressive growth strategy seem to have effectively substituted for a sustained buyers' market (see chapter 3 in this volume) in stimulating appropriate responses. The core of Number Two's competitive strategy was aggressive expansion of market share, even in a rapidly growing market, achieved through high investment and output growth as well as through development of the Dongfeng corporation. With such ambitious objectives, Number Two had to be responsive to the needs of customers and to the dictates of market demand, regardless of whether there was a temporary shortfall of demand in relation to total industry supply. Different aspects of Number Two's competitive strategy are explored in the following discussion.

Competitive Strategy

Number Two's competitive strategy was shaped both by its ambitious long-term objectives and by its market environment. The objectives included:

1. To become China's premier motor vehicle producer, through rapidly expanding production, through increasing market share, and through offering a superior product at a low price
2. To engage in comprehensive modernization of the enterprise's technology and production process
3. To move toward achieving full international competitiveness
4. To promote the rationalization and modernization of China's motor vehicle industry as a whole.

These objectives, combined with the aforementioned market situation and a dynamic management team, led to the development of a distinctive strategy that was essentially competitive in nature. Number Two's actions were increasingly oriented toward the market and toward customers, but its strategy was dynamic in that it did not take the current market situation, industrial structure, product structure, cost structure, or technology for granted. Instead the enterprise strove to move ahead in these areas and to build up and to maintain a lead over its main competitor, the First Motor Vehicle Manufacturing Plant.

The specific elements of Number Two's competitive strategy as it evolved in the 1980s were (1) an overriding concern for quality; (2) strong emphases on cost reduction and on competitive product pricing; (3) product improvement; (4) provision of postsale services and spare parts to customers; (5) aggressive product marketing; (6) development of new products and a wider range of product lines; (7) technological modernization, in large part through foreign collaborations; (8) an attempt to break into export markets for vehicles and for parts; (9) inculcation of a corporate ethos and pride in the work force; (10) partial relocation to a superior production site; and (11) development of close ties with related producers and suppliers through the Dongfeng corporation. With the exception of the last one, these elements are discussed in this section.

Good quality and other desirable product attributes allowed Number Two to position itself as China's best domestic truck producer; this position enabled the enterprise largely to avoid residual supplier status. Regardless of overall market conditions for trucks, Number Two was strongly motivated to come out with a product better than those of other domestic producers. From early on, Number Two laid great emphasis on quality control. In the early 1980s a focus on quality was built into the enterprise's internal management structure and incentives. Number Two's reputation for the quality and reliability of its products came to surpass that of the First Motor Vehicle Manufacturing Plant. Together with the higher load capacity of Number Two's trucks (5 tons as opposed to 4 tons) and their competitive price, this reputation for quality resulted in greater demand for Number Two's trucks.

Although additional research would be needed to permit a more definitive conclusion, on the surface it appears that Number Two paid great attention to cost reduction. That production costs declined sharply in 1975–80 is perhaps not surprising, because of the rapid growth of the plant's output over this period. Cost declines continued in 1981 and 1982, however, despite the much larger base of existing production in those years. Financial indicators suggest that cost declines may have been sustained subsequently, or at least that improved efficiency slowed the inevitable rise in costs that would have resulted from inflation. Moreover, production costs declined by a greater margin than would be expected solely from economies of scale, suggesting that Number Two was eliminating preexisting slack and waste, or was making genuine cost-reducing innovations, or both. The total decline in production costs of comparable products (a synthetic measure) between 1975 and 1982 was nearly 59 percent. The unit production cost of the Dongfeng 5-ton truck fell at an average annual rate of nearly 8 percent in 1978–83 (Jiang 1986, p. 298).

Falling unit costs permitted Number Two to reduce its ex-factory price by a considerable margin. Originally fixed at Y27,000 per truck, the price was reduced to Y25,000 in 1980, to Y23,000 in 1981, and finally to Y19,500 in 1982. These substantial reductions came largely at the initiative of Number Two. The enterprise made its own calculations and suggested a new price; approval by the relevant government agency, the State Price Bureau, appears to have been pro forma.[17] Prices were cut aggressively, by nearly 28 percent in 1980–82, to gain a competitive advantage over the First Motor Vehicle Manufacturing Plant. Number Two's price was still slightly higher than that of its main competitor in 1982, but it was offering a more modern, higher-capacity, and energy-efficient truck.

Marketing and a strong market orientation were very important in Number Two's competitive strategy. Before 1981 there had been virtually no marketing effort as such, given unified procurement of all output under the state plan. In 1981–82 the weak market for trucks forced Number Two to take stringent measures to promote sales, including emphasizing quality improvement and cost reduction, partly through new internal management incentives (see the ensuing discussion); improving fuel efficiency for truck engines (reducing gasoline consumption by 10 percent); increasing the number of product varieties offered; searching for new sources of demand, such as individual rural traders and transporters; making sales on credit, financed with additional loans from the People's Bank of China; and providing repair services and spare parts at numerous technical service centers established by Number Two around the country under the aegis of the Dongfeng corporation. These measures and, more generally, the strong customer orientation inculcated in the plant in the early 1980s were successful in easing demand constraints for Number Two, even when the domestic market was weak. Most of these practices and the plant's overall market orientation survived the return of the sellers' market for trucks in 1982–83.

The weak market of 1986 induced further changes in Number Two's approach to marketing. Previously the enterprise had relied on local government machinery and electrical equipment sales corporations to market its trucks in their localities, but these corporations turned out to be unreliable and inadequate when market demand was weak. Number Two in 1986 began setting up its own separate marketing network, a step that apparently required the approval of the State Planning Commission. The enterprise planned to establish marketing corporations in important cities and to convert some of its technical service centers in smaller cities into sales outlets. The new corporations would be under the joint supervision of Number Two's Dongfeng corporation and the local governments in the marketing areas they served. Unlike the machinery and electrical equipment sales corporations, these new entities would exclusively market Dongfeng products.

A distinctive feature of Number Two's market-oriented strategy was its emphasis on both product improvement (quality improvement and introduction of new features and varieties) and cost reduction. There seems to have been less emphasis on advertising, sales promotion through agents, and promotion at trade fairs in the strategy, although these mechanisms might have been used as well. Customer orientation and marketing strategy improved Number Two's competitive position over the longer run, and did not merely provide short-term benefits. Number Two also defended the interests of its customers, when the occasion arose, in conflicts with government agencies.

Another part of Number Two's competitive strategy was exports. Starting in 1982 Number Two gained the right to export its products directly, without having to go through the foreign trade bureaucracy.[18] Exports of trucks totaled 150 in 1982 and were said to have risen to about 1,500 vehicles a year in 1983 and 1984.[19] Number Two's total foreign exchange earnings from exports, including proceeds from export of spare parts, dies, and so forth, as well as vehicles, were $2.33 million in 1982, up from less than $1 million in 1981 and $285,000 in 1980. Annual exports in 1983–84 might have totaled about $10 million. By 1985 the enterprise's total value of export sales had surpassed Y45 million ($15.3 million valued at the average official exchange rate for that year). Exports accounted for a minuscule share in total output value, however—1.8 percent in 1985 (table 9.5). This share was nonetheless by far the highest among those of China's large motor vehicle producers.

Exporting not only tested the international competitiveness of Number Two's products but also brought in much-needed foreign exchange. Number Two was permitted to retain 40 percent of its foreign exchange earnings starting in the second half of 1983. (Previously the foreign exchange retention rate had been raised, first from 8–10 percent to 16 percent and then to 20 percent.) Retention of foreign exchange earnings was related to Number Two's status as an independent direct exporter, but its retention rate was much higher than were those allowed for other firms with similar export rights.

Modernization of technology formed another critical part of Number Two's competitive strategy. Modernization was motivated both by a general concern to promote technological advance in the Chinese motor vehicle industry and by Number Two's strong desire to expand its market share; it was also an integral part of the enterprise's rivalry with the First Motor Vehicle Manufacturing Plant. Modernization was linked with an aggressive pursuit of foreign collaborations. In the early 1980s Number Two complained that it was difficult for it to obtain approvals for joint ventures and other forms of collaboration with foreign companies. Constraints seem to have been eased enough subsequently to allow the enterprise to engage in a whole set of ventures to acquire technology from abroad. These ventures included a collaboration with Cummings Engine (of the United States) for diesel engine technology and assistance; the licensing of gearbox technology from a large German manufacturer; an equity joint venture with the Thomson company for production of thermostats; possible collaboration with the Ford Motor Company in the production of light trucks; and many others. With only one exception (the joint venture with Thomson) these associations involved licensing or other similar forms of technology acquisition, without equity investment by the foreign partner.

Number Two's foreign collaborations reflect its strong commitment to technological modernization as well as its decision to pick and choose technology from different sources so as to learn and to control the technologies acquired. Without additional research it is impossible to make a technical assessment of Number Two's modernization effort, but its ambitious yet seemingly well-thought-out character is evident. Number Two's own research and development base, of course, was not insignificant.

The enterprise's foreign collaborations also reflect its general strategy of developing new products and of broadening the product lines it offered. Number Two was moving into production of light trucks and wanted to develop automobile production, in addition to executing its plan to make heavy trucks. Foreign collaborations provided opportunities for the enterprise to enter new market segments with technologically advanced products. Number Two faced resistance from the government bureaucracy, however, to its attempts to develop automobile production.[20] Some important switches in production still required government approval.

A final aspect of Number Two's competitive strategy was related to its highly inappropriate initial location. Top management developed a long-term program for shifting activities from Shiyan to Xiangfan, another city in northern Hubei Province, 210 kilometers to the east of Shiyan, which has superior terrain, infrastructure, transport, and so forth. This shift occurred primarily through new investments at Xiangfan rather than through relocation of existing activities; Number Two's high investment and rapid output expansion meant that extreme measures, such as shutting down some of the existing activities at Shiyan, were probably unnecessary. It appeared that Number Two planned to locate the production facilities for a new, relatively advanced diesel truck model entirely at Xiangfan, and that it would continue to produce the 5-ton gasoline model at Shiyan. Light truck and automobile production, should they get under way, were definitely not to occur at Shiyan. Facilities to produce vehicles for export might be built in a coastal area. The heart of the enterprise's operations will gradually shift from Shiyan to Xiangfan, even if production at Shiyan is not abandoned. Number Two will improve its competitive position considerably by escaping to a large extent from its disadvantageous location.

Number Two's dynamism and aggressive expansion strategy are evident in the medium- and long-term plans it devised to guide its efforts in the 1980s (see Jiang 1986, pp. 76–100). It put together a perspective plan covering the period to the year 2000, a seven-year plan for the period 1984–90, three-year plans, and annual plans. Number Two's main objectives for the 1980s were to engage in technological modernization at the old Shiyan site and to build a new production base utilizing advanced technology at the Xiangfan site. It aimed to establish an annual production capacity of 200,000 vehicles by the early 1990s. Actual production in 1990 was to reach 140,000, a target that would not be hard to surpass because 1987 output already exceeded 100,000 units. Ten new vehicle types and 110 varieties of specialized vehicles were to be developed by 1990, including light trucks, automobiles, and buses. Diesel engine production was to be developed on a large scale. The plant also had ambitious goals pertaining to training and recruitment of engineers and technical personnel.

Despite these ambitious plans, Number Two seems to have been relatively responsible and market oriented in its investment behavior. Its expansion drive, although manifest, appears not to have been the typical blind expansion drive found in centrally planned economies. For example, in 1985 Number Two actually reduced its medium-term investment plans, from Y1.5 billion to something in the range of Y1.2 billion to Y1.36 billion, although the higher figure had already been approved by government authorities. Productive investments were cut back, as were nonproductive investments in workers' facilities, apparently with the approval or at least acquiescence of employees. More generally, Number Two seems to have been able to avoid the most blatant forms of worker-oriented or shortsighted behavior in its distribution of surplus.

Rivalry with Number One

The importance of market conditions and of Number Two's aggressive expansion in influencing enterprise behavior in the Chinese truck industry is shown in the experience of the First Motor Vehicle Manufacturing Plant (Number One). Number One's relationship with Number Two is perhaps best characterized as one of friendly rivalry. The two enterprises cooperated with each other in various ways. Number One provided extensive technical assistance and large amounts of skilled and professional manpower to Number Two during the latter's construction phase. Number Two helped Number One with engine design and with dies for Number One's new truck model that was put into production at the end of 1986. But Number Two's management asserted in 1987, however, that henceforth it would not provide substantial assistance to Number One.[21] From the late 1980s onward the relationship of the two enterprises may have been increasingly rivalrous.

By all indications, Number Two increasingly prevailed against Number One in competition in the domestic truck market. In 1980 Number One had a 29.7 percent share of total domestic motor vehicle production, Number Two only 14.2 percent. By 1985 Number Two had increased its share to 19.1 percent, while Number One's share had declined to 19.4 percent. In 1986 Number Two's production surpassed that of Number One for the first time, and in 1987 Number Two consolidated its position as China's largest truck producer; it had a share of 22.7 percent in total domestic motor vehicle output, whereas Number One's share slid to 13.1 percent. Until 1987 Number Two was offering a superior, price-competitive product, and its postsale services (maintenance, repairs, spare parts, and so forth) were probably also superior to those of Number One. Number One's new truck model, which appeared on the market in early 1987, undoubtedly helped to equalize the situation. Number Two had major investment projects under way, however, and was developing new products that probably would restore its superiority over Number One.

Number One in many ways typifies the traditional Soviet model of a large enterprise subject to central planning. Designed and constructed with massive Soviet assistance (including a large number of Russian advisers stationed at the site) in the 1950s, Number One became imbued with the orientation and culture of central planning, which was thoroughly ingrained in the following decades. Its shift to a market orientation came much later and was more hesitant, limited, and passive than was Number Two's. For example, Number One moved rapidly to put its new truck design into production only after the truck market became saturated and its old product became unmarketable in 1986. Faced with these extreme difficulties, Number One responded with alacrity and reconfigured its production line so that regular production of the new vehicle could begin within three months. The technological level of Number One's new truck was somewhat more advanced than was that of Number Two's 5-ton model, demonstrating that, under severe market pressures, Number One quickly made up a technological lag of thirty-odd years. It is not clear, however, whether Number One's belated market orientation was affected by the tightening market for trucks in 1987.

Number One also developed an enterprise group of its own, in imitation of Dongfeng. Number One's group seems, however, not to have been as successful as was Dongfeng, and Number One does not appear to have promoted its group very strongly until the national campaign to promote enterprise groups started in 1986. The obstacles Number One's enterprise group faced were similar to those Dongfeng faced (see "The Dongfeng Corporation," in this chapter), but Number One appears to have made less progress in overcoming them.

The rivalry between Number One and Number Two stimulated positive responses from both. There was no sign in the late 1980s of collusion between them to divide the Chinese truck market or to otherwise limit competition, although Number Two did avow it had no intention of putting Number One out of business. Number Two took on members for the Dongfeng corporation even in Number One's own backyard of Jilin Province, providing some indication of the rivalry between them. In this rivalry, Number Two typically was the aggressor and Number One took a defensive posture. The demise of AGC probably increased competition in the motor vehicle industry. Number Two's aggressive efforts to expand market share kept up competitive pressure on itself and on the other producers, even during periods of relatively tight market conditions.

Internal Management

Number Two's competitive strategy extended to internal management. In the early 1980s the enterprise decentralized internal management and provided financial incentives to lower-level units. In line with the profit-increase responsibility system promulgated in November 1982, Number Two instituted the so-called "two comprehensives" internal responsibility system on April 1, 1983, under which lower-level units were assigned targets for technical and economic indicators that were based on comprehensive quality control work on their part. This system made quality control a primary focus of internal management.

Targets were disaggregated down to the smallest work units and even to individuals. All rewards were to depend on quality control and on quality of output as preconditions. There were targets or quotas to be fulfilled in seven areas: (1) production and profit, (2) quality and variety, (3) technical standards, (4) technical innovation and modernization, (5) safety, environment, and workers' livelihood and education, (6) management standards, and (7) workers' attendance. Subunits also had to assure satisfaction of downstream work units or customers, services to and cooperation with other subunits, conformity with enterprise management standards, and fulfillment of special directives issued by the enterprise.

Specific arrangements were made with different kinds of work units. Production units were divided into three categories: commodity production plants, which sold finished goods inside or outside the enterprise; semifinished goods producers; and service units. Functional departments also were divided into three categories. Some schemes called for lower-level units to hand over a fixed amount of profits to headquarters, others for a fixed proportion of lower-level units' total profits to be remitted, or sometimes there was a higher retention rate from above-quota profits. Internal transfer prices had to be set for all goods transacted between subunits. No details are known about price determination, but it was cited as a source of friction between headquarters and subordinate units. By and large, subordinate factories and other units were to use 70 percent of their retained profits for reinvestment, 20 percent of them for workers' collective welfare, and only 10 percent for bonuses.

The two comprehensives system was modified into a system of three comprehensives at the beginning of 1984. The main change was the introduction of comprehensive technological progress and economic performance targets. There was also greater systemization and longer-term targeting in the new system. Number Two's headquarters signed seven-year contracts with each of its subordinate factories, covering the period 1984–90. Factories' profit remittances were to increase by 13 to 15 percent a year, much faster than Number Two's own remittances to the government. Stipulations on usage of retained profits by lower levels seem to have been left unchanged. The decentralization of incentives to work units that began under the two comprehensives scheme was systematically implemented. Workshops generally had simpler sets of targets and incentives than had the subordinate factories.

The new system emphasized two aspects: comprehensive technological modernization and level-by-level contracting and responsibility. The system was supported by significant expansion of Number Two's discretionary authority in 1984; by some important changes in mind-set (see Jiang 1986, p. 51) that focused greater attention on the goals of the system—quality control, technological progress, and economic performance; by further decentralization of decisionmaking authority to the subordinate factories; and by reduced and streamlined administrative procedures.

By the late 1980s Number Two's management was showing awareness that internal decentralization could pose severe problems if it were taken too far. Management recognized that profits of subordinate factories, based on transfer prices, did not necessarily coincide with the factories' investment needs. Hence control over substantial investments did not devolve to lower-level units. Factories' investments were financed in part by their own retained profits, but their projects had to be approved by headquarters. Only a small portion of subunits' retained funds (3 percent) was under their discretionary control. Headquarters also took control of subunits' bonus funds after 1984–85, when bonuses had threatened to go out of control. Thus, particularly after the mid-1980s, Number Two's internal decentralization was a measured, cautious, limited process.

Labor and Wages, Human Resource Development, and Corporate Ethos

Although Number Two, like other Chinese state enterprises, exhibited some manifestations of worker-oriented behavior, the family motive was not a driving force behind its strategies and actions. On the whole, Number Two's personnel, labor, and compensation practices appear to have been geared mainly toward furthering the enterprise's long-term strategic objectives rather than toward addressing workers' short-term interests. Evidence supporting this hypothesis comes from the findings of a survey, probably conducted in 1987, which indicate that 50 percent of a sample of Number Two's work force were not highly motivated and that more than 34 percent of it believed that workers' status in the enterprise had deteriorated.

Number Two's worker orientation was most obvious in its obligation to provide jobs for workers' children. In 1984 roughly a third of the enterprise's total labor force consisted of children of workers. Among the 1,500 new employees recruited in 1983 were at least 400 who were workers' children. (Two hundred others were hired "from society," 500 were university and vocational school graduates assigned to Number Two, and nearly 400 were demobilized People's Liberation Army soldiers; some of the workers in these categories may also have been children of workers.) Before 1979 Number Two had taken on some workers' children as "nonquota" workers, who worked alongside regular employees. This mixing was criticized by the central government, so the enterprise segregated the nonquota workers in a number of subordinate collective enterprises. By 1984 there were fifty-six such units, with a total of more than 9,000 employees, two-thirds of whom were children of workers, the remaining one-third peasants whose land Number Two had occupied. The contributions of the collective sector to employment and to output were, however, small in comparison with those of the collective sectors of large enterprises in northeast China (see chapters 5 and 8 in this volume).

Number Two provided good benefits and rapidly increasing wages to its workers (see table 9.7). The wage bill did not, however, represent much of a financial sacrifice for Number Two, because of the enterprise's rapid growth and fast-rising profits. Moreover, in the early 1980s management refrained from giving full bonuses allowed under state ceilings so as to allow gradual increases in bonuses over time.[22] Bonus payments in 1981 were equivalent to 2.5 months' average basic wages, 2.6 months' in 1982, and 2.9 months' in 1983. Management appears to have recognized that exclusive emphasis on individual material incentives is not the best method of strengthening worker motivation in a large, integrated enterprise.

The labor system at Number Two was basically similar to those of other large state industrial enterprises, and its evolution during the late 1970s and the early to mid-1980s was probably not too different from the norm. Number Two appears to have only dabbled in democratic forms of worker participation that did not mean much in practice. Management complaints about the rigidity of the labor system in the early 1980s were broadly similar to those voiced by other enterprises in the sample, but this rigidity did not hinder rapid growth and improved performance. As of 1987 Number Two had not yet implemented any scheme involving linkage between the size of its total wage bill and total enterprise profits and tax payments, presumably because such a scheme was not considered consonant with the profit-increase responsibility system. The enterprise wanted to be put under a linkage scheme, although in any case it was cautious about new hiring.

Number Two made strenuous efforts to improve the quality of its human resources, through education and training within the enterprise as well as through new recruitment. Management in the early 1980s perceived a severe shortage of professional and technical personnel, which it tried to ameliorate through various in-house training programs and through education in outside technical institutions for several hundred employees. Inadequacies in the quantity and quality of engineers and technicians were also problems (Ding and Xu 1983). Recruitment of qualified people was difficult, so there was great reliance on in-house training. Moreover, much new recruitment in the early 1980s consisted of workers' children, whose qualifications may not have matched management's desires. Finally, management objected to being forced to take on so many female workers, a complaint virtually universal among the enterprises in the sample. For the most part the objection was without foundation as regards work requirements, but extra leave and other benefits for women workers might have led managers to consider them a heavier financial burden.

Perhaps the most interesting aspect of internal management at Number Two were its broad approach to worker motivation and its conscious efforts to instill a corporate ethos in the work force. Workers were meant to internalize the goal of developing the best motor vehicle plant in China. Management also tried to instill in workers a long-term rather than a short-term orientation and a sense of pride. This approach is obviously related to the emphasis on quality control that permeated internal management from early on, but it was also applied more generally. Lower-level managers and professional personnel were encouraged to internalize an enterprise-oriented attitude. Because of the general attitudes of workers in Chinese state industry, Number Two probably faced an uphill battle in this area, but even the attempt to motivate workers in this way says a great deal about the vision and dynamism of the enterprise's top management.

The Dongfeng Corporation

The establishment of the Dongfeng Motor Vehicle Industry Associated Corporation and its successful development was the most visible reform at Number Two, and it received nationwide publicity. From a relatively small beginning in April 1981, the corporation expanded rapidly with regard to both its membership and its activities. It served not only as an instrument for increasing Number Two's market penetration and its stature but also as a mechanism for promoting partial rationalization of the truck industry. The development of Dongfeng also helped strengthen Number Two's autonomy from the government hierarchy, in that it was a new administrative structure under the enterprise.

Motivations for Establishment

Several motives for Number Two's establishing Dongfeng can be discerned, some of them based on the narrow self-interest of Number Two and of its associated firms and others not. The new corporation was seen by its members and by government authorities as a means of rationalizing the structure of the motor vehicle industry in China. In a situation in which it was extremely difficult to close down plants, Dongfeng could promote rationalization through specialization by smaller plants in the production of specific parts or in the assembly of customized vehicles. This specialization would help the industry move away from the excessive integration of activities within firms that was pervasive in the prereform period. The new corporation would, it was also hoped, reduce the insulation between different provinces and localities. Number Two itself was overly integrated in many respects, so a related goal of Dongfeng was to disperse part of Number Two's own production of certain parts and components.

A primary motivation of many small plants (and of the local governments to which they belonged) for joining Dongfeng was to improve the plants' performance and to stem the fiscal drain caused by their chronic losses (China Economic Yearbook Editorial Committee 1986, p. VIII-1). In the late 1970s and the early 1980s, many small-scale truck manufacturers faced extinction because of the lack of demand for their products. Providing some productive activities for these firms, such as assembly of trucks from kits provided by Number Two, was the immediate motivation for some initial associations formed even before 1981 (Jiang 1986, p. 59).

Another goal of Dongfeng was better coordination of the production and the flow of goods among firms. Trucks are assembled from a large number of parts and components that are made of many different materials, with many different processes. The specialized production of many of these parts and components by smaller firms would seem to be an economically efficient mode of organization, in view of international experience in the motor vehicle industry. In China, however, highly imperfect, administratively restricted markets gave rise to severe problems with coordination in situations in which numerous firms were involved in a particular production and assembly process. Thus a coordinating entity such as Dongfeng could play a useful role, while avoiding some of the inefficiencies usually associated with central planning.

Diversification of Number Two's product structure was still another important objective. Number Two saw the new corporation as a means of involving itself, at least indirectly, in the growing and lucrative market for specialized vehicles. These vehicles were built up from standard engine and chassis sets, and their superstructures were customized to fit their intended uses, such as fire fighting, street cleaning, watering or spraying, and various kinds of construction work. Specialized vehicles were typically produced in fairly short runs, in small operations that used labor-intensive methods. Number Two did not have a comparative advantage in this field, and its unpleasant experience with the production of dump trucks (see "Administrative Supervision," in this chapter) must have dissuaded it all the more from moving into this area. This activity was, however, suitable for Number Two's numerous smaller associated factories.

The establishment of Dongfeng undoubtedly was intended to improve Number Two's competitive position in the Chinese motor vehicle industry. The founding of Dongfeng had the effect of increasing Number Two's (direct and indirect) market share, as well as, at least potentially, the assets and the resources that the enterprise could bring to bear in market competition. Dongfeng also brought Number Two greater visibility and administrative clout. The corporation served as a useful counterweight against hierarchical supervision—the supervision Number Two itself faced and the local government interference the members of Dongfeng experienced.

Dongfeng became intimately related to the politics of economic reform in China. Its establishment was viewed as an important experiment with a new form of organization. Top government leaders praised Dongfeng at various times. The new corporation's success spawned a host of imitators and undoubtedly was a factor in convincing authorities to go ahead with national campaigns that promoted horizontal associations and enterprise groups (these enterprise groups, in particular, were modeled after Number Two) in 1986–87. In taking on responsibility for this experiment and especially in succeeding at it so well, Number Two built up considerable political capital.

As can be seen in this discussion, Number Two's motivations for its establishment of Dongfeng were complex and were not exclusively linked to its immediate short-run interests. On the contrary, Number Two made some financial sacrifices on behalf of Dongfeng in the short run. There is no evidence, however, that Number Two was pressured to start the new corporation against its will.

The short-run financial sacrifice of Number Two is most evident in its supply of engine-and-chassis sets to Dongfeng's associated factories at the relatively low price of Y14,000 each (as of 1983), compared with the (then-current) price of Y19,500 for a completed Dongfeng truck. The price charged for the engine-and-chassis sets probably exceeded the production cost by about 10 percent, so Number Two was still making profits in these deals. The enterprise's forgone profits were substantial, however, because the profit margin on complete trucks was about Y5,000 to Y6,000 a vehicle and that on many of the specialized vehicles was Y8,000 to Y10,000 a vehicle. In 1983 Number Two supplied a total of about 5,400 engine-and-chassis sets to associated factories of Dongfeng, 2,400 of these sets within the state plan and 3,000 of them outside the plan. Hence the financial sacrifice in forgone profits was about Y27 million (at Y5,000 a vehicle). Because the binding constraint on Number Two's own production in the early 1980s was its output of truck engines, this was a genuine sacrifice; although Number Two could not have produced large quantities of highly profitable specialized vehicles, it certainly could have increased production of standard trucks. The kits supplied to the associated factories for assembly before and during the early years of Dongfeng also were favorably priced. Number Two often paid other Dongfeng members higher prices for parts and components they supplied than its own cost of producing them. Finally, the technical assistance and guidance Number Two provided from its own resources undoubtedly had substantial costs.

Regardless of the precise costs Number Two incurred, Dongfeng turned out to be a highly successful investment, in that Dongfeng improved Number Two's competitive position, its market share, its coordination of production and supply, and its visibility in China's reform effort. Number Two also was not indifferent to the fortunes of the industry and particularly to those of its small associated producers.

Origins and Development, 1978–87

As early as 1978, when its own production of 5-ton trucks was just getting under way, Number Two's top leadership considered entering into associations with other firms. At the beginning of the year Number Two sent a team out to four provinces (Hubei, Sichuan, Guangdong, and Guangxi) to investigate the motor vehicle industries there and to hold discussions with factories and local supervisory bureaus. There was a general feeling that a reorganization of the industry's structure was needed. In June 1978 an initial meeting on associations was held by Number Two and authorities of the four provinces. The meeting came out with some suggestions for reform. Moreover, it made some preparations for an association for manufacture of motor vehicles. (These preparations predated the central government's policy of encouraging such relationships, which was promulgated in 1980.)

Assembly of kits supplied by Number Two was the initial activity of the associated enterprises. At first, eight firms participated: motor vehicle producers in Hangzhou, Guangzhou, Liuzhou, Hanyang, Guizhou, Yunnan, Xinjiang, and Chongqing. Number Two supported these firms by giving them a price preference of 10 percent in comparison with the price of finished vehicles. The assembled trucks carried the Dongfeng name, which at that time had not yet built up a good reputation. In subsequent years, the impetus for formalizing the relationship between Number Two and its associated enterprises and for setting up a corporation appears to have come from the eight associated factories as well as from Number Two itself; government authorities were not the driving force. On April 8, 1981, with the approval from the State Machine Building Industry Commission and other agencies, the Dongfeng Motor Vehicle Industry Associated Corporation was inaugurated, with nine members including Number Two.

Initially Dongfeng's main activity continued to be assembling from kits supplied by Number Two. Because there was a demand shortfall for Number Two's own vehicles during this period, however, the associated factories continued to face problems. Dongfeng engaged in a nationwide survey of vehicle users and found that although ordinary trucks were in excess supply, demand for various kinds of specialized vehicles still exceeded supply. Thus the associated factories were encouraged to move into production of specialized vehicles, which they did quickly. This shift solved the factories' demand problems and also ameliorated those of Number Two, which simultaneously gained a ready market for its engine-and-chassis sets.

After this initial success, numerous other small manufacturers of motor vehicles and producers of parts and components clamored for membership in Dongfeng. When Number Two was given a separate line item in China's state plan, demand for membership increased further. Dongfeng had to turn away applicants and could afford to scrutinize them very closely on financial viability and on development prospects. This selectivity strengthened the corporation as a whole.

As can be seen in table 9.11, the corporation developed rapidly after 1981, as regards membership, numbers of provinces included, and output. Member factories engaged in more activities, and there was an increase in the general level of specialization. Producers of parts and components also came to be included as members, and the original members of the group and other motor vehicle manufacturing plants that joined it later began to specialize in the production of different parts or subassemblies, such as engines and chassis. By 1987 the number of Dongfeng's associated factories had increased to 202 (including Number Two), located in twenty-four different provinces. Total employment was more than 150,000; GVIO was Y3.4 billion. Although as a group they were still dwarfed by Number Two, the other Dongfeng factories taken together formed a substantial part of China's motor vehicle industry. In 1984, for example, Dongfeng accounted for 28.4 percent of total Chinese motor vehicle production (including Number Two's share of 22 percent). By 1987, Dongfeng's total vehicle output had increased to more than 120,000 units. In the mid-1980s the medium-term objective for the Dongfeng corporation was production of 50,000 vehicles annually (excluding Number Two's output) by 1990.[23]

At least partly in recognition of its success, the Dongfeng corporation was given independent status in China's state plan in 1986. This status gave its subunits greater autonomy and more ability to adapt to the needs of the corporation. Independent status under the state plan was a rare privilege that most other enterprise groups formed in 1986–87 did not get.

Even discounting the tendency to exaggerate the achievements of a model entity in press reports, the history of the Dongfeng corporation has been a striking success story. In numerous cases its factories were able to move from financial losses and inadequate demand for their products to viable activ-

Table 9.11. Profile of the Dongfeng Corporation, 1981–87

Year	Enterprises (number)	Provinces (number)	Output of complete vehicles (units)[a]	Output of specialized vehicles (units)[b]	Employment (persons)	Original value of fixed assets (millions of yuan)	GVIO (millions of yuan)
1981	8	8	2,713	5,572	—	—	—
1982	34	14	3,828	7,577	—	—	—
1983	65	18	4,482	13,047	—	—	—
1984	108	20	15,586	15,038	—	—	—
1985	125	21	—	—	125,000	1,220	2,160
1986	163	24	—	—	—	—	—
1987	201	24	—	—	155,000	—	3,360

GVIO, gross value of industrial output.

— Not available.

Note: Data exclude the independent activities of Number Two.

a. Vehicles manufactured entirely by the associated factories.

b. Vehicles specialized for various purposes (fire trucks, street cleaners, refrigerated trucks, water trucks, and so forth) whose superstructures were added by associated factories, based on engine-and-chassis assemblies from Number Two or from other associated factories.

Source: China Economic Yearbook Editorial Committee 1986, pp. VIII-1, VIII-2; Jiang 1986, pp. 60, 70; information provided by the enterprise.

ities and increasing profits within a few years of having joined the Dongfeng corporation. One example is the Yunnan Motor Vehicle Factory in Kunming. Its own brand of truck was of poor quality and high in price, and production was halted in 1980. When it joined Dongfeng as one of the founding members, it gradually shifted to assembly of Dongfeng trucks and a truck especially built for use in mountainous terrain. It also helped thirty local factories in the Kunming area develop related production. Another enterprise, the Guizhou Motor Vehicle Factory, switched to specialized production of engines for Dongfeng trucks produced by the associated factories, and it built up an annual production capacity of 3,000 engines by the end of 1983. The Liuzhou Motor Vehicle Factory in Guangxi Province made losses of Y590,000 in 1981 that its membership in Dongfeng turned into profits of Y1.44 million in 1982 and of more than Y10 million in 1985.

Increasing specialization undoubtedly resulted in substantial cost reductions for the associated factories. The return on capital in the associated factories apparently was even higher than was that of Number Two. In 1985, GVIO generated per Y100 net value of fixed assets was reportedly Y151.6 at Number Two and Y271.9 in the associated factories. Profits per Y100 net value of fixed assets were Y39.5 at Number Two and Y46.9 in the associated factories. Labor productivity, however, was much lower in the associated factories, not more than half what it was at Number Two.

Dongfeng managers did not mention any serious problems hindering the corporation's further development. In its early stages, Dongfeng faced some difficulties because its brand name had a poor reputation, and it was difficult to expand membership. Some managers within Number Two apparently had opposed the formation of the new corporation, presumably on the grounds that it would drain resources or would distract Number Two from its own expansion effort.

There were also problems with local government authorities in charge of associated factories. Many of them did not want to give up control over their firms, and this led to frictions with the factories and with Dongfeng headquarters. Headquarters claimed that it took a low profile in these disputes. Probably the most important factor that led to the different kinds of associations that are described in the ensuing discussion was the varying attitudes of local authorities. Factories whose supervisory bureaus gave up control over them in order to stem the factories' fiscal drain tended to be the most closely associated with Dongfeng, whereas those whose higher-ups were concerned about maintaining their control and their prerogatives tended to be only loosely associated with Dongfeng.

Differences in tax treatment of associated factories and irrational pricing—controls over prices large enterprises could set, alongside increased freedom for small firms in setting higher prices in conjunction with local authorities—also were cited as difficulties in the early stages. Problems related to the lack of independence of the "head" of Dongfeng (that is, Number Two) must have been ameliorated over time, especially after Number Two became an entity directly under the state plan. The technical and managerial problems of organizing production and flows of materials and intermediate products between widely dispersed sites must have been considerable, but these problems were not mentioned by Dongfeng representatives in 1984.

Still other difficulties were by-products of success. By 1984 corporate headquarters had run out of specialized-vehicle types to assign to new members for production. Moreover, Number Two's supply of engine-and-chassis sets for specialized vehicles was falling short of the associated factories' demand. Dongfeng apparently also faced some problems in maintaining quality, although headquarters did conduct tests of quality and technical soundness. As of 1984, no member had been forced to leave the corporation, but several were warned that they had to improve quality and others were prevented from engaging in full-capacity production because of problems with quality.[24]

A final group of problems were really more in the nature of challenges for the future. It was believed in 1987–88 that further reform of the administrative environment of Dongfeng was needed to encourage a more unified, flexible structure for the corporation (for example, unification of the tax systems for the different associated factories). The fiscal relations between the corporation and the central and local governments needed to be clarified. It was suggested that the Dongfeng corporation as a whole be allowed to come under a profit-increase responsibility system similar to the one Number

Two was subject to. There was a plea for further loosening of what were still perceived as excessive government controls, despite the substantial de facto autonomy that had already been gained by Number Two and by Dongfeng.

Structure and Operations

The Dongfeng corporation's headquarters organizational structure was similar to that of Number Two. Each functional department in Number Two also served as the corresponding department in Dongfeng. This structure improved coordination and economized on staff costs. (In 1984, Dongfeng headquarters staff—those who did not simultaneously hold positions in Number Two—numbered only about twenty.) Except for the director of Number Two, who also served as general manager of Dongfeng, top leadership posts of the two entities were filled by different individuals. In addition, there were some departments that exclusively served Dongfeng headquarters.

At the apex of Dongfeng's control structure was its board of directors, composed of the director of Number Two, its chief engineer, and the directors of some of Dongfeng's associated factories. The board was mainly responsible for strategic decisions. Dongfeng's own organizational structure at headquarters consisted of six functional departments: the specialized production office, the associated enterprises office, the modified vehicles office, the associated products office, the parts and components office, and the technical service department, responsible for the numerous sales and technical service centers Dongfeng established throughout China.

The relations between Dongfeng headquarters and its associated factories are of interest. These factories can be broadly divided into four categories of members and two categories of nonmembers; the subordinate work units of Number Two itself formed another category. Of the 201 associated factories in Dongfeng at the end of 1987, 6 were "closely associated" with Number Two; 17 were "joint venture factories" that typically received investment funding from Number Two, from the associated factory itself, from the local government, and sometimes from other members of the corporation; 16 factories had "semiclose" relationships with Dongfeng; and 162 factories, the bulk of the total, had "loose" relationships to the corporation. In addition to the 201 members of Dongfeng, there were also 78 "fixed-point cooperating factories," which were not formally members of the corporation, and 213 sales and technical service centers.

Subordinate factories of Number Two had the closest relationships with Number Two and Dongfeng headquarters, but, with the institution of an internal responsibility system between headquarters and subunits (see "Business Environment, Strategy, and Practices," in this chapter), they did gain some discretionary authority. Two associated factories of the Dongfeng corporation apparently became subunits of Number Two in the late 1980s, on an experimental basis.

Closely associated factories were drawn for the most part from the original members of Dongfeng.[25] They had a status similar to that of Number Two's own subordinate factories, and only limited freedom of action. Their directors, deputy directors, party secretaries, and chief engineers were all appointed by Dongfeng headquarters. Headquarters maintained unified control over their personnel, finances, material supply, production, and marketing. Employment levels and wages were supervised by Number Two's labor department. The tightness of the control exerted by Dongfeng headquarters is shown by the limits it imposed on these factories' direct marketing of output: only 10 percent of output produced within the plan and only 20 perent of above-plan output could be marketed directly. In joining Dongfeng, the closely associated factories lost their fiscal and administrative ties to the local governments to which they had belonged.

Joint ventures were a new category that emerged apparently only after Dongfeng gained independent status under the state plan in 1986. There were seventeen joint ventures under the corporation by the end of 1987. Number Two, the associated factories themselves, local governments, and workers (in some cases) made investments in the joint ventures. Their relationships with headquarters were somewhat more distant than were those of the closely associated factories but perhaps were closer than were those of the next category, semiclose associations. It would appear that many of the joint ventures came from the ranks of semiclose associations, whose number declined in 1984–87.

Semiclose associations numbered only three in 1983 but twenty-five at the end of 1984. Subsequently their number fell to sixteen in 1987. The main difference between these units and the closely associated factories is that they preserved their original ownership, administrative subordination, and fiscal arrangements. Production operations, supply, and marketing for these factories were all under the unified control of headquarters; the factories' fundamental choices in the four primary areas of product orientation (kinds of products and kinds of customers), strategic planning and modernization, production planning, and management were guided by headquarters as well. There were stipulated profit-sharing arrangements involving semiclosely associated factories. In the Xinjiang Motor Vehicle Factory, 50 percent of profits went to its local government "owner," 30 percent was retained by the enterprise, and 20 percent was to be remitted to Dongfeng headquarters. At least through 1984, however, the corporation allowed factories such as Xinjiang to keep the headquarters share of profits for reinvestment. There was variation within this category in the degree of centralized control exerted by Dongfeng headquarters; overall, the category represented an intermediate stage of integration between close association and loose association.

Although members of the corporation in full standing, loosely associated factories maintained a considerable degree of independence from Dongfeng. This form of association mainly involved cooperation in production operations, according to contracts between the associated enterprises and corporate headquarters. Headquarters provided some technical assistance and supervised quality to ensure that the enterprises' products met standards for the corporation. Headquarters also helped with marketing of products. These enterprises typically had independent operations in addition to the tasks they did for Dongfeng. The corporation had little, if any, formal authority to intervene in management of these concerns.

Fixed-point cooperative factories were not formal members of the Dongfeng corporation. Otherwise the modes of interaction seem to have been broadly similar to those of the loosely associated factories. Headquarters may not have taken responsibility for the development of fixed-point cooperative factories, whereas for loosely associated members there may have been at least an implicit obligation in this respect.

Sales and technical service centers played an important role in promoting customer satisfaction. Their relationships with Dongfeng headquarters were probably fairly loose, although headquarters must have provided some technical assistance and incentives to improve quality, in addition to supplying spare parts.

Finally, there was another group of firms, whose number is difficult to gauge but may have been substantial, that had indirect relationships with Dongfeng through their membership in branch corporations set up by Dongfeng's closely associated members. Some of these firms were also members of Dongfeng, but many of them were not. A good example of this kind of indirect involvement is the Yunnan Motor Vehicle Factory's organization of thirty small local factories.

As regards activity, the 201 associated units were divided by Dongfeng's management into the following main types: 64 factories, the largest single category, produced specialized vehicles; 62 were suppliers of spare parts and components; 34 produced Dongfeng trucks and related products; 20 were involved in vertical dispersal of production; 14 made chassis-and-engine sets on which other associated factories could assemble vehicles; 6 were involved in backward integration; and 1 was a research and development unit.

A final issue concerns the relationship between Dongfeng and Number Two. Superficially it would appear that the corporation served as an arm of Number Two and, to a considerable extent, furthered Number Two's own objectives. Number Two, however, appears not to have exploited the associated factories for its own short-term gain; instead, it even made some financial sacrifices for the factories. Moreover, since 1986, Number Two management has emphasized that its departments should take a comprehensive view, handle well the business of the entire corporation, and not concentrate primarily on the activities of Number Two itself.[26] It may be most accurate to view Number Two and Dongfeng increasingly as two faces of the same entity, with little separation between the two in structure or in business decisionmaking.

Assessment

Dongfeng was obviously successful in meeting its most immediate goals: finding viable activities for small motor vehicle manufacturing firms, rationalizing production structure through specialization, facilitating modernization, increasing Number Two's market share, and so forth. The corporation became an important force in the motor vehicle industry and served as an inspiration for enterprise groups in other industries.

One question that must be addressed, even if it cannot be answered conclusively, concerns how Dongfeng was able to achieve and sustain success. What were the key ingredients, and to what extent could they be replicated? Many Chinese corporations were utter failures, and others had obvious and severe problems. Why was Dongfeng an exception? Some of the ingredients in Dongfeng's success were identical to factors in Number Two's own achievements (see "Conclusions," in this chapter) that were to some extent specific to Number Two or to the motor vehicle industry. Increasing independence from administrative authority and bureaucratic controls could, however, be achieved in ways different from those that applied in the cases of Number Two and Dongfeng.

One important factor in Dongfeng's successful development was Number Two's willingness to refrain from taking full advantage of its position in relation to the corporation in order to gain short-term financial or other benefits. By taking a long-term view, Number Two demonstrated to its members that it was not out to exploit them. This pattern became self-reinforcing, as the flood of applicants for membership in Dongfeng attests. Moreover, Number Two was quite flexible about the possible arrangements under which firms could become associated with Dongfeng. Overall, Number Two's initiative, creativity, and management skills were fully evident in the emergence, the structure, the operations, and the performance of Dongfeng; perhaps these manifest energies and capabilities should be considered the most important factors in Dongfeng's success.

Questions remain about the long-term viability of the Dongfeng corporation, despite its successful performance up to the late 1980s. If capacity in the motor vehicle industry catches up with long-term demand trends, many Dongfeng members may have trouble surviving without costly support from Number Two. It is not clear how long Number Two will be able or willing to continue resource transfers to associated factories. In the face of problems or more severe domestic competition, Dongfeng conceivably could become a serious drain on Number Two and could hurt Number Two's own development prospects. There was, however, no hint of the possible emergence of such problems in the late 1980s.

Top managers still perceived the need for greater centralization of authority within Dongfeng, even after the strengthening of the corporation's administrative status in 1986. Most Dongfeng member factories had only a loose relationship with headquarters; this structure may have led to problems with coordination and control. Hence came the requests for unified fiscal treatment of the entire corporation and for a profit-increase responsibility system, which probably would be lucrative enough to convince local governments to surrender more of their control over their firms to Dongfeng. The leadership of the corporation also perceived the need for greater flexibility and fungibility of capital.

A final question concerns the possibility of monopolistic tendencies in Dongfeng's behavior. Although the potential existed, there is no evidence that Dongfeng brought reduced competition to the Chinese motor vehicle industry. Any possible threat to competition depended on the relationships among Number Two, Number One, and the small handful of other relatively large plants in the industry. If the two largest producers did not collude with each other to reduce competition, it is extremely doubtful Dongfeng could have done anything to dampen it.

Conclusions

This section returns to the central questions posed at the beginning of this chapter: What were the essential ingredients in Number Two's successful evolution into a largely independent, business-oriented, dynamic, and successful entity, and to what extent and how might its experience be replicated in other Chinese state industrial enterprises?

The Ingredients of Success

There are a number of possible explanations for Number Two's successful performance in the turbulent 1980s. As a new concern whose production was just getting under way in the mid-1970s, Number Two benefited from subsequent rapid expansion and from moving down the learning curve. Because the Chinese planning and fiscal systems worked largely on the basis of constant or slowly increasing plan targets and fiscal levies, the enterprise could share disproportionately in the rewards from growth and improved financial performance. There was a natural tendency for directly marketed output, retained profits, and other benefits to Number Two to grow rapidly in the 1980s. Another advantage related to newness, as well as to Number Two's own early history, was the enterprise's failure to develop a stable hierarchical or patron-client relationship with a particular government supervisory agency. Finally, as a new enterprise, Number Two had a relatively young labor force and few retirees, so it had low pension costs.

Along with these advantages, Number Two also faced some severe problems as a new member of the industry, particularly in view of its poor location. These problems seem to have elicited strong positive responses, however, which perhaps even strengthened the enterprise's independent capabilities and orientation in the process. Nevertheless, as perceived in the late 1970s, these difficulties would have seemed to far outweigh any advantages that resulted from Number Two's newness.

Advantages of size and membership in a rapidly growing industry may have been significant. Number Two's size gave it some advantages as regards access to internally generated resources and administrative clout in the locality. Being a member of an important industry that had been singled out for emphasis in modernization and reform must also have conferred some benefits on Number Two. It is difficult, however, to gauge the importance of such advantages. Number Two's size also must have conferred disadvantages by rendering the enterprise more visible, accessible, and (once it had achieved a certain degree of success) tempting to the central government bureaucracy as a source of financial levies and other resources. That large enterprises tended in general to be less reformed than smaller ones in the mid-1980s suggests that size on balance carried some disadvantages.

A case can be made that Number Two's initial problems in establishing a reputation with customers and its subsequent market problems in 1981–82 propelled the plant toward independence from the government bureaucracy (see "Planning, Supply, and Marketing Controls," in this chapter). Indeed, market trends at certain critical junctures seem to have increased the enterprise's autonomy, by reducing incentives for involvement in Number Two's affairs by government supervisory agencies and by forcing the enterprise to take responsibility for marketing. Market conditions for trucks, however, were not dissimilar from those for products in numerous other industries, and, moreover, other truck manufacturers did not respond to those conditions in the same way Number Two did. There were periods of sustained strong demand that were typically longer than were those of excess supply. Therefore, the evolution of market conditions for trucks cannot have had a determining influence on Number Two's behavior.

There is no question that Number Two had unusually lucrative profit-sharing arrangements with the government, in part because of the rapid growth of the enterprise's aggregate profits but especially because of the profit-increase responsibility system, which became effective in 1983. Large retained profits undoubtedly bolstered Number Two's autonomy in decisionmaking in that they allowed it to finance a much larger share of its investment internally. Number Two also made extensive use of bank loans, however, to finance fixed investment from 1980 on. Moreover, the enterprise borrowed foreign exchange for investment from the Bank of China and the China Investment Bank.

Questions related to political patronage and favored treatment by the government naturally arise. Although Number Two seems to have maintained a partly antagonistic and rivalrous relationship with its immediate bureaucratic superiors, especially with AGC, the enterprise may well have had stronger patrons at the political level of the Chinese leadership. Because top political leaders visited China's largest industrial firms frequently and often had some involvement in major decisions that affected the firms (see Chapter 8 in this volume, for example), the outward trappings of political patronage at Number Two were not terribly unusual. High-level support seems, however, to have translated into certain important concrete concessions, most notably the profit-increase responsibility system, the authority to conduct foreign trade independently, and, subsequently, direct subordination to the state plan. These concessions provide indirect evidence of political patronage at a high level, that gave Number Two opportunities to increase its autonomy from the bureaucracy. Political patronage would not have been very helpful, however, if the strategic orientation and the ambitious competitive strategy of Number Two's top management were absent. Moreover, political patronage, to the extent that it occurred, was at least in part the result of Number Two's successful development rather than its cause.

Separation from the government administrative hierarchy was a crucial feature of the situation. Number Two never had a close, confining relationship with a particular government supervisory agency. Because Number Two's construction was part of the Third Front defense industrialization program and was apparently financed by the central government, direct involvement by the Hubei provincial government in the enterprise's affairs was less than might otherwise have been the case, even when Number Two was nominally under provincial control. The Ministry of Machine Building seems not to have been highly interventionist in its dealings with Number Two. The creation of AGC undoubtedly hindered Number Two's quest for increased autonomy, yet the enterprise emerged victorious from the resulting bureaucratic struggle. Perhaps the main reason why the dealings of AGC and Number Two developed into a rivalry rather than a patron-client relationship was that AGC's mandated economic role and partial business orientation made it into an economic competitor to Number Two (albeit one that competed largely on the basis of administrative decisions instead of becoming involved in genuine business competition), not merely a bureaucratic supervisor. Once it was apparent that Number Two could stand up to AGC successfully, the enterprise's autonomy was naturally further increased, well before the actual demise of AGC in 1987.

There is no denying that luck played some role in Number Two's success. The precise timing of Number Two's emergence in the industry, the evolution of market conditions, and other unpredictable events might have spurred the enterprise's move toward independence from the government bureaucracy at crucial points. The influence of these factors should not, however, be overemphasized. They demanded, at the very least, that Number Two recognize them as opportunities and respond to them appropriately and in a timely manner.

Dynamic, forward-looking management was important. The role of Number Two's top leadership, in particular of Huang Zhengxia, party secretary and director of the enterprise during much of its history, should not be underrated. Top management unfailingly kept a long-term strategic perspective and made vigorous efforts to implement ambitious objectives. The role of management was important in devising creative strategies, in setting ambitious but (in the event) feasible objectives, in carrying out these strategies with great success, in dealing adeptly with the government bureaucracy, in taking advantage of market opportunities and administrative openings, and in striving to instill a dynamic orientation in the enterprise and its personnel.

Psychological factors, in particular a self-image of independence, also were important in Number Two's evolution. The perceptions of enterprise leaders, first of Number Two's being "cast off" from administrative support and from state grants in 1979–80 and later of government supervisory agencies being brought down to Number Two's level (if not below it) by their narrowly self-interested behavior, must have stimulated a more independent mind-set and psychological separation from the government bureaucracy.

In coming to an overall assessment, it is difficult to disentangle the aforementioned factors and to come to even a preliminary judgment as to which ones were most important. Some of the specific benefits and advantages Number Two enjoyed were probably less important than they would appear to be at first sight; moreover, they were at least partly offset by some significant disadvantages, most notably poor location. Enterprise-specific and more general ingredients both played roles in determining Number Two's evolution.

Available evidence suggests that Number Two's break with the government supervisory bureaucracy was a critical prerequisite for its success (see "Administrative Supervision" and "Planning, Supply, and Marketing Controls," both in this chapter). How was the enterprise able to shed its bureaucratic shackles? Again, enterprise-specific and more general factors both seem to have been at work. Number Two's own objectives and strategies, as well as the market environment it faced, impelled it to strive for greater administrative autonomy, but numerous factors facilitated its gradual achievement of effective independence.

Replicability

There were some enterprise- and industry-specific factors in Number Two's success, but nevertheless a case can be made that the enterprise's evolution to a large extent could be replicated in other firms. As is suggested in the preceding discussion, the primary ingredient in Number Two's success seems to have been its emergence as an entity largely free from administrative ties to the government bureaucracy, which in turn can be traced to a number of causes.

1. The enterprise's failure to develop close patron-client relationships with any particular government supervisory agency
2. Its rivalry with its immediate supervisory body, AGC
3. Its relative independence in financial affairs, brought about by the 1980 deal and subsequent profit-increase responsibility system
4. Market problems, which forced the enterprise to make sales on its own
5. The enterprise's highly-skilled, dynamic cadre of management, with its independent self-image, its long-term strategic perspective, and its determination to carry out strategies boldly
6. Possibly some support and political patronage from the highest levels of the Chinese leadership.

Although the particular path to independence Number Two took may well be unique and impossible to replicate in most other firms, the removal of the shackles of administrative supervision was the crucial development, not the precise manner in which this occurred in the case of Number Two. Administrative supervision of state enterprises could be abolished or weakened in numerous ways. Thus the experience of Number Two, even if it were based to a large extent on nonreplicable factors, at least opens up possibilities for consideration in devising state enterprise reforms.

Whether the direct approach of simply removing supervisory agencies from the scene would work is questionable. In 1987, supervisory agencies for enterprises engaging in advanced reforms (various kinds of contractual responsibility systems) claimed to have stopped interference in the day-to-day business of their subordinate firms. Continuing involvement of functional government agencies (planning, supply, finance, banks, labor, and so forth), however, still impinged on enterprise autonomy. Hence abolishing state enterprises' bureaucratic superiors would not necessarily lead to real enterprise autonomy, because of the host of administrative matters that still would need to be dealt with, many of them related to the social responsibilities of state enterprises toward their employees and their dependents.

Thus simply abolishing supervisory agencies might not work well, although the potential improvements from such an approach could nevertheless be substantial.[27] A more indirect, multifaceted approach, including, but not limited to, abolition of enterprises' government supervisory agencies, could be more fruitful. Fundamental changes in the social responsibilities of enterprises, in particular their shedding responsibilities for housing, pensions, and social security, would also facilitate greater autonomy from the government bureaucracy.

Notes

1. This kind of development has been extremely rare in Chinese state industry as a whole and uncommon in the sample of tweny firms as well. The Mindong Electrical Machinery Corporation, one of the firms in the sample, sundered ties with its local supervisory bureau and relocated its headquarters from a remote area to the provincial capital. It also became highly export oriented, as early as the mid-1970s. Hence, on a smaller scale, Mindong exhibited entrepreneurial behavior.

2. Some of the following discussion is based on Lyons 1987a and 1987b.

3. Customers strongly preferred the Jiefang brand over others; many of the small factories simply copied the Jiefang design or assembled trucks from cannibalized or purchased Jiefang parts.

4. Motor vehicles comprised four line items in the state plan: trucks, vans, jeeps, and cars.

5. Rural individuals were sold trucks allocated through the state plan in the early 1980s. Thus the subsequent increase in the share of direct marketing of trucks was not solely a result of the change in truck ownership. The planning authorities may have found it difficult to handle sales of trucks to individuals, especially in rural areas, and therefore shed their responsibility in this area.

6. See Naughton 1988 for a detailed discussion of the Third Front and its effect on the Chinese economy, which includes some references to Number Two.

7. This discussion of the early history of Number Two is based mainly on Jiang 1986, pp. 1, 12–14.

8. Half a year would have been an incredibly short period of time to design and develop production of a new vehicle from scratch. Much of the design and preparatory work for the 5-ton truck had already been done. It appears that earlier, in the mid-1970s, Number Two was prevented from speedily developing the 5-ton truck by higher-level officials, who ordered the plant instead to concentrate on military vehicles.

9. One complaint was that Hubei Province for a time in the late 1970s had forbidden Number Two from going outside the province to seek suppliers of parts and components and instead had required it to use eighteen designated suppliers, all located within Hubei, exclusively. In 1981 or 1982 provincial banks went so far as to refuse to sanction Number Two's payments to suppliers outside of Hubei. The problem was resolved shortly afterward, however, and Hubei no longer opposed Number Two's use of suppliers from outside the province.

10. Number Two apparently never adopted the popular economic responsibility system, as did many enterprises in 1981–82, perhaps partly because it was under central rather than local government supervision.

11. This base figure does not correspond closely with actual remitted profits in 1982 of Y178.61 million. Enterprise management explained that about Y30 million of remitted profits in 1982 consisted of proceeds from collection of payments for vehicles sold on credit in 1981, and an additional Y8.6 million consisted of profit remittances "owed" from previous years. Despite this superficially plausible explanation, the possibility remains that the base figure was set at an artificially low level in order to allow Number Two to retain more profits in subsequent years.

12. At that time, these three important documents accompanied vehicles produced under the plan: gasoline ration certificate, license to operate, and authorization for bank financing. Trucks produced outside the plan did not carry these documents and hence presumably were available only to units with other channels of access to administrative approval and to gasoline. As the energy situation eased, these documents came to be provided for all trucks.

13. Although the mandatory plan target remained constant at 50,000 units, apparently 10,000 of these were actually sold by Number Two directly to transport companies, under a special program to encourage replacement of older gas-guzzling models. These sales may explain why reported direct marketing by Number Two in 1982 was 30,000 units rather than 20,000 (see table 9.9).

14. In April 1984 state enterprises were allowed to "float" prices of their production outside the mandatory plan upward by as much as 20 percent; in response, Number Two raised the price of its directly marketed trucks by 18 percent. This increase probably did not apply to trucks "exchanged" for raw materials.

15. Rolled steel consumption would have been 215,000 to 220,000 tons in 1983 and 270,000 to 275,000 tons in 1984. Thus only slightly more than 10 percent of Number Two's total rolled steel consumption in 1983 was obtained through exchanges, perhaps no more than 15 percent in 1984.

16. Data in the table are aggregates for all motor vehicles (as well as engine-and-chassis sets); becasue of data limitations it is impossible to construct a similar table for trucks and truck chassis alone. Hence table 9.10 provides only an imperfect indication of changes in the supply situation for trucks. For example, the surge of imports in 1984–85 consisted disproportionately of cars as opposed to trucks.

17. This pro forma approval contrasts with the experience of the Chinese watch industry, in which, despite emerging excess supply, price reductions in the early 1980s were delayed and inadequate to clear the market. Moreover, enterprises such as the Chongqing Clock and Watch Company were prohibited from cutting prices of their own volition (see chapter 3 in this volume).

18. This right was a coveted privilege; that it was conferred on Number Two provides still another indication of favorable treatment by central government authorities.

19. These figures, based on reports by the enterprise, conflict with national statistics on motor vehicle exports, which are shown in tables 9.2 and 9.10.

20. Apparently the First Motor Vehicle Manufacturing Plant received permission to produce cars on an experimental basis in the late 1980s. This permisssion was granted perhaps in part to counteract the competitive advantage of Number Two.

21. Apparently Number Two believed that by helping out with the new truck design, it had repaid the debt it owed to Number One from the construction period. Number One, for its part, asserted that a significant factor in its failure to modernize its own truck design for so many years was the diversion of its resources to help start Number Two.

22. This practice may have given workers the psychological satisfaction of receiving increasing bonuses over a period of several years, but of course it did not maximize the total value of bonuses workers received.

23. Twenty-five thousand of these were to be standard Dongfeng trucks; the other 25,000 were to be 3-ton trucks for agricultural use in rural areas.

24. Allocation of engine-and-chassis sets to associated factories by Number Two

probably served as a powerful instrument to pressure the factories to improve quality.

25. In 1982 there was only one closely associated factory in Dongfeng, the Yunnan Motor Vehicle Factory, but this category of membership increased to two in 1983, to five in 1984, and to six by 1987. At least until 1984, all closely associated factories were drawn from the founding members of Dongfeng.

26. This new emphasis suggests that before 1986 the functional management departments of Number Two may have to some extent neglected the affairs of Dongfeng.

27. At the very least, supervisory and related government agencies could be abolished as an experiment in some localities. The complexity of the problems involved need not serve as an excuse for inaction.

References

China Economic Yearbook Editorial Committee. 1986. *Zhongguo Jingji Nianjian 1986* (1986 China Economic Yearbook). Beijing: Jingji Guanli Chubanshe.

Ding Junfa and Xu Xin. 1983. "Di Er Qiche Zhizao Chang Gongcheng Jishu Renyuan Diaocha" (A Survey of Engineering and Technical Personnel at the Second Motor Vehicle Factory). *Jingji Diaocha* (Economic Investigations) 1 (March): 58–63.

Hubei Statistical Bureau. 1988. *Hubei Tongji Nianjian 1988* (Statistical Yearbook of Hubei 1988). Wuhan: Zhongguo Tongji Chubanshe.

Jiang Yiwei, ed. 1986. *Di Er Qiche Zhizao Chang Jingying Guanli Kaocha* (An Investigation of Business Management at the Second Motor Vehicle Factory). Beijing: Jingji Guanli Chubanshe.

Lyons, Thomas P. 1987a. *Economic Integration and Planning in Maoist China.* New York: Columbia University Press.

———. 1987b. "Spatial Aspects of Development in China: The Motor Vehicle Industry, 1956–1985." *International Regional Science Review* 11(1): 75–96.

Naughton, Barry. 1988. "The Third Front: Defence Industrialization in the Chinese Interior." *The China Quarterly*, 115 (September): 351–86.

State Economic Commission, Enterprise Management Department. 1983. *Gongye Jingying Guanli Jingyan Xuanbian 1982* (Selections on Experience in Industrial Administration and Management, 1982). Beijing: Renmin Chubanshe.

State Statistical Bureau. 1982. *Statistical Yearbook of China 1981.* Hong Kong: Economic Information and Agency.

———. 1983. *Statistical Yearbook of China 1983.* Hong Kong: Economic Information and Agency.

———. 1984. *Statistical Yearbook of China 1984.* Hong Kong: Economic Information and Agency.

———. 1985a. *Statistical Yearbook of China 1985.* Hong Kong: Economic Information and Agency.

———. 1985b. *1949–1984 Zhongguo Gongye de Fazhan* (Development of China's Industry, 1949–84). Beijing: Zhongguo Tongji Chubanshe.

———. 1985c. *Zhongguo Gongye Jingji Tongji Ziliao 1949–1984* (Statistical Materials on China's Industrial Economy 1949–84). Beijing: Zhongguo Tongji Chubanshe.

————. 1986. *Statistical Yearbook of China 1986*. Hong Kong: Economic Information and Agency.

————. 1987a. *Statistical Yearbook of China 1987*. Hong Kong: Orient Longman.

————. 1987b. *Zhongguo Gongye Jingji Tongji Ziliao 1986* (Statistical Materials on China's Industrial Economy 1986). Beijing: Zhongguo Tongji Chubanshe.

————. 1988. *Zhongguo Tongji Nianjian 1988* (Statistical Yearbook of China 1988). Beijing: Zhongguo Tongji Chubanshe.

————. 1989a. "Statistics for 1988 Socio-Economic Development." *Beijing Review* 32(10): I–VIII.

————. 1989b. *Zhongguo Gongye Jingji Tongji Nianjian 1988* (Statistical Yearbook of China's Industrial Economy 1988). Beijing: Zhongguo Tongji Chubanshe.

Xia Junbo. 1985. "Guanyu Banhao Qiche Maoyi Zhongxin de Jige Wenti" (Several Questions Concerning Handling of Vehicle Trading Centers). *Wuzi Guanli* (Materials Management) (April): 3, 4–5.

Index

Adjustment tax, enterprise-specific, 4

Administrative control, problems of, 55, 224 n35. *See also* Decentralization; Government and political interference and intervention; Supervisory agencies for firms

AGC. *See* China Automobile Industry General Corporation (AGC)

Anshan Iron and Steel Company, 44–46, 303; allocation of inputs for, 311, 325; annual steel production of, 304; appointment of top managers of, 311, 341–42; assets of, 304; bonuses at, 348–49; cement plant of, 336; centralization of management at (*1953–57*), 306–7; circumvention of financial constraints at, 325; collective enterprises for workers' children at, 353; collective workers and the collective economy at, 338, 353–55, 368 n29; compensation for price changes and, 318–19; conflict between production and profit targets and, 312; conflict with local authorities and, 313; continued dominance of mandatory planning at, 320–23; countertendencies to integration at, 331–32; Cultural Revolution and, 307, 342; delays and red tape during modernization of, 358; departments in headquarters of, 340; depreciation funds at, 340; depreciation rate of, 317; direct marketing by, 325–30; director responsibility system at, 341; diverse goals of supervisory agencies of, 312; electric power plants and, 336–37; employee goals and enterprise objectives at, 347–48; employment and wage trends at, 350; enterprise boundaries at, 329–30, 335, 339, 364–65; experimental stock system at, 319–20; financial dependence of collectives on, 355; financial incentives at, 316–20, 340, 345–46; financing of modernization of, 359–60; firing of workers and, 348; fundamental problems at, 339–40; funds from banking system and, 319; government interference at, 313; Great Leap Forward movement and, 307, 342; gross value of industrial output of, 304; historical background and supervision of (*1980s*), 309–11; housing depreciation and major repair funds, 352, 368 n28; incentives for vertical integration at, 330–31, 336; internal decentralization at, 305, 342–46, 363–64; internal financial management reforms at, 343; internal organization and management of, 340–46; internal transfer pricing at, 344–45; investment planning and

427

decisionmaking at, 311, 346; iron ore mines of, 332–33; issues and history of, 304–9; labor and wages at, 347–50, 352–55; labor force of, 367 n23; leadership system at, 341–42; magnesium mines and, 333–35; management's attitude toward workers at, 353, 363; mandatory planning and marketing controls at, 320–29; mandatory planning problems at, 322–23, 365; mandatory planning, sellers' markets, and reforms and, 361–62; marketing rights and practices of, 304, 323, 325–27, 328; multiheaded leadership at, 311–13; new construction company of, 337–38; oil refinery at, 337; ordering conferences and, 321–22; population of, 340, 367 n23; problems of ambiguity of property rights at, 339; production during modernization of, 357–58; profit retention at, 316–18, 340; profit tax and, 317–19; ratio of employees to dependents not employed by, 367 n23; renovation and modernization of, 356–61; rent seeking by, 328–29; repair funds at, 340; responses to mandatory planning at, 324–25; size of work force at, 304; as social service and welfare agency, 343, 350, 352–53; stock shares in steel-rolling plant sales at, 319; subsector responsibility system problems and, 304, 313–16, 324, 365; supervision of, 309–16; supply problems of, 304; vertical integration versus administrative fragmentation at, 329–40; wage and employment systems and enterprise objectives and, 362–63; wage system at, 348–50; worker organization as a constraint at, 363; worker participation in management at, 342; work for employees' children and, 331, 337, 338, 347, 353, 363

Anti-inflationary measures, 13
Antireform attitudes, 27–29
Asset management responsibility systems, 11
Automobile industry. See Motor vehicle industry

Bank branches, linkage between deposit and lending levels at local, 366 n9
Bank credit use as inflationary mechanism, 13
Bank loans, 51–52, 83–86; Anshan and, 319; Nanning's loan agreements and, 297–98; Northern Nonferrous Metals and Gold Associated Group and, 214; provisions for repayment of, 38, 43, 44; to Qingdao, 123, 143–44; to Qinghe, 238, 259–60. See also Loan repayments
Beijing Textile Bureau, 239
Bonuses for managers at Chongqing, 115 n17
Bonus system and bonuses for workers, 9, 30 n1, 43, 49; at Anshan, 348–49; at Chongqing Clock and Watch Company, 76–77, 78; at Nanning, 283, 284–85, 286, 297, 301 n7; at Qinghe, 247
Budget constraints, 51
Bureaucratic apparatus to supervise state enterprises, 18. See also Government and political interference and intervention
Bureaucratic restrictions and impediments, persistence of, 229, 320–23
Buyers' market, mandatory planning and, 48

Capital stock, 25
Capital taxation, 83–84
Case studies used in this book, 33–38, 40–47
Centralization, problems of, 54–55. See also Recentralization
Central planning. See Planning

Chemical fibers for textiles. *See* Synthetic fibers for textiles

China Automobile Industry General Corporation (AGC), 384, 385

China Nonferrous Metals Industry General Corporation, 193–95, 208; functions of, 217; nonferrous metals industry under control of, 216–17; profit-sharing and, 217, 218; progress in reform and, 217; regional corporations and, 219; Shenyang and, 195–96, 198

Chongqing Clock and Watch Company, 38, 40, 58–59; apprentices and entrants to technical school at, 115 n16; attitudes toward risk at, 84; changes in planning system and, 76–77; cost reductions at, 101–3; credit financing of fixed investment and, 74–75, 83; depreciation rate at, 115 n12; development of new products at, 98–100; developments after 1983 at, 111–14; employment and wage system reforms and, 77–79; goals for incorporation of, 69; growth and development of, during early 1980s, 111; history of, 64–68; implications of experience of, 103–11; incentives from financial reform and, 82–87; income tax computation at, 84; investment financing and, 108–10; involvement in associations and joint ventures of, 69–72; labor allocation and, 106–8; managerial benefits and turnover at, 80; manipulation of rules by, 94–96, 105–6; market as dominant influence on, 103–5; marketing and growth patterns and, 86; organizational reforms at, 68–72; output per worker at, 114 n7; performance of, 110–11; price reductions at, 100–101; product mix of, 77; profit target of, 77, 80; resources and natural advantages of, 66–67; response to reforms (1980–82) and, 87–88,

90–103; retained funds for fixed investment at, 73; retained profits for welfare benefits at, 79; sales promotion and marketing by, 75–76, 96–98; self-financed and loan-financed investment at, 86; tax system and, 72–75; uses of income of, 72–73; wage grades at, 115 n18; wages and company performance at, 78–79; welfare expenditures by, 72, 79; workers' benefits and bonuses and, 76–77, 78; workers' interest in increasing profits of, 80–81

Clock and watch industry, 59–64

Clock market, 38

Collective firms, 32 n32; at Anshan, 353–55, 368 n29

Collective versus state workers, 211

Consumer durables, 38

Contractual responsibility systems, 10–11, 14

Control over distribution of inputs, 2, 3, 53, 223 n21, 224 n33

Cost reductions at Chongqing Clock and Watch Company, 101–3

Cotton-blend textiles, 288, 294

Cotton cloth production in China, 271 n2

Cotton production in China, 231–32

Credit, inflation and, 13. *See also* Bank credit; Bank loans

Cultural Revolution, 122, 307, 342

Customer-oriented behavior, 47, 48. *See also* Market orientation

Decentralization, 41, 45, 53–54; Anshan's internal, 305, 342–44, 345–46, 363–64; Number Two's internal, 405; at Shenyang, 160, 167–71. *See also* Leadership; Reform of state enterprises

Decisionmaking autonomy, 2–3, 44; nationwide experiment to increase, 238

Depreciation, 115 n12; funding of, 131, 245, 366 n6

Development strategy in China, for-

eign technology in the, 64
Director responsibility system, 14; at
  Anshan, 341; at Nanning, 286, 294
Dongfeng (East Wind) corporation,
  46, 371, 407; AGC and, 384; assessment of, 417–18; coordination of
  production of parts by Number Two
  and, 394; difficulties and early problems of, 413; independence from
  AGC gained by, 385; independent
  status granted to, 411; Number
  Two's motivations for establishment
  of, 408–10; origins and development of, 410–14; quality problems
  at, 413; return on capital in factories of, 412; specialization of factories of, 412; structure and operations of, 414–17; as a successful
  investment, 410

Economic responsibility systems, 3–4,
  286
Efficiency, 27, 40
Electricity, 1; Anshan and, 336–37;
  conservation of, 179; prices for,
  224 n32; Qinghe and, 253. See also
  Shenyang Smelter
Employee welfare, firms' responsibility
  for, 4
Enterprise boundaries: administrative
  demarcation of, 53, 329–30; Anshan and, 339. See also State enterprises
Enterprise directors, progress toward
  autonomy for, 14
Enterprise groups, 225 n43. See also
  names of specific groups
Enterprise objectives, 49; constraints
  on, 50
Enterprise reorganization, stages in,
  272 n20. See also Reform of state
  enterprises
Environmental problems. See Pollution
  problems
Exports, 25, 30 n10, 43, 44, 124–25;
  from Nanning Mill, 281, 289–90;
  from Number Two, 400; Qinghe

and, 252; of woolen fabric, 235,
  257, 271 n5

Factor productivity, growth of, 27
Factory directors: increasing authority
  of, 10, 44; responsibility system of,
  286, 294, 367 n24; strengthened
  position of, 14
Family motive, 38; defined, 56 n5
Financial capital, 17–18
Financial discipline: financial incentives and, 5; weak, 18
Financial incentives, 3, 18; at Anshan, 316–20, 340, 345–46; financial discipline and, 5; at Qinghe,
  264. See also Incentives
Financial performance of state-owned
  industry, 25–26
Financial reforms, 3–5; incentives created by, 82–87
Firing of workers, 348
First Motor Vehicle Manufacturing
  Plant ("Number One"): independence from AGC granted to, 385; relationship between Number Two
  and, 402–4
Fixed investment: credit financing
  of, 74–75, 83; retained funds for,
  73
Floating wage system, 78–79, 80, 81

Government and political interference
  and intervention, 43, 52; at An-
  shan, 313; changing market condi-
  tions and, 38; at Number Two,
  382–86, 389–90, 391–92, 422; at
  Qingdao, 122
Government-owned enterprises. See
  State enterprises
Great Leap Forward movement, 121,
  307, 342
Gross value of industrial output
  (GVIO), changes in shares of, 16.
  See also Industrial output
Guangxi Autonomous Region, 276,
  279–81

Household registration in China, 301 n11

Housing for workers and staff, 12, 43, 49, 79, 81; at Anshan, 352, 368 n28; at Nanning, 282, 283, 284; at Qinghe, 263–64

Imported equipment, for textile processing and manufacturing, 277

Imported materials, allocation of, 249

Incentives: from financial reforms, 82–87; for loan-financing, 43, 51–52; managerial, 212; mechanisms to establish, 212–13; profit, 45; for workers, 9, 78–79; for work units, 212. See also Financial incentives

Industrial and Commercial Bank of China, 360

Industrial firms: categories of, 1–2, 30 n8; changes in size distribution of, 16; as communities, 49; supervision by major cities, 125. See also State enterprises

Industrial labor force, 24–25. See also Labor allocation; Labor productivity; Labor reforms; Workers in state-owned industrial enterprises

Industrial output, 27. See also Gross value of industrial output (GVIO)

Industrial performance (1978–88): capital and, 25; employment and wages and, 24–25; exports and, 25; factor productivity and, 27; financial performance and, 25–26; growth of output and, 18–19, 23; technological progress and, 26–27

Industrial producer goods, pricing of, 7–8

Industrial reform, 2, 11; achievements of, 14–16; common themes in study of, 47–56; problems of, 16–18. See also Reform of state enterprises

Inflationary pressures, 12–13

Innovation, stymying of, 215

Inputs, control over distribution of, 2, 3, 53, 165–67, 223 n21, 224 n33

Integration, vertical and horizontal organizational, 45

Investment and investment planning, 4–5, 17–18, 41, 51–52; at Anshan, 311; at Chongqing, 108–10; incentives for loans for, 38; at Number Two, 402; at Qingdao, 123, 131, 143–44; at Qinghe, 258–62; at Shenyang, 171, 173–75, 182–83, 209, 210. See also Fixed investment

Investment decisionmaking, 346

Investment financing: at Anshan, 311, 359–60; at Number Two, 402; at Qinghe, 258–62; at Shenyang, 171, 173–75, 182–83, 209, 210

Investment financing reform, 3; at Chongqing, 108–10

Jiao County Forging Machinery Plant, 122

Jobs for employees' children: at Anshan, 331, 337, 338, 347, 353, 363; at Number Two, 406; at Shenyang, 159–60, 175–76, 212

Joint ventures, 69–72

Jute, 301 n5

Kunming Watch Company, 71–72

Labor allocation, 77; effect on Chongqing of system of, 106–8; lack of control over, 262

Labor productivity: experiments in, 116 n27; watch industry national comparisons in, 62

Labor reforms, 8–9

Land acquisition, 52–53; urban, 222 n12

Leadership: at Anshan, 311–13; multiheaded system of, 40–41, 42. See also Decentralization; Management; Reform of state enterprises

Leasing as prelude to privatization, 12

Linen, 277

Living standards, urban and rural, 301 n11

Loan repayments: at Nanning,

297–98; from profits, 57 n10; at
Qingdao, 52, 145–46; at Qinghe,
259–60; treatment of, 83–86. *See
also* Bank loans
Local governments, enterprises and,
298–99, 300

Management, 42–43. *See also* Decentralization; Leadership; Reform of
state enterprises
Manipulation of rules: by Anshan,
325; by Chongqing, 94–96, 105–6;
by Nanning, 299
Market: as dominant influence on
Chongqing, 103–5; response to, 40,
44
Market conditions: Anshan and, 323;
importance of, 47–48
Marketing: at Anshan, 304, 323,
325–27, 328; at Chongqing, 86,
96–98, 103–5; at Nanning, 293–94;
at Number Two, 389–91; at Qingdao, 126–27, 129, 143; at Qinghe,
254–58, 267; at Shenyang, 185–88
Market orientation, obstacles to, 42.
See also Customer-oriented behavior
Market reform, 5, 7–8
Markets and marketlike mechanisms:
expansion of role of, 14; motor vehicles and rolled steel and, 395; response to changing, 42
Medals awarded for Chinese products,
273 n23
Methodology used in this study,
33–37. *See also* Case studies used in
this book
Mindong Electrical Machinery Company, 56 n4, 56 n7
Modernization, 45; at Anshan,
356–61; at Number Two, 400–401,
405
Motor vehicle industry: in China,
372–75; and Number Two's development, 376–82; reform of, 375–76,
384. *See also* Dongfeng (East Wind)
corporation; First Motor Vehicle
Manufacturing Plant ("Number

One"); Second Motor Vehicle Manufacturing Plant ("Number Two")

Nanning City, 276
Nanning Silk and Ramie Mill, 43–44;
background information on,
276–82; balance sheet of, 299;
blended textiles produced by, 294;
bonuses at, 283, 284, 286, 297,
301 n7; bonus tax and, 284; blurred
lines of responsibility and, 295,
298–99; budget of, 297; Construction Bank and, 297; contract workers at, 285, 300; control over personnel matters at, 281–82; demand
for ramie products of, 290; economic contract responsibility system
of, 286; exports by, 281, 289–90;
factory-director responsibility system
of, 286, 294; financial reforms at,
283–85; financing the expansion of,
293; general textile market trends
and, 288–89; golden era of, 292;
government supervisory changes
and, 287; housing at, 282, 283,
284; labor reforms at, 285; lessons
and implications of experience of,
299–300; limitations on enterprise
reforms and, 295–300; links with
other enterprises, 294; loan agreements of, 297–98; management reforms at, 285–86; manipulation of
financial arrangements of, 299;
marketing by, 293–94; market role
in performance of, 292, 295; as
model enterprise, 291; noncash subsidies for workers at, 284; output
mix decisions at, 286; People's Bank
of China and, 281, 293, 297;
phases in development of, 290–95;
as pilot plant in experimental reforms, 292; production targets for,
281; profits retained by, 283–84,
292, 296; ramie products of,
277–79, 290, 294; reforms and
changes at, 282–95, 299; response
to changes in demand and, 294; su-

pervisory agencies and, 295, 299–300; targets for, 287, 289; taxes and, 295; tax on profits of, 284; training of workers at, 285; welfare of employees and, 300; working capital for, 281

Nonferrous metals industry, 150–52; in China, 153–54, 156–59; imports versus domestic production and, 205; issues arising from recentralization and, 199–200; multiyear responsibility system and, 217–18; problems in, 192–93; recentralization of control of, 193, 196–97, 199–200; retained profits and, 218. See also China Nonferrous Metals Industry General Corporation

Northern Nonferrous Metals and Gold Associated Group, 213–15; scrap copper procurement by Revival Metallurgical Association Corporation and, 215–16

Number One. See First Motor Vehicle Manufacturing Plant ("Number One")

Number Two. See Second Motor Vehicle Manufacturing Plant ("Number Two")

Ordering conferences, 321–22

Pay, performance related to, 78
Pensions, 12, 282
People's Bank of China: Nanning branch of, 281, 293, 297; Number Two and, 387, 399; Qingdao and, 123, 131
Petroleum and petroleum products, exports of, 30 n10
Planned output targets, projection of, 395
Planning, 42, 48–49, 210; argument for, 58; inefficiency resulting from, 45, 252–53; mandatory, 42, 48–49, 210; problems stemming from, 214
Planning from the achieved level, 394–95

Political changes, economic consequences of, 27–28
Political crisis (May–June 1989), 13
Pollution problems, at Shenyang smelter, 164–65, 178–79, 198
Price reductions, at Chongqing, 100–101
Price reform, 3, 5–8
Pricing, of industrial producer goods, 7–8
Privatization, 12
Production, measure of efficiency in, 27
Productivity. See Labor productivity
Product mix, 40, 41, 43
Profit motive as source of problems in a bureaucratic system, 339
Profits, 49; collection of, 222 n17; link between wages and, 79–81; loan repayments from, 57 n10; motives for increasing, 40; orientation toward, 14; retained by Anshan, 316–18, 340; retained by Chongqing, 73; retained by Nanning Mill, 283–84, 292, 296; retained by Qingdao, 131; retained by Qinghe, 243, 246; retained by Shenyang, 210–11; retention by enterprises, 3, 30 n1, 218; taxes substituted by delivery of, 59, 284; uses of retained, 4; welfare benefits from retained, 79
Profit tax system, 4, 317–19, 368 n32

Qingdao Forging Machinery Plant, 40–41, 120–21; accounting systems at, 131–32, 145; bonuses at, 131, 132, 133, 140–41; customer service at, 128; customer views solicited by, 143; depreciation fund of, 131; difficulties due to supervisory structure of, 124–25; domestic and export sales responsibility at, 124–25; economic responsibility system and, 130, 139–40; expenses for product modification at, 132; as experimental unit promoting economic responsibility system, 130; financial relationship with government and,

133, 134; financial system reform at, 130–33; fuel and raw material costs of, 135; high quality of products of, 128; historical background of, 121–23; improving economic performance at, 130–35; interest rates paid by, 148 n2; labor and wage system at, 131, 132, 133, 135–41; loan problems at, 143–44; loan repayments and, 52, 145–46; as local government enterprise, 123; manipulation of rules and, 146–47; marketing reforms at, 126–27; market surveys used by, 129, 143; materials supply for, 123–24; new planning system for (early 1980s), 126; operations and management reforms at, 127–28; People's Bank of China and, 123, 131; personnel management system of, 124; planning and marketing reforms at, 126–30; poor economic performance of, 133–35; price setting at, 135; product mix changes at, 135; profits retained by, 131; research and development at, 128–30, 141–44, 146; self-made machinery at, 144–45; supervisory structure of, 123–26, 147; tax and profit collection from, 123, 133; training at, 136; unsalable and unwanted products of, 134; value of fixed assets at, 131; wages deducted for failure to fulfill quotas at, 131; worker benefits at, 141; work incentives at, 132; working capital of, 131, 134, 145

Qinghe Woolen Textile Mill, 42–43, 228–29; allocation of imported materials and, 249; alternative sources of supplies for, 253; authority over reforms at, 240; awards to, 256; bank loans of, 238; bonuses for workers linked to profits at, 247; bonus payments above official ceilings at, 248; bonus raises refused at, 243; bureaucratic interference and, 243, 253, 258, 262; calculation of profit retention rate at, 244; capital construction at, 260–61; computer use at, 251; contractual labor arrangements at, 265; cooperation between factories and, 268; cost management improvements at, 247; credit financing at, 267; critical role of the market for, 270; delinquent accounts of, 258; depreciation funds and, 245; direct marketing problems of, 257–58; economic responsibility system at, 244, 247, 251; electricity for, 253; emphasis on quality at, 255–56; employment and wage system of, 262–66; energy utilization by, 248; equipment at, 259, 261; expansion of production by, 243, 245; exports and, 257; fees paid out of retained profits of, 245; financial contributions to neighborhood improvement and upkeep by, 244; financial incentives at, 264; financial management problems at, 248; flexibility to set prices for own domestic sales at, 256; floating wage system at, 265; government intervention and, 242–43; history of, 236–38; housing at, 263; impediments to autonomy of, 243; implications of experience of, 269–71; improvement of top management at, 241–42; incentives created by tax system and, 267; incentives to raise skill levels at, 263; information-gathering to forecast demand and, 254–55; in-house bank at, 247; interference by party organization at, 242; investment financing and, 258–62; loan repayments and, 52, 259–60; low skill levels at, 265; maintenance and repair at, 265; marketing at, 254–58; marketing reforms at, 267; new management style at, 242; objectives and motivation at, 266–68; organization and leadership of,

239–43; overtime pay at, 264–65; planning and supply and, 249–54, 258; problems with second expansion project, 261; products for export and, 252; profit rate of, 246; profit retention by, 243, 246; raw materials supplies for, 251–52; relationship with supervisory agencies and, 270; response to changing environment and, 268–69; response to new financial incentives by, 243, 245; sales contracts and, 258; sales promotion by, 257; substitution of taxes for profit remittances by, 243, 244–45; supervision of, 239–41, 270; targets and, 250–51; taxes and, 243–46, 248; training of workers at, 265; use of management time at, 273 n22; use of retained funds by, 244, 245; worker absences at, 266; work force size at, 238; working conditions at, 261–62

Quality: emphasis on, 128, 255–56, 398, 405, 407; importance of, 180–81; inappropriately high, 42; poor, 413; prizes for, 211; at Qinghe, 255–56; at Qingdao, 128

Radical reform efforts after mid-1980s, 11–12

Ramie, 277–78

Ramie textiles: cotton-, 294; development of, 277–79; export demand for, 278, 290; linen-, 295; location of mills to produce, 279; polyester-, 277, 279, 291; tax on, 295

Ratchet effect, 73, 115 n13

Raw materials. See Inputs

Recentralization, 54; nonferrous metals industry and, 196–97, 199–200; Shenyang and, 193–97, 197–200

Reform of state enterprises: Chongqing's response to, 87–88, 90–103, 111; critical ingredient for, 48; decentralization and, 41, 45, 53–54; distortions from partial, 55–56; flaw in partial, 249; main elements of,

2–3; mandatory planning and, 48; organizational, 208; partial nature of, 269–70; primary goals of economic, 111; prospects for, 27–29. See also Financial reforms; Industrial reform

Regional branch corporations: control of and by, 199–200; nonferrous metals industry and, 195–96, 197–99; opposition to establishment of Shenyang's enterprise group by, 215

Rent seeking, Anshan and, 328–29

Research and development, 26; at Chongqing, 98–100; at Number Two, 401; at Qingdao, 128–30, 141–44, 146

Resource allocation, 2, 3, 53, 223 n21, 224 n33

Revival Metallurgical Associated Corporation, 215–16

Rules and regulations. See Manipulation of rules

Rural industrial enterprises, labor in, 9

Second Motor Vehicle Manufacturing Plant ("Number Two"), 46–47, 48; administrative supervision of, 382–86, 422; associations between smaller manufacturers and, 371; as best domestic truck producer, 398; bonuses at, 406; cautious internal decentralization by, 405; centralization and, 384; competitive strategy of, 397–402; conflicts between supply authorities and, 382, 389–90, 391–92; cost reduction and, 398–99; development of, 376–82; direct marketing by, 389–91, 399; discretionary authority expansion and, 405; Dongfeng corporation and, 371, 394, 407, 408–14; education and training at, 407; exchanges of output for inputs by, 392–93; exports by, 400; female workers at, 407; financial self-reliance at, 386–88; foreign exchange and, 394; forward-looking management of, 421; imported materials purchased by, 394; independence from government bureaucracy and, 382, 385–88; ingredients for success of, 418–21; internal responsibility system of, 404–5; investment behavior of, 402; jobs for children of workers at, 406; labor force of, 406; location of, 401; mandatory planning and, 388–95; market conditions and, 389, 390, 395–97; market orientation of, 399–400; new product development at, 401; profit margins at, 408; profit-increase responsibility system at, 387–88; profit retention by, 387–88; quality control at, 398, 405, 407; relationship between Number One and, 402–4; replicability of, 421–22; retained profit use by, 387, 405; return on capital at, 412; self-financed development at, 386–87; supply acquisition by, 392–94, 423 n9; technological modernization at, 400–401, 405; worker benefits and wages at, 406, 407; worker orientation of, 405–6

Sellers' market, mandatory planning and chronic, 48

Share ownership, 11–12

Sheep. *See* Wool for textile production

Shenyang Metallurgy Bureau: control of Shenyang Smelter and, 196; opposition to regional corporation and recentralization of smelter and, 219–20

Shenyang Regional Nonferrous Metals Industry Branch Corporation ("Shenyang regional corporation"): role of, 219; Shenyang Metallurgy Bureau and, 219–20; use of profits of Shenyang Smelter by, 219

Shenyang Smelter, 149–50; alloy production at, 188–89, 211; allocation of coke for, 223 n21; allocation of

retained profits of, 223 n22; backward integration and, 206–7; bonuses for workers at, 181, 223 n27; by-products of, 177–78; conflicting targets for, 167–69; control and leadership of, 161, 174, 193–96, 197–200; decentralization and, 160, 167–71; depreciation funds at, 210; direct marketing by, 185–88; employment of workers' children at, 159–60, 175–76, 212; energy conservation at, 179–80; enterprise group of, 213–15; financial manipulation and, 183–85; future strategy for, 220–21; history of, 159–64; investment and investment funds at, 171, 173–75, 182–83, 209, 210; location problems at, 161, 162–64, 174, 189–91; main problems of, 161–64; managers of, 222 n11; mandatory planning and, 210; multiheaded leadership at, 167–71, 174; organizational reforms at, 192–200; performance of, 200–201, 204; pollution and, 164–65, 178–79, 198; problems after 1983 of, 209–11; problems following recentralization and, 197–99; production management problems of, 176–77; profits and taxes at, 209, 210–11; quality at, 180–81; raw materials and energy supplies for, 165–67; recentralization and, 193–97, 197–200; recycling of scrap copper and, 165–66, 200; reform implementation at, 205–6; regional corporation and, 219; Shenyang Metallurgy Bureau and, 196; stagnant performance of, 209–11; subordinate collective enterprise and, 211–13; transfer of control of, 196–97; wages at, 185

Silk: blends with other fibers, 295; shortage of, 277

Sino-U.S. Agreement on Textile Trade, 290

Social services: provided by Chongqing, 72, 76–77, 78, 141; provided by Qingdao, 126, 141

State enterprises: bureaucratic subordination of, 18; classification of, 30 n8; easing social burden of, 12; involvement of government agencies in, 181, 422; lack of control over labor at, 262; main objectives and motivations of, 49; obstacles to relocation of industrial, 52; problems in upgrading of, 207–8; protection of backward, 204; reforms and supervising agencies of, 422; restructuring ownership of, 11, 55. *See also* Enterprise boundaries; Government and political interference and intervention; Industrial firms

State quality prizes, 211

Stock, raising money by issuing, 366 n9

Subsectoral responsibility system, 41, 45

Subsidized housing, 12. *See also* Housing for workers and staff

Supervisory agencies for firms, 2; Anshan and, 309–16; conflicting goals of, 312; Dongfeng corporation's escape from ties to, 47; self-interested behavior of, 391–92. *See also* Government and political interference and intervention

Synthetic fiber industry, investment in, 232

Synthetic fibers for textiles, annual production of, 232

Taxes: Chongqing Clock and Watch Company and, 72–74; collection of, 222 n17; enterprise-specific adjustment, 4; income, 75, 84; industrial-commercial sales, 73; kept by Guangxi government, 280; net product, 72; problems stemming from system of, 214; refusal to pay bonus, 44; substituted for profit delivery, 59, 284

Technological progress, 26–27

Technology, use of outdated, 40, 41.

See also names of individual firms

Textile firms in China: control over, 230; locations of, 231; sizes of, 301 n4

Textile industry in China, 232, 233; blended textiles and, 288, 291; development strategy for, 280; exports of, 232; Guangxi's contribution to, 280; subsections of, 229; synthetic fibers and, 288

U.S. textile and trade agreements with China, 290

Wage bill: of Chongqing Clock and Watch Company, 72; linkage between financial results and total, 9; productivity and, 50

Wage grades at Chongqing, 115 n18

Wages and wage reform, 8–9, 24–25; performance-related pay and, 9, 78–79

Watch industry in China, 59–64

Watches: market for, 38, 62; prices of, 61; production costs of, 114 n4

Woolen fabrics: experimentation, new product trial production, and market research and, 236; exports of, 235

Woolen textile industry in China, 232, 233

Wool for textile production, 233–35; blends of, 235; imported versus domestic, 252; sheep breeding for, 235

Worker-oriented behavior of enterprises, 43

Workers in state-owned industrial enterprises: contracts for, 8; financing of benefits for, 40; guaranteed jobs and incomes for, 14; housing for, 12, 43, 49, 79, 81, 263–64, 282, 283, 284; incentives for, 40, 78–79, 80; replaced by their children, 273 n26; social services for, 17, 49; training of, 265, 285. *See also* Collective versus state workers; Industrial labor force

Workers' interests, managers and, 50
Work force, using attrition to reduce, 9

Zhao Ziyang reform faction, 13

The complete backlist of publications from the World Bank is shown in the annual *Index of Publications*, which contains an alphabetical title list and indexes of subjects, authors, and countries and regions. The latest edition is available free of charge from the Distribution Unit, Office of the Publisher, The World Bank, 1818 H Street, N.W., Washington, D.C. 20433, or from Publications, The World Bank, 66, avenue d'Iéna, 75116 Paris, France.

DATE			